Foundations and
Strategies for Teaching
Children to Read

LOU E. BURMEISTER

University of Texas at El Paso

Foundations and Strategies for Teaching Children to Read

ADDISON-WESLEY PUBLISHING COMPANY
Reading, Massachusetts • Menlo Park, California
London • Amsterdam • Don Mills, Ontario • Sydney

Library of Congress Cataloging in Publication Data

Burmeister, Lou E.
   Foundations and strategies for teaching children to read.

   Bibliography: p.
   Includes index.
   1. Reading.   I. Title.
LB1050.B84   372.4'1   82-3949
ISBN 0-201-10802-X   AACR2

ISBN 0-201-10802-X
ABCDEFGHIJ-DO-89876543

To my students—past and present—
at the University of Texas at El Paso,
who have been, and continue to be,
a constant inspiration to me and to each other.

Reading—the quintessence, fullness, and variety of life may be found through it! Through reading, the wonders of the universe can be revealed to us. . . . The inmost thoughts of others can become known to us. . . . The plights, the fears, the joys, the failures and successes of a multitude of humans can be lived vicariously by us. And our own thoughts—once written down—can be relived, refined, enjoyed again, shared, and even criticized.

By reading, we can entertain ourselves and others. We can escape a trying world, take flights of fantasy to other spheres. Our lives can be enriched, enlightened by those who have unusual perception—who also have a gift with words—and who care enough to put these words, these thoughts, in print.

By reading we can learn the simplest things and the most complex. We can share thoughts of people we might never know but who might strengthen us in our convictions or who might lead us along other paths, who might form us anew. All this is possible through reading, as is much, much more.

Helping children learn to read, and to read better, is among the greatest gifts we can give. Giving children time to read materials of interest to them is a necessary correlative. And, in addition, broadening their horizons by providing new experiences to them helps complete the gift.

Reading is but one of the language arts. It evolves along with all the others: speaking, listening, and writing. All of these grow along with meaningful experiences. Reading and the other language arts do not compose an isolated entity. They are a part of a larger whole, composed of thoughts and feelings and perceptions.

There is almost a magical quality to reading. When reading is at its best, there's a rapport between reader and author . . . a constant interchange . . . a commonness of language, a "play" with thoughts, a sharing of feelings—perhaps an intimacy, perhaps a violent disagreement—but always an understanding on the part of the reader and a willingness and ability to "listen" and often to ponder and perhaps to change.

But the teaching of reading usually is not magic. It is a carefully planned step-by-step procedure based on a solid philosophy. It may progress from an emphasis on the development of perceptual skills and move from this to meaning and enjoyment. Or it may progress in the opposite direction, beginning with a stress on meaning, language development, and enjoyment and move toward the development of the perceptual skills thought necessary in such a program.

Within this book the reader will find an explanation of both types of programs: those that begin with an emphasis on the development of perceptual skills and on reading to "get the author's thoughts," frequently termed "bottom-up" or "text-bound" programs; and those that begin with the child's thoughts, language, and enjoyments, the recording of these, and the teaching of the perceptual skills necessary for the reading of these, frequently termed "top-down" or "concept-driven" programs. Another philosophy, or program, termed "interactive," moves between these two: the reader is driven by his or her thoughts (concepts) to predict the author's concepts (as recorded in the text) and to constantly test the quality, or match, of the predictions with the text.

Some of the activities and explanations in the present book are more appropriate for one of these sequences than for another. In many cases, such activities or explanations are labeled. It is the desire of the present author to present a wide range of activities to give the readers of this book—preservice and inservice teachers—basic understandings of several philosophies and their translation to the development of classroom experiences which will help children learn to read and to read with enjoyment.

Organization of This Book

This book is organized in three units which may be studied in any order. Unit One, called FOUNDATIONS, includes chapters in which the author provides

- definitions of reading given by children and by researchers
- explanations of factors that may influence the reading achievement of children
- descriptions of the range of reading achievement among age-mates and ways of adjusting to these differences

- descriptions of ways of developing reading readiness and of assessing readiness
- explanations of ways of promoting parental involvement to optimize learning

Unit Two, called STRATEGIES, includes chapters on

- recoding and decoding
- building vocabulary
- building literal and inferential comprehension
- developing critical reading abilities
- encouraging wide and in-depth reading
- developing appropriate rates of comprehension
- fusing the teaching of reading with the teaching of content

Unit Three, called APPROACHES, PROGRAMS, AND EVALUATION, includes chapters in which

- various approaches or programs are described and exemplified, including the Language Experience Approach, the basal reading approach, linguistic approaches, individualized reading, psycholinguistic implications for reading instruction, objective-based reading systems and approaches, and modified orthographies
- various ways in which reading performance can be evaluated

COMMENT

The very process of reading, which may make possible a world filled with delight and learning for some children, unfortunately also may lead to frustration, disenchantment, and disillusion for those who fail to learn to read or to learn to read well. It is hoped that those strategies explained in this book that are appropriate for use with specific children and groups of children will be used, modified, and supplemented to help make learning to read an enjoyable, successful experience for children.

Contents

UNIT THREE: APPROACHES, PROGRAMS, AND EVALUATION

APPENDIXES

INDEXES

Unit One

FOUNDATIONS

Unit One consists of five chapters:

Chapter 1 What Is Reading?

Chapter 2 Factors that Influence Reading Achievement

Chapter 3 Organizing for Individual Differences

Chapter 4 Reading Readiness and Early Reading

Chapter 5 Promoting Parental Involvement

Unit One has three basic purposes: *first*, to examine various definitions of reading in order to determine implications for teaching; *second*, to explore reasons for individual differences in achievement and interests, and to see how schools and teachers are grouping children in an attempt to adjust to these differences in order to maximize learning and interest for all children; and *third*, to suggest strategies for developing reading readiness and for promoting parental involvement to benefit preschool and school youngsters in ways that relate to the child's education. These are foundations necessary for understanding how reading can be taught in the elementary school.

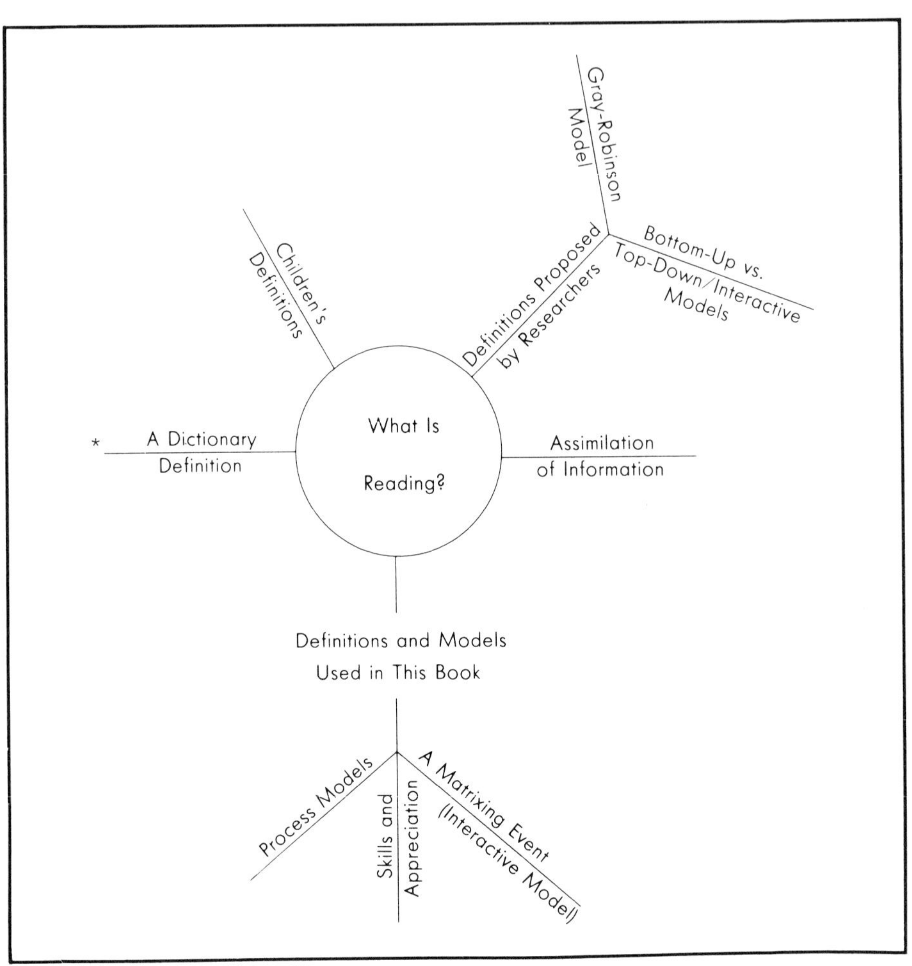

*Begin reading here and proceed in clockwise order.

- What insights does a dictionary definition give us about the meaning of reading?
- What do children's definitions tell us about how these children are being taught and about their attitudes toward reading?
- What skills does the Gray-Robinson model indicate are important in reading? Do you agree?
- When analyzing "bottom-up" and "top-down/interactive" process models of reading, try to determine why it is important for you as a teacher or future teacher to be able to distinguish between these. Consider each definition in terms of implications for an instructional program.
- How do people assimilate information?
- What definitions and models are used in this book? What is meant by calling reading "a matrixing event?"

CHAPTER 1

What Is Reading?

It may seem strange to the reader of this book that there should be a whole chapter dedicated to defining reading. After all, just about everyone knows what reading is, and those who don't could consult a good dictionary. However, things are really not that simple.

A Dictionary Definition

For example, one dictionary defines (to) read thus:*

read (rēd) *v.* read (rĕd), **reading, reads.** —*tr.* **1.** To comprehend or take in the meaning of (something written or printed). **2.** To utter or render aloud (something written or printed). **3.** To have the knowledge of (a language) necessary to understand printed or written material. **4.** To seek to interpret the true nature or meaning of (someone or something) through close scrutiny: *read the sky for signs of snow.* **5.** To ascertain the intent or mood of: *He read her mind.* **6.** To derive a special meaning from or ascribe a special significance to (something read, experienced, or observed): *"a tendency to read deep and nasty meanings into Robinson's words"* (Muriel Spark). **7.** To foretell or predict (the future). **8.** To perceive, receive, or comprehend (a signal, message, or the like): *I read you fine.* **9.** To study or make a study of: *read for a law exam.* **10.** To learn or get knowledge from (something written or printed): *He read that crime was rife.* **11.** To have or adopt as a reading in a particular passage: *For "colour" read "color."* **12.** To indicate, register, or show: *The dial reads 0°* —*intr.*

---

*Copyright 1980 by Houghton Mifflin Company. Reprinted by permission from *The American Heritage Dictionary of the English Language.*

At first glance, all of these definitions may appear to be reasonable. Yet, if you were to examine definitions and explanations given by professionals who have dedicated their careers to the study of and/or teaching of reading, you would find that each of these definitions is somewhat controversial as a component of the reading act or as a product of the act.

For example, some do not consider comprehension to be essential in reading. Most people would agree that when one reads, it is not necessary to "utter or render aloud" the passage; yet some program designers contend that this is all there is to reading. Similarly, a large percentage of people would concur with the idea that one must know the language of the printed material in order to read it; yet not all would agree with this (one might orally "read" a phonetic foreign language—if one knew its phonics—without understanding the passage).

Most, though not all, of the additional definitions (numbers 4–12) are broad in scope, in that they do not require that the message be in printed symbols. However, the message might be in a printed passage, and these definitions might suggest to some people a definition of high-level reading skills or competencies.

You may wish to ask yourself what reading means to you. What skills or competencies do you think are necessary for successful reading? Why do people read? What do people gain from reading?

Children's Definitions

Since most of us are teachers or are planning to be teachers, it might be interesting to see what some children think reading is. According to one study,[1] when school children were asked to define reading, the most common responses were:

- Reading is finishing the reader.
- Reading is work.
- Reading is going to reading class.

You might wonder about the reasons for the lack of enthusiasm toward reading evident in these definitions.

The following definitions were obtained from children in a local study conducted by the author of the present book: "Reading is important—so you can pass." "Reading is something so you can be a good girl or boy in school." "Reading is a bunch of letters." "Reading is learning to pronounce harder words." "Reading is studying." "Reading is where words are combined to tell you something." "Reading to me is understanding." "Reading is fun." "Reading is a class where you read and enjoy your book." "Reading is being able to take a whole bunch of words and being able to understand what they say." "Reading makes you think better." "Reading is looking at the words and imagining it." "Reading is something you have to learn to be a good man and have a good job." "Reading is being quiet and listening." "Reading is helping you learn nice things about the world." "Reading is thinking." "When there's nothing else to do, reading takes place." "Reading is gonna be in your life forever." "Reading is like seeing what other people are doing that you can't do. I think it builds your imagination."

"Reading is a way of killing time." "Reading is escaping from the real world to a fantasy world." "Reading is sitting down and relaxing." "Reading is being occupied, your mind out of something else." "Reading is fun and educational." "When I read, I don't pay that much attention to it unless it is a very interesting book." "Reading is boring because sometimes the story is not good. But sometimes the story is good and interesting." "When I read, sometimes my mind is not with me."

"I think (dream) of what I am reading." "Reading is like putting something in your mind about what you want to do or make." "I read, and then I get lost and start dreaming. . . . Reading is losing myself in a fantasy world (fiction). I try to 'step-into-the-shoes' of each character."

Here we have a wide variety of "definitions." Some include the child's idea of the process of reading (learning to pronounce words, changing words into meanings, looking at words and imagining it, putting something in your mind). Others include products of reading (understanding, fun, better thinking, learning nice things, building an imagination, escaping, relaxing, stepping into the shoes of a character). Still other definitions suggest that the child reads to satisfy others and/or to obtain goals set by schools or by himself or herself. (Reading is important—so you can pass. Reading is done to be a good boy or girl in school, to get a good job.)

Definitions Proposed by Researchers in Reading

Many reading experts, linguists, psycholinguists, and psychologists* have contributed definitions of reading and/or models for reading instruction. Those selected for inclusion here represent a wide variation—and often conflicting points of view. They are offered here to help you, the reader of this book, understand what may be going on in the mind of a person who is reading and to help you become aware of some philosophies that have governed and are now governing the production of reading materi-

---

Linguists study language in scientific ways. *Psycholinguists* study how people acquire language, e.g., reading ability, by combining mental (psycho) and language (linguistic) forces. *Psychologists* study human behavior.

als, and to give you some perspective for developing your own materials and lessons. These philosophies may give you insights into both the "process" of reading (the operations, systems of operations, actions, series of actions, and functions used to bring about ends and results) and into the "product" (the ends and results) of reading.

THE GRAY-ROBINSON MODEL[2]

The Gray-Robinson model is a frequently quoted traditional model used to explain skills the authors consider to be important in reading instruction. The original model, described by William S. Gray, was later expanded by Helen M. Robinson. The revised model is illustrated in Figure 1.1.

In this model, reading is defined as a "unitary" act, that is, an act in which all facets operate as a whole. The circle, or wheel, may be thought of as spinning, and the processes and products of reading constantly mesh. The five facets are described thus:

- *word perception* includes
  - word recognition skills
  - word meanings
- *comprehension* involves
  - literal meanings, i.e., getting a clear grasp of what the author is saying
  - implied meanings, i.e., determining the significance of the author's ideas beyond what is actually stated
- *reaction* involves
  - intellectual judgments, which require the reader to have an inquiring attitude and standards of judgment
  - emotional responses
- *assimilation* comes about through
  - the exercise of critical judgment
  - creative thinking
  - combining information secured from reading with one's previous experiences
- *rates* are flexible and are adjusted to
  - the reader's purpose, and
  - the nature of the material

According to this model, word perception includes more than what David Russell calls "word barking" or "barking at words." It also includes understanding the meanings of words. Comprehension includes clearly grasping statements made by the author and also understanding the "im-

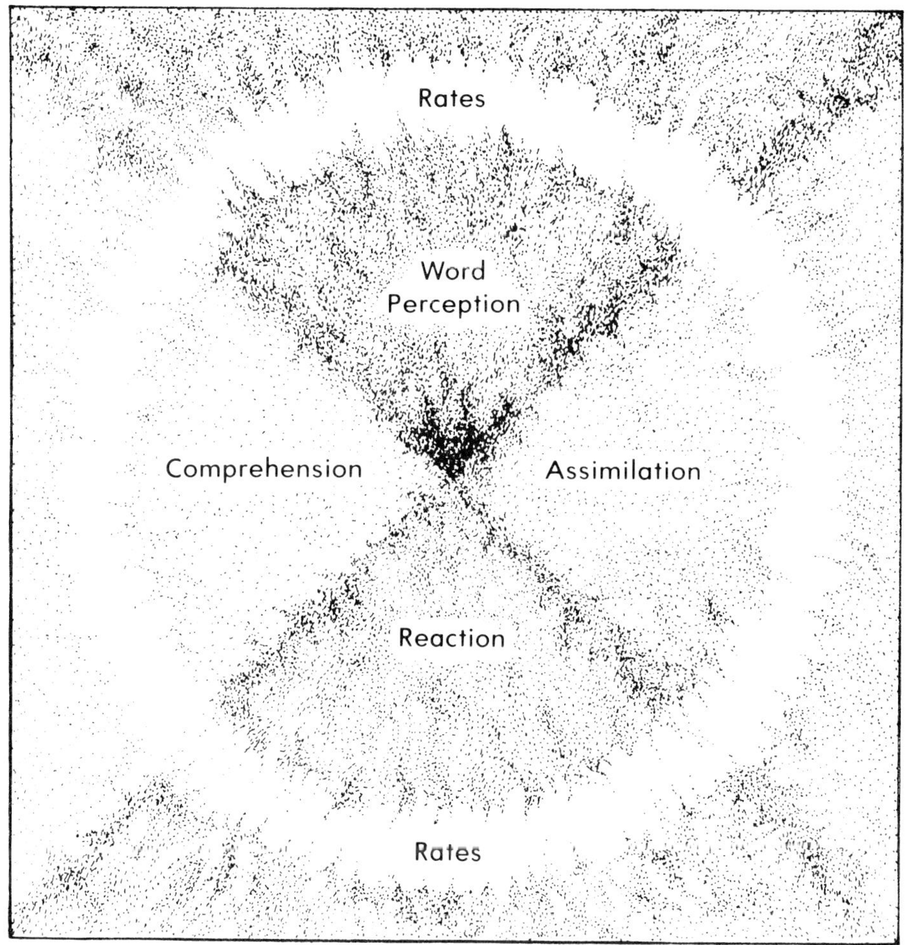

Fig. 1.1: Five major aspects of reading (Helen M. Robinson's revision of William S. Gray's model).

plications and significance of the author's ideas beyond those things actually stated." Reaction requires an inquiring attitude on the part of the reader, according to Gray, and the reader must have "standards or criteria of judgment" and must be able to reach conclusions. Both Gray and Robinson include the importance of an emotional response, i.e., an affective response to content. Many of the other models described later in this chapter omit this.

Assimilation, or fusion of new ideas with old, comes about as a result of the exercise of critical judgment. (Not everything is assimilated.) Creative thinking develops through assimilating, or synthesizing, old and new ideas, perhaps in typical or perhaps in unique, or divergent, ways.

This process may be similar to what J. P. Guilford[3] called convergent and divergent production, or thinking. This involves the combining of information secured from reading and other sources with one's previous experiences to produce for oneself a commonly held (convergent) concept or a new or unusual (divergent) concept.

Robinson includes the importance of rates, which according to her are adjusted to the reader's purpose and the nature of the material. Later in this chapter you will see a discussion of automaticity of decoding and/or the importance of maintaining meaning momentum in order that ideas may be assimilated by the reader.

Although the Gray-Robinson model provides a broad identification of the skills areas of reading, it does not include methodology for teaching reading. The illustration of the wheel that spins gives us insights into the authors' concept of the process of reading.

BOTTOM-UP VERSUS TOP-DOWN PROCESS MODELS

A major controversy in the field of reading today centers on whether reading is a bottom-up or top-down process. According to Constance Weaver,[4] today there are three popular characterizations of the reading process. They are:

> "1. Reading means pronouncing words. That is, reading means going from visible surface structure (written words) to audible surface structure (spoken words).
> 2. Reading means identifying words and getting their meaning. That is, reading means going from visible surface structure to deep structure (meaning).
> 3. Reading means bringing meaning *to* a text in order to get meaning from it. That is, reading means using deep structure to interpret surface structure."

Weaver describes the first two points of view as the "ink blotter" or "sponge" view of reading, in which the reader is passive. The third definition implies that meaning does not lie in the words, but in the people who are reading. She argues in favor of the third definition, saying that we must bring meaning to what we read and that reading is an interaction between the mind of the reader and the language of the text. The first two definitions describe the bottom-up (text-bound, text-driven) theory of reading. The third definition characterizes the top-down (concept-bound, concept-driven) theory, or what is called more recently by some an interactive theory.[5]

We might ask: Do readers look at the text, recode it to oral and/or aural language,* and then (perhaps) proceed to meaning (bottom-up, text-bound definition)? Those who define reading in a bottom-up way believe that the page supplies more information to the reader than the reader supplies to the page. The reader gathers information from the page and processes this information until it is understood.

Those who believe in the top-down (concept-driven) theory of reading, on the other hand, believe that the reader brings more information to the page than the page brings to the reader. They believe that the reader has in his or her mind information and concepts that enable the reader to make sense out of the discussion. They believe that readers begin with meanings** that are already in their experience storehouse, conjecture about the text before them while constantly interacting with the text. Readers proceed by combining memories of related previous experiences with the statements of the text in achieving meaning—perhaps, and perhaps not, to be followed by oral and/or aural reading.

The illustration in Figure 1.2 may help clarify these terms.

The definition we accept will have important implications for the way in which we will wish to teach reading. For example, if reading seems to us to be a bottom-up process, we would conclude that the first step in reading is word identification, which is usually achieved by systematically recoding and decoding[†] words using symbol-sound correspondences and spelling patterns and/or instant recognition of words as "sight" words.[6] Teaching phonics (or a spelling recoding system) would be an important component of such a program.

On the other hand, if we view reading as predominantly a top-down process, we would conclude that reading is hypothesis testing, dependent upon an active use of "sight" words, context cues, and background of experience.[7] Children would be taught to use context, to guess (hypothesize) about what is coming next, and to constantly test these hypotheses against the text.

An interactive model suggests that reading could be both bottom-up and top-down for an individual, and the approach might fluctuate from one to another. Many theorists in the past have argued against the possibility of such a combination. Calfee and Drum conclude: "We find ourselves at an unreasonable choice point: direct perception versus hypothesis testing; bottom-up versus top-down processing. . ."[8]

---

* Aural language is silent speech.

**For example, meanings of words, concepts, understandings about character actions, story-lines, organizational patterns, etc.

† Recoding here means going from code to code (e.g., graphic to oral or aural, while *decoding* means going from code (graphic, oral, or aural) to meaning. *Aural reading* is listening. When readers proceed from graphic symbols to their "aural" counterparts, they internally "listen" to the sounds represented by the graphic symbols.

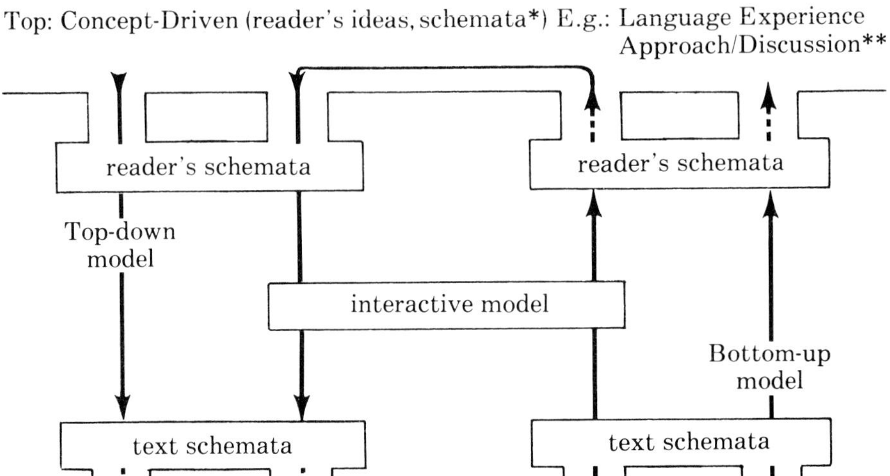

Figure 1.2

*   A *schema* is a main idea, a concept. *Schemata* is the plural. The reader's schemata are all the concepts (schema) the reader has in his or her long-term memory storage system. The text schemata include all the concepts (schema) the author relays on the printed page, i.e., in the text.
** In the Language Experience Approach, children learn to read what they have dictated to the teacher, who writes it for them.
***A Code Emphasis Approach is one that stresses grapho-phonic (symbol-sound relationships).

Bottom-Up Models

The following diagram demonstrates the general reading process model commonly called the bottom-up model. This model explains the steps a reader takes when reading, according to the major proponents of this model.

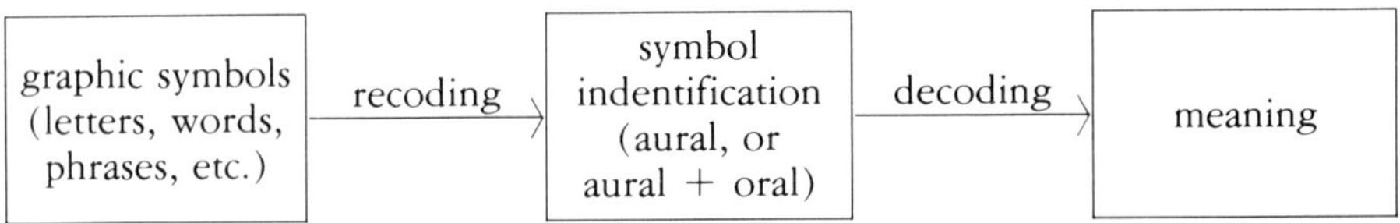

The graphic symbols may be letters, letter patterns, words, or phrases, or sentences. Recognizing these, or a mixture of these, may lead to aural reading (which may or may not lead to oral reading), which, in turn, (according to the proponents of this model) may trigger meaning. In the meaning phase, the reader may proceed through one or several stages (or levels of comprehension*) until meaning is partially or fully realized.

Following are several specific and unique theories that are of the bottom-up type.

Bloomfield-Barnhart and Flesch Models Two reading models include only the process of taking the reader from graphic symbols to oral reading. That is, reading is defined as recoding—going from visible language (print) to sound.

Leonard Bloomfield and Clarence Barnhart's *Let's Read*[9] series is a spelling to sound approach to teaching reading. There are no pictures and no comprehension activities. New words introduced are minimal linguistic contrasts of those already learned, e.g., cat → fat → rat . . . The following diagram describes the Bloomfield-Barnhart model of reading:

Bloomfield thinks that the child has such a difficult time seeing a relationship between letters and sounds that he or she can't attend to the meaning of what is read. He says that reading, per se, stops with the recognition of the oral counterpart of the printed symbol; however, listening skills may then take over and may be taught.

Rudolf Flesch, author of *Why Johnny Can't Read*, succinctly stated a similar philosophy: "Teach the child what each letter stands for and he can read." Thus, reading is equated with oral reading. Teachers who stress oral reading and teach little or no comprehension and enjoyment of reading are following this philosophy to a large extent.

Philip B. Gough Model[10] The Gough model was designed to explain what happens in one second of reading. Gough concluded that the beginning reader "plods through the sentence, letter by letter, word by word," and, of course, this takes much more time than one second. Gough con-

---

* For example, literal meanings, implied meanings, reaction, assimilation (Gray-Robinson); surface level, basic comprehension level, interpretive level (Perfetti).
**/kăt/, i.e. the sound of the word *cat.*

curs with Andrew Biemiller,[11] who says that, at least in the early stages of reading, oral reading errors are an indication that the child is avoiding the decoding problem, and thus a sign that the child is unable to identify what lies before him or her. Biemiller presents research findings that support the conclusion that the child's first task in learning to read is mastery of graphic information. To Gough, efficient reading even in later stages includes letter by letter, word by word skimming.

Gough believes that beginning readers usually know a great deal about spoken language in terms of vocabulary and sentence structure, and that they have the ability to understand spoken language. In the beginning stages of reading, "they must learn how to assign a phonological representation to the printed word." (It would be important here that the passage be linguistically similar to the child's dialect.) Biemiller adds that when there is evidence of the successful use of graphic skills (phonics, sight vocabulary), the teacher might teach the child to combine the use of graphic and contextual (meaning) information and teach the child to read faster.

Charles Perfetti Model[12] Charles Perfetti, a psychologist, describes his model by using three levels. They are:

Level I: Surface Level (Recoding) At this level phonological and acoustic (i.e., sounding and listening) properties are most prominent. (This is what Russell calls "word barking.") This level may be illustrated thus:

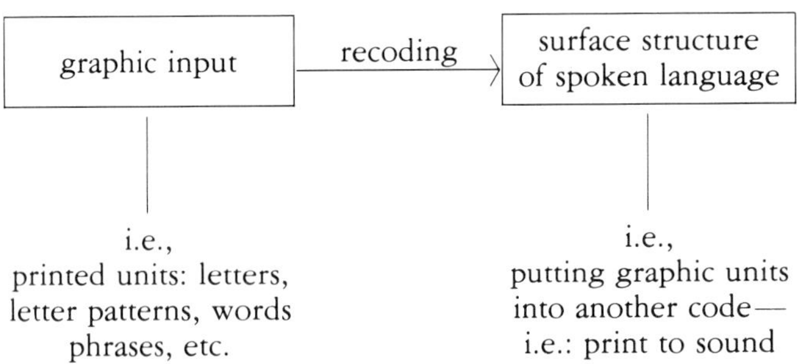

Perfetti hypothesizes that Level I (recoding) provides access to meaning; that is, meaning automatically accompanies recoding, provided that meanings are known. Perfetti suggests that a major difference between unskilled and skilled readers is that unskilled readers have a harder time recoding than do skilled readers. However, he states that both decode (attach meaning) at the same rate (holding I.Q., and background of experience, constant).

Levels II and III processing depend on Level I processing and cannot be accomplished without Level I processing. According to Perfetti, speeded recoding and decoding are intimately tied with skilled comprehension. "Level I serves as a holding action during brief periods that information is needed more or less verbatim in order to carry out higher levels of comprehension."[13]

<u>Level II: Basic Comprehension Level (Sentence Surfing)</u> At this level semantic (word and phrase meaning) and syntactic (sentence) properties take over, thus:

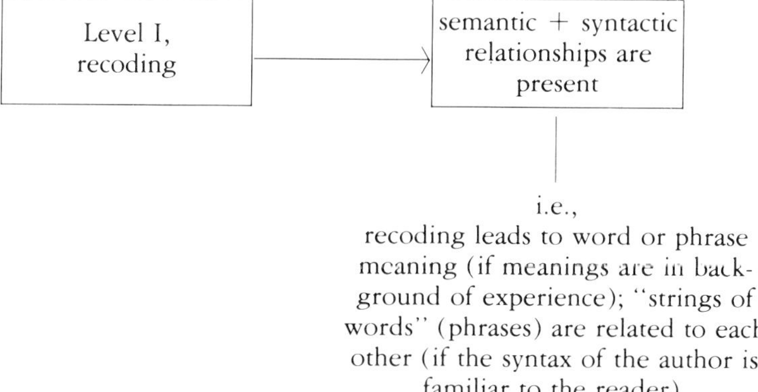

Answers to questions asked by the student or teacher are transformationally related to the passage read. (Answers simply incorporate word order changes and/or dialectal changes).

For example, if the textual passage is, "The admiral captured the bandit," and the reader knows the meanings of all the words in the passage, the reader could correctly respond to questions such as:

1. Who captured the bandit?
2. What did the admiral do?
3. Whom did the admiral capture?

Answering literal level questions of such types requires basic linguistic (language) competence. Perfetti calls reading at this level *sentence surfing*. He says, "Sentence surfers skim along the tops of sentences without getting deeper meaning."

> It might be noted here that sentence surfing questions can be an-swered even without the semantic (meaning) component. Take, for example, the sentence,"The snocker migged the gump Foosday."* Can you answer the following questions about this sentence?
>
> 1. Who migged the gump?
> 2. What did the snocker do?
> 3. Whom or what did the snocker mig?
> 4. When did the snocker mig the gump?

<u>Level III: Interpretive Level</u> Operating at this level requires the reader to know more than is in the immediate passage. This information may have been gained elsewhere in the story or may have come from the reader's background of experience. For example:

1. What bandit?
2. Captured how?
3. Why did the admiral capture the bandit?

A major contribution of this model is the term *sentence surfing* and its ex-planation. Literal level questions frequently are sentence surfing ques-tions. Explanations given here demonstrate that such questions can be an-swered without any understanding of the passage, although syntactic competence in the language being "read" is essential. According to Perfetti, additional higher comprehension levels may also be used in the reading process.

Kenneth Goodman's "Early Stages" Model[14] Kenneth Goodman, recognized as one of the leading proponents of the "top-down/interactive" theory (described later in this chapter), proposed the following "possible simpli-fied model" for reading in early stages:

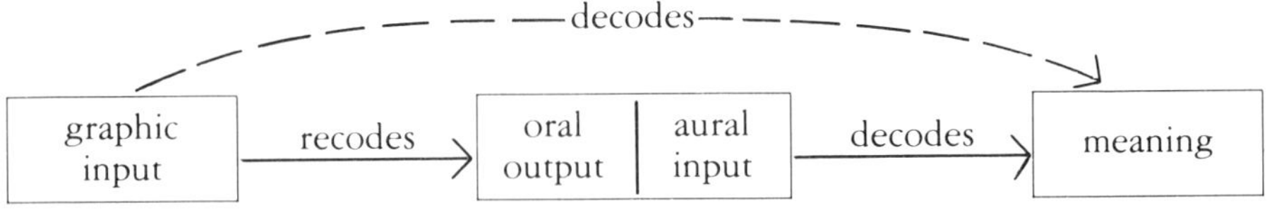

*Note that traditional English syntactic signals are present in this "nonsense" sentence: *The* tells us a noun is to follow, and *-er* frequently marks a noun (snocker, e.g. farm*er*, bak*er*, etc.). Also, *-ed* identifies a verb, specifically a verb in the past tense (migg*ed*, e.g., tilled). Again, *the* tells us a noun is to follow (gump, e.g., soil), perhaps preceded by an adjective (wampy gump, e.g., sandy soil). And, *-day* (Foosday) tells us when.

"The child here recodes graphic input as speech (either out loud or internally) and then, utilizing his own speech as aural input, decodes as he does in listening." It should be noted that Goodman's model assumes some direct decoding from print to meaning—even at the earliest stages.

Top-Down/Interactive Models*[15]

Contrasting with bottom-up theories, top-down/interactive process theories assume that grammatical transformations and/or meanings immediately follow the scanning of graphic input. If oral reading occurs, it follows the grasping of the transformation or meaning-getting process. Two models are presented here.

Frank Smith Model[16] Frank Smith rejects "bottom-up" reading theories. Using psycholinguistic terminology, Smith explains the steps in reading thus:

• oral reading proceeds in this way—

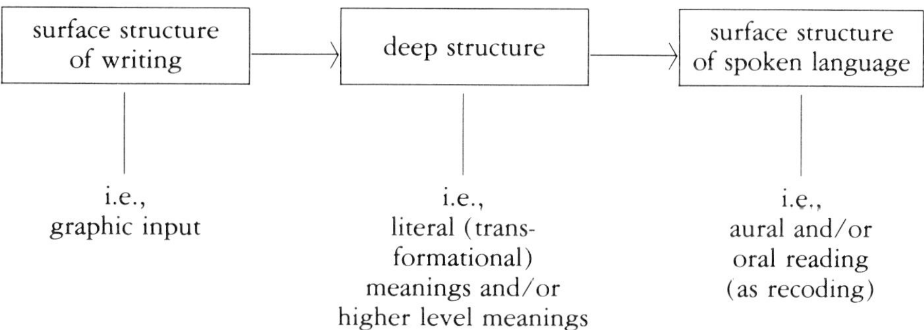

He cites as evidence that if one orally reads the following sentence correctly, meaning must have been in the reader's mind before the oral reading occurred: "We should *read* the *minute* print on the *permit*."

• silent reading proceeds in this way—

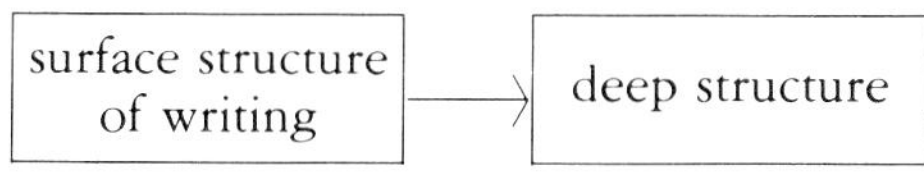

---

*Interactive models, but more top-down than bottom-up.

(There is no need for oral or aural reading, i.e., recoding, in silent reading.)

Kenneth Goodman Model[17]   Kenneth Goodman describes reading as a "psycholinguistic guessing game."* His model for proficient reading is:

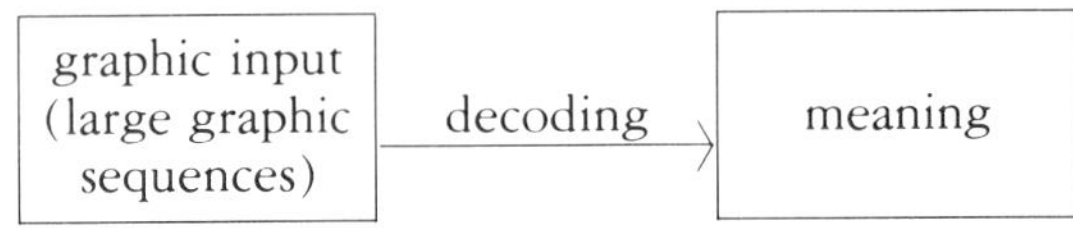

According to Goodman, "In silent reading, the reader sweeps ahead, sampling from the graphic input, predicting structures, leaping to quick conclusions about the meaning and only slowing down or regressing when subsequent sampling fails to confirm what he expects to find . . .

"Meaning is the constant goal of the proficient reader and he continually tests his choices against the developing meaning by asking himself if what he is reading makes sense. The process does not require that he perceive and identify every cue. In fact that would be both unnecessary and inefficient. But it does require that the reader monitor his choices so he can recognize his errors and gather more cues when needed."

Goodman continues, "Such traditional terms as *word recognition, sounding out*, and *word attack* stem from a view of reading as a succession of accurate perceptions or word identifications. Such a view is not consistent with the actual performance of proficient readers."

Comment—an Interactive Model

Research evidence is accumulating that describes the behavior of good, average, and poor readers as they are reading in terms of bottom-up and top-down theories of reading. Much more evidence is needed in order to draw definitive conclusions. A small portion of the research is summarized here.

The oral reading of children has been studied in terms of typical miscues different groups of children make. "Miscues" is a term popularized by Yetta Goodman and Kenneth Goodman and other psycholinguists. A miscue is a deviation from the expected oral response to a word of a passage, i.e., a reader makes a miscue if he or she orally reads something different from the words in print or reads them in a different order.

---

*Psycholinguistic: psycho = mind, thought, cognition and/or affect (interest, values); linguistic = language. A "psycholinguistic" guessing game would require the use of one's intellectual and/or affective abilities and language abilities.

According to Weaver,[18] when readers make miscues, poor readers are likely to make the type that suggest that they are attending mainly to the surface structure (visible language) of the text, suggesting that most miscues are made by poor readers in a bottom-up, text-driven, situation.

<table>
<tr><td>

For example, text: Patty and Jane had a dog.
         child: Patty and John had a dig.
         text: The dog had a bone.
         child: The dig had a bonny.

</td><td>

That is, typical errors
of poor readers
are text-bound
(bottom-up).

</td></tr>
</table>

On the other hand, most miscues of good readers suggest they are attending to deep structure (meaning), suggesting that most miscues are made by good readers in a top-down, context-driven, situation.

<table>
<tr><td>

For example, text: Patty and Jane had a dog.
         child: Jane and Patty had a dog.

         text: The dog had a bone.
         child: Their doll wore a bonnet.

         text: I can't find my ring.
         child: I lost my ring.

</td><td>

That is, typical errors
of good readers are
context-bound
(top-down).

</td></tr>
</table>

When looking at dialect related miscues, Barbara Hunt[19] found that the best readers (when they miscue) produce the most dialect-based miscues. That is, good readers, when they miscue, tend to express the author's deep structure in a surface structure which is partially their own.

<table>
<tr><td>

For example, text: Bobby doesn't care.
         child: Bobby don't care.

         text: Patty loved her dog and
                    brushed it every day.
         child: Patty love her dog and
                    brush it every day.

</td><td>

That is, typical errors of
good readers who speak
a dialect different from
the text are dialect-
based (top-down,
i.e., context-driven).

</td></tr>
</table>

In these situations good readers are less concerned with the exact words of an author than with meaning; i.e., they are reading in a top-down fashion.

In a similar vein, Robbins Burling,[20] author of *English in Black and White*, contends that children who convert book language to their dialect when reading orally—so long as they do not change meaning—show that they understand what they are reading. (That is, these children are efficient top-down readers). Such miscues give evidence of comprehension more than does the "accurate" recitation of words, according to Burling.

From the above, we might conclude that

1. *good readers' miscues* suggest that at the time of the miscue they are reading in a top-down fashion;
2. *poor readers' miscues* suggest that at the time of the miscue they are reading in a bottom-up fashion.

This conclusion relates only to the majority of miscues made by each type of reader.

Some researchers have concluded from this information that good readers tend to be top-down readers, and that poor readers tend to be bottom-up readers. Yet, is it possible that non-dialect based miscues may suggest another possible conclusion, or tentative conclusion?

Connie Juel,[21] who studied reading behavior of second and third graders when they orally read words in isolation, words in single sentences written to be "poor" in context clues, and words in single sentences written to be "moderate" in context clues,* found that in these situations good readers are predominantly text-driven, while poor readers are context-driven, and average readers fluctuate. She found that all readers appear to utilize context (meaning), but that better readers rely on context only when internal (graphic) word clues are weak. According to her, good readers usually are text-driven (are bottom-up readers) and they are context-driven (are top-down readers) only when words are of low frequency or are difficult to recode.

On the other hand, she found that poor readers benefit considerably from context for *all* types of words. Such readers are text-driven (i.e., they use phonics or recognize words by "sight") when they read word lists, but they are predominantly concept-driven when they read words in sentences. She found that poor readers do not ignore word structure when reading sentences, but that they are incapable of maximizing the use of word structure. Although poor readers are better at recognizing words in context than in isolation (for they use graphic clues poorly),

---

*For example:

Isolation	Poor Context	Moderate Context
bone	The man wants a bone.	The dog wants a bone.
pilot	In the house is a pilot.	In the airplane is a pilot.
cot	She wants a cot.	She sleeps on a cot.
hound	That is a hound.	That dog is a hound.
bisquets	We want bisquets.	We eat bisquets.

they do not use contextual information as well as good readers do (and good readers in her study used graphic information better than they used contextual information).[22]

The following may clarify the above statements:

1. *good readers used*
   first: graphic information (text-driven/bottom-up)
   second: contextual information (concept-driven/top-down)
2. *poor readers used*
   first: contextual information (concept-driven/top-down)
        but at a lower level than good readers did
   second: graphic information (text-driven/bottom-up)

A possible synthesis of the above findings might suggest that both good and poor readers make the majority of their non-dialect based miscues when using their own less favored mode of reading. (The majority of miscues made by good readers occur when they are reading top-down i.e., when they are using semantic and syntactic cues. The majority of miscues made by poor readers occur when they are reading bottom-up i.e., when they are using grapho-phonic cues.)

Biemiller's study[23] suggests that poor readers fail to progress because they rely on context for word identification rather than on graphic cues. This is an area of fertile research at the present time. Certainly more evidence is needed to substantiate any conclusions. Yet, the findings suggest the possibility of an interactive model: For the same person, reading may sometimes be bottom-up, and at other times it may be top-down.

Assimilation of Information

Learning to read apparently involves the formation of a large store of data in long-term memory. It also involves the retrieval of such data during the process of reading. Letters, letter patterns, words, phrases, clauses, a broad range of concepts and understandings (which are part of a person's background of experience) may be among the units or multiple-units stored and retrieved. Figure 1.3 represents an attempt to illustrate the process.

Recent research indicates that the short-term memory system of an individual is able to "hold" about 5 ± 2 or 7 ± 2 "chunks" of information at one time. (Young children, for example, may be able to "hold" three to five "chunks," and older youngsters five to nine "chunks.") Short-term storage can accept a new chunk of information about every

Reading involves:

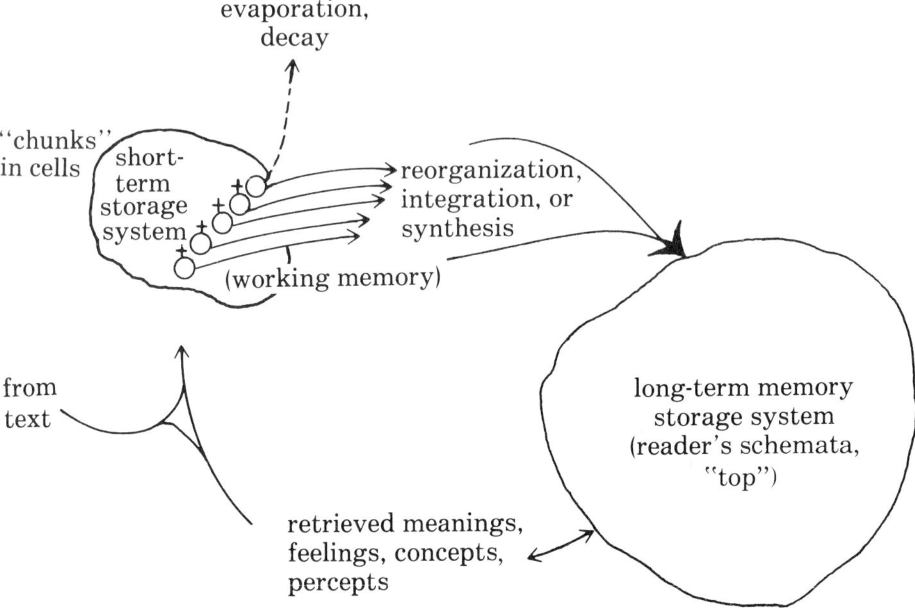

Figure 1.3

quarter of a second* and can hold such a chunk for a brief time—perhaps a few seconds.

The "working memory system," or short-term storage system, stores these chunks one to a cell or molecule. According to Waugh and Norman[24] any of the following might happen to a chunk:

1. If ignored it will decay rapidly.
2. Through rehearsal it can be renewed.
3. When the storage system is full, an item in a cell must be displaced if a new item is to enter.
4. It may be transferred to a more permanent memory system.

Gough[25] proposes that "items pass into secondary memory (long-term storage) only when they are related to one another, or integrated in some fashion akin to comprehension." According to Weaver,[26] long-term

---

*This may explain why eye fixations of efficient readers are frequently about 1/4 second in length.

memory can accept a new chunk of information about every three to five seconds. She cites psycholinguistic evidence that the clause is the major syntactic unit into which verbal material is initially rechunked for assimilation and that the clause is the major unit from which meaning is initially determined.

Knowledge of ideas similar to these has led many bottom-up advocates to a recognition of the need for "automaticity of decoding"—to be accomplished as early as possible for young readers. There are several reasons that such automaticity is important:

- If decoding (or recoding) takes too much time, the first part of a sentence or clause will slip away because decoding (or recoding) activities at the end of the sentence or clause require the use of the working memory. (It takes more time than is available to arrive at meaning.)
- The less work needed in the decoding (or recoding) act, the more room is available for comprehension and enjoyment.

One might wonder how large a "chunk" might be. The word *black* recoded (recognized) by individual letters might be five chunks (b + l + a + c + k). Recoded as *bl* + *ack*, it might be two chunks. Recoded as a word, *black* might be one chunk. On the other hand, *black* might be recoded as part of a phrase: *a black night*, and thus be only part of a chunk that might have meaning for a reader along with the rest of the sentence (clause) or sentences (clauses) needed for meaning to be determined (e.g.: "It was + a black night. + The moon + was hidden + behind the clouds." These sentences (or clauses), if understood, could then go into the long-term memory (or secondary memory) system. That is, they might go to the PWSGWTAU.*

Chunking was explained above in terms of letters and letter patterns, words, and phrases which might be synthesized into clauses or sentences (bottom-up theory). On the other hand, it is possible that units of meaning (semantic units—top-down theory) may determine chunk size. In either case, to encourage a larger chunk size, a strong argument can be made for reading at a good rate . . . for maintaining "meaning momentum."

Some reading experts have suggested that in order to encourage the chunking of larger units, we may have to relax the demand for accuracy. (These same experts, however, point out that the important growth of automaticity of decoding[27] takes place after the child has achieved accuracy of recoding or while he or she is attempting to gain speed by reading longer units.) They argue that "teachers who stress accuracy too strongly

---

*The <u>P</u>lace <u>W</u>here <u>S</u>entences <u>G</u>o <u>W</u>hen <u>T</u>hey <u>A</u>re <u>U</u>nderstood, according to Phillip B. Gough's theory.

may discourage children from developing sophisticated strategies of word recognition."

The need to maintain "meaning momentum" is apparent. However, at the present time, reading experts and teachers still debate positions on accuracy versus speed, and whether meaning follows or precedes recoding: Does recoding (pronouncing) make retrieval of meaning possible (provided that meaning is in the long-term storage system)? Or, does having meaning and retrieving it make recoding (pronouncing) possible when oral reading is engaged in, and also make recoding unnecessary in silent reading?

Definitions and Models Used in This Book

PROCESS MODELS: BOTTOM-UP AND TOP-DOWN

In the present text, both bottom-up and top-down processes are explained. This is done for several reasons:

- Experts in the field of reading do not agree as to whether the process of reading progresses in a bottom-up or top-down fashion, or is interactive, thus being some of both.
- The author of this text thinks that teachers and preservice teachers should be aware of a variety of techniques so that they may choose those that suit their philosophy of reading—which may be bottom-up, top-down, or interactive.
- Preservice teachers, especially, may not know what the philosophy of reading will be in the school in which they will teach in the future. They, therefore, should be aware of a broad range of types of activities from which they may choose when they do teach.
- The author of this text thinks that teachers may wish to choose the process or processes appropriate to the learning style of individual children, if such styles do vary.

Readers of this text are encouraged to question—whenever they consider designing and/or using a lesson plan or reading activity—whether the steps involve a top-down or bottom-up process, or perhaps both. When working with children, teachers should be aware of the choices available to them and should select techniques knowledgeably.

READING AS A MATRIXING EVENT (INTERACTIVE MODEL)

In considering both bottom-up and top-down reading processes, the author of this text finds it reasonable to consider reading as a mixture of both. Those who read with meaning must utilize concepts and images already in their thinking (long-term storage system) in order to both make sense out of the printed symbols the author supplies and to reason with the author. When vitally interested in and knowledgeable about a passage, a reader is likely to conjecture about, hypothesize about, and guess what the author will say next, and the reader will continually check these "guesses" against the text. However, when a reader is confronted with an unfamiliar passage, in terms of concepts and/or language, the reader may be text-bound, at least at times.

The following statement made by Richard Rystrom[28] suggests to the present author an interactive process model which can be illustrated to demonstrate the interaction of top-down (concept-driven) and bottom-up (text-driven) processes that may frequently occur in normal reading situations.

"Reading is a matrixing event between the reader and the text; the matrix is a framework, or latticework, in which there is a substantial percentage of unfilled squares, which can be thought of as information gaps. In the process of reading, the reader produces a small framework of meaning based upon the information on the page and his own stored information. If there is a match, he continues, slowly expanding the grid outward, sometimes by adding information from his own experiences, at others by filling the grid with information provided by the author."

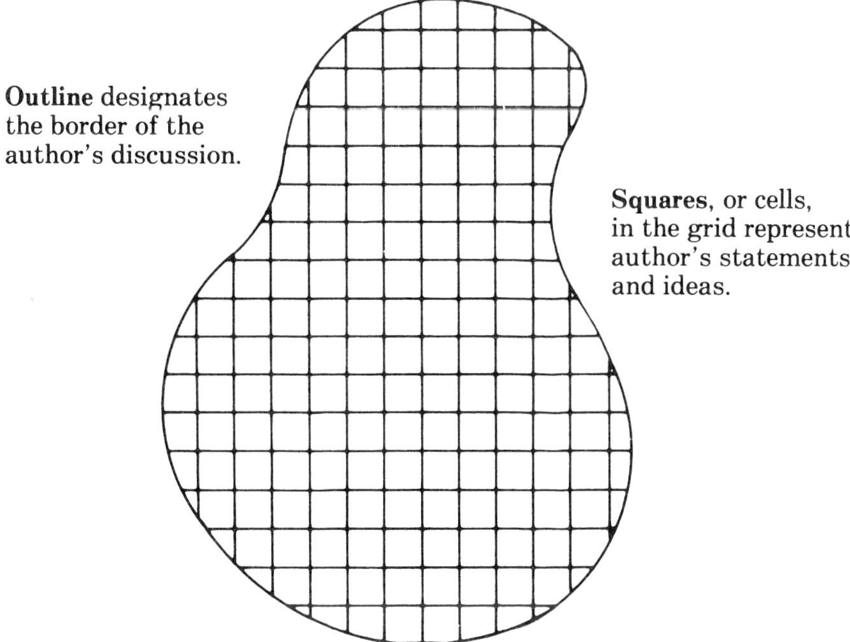

Figure 1.4

For the purpose of this discussion, let us consider a matrix to be a "latticework," a set of related "cells," those touching each other being most closely related, those farthest away from a cell being more remotely related to that cell. The cells are clustered together. In the illustration below, each cell represents one statement and/or concept the author has put in print. The border encloses the total passage.

Irene Athey[29] states, "Perhaps one of the first things a good reader does is to establish the dimensions of the subject with which he will be dealing in the paragraph, article, or volume." She suggests that the good reader uses all possible clues from the passage (title, opening sentences, headings) to establish the scope of the matrix (text-bound, author's schemata). While doing this, the reader fills in squares from his or her own experience *and* from what the author says (interactive). While reading, the reader operates on his or her knowledge of the probabilities of certain events occurring—physical, social, and linguistic events (concept-bound, reader's schemata). In other words, the reader hypothesizes.

Figure 1.5 shows this interaction of the reader's schemata with the text schemata:

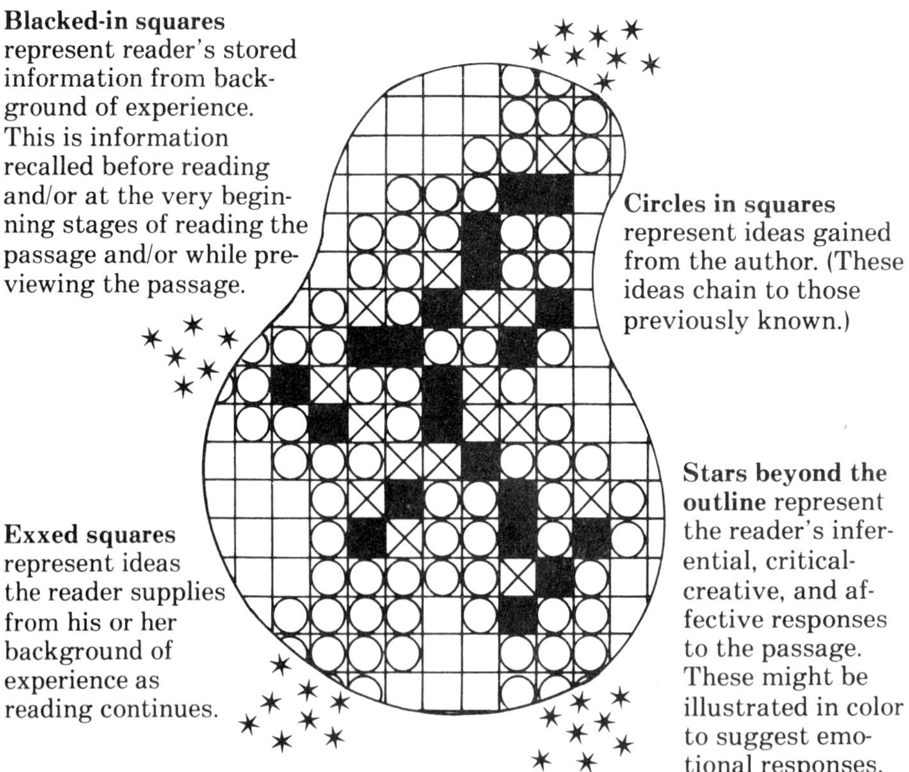

Blacked-in squares represent reader's stored information from background of experience. This is information recalled before reading and/or at the very beginning stages of reading the passage and/or while previewing the passage.

Circles in squares represent ideas gained from the author. (These ideas chain to those previously known.)

Exxed squares represent ideas the reader supplies from his or her background of experience as reading continues.

Stars beyond the outline represent the reader's inferential, critical-creative, and affective responses to the passage. These might be illustrated in color to suggest emotional responses.

Figure 1.5

Both the description and illustration indicate that what the reader brings to the passage (in terms of background of experience, concepts, understandings, etc.) is as important as what he or she takes from it. Note that what is newly learned clusters around the areas of background experience, i.e., the blacked-in and exxed squares. To be included here is the importance not only of conceptual commonalities but also of a linguistic "match" between an author and reader (that is, it is favorable if the reader and the author share linguistic schemata), which also promotes the reader's ability to process information—to literally comprehend an author's statements as well as to think beyond the author's stated ideas.

The process is illustrated in Figure 1.6.

Top: reader's schemata—focused in relation to the lesson

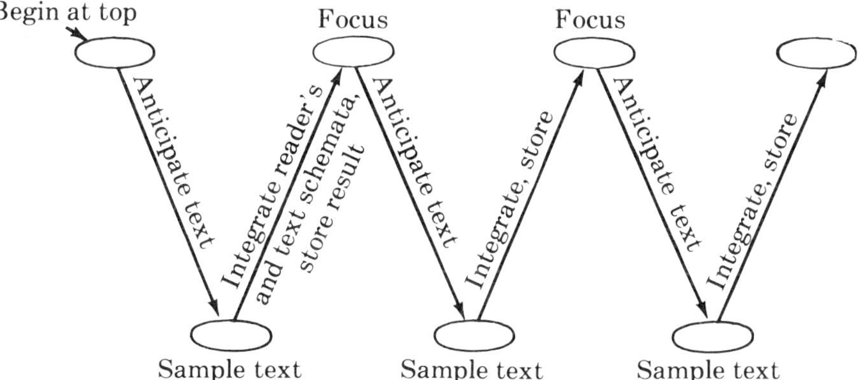

Bottom: text schemata, perception

Figure 1.6

SKILLS AND APPRECIATION

In addition to considering the process or processes used in reading and in learning to read, it is essential to decide upon the skills to be taught to help children read fluently and also to develop their enjoyment and appreciation of reading. In this book, in addition to Chapter 4, which in part describes strategies for developing reading readiness competencies, Unit Two is devoted to strategies that may be used for developing specific skills and appreciation and for uniting these in total content area lessons.

The titles of the Unit Two chapters somewhat parallel the Gray-Robinson model. They are:

Chapter 6: Recoding and Decoding: The Art of Using a Variety of
            Cue Systems

Although specific skills may be taught individually, in normal reading situations (when one is reading a story, a chapter, a book) reading is a "unitary" act—a holistic act in which all appropriate skills as well as appreciations operate together, and the processes and products of reading constantly mesh.

Summary

Many sources were used in an attempt to define reading. First, a dictionary definition was cited and analyzed. Next, children's definitions were given. These definitions usually included each child's ideas of either the process or products of reading. A few children even suggested that reading is done to satisfy goals set by schools.

Following this, definitions proposed by researchers in reading were given. Most of these were explained as models. Included were:

- The Gray-Robinson model, a traditional skills model in which the process of reading is explained as a "unitary" act composed of five facets: word perception, comprehension, reaction, assimilation of ideas, and rate, all of which constantly mesh.
- Bottom-up versus Top-Down process models, i.e., text-bound or text-driven, versus concept-bound, or concept-driven, models. A general model of the bottom-up type was first given, followed by unique models in this school of thought: Bloomfield and Barnhart's, Flesch's, Gough's, Perfetti's, and K. Goodman's "early stages" model. Top-down/interactive models explained were: Frank Smith's and K. Goodman's.

A comment relating research findings to bottom-up and top-down models concluded this section, with the statement of the possibility that an interactive model may explain the reading process. When one mode fails, the reader may transfer to the other mode. More miscues and/or comprehension errors may be made when using the less favored mode.

The next section of the chapter included a discussion of ways in which people may assimilate information. A person may hold a limited number of "chunks" of information in short-term memory before such information can be processed into long-term memory or before it evaporates from short-term memory. To increase the size and/or meaningfulness of each chunk and to promote the possibility of transferring information from short term to long-term memory, it appears that maintaining a good rate is important and is a worthwhile goal of reading instruction at an early age for children. Speed may be at the expense of accuracy, however, and therein lies a big debate.

The final section of the chapter included the explanation of the definitions and models used in this book. For reasons given in this section, activities for both bottom-up and top-down process models will be explained in the appropriate chapters later in the book.

Chapter 12: "Fusing the Teaching of Reading with the Teaching of Content" is designed to explain in some detail how reading can be taught as a "matrixing event," that is, by using an interactive model.

Questions and Activities

After answering the questions given at the beginning of this chapter, consider these questions and activities:

1. If reading is defined in this way: "Reading means pronouncing words . . . ," what kinds of activities would be stressed in a reading readiness program? in first grade? How important would oral reading be in the reading program at all grade levels? How important would comprehension be? interest in reading? How would reading achievement be evaluated? Describe classroom situations which you have observed that suggest that some teachers are defining reading in this way.

2. If reading is defined in this way: "Reading means identifying words and getting their meaning. That is, reading means going from visible surface structure to deep structure (meaning)," what kinds of activities would be stressed in a reading readiness program? in first grade? How important would oral reading be? vocabulary development? sentence understanding? literal comprehension? inferential comprehension? interest? How would reading achievement be evaluated? Describe classroom situations which you have observed that suggest that some teachers are defining reading in this way.

3. On the other hand, reading might be defined in this way: "Reading means bringing meaning *to* a text in order to get meaning from it." What are the implications of this definition in terms of a reading readiness program and a reading program? How important would it be to broaden children's direct experiences? Would it be important to discuss these experiences? Explain.

4. Which process model: bottom-up, top-down, or interactive do you favor? Why? Do you favor a different process model (or different emphases) for different grade levels? Explain.

5. What is "sentence surfing?" Is the ability to sentence surf a goal of any of the process models given in this chapter? If so, of which one(s)? Explain.

6. Consider ways in which meanings, feelings, concepts (even words) might be retrieved from a "long-term memory storage system." How do you recall meanings, feelings, concepts, etc., that you have stored? Consider experiences such as listening to music, dancing, looking at a picture, a scene, carrying on a conversation, seeing a word (or passage) in print, etc. Once former experiences are retrieved are they added to or changed by virtue of present experiences? Explain. Are some present experiences so fleeting that they evaporate before being integrated with previous experiences? Is reading just one way of adding to (or altering) our concepts in our long-term storage system?

7. In considering the definition of reading as "a matrixing event," how important are previous experiences and the retrieval of these before reading begins? While reading progresses? How can a teacher help a child build and retrieve experiences related to a reading assignment? What strategies might a child be taught that would enable him or her to retrieve concepts, etc., related to a reading passage without help from a teacher? What is the role of reviewing after an assignment is read? What is the role of diagnostic teaching?

NOTES

1. Jane King Lathum in a speech "Team Teaching, a Team Effort- Teacher and Administrator," given in El Paso, Texas, February, 1980.
2. See Helen M. Robinson in Selected References.
3. See J. P. Guilford in Selected References.
4. Constance Weaver, p. 132. See Selected References.
5. Kenneth Goodman, "The Know More . . . ," p. 659. See Selected References.

6. Connie Juel, p. 360. See Selected References.
7. See Robert C. Calfee and Priscilla Drum in Selected References.
8. *Ibid.*, p. 195.
9. Leonard Bloomfield and Clarence L. Barnhart. *Let's Read: A Linguistic Approach.* Detroit: Wayne State University Press, 1961.
10. See Philip B. Gough in Selected References.
11. Andrew Biemiller, p. 95. See Selected References.
12. See Charles Perfetti in Selected References.
13. *Ibid.*, p. 40.
14. Kenneth Goodman, "Behind the Eye . . . ," p. 481. See Selected References.
15. Kenneth Goodman, "The Know More . . . ," p. 659. See Selected References.
16. Frank Smith, pp. 70–73. See Selected References.
17. Kenneth Goodman, "Behind the Eye . . . ," pp. 482–483. See Selected References.
18. Constance Weaver, p. 127. See Selected References.
19. See Barbara Carey Hunt in Selected References.
20. Robbins Burling, pp. 158–159. See Selected References.
21. Connie Juel, p. 358. See Selected References.
22. *Ibid.*, p. 374.
23. See Andrew Biemiller in Selected References.
24. Philip B. Gough, *op. cit.*, p. 517.
25. *Ibid.*, p. 518.
26. Constance Weaver, *op. cit.*, p. 109.
27. David LaBerge and D. J. Samuels, pp. 570–573. See Selected References.
28. Richard Rystrom, in Athey, p. 87.
29. Irene Athey, p. 87. See Selected References.

SELECTED REFERENCES

Athey, Irene. "Syntax, Semantics, and Reading," in *Cognition, Curriculum, and Comprehension*, John T. Guthrie, (ed.). Newark, Delaware: International Reading Association, 1977, pp. 71–98.

Biemiller, Andrew. "The Development of the Use of Graphic and Contextual Information as Children Learn to Read." *Reading Research Quarterly*, VI, no. 1 (1970–71): 75–96.

Burling, Robbins. *English in Black and White.* New York: Holt, Rinehart and Winston, 1973.

Calfee, Robert C. and Priscilla Drum. "Learning to Read: Theory, Research, and Practice," an educational monograph sponsored by the Ontario Institute for Studies in Education. New York: John Wiley and Sons, Inc., 1978.

Clymer, Theodore L. "What Is 'Reading'?: Some Current Concepts," in *Innovation and Change in Reading Instruction, The 67th Yearbook of NSSE, Part II,*

Helen M. Robinson, (ed.). Chicago: The University of Chicago Press, 1968, pp. 7–29.

Fries, C. C. *Linguistics and Reading.* New York: Holt, Reinhart and Winston, 1963.

Goodman, Kenneth S. "Behind the Eye: What Happens in Reading," in *Theoretical Models and Processes of Reading, Second Edition*, Harry Singer and Robert B. Ruddell, (eds.). Newark, Delaware: International Reading Association, 1976, pp. 470–496.

——————————. "The Know More and the Know Nothing Movements in Reading, A Personal Response." *Language Arts*, 56 (September 1979): 657–663.

Gough, Philip B. "One Second of Reading," in *Theoretical Models and Processes of Reading, Second Edition*, Harry Singer and Robert B. Ruddell, (eds.). Newark, Delaware: International Reading Association, 1976, pp. 509–535.

Guilford, Joy P. "Frontiers in Thinking That Teachers Should Know About." *The Reading Teacher*, 13 (Feb. 1960): 176–82.

Hunt, Barbara Carey. "Black Dialect and Third and Fourth Graders' Performance on the Gray Oral Reading Test." *Reading Research Quarterly*, X, no. 1 (1974–75): 103–123.

Jones, Linda L. "An Interactive View of Reading: Implications for the Classroom." *The Reading Teacher*, 35 (April 1982): 772–777.

Juel, Connie. "Comparison of Word Identification Strategies with Varying Context, Word Type, and Reader Skill." *Reading Research Quarterly*, XV, no. 3 (1979–80): 358–376.

La Berge, David and S. J. Samuels. "Toward a Theory of Automatic Information Processing in Reading," in *Theoretical Models and Processes of Reading, Second Edition*, Harry Singer and Robert B. Ruddell, (eds.). Newark, Delaware: International Reading Association, 1976, pp. 548–579.

Lapp, Diane, James Flood, and Gary Gleckman. "Classroom Practices Can Make Use of What Researchers Learn." *The Reading Teacher*, 35 (February 1982): 578–585.

Lefevre, Carl. *Linguistics and the Teaching of Reading.* New York: McGraw-Hill, 1964.

Perfetti, Charles A. "Language Comprehension and Fast Decoding: Some Psycholinguistic Prerequisites for Skilled Reading Comprehension," in *Cognition, Curriculum, and Comprehension*, John T. Guthrie, (ed.). Newark, Delaware: International Reading Association, 1977, pp. 20–41.

Robinson, Helen M. "The Major Aspects of Reading," in *Reading: Seventy-Five Years of Progress*, (Supplementary Educational Monographs, No. 96), H. Alan Robinson, (ed.). Chicago: University of Chicago Press, 1966, pp. 22–32.

Rumelhart, David. *Toward an Interactive Model of Reading.* Center for Human Information Processing, Technical Report No. 56. University of California, San Diego, 1976.

Rystrom, Richard. "Reflections of Meaning." *Journal of Reading Behavior*, 9 (Summer, 1977): 193–200.

Strange, Michael. "Instructional Implications of a Conceptual Theory of Reading Comprehension." *The Reading Teacher*, 33 (January, 1980): 391–397.

Smith, Frank. *Understanding Reading, a Psycholinguistic Analysis of Reading and Learning to Read, Second Edition.* New York: Holt, Rinehart and Winston, 1978.

Weaver, Constance. *Psycholinguistics and Reading: From Process to Practice.* Cambridge, Mass.: Winthrop Publishers, 1980.

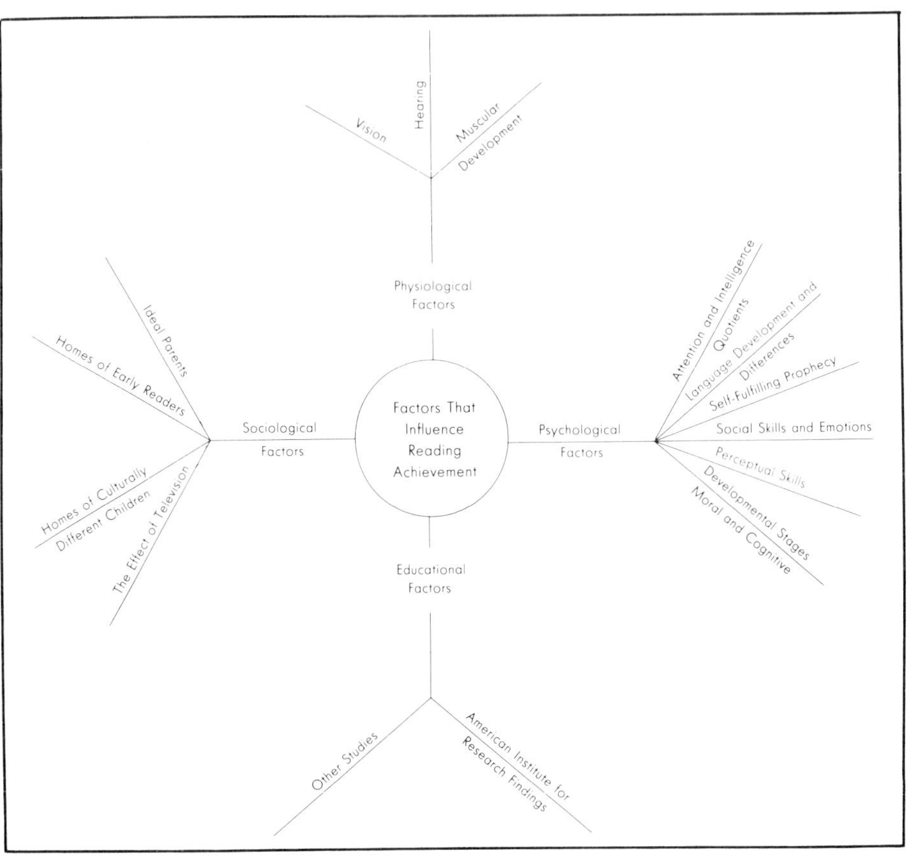

- Sociological factors relate to the home and community of the reader. What have some parents done that have helped ready their children for reading? How can we describe homes of children who read early? (What do they have in common?) What are some advantages and disadvantages of homes of culturally different children? How does T.V. affect reading ability?

- How do vision and hearing affect readiness for reading at all levels, as well as the child's ability to profit from class instruction? What are some good vision tests for reading purposes? What are the implications for the classroom teacher of the fact that much of young children's increase in weight is related to muscular development?

- How does attention affect the development of I.Q.? How does the child's language affect his or her ability to read? Do teachers' expectations affect a child's ability to perform in school? Why are social skills and the child's emotions important in learning to read? What perceptual skills are important in reading? How do Piaget's cognitive developmental stages relate to the child's ability to learn to read? Do children also progress through moral stages when maturing? If so, how does the child's moral level relate to reading?

- What does research tell us about schools that produce good readers?

CHAPTER 2

Factors That Influence Reading Achievement

You might wonder why some children read well and others read poorly. In reality, many factors affect the level of achievement that children have in reading and in reading readiness, as well as the level of interest that children display toward reading. These factors can be classified in four major categories: sociological, physiological, psychological, and educational factors. There is some overlapping among these categories. Major factors in each of these categories will be discussed in this chapter.

Sociological Factors

Sociological factors that relate to reading are those characteristics that are associated with the home, the neighborhood, and community of the child. These include characteristics of parents of the child, the home environment, and the availability and use of the library and the mass media: television, newspapers, the radio, etc.

The home and community affect the child's school achievement at all grade levels. Robert Thorndike notes that the cultural opportunities of the home are the best predictors of reading comprehension scores.[1] Both American educators and the general public have been looking more and more at the home for clues that can be used to explain in part why some children achieve to a higher degree than others. As a result of this search we know more about important factors in the home that affect reading achievement than we knew in the past. Many school systems are using these findings in formulating programs that involve parents in improving children's opportunities. Some ways of involving parents are discussed in Chapter 5 of this book.

Ideal Parents

For example, Burton White[2] and others at Harvard University found that the best parents (or other home-based adults) are not those who are constantly helping the child. Rather, the best parents are those who are regularly available as consultants or facilitators. The ideal parent is not a "stimulator," one who constantly works with the child—talking, playing, helping, advising. Instead, the ideal parent answers questions when asked, supplies materials when needed, helps solve problems the child has encountered, and offers an occasional suggestion. The ideal parent does not create situations for the child but, instead, when asked, responds to the situations created by the child. The ideal parent provides an environment that enhances, or facilitates, "learning by doing" but does not teach or "do for" the child.

Next in importance, according to White, is that ideal parents "supply a series of relevant models which have an orienting or motivating effect, rather than an intellectual effect" on the child. For example, an ideal parent is seen reading, enjoys discussions, and leads the child toward the expectation that school is to be used as a resource.

Homes of Early Readers

When Dolores Durkin[3] studied the backgrounds of children who read before entering school, she found some very interesting characteristics of these children and also of their homes. She found that early readers were inquisitive about written language, asking questions such as:

"What does that sign say?"
"Where does it say that?"
"Make me my name."
"How do you make a *b*?"

And she found that parents responded positively to these questions.

Not unexpectedly, she found that early readers come from homes in which people read and that at least one parent was a frequent reader. She found, also, that early readers had been read to regularly—often from a very early age.

Dr. Durkin also found that parents in these homes enjoyed their children—frequently taking them places, discussing with them what had been seen, and answering questions the children asked and sometimes stimulating more questions. And she found that "deliberate attempts on the part of parents to teach their preschoolers to read were uncommon." The help given to the child was in response to the child's questions and requests for help.

She also found that adults provided materials of interest to children and an environment that promoted questioning and learning. Such materials as the following were found to arouse curiosity: books, calendars (words, numbers, pictures), games for which directions had to be read, labels on boxes and canned goods, etc. She did find that an older sister of the child who learned to read early often played school with the child —teaching the child as she was being taught in school. This sister was about two years older than the child.

HOMES OF CULTURALLY DIFFERENT CHILDREN

Homes of culturally different children may offer these children some advantages. For example, Frank Riesman[4] suggests the following benefits: cooperativeness, security, and mutual aid among children and adults, which frequently characterize members of an extended family. He also indicates that there is likely to be a lessened sense of rivalry, as well as the avoidance of strain that frequently accompanies competitiveness among middle class children.

These advantages, however, may be counter-balanced by the following disadvantages, given by James Laffey and Raymond Morgan:[5]

1. The language used in the homes of these children is usually different from the language the children encounter in their schools. It has been estimated that the comprehension vocabulary of the disadvantaged child in the initial years of school is between one-third and one-half of that of the middle class child.
2. Culturally different children frequently come from crowded and noisy homes in which they are afforded little or no privacy. In order to survive in such an environment, they often psychologically shut out many stimuli. As a result, they miss many experiences, and they find it difficult to reverse the procedure and "tune-in" in school.
3. For the above reasons, plus others, school activities frequently do not hold the attention of culturally different children, and these children frequently become discipline problems. Also, their parents may be more used to defeat than to success, and these parents may have done poorly in school. As a result, they may not provide an example of success in education for their children. Also, these parents may be unable or unavailable to control their children. In addition, the child's sense of individualism or ethnic pride may prevent him or her from conforming to middle class standards.

In a highly informative study done by Ronald Henderson, family variables were measured among a sample of Mexican-American children when they entered first grade. When these children completed third grade, it was found that achievement press (parental pressure for their child's achievement) was the highest correlate of reading success among these children and that it predicted reading status for these children more accurately than did most reading readiness and I.Q. tests.[6]

THE EFFECT OF TELEVISION

One might expect television to have a wide and strong impact on reading achievement, especially among young children. Virtually every child in the United States can watch television if he or she wishes, and most do watch regularly. One might also expect television to have the greatest impact on children whose home language differs from the language used in schools, for the language of television approximates school language, it seems. Yet, culturally different children may not benefit much or at all from watching T.V. This is true even when we consider the viewing of Sesame Street and The Electric Company.

According to Pose Lamb,[7] "simply watching a T.V. lesson brought by the letter H is not enough." The greatest benefits accrue when the T.V. lesson is supplemented by work with parents, teachers, or aides. She also argues that preparation for listening and viewing is needed. When T.V. is viewed at home, it is more likely that middle class parents, rather than lower class parents, will discuss programs with their children.

Reports about schools suggest that frequently when educational television is watched in schools, teachers feel the program does it all. Often no introduction or summary is given, and no extension activities are used. In fact, the teacher frequently leaves the class alone to view the program, so he or she does not even know what was included in the program.

Many educators think that the content of Sesame Street is too narrow in scope to be of real value, for perceptual skills, rather than concept development or problem solving, are given major attention: children are taught letters, numbers, and object-matching skills. Both Sesame Street and The Electric Company might make a more significant contribution by developing higher level cognitive skills and critical-creative thinking, and by exposing children to a wide variety of children's literature and authors, rather than by concentrating on perceptual skills, according to Lamb.[8] However, some other programs such as Mr. Rogers do help children in the development of self-concept and social skills, and Captain Kangaroo provides for concept development.

Robinson, Strickland, and Cullinan,[9] as well as others, have made important observations about television and its effect on the language development of young children. They note that young children who watch much television have not demonstrated unusual language control. They use the terms *active* and *passive* use of language. As Pose Lamb indicated, they, too, argue that "models without participation and active use by children have a limited effect." The active language of the culturally different child is not the language of T.V. In other words, the language the child uses regularly is not T.V. language. Children are involved in the use of their language, and they only passively watch and listen to T.V. unless someone involves them.

Even for children in the cultural mainstream of American life, the effect of television on positive reading achievement is less than the effect of children's books read to or by them. When comparing the language of television with that of books, it is obvious that television frequently uses short, fragmentary sentences while books use longer and more complex constructions. So, reading books to children prepares children for the syntactical structures found in the books they read, or will read, better than listening to television does. Book reading also promotes an active use of the imagination, whereas television frequently supplies all of the pictures. In television, almost everything is given.

According to Nancy Larrick,[10] the average American child has viewed television for 5,000 hours by the time she or he enters first grade. From this time on, more time is spent watching T.V. at home than is spent in school. Because of T.V. these children are "habituated to instant gratification, quick change of scene and situation, sharp emotional impact, (and) continuous sound . . ." All this requires little or no effort on their part and very little intellectual commitment. Marie Winn[11] calls T.V. the "plug-in drug" and points out that the pace of television programs restricts the opportunity of viewers to use their imagination.

Yet, T.V. is not without value. Larrick[12] cites the fact that I.Q. scores are rising among preschool children. (In 1972 four-year-olds averaged scores of 110 based on 1960 standard scores, and 5½ -year-olds averaged 111 based on these same standard scores, both of which were 100 in 1960.)

Pauline Gough[13] suggests that we might ask any children's librarian which books rarely gather dust on the shelves. She says that one answer will be "books that are television related." Gough also makes a strong point for instructional television (ITV): "ITV's advantage is that it can bring skilled, professional storytellers into every classroom . . . it can dramatize exciting excerpts to make a book come alive . . . it can give viewers a personal brush with a book's creator . . . (it) is able to use a wide variety of related arts: paintings, drawings, pantomime, puppetry, dance, background music, sound effects." In her article, she describes specific ITV programs that motivate.

Physiological Factors

Among the most important physical factors that relate to reading are vision and hearing. Another physical factor deserving strong attention at the readiness and beginning reading stages is that of muscular development. These are discussed in this section.

VISION

Visual defects that may affect reading achievement are hyperopia, extreme myopia, poor binocular coordination, and poor fusion. A person who is hyperopic (far-sighted) has poor near-point acuity and, therefore, will find it difficult to see sharp images when reading a book. A person with extreme myopia (near-sightedness) may have to hold the book too close to the eyes for physical comfort, and will have difficulty reading the board.

Normally the two eyes are used together in reading. If both eyes do not focus simultaneously on the same object, the image may be blurred. Also, the eye lenses must focus with precision on an object if the images seen by the two eyes are to fuse so that only one object is seen.

The Snellen test is the visual test used most frequently in schools. However, it will screen out only those children who have myopia, and myopia, if it is not extreme, does not negatively affect reading achievement, except in cases where reading may be done at a distance—as when reading the board or overhead projections or charts at a distance. Children with hyperopia normally pass the Snellen test, as do children with binocular defects. The following tests are better for screening vision for reading purposes:

Massachusetts Vision Test
AO School Vision Screening Test
Keystone Visual Survey Test
Ortho-Rater[14]

To be considered also is the impact that poor vision may have on concept development, that is, on the development of the child's schemata. Children who cannot see well may be limited in their ability to learn from their environment—both in reading and in nonreading situations. Preschool and school children frequently read traffic signs, store signs, T.V. ads, etc. Myopic children may have visual problems that hinder them in these areas. Also, all people learn a great deal by looking at things and visually examining them, and they frequently enjoy such experiences. The child with limited visual ability may not benefit as much from such experiences as the child with normal vision will.

HEARING

Poor hearing may be a contributing factor in reading disability because: *First*—children normally learn to speak through listening. So, both the vocabulary and sentence patterns of children who hear poorly are likely to be inadequate. In addition, these children will not have been able to benefit in other ways from listening experiences—being read to, reasoning with others, enjoying conversations, etc. *Second*—children may be taught to read through an oral approach. Those who cannot hear well will have difficulty in auditorily perceiving differences in sounds, and, therefore, they may not learn to read well. (These children, however, could learn to read by using another approach.) *Third*—children who cannot hear well cannot benefit from class discussions, nor can they follow oral directions given by the teacher.

Children who are hard of hearing may not be aware that they hear any differently than other children do, for they have no standard against which to judge. It is extremely important for children to hear well in school if it is possible. Therefore, the teacher should be alert to detect any signs of hearing loss, such as inattentiveness, poor pronunciation, frequent misunderstanding of simple directions, turning one ear toward the speaker, etc.

Children probably have been tested for hearing losses, but teachers often do not know how to interpret the results of an audiometer test. According to Harris and Sipay, "a hearing loss of over 25 decibels is almost certain to handicap a child in hearing in classroom situations and is usually accompanied by some indistinctness in speech."[15] A child who exhibits a significant hearing loss probably needs professional help.

MUSCULAR DEVELOPMENT

According to Robinson, *et al.*,[16] 75 percent of a five-year-old's increase in weight is due to muscular development. That is one reason why five-year-olds are so physically active. The authors suggest that because of this high activity level, "any instructional period of more than fifteen minutes should include physical activity. Games, such as 'clapping games,' and the use of manipulative materials meet the young child's action needs in reading-related instruction." Many activities suggested in this book for reading instruction at the readiness and primary levels include physical activity.

Psychological Factors

Psychological factors that relate to reading are diverse. A few of these will be discussed here. Included are: attention and I.Q., language development and language differences, the self-fulfilling prophecy, social skills and emotions, perceptual skills related to reading, and developmental stages of the child—moral and cognitive. Interest, related to some factors discussed in this section, will be discussed in a later chapter.

ATTENTION AND INTELLIGENCE QUOTIENTS

According to Jean Mackworth,[17] the best learners are not only in a suitable physiological state of alertness, but also are ready and able to direct their attention toward the task at hand. Children may lack alertness and, therefore, lack attention because of over- or understimulation. For example, overstimulated children may be unable to pay attention to a task because they are preoccupied in thinking about their problems, fears, hunger, excitement, anger, etc. Understimulated children may be drowsy, uninquisitive, and uninterested. It may be extremely difficult to arouse these children and to gain their attention.

Children who have built up a large store of information and concepts in their long-term memories have done so through active participation, which requires attention, motivation, and a wide range of experiences. Slowness in building this long-term storage system has a cumulative effect on learning. Children who are less competent in building their long-term memory systems—perhaps because of lack of motivation and opportunity—fall further and further behind because they have less and less to build upon. Even after such children begin to read, the less skilled readers fall further and further behind because they read less than do other children and, therefore, never build up the highly over-learned associations that help them decode and recode and/or predict probabilities of what will come next in the text (that help them maintain reading momentum and interact with the author).

Belmont and Butterfield[18] suggest that "long-term mental storage may be adequate in retardates but that their difficulty may be in coding the material into store." Such coding refers to understanding and enjoying a wide range of experiences as well as language. They continue: "Since coding depends on familiarity with the code, slowness has a highly cumulative effect." School-age children who have not "broken the code" in reading (who do not recode and/or decode as easily as do other children and/or are not familiar with the meanings of the words and concepts.) or who are reading a language whose syntax doesn't match theirs (and, therefore, find it difficult to break the syntactical code of the text) are at a definite disadvantage in transferring information in reading situations from short-term to long-term memory. It has been hypothesized that some children may have difficulty in coding into long-term memory, whereas others may have problems in retrieving information from long-term memory. Those children who are termed intelligent by present-day standards have been found to use a wide range of strategies to build their long-term memories.[19]

Several additional related findings are worthy of the consideration of teachers. Albert J. Harris,[20] in a recent article in *The Reading Teacher*, cites evidence from the research of others that the easier the reading material is in relation to a child's reading achievement, the better the child's classroom behavior is likely to be. That is, the greater attention the child will give to the reading task, and the less the child is likely to distract others. He also cites evidence that teaching that encompasses the use of warm praise and encouragement and avoids scolding, sarcasm, and other expressions of strong disapproval helps motivate children to learn.

I.Q. tests have been designed to measure the cognitive (intellectual) ability of people to function in a particular culture. The question asked is: To what degree does the child have in his or her long-term storage system language, experiences, and thinking skills that will enable him or her to intellectually function in that culture? Many educators today seriously question the validity of I.Q. test scores for children who live predominantly in one culture (i.e., home culture) but are tested using the standards of another culture (e.g., the school culture, the middle class culture). Though you may not consider it apropos to cite the following example,[21] perhaps it will help clarify the concept.

Koko, perhaps the first gorilla to "talk" (by means of a sign language) with a person on a regular basis, was given the Stanford-Binet Intelligence Test three times between the ages of three-and-a-half and about four-and-a half years. Each time she scored between 84 and 95, just below the average for humans. However, her responses to several questions were quite logical for her, but were marked wrong because they did not reflect correct responses in human culture, which indicates how the test must be scored. In response to the question: "Point to two things that are good to eat" (a block, an apple, a shoe, a flower, an ice cream sundae), Koko pointed to the apple and the flower, quite appropriate for a gorilla. Another question asked her to pick where she would run in the rain (a hat, a spoon, a tree, a house). Koko chose the tree. Koko made many other similar "errors" and was penalized for them. Koko might have scored in the genius category had her responses that were logical in her culture been scored as correct on the test. But, then, Koko is probably a very bright gorilla since she is the first gorilla to learn and to use a human sign language.

Human children make similar "errors." They frequently respond logically in terms of their culture, but illogically in terms of the mainstream. For example, look at the following items from different I.Q. tests:

- Put these into two categories: orange, cucumber, onion, banana. (The only "correct" answer is fruits and vegetables. Middle class children usually classify by function. Culturally different children often classify by color or shape.)
- Point to the one
  - we carry when it's raining. (given at age 4 and later. Many desert children who have not traveled have never seen an umbrella.)
  - we use to iron clothes. (given at age 3½ and later. Nowadays many people never iron.)

- that catches mice. (given at age 4 and later. This may be more fair for lower class youngsters than for middle class children.)
- that gives us milk. (given at age 4 and later. There is no picture of a supermarket, etc.)
- What is the thing to do if someone hits you?
(The "correct" answer is walk away.)

Scores on such tests may suggest success or failure in school if the children are taught in terms of the mainstream. Needless to say, I.Q. tests are extremely unfair to culturally different children. Also, written I.Q. tests are extremely unfair to poor readers, since such children cannot read the tests. Joel R. Levin[22] notes that correlation between I.Q. and learning ability is strong for middle class children but is weak for lower class children. He says that middle class children with low I.Q.'s probably are slow learners as well. The same cannot be said of lower class children.

For many middle class Americans, I.Q. scores may indicate potential for cognitive learning for a brief period of time after the test is given. A score of 95–105 (or 90–110) suggests average potential for achievement. (The child should be reading approximately at grade level and should make normal progress.) A score above this indicates that better than average potential and achievement should be expected. And a score below 95 or 90 indicates that it is likely that the child will be achieving at a grade level lower than average and will learn more slowly than average.

There are two full-scale I.Q. tests (including verbal and nonverbal subtests) that might be given to children and young people. They are the Stanford-Binet Intelligence Scale and the Wechsler tests (WPPSI— Wechsler Preschool and Primary Scale of Intelligence, WISC-R— Wechsler Intelligence Scale for Children-Revised, and the WAIS— Wechsler Adult Intelligence Scale). These tests can be given only by trained psychometrists. Other individual "intelligence tests" include the Slosson Intelligence Test, Peabody Picture Vocabulary Test (PPVT), and the Goodenough-Harris Drawing Test.[23] In addition, there are group tests that may be given to children, but most, or all, of these require reading achievement comparable to the level of the test.[24]

Language Development and Language Differences

Oral language competence is of paramount importance in reading development for most children. Except for the deaf or hard-of-hearing child or the person learning to read a foreign language who never plans to speak it, oral language is normally considered the primary language. (Written English is, for example, a phonic or alphabetic recoding of oral English.)

In "bottom-up" reading programs, children learn to recode print to sound. In "top-down" programs, deep structure (meaning) is normally assumed to be present. (In some top-down programs, e.g., the Language Experience Approach,* the teacher or child recodes sound to print; next the child learns the print to sound associations.) Before reading begins and as it progresses, children build this deep structure through having experiences, discussing these experiences, and through listening. Without an understanding of the meanings of words and strings of words, no meaning can be attached to symbols in print. Except in the most extreme bottom-up programs, this would mean failure in reading even though words might be pronounced correctly (through the use of phonics, or other recoding approach, and the use of a sight vocabulary).

If you accept (or consider for acceptance) the model given in Chapter One of this book concerning the assimilation of ideas, you will consider the idea that meanings are both retrieved from and new ones added to the long-term memory system (assimilated) through the reading act. Without the retrieval of meanings, what may be "read" has no meaning.

Children learn language partly through imitation. They listen to and copy what they hear—hence the importance to children of having the opportunity to hear language from the earliest age. Children also learn language through their ability to generalize. The ability to generalize is in part dependent upon the child's opportunity to listen.

Upon listening, children form their own rules about grammar. In the initial stages these rules may not be completely consistent with the grammar of the language to which the children listen. This is especially evident when we look at children's tendency to regularize irregular forms. For example, the plural of *foot* may be expressed thus: *foots, feets, feetses,* and finally *feet.* Similarly, children may show evidence of active grammatical construction (of generalizing) when using forms such as "He goed" and "I taked it." In these cases, the child has overgeneralized.[25]

According to Robert Ruddell,[26] ". . . the child's ability to generalize and extend production of language forms is basic to language learning. Imitating an appropriate adult model is important in language learning, but the child's ability to form generalizations about language patterning appears to be central. The fact that the child comprehends adult language utterances considerably before he can produce such utterances also lends support to the importance of internalized grammatical generalizations that are basic to comprehension and production." By kindergarten or first grade, most children do comprehend sentences and can produce expanded and elaborated sentences, but they must also be helped to continue developing this ability in the elementary school, for some complex subordination forms are not known at the early ages.

---

*See Chapter 13 for a discussion of this approach.

Individual children vary greatly in their ability to produce and understand language principally because of variables in the home situation—their opportunities to observe and use language at home, their opportunities to interact with others, to reason with others. Also, the type of language used at home is important. Is it the same language that is used in school? In addition to variables considered in relation to children reared in homes in which middle class English is spoken, it is necessary to consider language variables related to children brought up in homes in which variant dialects are spoken and in which foreign languages are spoken. You may wish to see Ruddell's excellent treatment of this topic in the source cited above.

Language variations should not be considered deficits. Rather, they should be viewed as differences. Children usually are competent in their own language, but their language may not be the language of the school they attend or of the teacher who teaches them. For the benefit of the child's self-concept, it is extremely important that the teacher respect the child's home language.

THE SELF-FULFILLING PROPHESY

Teachers must guard against their own biases, prejudices, and value systems. From kindergarten and first grade on, children frequently become victims or benefactors of these biases. A great deal has been written recently about what is sometimes called "Pygmalion in education," or the "self-fulfilling prophecy." Such books and articles merit the attention of educators.[27]

Frequently teachers are found grouping children in kindergarten and first grade according to the degree to which each child approximates (or fails to approximate) the teacher's "ideal type." Children in kindergarten and first grade may thus be grouped on the basis of the father's and/or mother's occupation, the neatness and variety of clothing, grooming of hair and body, ease of interaction with adults, degree of verbalization in "Standard American English," and anything else that relates to the teacher's model of the "ideal type" of child, including sex stereotypes. Teachers may designate some children as "fast learners" (and others as "slow learners"), may give the favored children more of their time and attention, and may reward their behaviors in positive ways (and reward the other children's behaviors in negative ways).

Children thus grouped soon "learn their place" because of the differential treatment of the teacher toward the children in the various groups. If such treatment persists from September to May of the child's first year in school, it frequently continues into successive years—where the next teachers continue to use similar grouping patterns. (Even cumulative folders follow a child when transferred to another school.) Also, the children have learned what to expect from themselves and their peers. Thus the teacher's prophecy is frequently fulfilled.[28] The die is cast at a very tender age as a result of the biases and prejudices of the teacher, not as a result of the child's qualities, except as they relate to the teacher's value system.

The chart in Fig. 2.1 illustrates the system in action.

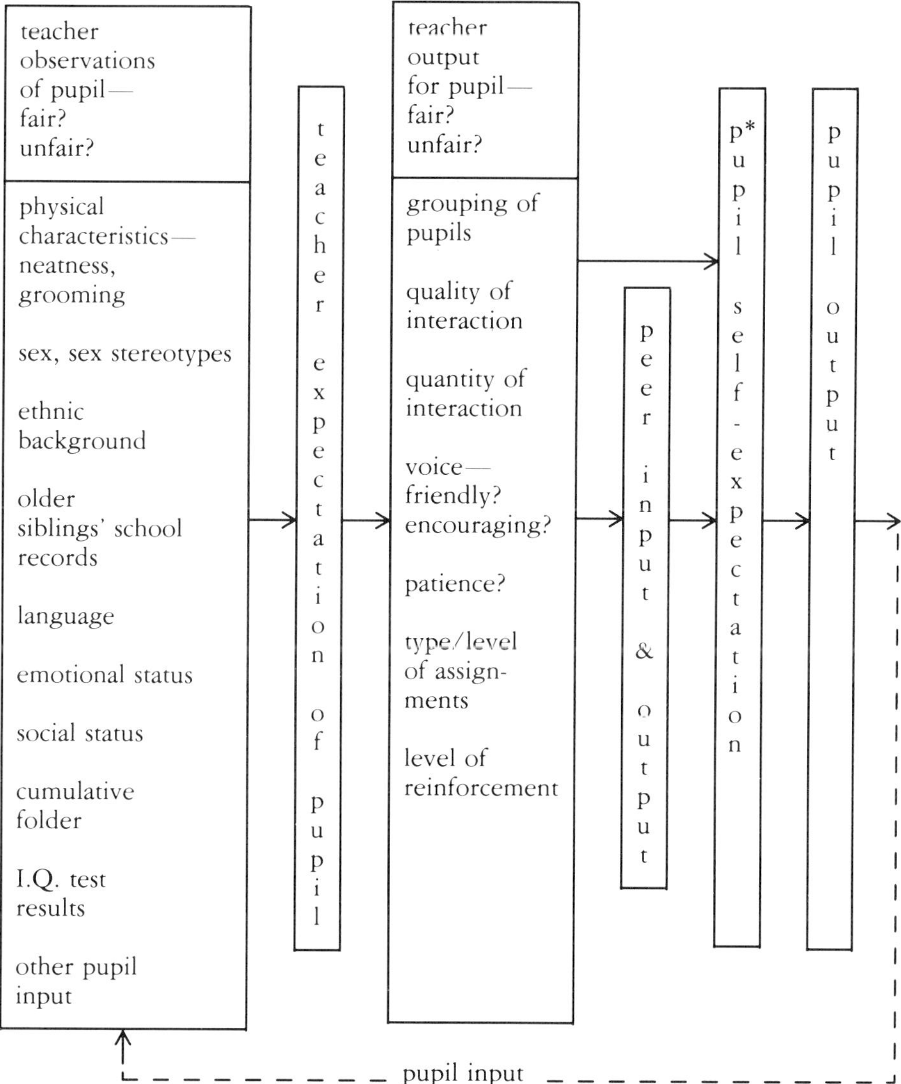

Figure 2.1: The "self-fulfilling prophecy" or "Pygmalian in education" process.

*Pupil self-expectation may be strongly (or weakly) affected by factors outside of the classroom also. In some cases this may weaken or even negate the influence of the teacher and/or peers—for good or for bad.

Of major concern to educators should be the school's role in promoting equal opportunity for all children and young people. However, it is undoubtedly true that teachers—including good teachers—will have different expectations for different children. The important point appears to be whether or not these expectations "are based on accurate perceptions of pupil behavior and whether they are flexible or rigid."[29]

Social Skills and Emotions

Poor social skills may interfere with learning at any age. Some children find it difficult to cooperate with others, to participate fairly with children in games and other activities, to share ideas with others, or to work along with a teacher. Without such social behaviors, children may have difficulty functioning in group settings typical of school learning.

Sometimes emotional problems contribute to reading disability. Such problems should be carefully considered if some evidence of them seems apparent. It is quite possible that professional help may be needed in solving severe emotional problems. Types of problems a teacher might be alert to detect are:[30]

1. *conscious refusal to learn.* The child may refuse to learn because he or she is imitating an admired parent, sibling, or other adult who shows contempt for "book learning."
2. *displacement of hostility.* The child may be jealous of a brother or sister who is a good reader, and this hostility may be transferred to the act of reading, the sibling's strong point. Similarly, a child may be unable to express hostility in an open fashion toward a parent or teacher who is an avid reader and believes reading to be important, and may instead express the hostility by refusing to learn to read.
3. *clinging to dependency.* The overprotected child may prefer to remain helpless. Learning to read may suggest to a child self-reliance, a step for which the child may not be ready. To some children, success is dangerous.
4. *extreme distractability or restlessness.* The child may be restless and easily distracted, perhaps because of neurological deviation or because of the need for physical activity or because of poor nutrition.
5. *absorption in a private world.* The child may be preoccupied with concerns beyond the school or with daydreams. According to Harris and Sipay, "Some of these children, who seem merely to be inattentive so far as the teacher is concerned, are found to have severe mental disturbances . . ."

George Dennison[31] adds an additional example: "Jose's reading problem is Jose . . . Jose hates books, schools, and teachers, and among a hundred other insufficiencies—all of a piece—he cannot read. Is this a reading problem?"

It is not enough to detect and seek treatment for problem situations, however. Teachers are responsible for providing a healthy atmosphere in the classroom. Each child deserves to be in a completely safe environment—one in which he or she is a valued person, no matter what his or her idiosyncracies might be. Each child deserves positive reinforcement, too, and an opportunity to grow up.

PERCEPTUAL SKILLS RELATED TO READING

Perceptual skills are usually classified in the psychomotor domain (i.e., they require both psychological, or mental, abilities and also motor, or physiological, abilities). Harris and Sipay list the following perceptual skills as important to reading:[32] figure and ground, closure, sequence, learning, set, and discrimination.

Figure and ground applies to both auditory and visual perception. A person with satisfactory figure-ground auditory perceptual ability is able to isolate, or identify, from the complete background of sounds the ones that are appropriate to concentrate on. For example, there may be the sound of a jet, background music, children playing next door, yet the child can concentrate on what the teacher is saying. This requires the ability to "mask" out unrelated or inappropriate sounds. A person with satisfactory figure-ground visual perceptual ability is able to, for example, isolate, or identify, from everything in his or her visual field the symbols or words necessary in a specific learning situation.

Closure applies to auditory, visual, or motor perceptual skills. A person with closure ability is able to complete something that is incomplete. For example, a child may hear only part of a word or sentence and may be able to complete it satisfactorily using his or her background of experience. A child may see (or visually recognize) only part of an object, sentence, or word and be able to complete it satisfactorily by using her or his background or experience (e.g., the Canadian flag is red, ____, and blue). Using visual-motor skills, a child may be able to complete "prompts" when learning to form letters, or complete pictures that are incomplete.

$$(\text{E.g., } \downarrow\!\lfloor\_ \rightarrow \lfloor .)$$

Sequence means order or organizational pattern. A person with the ability to sequence, for example, may be able to put letters together in the proper order to compose words, may be able to put words together to form phrases and sentences, and may be able to put sentences together to create paragraphs, etc. Or the person may be able to recognize that this has been done by others. (The reader is synthesizing information.) Conversely (analyzing information), the person may be able to start with larger units and proceed to ordering the parts. When reading English another sequential ability is necessary: the ability to move one's eyes from left to right.

Learning is dependent on a background of experience, and the learner proceeds to extend that background. Reading as a "matrixing event"* helps to explain such learning.

Set, or "mindset" is also explained in the reading as a matrixing event theory. It is helpful, perhaps necessary, to anticipate or to hypothesize about what one is learning or is about to learn. According to the top-down, concept-bound, theory of reading, the active reader is always generating guesses or hypotheses about the text and is operating on his or her "knowledge of the probabilities of certain events occurring. . . ."

Discrimination refers to the development of auditory, visual, and visual-motor (kinesthetic) skills and the integration of these. Recoding means going from one code (e.g., visual) to another code (e.g., auditory). Children progress in their ability to discriminate as they become better readers.

DEVELOPMENTAL STAGES OF THE CHILDREN: MORAL AND COGNITIVE

G. Robert Carlsen, author of *Books and the Teen-Age Reader,*[33] says that teenagers frequently choose to read books in which the major characters are one step beyond their (the reader's) stage of development. For example, juniors and seniors want to know what it's like to be out of school, to have a job, and to be married.

Lawrence Kohlberg[34] lists and explains six stages of moral reasoning** that children pass through to adulthood. Kohlberg has found that a child's highest stage of moral reasoning sets the limits on what he or she can comprehend. When asked to state resolutions to moral dilemmas, children usually can do so only if the dilemma can be solved at their highest stage of moral reasoning or below that stage. The child's level of ability to state or restate the resolution is called the child's "production stage."

---

* See Chapters 1 and 12 of this book.
**See the discussion of these stages in Chapter 9.

Bernard Rihn[35] indicates that children, however, "instinctively prefer as better resolutions those which are one stage above their production stage, i.e., their 'comprehension stage.'" He adds: "Children generally do not understand, and thus cannot produce, resolutions two stages in advance of their production stage." Rihn suggests that it might be of value to explore as an interest factor the moral reasoning level of a protagonist in a story and its relationship to a child's developmental level of moral reasoning.

Besides passing through stages in moral development, children also progress through stages in cognitive (intellectual, including perceptual) development. These have been thoroughly researched and explained by Piaget.[36] The following chart gives a general description of the stages and the usual age levels characteristic of each stage. Included, also, are some suggested activities.

Photo courtesy of Frank Ainsa.

Piaget's stages of cognitive development

Stage + Age	*Description and Possible Implications*
Sensorimotor period *ages 0-2* *Preoperational period*	Children use physical manipulation to recognize objects, progressing through these stages:

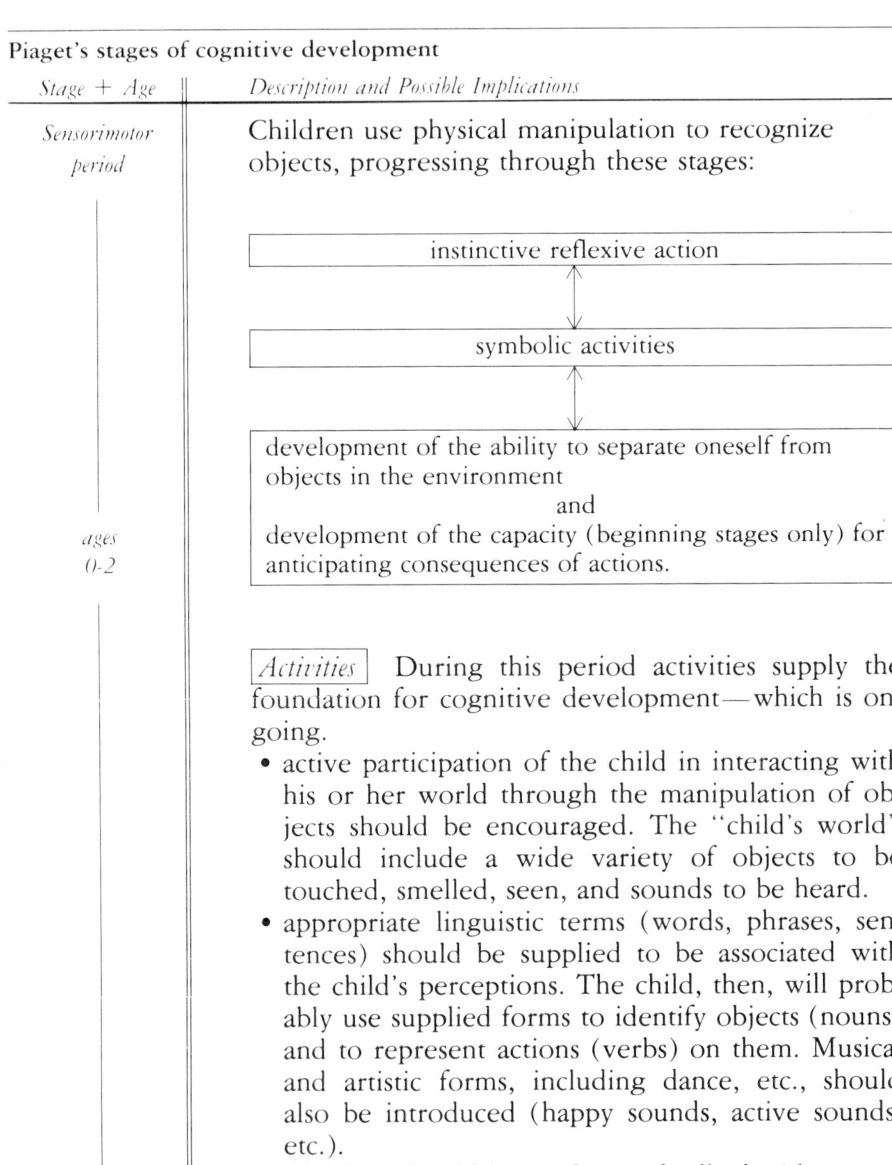

	<u>*Activities*</u> During this period activities supply the foundation for cognitive development—which is on-going.

- active participation of the child in interacting with his or her world through the manipulation of objects should be encouraged. The "child's world" should include a wide variety of objects to be touched, smelled, seen, and sounds to be heard.
- appropriate linguistic terms (words, phrases, sentences) should be supplied to be associated with the child's perceptions. The child, then, will probably use supplied forms to identify objects (nouns) and to represent actions (verbs) on them. Musical and artistic forms, including dance, etc., should also be introduced (happy sounds, active sounds, etc.).
- Children should be read to and talked with.

The child's ability to think continues to be refined. Two stages have been defined, corresponding with progressing chronological ages. During both of these stages, the child is characterized by

- *egocentricity*. The child feels that his or her viewpoint is the only one. The child is unable to take another's viewpoint or to see that he or she might be incorrect.

ages
2 to 6 or 7

- *inability to reverse.* The child has not attained the ability to go back and forth in a situation. The child has trouble seeing cause and effect relationships.
- *inability to conserve.* The child is unable to recognize that quantities, or characteristics, remain stable even when put in another form. A cup of soil in a small container appears to be less than a cup of soil spread over the surface of several large flower pots, even though the child watches the spreading of the soil. A clay ball seems to be smaller than the same mass formed into a flat plate.
- *centration.* The child focuses (or centers) on one characteristic of an object or idea and ignores other facets or characteristics.
- *inability to seriate.* The child is unable to arrange objects in order (e.g., according to height) and is unable to determine where an object belongs in an arrangement. The child finds it difficult to arrange objects in classes (e.g., pets vs. wild animals) and finds it especially difficult to see how one object can belong to several classes at the same time (e.g., a person can be a resident of Chicago and Illinois and the United States at the same time).

First stage:

preconceptual thinking

ages
2-4

- The child is concerned with individual things, but is unable to group objects. . .
- The child is able to use symbols (e.g., words) to deal with problems. The child learns that one thing may stand for another, e.g.,
  - a word represents an object or movement
  - a three-dimensional stuffed animal represents a real animal
  - a picture represents an object
  - writing represents meaning
  - musical tones, phrases, sentences represent objects, movements, thoughts, feelings

ages
4 to 6 or 7

Activities   During this period activities supply the opportunity for cognitive, including language, development—which is on-going, beginning at birth and continuing through a lifetime.
- rich and varied concrete (real) experiences are essential, including experiences in manipulating objects. To develop the symbolic function, language must be associated with these experiences. Children should be talked with, played with. . . music, art, dance should be included.
- children should be read to.

Second stage:

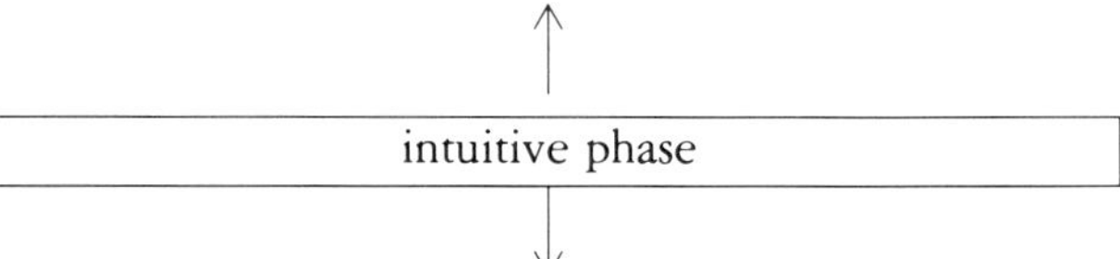

- The child continues to develop reasoning abilities and begins to be able to:
  - group objects into classes, but still has difficulty seeing that an object can be classified in two or more groups at the same time.
  - form "family name" concepts for groups (e.g., cats, dogs, and cows are animals)
  - use logical thought
- The child
  - uses the grammar (syntax) of the language of his or her environment.
  - continues to develop vocabulary
  - learns some time and space relationships and has some idea of cause-effect relationships. (Such relationships, however, are frequently erroneous because of the child's likelihood of focusing on only one characteristic or quality of an object or idea, i.e., of centrating).

Activities   Activities and experiences during this period continue to influence the child's cognitive, including language, development. Previously suggested activities should be continued and enriched. Also:
- abstract terms (e.g., family names) should be included in talking with children, e.g., baseball is a sport.

- children should be reasoned with. Explanations for requests and actions should be discussed. Children should be told why they should or should not do things.
- analytical thinking may be fostered (e.g., a cat may be a pet, an animal, a Siamese, a feline, a mammal, etc.; a T.V. show may be fun to watch but a waste of time, etc.; advertisements entice a person to buy, but the object may not deliver on the promise; etc.)

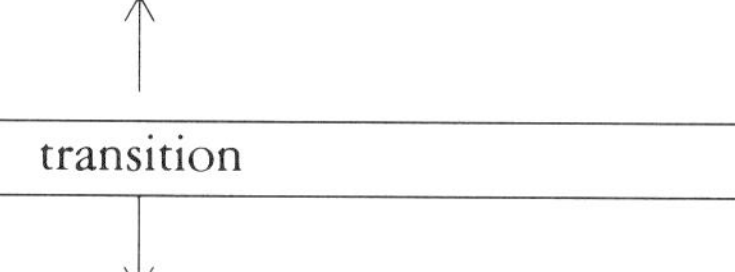

- The child is gradually moving into the next period: concrete operations. As in all phases, some children move in this period before others do. Children still in the preoperational period have not achieved the ability to
  - *conserve* (the ability to understand that slightly altered situations, symbols or forms, may represent the same concept, e.g., G, g, ɡ, or A, a, ɑ, or B, b, etc., are virtually in the same class).
  - *reverse* (the ability to go back and forth in an operation, e.g., from oral symbol to graphic symbol to oral symbol, etc.).
  - *decentrate* (the ability to simultaneously coordinate several characteristics of a situation, e.g., to simultaneously recognize a graphic symbol, the sound it represents, and its meaning).
  - *seriate or classify*, except in a very elementary way. (In phonics, the child must learn that symbol-sound relationships may be complex, e.g., <a> represents different sounds in cap, able, car, alone, father, etc., and /ā/ may be spelled with various symbols, e.g., maid, pay, cafe, steak, cake, etc.)

(transition)

Concrete Operations

conservation, reversability, decentration
multiple classification (and seriation)

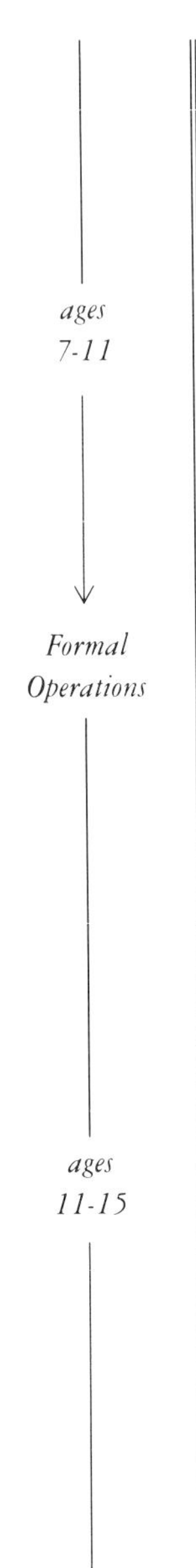

The child is gradually developing and refining the abilities to conserve, reverse, decentrate, and classify. The child learns about the *order* of things, e.g., the order of letters in a word, words in a sentence, transformations of sentence patterns, ideas in a passage. Children who are poor readers in the primary grades may develop these abilities at later ages than normal.

| *Activities* | Activities in the present book suggest ways of developing these abilities.

logical, hypothetical, conceptual reasoning

The person learns to reason hypothetically, to function on an abstract level, to conceptualize. The person increases in the ability to
• analyze logically
• consider the possible, as well as the concrete
• use deductive reasoning
• reason about concepts and ideas not in her or his direct experience
When faced with a difficult and complex situation, the youngster is able to hypothesize about casual and/or related factors and test and evaluate these hypotheses. The youngster is able to think beyond his or her own direct experiences. (Not everyone reaches this stage.)

| *Activities* | Activities in the present book suggest ways of developing some of these abilities. As in other stages, some children move into this stage at earlier chronological ages than do others. The teacher must be aware of individual differences and provide opportunities for learning as appropriate to each child.

Although all children progress through these stages in order, some do so more rapidly than others. Some research studies indicate that those children who succeed in learning to read at early ages have progressed into the stage of concrete operations by the time they are reading.[37]

Educational Factors

The discussion of educational factors that promote reading achievement is the province of most of this book. Discussed in this section will be the findings of two studies that describe characteristics of schools that have been successful in developing good readers. The first includes the findings of the American Institute for Research (AIR).

In 1969 the United States Office of Education commissioned AIR "to study the effects of innovation on the education of young Americans." In the September, 1977, *Language Arts* journal, Donald H. Graves summarizes these findings in "Research Update: What's New May Not Be Good."[38] According to Graves, "The most significant correlate with reading success in grade two was the amount of time students spent on language arts—113 minutes per day for higher achievers as opposed to 85 minutes for lower achievers. This growth for high achievers established in grade two continued to hold up in grade three even if they were exposed to less teaching time in the language arts. Other studies have verified this finding at additional grade levels.[39]

Another high correlate with reading success was student performance on a "Reading Interest Scale." Children who showed a higher level of interest were higher achievers.

A major finding was that "moderate innovation," rather than extensive innovation or no innovation, makes the real difference in student learning:

In a number of cases, innovative programs had some impact in the first year. But as the program grew older and involved older students, improvements diminished. Furthermore, a large outlay of funds (as intensive innovation is defined) is not only wasteful but often implies prodigious beginnings that belie effective change in the long run. Change is more by decree than by grass-roots development. The teachers who must carry out the program in the long-run are not involved at the start, especially when programs are funded on a yearly basis with less thought to the long-haul. A project is written in the front office and teachers are brought in on the implementation later.

Moderate innovation implies a different pace from the start. Changes are more gradual, funding judiciously shared, and teachers more easily join the effort. With high funding, programs are often more ambitious, contain more components, use elaborate evaluation schemes, and cannot be digested by teachers as quickly as project directors might like. There is enough energy to sustain the first year, and the impact may be high, but the staff cannot maintain the level of effort desired, especially if it was not their idea in the first place.*

Each of these major points has strong implications for the school administrator and the school reading program: *First*—the best programs progress and change at a moderate rate—and with faculty cooperation. The impetus for change comes by joint effort of the faculty and administration. Buying expensive machinery, equipment, and materials and expecting these to do the job of teaching is unrealistic and detrimental to a reading program.[40] *Second*—time must be provided for reading and language arts instruction. And this time must be used for such instruction. *Third*—interest is extremely important. How can a child be interested in reading if books are too hard, too easy, dull, unorganized, etc., and if time isn't provided for reading for pleasure? And how can one read for pleasure if there aren't enough interesting books to read?

Richard Venezky[41] gives additional clues in describing schools that were successful in producing good readers. He says that these schools

- had strong leadership that worked well with teachers.
- were achievement oriented rather than human relations oriented;* i.e., they delivered appropriate instruction.
- were "client centered" in the delivery of services; i.e., they coordinated the services that were extended to the children. For example, the reading teacher might work with teachers and also with children in their regular classrooms, helping the children use the materials of these classrooms and learn the concepts needed in these classes. The reading teachers in these schools were not remedial reading or reading centered oriented.

Jean Mackworth[42] makes another important observation when she says that if the general environment of the school is dull and unattractive, the child might connect the reading process—as well as all learning—with this dreary place and lose all interest.

Summary

There are many factors that influence reading achievement. These factors are frequently classified into four major categories: sociological, physiological, psychological, and educational factors. Each of these major categories was discussed in this chapter.

Among the sociological factors discussed were those that relate to the homes of children. "Ideal parents" were found to provide an environment that facilitates learning by doing; however, they do not actively

---

*This is not to say that teacher warmth and encouragement are unimportant. But warmth and encouragement without the delivery of instruction is empty.

stimulate their children. Parents of children who read early did not usually make deliberate attempts to teach their children to read, but they did respond positively to questions asked by children about written language. They also enjoyed their children, took them places, and talked with them.

Culturally different children have some distinct advantages, particularly those that characterize members of an extended family. They frequently also have disadvantages, e.g., language differences, lack of privacy which may cause them to "tune-out" many experiences, and lack of a model for success in education.

The effect of television was also discussed. A major finding was that for the culturally different child, T.V. language is a passive language. Children benefit from T.V. (e.g., "Sesame Street") to the extent that they discuss the programs with adults. Other effects were also discussed, as were possible advantages of the use of instructional T.V.

Among the physiological factors discussed were vision and hearing. Not only for reading purposes but also so that children can benefit as fully as possible from all of their experiences, it is important that vision and hearing be checked and corrective measures be taken if necessary. Children have periods of rapid muscular development during which time they tend to be physically active. Schools should provide for this by including physical activities in their regular programs.

Psychological factors discussed included attention and I.Q. Children who have built up a large store of information and concepts in their long-term storage systems have done so because of active participation, which requires attention, motivation, and a wide range of experiences. Possession of such information and the ability to think about such information is reflected in scores children receive on I.Q. tests if the I.Q. tests are appropriate to the children's culture. If the I.Q. tests are inappropriate to the children, they are inappropriate for use in predicting school success or failure.

Language development and language differences were also discussed. Children learn language through imitation and generalization, and most children enter kindergarten or first grade with the ability to use most basic grammatical forms of their home language. In order to attach meanings to printed symbols, they must understand the meanings of the words and strings of words (phrases, clauses, sentences) used. Children who speak languages or dialects other than those used in their schools need special attention.

Other psychological factors discussed were the "self-fulfilling prophesy," social skills and emotions as they relate to school success, perceptual skills related to reading, and developmental stages of children: moral and cognitive. A chart was included titled "Piaget's stages of cognitive development." Each stage was described and was followed by suggested activities appropriate to the stage.

Finally, several important research findings related to educational factors were presented. Among the important findings were: the amount of time spent on language arts instruction is the most significant correlate of reading success. Also important is the child's interest in reading. Moderate innovation in school programs is better than extensive innovation or no innovation. Schools that were successful in producing good readers had strong leadership that worked well with teachers, were achievement oriented, and were "client centered" in the delivery of instruction—special services were extended to the children in need in their regular classrooms.

All of these factors—sociological, physiological, psychological, and educational—interact for a youngster, and they interact in a unique way for each child. One characteristic thought to be highly negative and found in the experiences of several children may affect some of these children far more strongly than others. The same is possible with highly positive characteristics. It is the total of all experiences, as "interpreted" by the child, that determines the child's status.

Not discussed in this chapter are two extremely important factors: the content of the child's reading program in school and the teaching methods or approaches used by the child's teachers. Obviously, these are extremely important to the success or failure of each child. Much of the remainder of this book is a discussion of these elements.

Questions and Activities

After answering the questions given at the beginning of this chapter, consider these questions and activities:

1. Plan and participate in a skit in which an "ideal parent" has made available many activities for a child and in which the child responds to one or more of these available activities. You may wish to have the child then interact with the parent(s). Another group in the class might plan and perform in a skit in which a parent is a constant stimulator and is always "doing for" the child. Compare the effects of each on the child.
2. Demonstrate how an adult (parent, teacher, or other adult) might interact with a child before or/and after a T.V. program to enhance the value of the program for the child.
3. If one of the better vision tests mentioned in this chapter is available for your use, you might wish to learn to give it.
4. Analyze the proposition that the ability and desire to pay attention to experiences helps to develop a person's intellectual potential, as measured by an I.Q. test. Do you think the proposition is valid?

Consider the implications in terms of the home and school of a child. How can we promote the child's ability and desire to pay attention? Relate this to classroom discipline, to the child's emotional state, to the quality and types of experiences available to the child.

5. How do children acquire language? What is meant by the child's ability to form generalizations about language patterning? How do you feel about the language variations you will meet (or have met) in the classroom when you teach? How will you (or do you) view a child whose dialect is very different from yours? What effect do you think your attitude will have on the child?

6. Give one example of an activity for developing each of the following perceptual skills: figure and ground, closure, sequence, learning, set, and discrimination. Share these with some of your classmates, who may give additional examples.

7. Consider Piaget's stages (and ages) of cognitive development and their relationship to a child's ability to learn to read. Is Piaget's account the result of his observations? Does such a report suggest the present status of children in relation to cognitive development? Does it suggest limitations to the potential of children at specific ages at the present time? in the future?

8. Consider the value of a reading "specialist" in a school situation. Would the specialist's time be used best in teaching groups of children or in serving as a resource person in helping teachers and perhaps at times in team teaching in a regular classroom situation?

NOTES

1. Constance McCullough, p. 3. See Selected References.
2. Asher Cashdan, pp. 82–83. See Selected References.
3. Dolores Durkin, p. 2. See Selected References.
4. Frank Riesman, p. 48. See Selected References.
5. James L. Laffey and Raymond Morgan, pp. 57–58. See Selected References.
6. According to Harris and Sipay, Seventh Edition, 1980, p. 313. From Ronald W. Henderson. "Environmental Predictors of Academic Performance of Disadvantaged Mexican-American Children." *Journal of Consulting and Clinical Psychology*, 38 (April 1972): 297.
7. Pose Lamb, p. 372. See Selected References.
8. *Ibid.*, p. 373.
9. Violet B. Robinson, Dorothy S. Strickland, and Bernice Cullinan, pp. 35–36. See Selected References.
10. Nancy Larrick, p. 72. See Selected References.
11. Marie Winn. See Selected References.

12. Nancy Larrick, *op. cit.*, pp. 69–70.

13. Pauline B. Gough, pp. 458–459. See Selected References.

14. Massachusetts Vision Test and AO School Screening Test, from American Optical Co., Southern, Mass. Keystone Visual Survey Test, from Keystone View Co., Meadville, Pa. Ortho-Rater, from Bausch and Lomb Optical Co., Rochester, N.Y.

15. Albert J. Harris and Edward R. Sipay, p. 288. See Selected References.

16. Violet B. Robinson, *et al.*, *op. cit.*

17. Jean Mackworth, pp. 707–720. See Selected References.

18. See *Ibid.*, p. 727.

19. See *Ibid.*

20. Albert J. Harris, pp. 137–138. See Selected References.

21. Francine Patterson. "Conservations with a Gorilla." *National Geographic*, 154 (October 1978): 438–465.

22. Joel R. Levin, p. 324. See Selected References.

23. Stanford-Binet Intelligence Scale from Houghton Mifflin Co.; Wechsler Intelligence Scales from Psychological Corp.; Slosson Intelligence Test from Slosson Educational Publications; Peabody Picture Vocabulary Test (Revised) from American Guidance Service, Inc.; Goodenough-Harris Drawing Test from Harcourt Brace Jovanovich.

24. E.g.: Lorge-Thorndike Intelligence Tests from Houghton Mifflin Co., California Short-Form Test of Mental Maturity and California Test of Mental Maturity Long Form from California Test Bureau.

25. See Ed Labinowicz, p. 112. See Selected References.

26. Robert Ruddell, p. 90. See Selected References. In the same book you may wish to see the following sections: "Conflict Points between Standard and Nonstandard Dialects," pp. 267–273, and "English and Second Language Conflict Points" (Spanish and Chinese), pp. 273–281.

27. E.g., see Robert Rosenthal and Lenore Jacobson. *Pygmalion in the Classroom: Teacher Expectation and Pupil's Intellectual Development.* New York: Holt, Rinehart and Winston, 1968; Ray C. Rist. "Student Social Class and Teacher Expectations: The Self-Fulfilling Prophecy in Ghetto Education," in *Harvard Educational Review*, 40, no. 3 (August 1970): 411–451; also Jean José and John J. Cody. "Teacher—Pupil Interaction as It Relates to Attempted Changes in Teacher Expectancy of Academic Ability and Achievement," in *American Educational Research Journal*, 8, no. 1 (January 1971): 40–49. There are numerous other sources.

28. Ray C. Rist. See Selected References. As a result of recent laws, e.g., Bradamous, the student and parent have a right to see school records.

29. Albert J. Harris, *op. cit.*, p. 138.

30. After Albert J. Harris and Edward R. Sipay, *op. cit.*, pp. 301–305.

31. In James Macdonald (ed.) p. 38. See Selected References.

32. Harris and Sipay, *op. cit.*, pp. 250–251.

33. G. Robert Carlsen. *Books and the Teen-Age Reader.* New York: Bantam, 1972.

34. Lawrence Kohlberg. See Selected References.

35. Bernard Rihn. "Kohlberg Level of Moral Reasoning of Protagonists in Newberry Award Winning Fiction." *Reading Research Quarterly*, XV, no. 3 (1980): 379.

36. J. Piaget and B. Inhelder. *The Growth of Logical Thinking: From Childhood to Adolescence.* New York: Basic Books, 1958.
37. See, for example, David Elkind, p. 334, in Selected References. Also see C. Breggs and D. Elkind "Cognitive Development in Early Readers" and "Characteristics of Early Readers" in Selected References.
38. Donald H. Graves, pp. 708–713. See Selected References.
39. See A. J. Harris, *op. cit.,* p. 136.
40. See Harry Singer in Selected References.
41. Richard Venezky in a Leadership Conference sponsored by Ginn and Co. in Austin, Texas, 1979.
42. Jean Macworth, p. 708. See Selected References.

Selected References

Bean, Rita M. and Robert M. Wilson. *Effecting Change in School Reading Programs: The Resource Role.* Newark, Delaware: International Reading Association, 1981.

Briggs, C. and David Elkind. "Characteristics of Early Readers." *Perceptual and Motor Skills,* 44 (1977): 1231–1237.

——————————————. "Cognitive Development in Early Readers." *Developmental Psychology,* 9 (1973): 279–280.

Cashdan, Asher. "Who Teaches the Child to Read?" in *New Horizons in Reading,* John E. Merritt (ed.). Newark, Delaware: International Reading Association, 1976, pp. 82–83.

Durkin, Dolores. "Facts about Pre-First Grade Reading," in *The Kindergarten Child and Reading,* Lloyd O. Ollila (ed.). Newark, Delaware: International Reading Association, 1977, pp. 1–12.

Elkind, David. "Cognitive Development and Reading," in *Theoretical Models and Processes of Reading, Second Edition,* Harry Singer and Robert B. Ruddell (eds.). Newark, Delaware: International Reading Assoc., 1976, pp. 331–340.

Gough, Pauline B. "Introducing Children to Books Via Television." *The Reading Teacher,* 32 (January 1979): 458–462.

Graves, Donald H. "Research Update: What's New May Not Be Good." *Language Arts,* 54 (September 1977): 708–713.

Harris, Albert J. "The Effective Teacher of Reading, Revisited." *The Reading Teacher,* 33 (November 1979): 135–140.

—————————————— and Edward R. Sipay. *How to Increase Reading Ability, 6th ed.* New York: David McKay, 1975.

Henderson, Ronald W. "Environmental Predictors of Academic Performance of Disadvantaged Mexican-American Children." *Journal of Consulting and Clinical Psychology,* 38 (April 1972): 297.

Kohlberg, Lawrence. "Stage and Sequence: the Cognitive-Developmental Approach to Socialization," in *Handbook of Socialization Theory and Research.* Chicago: Rand-McNally, 1968, pp. 347–480.

Labinowicz, Ed. *The Piaget Primer—Thinking, Learning, Teaching.* Menlo Park, California: Addison-Wesley Publishing Co., 1980.

Laffey, James L. and Raymond Morgan. "Sociocultural Bases," in *Teaching Reading—Foundations and Strategies, Second Edition*, Pose Lamb and Richard Arnold (eds.). Belmont, California: Wadsworth Publishing Co., 1980, p. 57–58.

Lamb, Pose. "Reading and Television in the United States," in *New Horizons in Reading*, John E. Merritt (ed.). Newark, Delaware: International Reading Association, 1976, p. 372.

Larrick, Nancy. "The Impact of Television on Children's Reading," in *Inchworm, Inchworm: Persistent Problems in Reading Education*, Constance M. McCullough (ed.). Newark, Delaware: International Reading Association, 1980, pp. 65–74.

Levin, Joel R. "Comprehending What We Read: An Outsider Looks In," in *Theoretical Models and Processes of Reading, Second Edition*, Harry Singer and Robert B. Ruddell (eds.). Newark, Delaware: International Reading Association, 1976, pp. 320–330.

Macdonald, James B. (ed.). *Perspectives in Reading No. 17: Social Perspectives on Reading: Social Influences and Reading Achievement.* Newark, Delaware: International Reading Association, 1973.

Mackworth, Jane. "Some Models of the Reading Process: Learners and Skilled Readers," *Reading Research Quarterly*, VII, no. 4 (Summer 1972): 701–733.

McCullough, Constance. "Straws in the Wind," in *New Horizons in Reading*, John E. Merritt (ed.). Newark, Delaware: International Reading Association, 1976, pp. 2–7.

Pertz, Doris L. and Lillian R. Putnam. "An Examination of the Relationship between Nutrition and Learning." *The Reading Teacher*, 35 (March 1982): 702–706.

Rest, J. and E. Turiel and L. Kohlberg. "Level of Moral Judgment as a Determinant of Preference and Comprehension of Moral Judgments Made By Others." *Journal of Personality*, 37 (1969): 225–232.

Riesman, Frank. *The Culturally Deprived Child.* New York: Harper and Row Publishing Co., 1962.

Rist, Ray C. "Student Social Class and Teacher Expectations: The Self-Fulfilling Prophecy in Ghetto Education," in *Harvard Educational Review*, 40, no. 3 (August 1970): 411–451.

Robinson, Helen M. *Why Pupils Fail in Reading.* Chicago: University of Chicago Press, 1946.

Robinson, Violet B., Dorothy S. Strickland, and Bernice Cullinan. "The Child: Ready or Not?" in *The Kindergarten Child and Reading*, Lloyd O. Ollila (ed.). Newark, Delaware: International Reading Association, 1977, pp. 13–39.

Ruddell, Robert B. *Reading-Language Instruction & Innovative Practices.* Englewood Cliffs, New Jersey: Prentice Hall, Inc., 1974.

Samuels, S. Jay. "Characteristics of Exemplary Reading Programs," in *Comprehension and Teaching: Research Reviews*, John T. Guthrie (ed.). Newark, Delaware: International Reading Association, 1981, pp. 255–273.

Singer, Harry. "Resolving Curricular Conflicts in the 1970's: Modifying the Hypothesis, It's the Teacher Who Makes the Difference in Reading Achievement." *Language Arts*, 54 (February 1977): 158–163.

Winn, Marie. *The Plug in Drug.* New York: Viking Press, 1977.

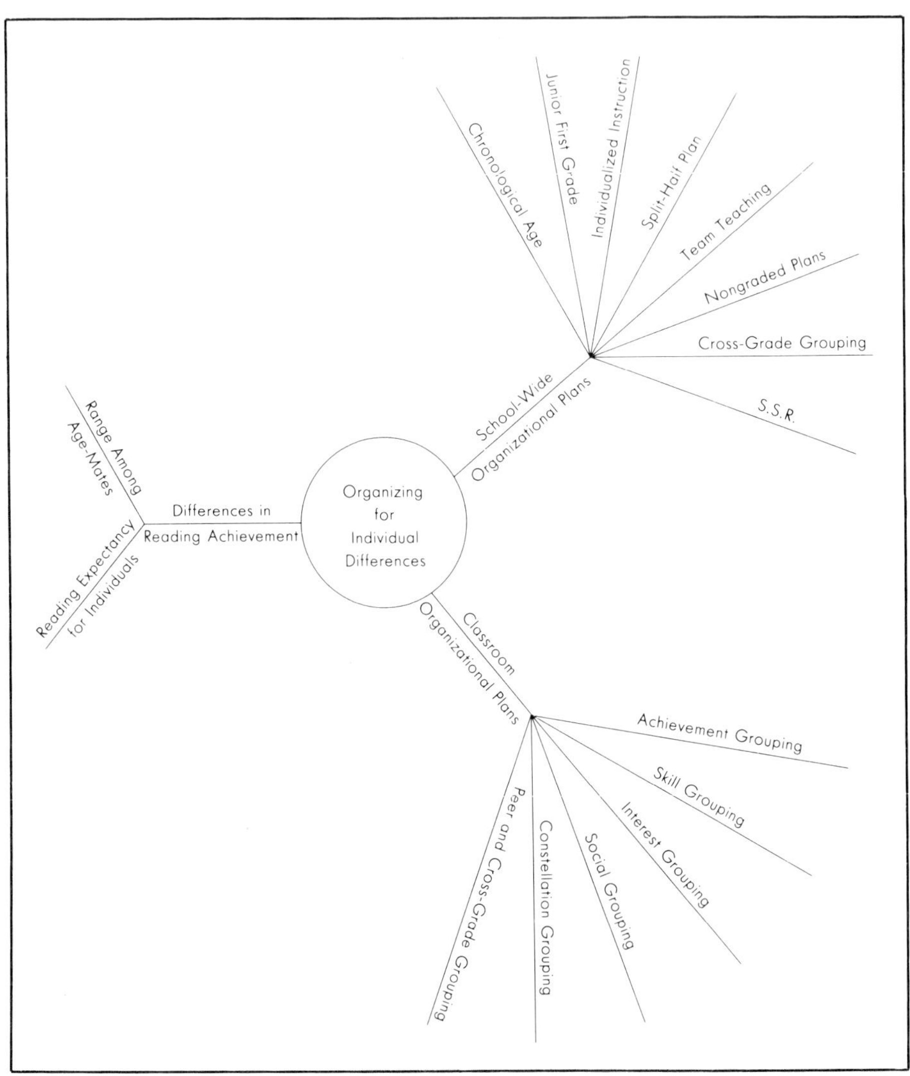

- What is the range in reading achievement (or in readiness to read) in a typical classroom? How well should we expect individual children to read?

- What are some commonly used school-wide plans for grouping children? What are the strengths and weaknesses of each plan?

- How do teachers group children in their classrooms? What is the purpose for each type of grouping plan?

CHAPTER 3

Organizing for Individual Differences

Anyone who has been in a classroom and is at all observant realizes that there are differences in achievement levels of children found in the same class. What may be surprising is the vastness of these differences.

Differences in Reading Achievement

RANGE IN READING ACHIEVEMENT AMONG AGE-MATES

In a typical American classroom in which children are grouped according to chronological age, the expected range in reading achievement (or range in readiness for beginning reading) can be expressed by the following formula:

$$\text{Range} \begin{bmatrix} \text{in reading achievement} \\ \text{in a typical classroom} \end{bmatrix} = 2/3 \text{ C.A. of the average child.} \quad [1]$$

To find the expected achievement level of the poorest and best readers in a classroom, the following translation of the formula might be used:

$$\text{Range} = \text{grade level} \pm \frac{\text{C.A. of average child}}{3}.$$

Using the above formula, we find that:

- at the beginning of first grade,
  - the most poorly prepared children will be about as mature in terms of readiness for reading as the average four-year-old, while
  - the best prepared children will be reading at the 3.0 grade level, or if not taught will have the potential for reading at that level.

  That is, the expected range in grade 1.0 is:

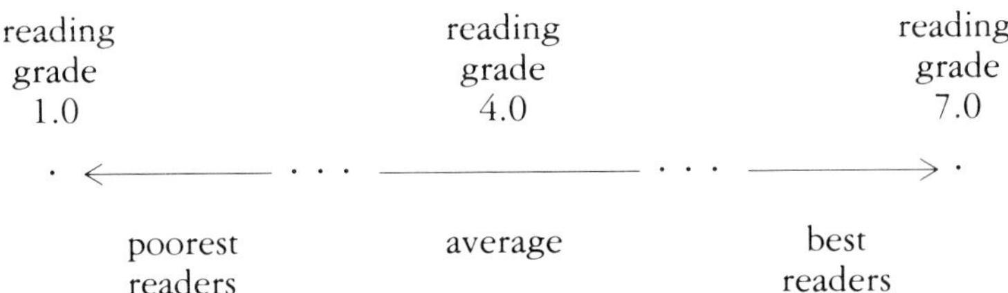

- at the beginning of fourth grade (at the end of the primary grades),
  - the poorest readers will be reading at the first grade level, while
  - the best readers will be reading at the seventh grade level.

  That is, the expected range in grade 4.0 is:

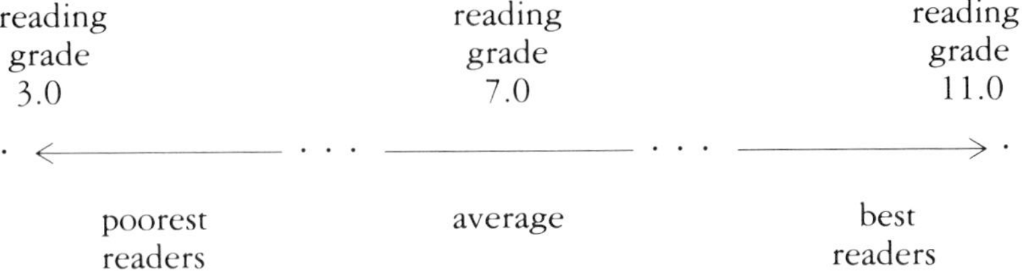

- at the beginning of seventh grade (at the end of elementary school),
  - the poorest readers will be reading at the third grade level, while
  - the best readers will be reading at the eleventh grade level.

  That is, the expected range in grade 7.0 is:

Examination of the above information indicates that:
- the range in reading achievement in a classroom in which children are grouped according to chronological age increases as the children grow older; i.e., the slower children fall further and further behind

the average, while the brighter children go further and further ahead of the average.

- the range continues to be in the same ratio to the chronological age of the children (Range = 2/3 of C.A.) throughout the school years K-12.

- the poorest readers (or in first grade, the most poorly prepared children) gain about two-thirds of a year per year in reading achievement (or in readiness for reading achievement). This begins at birth and continues throughout the school years. By the time the children of this category reach first grade (C.A. = 6 years), they are as ready for reading as the average four-year-old. By the time they are in fourth grade (C.A. = 9) they are reading as well as an average six year old, etc.

- the average readers (or in first grade, those who are intellectually average) gain about one year per year in reading achievement (or in readiness for reading achievement). This, too, begins at birth and continues throughout the school years. By the time the children in this category reach first grade (C.A. = 6 years), they are frequently almost ready to begin to read. As they continue through school, they remain at grade level.

- the best readers (or in first grade, those best prepared to learn to read if they haven't already learned) gain about 1 1/3 years per year in reading achievement (or in readiness for reading achievement). This 1 1/3 years per year gain begins at birth and continues throughout the school years. By the time the children in this category reach first grade, they may already be reading at the second or third grade level. By the time they are in fourth grade (C.A. = 9) they are reading as well as an average 12 year old, etc.

It should be noted at this point that individual children may move from one category to another (up or down) during preschool years and as they grow older and receive reading instruction in a school situation.

Table 3.1 shows the typical range according to grade level of the children. When children are grouped in a classroom at random by chronological age, this range is what a teacher might expect to find in his or her classroom.

It might be noted that according to Table 3.1 the best readers in first grade read about as well as the average readers in third grade and as well as the poorest readers in seventh grade. It is necessary to be very cautious in interpreting such data. What is usually meant is that a first grader may score 3.0 grade on a primary level reading test. (All material in the test is at the lower primary level). An average reader in third grade will score about 3.0 on a third grade reading test. (All material on the test is likely to be approximately at the second, third, and fourth

TABLE 3.1: Expected range in reading achievement of children by grade level

Grade level of children	reading achievement (or reading readiness) level												
	Pre-school	K	1.0	2.0	3.0	4.0	5.0	6.0	7.0	8.0	9.0	10.0	11.0
1.0	(pre) ←——— * ———→ (3.0)												
2.0	(pre) ←——— * ———→ (4.3)												
3.0	(K) ←——— * ———→ (5.7)												
4.0	(1.0) ←——— * ———→ (7.0)												
5.0	(1.7) ←——— * ———→ (8.3)												
6.0	(2.3) ←——— * ———→ (9.7)												
7.0	(3.0) ←——— * ———→ (11.0)												

*Indicates average, or midpoint scores; 50 percent of a typical class will score above this and 50 percent below.

grade levels.) A poor reader in seventh grade may score about 3.0 on a reading test designed for seventh and eighth graders. (All material on the test is likely to be approximately betweeen the fifth and ninth grade levels in difficulty.) When comparing these tests one can see that there are differences in reading difficulty (readability) of the tests and in assumed background of experiences of readers at different age levels for which the tests were designed, so test score grade levels are not precisely equivalent from one level of a test to another.

Yet it is also obvious to observant teachers that some bright younger children do perform in some reading tasks as well as much older children who are average in reading achievement, even when both groups use the same materials. The younger children, however, usually lack the wider range of experiences that comes through age, including classroom experiences. However, as school programs for the gifted and talented gain in popularity, the better students may progress through programs that are rapidly paced and enriched. Then gifted and talented younger students may have classroom experiences comparable to (and perhaps superior to) those of average students who are older. These younger students might then outscore older average students on the same tests. (In fact, this is not unusual even now.)

READING EXPECTANCY FOR INDIVIDUAL CHILDREN

It is one thing to consider groups of children and another to consider individuals. One might wonder what to expect of an individual child in reading achievement. It is common practice to relate the expected reading achievement level of an individual child to his or her mental age (M.A.), or intelligence quotient (I.Q.) score. This practice supplies a limited amount of information that many teachers might find useful.

There are several formulas that are frequently used in estimating the expected achievement of individual children.[2] Two of them are:

$$\text{Reading Expectancy (grade)} = \text{M.A.} - 5.2 \text{ (or 5.0, for ease)}$$

and

$$\text{Reading Expectancy (grade)} = \frac{2\ \text{M.A.} + \text{C.A.}}{3} - 5.2$$

If we use the first (and easier) formula, we see that we expect a child to read at the same level he or she scores on an I.Q. test, with I.Q. translated into M.A.* For example, if a child's M.A. = 9.5, we would expect the child to read as well as the average child who is 9.5 years old (i.e., at grade level 4.3: 9.5 − 5.2**). The second formula, in addition, uses the chronological age factor in estimating expectancy. The expectancy levels for children according to these formulas are given in Tables 3.2 and 3.3.

Table 3.2, composed by using the first formula, gives the approximate expectancy grade-level scores for children of various chronological ages and I.Q.'s. (Rounded C.A. scores are used.)

The second formula "gives priority to the importance of intelligence, but also recognizes the presence of other age-related characteristics in

---

*The following formulas tell how to convert these scores:

$$\text{M.A.} = \frac{\text{I.Q.}}{100} \times \text{C.A.} \qquad \text{and I.Q.} = \frac{\text{M.A.}}{\text{C.A.}} \times 100$$

**The difference between age and grade is approximately 5.2 years. The average child is 6.2 years old in grade 1.0.

TABLE 3.2 Reading expectancy scores according to I.Q. and C.A., using the formula R.E. (grade) = M.A. − 5.

Usual grade placement	C.A.	I.Q.						
		80	90	100	110	120	130	140
1.0	6.0	R*	R*	1.0	1.6†	2.2†	2.8†	3.4†
2.0	7.0	R*	1.3	2.0	2.7	3.4	4.1	4.8
3.0	8.0	1.4	2.2	3.0	3.8	4.6	5.4	6.2
4.0	9.0	2.2	3.1	4.0	4.9	5.8	6.7	7.6
5.0	10.0	3.0	4.0	5.0	6.0	7.0	8.0	9.0
6.0	11.0	3.8	4.9	6.0	7.1	8.2	9.3	10.4
7.0	12.0	4.6	5.8	7.0	8.2	9.4	10.7	11.8
8.0	13.0	5.4	6.7	8.0	9.3	10.6	12.0	13.2
9.0	14.0	6.2	7.6	9.0	10.4	11.8	13.3	14.6
10.0	15.0	7.0	8.5	10.0	11.5	13.0	14.7	
11.0	16.0	7.8	9.4	11.0	12.6	14.2		
12.0	17.0	8.6	10.3	12.0	13.7	(mature college level)		
12.99	17.99	9.4	11.2	13.0	14.8			

*R = reading readiness
† It would be unrealistic to expect untaught children to be reading at these levels upon entering school.

reading expectancy."[3] One of these is the opportunity to have experiences. (The number of these experiences increases with age.) Table 3.3, composed by using this formula, gives the approximate expectancy grade-level scores for children of various chronological ages and I.Q.'s.

TABLE 3.3 Reading expectancy grade scores according to I.Q. and C.A., using the formula R.E. (grade) = [(2 M.A. + C.A.)/3] − 5.2

Usual grade placement	C.A.	I.Q.						
		80	90	100	110	120	130	140
1.0	6.2	R*	R*	1.0	1.3†	1.7†	2.2†	2.6†
2.0	7.2	1.0	1.5	2.0	2.4	2.9	3.4	3.9
3.0	8.2	1.9	2.4	3.0	3.5	4.1	4.6	5.1
4.0	9.2	2.7	3.4	4.0	4.6	5.2	5.8	6.4
5.0	10.2	3.6	4.3	5.0	5.7	6.3	7.0	7.7
6.0	11.2	4.5	5.2	6.0	6.7	7.5	8.2	8.9
7.0	12.2	5.3	6.2	7.0	7.8	8.6	9.4	10.2
8.0	13.2	6.2	7.1	8.0	8.9	9.7	10.6	11.5
9.0	14.2	7.1	8.0	9.0	10.0	10.9	11.8	12.7
10.0	15.2	7.9	9.0	10.0	11.0	12.0	13.0	14.0
11.0	16.2	8.8	9.9	11.0	12.1	13.1	14.2	
12.0	17.2	9.7	10.8	12.0	13.2	14.3		
12.99	18.19	10.5	11.8	13.0	14.3	(mature college level)		

*R = reading readiness
† It would be unrealistic to expect untaught children to be reading at these levels upon entering school.

It might seem quite shocking to find that children vary so much in reading achievement. However, they vary as much—or almost as much—in mental age, and also in achievement in arithmetic, social studies, science, art, music, etc. One need only observe children throughout the school day in all classes and also when playing on the school grounds, when drawing pictures, singing songs, etc., to note that this wide variation is found not only in reading.

Schools have tried to adjust to these differences through administrative grouping plans and through grouping children within classrooms. The following sections describe some of these plans.

School-Wide (Administrative) Organizational Plans

In an attempt to adjust to individual differences among children—sometimes by minimizing them and other times by maximizing them—different administrative organizational plans have evolved. Some of these are briefly described below.

SELF-CONTAINED CLASSROOM/GROUPING BY CHRONOLOGICAL AGE

By far the most popular organizational plan for elementary schools is the self-contained classroom in which children are grouped homogeneously by chronological age and heterogeneously according to many other characteristics. Six-year-olds are first graders, seven-year-olds are second graders, eight-year-olds are third graders, etc. The plan is popular for social reasons and because of tradition.

Children of similar chronological ages frequently have interests in common. These interests seem unaffected by I.Q. or mental age, although children of higher I.Q.'s tend to desire to learn in greater depth and at a higher level than do children of lower I.Q.'s. Yet, their basic interests are the same.

Although there are similarities in chronological age (though there may be about a year's difference in age among the children in schools that promote only once a year), and similarities in interests (or stage of development in interests), and other factors, there are vast differences in level of achievement among these children. As in all classrooms, teachers must adjust to these differences. Some ways of doing so are discussed later in this chapter.

JUNIOR FIRST GRADE

Some school systems are now providing a "junior first grade" for six-year-olds who may have completed kindergarten but are not yet ready to enter the school's first grade classes. Children in these junior first grade classes are provided additional time for maturation and for extended reading readiness experiences, including language development. After a semester or a year in such a program, the children enter first grade.

INDIVIDUALIZED INSTRUCTION

Individualized instruction is designed to meet the needs and interests of each child. Frequently when we describe individualized reading we mean the kind of program that can be characterized by using these descriptive terms: seeking, self-selection, and pacing. The children seek their own interests, select their own materials, and pace themselves. The reading skills the children are taught are those that are needed to understand the materials the children have selected. Other types of individualized programs are also used. Several of these are discussed in a later chapter in this book.

Older, and less successful, individualized plans involved differentiated pacing only. All children did the same things, but they did them at different stages, i.e., when it was felt they were ready to do them. Such was the Winnetka plan. The Dalton plan involved "units" of work, somewhat like modern "modules." Children contracted to do as many units as they wished—so that a bright child might do five units in the time a slower child did two or three. But, materials within a unit were the same for all children. A bright child, of course, can work at a faster pace than a slower child, but also at a higher level. Level accommodations were not made in these units.

Many teachers find it difficult, if not impossible, to differentiate or individualize instruction when classes are large. Perhaps if school enrollments decrease and faculties are maintained, such instruction may be possible. The following plan describes how some schools have already made some adjustments.

SPLIT-HALF PLAN

A rarely used plan, but one worthy of consideration, is the split-half plan. In this plan, the classroom teacher teaches half of the class at one time and the other half at another. The children not being instructed by the classroom teacher are not present in the classroom while the other children are being taught. In some schools, half of a class comes early in the morning for their reading instruction, and the other half stays later in the afternoon for their instruction. In other schools, during the regular school day half of the class is taught reading by the classroom teacher while the other half may join another group of children for instruction in art, music, physical education, or some other course elsewhere. Then the other half returns for reading instruction, which is given by the regular classroom teacher, and the first half is instructed elsewhere. Figure 3.1 illustrates how such splitting might proceed.

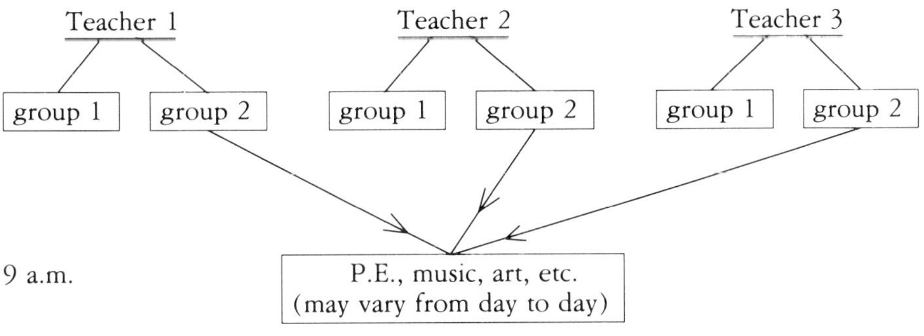

Group 1 children stay with their classroom teacher.

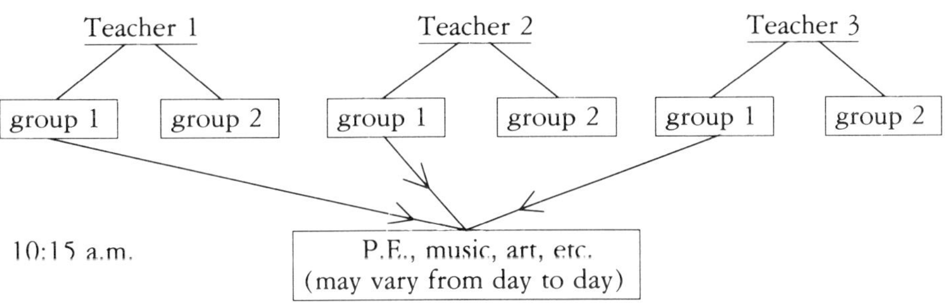

Group 2 children return to their classroom teacher.

Figure 3.1: An example of how the Split-Half Plan works.

A brief report of this plan in action in Denmark is available.[4] Here, the splitting of the class is random, taking no account of sex or achievement. The splitting has been done for native language instruction (language arts instruction, including reading) in grades one to four, for mathematics in grades one and two, also for foreign language instruction and other subjects at other grade levels. The author states that this splitting at the lower grade levels "enabled many slow learners to benefit from instruction while remaining in their own classes, instead of immediately being segregated for special education treatment."[5] In the United States, this might have strong implications for mainstreaming.

The author states that when compared to full-class instruction, where reading usually took the form of round robin reading,* in the split-half classes there was differentiated teaching, and assignments and materials were adapted to individual pupil's reading skills, interests, and working capacities. The author stresses the importance of the teacher's knowledge of different forms of teaching (methods and/or approaches) for diversification of instruction to occur.

TEAM TEACHING

Team teaching involves the sharing of responsibility among teachers for teaching a group of children. Team teaching can take many forms, one of which might involve the school's special reading teacher, who might work with classroom teachers in helping them become more knowledgeable about incorporating the teaching of reading in all classes, including reading class itself.

For example, a real burden a classroom teacher might have when trying to differentiate instruction by using multilevel materials is placing individual children in the proper materials. The special reading teacher could help the classroom teacher do this.

The special reading teacher, also, might work with children in skill and interest centers and/or in individualizing instruction for the children within their regular classrooms. Instead of taking children out of their classrooms for special reading instruction, the special reading teacher would join children in their regular classrooms and correlate the teaching of needed reading skills with the content of these classrooms. And the special reading teacher could help the classroom teacher in designing lessons and activities for all children.

For example, some children might need additional help in vocabulary as it relates to a unit in a reading or social studies class or any other class. The reading teacher could work with the classroom teacher in identifying difficult terms and then help develop a balanced variety of activities to teach these terms. The same might be true for activities for teaching phonics (if phonics is taught), concept development, critical reading, rate, and other skill areas the classroom teacher or reading teacher identifies.

Once the skill centers are set up, the reading teacher could work with children in one center while the classroom teacher may work in another. In still another, the children might work on their own.

Interest centers could also be set up and used in the same way. Thus the reading teacher would help children in their regular classrooms, by

---

*In round robin reading all children have their books open while one child, then another, and yet another—in order—reads orally.

utilizing ideas and materials that are basic to or that supplement the on-going efforts of classroom teachers.

Some school systems provide a materials preparation center to help teachers produce materials for classroom use. The special reading teacher could help coordinate the efforts of teachers in the use of such a center. Also the special reading teacher could coordinate the efforts of the librarian in working with teachers in selecting materials for use in classrooms.

Nongraded Plans

Some school systems use nongraded plans, especially at the primary level. A nongraded plan is one in which grade levels are not designated and in which children are grouped into self-contained classrooms. There are several forms that are used. Three are discussed here.

Multi-age Plan

In the multi-age plan, children of different chronological ages are grouped together in one classroom. The idea is like that of the old country school house. In a primary plan, one might find in one classroom about one-third of the children to be six years old, one-third seven, and one-third eight. Those who favor this plan contend that it is life-like, for children normally mingle freely with other children of many ages. This plan stresses differences, rather than likenesses, in achievement and age, making it a normal grouping situation—like the home and the neighborhood in which the children live.

Each child remains with the same teacher for three years, or possibly longer for those who learn slowly. Each year, the teacher loses one-third of the class (who "graduate" to fourth grade), and picks up another third, new six year olds. So the relationship between each child and the teacher is extended over three years. It is truly an in-depth relationship—marvelous if the teacher is excellent, and rather awful if the opposite is true.

The plan is frequently used in a modified form at other grade levels, for example, when a course is offered—say graphic design in art—and anyone in the school may take it. The newspaper staff and clubs are usually organized in this way, too.

Homogeneous Grouping By Achievement

Some nongraded plans involve grouping children into self-contained classrooms homogeneously according to achievement. In some schools, the achievement area by which children are grouped is reading. In other schools, it is reading and arithmetic. Frequently such nongraded plans are found at the primary level, followed by more traditional self-contained classrooms or departmentalized programs beginning at the fourth grade level.

In a primary plan, individual children may be labeled thus: P_1 (primary, first semester), P_2 (primary, second semester), P_3 (primary, third semester), etc. But the children are grouped in classrooms by achievement level. Thus in a classroom for those achieving, for example, at levels 1.0–1.4, we might find many P_1's, but also P_2's, P_3's, P_4's, etc. In a classroom for those achieving at levels 1.5–1.9, we might find some P_1's, P_2's, P_3's, P_4's, P_5's, etc. When we look at those achieving at levels 3.5–3.9, we might find a rare P_2, plus P_3's, P_4's, P_5's, P_6's and even P_7's and P_8's. When children achieve at the fourth grade level, they move into the upper elementary (or middle grade) plan.

Thus children who progress rapidly may continue in this type of nongraded primary plan for two or two-and-a half years, whereas the average child would remain in the plan for three years, and the slower child might stay in the plan for three-and-a-half or four years. Both rapid progression and slow progression are not obvious in this plan, and a slow learner is not stigmatized by slower than average progression. Even in this plan, teachers must differentiate instruction in the classroom because subskill levels and interests differ.

Homogeneous Grouping By Achievement—With Overlap

Similar to the above plan, but perhaps more realistic, flexible, and functional, is a homogeneous grouping plan that provides for "overlap" in achievement among or between classes of essentially different levels. Table 3.4 shows a possible plan for level distribution among teachers.

TABLE 3.4   **A sample homogeneous grouping plan with overlap.**

Teacher	Achievement levels of children									
Teacher A	r^1	r^2	pp*							
Teacher B			pp	p	1					
Teacher C					1	2^1	2^2			
Teacher D							2^2	3^1	3^2	
Teacher E									3^2	4^1	4^2
										(or enrichment)

*r^1 = readiness, first semester, r^2 = readiness, second semester, pp = preprimer level, p = primer level, 2^1 = first semester second grade, etc.

Like the previous plan, this is usually a primary plan, and children remain in the plan until they reach fourth grade level in achievement, although some precocious younger children may remain (e.g., with

Teacher E) for enrichment until they are judged to be old enough to enter fourth grade (or a middle grade plan similarly designed).

Children who reach the top level in a classroom are considered for transfer to the next class. The child who demonstrates achievement in all (or most) subareas of reading and content area achievement are usually transferred upon reaching the top level. However, the child who is weak in some areas may remain for a longer time in order to have an opportunity to improve in these areas.[6]

CROSS-GRADE GROUPING FOR READING

The Joplin plan, introduced in Joplin, Missouri, was designed to accommodate differences in level of reading achievement during reading class time. Although children remained in their self-contained classrooms for other subjects, for reading, they were grouped homogeneously according to reading achievement. Thus, for example, children who read at grade levels 1.0–1.4 were grouped together for reading class, though they might be six, seven, or eight years old or even older. Similarly those who read at grade levels 1.5–1.9 were grouped together—also 2.0–2.4, 2.5–2.9, 3.0–3.4, 3.5–3.9, etc. The plan is frequently called "the ring and run plan," because at a specified time each day, the school bell rang, and children supposedly ran to their reading classes.

Although the classroom teacher taught children most of their other subjects, it was usually another teacher who taught them reading. There may have been several problems because of this. For example, reading instruction was isolated from the classroom teacher and, therefore, it was difficult for the classroom teacher to understand the reading strengths and weaknesses the children had when reading their content area assignments. Also, the assumption tended to be that differentiated instruction was necessary in reading class but not in other classes. (A third grade child might be in a first grade reading class, but he or she often was expected to read science, arithmetic, etc., at third grade level along with his or her regular classmates in the homeroom setting.)

SUSTAINED SILENT READING

Any discussion of school-wide plans would be incomplete without a discussion of USSR's (Uninterrupted Sustained Silent Reading) or SSR's (Sustained Silent Reading). SSR is described in more detail later in this book. Briefly, the plan includes setting aside time—perhaps once a week or even every day—during which everyone reads for pleasure—the teacher, principal, nurse, janitor, and, of course, the children. Adults serve as models for children, who may otherwise never see adults enjoying reading.

Classroom Organizational Plans

Although school-wide grouping plans may lessen differences in achievement in a classroom, they do not eliminate such differences. Teachers must still individualize instruction at times and group children at other times. Some common classroom grouping plans are briefly discussed below. Each of these plans is discussed in an appropriate section elsewhere in this book.

ACHIEVEMENT GROUPING

Children are frequently grouped in reading class (and perhaps in content area classes also) according to their level of reading achievement. A three-group plan is often used.

Some authors use the following terms for children in these three groups:

- accelerated readers—those children who make more than a year's progress in a year. These children are given materials above grade level, suitable to their reading levels. Pacing is more rapid than it is for the other groups, as these children should continue to gain more than one year per year.
- average readers—those children who gain approximately one year per year. These children are given materials approximately at grade level, i.e., at a level suitable for them. Pacing is average, as these children usually gain one year in achievement each year.
- below average readers—are in groups sometimes called "adapted" reading groups. The children in these groups are given materials below grade level, suitable to their achievement levels. These children usually progress through these materials at a rate slower than one year per year.

    Table 3.5 may help you understand how a teacher who uses basal readers might provide for group work during one hour per day of *reading class time.*

If a classroom is divided into only three groups of children, the differences within each group are still quite broad. For example, in third grade the range for the low group might be from grade 1.0, or even lower, to grade 2.4. The average group of children might have reading scores ranging from 2.5–3.5. The fastest group might range from 3.6–5.7, or even higher.

Individual children, themselves, may have noticeable differences in their reading achievement in different reading skills. One child may be

TABLE 3.5:   Illustrative chart showing how three different groups of children might be engaged in reading activities during one hour of their daily reading time.* The plan might change each week.

	Time	Monday	Tuesday	Wednesday	Thursday	Friday
Group 1 (adapted)	9:00-9:20	free reading	play reading	sharing activities	echo reading, with group 3	free reading
	9:20-9:40	basal** reading	basal reading	basal reading	basal reading	basal reading
	9:40-10:00	correlated skills***	echo reading, with group 2	correlated skills or interests	free reading	correlated skills or interests

	Time	Monday	Tuesday	Wednesday	Thursday	Friday
Group 2 (average)	9:00-9:20	basal reading	basal reading	basal reading	basal reading	basal reading
	9:20-9:40	correlated skills	correlated skills or interests	free reading	correlated skills or interests	free reading
	9:40-10:00	free reading	echo reading, with group 1	free reading	sharing activities	play reading

	Time	Monday	Tuesday	Wednesday	Thursday	Friday
Group 3 (accelerated)	9:00-9:20	free reading	play reading	sharing activities	echo reading, with group 1	free reading
	9:20-9:40	correlated skills	correlated skills or interests	free reading	correlated skills or interests	sharing activities
	9:40-10:00	basal reading	basal reading	basal reading	basal reading	basal reading

*   Additional reading time would be spent in other activities, perhaps class-wide, e.g., language experience, teacher reading to the class, sustained silent reading, choral reading, sharing, etc. All of these are explained later in this book.

** Assuming a basal reading program is being used. Basal reading is explained in Chapter 13.

***That is, skill development related to the basal lesson and/or skill development diagnosed as necessary for individual children.

relatively good in science vocabulary but may be weak in social studies vocabulary; he or she may be a bottom-up reader and may grasp details well but may have trouble with generalizing; he or she may believe everything read, including advertisements. Another child might score the same on the total score of a reading test (or on an Informal Reading Inventory* given by the teacher) but may display a different profile in skill development. He or she may have a poor science vocabulary because of lack of interest or exposure to science terms but may have an excellent vocabulary in sports terms; he or she may be a top-down reader and may grasp general concepts well but may have problems with details; he or she may be skeptical about many ideas presented in reading materials.

If, in *content area classrooms,* children of different achievement levels read books not only of different difficulty levels but also by different authors, these books may contain similar basic information but very different examples and elaborations. Children in all groups would be able to share learnings. Even the children in the lower group would be able to contribute ideas to the class discussion not found in the higher level books.

Within these three groups, teachers make adjustments in teaching individual children. Also, other groups that are more fluid in nature are frequently formed. These are discussed in the following sections.

If the special reading teacher team teaches with the classroom teacher, he or she may help identify the best group and activities for each child.

SKILL GROUPING

Some children from several achievement level groups may need help in developing a specific skill. These children are brought together in a group to learn this skill. As soon as they have learned the skill, the group is dissolved.

For example, in a science class, those children who don't know how to use a microscope may be taught to use one. Also in a science class, those who do not have satisfactory vocabularies in a unit being taught, say in space travel, may be given special help with terms related to space travel. Those who need special help in mapping trips made in space may be given this help. Skill groups can be formed in any class to develop skills needed in that class.

In reading, skill groups might be formed to help certain children learn how to syllabicate words if this is the kind of help they need. Or, chil-

---

*See Chapter 14 for a discussion of Informal Reading Inventories.

dren might be grouped to learn when <c> represents /s/, as in city, certain, cycle, and when it represents /k/, as in cake, cloud, coat, crowd, and cup. And children who need help in automaticity of decoding could be given such help in a group.

If the special reading teacher team teaches with other teachers, he or she might form or help form such skill groups in regular reading classes and in content area classes. Teaching would be done using the vocabulary and materials of that classroom to teach reading skills. These groups may be very temporary in nature, for they exist only until their purposes are achieved.

INTEREST GROUPING

Children with various achievement levels may be interested in the same things—and other children in other things. For example, if in a social studies class there is a unit on children of the world, some children may wish to read about Mexican children while others may wish to study Canadian children—or British, or African, or Japanese, or Norwegian, etc. Some children may wish to read poetry written about or by children, while others may wish to get involved in a pen pal situation. Still others might wish to read whole books, and others may wish to gather and read information from travel bureaus about countries around the world. Some children may wish to read about the celebration of holidays around the world.

Often there may be no need for everyone to study the same thing. Children can work individually or in groups related to their strongest interests. This is true in any class.

If the special reading teacher team teaches with the classroom reading teacher and content area teachers, he or she may help in the identification of a wide variety of materials useful for specific units and may help coordinate the services of the school librarian with teachers who have specific needs.

SOCIAL GROUPING

Some children may wish to work together because they enjoy each other's company. At other times, children might work together to get to know each other better—perhaps children of different cultural backgrounds. Schools can provide for social development by the use of social grouping within a variety of contexts.

For example, if studying holidays around the world, children of different backgrounds might explain to each other about how a holiday—or birthday—is celebrated at their homes. Children who enjoy different kinds of music or poetry might share their favorites, and, together, children might grow to appreciate the values of others. To promote cooperation, a group of children might meet to distribute responsibilities for a week in the classroom: one might decide to water plants; another might keep the library shelves in order; another might read announcements to the class, etc. All might share in decorating the bulletin board or in making a mobile, etc.

CONSTELLATION GROUPING

All, or most, of the above procedures might flow from a unit plan. Figure 3.2 shows how this plan might operate in a content area classroom.

PEER AND CROSS-GRADE GROUPING

Sometimes individual children enjoy tutoring their classmates. Sometimes even children in an adapted group can teach something to another child in a more advanced group in the same classroom. This could help both children.

What some schools do is make provisions for older youngsters who are poor readers to visit lower grade level classrooms to read to younger children. Thus a sixth grader who reads at the third grade level might visit a second or third grade classroom to read to a child or several children in that classroom. The older child feels worthy and becomes proud of his or her reading ability. And the younger children enjoy being read to. There may also be a positive side-effect to this. Since these older children have gained successful experience in reading to younger children, they may at a much later date enjoy reading to their own children, a very desirable parental habit!

Summary

Vast differences in reading achievement (or readiness for reading achievement) exist among children at all ages. In fact, the range in reading achievement in a typical class of age-mates is two-thirds the chronological age of the average child. When children are six years old, the

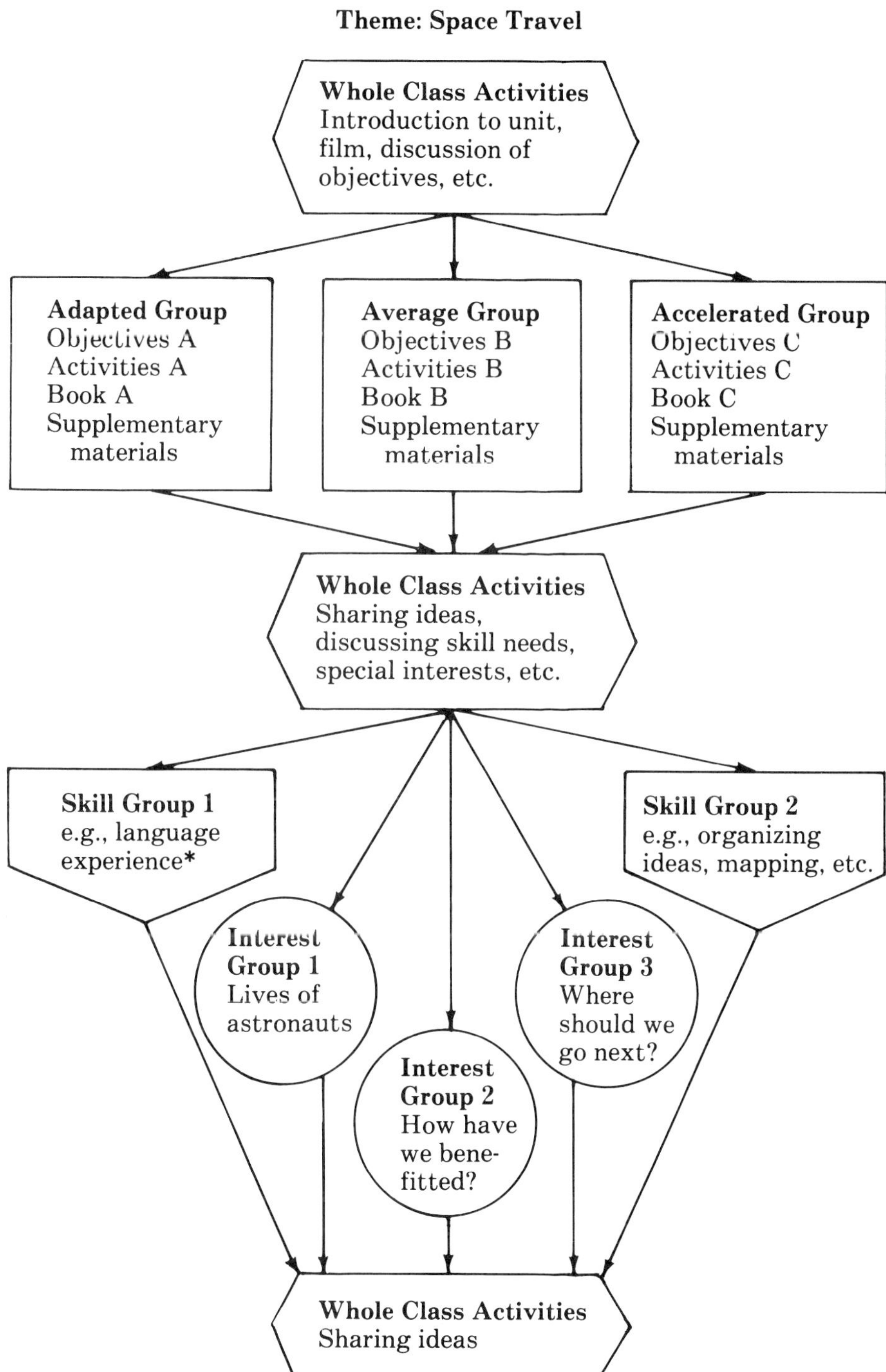

*Discussed in Chapter 13 of this book.

Figure 3.2: Constellation grouping.

range is already four years, and by the time they enter seventh grade, it is eight years. Knowledge of this tells us that schools and teachers must make adjustments to accommodate this span.

Two formulas were given, either of which might be used to aid teachers in gaining an idea about how well individual children might be expected to read. One of these formulas is expressed by the following equation:

$$\text{Reading Expectancy (grade)} = \text{M.A.} - 5.2$$
$$\text{or, for ease,}$$
$$= \text{M.A.} - 5.0$$

the other is

$$\text{Reading Expectancy (grade)} = \frac{2\,\text{M.A.} + \text{C.A.}}{3} - 5.2$$

Such formulas help the teacher understand the possible potential level for individuals. It should be understood, however, that not all children read at their potential levels. (In Chapter 14, ways of determining the level(s) at which individual children do read will be explained.)

School-wide (administrative) organizational plans were next discussed. Among these were:

- self-contained classrooms/grouping by chronological age
- junior first grade
- individualized instruction
- split-half plan
- team teaching (classroom teacher and special reading teacher)
- nongraded plans of these types: multi-age, homogeneous grouping by achievement, and homogeneous grouping by achievement—with overlap
- cross-grade grouping for reading
- SSR's (or USSR's)

Classroom organizational plans were also discussed. The following types were included:

- achievement grouping
- skill grouping

- interest grouping
- social grouping
- constellation grouping
- peer and cross-grade grouping

It must be understood that even if variations among children in classes are minimized, provisions must be made for grouping and individualizing instruction in these classes.

Questions and Activities

After answering the questions given at the beginning of this chapter, consider these questions and activities:

1. In viewing the range in reading achievement found in a typical classroom, it might be well to make informal comparisons with achievement in other areas of children's and adult's lives. Consider the last time you listened to a group of people singing—perhaps the National Anthem at a sports event. Did you notice the range in vocal ability? Have you watched a Little League baseball game? Did you notice the range in playing ability? Perhaps you can cite other examples in which the range in achievement is as broad as it is in reading.
2. What do you consider to be the strengths and the weaknesses of each of the administrative organizational plans discussed in this chapter? Which plan(s) do you view as most desirable? least desirable? Explain.

NOTES

1. John J. Goodlad. *School, Curriculum, and the Individual.* Waltham, Mass.: Blaisdell (Ginn) Publishing Co., 1966, p. 34.
2. See Albert Harris in Selected References. Also see George Spache in Selected References.
3. Albert J. Harris and Edward R. Sipay. *How to Increase Reading Ability, Sixth Edition.* New York: David McKay, 1975, p. 152.
4. Flemming Lundahl, p. 428. See Selected References.
5. *Ibid.*
6. Helen N. Driscoll, pp. 18–32. See Selected References.

Selected References

Anderson, Robert H. and John Goodlad. *The Nongraded Elementary School, Revised Edition.* New York: Harcourt, Brace & World, Inc., 1963.

Bean, Rita M. "Role of the Reading Specialist: A Multifaceted Dilemma." *The Reading Teacher,* 32 (January 1979): 409–413.

Cohen, Elizabeth G., Jo-Ann K. Intili, and Susan Hurevitz Robbins. "Teachers and Reading Specialists: Cooperation or Isolation?" *The Reading Teacher,* 32 (December 1978): 281–287.

Driscoll, Helen N. "In-Class Grouping," in *Organizing for Individual Differences,* Wallace Z. Ramsey (ed.). Newark, Delaware: International Reading Assoc., 1967, pp. 18–32.

Finkelstein, Miriam G. "What I Do (and What I Used to Do) as a Reading Specialist." *The Reading Teacher,* 32 (December 1978): 288–291.

Guthrie, John T. "Research Views: Grouping for Reading." *The Reading Teacher,* 32 (January 1979): 500–501.

——————————. "Research Views: Recreating Successful Reading Programs." *The Reading Teacher,* 30 (May 1977): 952–953.

Harris, Albert. "A Comparison of Formulas for Measuring Degrees of Reading Disability," in *Diagnostic Viewpoints in Reading,* Robert E. Leibert (ed.). Newark, Delaware: International Reading Assoc., 1971, pp. 113–120.

Horn, Janis L. "The Reading Specialist as an Effective Change Agent." *The Reading Teacher,* 35 (January 1982): 408–411.

Lapp, Diane (ed.). *Making Reading Possible Through Effective Classroom Management.* Newark, Delaware: International Reading Assoc., 1980.

Lundahl, Flemming. "Split-Half Classes," in *New Horizons in Reading,* John E. Merritt (ed.). Newark, Delaware: International Reading Association, 1976, pp. 428–433.

Moss, Jeanette K. "Alternatives: Four Schools of Choice." *Teacher,* 91 (June 1976): 33–38.

Ramsey, Wallace Z. (ed.). *Perspectives in Reading No. 9: Organizing for Individual Differences.* Newark, Delaware: International Reading Assoc., 1967.

Rauhala Ritva A. I. "Remedial Teacher as Cooperator—Finland." *The Reading Teacher,* 35 (January 1982): 412–417.

Robinson, Richard D. and Neila T. Pettit. "The Role of the Reading Teacher: Where Do You Fit In?" *The Reading Teacher,* 31 (May 1978): 923–927.

Sartain, Harry W. "Organizational Patterns of Schools and Classrooms for Reading Instruction," in *Innovation and Change in Reading Instruction,* Helen M. Robinson (ed.), N.S.S.E. Yearbook, Part II. Chicago, University of Chicago Press, 1968, pp. 195–236.

Singer, Harry. "Resolving Curricular Conflicts in the 1970's: Modifying the Hypothesis, It's the Teacher Who Makes the Difference in Reading Achievement." *Language Arts,* 54 (February 1977): 158–163.

Smith, Richard J., Wayne Otto, and Lee Hansen. *The School Reading Program.* Boston: Houghton Mifflin Co., 1978.

Spache, George. "Estimating Reading Capacity," in *The Evaluation of Reading,* Supplementary Educational Monographs, No. 88, Helen M. Robinson (ed.). Chicago: The University of Chicago Press, 1958, pp. 15–20.

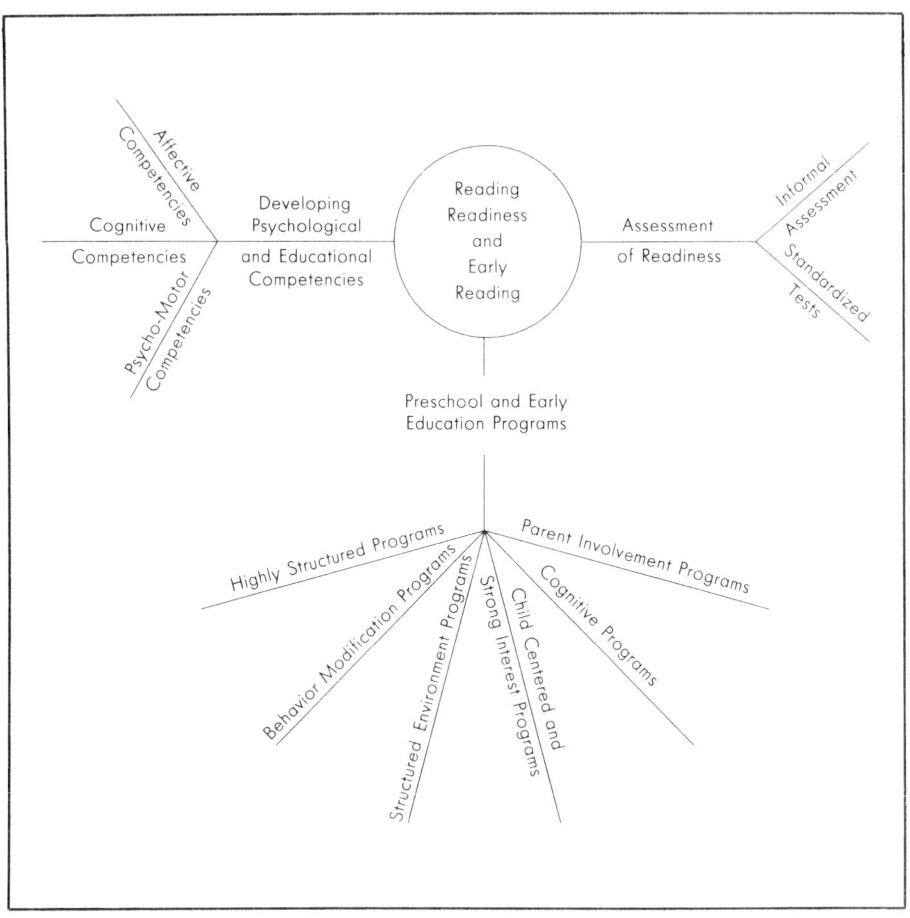

- What are major requirements for successful beginning reading?

- What are some major concerns and recommendations for pre-first grade reading and readiness instruction?

- What are the major affective, cognitive, and psychomotor competencies important in beginning reading? How can each be developed?

- How can we assess a child's readiness for learning to read through using informal (nonstandardized) techniques? What are some standardized tests available for use?

- How can we describe some major preschool and early education model programs? What have we learned from some of these programs?

CHAPTER 4

Reading Readiness and Early Reading

Often educators are asked, "When is the optimal time for beginning reading instruction?" Apparently there is no definitive answer to this question, for the answer varies according to two major factors and the interaction of these factors:

- what the capabilities and interests of the children are, and
- how the children are to be taught.

There is no magic age for the beginning stages of reading instruction. Some rather average children have learned to read at the age of two or three. Many early readers showed strong signs of readiness at the age of four. In some countries children are expected to learn to read at five. In the United States six or six-and-a-half have been target ages for teaching beginning reading. In other countries, the teaching of reading is normally delayed until the child is seven.

David Elkind[1] states that there are at least four requirements for successful beginning reading. They are

- a rich language environment,
- attachment to adults who model and reward reading behavior,
- attainment of Piaget's concrete operations stage, and
- an instructional program.

Some of these can be provided by schools, although home environment also plays an important role. Perhaps Piaget's stage is maturational.

Custom, or tradition, is a strong factor in deciding when most schools expect children to be ready. Yet, in reality, there seems to be no special time according to the rhythms of the world of children—when we think of children collectively. Like most other characteristics of children, the optimal age for beginning reading varies greatly from child to child.

According to some authors, the degree of readiness that a child exhibits for beginning reading can best be measured in relationship to the way in which the child is to be taught. Readiness for reading is not an abstract factor. One might best ask: Is this child ready to benefit from the Language Experience Approach? (And one might find out by trying that approach to see if it works with the child.) Or one might ask: Is this child ready to benefit from a certain basal reader approach? from individualized reading? other child language approaches? a very structured approach? etc.*

In reading readiness classes, the teacher should consider the way in which the child is to be taught to read, for those reading readiness activities that approximate the activities of the child's beginning reading program are most valuable. A major way to decide upon the activities that are appropriate for reading readiness is to know what the child is being prepared to do.

But, of course, there is more to reading readiness than "program readiness" or program related factors. Some of these additional factors are sociological, some are physical, and some are psychological. Major factors in these areas were discussed in Chapter 2.

The present chapter emphasizes ways of developing psychological and educational competencies that are commonly developed in school and preschool programs and through informal experiences that, according to many current philosophies, are related to a child's ability to begin to learn to read and to make progress in a reading program. These are:

- affective competencies
  - social skills: Since much work and play in schools involves group activities, a spirit of cooperation and sharing with other children and the teacher is essential. Consideration of others is also necessary when children work independently.
  - self-concept: Children need a feeling of self-esteem and self-confidence in order to progress. Teachers must be genuine in showing respect for children and their backgrounds, including their language, in order for learning to progress with as little stress as possible. Teachers should be personal in praising children for the progress they are making in class.
  - interests and language competencies: Children are easily motivated

---

*These approaches are discussed in Chapter 13.

to read if they are aware of the fascinating ideas that are found in books and if they are encouraged to respond personally to these ideas when they read or are read to. They need to understand that "book language" often differs from spoken language.

- cognitive competencies
  - oral language and concept development: Children need to understand meanings of words and "strings of words" and have "sentence sense" in order to understand and enjoy what they're reading. They need "pictures in their minds" to relate to authors' passages. When reading, they both use images they already have in their long-term memory storage systems and they add to these images.
  - story sense, story and text schema: Children need to understand the flow of stories—they need to sense the ways stories and other longer passages are organized so they can grasp major relationships when listening and reading.
  - following directions: Children must be able to follow the teacher's directions when being taught, and often they must follow an author's directions, or instructions, to complete assignments.
- psychomotor competencies: perceptual skills
  - auditory discrimination: Children need to distinguish—orally and aurally—one word from another and one sound from another both to learn through listening and to succeed in a phonics program.
  - visual discrimination: Children need to visually distinguish one object from another, one word or phrase from another, and one letter from another to learn through seeing and to succeed in developing a sight vocabulary and in recognizing visual-auditory relationships in a phonics program.
  - auditory-visual integration: Children need to auditorily recognize names of things they see. In a phonics program, they need to learn to associate words in print with their oral counterparts.
  - visual-motor skills: Children must learn to move their eyes from left to right and to make a return sweep to the next line in order to read. They must also learn to write words to successfully participate in a total language arts program.

This chapter also includes sections on the appraisal of reading readiness and on some recent and current preschool programs. The following chapter contains a discussion of ways of promoting parental involvement to help preschool and school youngsters.

Before discussing the above competencies, it might be well to examine "A Joint Statement of Concerns about Present Practices in Pre-First Grade Reading Instruction and Recommendations for Improvement," sponsored by several professional educational associations. (See Fig. 4.1).

Reading and Pre-First Grade

A Joint Statement of Concerns about Present Practices in Pre-First Grade Reading Instruction and Recommendations for Improvement

Sponsors: American Association of Elementary/Kindergarten/Nursery Educators; Association for Childhood Education International; Association for Supervision and Curriculum Development; International Reading Association; National Association for the Education of Young Children; National Association of Elementary School Principals; National Council of Teachers of English

A PERSPECTIVE on pre-first graders and the teaching of reading

Pre-first graders need
- opportunities to express orally, graphically, and dramatically their feelings and responses to experiences.
- opportunities to interpret the language of others whether it is written, spoken, or nonverbal.

Teachers of pre-first graders need
- preparation which emphasizes developmentally appropriate language experiences for all pre-first graders, including those ready to read or already reading.
- the combined efforts of professional organizations, colleges, and universities to help them successfully meet the concerns outlined in this document.

CONCERNS

• A growing number of children are enrolled in pre-kindergarten and kindergarten classes in which highly structured pre-reading and reading programs are being used. • Decisions related to schooling, including the teaching of reading, are increasingly being made on economic and political bases instead of on our knowledge of young children and of how they best learn. • In a time of diminishing financial resources, schools often try to make "a good showing" on measures of achievement that may or may not be appropriate for the children involved. Such measures all too often dictate the content and goals of the programs. • In attempting to respond to pressures for high scores on widely-used measures of achievement, teachers of young children sometimes feel compelled to use materials, methods, and activities designed for older children. In so doing, they may impede the development of intellectual functions such as curiosity, critical thinking, and creative expression, and, at the same time, promote negative attitudes toward reading. • A need exists to provide alternative ways to teach and evaluate progress in pre-reading and reading skills. • Teachers of pre-first graders who are carrying out highly individualized programs without depending upon commercial readers and workbooks need help in articulating for themselves and the public *what* they are doing and *why.*

RECOMMENDATIONS:

1. Provide reading experiences as an integrated part of the broader communication process that includes listening, speaking, and writing. A language experience approach is an example of such integration.
2. Provide for a broad range of activities both in scope and in content. Include direct experiences that offer opportunities to communicate in different settings with different persons.
3. Foster children's affective and cognitive development by providing materials, experiences, and opportunities to communicate what they know and how they feel.
4. Continually appraise how various aspects of each child's total development affects his/her reading development.
5. Use evaluative procedures that are developmentally appropriate for the children being assessed and that reflect the goals and objectives of the instructional program.
6. Insure feelings of success for all children in order to help them see themselves as persons who can enjoy exploring language and learning to read.
7. Plan flexibly in order to accommodate a variety of learning styles and ways of thinking.
8. Respect the language the child brings to school, and use it as a base for language activities.
9. Plan activities that will cause children to become active participants in the learning process rather than passive recipients of knowledge.
10. Provide opportunities for children to experiment with language and simply to have fun with it.
11. Require that pre-service and in-service teachers of young children be prepared in the teaching of reading in a way that emphasizes reading as an integral part of the language arts as well as the total curriculum.
12. Encourage developmentally appropriate language learning opportunities in the home.

Fig. 4.1: Used by permission of the International Reading Association.

Developing Psychological and Educational Competencies

Psychological and educational factors that affect reading readiness and reading achievement at all levels can be classified in three domains: the affective domain, the cognitive domain, and the psychomotor domain. Activities in these domains overlap, but each will be described independently here. When possible, activities for building reading readiness in subareas will be discussed briefly and sequenced from easy to more difficult.

Activities appropriate to this section are so broad that they encompass the total preschool curriculum. In this chapter, discussion will be limited to those aspects of readiness that deal principally with readiness for reading itself, and within these limits, to those activities that are closest in level to reading.

AFFECTIVE COMPETENCIES

Social Skills

Children need social skills so that they can work with teachers and with other children. Children must learn the values and joys of sharing and of helping others. They must learn to work in a group situation, to share responsibilities, to attend to a task, and also to work independently both to learn and to contribute to the whole.

Many activities can be used to develop social skills. For example, when playing games, children learn to take turns, to lead and to follow, to help their teammates (and even their "opponents"), to be patient in waiting for another child to take his or her turn, to comfort children who feel they have not done a good job and to accept such comfort themselves, to give reasons for a response and to listen to pros and cons for responses of other children, and to think of unique ways of responding to and solving problems.

Special occasions offer children the opportunity to work and plan together. In kindergarten and first grade, children might decide that they wish to celebrate each child's birthday, or they might decide to have one celebration each month for all of the children whose birthdays fall during that month. Each child might decide about the contribution he or she will make for each celebration. Some children might make cards, and they might dictate messages for the teacher to write on them. All children might learn to read these messages. Others might work together in making gifts. Some might work on a short program of perhaps music, dancing, reciting a verse, and/or playing a game that the birthday children would especially enjoy. Each child should be helped and encouraged in making the kind of contribution he or she wishes to make. And the teacher might contribute by reading a special story to the class for each party. Children might also wish to join together in celebrating holidays. They may wish to find out how holidays are celebrated by different cultural groups and may wish to plan a celebration that is representative of a group of children within their class.

On a regular basis, certain "chores" may need to be done daily or weekly. In a discussion, children might be made aware of these and might volunteer to help in doing them. For example, children might see that the fish have to be fed, the plants have to be watered, the milk or juice must be served, the waste basket has to be passed for debris to be thrown in, etc. Children might like to set up a schedule for doing these things. To help, the teacher might work along with the class in writing an experience chart with pockets in it for children to insert their names when they volunteer for duties, as illustrated in Fig. 4.2.

Figure 4.2

Self-Concept

Children need positive personal reinforcement. They need a feeling of worth, or value. The teacher is in an excellent position to build a child's feeling of self-esteem.

Teachers should look for characteristics each child exhibits that are worthy of praise, and should compliment children for their efforts in a personal way. (Yet, the teacher should avoid stereotyping children, e.g.:

Maria is smart. Yolanda is polite. Bruce is friendly.) Instead of saying, "The juice was served well today," the teacher should say, "*Clide* and *Wanda* served the juice well today . . . *Johnny* and *Jane* also served it well yesterday." Instead of saying, "What a nice story," the teacher should say, "*Your* story is interesting. *You* told us such a nice story, *Bobby*." Such personal comments help build the child's self-confidence.

Teachers' attitudes are readily recognized by children, and no child will be happy or confident if the teacher's attitude toward his or her language is negative. The child's language reflects his or her home, and even a very young child is aware of this. To criticize a child's speech (even in thought only) strikes at the totality of the child. The child may wilt or become defensive.

Robinson, *et al.*,[2] recommend that a teacher adhere to the following guidelines in relation to the child's language:

- the child's dialect should be accepted as readily as the "school-like" dialect during sharing time, storytelling, creative dramatics, and any other oral language experiences that might be provided for.
- when the teacher records for the children, as in the Language Experience Approach, standard spelling should be used, but grammatical variations should be recorded as dictated, or expressed, by the child or children. E.g., Billy might tell a story that sounds like this:

Recorded thus:

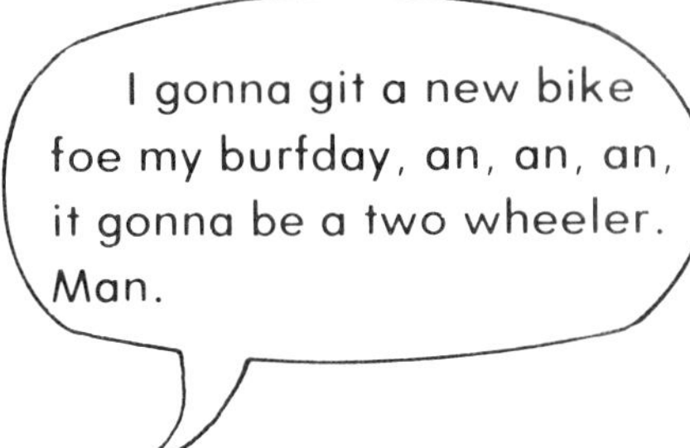

I going to get a new bike for my birthday. And it going to be a two wheeler. Man.

Thus the story is recorded grammatically as Billy told it, but the spelling is what he will see when he sees these words in print.

Interests and Language Competencies

A wide variety of activities can be used to build interest and cognitive competencies in reading during reading readiness years and later years. Children should be read to regularly—so that they can see the fascinating ideas that are in books and also so that they will understand "book language" and organizational patterns of stories (story schema). Besides reading traditional favorites to children, teachers might wish also to read children's choices of favorite books.* Teachers should always look for books that especially appeal to the child or children being read to.

Encouraging children to respond to stories is of extreme importance, although it is not always necessary. (Sometimes just listening is enough.) In discussing the response one might hope to get from a child, Charlotte Huck comments, "Always, I would begin with the child's response to the story, the way the story makes him feel, its meaning for him."[3] Such a response might be given in conversation—or in many other ways: through child acting, art work, music, etc.

Children should be encouraged to handle books, to page through them, to examine them. At school, books should be placed around the room in handy places for children. Perhaps an interesting area could be arranged in the room for reading materials . . . with a rug on the floor and soft pillows to sit on. One classroom used a water bed in a corner. Another had an African tree house—elevated above the floor.

When children page through picture books, they might wish to make up stories to accompany the pictures. At times, the teacher might record these on experience charts to show children that their speech can be written down. These stories could be read and reread at later dates and even sent home with the child with a note saying the child had made up the story.

---

*See Appendix C and the annual October issues of *The Reading Teacher*.

Children might "read along with" little books that have accompanying tapes. They might be encouraged to tell their stories to a child or a group of children. Together, children might dramatize stories. They might pantomime stories, or a character's role, use puppets and finger puppets, and have other children guess who they are.

The teacher might read poems to the class, and have children, through choral speaking, join in the refrain. Children can also ring bells, purr, meow, bark, play tambourines, maracas, etc., as appropriate to the verse or story the teacher is reading.

Cognitive (Intellectual) Competencies

Oral Language and Concept Development

Infants and preschool children enjoy being read to even when they don't understand all of the words. The rhythm of the voice intrigues them, and children learn new words and the "melody of language" through listening. But children also need real experiences in order to grow in language acquisition and concept development. They learn by listening, by doing, and by talking about things that interest them. A possible sequence for working with children follows. The "easier" experiences might be utilized at all ages, but the more difficult experiences would not be introduced until the child had succeeded with the easier ones.

Easy

- Children learn words, "strings of words," "sentence sense," and story schema,* plus much more, by being read to regularly—each day. They learn even more if they actively use this language in conversation, creative dramatics, choral speaking, puppetry, story telling, role playing, discussions, etc.[4]
- Children should be talked with regularly.
- Children expand vocabulary through broadened experiences—if words are given and explained to them. These experiences can be direct or vicarious. Usually direct experiences are most helpful. Being able to see and touch real objects promotes basic and necessary understandings. Later, pictures and films are helpful, if explained and discussed. Children should be taught names of objects they show an interest in and should be helped in describing the objects. If a bowl

---

*Story schema: essential elements of stories and organizational patterns of stories, discussed in the next section of this chapter.

of guppies sparks a child's interest, tell the child they are guppies—
and that they have another name—millionfish. They're fresh water
fish originally from the West Indies or northwest South America.
(You may wish to show the child the place on the map.) . . . Ask the
child what colors the guppies are . . . "Would you say they're small?
. . . tiny? . . . petite? . . . When the guppies reproduce explain to the
child why the babies are separated from the parents.
- Children need experiences in classifying. They should begin by classifying real objects, e.g., sea shells, flowers in a garden, buttons, anything they're interested in. They might be urged to name: What's
round? Point out things that are round. What's square? What's soft?
What's hard? What's yellow? What tastes good? smells good? feels
nice? etc. Later they can classify pictures, and much later, words.
- The Language Experience Approach and/or syntactical (sentence patterns) linguistic approaches* help children build vocabulary and sentence sense in the beginning stages of reading, as well as later.
Teachers must be alert to sense opportunities to teach new words
when children struggle to describe objects and feelings.

- Children may have to learn about word order in sentences. Sentences
can be broken into phrases or single words, which are written on
cards. Then children can be shown that these can be combined in
various ways. E.g., if we took sentences dictated by children and

---

*Explained in Chapter 6.

written by teachers and then separated them into single words, children might arrange the words as dictated and then attempt variations:

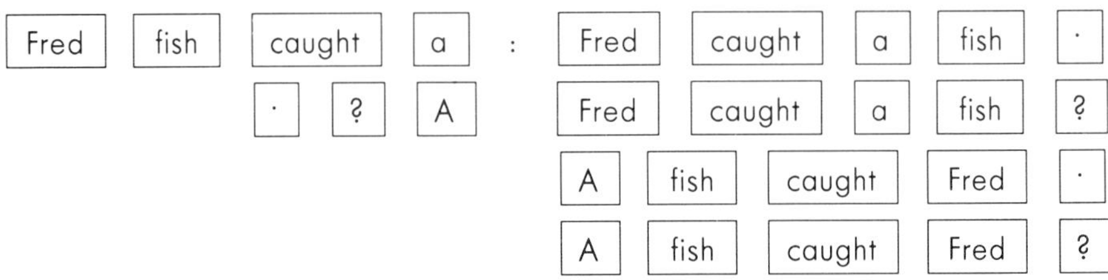

The meaning of each sentence should be discussed.
- Children need to learn about other syntactical elements, e.g., *signal words* (markers, structure words).* The teacher might take a sentence dictated by a child and write it down. The teacher might help the child in substituting words that make sense in the sentence. This could be done orally and then in writing. E.g.:

The fish	was swimming	in the river.
The boy	was playing	in the park.
The bird	was flying	in the sky.

- Children enjoy varying intonation patterns in sentences. Again, the teacher might take a sentence dictated by the children. Each of the words should be printed on a card and each given to a different child. The children line up and read the sentence orally, each child pronouncing her or his word. The first time, one word is stressed, and the child holding it steps forward. Then another word is stressed, etc. The children should discuss the different meanings of the sentence as different words are stressed.

Marcie swam across that river.	(Marcie, not Jodie.)
Marcie **swam** across that river.	(swam, not rowed.)
Marcie swam **across** that river.	(all the way!)
Marcie swam across **that** river.	(that river, not this one.)
Marcie swam across that **river**.	(river, not lake.)

> In all these activities, words, or strings of words, a child especially likes should be written on separate cards for the child to keep. These cards can be used in additional activities explained later in this chapter and book.

---

*Discussed more fully on pages 215–216.

• Children need to learn about sentence expansion. E.g., If a child dictates a sentence such as the following:

The dog was barking.   he or she can be helped in using modifiers:

The _____ dog was barking _____.
The huge dog was barking loudly _____.
The huge dog was barking loudly in the yard.
For this sentence, a picture of a dog might be drawn by the child or cut from a magazine, and descriptive words might be written around it. The child would circle those words that are appropriate to the sentence and picture. E.g.:

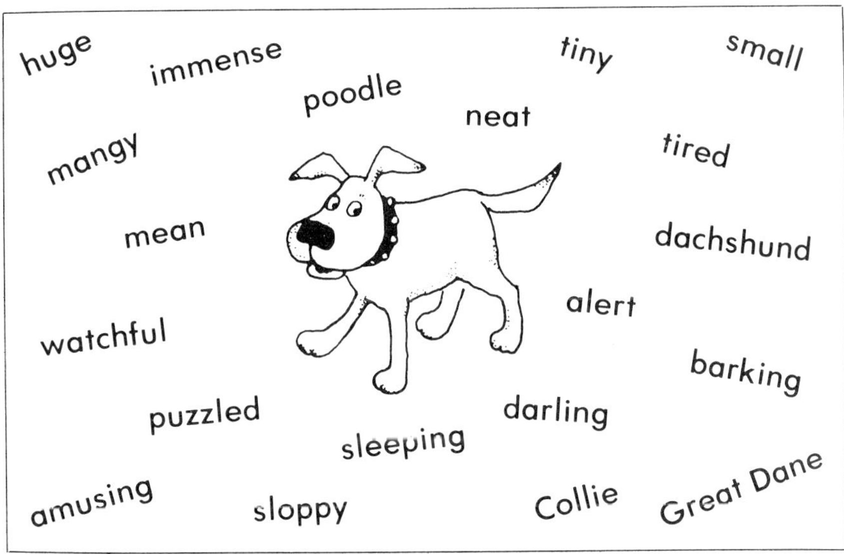

• Children need increased direct experiences and listening experiences—to learn more words, and to improve sentence sense, and story-line (story schema) understanding. Songs and nursery rhymes should be included.

More
Difficult

Story Sense, Story Schema, Text Schema

Story sense (understanding sequence and being able to anticipate) is essential to reading success. "Story schema" is a term frequently used to designate story-line and other essential elements of a story. By analogy, "text schema" explains organizational patterns of some other types of writing, like textbook writing.

Following are suggestions to help develop story sense. These are not sequenced in order of difficulty.

- Children learn *time-order sequences* by relating them to their everyday lives, e.g.: What does the child do in order between getting up and coming to school? What does the child do during a school day? on a day off?
- Children learn to pick out important events in stories that are read to them. And they are taught to put these in order, perhaps on a time line or flow chart or perhaps in a play. They may wish to use puppets or flannel-board characters to tell (or retell) a story. They listen to a part of a story and anticipate what will happen next. They might draw a picture depicting a story ending. Also they might guess what happened before the story began.

- Children learn *space-order sequence* by relating it to everyday life also. E.g., how does the child come to school? go to the store? go elsewhere? Where are important things in the classroom? in the library? on their bicycles? Etc. They are taught to describe and to draw "maps," perhaps working from three-dimensional models.
- Children learn to see spatial patterns in pictures in books and also to understand where things are that are described in stories. Participating in a play might help clarify such concepts. Children can sketch their own pictures from stories, with help from the teacher.

- Children learn about *text-schema* or logical reasoning by gathering information about different facets of something they enjoy. E.g., they tell why they like to swim—several reasons, why they enjoy a T.V. show. They are taught to explain, to analyze.
- Children learn to inquire for information and for directions. They use the information (e.g., in a skit) and to follow the directions given.
- Children learn to compare, but they must understand meanings of comparative terms. These meanings often must be taught to kindergarten children, e.g.: before/after, more/less, older/younger, bigger/smaller, etc.
- Children might listen to the teacher read aloud names of different objects. One child might be asked to remember one type, e.g., animals; another child might remember another type, e.g., flowers; etc.
  Teacher: "lion, tiger, daisy, elephant, banana, violet, dog, rose, orange, plum, . . ."
  The teacher might show pictures of objects of different colors, and one child might remember the green things (e.g., grass, trees); another might remember yellow things (e.g., a daisy, a pillow); etc.

Following Directions

Children must learn to follow directions for many reasons. (They must also know when *not* to follow directions, e.g., if a stranger asks them to get in a car.) Children must follow teachers's directions when being taught in school. Following are some techniques for teaching children to follow directions.

Easy

- Children play Simple Simon, Candyland, and other games.
- Children learn by doing simple activities, like folding and cutting paper, following directions given by the teacher or another child . . . one step at a time. They learn to hang up their coats in the proper place, etc.
- Children learn by being given one instruction to follow, and they follow it, e.g.: "Sharpen your pencil." Also: "Color the grass green." Wait until they finish. Then say, "Color the sky blue." Etc.
- Children then are ready to be given *two* instructions to follow, and they follow them in order, e.g.: "Go to the library, and pick out a book about animals." Also: "Color the grass green and the sky blue."
- Next they learn to follow *three* instructions, e.g.: "Take this note to Mrs. Green. Wait for an answer. Then take it to Mr. Klinger." Also: "Color the grass green . . . the sky blue . . . and the sun yellow." Etc. They might make up recipes and follow them.

More
Difficult

PSYCHOMOTOR COMPETENCIES: PERCEPTUAL SKILLS

The psychomotor domain is the realm in which motor (physical) skills and psycho- (mental) skills are integrated. Frequently the term "perceptual skills" is used to designate those psychomotor skills thought by many to be necessary for reading. These relate especially to "bottom-up" programs.

Perceptual skills that may affect reading achievement include auditory discrimination, visual discrimination, auditory-visual integration, and visual-motor skills. Each of these is a usual and/or necessary concomitant of beginning reading instruction.

Auditory discrimination involves the oral recognition of the alphabet, words, phrases, and longer units and is frequently taught by contrasting names of letters, phonemes* or strings of phonemes, sounds of whole words, and longer units.

Visual discrimination involves the visual recognition of the letters of the alphabet, graphemes** and strings of graphemes, words, phrases, and longer units and is frequently taught by contrasting letters, graphemes or strings of graphemes, words, phrases, and longer units.

Auditory-visual integration involves recognizing the relationships between auditory and visual forms of the same unit. This is frequently taught by correlating phoneme-grapheme (sound-symbol) relationships and by building a "sight vocabulary" of words and phrases.

Visual-motor skills are those that relate visual discrimination with bodily movement skills. A person uses visual-motor skills in handwriting, in focusing the eyes on parts of words, whole words, and phrases and in making saccadic movements, frequently called left-to-right eye movements.

Auditory discrimination and auditory-visual integration skills are not necessary in reading, but when a person reads a language he or she knows orally, these skills may help the reader relate the words being read to the words known orally (bottom-up theory). Since the oral vocabularies of young children are usually much larger than their reading vocabularies, this is usually viewed as a real boon. However, children who are extremely hard of hearing or deaf can learn to read without these skills. In these cases, sign language might be used by some as a substitute for auditory skills. People who read foreign languages frequently do so without recognizing oral counterparts for printed words.

Much of what is learned by humans is learned through visual, auditory, and motor perception, that is, through the trained use of physical senses. But what a person does with this learning is more often cognitive and/or affective, rather than perceptual. Also, what one is willing and able to learn through perception is controlled by cognitive and/or affective factors. Therefore, to conceive of a learning situation—such as reading—as wholly or principally perceptual appears to many reading experts to be very limited in scope. Yet, many reading readiness programs, including Sesame Street, deal principally with the development of perception as do some "bottom-up" reading programs. It should not be surprising to find that Sesame Street and other perceptual programs have little impact on those children who are not fortunate enough to have someone relate the lessons to them by introducing the lessons, discussing them afterwards, and extending them through related activities.

You may recall that in Chapter 2 of this book the following additional

---

* Phonemes are the smallest units of sound; e.g., the word *pat* has three phonemes: /p/ + /ă/ + /t/. Two possible "strings of phonemes" for this word are /pă/ and /ăt/.
**A grapheme is used to spell a phoneme; e.g., *pat* has three graphemes: <p> + <a> + <t> and two possible strings of graphemes: <pa> and <at>.

skills were discussed in the section titled "Perceptual Skills Related to Reading": figure and ground, closure, sequence, learning, and set. The teaching of these is integrated with the teaching of discrimination skills discussed in this section. The development of these skills is also included in later parts of this book.

Auditory Discrimination

For reading readiness and reading purposes, the teacher should work with children as closely as possible to the more difficult levels of these activities. The activities should be as close as possible to auditory discrimination activities needed in the types of lessons the children will have in their reading program, e.g., such as those given in the chapter on recoding and decoding in order to teach a complete phonics lesson (auditory discrimination, plus visual discrimination, plus blending, plus contextual application, i.e., vocabulary development). Following are some auditory discrimination activities graded from easy to difficult (or approximately so graded).

Easy

- Children point to the origin of a given sound (figure and ground).
- Children distinguish sounds in their environment: a jet, a helicopter, a car stopping, a train, a bird singing, a door closing, etc. Children might enjoy making a tape on which they record a variety of sounds for other children to identify (figure and ground).
- The teacher or a child taps a rhythm with a pencil. Children repeat it (sequence).
- The teacher plays a tune on the piano or other musical instrument. Children identify it and/or repeat the tune (sequence) and complete it (closure).
- Children listen for repetitions, e.g., when the teacher reads poetry. Children ring a bell, clap their hands, or orally mimic the repetition.
- Children play simple percussion instruments (gourds, symbols, rhythm sticks, chimes, bells, etc.) in rhythm with music to which they are listening.
- Children listen for special sounds of nature and learn to describe them, e.g., the wind howling, a brook bubbling and flowing, a bird chirping or urging its young to fly for the first time, a dog barking, a cat purring, etc. (figure and ground, and sequence).
- Children comment about loudest and softest sounds, longest and shortest sounds, high sounds, low sounds, etc., when listening to jets, cars, trucks, drum beats, piano music, etc.

══ readiness for phonics:

- Children listen for rhyming words, e.g., when the teacher reads poetry. They raise their hands when they hear these.
- Children produce, or volunteer, rhyming words.
- Children learn sounds of the letters of the alphabet, perhaps by listening for words that begin alike, e.g., when the teacher reads poetry that contains alliteration or lists of words. They tap their desk with a pencil, or they hold up the green side of a paddle when they hear these and the red side when they don't.
- Children produce, or volunteer, words that begin alike. They may correlate the names of the letters of the alphabet with their sounds. E.g., they may be asked to name words that begin with the letter b (analytic approach to phonics).

More
Difficult

Visual Discrimination

For reading readiness and reading purposes, the teacher should begin as close as possible to the visual discrimination activities given in the chapter on recoding and decoding. Following are some visual discrimination activities graded from easy to difficult (or approximately so graded).

Easy

- Children identify objects in real life and in pictures from clues given by the teacher. E.g., they point to a bird; they color or outline all of the balloons in a picture (or more simply, just check them), etc. (figure and ground).
- Children group like objects (dolls, apples, oranges, balls, etc.) together. Or they color all apples in a picture red, all oranges orange, all grapes purple, etc. (figure and ground).
- Children compare and contrast objects according to color, size, or shape, etc.
- Children group pictures together—similar pictures; later they compare and contrast pictures.
- Children classify and compare geometric forms—three dimensional, flat, etc., triangles, circles, squares, etc. They may group like items together, unlike items together, create pictures using these objects, etc.
- Children find likenesses and/or differences in geometric forms drawn on paper, e.g.:

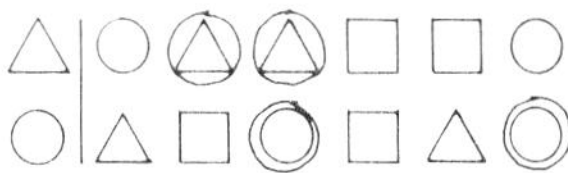

==readiness for phonics:

- Children indicate likenesses and/or differences in letters, e.g.:

  a | b   f   g   r   (a)
  d | k   m   (d)   s   p

- Children classify words from their word-banks.* E.g., they select all words that begin with <b> or <B>. They may share these with each other. The class might have a "B day," or a "F day," etc.
- Children indicate likenesses and/or differences in short words, e.g.:

  dog | pal   cat   (dog)   rag   fat
  sun | fun   run   pun   (sun)   sud

- Children may be asked to put letters or words in alphabetical order by their first letters. (sequence) These words might be from their own word banks.

More
Difficult

Auditory-Visual Integration

Children usually begin by reading some (or many) letters, also words and strings of words at "sight," i.e., they learn to recognize these without analysis, or without apparent analysis. That is, children build what is called a sight vocabulary.**

Easy

- Children learn letters, words, and strings of words at sight that they ask to learn, plus their own names. The teacher writes these for the children. They keep word-banks containing these, and they may play games or do other activities with them (top-down theory).†
- Children learn to read names of objects in the room from labels the teacher attaches to them. These must be discussed in class.
- Children may learn to read words, phrases, and sentences from their Language Experience charts (top-down theory).

---

* A child's word-bank cards are cards with words on them that the child recognizes at sight. See Chapter 13.
**See Chapter 6.
† See Chapter 13.

- Children may learn "empty" words, e.g., signal words (like a, an, the, these, is, was, of, etc.) and other bland words as parts of phrases and/or sentences, rather than as individual words. E.g., a boy, a girl, an apple, an orange.

More
Difficult

Later, or accompanying the above steps, children learn to integrate sound-symbol relations for parts of words if phonics is taught. This is explained more fully in Chapter 6.

In some programs, consonant and vowel phonemes (sounds) are isolated and contrasted before sounds of words are contrasted (synthetic approach). E.g.:

Thought to be easier

- Children contrast sounds of letters, e.g., /b/ with /f/ and /m/ and /n/ and /p/, etc. They associate the sound /b/ with the letter <b>, etc. They blend letter sounds, e.g., /b/ + /ă/ + /t/ to arrive at the sound of the word.
- Children compare and contrast whole words, both in sound and in written form.

Thought to be more difficult

However, in other programs, children do not listen to or produce sounds that consonants represent in isolation, though they may produce vowel sounds in isolation. They begin with words (analytic approach). E.g.:

Thought to be easier

- Children are asked to say and to view complete words that begin, e.g., with <b>, like *bat, ball,* etc., to learn the initial sound-symbol relationships for the initial b.
- Letter substitution is usually used to learn new words, e.g., bat→_at →cat, or bat→ba_ →bad, or bat→b_t→bit, etc.

Thought to be more difficult

Visual-Motor Skills

Left-to-Right Orientation and Ocular Control To read English as it's written, children must learn to move their eyes from left to right and to make the return sweep to the next line. The following activities relate to this skill.

Easy

- Children learn to differentiate the left side of their body from the right side to give orientation in space. Often they play "Simon Says" for reinforcement.
- Children arrange two, then three, then four objects, pictures, or cartoons from left to right to tell a story. They may arrange the letters of the alphabet from left to right.
- Children may arrange strings of words from their Language Experience charts, going from left to right. E.g.:

- Children arrange words from their Language Experience charts, going from left to right. E.g.:

- Children might work timed exercises like those given in the chapter on rate. E.g., they underline the letter in the series at the right that matches the letter in the left column. They are timed when they do this and compete only with themselves.

X	O	O	*X*	O
O	X	X	X̲	*0*
X	O	O	*X*	O̲
X	O	O	X̲	O

etc.

More
Difficult

Pre-Handwriting Visual-Motor Skills General visual-motor skills help children understand their environment. Looking at an object while feeling it, smelling it, listening to it, and possibly tasting it add to children's understanding of the world. Certain of these activities, such as those listed below, help prepare children for handwriting.

Easy

- Children collect "treasures" from their environment. They may wish to select fall leaves and mount them in interesting patterns. They may enjoy drying flowers and arranging them, etc. They may make collages using pictures from magazines.
- Children shape clay into interesting forms. They may enjoy shaping playdough, using a variety of colors.
- Children fingerpaint.
- Children supply missing details in one picture which otherwise is like another (closure), e.g.:

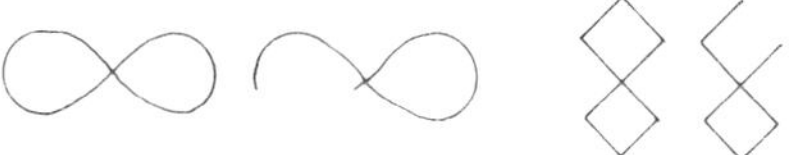

- Children might copy designs, e.g.:

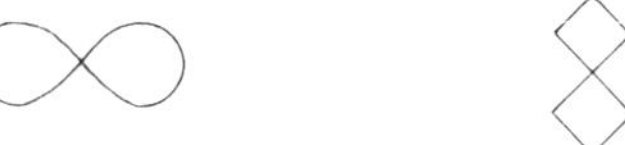

- Children make interesting shapes—and even letters, using blocks. They may also use pegs, pegboards, and geoboards. They may roll playdough into tube forms and make letters from these.

More
Difficult

Handwriting In most reading programs the four language arts (reading, writing, listening, and speaking) are used in a coordinated fashion. Children normally learn manuscript writing before they learn cursive writing because manuscript writing is what they see in the books they read. Writing their own alphabetic letters, words, and sentences helps them reinforce visual images, helps them remember what they've listened to, and enables them to produce messages that both they and others may read.

Easy

- Children learn letters (either capital or lower case) by using prompts. Steps in making the letters are numbered, e.g.:

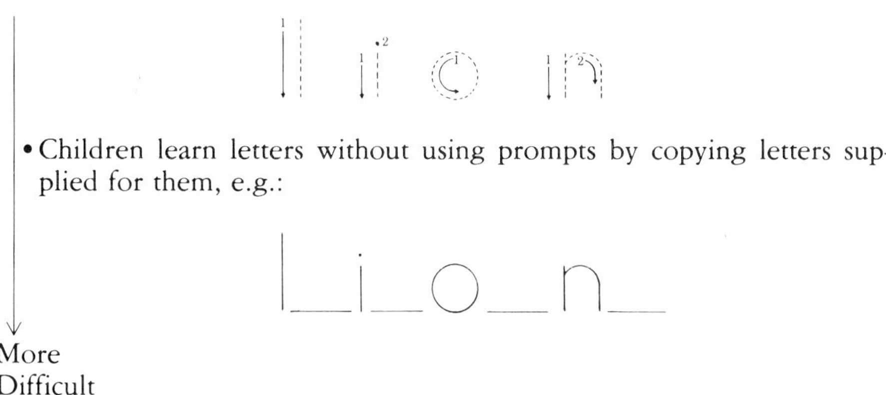

• Children learn letters without using prompts by copying letters supplied for them, e.g.:

More
Difficult

In bottom-up programs, children learn these letters in a predetermined order, e.g., alphabetical order, or according to shapes—straight letters first, then slant letters, round letters, curved letters.

In top-down programs, children learn these letters in order of their choice, e.g. the letters of their names and of words they want to learn.

Assessment of Readiness

When answering the question, when is a child ready to learn to read, sage advice might be: A child is ready to learn to read when he or she can do so without undue pressure. Harris and Sipay[5] say: "Readiness for reading . . . depends . . ., in part, on the fit between the child's abilities and the way he is taught. Thus a child of below-average intelligence may fail in a fast-moving group or succeed in a group taught slowly and patiently; and children with visual defects may learn to read normally if the print is made large enough." Some children may be ready to learn if the approach is highly structured, while others may only be ready for a free or creative approach.

Dolores Durkin[6] says: ". . . the readiness of children to read can be assessed most accurately by giving them varied opportunities to begin." She adds, ". . . careful attention must be given to the quality of these opportunities." Brzeinski and Elledge[7] add: "The question of readiness is being viewed as a *propaedeutic* function; namely, that when a child learns to read, he does so a step at a time—the vital requirement being that he is ready to learn the first step which, in turn, prepares him to be ready for the second step."

The teacher might recognize that it is an appropriate time to attempt to begin teaching the child to read through using both informal and standardized assessment procedures. These will be explained briefly below.

Informal Assessment

There is a fine line between reading readiness and the beginning stages of reading. Indeed, many "reading readiness" procedures continue to be used during the stages of early reading. While a child is learning to read words, strings of words, and/or sentences, he or she usually will also be continuing to work on readiness activities such as those described in the previous section of this chapter. Ideally, the "readiness" procedures blend with the "reading" procedures in a unified whole. One does not stop working on reading readiness in order to begin reading instruction.

Some teachers may feel comfortable in assessing readiness by identifying the child's position on a scale in each, or most, of the areas the teacher feels are important in reading readiness. Charts such as those given in the previous section of this chapter—in which the scales are an attempt to rank activities from easy to difficult—may be prepared by the teacher or by several teachers working together in a school situation. Such charts should relate to readiness factors that are important in relation to a specific program, or to specific programs, that might be used in the classroom. (Bottom-up programs stress psychomotor competencies, while top-down programs stress cognitive competencies. Both programs need some of each, plus affective competencies.) The higher the child is on a majority of these scales, the more ready he or she probably is for beginning reading. The lower the child is on several or many of these scales, the more he or she may need continued readiness activities, rather than reading activities, *per se*.

Some teachers or schools may feel comfortable in using a check list on which the mature points of each of the appropriate charts are listed. The teacher could simply check the attainment or nonattainment in each top level pre-reading area. When the top points of the majority of the areas are satisfactorily attained by a child, the teacher may feel comfortable in moving into the reading situation while continuing to work on readiness in the remaining areas.

If several programs or approaches are available for use in a classroom, the teacher might compare the relative readiness of individual children for particular programs or approaches by trying these on the children. Thus several children may be found to be "ready" to benefit from a child language or Language Experience approach, while others may be "ready" for a basal approach, perhaps of the type that emphasizes phonics, and still others for an individualized approach, or highly structured approach, etc.

Children might be identified who easily remember whole words or phrases. These could be taught by using a whole word approach, at least in the beginning stages. Other children may be identified who, instead, find it easier to learn words through writing, spelling, and sounding, while others may be identified who find the use of motor skills and phonics a most difficult task. In all cases, it would seem desirable to assess child preferences and interests also. But how can a child prefer something or be interested in it if he or she is not exposed to it? So, we return to a statement made earlier in this section. ". . . the readiness of children to read can be assessed most accurately by giving them varied opportunities to begin . . . careful attention must be given to the quality of these opportunities."

Published Informal Assessment Instruments

Published nonstandardized check lists and tests are available. Figure 4.3 is an example of a nonstandardized reading readiness check list. This

BARBE READING SKILLS CHECK LIST
READINESS LEVEL

(Last Name)   (First Name)   (Name of School)

(Age)   (Grade Placement)   (Name of Teacher)

I. Vocabulary:
   A. Word Recognition
      1. Interested in words _____
      2. Recognizes own name in print _____
      3. Knows names of letters _____
      4. Knows names of numbers _____
      5. Can match letters _____
      6. Can match numbers _____
      7. Can match capital and small letters _____

   B. Word meaning
      1. Speaking vocabulary adequate to convey ideas _____
      2. Associates pictures to words _____
      3. Identifies new words by picture clues _____

II. Perceptive Skills:
   A. Auditory
      1. Can reproduce pronounced two and three syllable words _____
      2. Knows number of sounds in spoken words _____
      3. Can hear differences in words _____
      4. Able to hear length of word (Which is shorter? boy-elephant) _____
      5. Able to hear sound:
         At beginning of word _____
         At end of word _____
         In middle of word
      6. Hears rhyming words _____
      7. Aware of unusual words _____

   B. Visual
      1. Uses picture clues
      2. Recognizes:
         Colors _____
         Sizes (big, little; tall, short) _____
         Shapes (square, round, triangle) _____

      3. Observes likenesses and differences
         in words _____
         in letters _____
      4. Left-right eye movements _____

III. Comprehension:
   A. Interest
      1. Wants to learn to read _____
      2. Likes to be read to _____
      3. Attention span sufficiently long _____

   B. Ability
      1. Remembers from stories read aloud:
         Names of characters _____
         Main ideas _____
         Conclusion _____
      2. Can keep events in proper sequence _____
      3. Uses complete sentences _____
      4. Can work independently for short periods _____
      5. Begins at front of book _____
      6. Begins on left hand page _____
      7. Knows sentence begins at left _____

IV. Oral Expression:
   A. Expresses self spontaneously _____
   B. Able to remember five word sentence _____
   C. Able to make up simple endings for series _____
   D. Able to use new words _____

Teacher's Notes:

Fig. 4.3: Barbe Reading Skills Check List, Readiness Level. Copyright 1975. Used by permission of Walter B. Barbe. Individual copies may be obtained from Dr. Walter B. Barbe, 823 Church St., Honesdale, PA 18431.

might serve as a guide to help teachers formulate their own lists.

Another list, based on the research of Marie Clay, a New Zealander, is shown in Fig. 4.4. The check list was written by teachers in the Fairfax County Public Schools, Springfield, Virginia. It is an attempt "to help teachers recognize the relationships between oral and written language that children must discover" in order to learn to read. The list is not an attempt to sequence understandings. The letters in the diagram are keyed to the explanations that follow.

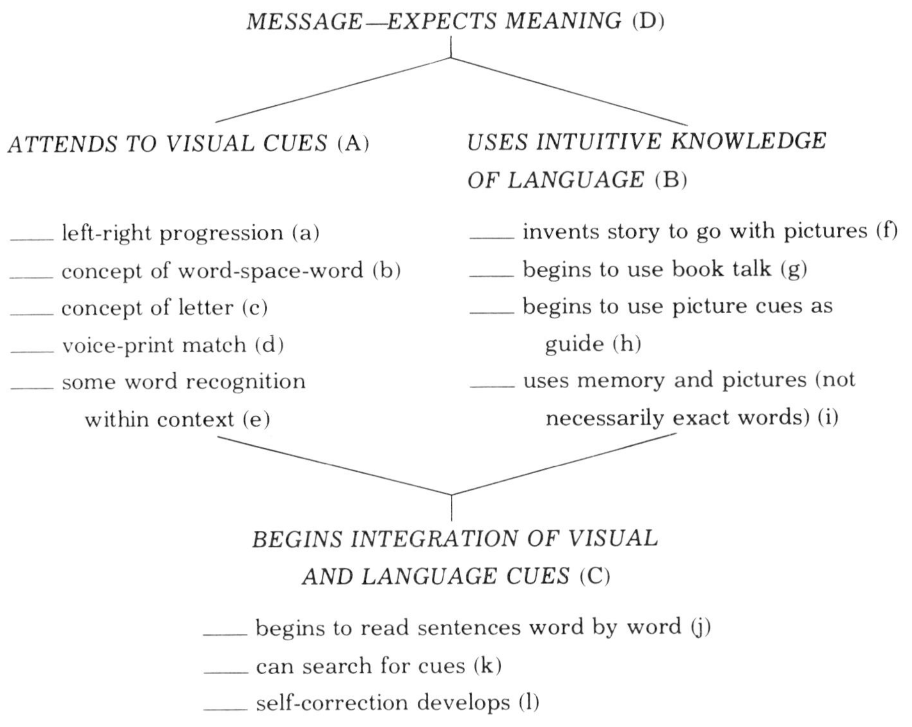

A. Does the child attend to the visual cues of print?
   - If I am reading a story, can the child tell me where to start and where to go next? (a)
   - Is the child able to point to words as I read them, thereby demonstrating knowledge of directional patterns of print? (d)
   - Does the child understand the concept of words and letters? Can he or she circle a word and letter in the book? (b & c) To eliminate the good guesser, this ability should be demonstrated several times.

B. Does the child use his/her intuitive knowledge of language?
- Can the child look at a picture book and invent a story to go with the pictures? (f)
- Does the invented story, when the teacher begins to write it down, indicate the child is using a more formalized language that approximates the language used in books (book talk) rather than an informal conversational style? (g)
- Does the child recognize that the print and the pictures are related? (h)
- Can the child "read the words" of a memorized text such as a nursery rhyme, even though the spoken words are not completely accurate matches for the print? Is this recall stimulated or changed by the pictures? (i)

C. Is the child beginning to show signs of integrating the visual and language cues?
- Is he/she beginning to read single sentences word by word, pointing to each word with a finger while reading? (j)
- Can the child use all the cues available to a reader: the predictability of language, word order, a beginning sound, and an appropriateness to context while reading? (k)
- Does he/she stop and correct, without prompting, when a visual-vocal mismatch occurs? (l)

D. Does the child expect meaning from print?
- Does he/she demonstrate that a message is expected by relating a sensible story?

Fig. 4.4: Reading readiness check list. From Gloria M. McDonell and E. Bess Osburn. "New Thoughts about Reading Readiness." Language Arts, 55 (January 1978): 26–29. Copyright 1978 by the National Council of Teachers of English. Reprinted by permission of the publisher and the authors.

The authors add the following words of caution:

Although this checklist can help teachers diagnose which areas a child needs to develop, teachers found that individual items could not be successfully taught separately. Rather, a diagnosis of weakness in any area usually indicates that the child needs more exposure to print in the form of choral reading, story writing, assisted reading, and so on. Certainly, just explaining the concepts is ineffective. To tell a child the meaning of "word" does not cause learning. An activity such as matching words on a word card to a chart containing a story, or matching a sentence strip and then cutting the sentence into words, involves the child in the learning process and is more likely to result in a clear understanding of the concept.

Standardized Assessment Instruments

Several standardized reading readiness tests are available for use in schools. Some of these are listed and briefly described below. Like informal instruments, a standardized test that includes readiness factors related to one type of program or approach may not be equally useful in indicating readiness for another program or approach.

Clymer-Barrett Prereading Battery (Santa Barabara, Calif: Chapman, Brooks and Kent.) Includes tests of visual discrimination, auditory discrimination, and visual motor skills.

Gates-MacGinitie Readiness Skills Test (New York, N.Y.: Teachers College Press, Columbia University) Includes tests of auditory discrimination, visual discrimination, following directions, letter recognition, visual-motor coordination, auditory blending, and word recognition.

Harrison-Stroud Reading Readiness Profiles (Hopewell, N.J.: Houghton Mifflin Co.) Includes tests in using symbols, visual discrimination, using context, auditory discrimination, using context and auditory clues, and letter names.

Lee-Clark Reading Readiness Test (Los Angeles: California Test Bureau) Includes tests of visual discrimination of letters and words, and of vocabulary and concepts.

Metropolitan Readiness Test (New York, N.Y.: Harcourt Brace Jovanovich) Includes tests of auditory discrimination, visual discrimination, school language, including a test of "reception of varied sentence patterns"), listening comprehension, and a "draw a person" test or an assessment of handwriting test.

Monroe Reading Aptitude Test (Hopewell, N.J.: Houghton Mifflin Co.) Includes tests in visual perception, auditory perception and memory, motor control, speed and articulation of speech, and language development.

Murphy-Durrell Reading Readiness Analysis (New York, N.Y.: Harcourt Brace Jovanovich) Includes tests of visual discrimination, auditory discrimination of phonemes, letter names, and learning rate.

Preschool and Early Education Programs

Some preschool and early education programs merit attention here because they are often discussed and because the findings of research studies related to some of them may be significant. These programs can be categorized roughly into six groups, with frequent overlappings among groups.

PARENT INVOLVEMENT PROGRAMS

Some programs stand out as programs designed to encourage parent involvement. The number of such programs is growing rapidly. Three such programs are briefly described here, but periodical literature should be consulted for more information about newly developing programs.

Denver Studies Two Denver studies point to important observations. One of these is a television study. This study was designed for children who were at least four-and-one-half years old. Sixteen television lessons were presented. Accompanying these lessons was a guidebook for parents to use with their children. Results were positive for those children who practiced 30 minutes or more per week. According to Brzeinski and Elledge, "The amount a child learned depended directly on the length of time someone practiced the beginning reading activities with him."[8] (You will recall that results of "Sesame Street" suggest the same conclusion.)

Another Denver study provided reading instruction to 4,000 kindergarten children, many of whom learned to read satisfactorily at this age. When these children entered first grade, some were placed in Denver's traditional first grade program, whereas others received adjusted instruction. When these children reached fifth grade, "early readers who had the adjusted instruction scored significantly higher on tests of reading vocabulary, comprehension, rate, and study skills than did their counterparts who began reading in first grade." The early readers who were placed in classes where the program was traditional "lost their early advantage and scored similarly to those who began reading in first grade."[9]

We might conclude that permanence of early reading appears to depend upon the type of instruction that follows it. Durkin,[10] when talking with parents of children who read early, found that some of them felt guilty, for they felt that their children might be bored or confused in first grade, no doubt fearing that they would be retaught those things they already knew.

DARCEE The Demonstration and Research Center for Early Education (George Peabody College for Teachers)[11] provides a program for three-, four-, five-year-old children and a training program for parents. Parents may be trained at home by a visitor or in the demonstration school to learn how to capitalize on common home situations for teaching children. Prominent objectives for the children are in the areas of sensory skill development, abstracting skills, and response skills.

Head Start Project Head Start[12] evolved from the national Economic Opportunity Act of 1964. It was designed to help four- and five-year-old children from the lowest socioeconomic levels, who, it was recognized, usually had disadvantages that deterred adequate school achievement. It had a strong parent component in that each local program had its own advisory committee that was composed of parents, and parents and other community members served in the program as volunteers or paid assistants and worked under the supervision of trained teachers.

The program had five components: It offered medical and dental services for children, social services and parent education, and services designed to help children develop psychologically. Also it included the use of volunteers within the program setting and provided for school readiness.

COGNITIVE PROGRAMS

Cognitive models are characterized by having clearly stated goals designed to promote specific cognitive and language development skills. A well-known model in this field is the *Ypsilanti Early Education Project.*

In Ypsilanti, Michigan, children beginning at the age of three or four attended a modified Piagetian preschool for two years. The program stressed the learning of skills and concepts necessary for classifying concrete objects by shape, size, and use, followed later by classifying abstract symbols. Also stressed was verbal interaction and sociodramatic play. Families of the children were visited weekly and were encouraged to participate in instruction.

At the end of second and third grade, these children outscored the control group children, who were in a traditional program, on the California Achievement Test, and their teachers rated them higher in academic, social, and emotional development.

CHILD CENTERED AND STRONG-INTEREST PROGRAMS

Many programs are child centered, in that the children are encouraged to express their own interests, and the development of the whole child is of utmost importance. In these programs attention is usually given to social, emotional, and academic development. These programs tend to weave learning experiences around a child's preferred activities. A few of these programs are briefly described in this section.

Open Education Model The Open Education Model[13] of Newton, Massachusetts, is based on the practices of British infant schools. The child's curiosity and interests are prized, and learning is designed in such a way as to respond to these. Communication skills and cooperation are emphasized when children work together.

TEEM The Tucson Early Education Model,[14] first designed for Mexican-American children in the primary grades, is now a preschool and elementary grades model for children of all backgrounds. Four facets characterize the program: language competence, intellectual base (recall, planning, organizing), motivational base, and societal arts and skills (reading and arithmetic).

The classrooms are organized in interest areas. Children who choose a common project, such as growing plants, work together learning new words and concepts about plants, learning to follow directions in caring for the plants, learning to measure, and other appropriate skills. They learn to cooperate with each other and with the teacher.

Bank Street The Bank Street Model,[15] of Bank Street College of Education, New York, emphasizes the nourishment of a positive self-image together with the development of the ability for self-direction. Learning experiences are usually based on children's play activities.

A rich environment is provided in which the child is given much freedom in choosing individual and group activities, which are used to provide for learning appropriate concepts and social skills.

Responsive Model Learning episodes of the child's choice highlight the Responsive Model program. The teacher provides materials, from which each child may choose what is of greatest interest to him or her. The teacher then helps with the vocabulary and other necessary skills, and the child is allowed to explore. Problem solving and the development of a healthy self-concept are stressed, and adults respond to children's needs rather than initiate learning. This program was developed by the Far West Laboratory for Educational Research and Development in San Francisco.

STRUCTURED ENVIRONMENT PROGRAMS

In structured environment programs, the child achieves growth through organizing his or her environment rather than from interacting with the teacher. Probably the best known program of this type is the *Montessori*[16] program.

Maria Montessori, an Italian medical doctor, worked successfully in teaching Italian children of low measured intelligence at the turn of the century. She then began teaching normal children who were three to five years of age and achieved worldwide recognition for these efforts and successes. In time, however, interest waned, but has again been revived, somewhat. Many American communities today have modified Montessori type preschools and schools.

In the nonmodified Montessori schools that maintain the old tradition, children tend to spend much time working alone on very structured and convergent activities. There is a heavy emphasis on perception, with little attention given to social or emotional development or creative problem solving. Materials include a movable alphabet and sandpaper letters for a tactile (touch) approach. However, in addition, the teacher frequently reads to the children, and books are available to the children for their own reading. Many children in these schools do learn to read before the age of six.

BEHAVIOR MODIFICATION PROGRAMS

Behavior modification models focus on reinforcing desired behaviors through the use of rewards. The *Behavior Analysis Model* focuses on teaching children to complete tasks, to work independently, and to pay attention through the use of rewards. These rewards can be used to "buy" something the child wants, such as time to listen to the teacher read a story. Necessary skill development in reading readiness and reading might also be taught and carefully measured and rewarded. This program stems from the Department of Human Development, University of Kansas at Lawrence.

HIGHLY STRUCTURED PROGRAMS

Highly structured learning models are characterized by carefully sequenced steps in learning, the regular checking of these steps, and immediate reteaching of steps missed. Two much discussed models are included here.

Talking-Typewriter Omar Khayyam Moore, of Yale University, experimented in teaching two- and three-year-old children to read by using a "talking typewriter."[17] In the sequence of teaching, when a particular letter was to be learned, all keys on the typewriter were locked but the key for that letter. When the child touched that key, say *b*, a *b* flashed on a screen, along with the name of the letter spoken by an unseen attendant. If a word was to be learned, the first letter was unlocked first, e.g., *c*; then the second, e.g., *a*; then the third, e.g., *t*. Then the word was pronounced.

Young children did learn to read by using this machinery, the price of which was said to have been $32,000—apiece.

It was reported that once a little girl pressed a *b*, and a *c* came on the screen, and the voice said *C*. She pressed the *b* two or three times again, with the same response. Then she got up, kicked the machine, pressed *b*, and the voice said *B*. She responded, "That's right, typewriter."

Engleman-Becker Model: Distar Siegfried Engleman and Wesley Becker[18] of the University of Oregon, Eugene, developed a highly structured program for low income children from preschool age to grade three. Attention is strictly focused on the subskill being taught with no deviations allowed. The curriculum, called Distar, has been designed to teach reading, language, and arithmetic. Children are taught in small groups of about five children.

COMMENT RELATED TO ALL EARLY INTERVENTION PROGRAMS

Many early intervention programs have been designed to help the future educational performance of minority and lower-class children. In an article titled "Effects of Early Intervention Programs," Doris Roettger[19] discusses some of the important programs and highlights findings related to language deprivation. She reports that Martin Deutsch observed that low socioeconomic children "lack knowledge of context" (i.e., background of experience, meanings) "and of syntactical regularities which lead to comprehension of language sequences." This, of course, is related to concept development—which is achieved through "learning by doing" in a rich environment and through learning by being read to and spoken with.

Dr. Roettger also comments: ". . . children from birth through five years of age will spend a relatively small amount of time in intervention programs. Thus, these programs in themselves cannot totally offset the results of deprivation. Parents must become involved to change the home environment of the child."[20] Another very cogent observation was made: Many of the intervention programs have been designed to prepare children for the kinds of primary level programs that now exist in our schools. Instead, what is needed, according to Dr. Roettger, is that the curricula of elementary schools must be adjusted to the needs of these children.

Summary

Although it may be tempting to decide that there is a magic age for beginning reading instruction, such is not the case. Children learn to read at different ages, because they are ready to learn to read at different ages. Part of this readiness, however, is determined by the way in which the children are taught. Average children can learn to read at very young ages if they are given much individual attention and if they concentrate much effort on learning. In order to read with meaning (i.e., beyond the recoding stage) they must also have had the necessary experiences for concept development (and cognition) to occur.

There are many factors that affect children's readiness for reading and their success (or lack of it) in reading. Among these are educational, sociological, physical, and psychological factors. Many of these were discussed in Chapter 2. The degree of readiness that children exhibit for beginning reading can be measured best in relationship to the way in which the children are to be taught.

Because psychological and educational competencies are extremely important in the school situation, strategies for developing these have been suggested in this chapter. These have been classified in three domains: the affective domain, the cognitive domain, and the psychomotor domain. Affective competencies discussed include the development of social skills, self-concept, and interests. Cognitive competencies discussed include the development of oral language and concepts, story sense or story and text schema, and following directions. Psychomotor competencies discussed include auditory discrimination, visual discrimination, auditory-visual integration, visual-motor skills (left-to-right orientation and ocular control, pre-handwriting, visual-motor skills, and handwriting).

Next, the assessment of readiness was discussed. Included was a rationale for encouraging informal assessment in relation to the program or programs to be used in beginning reading. Two published informal assessment check lists were included, which might be used as guides to help teachers compose their own lists. Also, some standardized reading readiness tests were named and briefly described.

Some preschool and early education programs were described next. These were discussed in the following categories: parent involvement programs, cognitive programs, child centered and strong-interest programs, structured environment programs, behavior modification programs, and highly structured programs. A final comment in this section included the finding that parents and homes of children are of extreme importance and that parental involvement is of prime importance.

Questions and Activities

After answering the questions given at the beginning of this chapter, consider these questions and activities:

1. Why is each of these necessary for successful beginning reading:
   - a rich language environment
   - attachment to adults who model and reward reading behavior
   - attainment of Piaget's concrete operations stage, and

- an instructional program?

Are all of these necessary for "bottom-up" reading programs? for "top-down" reading programs? Explain.

2. Do the recommendations given in the "Joint Statement about Concerns . . ." (p. 000) reflect a bottom-up, top-down, or interactive philosophy of reading?

3. Pair-off with another student. One of you may role play as a child with a variant dialect and may dictate a brief experience story (and write it as dictated). The other person will role play as a teacher and will write the story as a teacher would for a child. Compare the two written versions and judge the value of the recommendation given in this chapter that standard spelling should be used but the child's grammar. Consider the child's ego and the transferability of skills to reading assignments to be given later.

4. Do you agree with Charlotte Huck's recommendation for discussing a story that, "Always, I would begin with the child's response to the story, the way the story makes him feel, its meaning for him"? Explain. How might such a response be given by a child besides through discussion?

5. Review suggestions concerning oral language and concept development. Can you add to these suggestions? Try to develop additional examples for those basic strategies you think are important. Share these with your classmates. Are these suggestions principally for bottom-up or top-down programs? Explain.

6. Elaborate on suggestions for building story sense, story and text schema. Share these with your classmates.

7. Elaborate on suggestions for developing the ability to follow directions. Share these with your classmates. Why must a child be able to follow directions in order to learn to read?

8. How much emphasis would be given to developing psychomotor competencies in preparation for a "bottom-up" reading program? for a "top-down" reading program? Explain.

9. Try to develop additional types of auditory discrimination activities that prepare a child for phonic instruction . . . visual discrimination activities that prepare a child for phonic instruction . . . auditory-visual integration activities . . . visual-motor skills. Share these with your classmates.

10. Compare the two informal assessment instruments (checklists) given in this chapter. How are they alike? different?

11. What two important conclusions can be drawn from the Denver studies? What important findings does Doris Roettger (pp. 00) emphasize as related to early intervention programs? Consider these findings in relation to the importance of parent involvement recommendations given in Chapter 5.

NOTES

1. David Elkind, p. 335. See Selected References.
2. Violet B. Robinson, Dorothy S. Strickland, and Bernice Cullinan, pp. 31–32. See Selected References.
3. Charlotte Huck, p. 42. See Selected References.
4. Bernice E. Cullinan, Angela Jaggar, and Dorothy Strickland, pp. 98–112. See Selected References.
5. Albert J. Harris and Edward R. Sipay. *How to Increase Reading Ability, Sixth Ed.* New York: David McKay, 1975, pp. 18–19.
6. Dolores Durkin, 1967, p. 33. See Selected References.
7. Joseph R. Brzeinski and Gerald E. Elledge, pp. 73–74. See Selected References.
8. *Ibid.*, p. 70.
9. Lloyd O. Ollila, 1972, p. 55. See Selected References.
10. Dolores Durkin, *op. cit.*, p. 1.
11. George Peabody College for Teachers, Nashville, Tennessee.
12. See S. Moore in Selected References, also E. Zigler.
13. See G. Engstrom (ed.) in Selected References.
14. Arizona Center for Early Childhood Education, University of Arizona, Tucson.
15. See Barbara Biber in Selected References.
16. See Maria Montessori in Selected References, also *Montessori in Perspective.*
17. See the following authors in Selected References: E. S. Hirsch, also S. Moskowitz, also J. E. Brzeinski, "Early Introduction to Reading."
18. See Carl Bereiter and Siegfried Engleman in Selected References.
19. Doris Roettger, pp. 464–471. See Selected References.
20. *Ibid.*

SELECTED REFERENCES

Anselmo, Sandra. "Improving Home and Preschool Influences on Early Language Development." *The Reading Teacher*, 32 (November 1978): 139–143.

Aukerman, Robert C. (ed.). *Some Persistent Questions on Beginning Reading.* Newark, Delaware: International Reading Association, 1972.

Barufaldi, James P. and Jennifer Wallenfels Swift. "Children Learning to Read Should Experience Science." *The Reading Teacher*, 30 (January 1977): 388–393.

Bereiter, Carl and Siegfried Engleman. *Teaching Disadvantaged Children in the Preschool.* Englewood Cliffs, N.J.: Prentice-Hall, 1966.

Biber, Barbara. "Goals and Methods in a Preschool Program for Disadvantaged Children." *Children* (Feb. 1970). Also in *Early Childhood Education*, Bernard Spodek (ed.). Englewood Cliffs, N.J.: Prentice-Hall, 1973, pp. 249–262.

Briggs, C. and David Elkind. "Characteristics of Early Readers." *Perceptual and Motor Skills*, 44 (1977): 1231–1237.

Brzeinski, Joseph. "Early Introduction to Reading," in *Reading and Inquiry*, J. A. Figurel (ed.). Newark, Delaware: International Reading Assoc., 1965, pp. 443–446.

——————————— and Gerald E. Elledge. "Early Reading," in *Some Persistent Questions on Beginning Reading*, Robert C. Aukerman (ed.). Newark, Delaware: International Reading Association, 1972, pp. 65–76.

Carlton, Lessie and Robert H. Moore. *Reading, Self-Directive Dramatization and Self-Concept.* Columbus, Ohio: Chas. E. Merrill, 1968.

Clark, M. M. *Young Fluent Readers.* London: Heinemann Educational Books, 1976.

Clay, Marie M. *Reading: The Patterning of Complex Behavior.* Aukland, New Zealand: Heineman Educational Books, 1972.

Corcoran, Gertrude B. *Language Experience for Nursery and Kindergarten Years.* Itasca, Illinois: P. E. Peacock Publications, Inc., 1976.

Cox, Mary B. "The Effect of Conservation Ability on Reading Competency." *The Reading Teacher*, 30 (December 1976): 251–258.

Cullinan, Bernice E., Angela Jaggar, and Dorothy Strickland. "Language Expansion for Black Children in the Primary Grades: A Research Report." *Young Children*, 29 (January 1974): 98–112.

Deutsch, Martin, *et al. The Disadvantaged Child.* New York: Basic Books, 1967.

Durkin, Dolores. "Informal Techniques for the Assessment of Pre-reading Behavior," in *Perspectives in Reading #8: The Evaluation of Children's Reading Achievement*, Thomas C. Barrett (ed.). Newark, Delaware: International Reading Association, 1967, pp. 27–34.

——————————. *Reading and the Kindergarten, An Annotated Bibliography.* Newark, Delaware: International Reading Association, 1969.

——————————. "A Six Year Study of Children Who Learned to Read in School at the Age of Four." *Reading Research Quarterly*, 10 (1974–1975): 9–60.

Dykstra, Robert. "The Use of Reading Readiness Tests for Prediction and Diagnosis: A Critique," in *Perspectives in Reading #8: The Evaluation of Children's Reading Achievement*, Thomas C. Barrett (ed.). Newark, Delaware: International Reading Association, 1967, pp. 35–52.

Elkind, David. "Cognitive Development and Reading," in *Theoretical Models and Processes of Reading, Second Edition*, Harry Singer and Robert B. Ruddell (eds.). Newark, Delaware: International Reading Assoc., 1976, pp. 331–340.

Engstrom, G. (ed.). Open Education: *The Legacy of the Progressive Movement.* Washington, D.C.: National Association for the Education of Young Children, 1970.

Frost, J. L. and B. L. Klein. *Children's Play and Playgrounds.* Boston: Allyn and Bacon, 1979.

Hess, Robert D. and Doreen J. Croft. *Teachers of Young Children, 2nd Edition.* Boston: Houghton Mifflin Co., 1975.

Hirsch, E. S. "What Are Good Responsive Environments for Young Children? A Critical Discussion of O. K. Moore's Theoretical Foundations." *Young Children*, 28 (1972): 75–80.

Huck, Charlotte S. "Strategies for Improving Interest and Appreciation in Literature," in *Reaching Children and Young People Through Literature*, Helen W. Painter (ed.). Newark, Delaware: International Reading Assoc., 1971, pp. 37–45.

King, Ethel M. "Prereading Programs: Direct versus Incidental Teaching." *The Reading Teacher*, 31 (February 1978): 504–510.

King, Viola. "Dialect Awareness in Preschoolers." *Language Arts*, 53 (March 1976): 248–250.

Leeper, Sarah Hammond, Dora Sikes Skipper, and Ralph L. Witherspoon. *Good Schools for Young Children, Fourth Edition*. New York: Macmillan Publishing Co., 1974.

Lesiak, Judi. "Reading in Kindergarten: What the Research Doesn't Tell Us." *The Reading Teacher*, 32 (November 1978): 135–138.

Lindberg, Lucile and Rita Swedlow. *Early Childhood Education: A Guide for Observation and Participation*. Boston: Allyn and Bacon, Inc., 1976.

Lloyd, Mavis J. "Teach Music to Aid Beginning Readers." *The Reading Teacher*, 32 (December 1978): 323–327.

Lorton, John W. and Bertha L. Walley. *Introduction to Early Childhood Education*. New York: D. Van Nostrand Co., 1979.

MacGinitie, Walter. "Evaluating Readiness for Learning to Read: A Critical Review and Evaluation of Research." *Reading Research Quarterly*, 4 (1969): 396–410.

——————————. "When Should We Begin to Teach Reading?" *Language Arts*, 53 (Nov./Dec. 1976): 878–882.

McDonald, Dorothy. "Music and Reading Readiness." *Language Arts*, 52 (September 1975): 872–876.

Merritt, John E. (ed.). *New Horizons in Reading*. Newark, Delaware: International Reading Association, 1976.

Montessori, Maria. *The Montessori Method*. Cambridge, Mass.: Robert Bentley, Inc., 1912 and 1965.

Montessori in Perspective. Washington, D.C.: National Association for the Education of Young Children, 1966.

Moore, S. "The Effects of Head Start Programs with Different Curricular and Teaching Strategies. *Young Children*, 32 (1977): 54–61.

Moskowitz, S. "Should We Teach Reading in the Kindergarten?" *Elementary English*, 42 (1965): 798–804.

Ollila, Lloyd D. (ed.). *The Kindergarten Child and Reading*. Newark, Delaware: International Reading Association, 1977.

__________. "Pros and Cons of Teaching Reading to Four- and Five-Year Olds," in *Some Persistent Questions on Beginning Reading*, Robert C. Aukerman (ed.). Newark, Delaware: International Reading Association, 1972.

Past, Kay Cude, Al Past, and Scheila Bernal Guzmán. "A Bilingual Kindergarten Immersed in Print." *The Reading Teacher*, 33 (May 1980): 907–913.

Pines, Maya. "How Children Learn to Talk." *Redbook*, (November 1979): 35ff

Read, Katherine and June Patterson. *The Nursery School and Kindergarten—Human Relationships and Learning, 7th Edition.* New York: Holt, Rinehart and Winston, 1980.

Roberts, Kathleen Piegdon. "Piaget's Theory of Conservation and Reading Readiness." *The Reading Teacher*, 30 (December 1976): 246–250.

Robinson, Violet, Dorothy S. Strickland, and Bernice Cullinan. "The Child: Ready or Not?" in *The Kindergarten Child and Reading*, Lloyd O. Ollila (ed.). Newark, Delaware: International Reading Association, 1977, pp. 13–39.

Robison, Helen F. *Exploring Teaching in Early Childhood Education.* Boston: Allyn and Bacon, 1977.

Roettger, Doris. "Effects of Early Intervention Programs," in *New Horizons in Reading*, John E. Merritt (ed.). Newark, Delaware: International Reading Association, 1976, pp. 464–471.

Rosen, C. E. "The Effects of Socio-Dramatic Play on Problem-Solving Behavior among Culturally Disadvantaged Pre-School Children." *Child Development*, 45 (1974): 920–927.

Sebesta, Sam. "Why Rudolph Can't Read." *Language Arts*, 58 (May 1981): 545–548.

Seitz, Victoria. *Social Class and Ethnic Group Differences in Learning to Read.* Newark, Delaware: International Reading Association, 1977.

Smith, Helen K. (ed.). *Perception and Reading.* Newark, Delaware: International Reading Association, 1968.

Vernon, Magdalen D. *Visual Perception and Its Relation to Reading: An Annotated Bibliography.* Newark, Delaware: International Reading Association, 1973.

Waller, T. Gary. *Think First, Read Later! Piagetian Prerequisites for Reading.* Newark, Delaware: International Reading Association, 1977.

Wanat, Stanley F. (ed.). *Issues in Evaluating Reading.* Linguistics and Reading Series: 1. Arlington, Va.: Center for Applied Linguistics, 1977.

Whiren, A. "Table Toys: The Underdeveloped Resource." *Young Children*, 30 (1975): 413–419.

Willems, Arnold and Wanda L. Willems. "Please, Read Me a Book." *Language Arts*, 52 (September 1975): 831–835.

Zigler, E. "America's Head Start Program: an Agenda for Its Second Decade." *Young Children*, 33 (1978): 4–11.

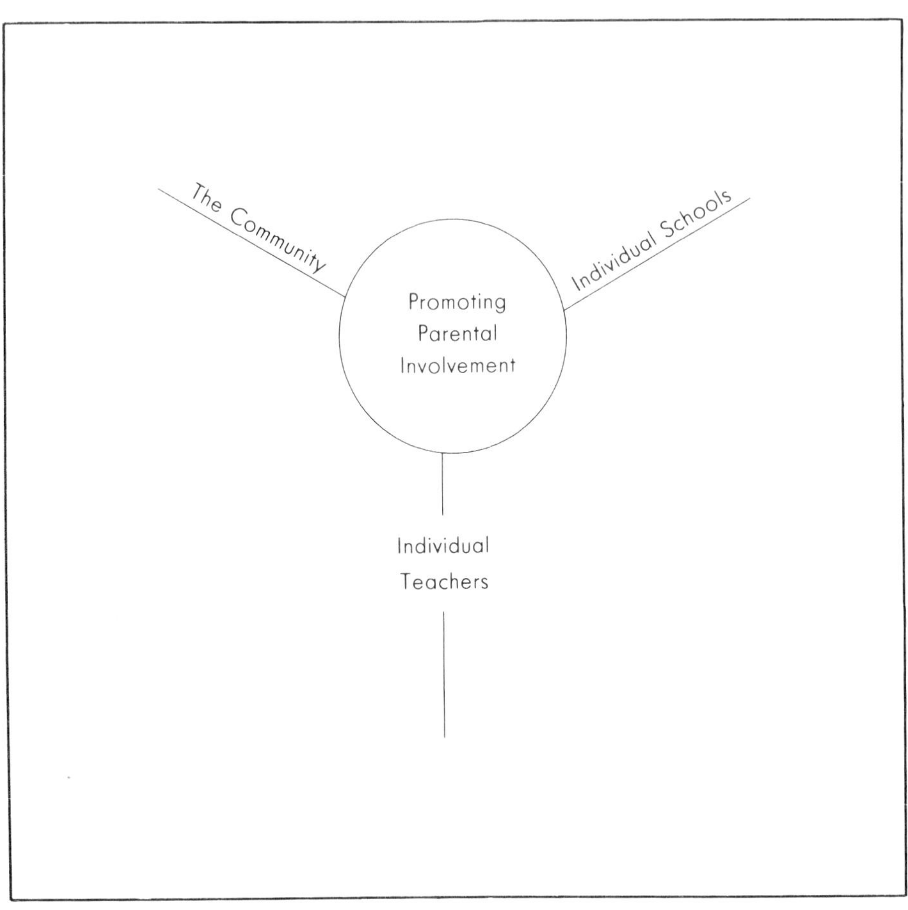

- Why is the home of the child of vital importance in developing his or her reading readiness and reading achievement?

- What can best be done on a community-wide basis that will promote parental awareness and help in developing reading readiness and reading interest and achievement?

- What can best be done in individual schools to promote parental awareness and help in developing reading readiness and reading interest and achievement?

- What can best be done by the child's teachers to promote parental awareness and help in developing reading readiness and reading interest and achievement?

CHAPTER 5

Promoting Parental Involvement

In the last decade, much attention has focused on the importance of the home and preschool years in later school achievement. Children spend most of their time during their preschool years at home, and during their school years they spend much more time at home or around home than they spend in school.

Since the home of the child stands out as a vital influence in reading readiness and reading achievement of children of all ages, it is of extreme importance that schools do all they possibly can to

- provide for parental awareness of this importance
- suggest ways in which parents can help children in their development, and
- when possible, work along with parents in providing for such development.

The Parents and Reading Committee, an ad hoc committee of the International Reading Association, has provided guidelines meant to facilitate parental awareness and to suggest ways in which parents can help their children. These guidelines follow.

Parents and Reading—How Can I Help My Child?*

1. Develop an appreciation of books by (1) setting up a library shelf, (2) making *regular* trips to the library, (3) asking the librarian to recommend books, (4) giving books as gifts, and (5) letting your child see *you* read.

---

*Parents and Reading Committee of the International Reading Association, Pat Koppman, Chairman, 1979. Used by permission of the IRA.

2. Read. Let your child see you read. Children learn by imitating.
3. Read *to* your child *often*. Make it a good experience.
4. Accept your children as they are. Seek out their strengths and capabilities, and be ready with praise when they do well. Avoid comparing.
5. Relate reading to everyday life situations (billboards, traffic signs, menus, T.V. guide, catalog, labels, maps).
6. Play games with the child that require concentration. Often such games can help increase intellectual capacity and vocabulary.
7. Take your child shopping with you. Early experiences in reading and mathematics can develop from such trips.
8. Have good conversations at the dinner table with thought-provoking questions, but don't make it a question-and-answer session. Be a good listener.
9. Control T.V. Pick out good T.V. programs and discuss them casually with your child.
10. Encourage play with manipulative toys. Let children experiment with typing, cooking, building and sewing. Children learn best by doing.
11. Take trips to points of interest. Visits to museums, planetariums, art displays, concerts, and sporting events are enriching experiences. Other points of interest: the airport, a farm, city hall, zoo, and amusement parks.
12. Let children make decisions: by giving them choices and letting them choose how they want to celebrate a birthday, the color of their bedroom, what they want to wear. Then abide by their choices.
13. Take advantage of daily learning situations: point out colors, numbers, letters, and words. Count with your child the number of plates on the table; talk about the colors in the striped shirt he or she is wearing; discuss comparative sizes of blocks.

The Committee stresses that it is not enough to simply circulate these guidelines, for they are general, and parents who need help most need more guidance in using the guidelines. They must be shown how to do these things.*

It might be well at this point to recall a research project cited in Chapter 2, one done by Ronald Henderson.[1] In a sample of Mexican-American children who were studied at the beginning of first grade and again at the end of third grade, the author found the best predictor of reading

---

*For example, if it is suggested that parents set up a library shelf, they might be given a sketch, or actually shown, how to use cement blocks and planks in so doing. If it is suggested that parents give books as gifts, suggestions of actual books might be made.

success to be parental press for achievement. Significant correlations with achievement at the end of third grade were also found for "language models, academic guidance, activeness of family, range of social interaction, intellectuality in the home, identification with models, and perceived value of education." Harris and Sipay[2] report that " . . . parental pressure for their child's achievement predicted third-grade reading a little more accurately than most readiness and intelligence tests for first graders can." They conclude that "Factors such as parental desire for their children to be educated, guidance without strict domination, emotional support, and parental intellectuality and interest in reading help to determine which children in a disadvantaged* group will succeed in school and which will fail."

In the last section of the previous chapter, it was stressed that it is necessary to reach parents of preschool children as well as parents of children already attending school. For such efforts to bear fruit, a well-organized program is essential. It might be organized on three levels: the community, individual schools, and individual classrooms. Suggestions for each of these follow.

The Community

To reach parents of preschool children as well as parents of school-age children in the whole community, community-wide efforts are essential and must be coordinated. It would be wise to designate a person to head such a program.

A community-wide program might include the following facets:

- the use of the mass media, e.g.:
  - spot announcements on the radio
  - a one or two minute spot on a local T.V. channel once or twice a week
  - a newspaper column in a local paper once or twice a week
- community-wide informational and promotional activities, e.g.:
  - workshops, seminars, colloquia, and noncredit courses offered by school or college personnel
  - printing and distribution of booklets, fliers, etc.
  - promotion and scheduling (perhaps providing bussing for) visitations by parents and children at local points of interest, e.g., at art museums, libraries for "story time" and other occasions, the airport, the zoo, petting zoo, science museums, plays for children, etc.

---

*I.e., "disadvantaged" in socioeconomic class, advantaged perhaps in the characteristics listed here.

Following are some examples of ways of using the mass media.

□ *A Radio Spot* "Have you read to your preschool child today? Did you know that by listening to a child speak, it is possible to tell the difference between a child who has been read to regularly and one who has not been read to by the time the child is 18 months old? Read something to your child of interest to both of you today, and read again tomorrow and every day.

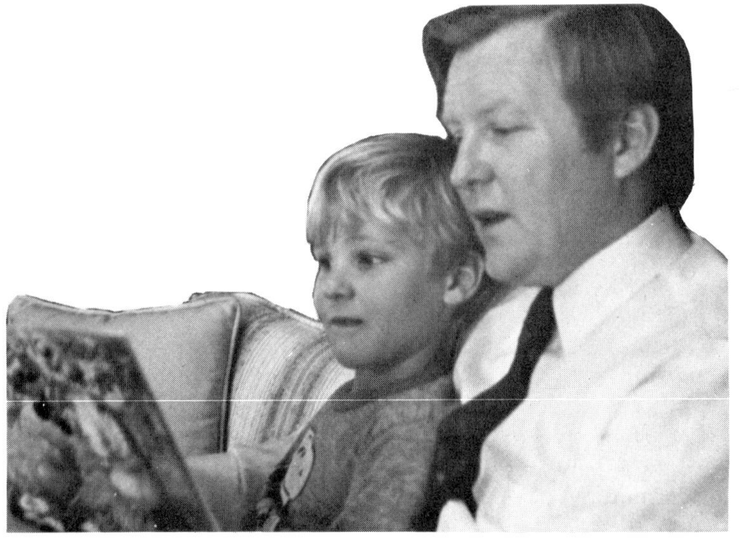

Photo courtesy of Frank Ainsa.

"Both the school in your district and the Children's Room of the Public Library have books that you may borrow, and librarians there can help you in the selection of books that your child will like. Tapes and records are also available that you may take home and play to your child and discuss with him or her.

"You, the parents as well as older brothers and sisters, are encouraged to participate. Let the child sit on your lap and watch the book as you read. Point out words to the child. If you're listening to a tape or record, or reading to your child, ask what he or she especially liked about the story . . . or didn't like about it. Ask your child what she or he would like to listen to tomorrow. Remember that children often wish to listen to a favorite story over and over."

□ *A Radio Spot* "When was the last time your child invited you to go on a walk or to go out in your yard? Did you go? Why not go today? If your child points out something that's alive, talk about it together. Ask if it is an animal . . . a plant. How big is it? What color is it? Is it smooth? fluffy? round? oval? tall? short? Is it pretty? Is it full grown? If possible, let the child touch it, smell it, and even name it.

"Yesterday my daughter found a snail in our yard. She said it was icky. I added slimey. But she said it was pretty, too—rounded, brown and grey, and little. It smelled funny, she said—I suggested musty, rancid, from the wet soil. She laughed. She said she'd call it Herman, and then she put it back. Then we had a conversation about what Herman could see from where he was in the yard."

Then an announcement: "Children learn by touching, smelling, looking, listening—and even tasting, and also by imagining. Help your child explore in your yard and in the neighborhood. Encourage your child to notice flowers and plants and animals. Help him or her describe these. When necessary, caution him or her about touching and tasting. Have fun together outdoors. Today's and tomorrow's adventures will make your child a more interested and interesting person—and a better student."

□*A T.V. Spot* might show a parent reading a few sentences to a child who is sitting on the parent's lap, then asking the child one or a few interesting questions, e.g., "Did you like the story? . . . (child answers) . . . Did you like Whimpy the Frog? . . . What would you say to Whimpy if you could talk to him? . . . Should I read this story to you again tomorrow? . . . (child answers) . . .

Then an announcement: "Did you read to your child or children today? Children enjoy being read to. Their oral language improves when they're read to. And their imaginations grow. Try to read to your child every day . . . You'll enjoy it too."

□*A T.V. Spot* zeros in on a child watching an educational T.V. program alone. A voice says, "Do you encourage your child to watch 'Sesame Street' (etc.)? Why not listen along with your child? Then you'll be able to talk with her or him about it."

The next view is of a parent watching with the child. When the program is over, the parent is shown discussing a highlight of the program, e.g.: "What things in this room begin with the same sound as *pumpkin?*" The child responds, "picture, pillow." The parent adds, "plant, pen." The parent says, "Let's make up a sentence with these words." The child and parent come up with, "Let's sit on the pillow and draw a picture of a plant with our pen."

Then an announcement: "Children learn when someone talks with them about the T.V. programs they watch. This includes programs on Educational Television. Usually they learn little or nothing if they watch alone. Help your child by talking with him or her about programs on television."

□*A Newspaper Article.* Do you have a hobby? Is your child interested in it? When your child shows an interest in your hobby, do you discuss it with him or her? For example, if you enjoy cooking, has your child "caught" your enthusiasm? If so, you may wish to show your child how to bake a cake, make popcorn, or even prepare a roast.

If your child shows an interest, you might teach your child about different ingredients, about proportions and how to measure things, and about following directions in order. You could even take your child to the store to help you select items. You might teach your child how to classify, or group, ingredients. e.g.: cut out the pictures below, and help your child group together the items used in baking a cake. (Better still, use the real things if you have them at home.) Then have him or her group together those used in making popcorn. Then have him or her group together those used for a roast. Then you might ask your child to make up a recipe using some of these ingredients. Ask your child to give it a name.

□*A Newspaper Article* On a weekly schedule, a local newspaper might include a question and answer column authored by a local, state, or national reading expert.

Next are some suggestions for community-wide informational and promotional activities.

□ *Workshops, Seminars, Colloquia, Noncredit Courses* School personnel and college professors might be encouraged to offer short workshops, seminars or colloquia or longer noncredit courses on subjects of interest to parents, e.g.:

• a workshop showing educational toys, games, read-along books with tapes, etc., to parents.
• a seminar or colloquium in which ideas can be shared about community resources such as museums, the zoo, plantetarium, etc., about reading aloud to children, etc.
• a noncredit course, e.g., on children's literature.

□*Printing of Booklets and Fliers.* Some school systems print booklets and fliers for parents. One flier prepared by the El Paso Independent School District if reproduced in Fig. 5.1.

Fliers might also be distributed naming points of interest and special events in a local community: as shown in Fig. 5.2.

reading corner

books

Children's Choices for 1979, a list of children's favorite books from 1978 is available from the Children's Book Council. The list of more than 100 books reflects the choices of children throughout the United States. The books are arranged alphabetically and by age level, and each is briefly described. Single copies of this list can be obtained free by sending a self-addressed 6 x 9 envelope with a first class postage for two ounces (\$.28) to the Children's Book Council, 67 Irving Place, New York, New York, 10003, U.S.A. Attn: Children's Choices. The list was compiled under the direction of the International Reading Association Children's Book Council Joint Committee.

games

Question: I read to my child often when she was young. Now that she has begun school, I feel it is more worthwhile for her to read to me. She's quite upset that I no longer read to her. What should I do?

Answer: Many parents make it a habit to read bedtime stories to their infants and toddlers but depart from this when their children go to school. Many parents, like you, try to help their children by listening to them read and supplying the unknown words. This often results in impatient parents and tearful embarrassed youngsters.

A more pleasureable experience would be to continue the childhood ritual of the child being read to. This does not need to be a daily activity. Instead, whenever the parent reads something especially entertaining or interesting he should share it with the child, this would sometimes be a newspaper clipping, magazine article or segment of a book.

I would also encourage you to continue reading story books to your child. Your child obviously sees reading as a positive experience; do nothing to discourage that.

questions

Penny Hirshman of the IRA Parents and Reading Committee suggests the Yellow Page Alphabet Hunt as a pleasant game to help preschoolers learn to recognize various letters. The game goes like this:
1. Tear a page from an old Yellow Pages section of the telphone book.
2. Choose any capital letter, and print it at the top of the page.
3. Have your child circle every capital B that he or she finds on the page.
4. You can repeat in the same fashion with other capital letters, or you can vary the game by using lower case letters.
5. Give praise and encouragement!

Climbing Higher

Alma Harrington suggests an activity for primary age children.

After a child has been introduced to a word in the school situation, he may find it helpful to practice these words at home. Write each word on a two by four inch piece of cardboard. Using a set of steps or stairs or a sequence of floor tiles tape one word to each stair or tile. Let the child step on a stair or tile if he can say the word correctly. The child may enjoy seeing how far he can go without making a mistake.

Figure 5.1

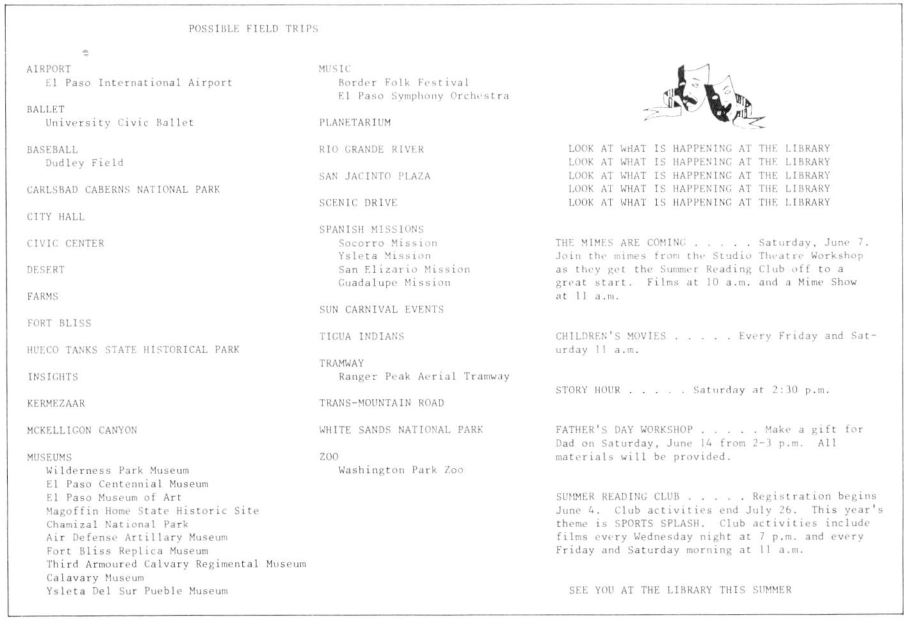

Figure 5.2

□ *Promotion and Scheduling Visitations by Parents and Children at Local Points of Interest* The local art museum might be having a show of special interest to children. An announcement might be placed in local newspapers, and there might be announcements on radio and T.V. Tours might be conducted every two hours. Scheduling might be coordinated by the school district and, if possible, bussing might be provided. (If field trips can be scheduled during the school day, arrangements would be facilitated for child involvement. It would be well to encourage parents to attend along with their children. However, to promote parent involvement, perhaps such trips should be scheduled on weekends or after school.)

Individual Schools

Individual schools should organize and publicize efforts that are particularly appropriate for the school district. It is necessary to have someone in the school itself—like the principal, assistant principal, guidance counselor, or reading teacher—coordinate these efforts and the publicity related to them.

Many schools seek parental and senior citizen participation on an ongoing basis. Sometimes parents, and senior citizens serve as classroom volunteers, devoting a few hours per week to reading with children in the classroom or helping in some other way. Some schools have scheduled visitation days, and others have an open-door policy so adults and others, can come whenever they wish.

Individual schools might offer workshops and seminars for parents, during which time the school reading program might be explained, ways of extending classroom activities might be explained, ways of building the experiences of children might be explained, etc.

Some schools have resource centers stocked with materials that parents and others may check out and where adults may meet informally with teachers.

General principles that apply to most reading situations might be discussed during programs held at the school. During these programs adults should be encouraged to interact with the presenters.

> □*A School Program* A brief description of the content of one possible program follows. This program would be appropriate for parents of preschool and school children.
>
> Theme: How Parents Can Help Their Children Comprehend Print
>
> The program might begin with a definition of comprehension, such as Barbara Swaby's[3]: ". . . Comprehension is building a bridge between the known and the unknown." Understanding the importance of this relationship is crucial. ". . . We comprehend by relating incoming information to what we already know. There is little or no comprehension without that already existing body of information with which to interact." It is for this reason that the more information we have to relate new information to, the better our chance of comprehension. According to Swaby, this explains why the child who knows almost everything there is to know about dinosaurs is able to read with ease a relatively difficult book about dinosaurs while at the same time the child struggles with a book on a less interesting (to him or her) topic. Implications are:*
>
> • Make available rich and varied experiences for your children. Then discuss with your children the experiences they choose to have. Listen carefully to your children and interact with them. Discourage baby talk and encourage them to use complete sentences when possible. Encourage your children to ask questions.
> • Build a wide range of experiences with print. Read to children often. They will discover that reading makes sense. Point out words and phrases to them, even run your finger under lines

---

*Each of these should be exemplified in some detail.

from left to right as you read to preschoolers and first graders. They will enjoy print, learn words, phrases, sentence patterns—book language. Share newspaper articles with them too. Get them their own library card.

- Help children become active participants when you read to them. It's not necessary that your children remember such details as a boy's name in a story. But it is important to find out such things as whether or not they liked the boy, agreed or disagreed with him, whether they had a favorite character, whether they liked the ending, etc.[4]
- Encourage children to read using their knowledge. Encourage your children to predict: What do you think comes next? What do you think the title means? Would you prefer a different ending to the story? Etc. Do you agree with what the author said?
- At times, choose books with a "strong and contagious" language pattern. Swaby suggests books such as those by Dr. Seuss or Bill Martin. She explains the use of Bill Martin's *Brown Bear, Brown Bear*[5] thus: Read "Brown Bear, Brown Bear, What do you see? I see Yellow Duck looking at me. Yellow Duck, Yellow Duck, what do you see? I see Green Frog looking at me." After having read the book, ask the child, "What if you didn't want to say Brown Bear? Could you say 'Mother, Mother, what do you see? I see Johnnie looking at me'?" Explore this idea with them, and as they create, you might write down what they say.* Help them reread it and illustrate it. Post the story in your home.

Individual Teachers

The classroom teacher is in a unique position in working along with parents of the children in his or her classroom. The classroom teacher is familiar with each child and should know each child's interests, abilities,

---

*Parents might be given a handout like this one showing manuscript lettering so that they write their letters similar to those used in school. Consistency is important, especially for the child who is in Piaget's preoperational period.

and needs. Also the teacher knows exactly what the children are being taught at a specific time and, therefore, is in a position to make valuable suggestions to parents as well as to commend children when they have achieved something special.

Classroom teachers have many opportunities to get to know parents of their children well. Such opportunities can be part of the school-wide program but should also supplement this. Teachers, for example, might invite parents to come for conferences, might phone parents, and might —if invited—visit in the home. Teachers are in a position to send home notes, which might help promote parental involvement. These notes might be notes of praise, e.g.:

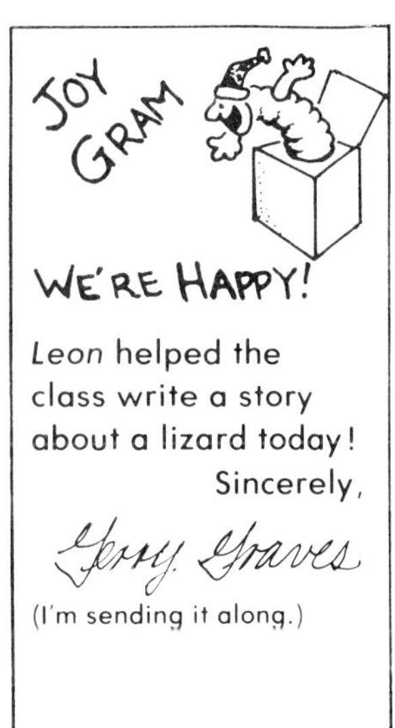

The teacher might have plain note paper on which stars or seasonal stickers could be placed.

Parents who know what is going on in school—from receiving such notes or from listening to their children talk about school—are in a position to regularly reinforce and extend daily learnings. The parent who has found that Bonnie learned to read *Halloween, pumpkin,* and *broomstick* might show the words to Bonnie again and ask her to repeat them. Bonnie might suggest another word, like *witch,* that she'd like to learn also, and she might be taught that at home. She might be asked if she knows what a *goblin* is. She might be told why some children collect money for UNICEF on "beggers night." Etc. Children of parents who don't know what's going on in school are in no position to have their school learnings reinforced and extended. Instead of learning a little more in the evening, they may slip back a bit.

A classroom teacher can also suggest activities that are especially appropriate for the children in his or her class and their parents, and might send fliers home about these.

Nicholas P. Criscuolo[6] suggests these as examples:

- The teacher selects a letter or letters a child needs to work on and sends home the following directions:
  1. Working with one letter at a time, show your child the letter and ask your child to name the letter and then draw a picture of a word that either begins or ends with that letter.
  2. Ask your child to name other words that either begin or end with that letter.
  3. Ask your child to find a picture of an object whose name begins with the letter sound.
- The teacher gives the parent four pictures that depict sequentially an event or story, along with the following directions:
  1. Ask your child to look at all four pictures.
  2. Ask your child to tell you what happened first, second, third, fourth. Ask him or her to arrange these in left to right order.
  3. Then ask your child to tell a story about the picture.
  4. Ask the child if the pictures can be arranged in another order to tell another story. If so, proceed as above.
- Send home step-by-step "recipes," or directions, e.g.: "ABC dusting."
  objective: to reinforce alphabetical order
  ingredients: room to be dusted, paper and pencil
  procedure: Make a list of things in a room to be dusted. Instruct the child that you would like to dust each object by order of the alphabet. Using the list, ask your child, "What should we dust first? Second? At first work along with your child. Later give your child the list to work on alone.

Examples of prepared fliers follow.[7]

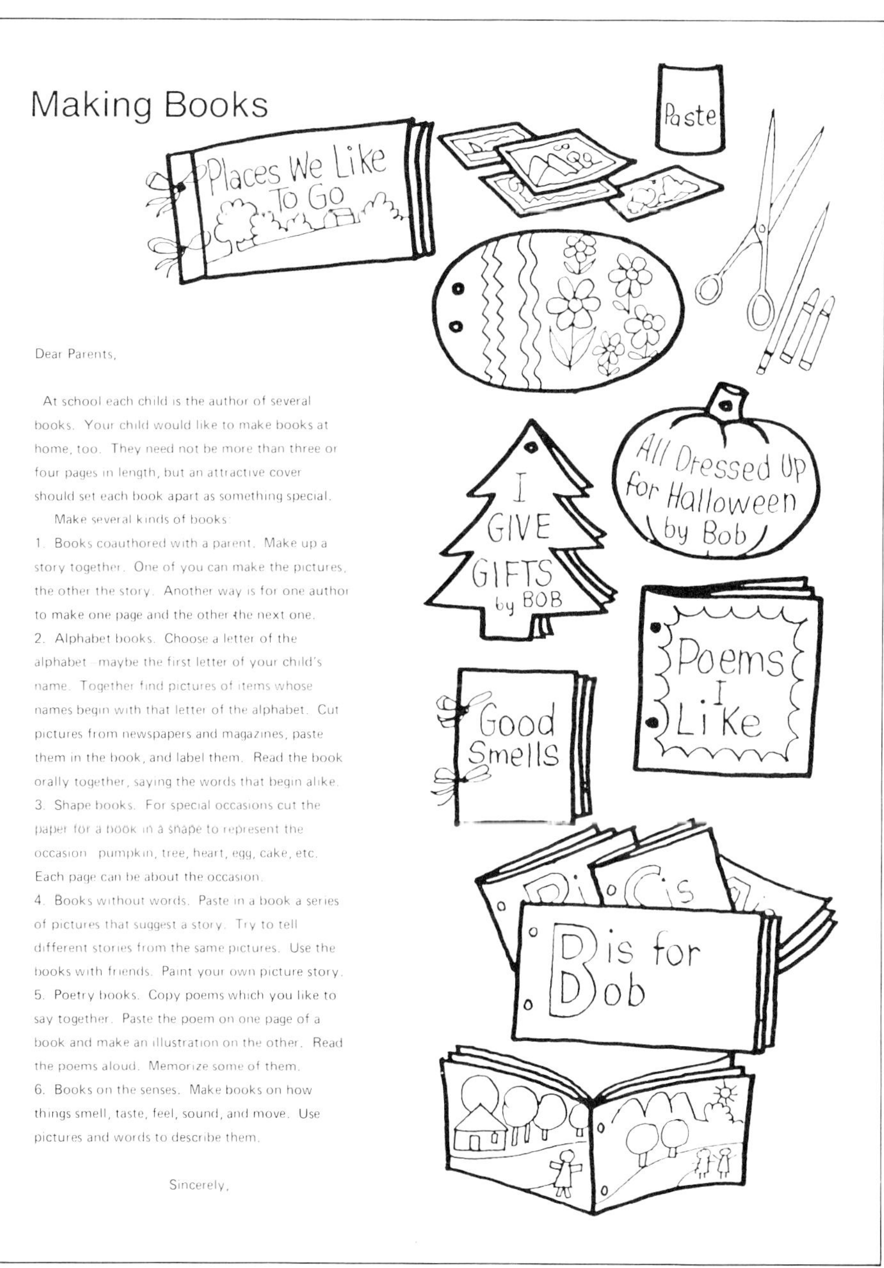

Making Books

Dear Parents,

At school each child is the author of several books. Your child would like to make books at home, too. They need not be more than three or four pages in length, but an attractive cover should set each book apart as something special.

Make several kinds of books:

1. Books coauthored with a parent. Make up a story together. One of you can make the pictures, the other the story. Another way is for one author to make one page and the other the next one.

2. Alphabet books. Choose a letter of the alphabet—maybe the first letter of your child's name. Together find pictures of items whose names begin with that letter of the alphabet. Cut pictures from newspapers and magazines, paste them in the book, and label them. Read the book orally together, saying the words that begin alike.

3. Shape books. For special occasions cut the paper for a book in a shape to represent the occasion—pumpkin, tree, heart, egg, cake, etc. Each page can be about the occasion.

4. Books without words. Paste in a book a series of pictures that suggest a story. Try to tell different stories from the same pictures. Use the books with friends. Paint your own picture story.

5. Poetry books. Copy poems which you like to say together. Paste the poem on one page of a book and make an illustration on the other. Read the poems aloud. Memorize some of them.

6. Books on the senses. Make books on how things smell, taste, feel, sound, and move. Use pictures and words to describe them.

Sincerely,

Roach Van Allen, *Language Experience in Reading*. Chicago: Encyclopaedia Britannica Educational Corp., 1970, 1966. Used by permission of Encyclopaedia Brittanica Press Inc.

ANIMALS

Dear Parents:

** Next week is National Animal Week (September 22–28)

**Free Zoo Day: Friday from 10 a.m. to 6 p.m.

**TV Special: Those Amazing Animals, Saturday, Sept. 28
6 p.m., Channel 13

** Game: Parents are allowed to help.

**Instructions: There are many kinds of animals in the animal kingdom. Ask your child if she or he can name those pictured below. You may wish to help your child put the correct animal name in the space below each picture. For fun, your child might like to color each animal. Maybe your child will be able to tell you where each lives in the wild. . . . We've studied these animals in class.

Dear Parents:

Your child has had an enjoyable time learning about maps and how to read them. The following activity is one that the class had a great deal of fun with, and perhaps you may enjoy sharing with your child. The attached map is like one we used in class.

* * * * * * * * * * * *

Plan an imaginary trip. A trip from El Paso to Santa Fe has many possibilities. Find two or three routes, and trace them in different colored crayons. You may wish to take the most direct route going and then a longer one coming back.

* * * * * * * * * *

You may wish to visit the ski country of Ruidoso, Old Town in Albuquerque. Perhaps you would like to visit the Santo Domingo Indians, near Santa Fe. You may wish to plan a visit to the Santa Fe Opera House.

Reading about these places will add to the enjoyment and education of your child. Enjoy this happy sharing experience.

Dear Parents:

Our 5th grade class is studying about our early Southwest history. You may wish to take your children to visit

The Wilderness Park Museum

Enjoy Picturesque Dioramas and Ancient Artifacts of This Area's Earliest Known Inhabitants

The Wilderness Park Museum is located at
2000 Trans-Mountain Road at Gateway South

Admission is Free

Tuesday–Saturday   9:30 a.m.–5:00 p.m.

Sunday   1:00 p.m.–5:00 p.m.

Closed on Monday

Parents:

BATTERS UP!

FOR READING

Score a hit with your children by helping them select biographies of famous athletes in their favorite sports at the library or bookstore.

Some examples:
Young Olympic Champions, by Steve Gelman

Roger Maris at Bat, by Maris and Ogle

Famous American Women Athletes, by Helen Hull Jacobs

The Jim Ryun Story, by Cordner Nelson

Famous Pro Football Stars, by Heuman

Sports Titans of the 20th Century, by Al Silverman

Famous Negro Athletes, by Arna Bontemps

Here are some questions you might want to discuss with your children after they read a book:

1. What factors does the book say contributed to the athlete's success?

2. What was the athlete's life like before she or he became so successful? What is it like now?

3. Has the athlete had to give up certain things in order to achieve his or her goals? Has it been worth it?

4. Would you like that kind of life?

Summary

It is becoming increasingly obvious that the home plays an important role in school achievement. Because of this role it is important that schools do all they can to

- provide for parental awareness of this importance
- suggest ways in which parents can help children in their development, and
- when possible, work along with parents in providing for such development.

This chapter contains suggestions of ways of implementing these goals.

Community based projects are of importance in reaching parents of children of all ages. Such projects might include the use of the mass media and providing for community-wide informational and promotional activities. Examples involving the use of the radio, T.V. and newspaper articles were given, plus providing for workshops and seminars, etc., the use of booklets and fliers, and the scheduling of visitations to local points of interest.

The place of individual schools in providing for parental and senior citizen participation was discussed next. Individual schools may seek parental and senior citizen participation on an on-going basis and also for special projects and meetings. Some schools encourage parents of preschool and school children to borrow materials that might be used with their children.

The classroom teacher is in a unique position for working along with parents of children in his or her classroom. Teachers might invite parents to have conferences and to visit the classroom. They might send notes home in praise of a child's accomplishments and might also send home notes or fliers suggesting activities that correlate with classroom learnings.

Questions and Activities

After answering the questions given at the beginning of this chapter, consider these questions and activities:

1. Select one or more of the suggestions given in the guidelines developed by The Parents and Reading Committee of I.R.A. and tell specifically how you would explain the suggestion to a group of parents who don't understand what to do or how to do it. You may wish to prepare model games or activities, fliers to be sent

home, a workshop for parents, etc. Share your information with your classmates.

2. Prepare a spot announcement for radio or T.V. or a newspaper column, perhaps with other members of your class. Or outline a workshop, seminar, etc., that might be developed for use on a community-wide basis. Share these with your classmates.

3. Help design a program or other activity—or tell how a resource center might be equipped and used—at an individual school.

4. Try to add to the suggestions for individual teachers. Why is it so important for teachers to communicate with parents?

NOTES

1. Ronald Henderson, p. 297. See Selected References.
2. Albert J. Harris and Edward R. Sipay, pp. 313–314. See Selected References.
3. Barbara Swaby, p. 281. See Selected References. Also see Chapters 1 and 12 of the present book: reading as a matrixing event.
4. *Ibid.*, pp. 281–282.
5. Bill Martin, Jr. *Brown Bear, Brown Bear.* New York: N.Y.: Holt, Rinehart and Winston, 1971.
6. Nicholas P. Criscuolo, January 1979, pp. 418–419. See Selected References.
7. The author wishes to express gratitude to the following students at the University of Texas at El Paso for contributing these fliers: Cheryl Dickey, Ramona Carter, Jo Ann Trejo, and M. Kay Roy.

SELECTED REFERENCES

Allen, Roach Van. *Language Experience in Reading.* Chicago: Encyclopaedia Britannica Educational Corp., 1970.

Anselmo, Sandra. "Improving Home and Preschool Influences on Early Language Development." *The Reading Teacher*, 32 (November 1978): 139–143.

Cassidy, Jack and Carol Vukelich. "Survival Reading for Parents and Kids: A Parent Educational Program." *The Reading Teacher*, 31 (March 1978): 638–641.

Criscuolo, Nicholas. "Activities that Help Involve Parents in Reading." *The Reading Teacher*, 32 (January 1979): 417–419.

_______________. "Effective Ways to Communicate with Parents about Reading." *The Reading Teacher*, 34 (November 1980): 164–166.

Freshour, Frank W. "Beginning Reading: Parents Can Help." *The Reading Teacher.* 25 (March 1972): 513–516.

Granowsky, Alvin, Frances R. Middleton, and Janice Hall Mumford. "Parents as Partners in Education." *The Reading Teacher*, 32 (April 1979).

__________. *A Guide for Better Reading.* Englewood Cliffs, New Jersey: Scholastic's Readers' Choice, 1977.

Harris, Albert J. and Edward R. Sipay. *How to Increase Reading Ability, Seventh Edition.* New York, N.Y.: Longman Inc., 1980.

Henderson, Ronald. "Environmental Predictors of Acceptance Performance of Disadvantaged Mexican-American Children." *Journal of Consulting and Clinical Psychology*, 38 (April 1972): 297.

Hoskisson, K. "Should Parents Teach Their Children to Read?" *Elementary English*, 51 (February 1974): 295–299.

Quisenberry, Nancy L., Candace Blakemore, and Claudia A. Warren. "Involving Parents in Reading: An Annotated Bibliography." *The Reading Teacher*, 31 (October 1977): 34–39.

Rhaten, Juliana. "Helping Parents to Develop the Language of Preschool Children." *Language Arts*, 55 (May 1978): 612–614.

Sebesta, Samuel. "Why Rudolph Can't Read." *Language Arts*, 58 (May 1981): 545–548.

Swaby, Barbara. "How Parents Can Foster Comprehension Growth in Children." *The Reading Teacher*, 34 (December 1980): 280–283.

Teale, William H. *Early Reading-An Annotated Bibliography.* Newark, Delaware: International Reading Association, 1980.

__________. "Positive Environments for Learning to Read: What Studies of Early Readers Tell Us." *Language Arts*, 55 (Nov./Dec. 1978): 922 –932.

STRATEGIES

Unit Two consists of seven chapters:

Unit Two focuses on ways of developing skills necessary for understanding reading materials, on ways of developing interests, and on ways of integrating the teaching of reading with the teaching of content. Conceptual frameworks are provided, followed by strategies, or techniques, that are recommended for classroom use.

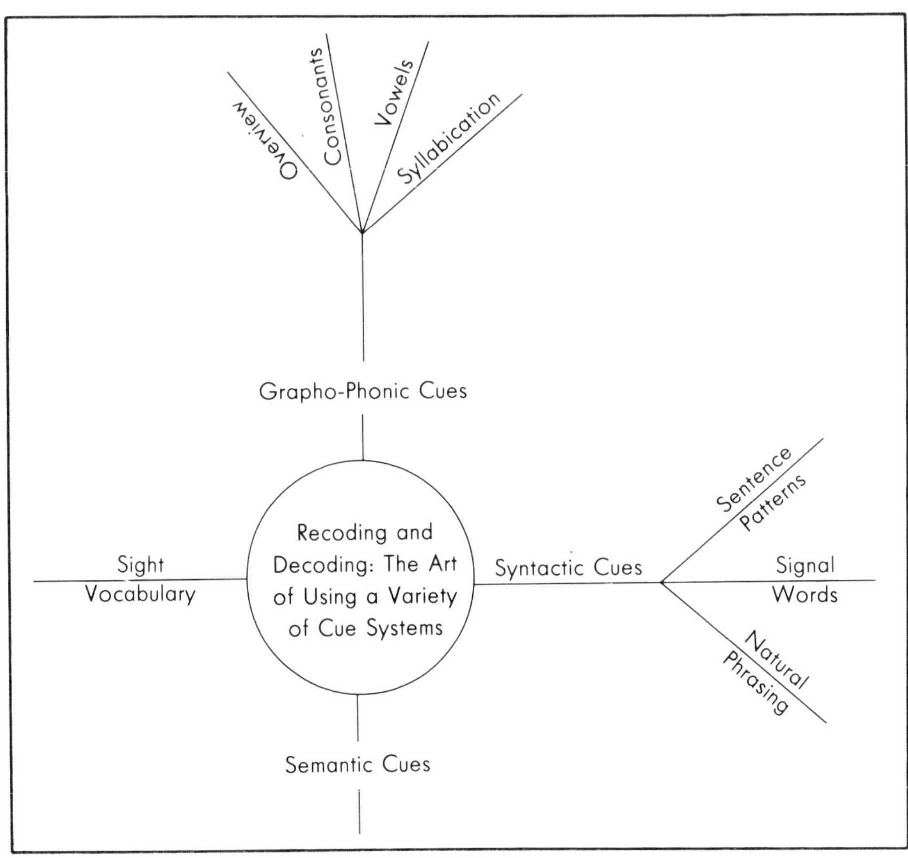

- What cue systems do good readers use when reading? Is it important to be able to use four different cue systems when reading? Why or why not?

- What is meant by "sight vocabulary"? What sight words should a child be taught? How should these words be taught?

- What is meant by "grapho-phonic" cues? How consistent are consonants in representing their own (or consistent) sounds? What are consonant digraphs? How many "vowel patterns" are there in English? What are they? What sounds do different vowels or vowel clusters represent in each pattern? What are the components of a complete phonics lesson? When teaching a phonics lesson, is it always necessary to include all of the components? Why or why not? What is morphological syllabication? phonic syllabication? What are the generalizations for morphological syllabication? for phonic syllabication? In your opinion, how important for reading purpose is it to divide words into syllables exactly as the rules (or a dictionary) suggest? Why?

- What is meant by "syntactic" cues? How can we teach children to use syntactic cues of the sentence pattern type? How can we teach children to recognize and use signal words? to phrase naturally?

- What is meant by "semantic" cues? How can we help children use semantic cues?

150

CHAPTER 6

Recoding and Decoding:
The Art of Using a Variety of Cue Systems

How does a reader interact with the printed page to add meanings to his or her long-term storage system? It has been found that good readers use a variety of cue systems when reading printed messages. Less able readers, and beginning readers, may use fewer systems—until they are able to deal with more systems. The diagram on p. 152 suggests cue systems that might be used and the way in which they might be used.

Some psycholinguists tell us that "comprehension and word attack skills are complementary and mutually dependent, i.e., word attack skills help students attain comprehension skills, while comprehension skills help them with decoding."[1] According to Weaver, "Effective reading involves a constant interaction between the mind of the reader and the language of the text."[2] Such an interaction is illustrated in the chart above, when the reader is dealing with surface structure (graphic) cues and meanings which may (or may in part) already be in the reader's mind (i.e., long-term memory storage system). If meanings are already in the reader's mind—or are building in the reader's mind—the reader will be able to hypothesize about what is coming next and test semantic, syntactic, grapho-phonic, and sight cues against his or her hypothesis to see if sense is being made. If sense is not being made, the reader may go back and try cues other than the one(s) originally used until meaning is achieved.

Beginning readers may not be at the point where they can use all of these cue systems—perhaps because they have not as yet learned all of these cue systems and/or perhaps because they cannot process cues with the speed necessary to be able to use multiple cues. For them, reading and learning to read may mean using, and learning to use, these cues singly and then in combination.

Reading involves:

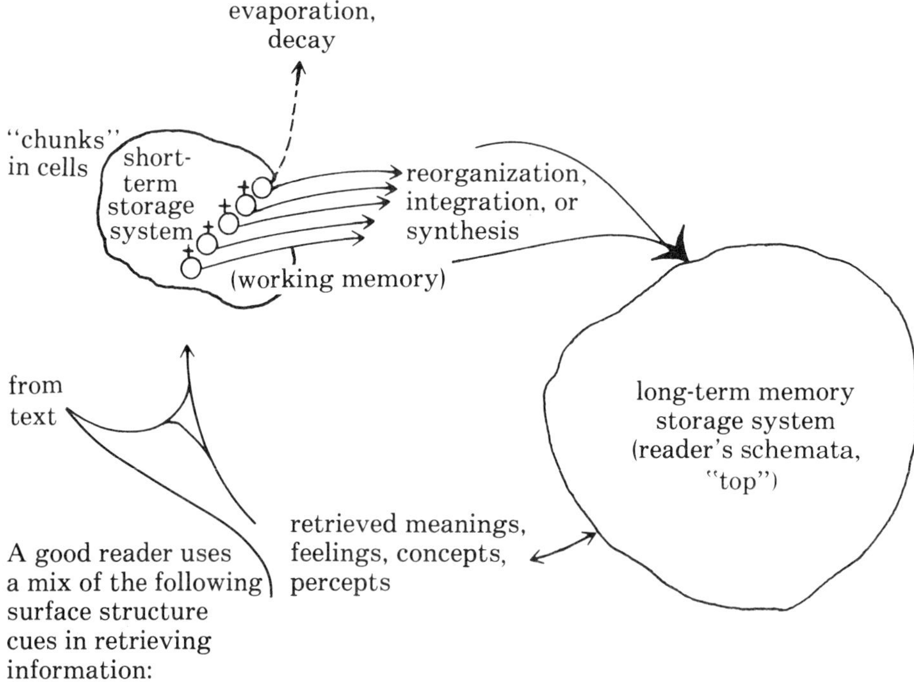

Readers may begin by going from deep structure (or meaning) to surface structure (graphic symbols), as in the Language Experience Approach (top-down). (See Chapter 13.) Or they might begin with surface structure (graphic symbols, the text) and progress to meaning, by using text centered materials and approaches (bottom-up). In many cases, they may use top-down and bottom-up approaches in a complementary manner.

This chapter is designed to show ways of promoting the acquisition of a sight vocabulary, of teaching the utilization of grapho-phonic cues, syntactic cues, and semantic cues. (The latter two cue systems are only briefly described in this chapter because there are additional discussions in several other places in the text.) These terms can be defined thus:

- *sight vocabulary:* a person's sight vocabulary is composed of the words, phrases, and longer units that he or she recognizes as a Gestalt, i.e., with no apparent analysis. These are "automatically" recognized.
- *grapho-phonic cues* are those cues related to graphic symbols and their corresponding sounds.
- *syntactic cues* are those cues related to the sentence as a unit. A syntactic cue might suggest that a verb fits in these blanks: Jane _____ for two hours. Did Jane _____ for two hours?
- *semantic cues* relate to meanings. For example, what possible words could fit in this blank: The _____ chirped while pulling a worm out of the ground. An added grapho-phonic cue would narrow the choice: The r_____ chirped while pulling a worm out of the ground.

Sight Vocabulary

Words that children learn to read first should be highly interesting to them—and what's more interesting than their names and words they ask to learn to read? Such words might be the first words in their sight vocabularies. To these might be added words and strings of words that the teacher considers important for the child to learn, e.g., boys room, girls room, stop, go, and words that will be used later in basal reader lessons.

Teachers normally don't just stop with teaching the sight recognition of such words. They teach children to use these words and strings of words in building sentences or stories. Sometimes teachers use children's words for initial phonics lessons. They may also use these words and the concepts the children have in relationship to the words to extend the vocabularies of the children. Such lessons occur at all grade levels. Suggestions for implementing such a program follow.

□ *Child's Name* All children want to be able to read their own names as well as the names of the other children in the classroom. In kindergarten or first grade, the teacher should print each child's name on a card of an interesting shape and color, such as a red or yellow car, a pink, yellow, red or blue flower, a white or tan baseball or football, etc. (Each child could choose a favorite card.)
The card then is pinned on the child's clothing. Soon after, a duplicate name card is made for each child.

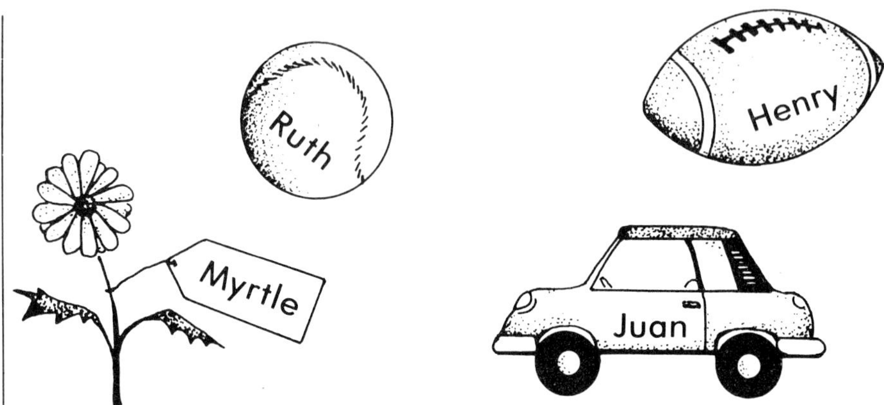

These duplicate cards can be mixed together on a table, after which each child would select his or her own card. The cards can be returned and mixed again, and each child would be asked to select the name card of the child or children sitting next to him or her, or across the room, etc. This can be done by visually matching the names and/or shapes and colors of the cards the children are wearing. Later the cards can be removed from the children's clothing, and card selection would be done by memory. Many repetitions may be necessary for children to learn some of the words.

Children can be taught simple phonics lessons by using these cards. For example, to teach sound-symbol relations for the initial letter "B", the teacher might show the class Betty's card and ask the children to find all other cards that begin like Betty, e.g., Billy, Bob, Brian. The teacher would point out that the names on all of these cards start with "B" and that all of the names sound the same at the beginning. A chart could be made to reinforce this:

<pre>
            B |
        ─────────┼─────────
          Betty |
          Billy |
          Bob |
          Brian |
                 |
</pre>

Then the teacher could ask the class to suggest other words that begin like Betty. Children might suggest ball, bat, beg, banana (auditory discrimination). The teacher would add these to the chart, stressing that the initial letter is the same in all of these words (visual discrimination).

B	b
Betty	ball
Billy	bat
Bob	beg
Brian	banana

□ *Child's Word Choice* Most children have favorite words they would like to learn to read. How exciting it would be for them to be able to go home the first day of school with their cards and be able to read them!

On the first day of school, and regularly thereafter, the teacher might ask each child for one word, or perhaps several words, each would like to learn to read.* The teacher would print each word on the bottom of a 3 × 5″ or 4 × 6″ card while the child is watching. Then the teacher would point to each word, say it along with the child, and ask the child to illustrate the meaning above it. Next, the teacher would cut the card into a two piece puzzle with the word on one part and the illustration on the other. Then the teacher would also print the word for the child on a small rectangular card. E.g.:

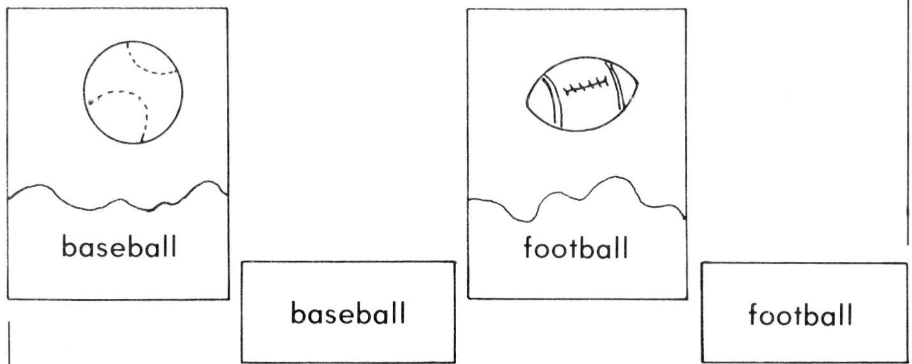

Later, children could form into small groups and learn each other's words. After a little practice, they might wish to play a game

---

*If this is too time-consuming, the teacher might ask the whole class to suggest a few words they would like to learn to read. The teacher could write these on a ditto master and give each child a copy to illustrate and take home.

such as tic-tac-toe. The children's words would be printed on a card, e.g.:

baseball	dad	tiger
dog	house	mother
mouse	football	fire

One team would be given "O" tokens, and the other team would be given "X" tokens. To be allowed to place a token on a word, the children in the group would have to do something that would be a slight challenge to them at their stage of development. At the readiness stage, children might simply match a word on a rectangular card that they draw from a pile with its counterpart on the tic-tac-toe board (visual discrimination). More mature children might have to say the word to cover it (visual-auditory integration). Children even more mature would say the word and define it or use it in a sentence (visual-auditory integration, plus meaning).

Following this, the picture parts for a larger group of children or for the whole class could be arranged on a table or on a bulletin board, and each child would select from a hat or box one word puzzle part, match it with the picture puzzle part, and say the word. Finally, the children would just pick the words on the rectangular cards, say them and tell what they mean, if possible. If they don't recognize the word, they would (through visual discrimination) match it with the word puzzle part and match the puzzle part with the illustration to recognize the word, thus:

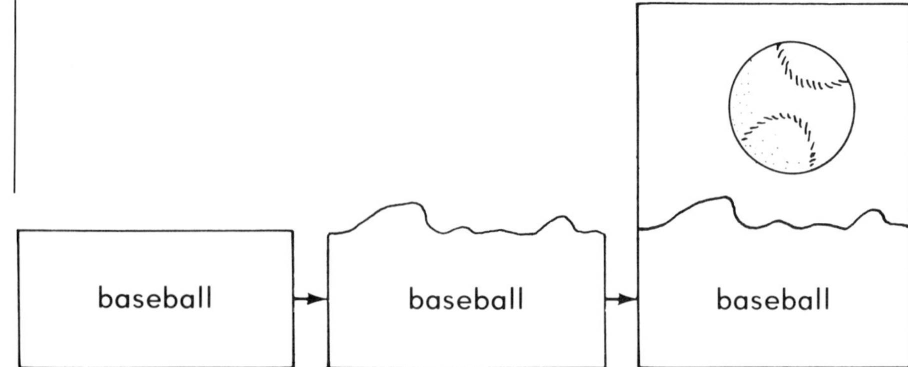

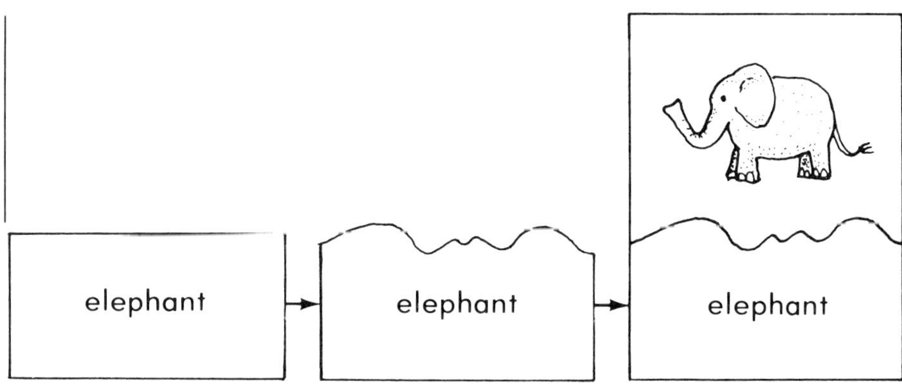

Children, individually or in groups, might be encouraged to compose sentences using some of these words. For individual work, the teacher would print the sentence and give the child a copy. For group work, the teacher could print the sentence on a ditto master, quickly duplicate it, and give each child a copy. (The children could take the copy home and read it to their families.)

In time, each child would have many "personal cards." Each child could file these in alphabetical order, group them in a variety of ways, and/or make an individual picture dictionary, or a group or classroom picture dictionary could be made.*

These cards later could also be used for teaching simple phonics lessons, such as initial or final consonant sound-symbol relations, vowel sound-symbol relations, or syllabication. For example, if cards like the following are available, this generalization might be taught (one vowel at a time): A single vowel in a closed syllable (a syllable that ends with a consonant) usually represents its own short sound:**

a	*e*	*i*	*o*	*u*
cat	pet	hit	hop	cub
map	bed	dig	pot	cut
hat	red	ink	top	tub
bat	met	pig	cop	hug

---

* See Chapter 13, for further suggestions.

**Children need not be able to state the generalization. They should only be able to apply it; i.e., when they see a one syllable word that has one vowel in it and ends with a consonant, they should try the short sound of the vowel.

□ *Organic Reading Approach* Sylvia Ashton-Warner, author of *Teacher*, a book in which she describes her experiences in teaching Maori children of New Zealand, used the innermost thought-language of these children in teaching them to read. She found that the feelings of fear and hate were keys to these children's inner-selves, and she used words of intense meaning to the children to build their reading "key-vocabulary." Maori children had many fear words that they wished to learn. Among them were: *fight, ghost, cry, wild, growl, bomb, tiger.*

Miss Ashton-Warner explained:

"First words must have an intense meaning.
First words must be already part of the dynamic life.
First books must be made of the stuff of the child himself, whatever and wherever the child."[3]

The child told Miss Ashton-Warner the word to be learned and watched her print it on a card. The two of them then said the word, and then the child traced it with a finger. Next the children worked in pairs, and learned each other's words. Then Miss

Ashton-Warner put all of the words together on a table, and all children found their own words.

Next, the child wrote or dictated a sentence using one of the key words, e.g.:

She described the sentences as "captions to the pictures in the mind," for they described the strong feelings of the children. The child then learned to read the sentence and finally put several sentences together to make a story.

Miss Ashton-Warner called the cards "One-Look" cards. She found that pictures or illustrations were unnecessary on these cards. The child had to see the card only once to know it because each card had a word on it with such intense meaning to him or her. She said that children could learn as many of their own words in four minutes as they could learn in four months in a basal reader program.

□ *Extending the Child's Vocabulary and Experiences* A child or several children of any age, or perhaps a whole class, might be particularly interested in a specific subject. Young children might be interested in animals, including pets, but they might have a limited acquaintance with them. They might know the words *cat, dog, bird, fish* and know a few members of each of these families but might be interested in knowing more of the members.

For example, from the cat family they might learn about specific types of domestic cats: Persian, Siamese, Manx, Burmese, Tabby, Calico, etc., and they might learn about wild felines: lion, tiger, leopard, snow leopard, etc. They might learn to read the words, to match pictures with the words, and to learn of the habitats of the wild felines and characteristics of each type of cat.

They might be encouraged to write or dictate a verse, such as Haiku,* about one or more of these animals:

> Cats mysterious:
> Persian, Siamese, Burmese—
> Foreign, kind, loving.

In extending their knowledge about animals, children might wish to learn about groups of animals. They might study about the following animals and match each animal with the name of its group. E.g., from the right hand column, the teacher would help the children select a group name for the following animals, and write that name in the blank: (For very young children, this would be done orally.)

---

*Haiku is a Japanese verse form, and writing it is popular with children once they try. It is meant to convey a mood. The first line has five syllables; the second line has seven syllables, and the third line has five syllables.

<table>
<tr><td>1. a _pack_ of wolves</td><td>flock</td></tr>
<tr><td>2. a _______ of bees</td><td>gaggle</td></tr>
<tr><td>3. a _______ of quail</td><td>swarm</td></tr>
<tr><td>4. a _______ of fish</td><td>litter</td></tr>
<tr><td>5. a _______ of geese</td><td>herd</td></tr>
<tr><td>6. a _______ of cattle</td><td>pride</td></tr>
<tr><td>7. a _______ of sheep</td><td>pack</td></tr>
<tr><td>8. a _______ of puppies</td><td>school</td></tr>
<tr><td>9. a _______ of lions</td><td>brood</td></tr>
<tr><td>10. a _______ of young birds</td><td>covey</td></tr>
</table>

All of the words the children decide they wish to learn to read could be printed on cards for them. If groups of children wish to learn the same words, the teacher could run off dittoed copies for them. Games then could be played to reinforce the recognition and meanings of the words,* and the cards could be added to the children's word banks.

In addition to teaching children words they choose to learn, the teacher may wish to teach words the children will frequently meet in their reading. Lists of high frequency words that many reading experts think children should know at sight are available.[4] Among these is "The New Instant Word List," by Edward Fry, shown in Figs. 6.1–6.3.**

Fry comments: "Teachers can use the list in many ways. They can teach just the base word or they can teach the common variants with very little extra effort at the same time that they are teaching the base word."

"If teachers teach only the base words, it might be helpful for them to know that the vast majority of the variants are caused by just six suffixes: -s, -ing, -ed, -er, -ly, -est. The variants given in the list are not all that are possible; they are just the most common ones.

"Teachers can use the Instant Words as an oral reading diagnostic test of a student's knowledge of the most common words. This test can be either an oral sight reading test or a spelling test. In other words, if reading is the goal, just ask the student to read them aloud; and if spelling is the goal, ask the student to write the word or spell it aloud."

Fry warns against trying to teach too many of these words at one sit-

---

* Rationale and additional examples are given in Chapter 13.
**Edward Fry. "The New Instant Word List." *The Reading Teacher*, 34 (December 1980): 284–289. Used by permission of the International Reading Association and of Edward Fry.

The Instant Words: first hundred

First 25 Group 1a	Second 25 Group 1b	Third 25 Group 1c	Fourth 25 Group 1d
the	or	will	number
of	one	up	no
and	had	other	way
a	by	about	could
to	word	out	people
in	but	many	my
is	not	then	than
you	what	them	first
that	all	these	water
it	were	so	been
he	we	some	call
was	when	her	who
for	your	would	oil
on	can	make	now
are	said	like	find
as	there	him	long
with	use	into	down
his	an	time	day
they	each	has	did
I	which	look	get
at	she	two	come
be	do	more	made
this	how	write	may
have	their	go	part
from	if	see	over

Common suffixes: *s, ing, ed*

Figure 6.1

ting and suggests that teachers use their own judgment and try to teach only as many as the student can do without fatigue or boredom.

He adds: "Learning a list of words can be a boring lesson, so liven it up with your entire bag of tricks: oral reading, silent reading, games, flash cards, spelling lessons, writing lessons, easy reading material, and anything you can think of for fun and variation. However, teaching this list of words can also be efficient instruction. It saves time, and it teaches students the words they really need to know most."

The following activities are suggested to help children learn these words:

□ *Use Word Blocks* For young children, prepare blocks of different colors—each color representing a different position in the sentence pattern to be used. E.g., for a noun-verb sentence, nouns

The Instant Words: second hundred

First 25 Group 2a	Second 25 Group 2b	Third 25 Group 2c	Fourth 25 Group 2d
new	great	put	kind
sound	where	end	hand
take	help	does	picture
only	through	another	again
little	much	well	change
work	before	large	off
know	line	must	play
place	right	big	spell
year	too	even	air
live	mean	such	away
me	old	because	animal
back	any	turn	house
give	same	here	point
most	tell	why	page
very	boy	ask	letter
after	follow	went	mother
thing	came	men	answer
our	want	read	found
just	show	need	study
name	also	land	still
good	around	different	learn
sentence	form	home	should
man	three	us	America
think	small	move	world
say	set	try	high

Common suffixes: *s, ing, ed, er, ly, est*

Figure 6.2

could be printed on a yellow block and verbs on a blue block. The children would be instructed that normally the yellow block comes first and the blue block second. They toss the blocks, arrange them in left-to-right order, and then get a point if they can read the sentence. E.g.:

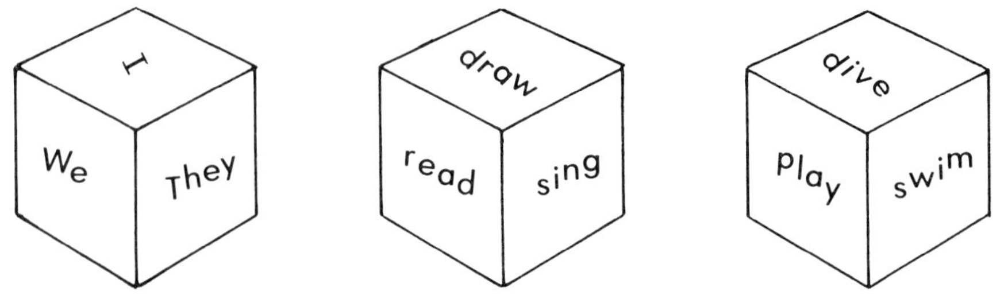

The Instant Words: third hundred

First 25 Group 3a	Second 25 Group 3b	Third 25 Group 3c	Fourth 25 Group 3d
every	left	until	idea
near	don't	children	enough
add	few	side	eat
food	while	feet	face
between	along	car	watch
own	might	mile	far
below	close	night	Indian
country	something	walk	real
plant	seem	white	almost
last	next	sea	let
school	hard	began	above
father	open	grow	girl
keep	example	took	sometimes
tree	begin	river	mountain
never	life	four	cut
start	always	carry	young
city	those	state	talk
earth	both	once	soon
eye	paper	book	list
light	together	hear	song
thought	got	stop	leave
head	group	without	family
under	often	second	body
story	run	late	music
saw	important	miss	color

Common suffixes: *s, ing, ed, er, ly, est*

Figure 6.3

If two verb blocks are used, two points would be given if the child could read two sentences.

□ *Stress Configuration Clues* Some authorities suggest that children be taught to notice shapes of words, although the value of this appears to be limited because so many words have the same shape. In the initial stages of reading, noting differences in shapes (ascending and descending letters) might prove helpful. Note the shapes of these:

best   many   oh   sleep   them

After more words are learned, however, it will become apparent that other words have the same shapes, e.g.:

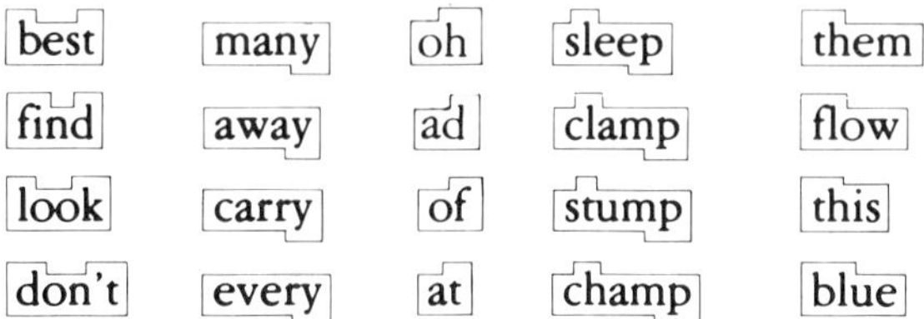

□ *Use Verses* Shirley Hollingsworth[5] suggests using a limerick to teach some of the Dolch words.* In the following limerick, high frequency words (18 different words from the Dolch list, i.e., 6 percent of the Dolch words) are combined with rhythm and rhyme to teach basic sight vocabulary with a bit of humor. Notice that the words are taught in context, rather than in isolation.

I've got a dog as thin as a rail,
He's got fleas all over his tail;
Every time his tail goes flop,
The fleas on the bottom all hop to the top.

Unknown

After reading the verse—perhaps in choral reading—strings of words from each line might be written on cards, and the children might arrange these in order of the verse, e.g.:

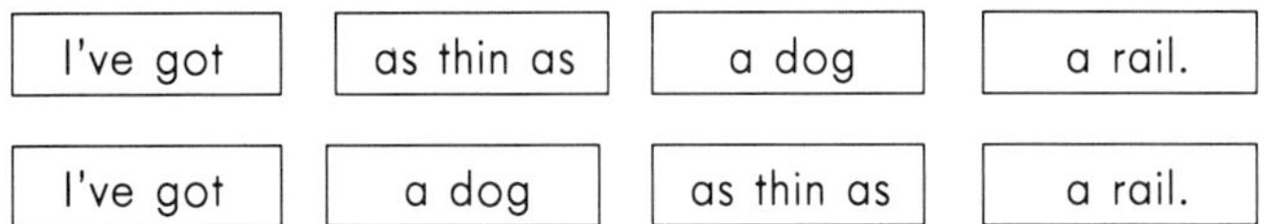

After this, each string would be cut into individual words and these arranged in order:

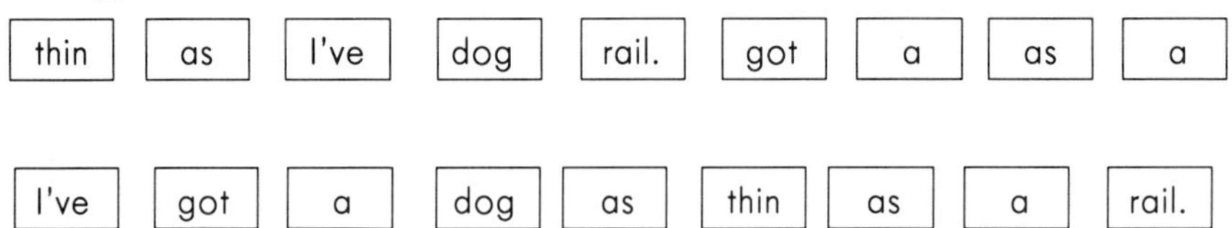

The following verse contains 21 different Dolch words, used a total of 56 times.

When did I get my pretty blue ball?
Did I get it in spring? Did I get it in fall?
When will you bring your pretty green ball?
Will you bring it in spring? Will you bring it in fall?
When you bring your green ball, we will play with two balls.
We will play with your green ball and with my blue ball.

---

*The Dolch list is a commonly used word list. See note 4.

S. Jay Samuels[6] sounds a note of caution when discussing sight words. He points out that learning is rapid at first, but that soon the rate of learning new words slows down drastically. He notes that in the initial stages many simple strategies provide cues for word recognition, but that "only so many words can be recognized by length, shape, and single letters before the strategies prove ineffective." When this happens, the learner remains on a plateau, according to Samuels, "until he learns a rational system for decoding words from symbols to sounds."* Samuels points out that "a strategy of learning to read using word shape and length provides a poor basis for transfer to reading new words. . . For the objective of transfer to reading new words, knowledge of letter-sounds, ability to recognize higher-order units such as digraphs and blends and knowledge of their sounds, as well as the ability to blend these sounds into words are required."

Grapho-Phonic Cues

Overview

The teaching of symbol-sound relationships in words is viewed as relatively important or unimportant, depending upon whether one views the reading process as bottom-up or top-down. Yet, even those who view reading according to a top-down model may agree that symbol-sound cues do help in recognizing an author's word when several choices may be possible semantically and syntactically.

A. Steil Artley[7] supplies the following example as an argument, or justification, for teaching consonant symbol-sound relationships. The reader comes across this sentence: "The postman put a ______ in the mail box." Artley comments that the unknown word might be *package*, *letter*, or *message*. If the reader notes that the unknown word begins with p, which represents the p sound, i.e., /p/, this tells the reader the word is *package*. One might wonder how a beginning reader would know all of the other words of the sentence—unless they were all in his or her sight vocabulary.

Those reading experts who believe in the bottom-up theory—at least for beginning readers—might agree that a child would have to know much more about phonics than initial letter symbol-sound relationships to recode or decode this sentence. Indeed, for the above sentence, /p/ might signal, besides package: parcel, packet, paper, pamphlet, periodical, picture, portrait, poster, present, prize or many other words for the imaginative reader. Artley does concede, however, that readers need to

---

*Phonics, of course, is not always effective either.

know more about phonics than consonant symbol-sound relationships. How much more is frequently a matter of debate.

Samuels[8] pointed out that children frequently discriminate between words using the minimum number of visual cues, and using first letters as their preferred cue, i.e., they centrate on first letters. He argues, then, that in order to encourage children to identify new words correctly, it is necessary to train them to discriminate among words by looking at whole words. This can be done, he says, by requiring discrimination among words in which the first letter or letters are the same and later letters are different.

Rationale

According to bottom-up and some interactive theorists, beginning readers are still working on identifying words automatically, and phonics is taught to help them do this.[9] Utilizing grapho-phonic cues (and other surface structure cues) to them is a basic component of the reading act. They reason that without phonic skills, most people would find it difficult to read, although most agree that reading involves much more than phonic analysis.

Although phonic processing skills may be basic to reading for many readers, an over-emphasis on phonics (especially without coordinating the use of phonics with the use of syntax and semantics) produces plodding readers. But readers without phonic skills would probably be more plodding if they had to look up many new words in a glossary or dictionary. The challenge is to find a balance between the use of too much and too little phonics and to raise phonic awareness to the level of automaticity.

Another recognition is essential. Phonics deals with relationships between printed symbols and sounds. Phonics will be of no help to the reader interested in getting meaning unless the reader orally knows the words being "attacked." That is, if the oral or aural counterpart of the printed symbol is used to probe the long-term memory system for meaning and no meaning is there, no communication between the author and reader can result. (If, on the other hand, the printed symbol, itself, is used for this probe, also no communication will result unless the meaning is in the long-term storage system.) The oral symbol is often used because it is thought that a child's oral language is better developed than his or her understanding of written language is.

You may feel that learning phonic generalizations will be very difficult for you. It is doubtful that this will be true—if you're not afraid of phonics. In fact, it is quite likely that you already know most, if not all, of the generalizations and symbol-sound relationships you may need to teach. However, you may have internalized your know-how and may not recognize these relationships at the level of "conscious awareness." To see if you know the major recoding relationships, try to pronounce the following nonsense words:

nad   pef   rill   tob   gup

Compare your pronunciation with a friend's. Are they alike? Try these:

nade   pefe   rile   tobe   gupe

And these:

tain   peef   roif   toan   spow
tay   tead   koy   poub   kaw

And these:

jenty   aimsel   wankle   loashoo

Look back at these when you finish the chapter to see if you gave probable consonant sounds, vowel sounds, and syllabicated the words in the last group in the probable ways. It is quite likely that you already know the symbol-sound relationships but that you need help in learning how to teach them.

The Evolution of Modern Generalizations

It might be well to briefly look at the recent history of phonic generalizations. Not too long ago—as late as the 1950's and 1960's, teachers and children felt overburdened with vast numbers of phonic principles to be learned. As many as 140 were taught, most of which had limited usefulness, in that they applied to only a few words that children read, or were invalid, in that there were more exceptions to the generalizations than there were instances of application. When being queried by an observant youngster, the teacher too frequently was forced to admit, "That word, Carol, is an exception to the generalization."

The thousands of Carols and Freds led several reading researchers, e.g., Theodore Clymer, Mildred Bailey, Robert Emans, and the present author, to supply objective evidence to publishers and teachers that, indeed, our phonics programs had gone far astray. Such evidence gave impetus to the growing demand for revised programs.

The generalizations in this chapter have been formulated as a result of this research. At the present time, they describe symbol-sound relationships of General American English. Several times, when there are dialectal differences, this is indicated. Also, when a symbol frequently represents more than one sound, this is also indicated.

It is important for the teacher to recognize that phonics is taught to help the reader recognize the oral counterpart of the printed word which the reader presumably knows orally. Phonics is not taught to correct the reader's pronunciation of a word. Few, if any, phonic generalizations are 100 percent accurate. So, if usage differs from the "rule," the usage is satisfactory, and the "rule" is limited.

Terminology

It is necessary for you to understand several terms in order to understand this chapter. Some of these are recently coined linguistic words. Among them are:

- phoneme—smallest unit (*eme*) of sound (*phon*)
- grapheme—the writing, or spelling, of the phoneme, literally smallest unit (*eme*) of writing (*graph*)
- morpheme—smallest unit (*eme*) of meaning (*morph*) (further defined later in chapter)

Here are some examples to help you clarify the definitions of phoneme and grapheme. Fill in the blanks. Then check your answers.

Word	Phonemes	Graphemes
1. cat	3 — /k/ + /ǎ/ + /t/	3 — <c> + <a> + <t>
2. hen	3 — /h/ + /ě/ + /n/	3 — <h> + <e> + <n>
3. man		
4. main		
5. mane		
6. Maine		
7. be		
8. bee		
9. boy		
10. photo		
11. child		
12. shame		

Answers:
man   (3 phonemes: /m/ + /ǎ/ + /n/, 3 graphemes: <m> + <a> + <n>
main   (3 phonemes: /m/ + /ā/ + /n/, 3 graphemes: <m> + <ai> + <n>

mane   (3 phonemes: /m/ + /ā/ + /n/, 3 graphemes: <m> + <a-e> + <n>

Maine   (3 phonemes: /m/ + /ā/ + /n/, 3 graphemes: <m> + <ai-e> + <n>

be   (2 phonemes: /b/ + /ē/, 2 graphemes: <b> + <e>

bee   (2 phonemes: /b/ + /ē/, 2 graphemes: <b> + <ee>

boy   (2 phonemes: /b/ + /oi/, 2 graphemes: <b> + <oy>

photo   (4 phonemes: /f/ + /ō/ + /t/ + /ō/, 4 graphemes: <ph> + <o> + <t> + <o>

child   (4 phonemes: /ch/ + /i/ + /l/ + /d/, 4 graphemes: <ch> + <i> + <l> + <d>

shame   (3 phonemes: /sh/ + /ā/ + /m/, 3 graphemes: <sh> + <a-e> + <m>

Organization of the Content and Methodology Parts of this Section

The remainder of this section on grapho-phonic cues is divided into three main parts. The first part deals with consonant grapheme to phoneme relationships. The second part deals with vowel grapheme to phoneme relationships. And the third part deals with syllabication. Each of these major sections is subdivided. In each subsection, what is to be taught (content) is explained first, followed by "model," or sample, lesson plans for teaching a small part of the content that has been given.

Lesson plans are of the following types:

- *five-part plans.* Each of these plans explains the teaching of grapheme to phoneme relationships by using the following steps:
  - auditory discrimination
  - visual discrimination
  - auditory-visual integration
  - blending
  - contextual application (meaning)

Combinations of these are also included; e.g., meaning might be a part of any step.

Teachers frequently follow such plans when teaching phonics extrinsically, that is, as independent of the children's reading assignments, such as when they are scheduled to teach specific phonics elements over a semester's or year's time. Such plans, however, could also be coordinated with the teaching of basal lessons, content area lessons, or Language Experience lessons.

- *shorter, intrinsic plans.* These plans are designed to show how a teacher might weave the teaching of phonics principles into the fabric of a total reading assignment. Such teaching may not include all of what some people consider the basic steps. These plans suggest ways of reviewing or reinforcing lessons previously taught and/or ways of teaching children who do not require all of the steps.

- *reinforcement activities.* These activities are designed to exemplify techniques for strengthening a particular skill or subskill.

Some definitions may be helpful here:

- *auditory discrimination* is the oral (or aural) recognition of the phoneme(s) for the grapheme(s) being taught. . . . or the oral (or aural) recognition of syllables in the syllabication section.
- *visual discrimination* is the recognition of the printed symbol(s), or grapheme(s), being taught. . . . or the visual recognition of syllables in the syllabication section.
- *auditory-visual integration* is the synthesizing of the oral (or aural) and visual recognition of the same unit, e.g., that the symbols <no> represent the sound /nō/. This is the act of recoding, i.e., moving from one code to another.
- *blending* may be explained in either, or both, of these ways:
  - *analytic blending*—in which minimal contrasts are used. Usually children are shown how words being taught are similar to and different from words they already know. E.g., the child may have the word <u>man</u> in his or her sight vocabulary. By using minimal contrasts the child could learn:

man	man	man
_an	ma_	m_n
tan	mat	men
fan	mad	mean
ran	map	main
etc.	etc.	etc.

- *synthetic blending*—in which phonemes are blended (or synthesized) to compose a word, e.g.:

/m/ + /ă/ + /n/ → /măn/
/ t / + /ă/ + /n/ → / tăn/
/m/ + /ā/ + /n/ → /mān/, spelled mane or main or Maine

or e.g., for

<man>	<mane>	<main>
/ ă /	/ ā /	/ ā /
/mă /	/mā /	/mā /
/măn/	/mān/	/mān/

or

/ ă /	/ ā /	/ ā /
/ ăn/	/ ān/	/ ān/
/măn/	/mān/	/mān/

- *contextual application/vocabulary development* is the decoding phase. This is the teaching or reinforcing of meanings of words taught in the lesson.

It must be pointed out here that in an actual teaching situation, it may not be necessary to teach all of these steps in a lesson. It might be advisable for the teacher to teach as much (or as little) as is necessary to assure recoding and decoding ability.

Sequencing of Teaching of Phonics

Some teachers teach phonics skills in the order in which children need them so that the children may decode words found in specific assignments. Teachers who use an Individualized Reading approach normally teach a child or a group of children as the need presents itself.

One of the characteristics of basal reading programs is controlled vocabulary. A major kind of control is graphemic: only certain specific graphemes (or graphemic patterns, i.e., spelling patterns) are introduced at each level of a series. Those patterns taught at previous levels are also reinforced at higher levels. One of the reasons for this is that the authors think that the teaching of phonics generalizations needs to be spaced-out so that children are not overwhelmed with too many generalizations, or new grapheme to phoneme relationships at one time.

When using basal programs, teachers may find that lesson plans like those given in this chapter may be coordinated with the order of introduction of new phonic elements in basal readers. Thus if one basal series introduces words like cape, cake, make, take, wake, tape, etc., in a first grade reader, the grapheme-phoneme relationships covering this situation may be taught to the children who are reading this book. In another basal series such words may be introduced in the 2-1 reader. The children using this series may be taught these relationships when they use the second grade book.

In some school systems, the teaching of phonics is sequenced independently of the other reading program or programs the children are using. Some of these school systems use phonics workbooks or packaged materials that have their own sequential patterns. Sometimes teachers, themselves, plan their own sequence and design their own lessons, which may resemble those plans given in this chapter.

TABLE 6.1 **Commonly used sequential pattern for the achievement of phonic skills**

Grade	Phonic Analysis — Content
K	Is able to identify sounds in the immediate environment Learns the alphabet (basis for phonics) Learns to auditorily discriminate words that rhyme Learns to auditorily discriminate initial consonants Is able to sort pictures according to rhyming sounds or initial consonants Is aware that there is a relationship between the printed word and the sound it represents

1	Learns phoneme to grapheme (and grapheme to phoneme) relationships for:
	    a) initial and final consonants
	    b) consonant blends of the families -r, -l, s-
	    c) common final consonant clusters
	    d) short vowels in closed syllables of the cvc pattern, e.g., cap, pet, bit, hop, cut
	    e) consonant digraphs: ch, sh, th, ph, -ng
	Combines the use of phonics with syntax and semantics

2	Learns phoneme to grapheme (and grapheme to phoneme) relationships for:
	    a) long vowel sounds in the cvce pattern, e.g., cape, Pete, bite, hope, cute
	    b) the following vowel pairs: ai, ay, ee, ea, oa, ow
	    c) "r modified" vowels, e.g., car, care, her, here, fir, fire, for (fore), hurt
	    d) the two sounds of c and the two sounds of g
	    e) three sounds of y (yes, my, baby)
	    f) the following vowel pairs as dipthongs: ou, ow, oi, oy, (and possibly au, aw); and the two sounds represented by oo (rooster, book)
	Is introduced to the schwa sound
	Is introduced to the syllabication of two syllable words in the patterns: vc/cv (for/mer), v/cv (ra/zor), vc/v (lemon)
	Combines the use of phonics with syntax and semantics

3	Learns phoneme to grapheme (and grapheme to phoneme) relationships for:
	    a) the vowel pairs: au, aw (auto, awful) and ei and ie
	    b) the vowel pair io, as in suffixes: -cion, -tion, -sion
	Continues to refine syllabication skills in the patterns vccv, vcv, and learns the final -cle generalization (ca/ble, un/cle)
	Is aware of stress in polysyllabic words
	Combines the use of phonics with syntax and semantics

4 5 6	Is taught phonics concepts that were not learned earlier (diagnostic teaching) Some phonic concepts may be reinforced for most children, especially the c and g generalizations, phonic syllabication (and morphological syllabication), and vowel pairs Stress is placed on combining phonic analysis with syntax, semantics and morphology

172

A survey of six published phonics programs indicates that the sequence shown in Table 6.1 is commonly used.

CONSONANTS—CONTENT

Consonant grapheme to phoneme relationships are, in general, highly consistent in English. This section explains and exemplifies these relationships in two major subsections:

- *single consonants,* that is, consonants that do not have another consonant at either side (though they surely do have a vowel at at least one side)
- *consonant clusters,* that is, consonants that appear side-by-side.

Figure 6.4 shows single consonant sound-symbol relationships, with examples.

Figure 6.5 shows consonant clusters that represent blends,* by families.

Consonant clusters that represent one sound each, but three different kinds of relationships are shown in Fig. 6.6.

CONSONANTS—METHODOLOGY

□ *Five-Part Plan: Teaching About Single Consonants in the Initial Position in Words*

- *Objectives*: 1) to teach grapheme → phoneme relationships for the consonant < d > using the analytic (whole word) approach.

   2) to teach, or reinforce, meanings of the words phonically taught.
- *Words to be taught*: words suggested by the children, words that are interesting and that are minimal contrasts of words on a high-frequency word list that the children know, words that are minimal contrasts of children's word-bank words, and/or words from a current reading assignment.
- *Auditory discrimination*: The teacher says, "I'm thinking of someone whose name begins like Donald. Who is it? Children respond: "David, Dianne, Darrell, Dorothy, Dick . . ."

   The teacher says, "I'm thinking of something that David or Dianne or Darrell or Dorothy or Dick might do. The word be-

---

*In consonant blends, each consonant represents its own sound.

b	/b/	bad	k	/k /	king	s	/s /	sun
c	/k/*	cat	l	/l /	lad		/z /	music
	/s /	city	m	/m /	map	t	/t /	top
d	/d/	dad	n	/n /	nut	v	/v /	van
f	/f /	fat	p	/p /	pen	w	/w /	wig
g	/g/**	goat	q(u)	/kw/	quail	x	/ks /	six
	/j/	gypsy		/k /	bouquet		/g+z/	exam
h	/h/	house	r	/r /	red	y	/y /	yes
j	/j/	jet				z	/z /	zoo

* <c> represents /k/, except when followed by <e>, <i>, or <y>.
  <c> represents /s/ when followed by <e>, <i>, or <y>.

** <g> represents /g/, except when followed by <e>, <i>, or <y>.
  <g> represents /j/ when followed by <e>, <i>, or <y>.
(Exceptions: Anglo-Saxon words, e.g., give, get, girl, tiger, finger, forget, forgive.)

Fig. 6.4: Single consonants

1- family		
bl-	/bl /	blue
cl-	/kl /	clown
fl-	/fl /	flag
gl-	/gl /	glass
pl-	/pl /	please
sl-	/sl /	sleep

also		
-ft	/ft /	raft
-lt	/lt /	salt
-nt	/nt /	dent
-ld	/ld /	cold
-nd	/nd /	wand
-mp	/mp/	ramp

r- family		
br-	/br /	brown
cr-	/kr /	crab
dr-	/dr /	drive
fr-	/fr /	frog
gr-	/gr /	green
pr-	/pr /	prune
tr-	/tr /	tree
str-	/str/	stream
thr-	/θr /	three

s-,-s family		
sc-	/sk /	scarf
sk-,-sk	/sk /	skunk, risk
sl-	/sl /	slow
sm-	/sm /	smile
sn-	/sn /	snow
sp-,-sp	/sp /	spin, wasp
st-,-st	/st /	star, test
sw-	/sw /	swim
sch-	/sk /	school
scr-	/skr/	screen
spl-	/spl/	splash
spr-	/spr/	spring
str-	/str /	street

Fig. 6.5: Consonant clusters-blends

consonant digraphs (two unlike letters, one sound; the sound is different than the sound of either letter):

ch   /ch/   child, chop
      /k /   chorus, orchid
      /sh/   chef, mustache
 	
sh   /sh/   should, ship
 	
ph   /f /   elephant, photo
	th /δ / this, they (voiced)
	      /θ / think, youth (voiceless)
	
	-ng /θ / sing, young
	
	wh /hw/* white, when

———————

*dialectal

consonant twins (two like letters, one sound: the sound is the same as the sound of the letter):

bb	/b/	ebb, robber	ll /l / ball, hello
cc	/k/	raccoon success(/k/ + /s/)	mm /m/ hammock nn /n / inn, bunny
ck	/k/	chick, pocket	
dd	/d/	odd, daddy	pp /p / puppy
ff	/f /	off, giraffe	rr /r / arrow
gg	/g/	egg, toboggan suggest(/g/ + /j/)	ss /s / boss, blossom tt /t / mitt, cotton

"silent" consonants (two unlike letters; the sound is the same as the sound of one of the letters):

kn-	/n/	knee, knife	-dg(e) /j / badge, lodge
ps-	/s /	psalm, pseudo	-lm /m/* palm, almond
wr-	/r /	wrong, wren	-mb /m/ lamb, bomb
gn-/-gn	/n/	gnat, sign	-tch /ch/ ditch, match

———————

*dialectal

Fig. 6.6: Consonant clusters that represent one sound each–digraphs, twins, "silent" consonants

gins like <u>d</u>ig." Children respond: "dive, dance, deal (cards), doodle."

The teacher says, "I'm thinking of the name of something that begins like <u>d</u>og." Children respond: "doll, dime, diner."

- *Auditory-visual integration:** The teacher writes these words on the board (or on an overhead transparency, which may be kept for future use), thus:

D	d	
David	dive	doll
Dianne	dance	dime
Darrell	deal	diner
Dorothy	doodle	dinghy
Dick	dig	dog
Donald		

The teacher points out that all of these words sound alike at the beginning and that all of them begin with the same letter.

- *Auditory discrimination-diagnosis*: To determine which children can auditorily discriminate the initial /d/, the teacher gives each child a paper paddle. One side is green, and the other side is red. Each child is to show the green side when the teacher reads a word that begins like "dog" and the red side when the teacher reads a word that does not begin like "dog." Color blind children might have a smiling face on the green side and an "X" on the red side of their paddles. The teacher can easily spot the children who are confused. Following is a list the teacher might read. (The teacher might have selected these words from a story the children are about to read.)

boat	do	ball	did
dog	Betty	doughnut	dance
dig	Tom	Harry	big
pig	dandy	Don	dove

The teacher might slowly read a short paragraph to the children, asking children to respond in the same way. The paragraph might have been selected from a story the children are about to read.

Those children who are confused should be given extra help in auditory discrimination of the initial /d/. E.g., they might be given a box of objects and asked to sort those whose names begin like "dog" from those whose names begin in other ways. Or pictures might be used. (The assumption here is that children know the names of the objects or pictures.) For auditory discrimination, names are not written out.

- *Visual discrimination*: Children are given a thermofax copy of two pages from a story they are about to read, or they are given

---

*You may prefer to do this step after Auditory discrimination–diagnosis (the next section).

part of a newspaper article. They are told to circle words that begin with <d>:

The (dog) barked and (dove) at the bone. (Don) really (did) not know what he would (do) next . . . (If a book itself is used, children may be asked to write such words on a piece of paper.)

• *Visual discrimination-diagnosis*: When checking the above exercise, the teacher can easily see who is successful and who is not. Those needing special help should be given such help now. E.g., if the children have their own word-bank cards of words they chose to learn, they might sort out the cards that begin with <d>. Otherwise the teacher might give them a set of cards he or she has. Or the teacher might give them an activity such as the following: Circle each <u>d</u> in the following list:

d   a   b   c   d   f   g   m   p   d   l   r   d,   etc.

Circle the words that begin with <u>d</u>: The first word in each line begins with d:

dog	did	ball	put	do
dig	fun	pill	dove	sun
Don	Tom	David	Harry	Dick
etc.				

• *Blending, i.e., minimal contrasts*:* Sometimes it is helpful to show children that they know words that are similar to the ones they are learning, but differ in spelling only in the element being taught. E.g., the teacher might say, "You know the word <u>big</u>." She or he writes it on the board:

big

Then she or he says, "Let's take off the letter <u>b</u> and put on the letter <u>d</u>. What word do we have?

big → _ig → dig

Then the teacher might say, "Let's use both of these words in a sentence." Children might respond:

"We will dig a big hole."

---

*In a top-down reading program, and even in some bottom-up reading programs, this would be step one of a phonics lesson. In a top-down program, word-bank cards would probably be used for known words.

Other examples of minimal contrasts:

from the first hundred Instant Words on the Fry list to common words that begin with <d>

had → _ad → dad
not → _ot → dot
may → _ay → day
can → _an → Dan
him → _im → dim
time → _ime → dime
way → _ay → day
part → _art → dart
like → _ike → dike
long → _ong → dong

from word-bank cards to interesting words for the child to learn

poodle → _oodle → doodle
meal → _eal → deal
must → _ust → dust
miner → _iner → diner

from known words to words in the children's next reading lesson

big → _ig → dig
to → _o → do
hid → _id → did
log → _og → dog
cove → _ove → dove
Ron → _on → Don

The Fry words and/or word-bank words and/or other known words could be printed on cards, and the d__ words could also be printed on cards. The pairs could be matched in a game of concentration. The child could keep the pair if he or she could pronounce each word and use each in a sentence.

- *Vocabulary development and diagnosis*: There seems little reason to teach children to pronounce words they do not understand. Although many of the words had to be known to be used in this lesson, perhaps they were known only by the children who suggested them. Children may also know the meanings of many of the Fry words. To teach and/or reinforce meanings, picture cards might be added to correspond with the words used in the blending activity above, and rummy might be played with books of four. Examples of books:

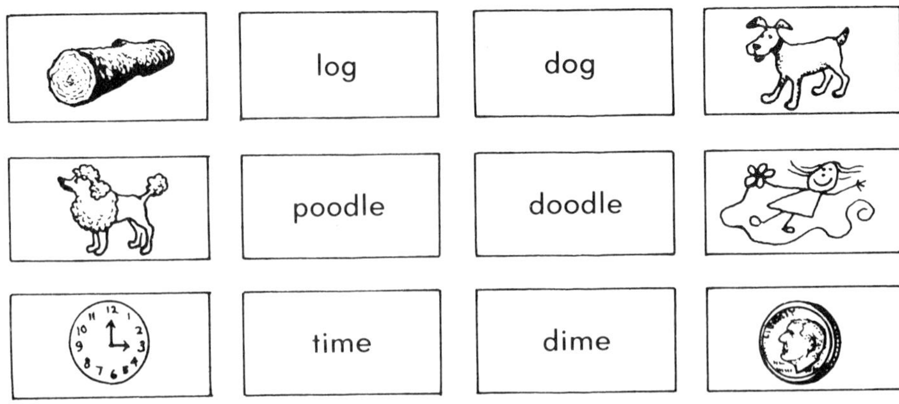

Children having trouble should be given extra help, perhaps in terms of reinforcement activities given at the end of this section.

• *Variation.* The same type of activity, or a similar activity, could be used with other initial consonants.

□ *Reinforcing the "C Generalization" in a Science Lesson*

• *Objectives*: 1) to inductively elicit the generalization for the pronunciation of <c>. Many words containing <c> appear in a lesson the children are to read, and children will have to decode them to uderstand the lesson.

2) to teach, reinforce, or set the stage for understanding the meanings of these words.

• *Words to be taught*: words taken from a chapter in the children's science books.

• *Step one—auditory discrimination*: Children are asked to give several words that contain the letter c (not ch), e.g., city, cat, active, lace. They are asked what sound the <c> represents in each word.

The teacher prepares a chart like the following:

<c> → /s/	<c> → /k/
1. city	cat
2. lace	active
.	
.	
.	
10.	

Children are asked to copy the chart and to complete it with words from the lesson in their book. Every word with a <c> in it will fit in one column or the other. They are also to compile a list of <c> words from these pages that they can't pronounce and, therefore, are unable to put in a column.

One child's paper might look like this:

<c> → /s/	<c> → /k/	unsure
1. city	cat	cultivate
2. lace	active	produce
3. cereal	corn	commerce
4. rice	cocoa	arc
5. spice	coffee	
6. certain	cotton	
7. race	tobacco	
8. century	agriculture	
9. province	crops	
10. cyclone	cattle	

- *Step two—visual discrimination* of the unit that indicates the sound <c> represents:

  Children are asked to list the letter that follows each <c>:

<c> → /s/		<c> → /k/		unsure	
1. city	i	cat	a	cultivate	u
2. lace	e	active	t	produce	e
3. cereal	e	corn	o	commerce	o,e
4. rice	e	cocoa	o,o	arc	—
5. spice	e	coffee	o		
6. certain	e	cloud	l		
7. race	e	tobacco	c,o		
8. century	e	agriculture	u		
9. province	e	crops	r		
10. cyclone	y	cattle	a		

Children are asked what letters follow a <c> when it represents /s/ (i, e, y).

Then they are asked if i, e, or y follows a <c> when it represents /k/.

No, but any other letter could, or no letter.

Next, they are asked to formulate a rule: "<c> represents /s/ when followed by e, i, or y. Otherwise <c> represents /k/."

- *Step three—application:* The words the children were unsure of are now examined:

cultivate	— <c> followed by u → /k/
produce	— <c> followed by e → /s/
commerce	— <c> followed by o → /k/
	<c> followed by e → /s/
arc	— <c> followed by - → /k/

  (words from other lists are added also)

Children in the class are asked to try to pronounce these words. (More knowledge is needed than just the sound of the <c>, e.g., syllabication. Therefore this activity is suitable for older children. The same type of activity could be used with younger children and/or for those reading an easier book. The words, then, would be simpler.)

- *Step four—vocabulary development:* The words for this activity have been taken from the children's science textbook. Now they are to read the chapter. One of the objectives in reading this chapter is to learn the meanings of these words. If the author gives meanings, the children should probably be asked to try to figure out the meanings from context, i.e., from the reading assignment. The teacher might write certain of these words on the board and ask the children to read to find their meanings, e.g.:

arc   commerce   produce
cultivate   cyclone

- *Step five—checking and reinforcing word meanings*: First, the teacher may ask children the meanings of the above words. Next, he or she may give them a little quiz on the meanings in order to determine who needs more teaching. The teacher may wish to include some words from a previous chapter, e.g.:
     Choose a word from the top of the page to complete each sentence below.

cyclone   exhale   flammable   produce
inhale   arc   cultivate   atom
commerce   fertilizer

1. Gardeners and farmers mix ____________ into soil to improve its condition.
2. Seeds are often planted in a(an) ____________ to help prevent erosion.
3. When we breathe in, we ____________.
4. When we breathe out, we ____________.
5. Oil and gas burn easily. They are highly ____________.
6. If a(an) ____________ sweeps through an area, crops may be destroyed.
7. Farm products may be called ____________.
8. The buying and selling of goods is known as ____________.
9. If a farmer expects a crop to grow, he must ____________ it.
10. Until recent times, it was thought that a(an) ____________ could not be split.

Children who do poorly here need appropriate reinforcement activities. See next chapter.

- *Variation*: The same type of activity could be used for <g>.

□ *Reinforcing Auditory-Visual Discrimination of Specific Consonants*

- *Objectives:*   1) to reinforce auditory discrimination and visual discrimination of the consonants d, b, p, f, and t.

	2) to reinforce and develop word meanings.
• *Materials:*	1) a marker of a different color for each child
	2) a board, like that below
	3) small cards, on which are written words for children—perhaps from their reading assignments—beginning with one of the above letters, e.g.: dog, dig, doodle, dinghy, book, boat, bat, ball, pig, porcupine, etc.
	4) additional cards are added giving directions: go back five spaces, go back to the previous <b>, advance two spaces, etc.
• *Participants:*	from two to six children, playing individually or in teams.
• *Directions:*	1) The first child picks a card, says the word, places his or her marker on the first letter that matches the initial letter of the word and remains there if he or she can use the word in a sentence that makes sense.
	2) If the child picks a "direction" card, he or she must follow that direction instead.
	3) The first child or team to place in the "winner" area wins.

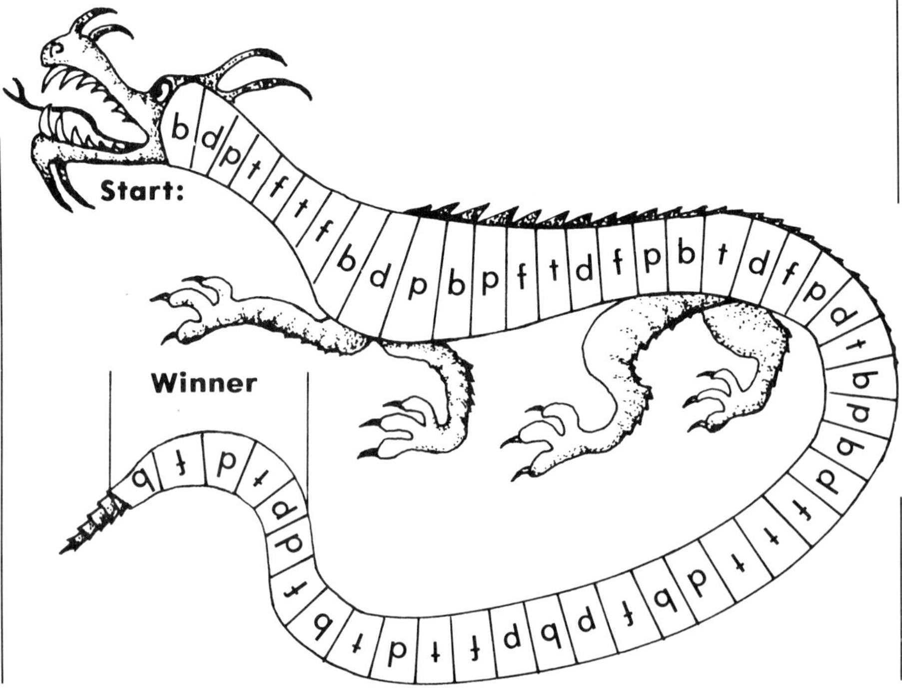

- *Variations*: The same activity might be used for any consonant or combination of consonants, for soft and hard c and/or g, for consonants in any position in the word: initial, medial, final.

□ *Reinforcing Auditory-Visual Integration of Consonants*

- *Objective*:   to reinforce auditory-visual integration of initial consonant sound-symbol relationships.
- *Materials*:   1) Each child folds an 8½ × 11″ paper into 9 or 16 rectangles and writes 9 or 16 of the following letters on it —one in each rectangle: b, d, f, h, j, k, l, m, n, p, r, s, t, v, w, y, z. (c and g may be added if the two sounds of each have been taught.)
                    2) The teacher has a box of cards, each card having one of the above letters on it.
                    3) Each child has about a dozen chips.
- *Participants*: two or more children
- *Directions*:   1) This game, known as "Wordo," is played like bingo. Before beginning each game, it is announced what must be covered to win: diagonal or vertical column, four corners, picture frame, etc.
                   2) The teacher picks a letter card and says a word beginning with that letter.
                   3) Children who have that letter on their cards cover it.
                   4) The first child to have designated rectangles covered calls "Wordo". The child reads the letters covered. (The teacher may wish to ask the child to give a word beginning with each letter.)
- *Variations*: The same activity might be used with final consonants (eliminate h, j, v, as they do not appear or rarely appear in final positions, and eliminate w and y because they are vowels when final in a word). Children will have to repeat one letter if 16 spaces are used.

□ *Reinforcing the use of Consonant Digraphs*

- *Objective*: to reinforce the use of consonant digraphs.
- *Materials*: Each child is given a sheet of paper with the following, or a similar, activity.

- *Directions*: The digraphs you are to use are listed at the top of the page. Insert one in each blank provided on the page.

    ch   sh   ph   th   ng

1. __irley went to __ur__ last Sunday.
2. Do you like taki__ __otogra__s?
3. Do you __ink you __ould go?
4. __ould we __ow her where it is?
5. We will __ill the juice before drinki__ it.

- *Variation*: If this is too difficult, the teacher could read all of the words except those that need a digraph added and ask the children to add the digraph.

☐ *Reinforcing the Use of a Specific Blend Family*

- *Objective*: to reinforce the use of the <l> family of consonant blends.
- *Materials*: The teacher has an exercise duplicated on paper for each child, like that following.
- *Directions*: 1) The teacher writes the following words on the board:
    lock   last   lass   low   lump
    leek   lot   lane   lap   lame
  2) Together, the children pronounce these words.
  3) The children are given the written exercise and told to fill in the correct consonant to make a new word that makes sense in each sentence.

Activity:

1. The wind will __low hard today.
2. The light will __low in the dark.
3. The children will __lap at the program.
4. Do not __lap your dog.
5. John dug up a __lump of earth to plant the seed.
6. Children who eat a lot may become __lump.
7. What __lass are you in?
8. Do you drink a __lass of milk each day?
9. Joan and Gerry live on the same __lock.
10. In the country we saw a __lock of sheep.
    Etc.

- *Variation*: If some of the words in the sentence are too difficult, the teacher could read the words, including the given words that need the letter added to complete the blend. Any family of blends could be used or even a combination of families.
- *imaginative variation*: The teacher may wish to write a verse using the blends being taught. The class might engage in choral reading or echo reading to learn the verse, and thus the phonic elements being reinforced. An example is shown in Figure 6.7.

☐ *Recognizing Silent Consonants*

- *Objective*: to reinforce the understanding of "silent" consonants.
- *Materials*: chalkboard and chalk
- *Directions*:   1) The teacher writes words on the board that contain consonants that are not pronounced, e.g.:

puppy	knee	badge	comb
tennis	psalm	gnaw	write
saddle	wren	calm	lamb
corral	sign	fudge	knife

  2) The children come to the board to cross out the "silent" consonants. (In the case of like consonants, it doesn't matter which of the two is crossed out.)

  3) As the child crosses out the silent consonant, he or she says the word and then uses it in a sentence.

☐ *Building Words by Using Common Phonograms*

- *Objectives*: to teach work building by the use of common phonograms by combining them with initial consonants and consonant blends. Also: to teach, or reinforce, meanings of words that are built.
- *Materials*: A hand tachistoscope on which are typed one or more of the following common phonograms: _all, _ain, _ail, _and, _ate, _ay, _ake, _eep, _eel, _ent, _est, _ick, _ill, _ing, _ock, _ide, _ine, _it. Each phonogram has a rectangular opening before it. A tape is inserted to show through the rectangle(s). The tape has typed on it the following single consonants and consonant blends: b, d, f, h, l, m, p, qu, r, s, t, v, w, bl, fl, sl, br, tr, st. These are blended with the phonogram(s) to compose words or nonsense words. E.g.:

Figure 6.7

186

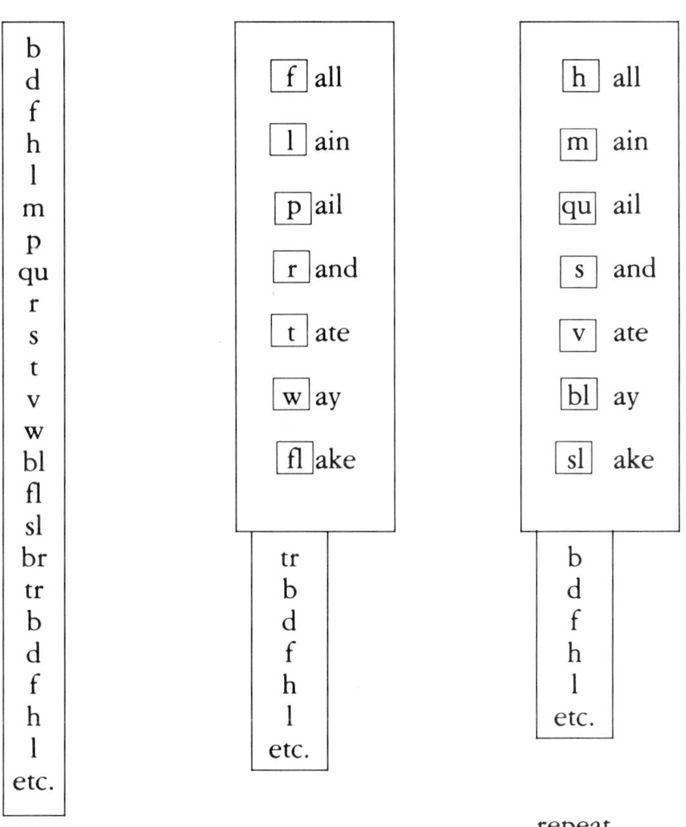

The teacher may compose lists of real words that can be made for each phonogram, e.g., for
_all: ball, fall, hall, tall, wall, stall,
_ain: lain, main, pain, rain, slain, brain, train, stain
_ail: bail, fail, hail, mail, pail, quail, rail, sail, tail, wail, flail, trail
Etc.

- *Participants*: the teacher (or peer leader) with one or more children.

- *Directions*: If the tachistoscope is poster size, one may be used for the whole group. Small individual tachistoscopes may be used by individual children instead.
    1) The teacher teaches the pronunciation(s) of the phonogram(s) to be used. E.g., _all → /ôl/.
    2) The tape is inserted. One letter or blend is seen at a time with each phonogram. The teacher teaches the children to blend the initial consonant or consonant blend with the phonogram, e.g.:

$$/ôl/ \rightarrow /bôl/$$
$$/ôl/ \rightarrow /dôl/$$
$$/ôl/ \rightarrow /fôl/$$
$$/ôl/ \rightarrow /hôl/$$

Each time the teacher asks if the children recognize the oral word . . . and if it is a real word. If it is a real word, the children are asked to use it in a sentence.

- *Variations*: As children mature, several or many phonograms may be used together in the same lesson, e.g., all of those as shown on the tachistoscope in the materials section above. Children may work together as teams. Games may be used. E.g., a spelldown, in which the child must recognize all real words in one exposure of the tachistoscope and tape, e.g., as shown in materials section: fall, lain, pail, way, flake. The next child might recognize: hall, main, quail, sand, slake. Etc.

Vowels—Content

Although consonants—in almost all situations—are highly consistent in the sounds they represent, such is not the case with vowels in English. However, vowel grapheme to phoneme relationships are far more consistent than we thought in the past, for in the past we were frequently teaching the wrong thing.

A major recognition has been that spelling *patterns* are important in describing the sounds vowels represent. We have only three major vowel patterns in English. Each pattern requires a different set of descriptors. These patterns are:

- *a single vowel* (i.e., a vowel without another vowel at either side and not a final vowel-consonant-e, e.g., not *rate*). Single vowels can be found in open or closed syllables. An open syllable ends with a vowel. A closed syllable ends with a consonant. E.g.:
  - open (cv)*: be, my, the, ma, hi, so, to, sly, etc.
  - closed (vc): cat, pet, kill, not, cut, cub, etc.
- *final vowel-(consonant)-e:* cake, Pete, hide, hope, cube, etc.
- *vowel pairs* (or adjacent vowels): main, sleep, out, cow, snow, boy, coin, say, saw, etc.**

To see if you understand this, indicate the vowel pattern(s) each of these words contains. Use the symbols given above the chart. Then check your answers.

---

* "c" represents any consonant; "v" represents any vowel.
**"y" and "w" are vowels when they follow a vowel, e.g.: ay, oy, aw, ow.

s = single vowel		-e = final v-(c)-e		p = vowel pair

word	pattern(s)	word	pattern(s)
1. be	s	11. kitchen	
2. bee	p	12. apron	
3. kite	-e	13. elephant	
4. cat		14. moody	
5. coat		15. secret	
6. met		16. poodle	
7. mete		17. table	
8. cow		18. balloon	
9. pray		19. remain	
10. soul		20. complete	

Answers: 3, -e; 4, s; 5, p; 6, s; 7, -e; 8, p; 9, p; 10, p; 11, s and s; 12, s and s; 13, s and s and s; 14, p and s; 15, s and s; 16, p and s (this is a final consonant +1+e, not a final vowel-(consonant)-e; 17, s and s; 18, s and p; 19, s and p; 20, s and -e.

Also, some definitions are necessary here. We must understand the terminology for vowel sounds used in this chapter.

1. a *long vowel sound* is the same as the name of a vowel letter: cake, Pete, hide, hope, cute.
2. a *short vowel sound* is far from this. The following words have short vowel sounds: cap, bed, hid, hop, cut.
3. a *schwa* (ə) is an extremely short vowel sound. (It is both short in duration, and it is far from any long vowel sound.) Schwas can be spelled with any single vowel and with some vowel pairs: about, parent, pencil, lemon, circus, dangerous, etc. The schwa is the most common vowel sound in modern English.
4. *diphthongs* are speech sounds that begin with one vowel sound and end with another in the same syllable (di = 2): coin, boy, cow, mouse.

These are the major types of vowel sounds of English.

The charts on pages 190 and 191 describe the usual sounds vowels represent when they are found in specific letter combinations, or spelling patterns.

Vowels—Methodology

□ *Five-Part Plan: Teaching about Single Vowels in Closed Syllables*

• *Objectives:*   1) to teach grapheme → phoneme relationships for the single vowel <a> in a closed syllable pattern in one syllable words.

(*continued on page 192*)

1. *Single vowels*[10] usually represent their own short, long or schwa sounds. In closed syllables single vowels usually represent short or schwa sounds.* (Children should be instructed to try each of the sounds until they recognize the word.) E.g.:

• *closed syllables* (short sound)

cap	pet	hid	hop	cut	/ hymn
man	bed	bit	rob	hug	/ gym
hat	hem	fin	not	cub	/ synonym

• *closed syllable-unstressed* (schwa sound)

sandal	gravel	April	second	circus
slogan	earthen	edible	parrot	awful

• *"r" modification* (when "r" follows a vowel, the sound of the vowel is modified):

car	her	fir	for	hurt
arm	fern	bird	corn	burn

• *open syllables*** (usually long or schwa sound):

(one syllable) a/ā/or/ə/	me	hi	no	—
(long) ra/dar	e/go	pi/lot	so/lar	u/nite
(schwa) a/bide	com/e/dy	jan/i/tor	mem/o/ry	u/pon

• *final y**** (long i in one syllable words): my, try, fry, cry, shy, thy, dry, spry, etc.

• *final y* (long e—or short i—in longer words): candy, hazy, melody, baby, fifty, etc.

2. When a word ends in *single vowel-consonant-e,* the <e> is silent, and the vowel represents its own long sound:[11]

cape	Pete	hide	hope	cute
mane	theme	bite	robe	huge
hate	cede	fine	note	cube

---

* A single vowel in a closed syllable (pattern cvc-) usually represents its own short sound (or /ə/ in a polysyllabic word, unstressed syllable.)

** If the single vowel in an open syllable (pattern cv-) is an <e>, <o>, or <u>, it usually represents its own long sound; if the vowel is an <a>, it may represent /ə/ –53%; /ā/–32%, /ă/–12%; if the vowel is <i>, it may represent /ə/–49%, /ĭ/–37%, or /ī/–14% of the time.

***If a one syllable word ends in a consonant + <y>, the <y> will represent /ī/. If a polysyllabic word ends in a consonant + <y>, the <y> will represent /ē/.

The following primary level* words are exceptions to this generalization:

a-e: have; are; purchase; average, courage, manage, message, passage, village, advantage; surface, palace; senate, separate

e-e: there, where; were; college

i-e: live, give, office, active, notice, native, justice, practice, service, promise, examine, favorite, determine, opposite, representative; machine, magazine, police, automobile; engine

o-e: purpose, welcome; lose, improve, move, movement, remove, whose; gone; above, come, become, done, love, lovely, none, some, something, sometimes, somewhat, somewhere; one

u-e: rule, conclude, include; measure, pleasure, treasure; sure, assure

3. *Vowel pairs* represent a variety of sounds.[12] The most common sounds for the most frequently appearing vowel pairs are given below.

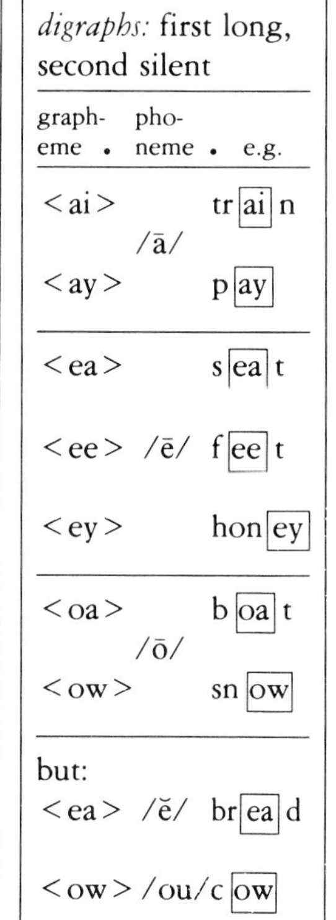

digraphs: first long, second silent		
graph-eme	pho-neme	e.g.
<ai>		tr|ai|n
<ay>	/ā/	p|ay|
<ea>		s|ea|t
<ee>	/ē/	f|ee|t
<ey>		hon|ey|
<oa>		b|oa|t
<ow>	/ō/	sn|ow|
but:		
<ea>	/ĕ/	br|ea|d
<ow>	/ou/	c|ow|

dipthongs: union of two vowels		
graph-eme	pho-neme	e.g.
<au>		|au| to
<aw>	/ô/	p|aw|
<a+ll>		b|all|
<oi>		c|oi|n
<oy>	/oi/	b|oy|
<ou>		h|ou|se
<ow>	/ou/	c|ow|
but:		
<ou>	/ə/	danger|ou|s
<ow>	/ō/	sn|ow|

other		
graph-eme	pho-neme	e.g.
<oo>	/ōō/	r|oo|ster
	/ŏŏ/	b|oo|k
<ei>	/ā/	w|ei|gh
	/ē/	c|ei|ling
<ie>	/ē/	bel|ie|ve

*primary level—grades 1–3, according to the Thorndike-Lorge word list gradings.

2) to teach, or reinforce, meanings of the words phonically taught.

- *Words to be taught*: cat, plus other words in the children's next few lessons, and any additional words the children suggest.
- *Auditory discrimination*: The teacher has placed many pictures and/or objects around the room whose names are spelled in the pattern: consonant-a-consonant. The teacher says the word "cat," then asks the children to find real objects or pictures of objects in the room that have the same vowel sound as "cat." Children might find: rat, mat, hat, bat, pan, can, fan, cap, map, etc. (There may be multiple objects or pictures of each.) The teacher asks all the children to say the words.
- *Auditory-visual integration*:* As the children say a word, the teacher writes the word on the board. The teacher asks the children if they know any other short words with the same vowel sound, e.g., fat, tan, ran. These are also written on the board.

  The teacher asks the children if they see similarities in all of the words. "What is alike in all of these words?" (They have a *short a* sound, and they are spelled with a consonant before and after the <a>.)
- *Auditory discrimination-diagnosis*: The teacher asks the children to number from one to twenty-five on a piece of paper. Then the teacher reads 25 words, each preceded by its number. Children put a smiling face if the word contains /ă/ and an "X" if it does not. E.g.:

Teacher's paper

1. cat	6. is	11. map	16. ton	21. rat
2. fat	7. hot	12. one	17. cut	22. sit
3. plum	8. cap	13. hat	18. can	23. mat
4. big	9. fan	14. ham	19. bat	24. cab
5. pan	10. fun	15. come	20. top	25. had

Child's paper

1. ☺	6. X	11. ☺	16. X	21.
2. ☺	7. X	12. X	17. X	22. X
3. X	8. ☺	13. ☺	18. ☺	23. ☺
4. X	9. ☺	14. ☺	19. ☺	24. ☺
5. ☺	10. X	15. X	20. X	25. ☺

---

*You may wish to do this following the next section (after Auditory discrimination-diagnosis).

The teacher can easily identify the children who need additional help.

- *Visual discrimination-diagnosis*: Children are given a copy of the teacher's paper, above, and asked to circle words of the c-a-c pattern and to "X" all other words.

The teacher can easily identify the children who need additional help.

- *Blending, using minimal contrasts (analytic approach)*:* The teacher may wish to show children that they already know some words that are like the new words being learned but differ only in the element being taught. The teacher may write the following on the board:

      cut

Then says, "Let's take out the <u> and add an <a>:

      cut → c_t → cat

The teacher asks for a sentence:

      "The <u>cat</u> <u>cut</u> its foot."

Other possible minimal contrasts are

(from known words to words in the lessons):

pen → p_n → pan
cup → c_p → cap
mop → m_p → map
but → b_t → bat
cub → c_b → cab

(from Fry's first hundred words to words in the lessons):

but → b_t → bat
did → d_d → dad
him → h_m → ham
his → h_s → has
then → th_n → than

Sentences might be composed orally, using these words.

- *Blending—synthetic approach*: The teacher may prefer to use a synthetic approach to blending. Since we are working with short a, i.e., /ă/ here, we will begin with that as the first constant in all words, e.g.:

words:	cat	or	cat	fat	or	fat
step 1:	/ ă /		/ ă /	/ ă /		/ ă /
step 2:	/că /		/ ăt/	/fă /		/ ăt/
step 3:	/căt/		/căt/	/făt/		/făt/

- *Vocabulary development and diagnosis*: Each of the words being taught (cat, fat, rat, mat, hat, bat, pan, can, fan, cap, car, star, map, etc.) would be printed on a card. Children who are able to

---

*In a top-down program, this might be step one of this lesson. The known words might logically be the children's word-bank words. It might be step one in a bottom-up program also.

would take a card and match it with the picture or object the teacher has provided for the auditory discrimination activity. Then these children would show the class the matched pair and even describe the object briefly.

Then the teacher would have the children number on their papers. In some cases, the teacher would hold up a word card, e.g., "hat" and the children would draw a picture. In other cases, the teacher would hold up the picture or object, e.g., "fan" and the children would write the word. (If writing the words is required, it is assumed that the children have already studied the appropriate consonants.)

The teacher can easily identify those children who need additional help.

- *Variation*: A similar activity can be used for all single-vowels in a medial position, for vowel pairs, and even for final vowel-(consonant)-e.

□ *Using Analytic Blending to Teach Additional Vowels in a Closed Syllable Pattern*

- *Objective*: to teach monosyllabic *short i* words, after having taught monosyllabic *short a* words. Use sentences such as the following:

    1. Mary has a <u>fan</u>, but the fish has a <u>f_n</u>.
       (fan → f_n → fin)
    2. Harry wore a <u>hat</u> when he <u>h_t</u> that ball.
       (hat → h_t → hit)

Other contrasting pairs that can be used are:

bat - bit	pan - pin	bad - bid
ham - him	jam - Jim	lap - lip
nap - nip	rag - rig	sap - sip

- *Objective*: to teach monosyllabic *short e, short o, short u* words after having taught *short a* and *short i* words:

    1. The <u>cat</u> jumped up on the <u>c_t</u>.
       (cat → c_t → cot)
    2. Sue <u>hit</u> the ball. What a <u>h_t</u> shot!
       (hit → h_t → hot)

Other contrasting pairs that can be used are:

a → e	a → o	a → u
man - men	cab - cob	bat - but
bag - beg	cap - cop	back - buck
band - bend	flap - flop	cab - cub

a → e	a → o	a → u
Dan - den	pad - pod	cat - cut
sat - set	jab - job	ham - hum
land - lend	pat - pot	lamp - lump
mat - met	rack - rock	mad - mud
pack - peck	rat - rot	rat - rut
fad - fed	tap - top	tag - tug

i → e*	i → o	i → u
bit - bet	hit - hot	bit - but
him - hem	flip - flop	him - hum
pin - pen	pit - pot	rig - rug
bid - bed	Rick - rock	bid - bud
big - beg	tip - top	sip - sup
sit - set	hip - hop	fin - fun
pick - peck	rid - rod	hit - hut

□ *Reinforcing the "Final y" Generalization*

- *Objective*: to reinforce the "final y" generalization: "Final y in a one syllable word represents /ī/; in a polysyllabic word it represents /ē/ (or /ĭ/).
- *Materials*: The teacher prepares 3 × 5″ cards, each with a *final y* word on it, e.g.:

    long i: by, my, try, fry, cry, dry, spy, why, sly, sky, fly, pry (Multiple copies may be made.)

    long e: army, baby, berry, buggy, city, chilly, sunny, cooky, copy, cozy, daily, dandy, dolly, dusty, weedy, easy, empty, enemy, foxy, hobby, ivy, lily, woody, merry, plenty, ready, puppy, ruby, sleepy, sorry, story, etc.

- *Participants*: About 6–8 children, in teams.
- *Directions*:   1) Cards are dealt face down to the children.
    2) Children take turns in order. The player turns up the top card in his or her stack. If she or he can pronounce it, use it in a sentence, and place it in the *long i* or *long e* stack correctly, the player is rid of the card. Then the next player goes. If the player fails, the card is placed at the bottom of the stack of his or her partner to the left. The first team to be out of cards wins.

---

*Some dialects do not contrast these sounds.

□ *Reinforcing the Final Vowel-(consonant)-e Generalization in a Mathematics Lesson*

- *Objectives*:   1) to teach children grapheme → phoneme relationships for words ending in v-c-e that are in their next arithmetic assignment.
  2) to set the stage for the children to learn the meanings of these words as used in the assignment. Common meanings of these words may be discussed before the children read the assignments.
- *Words to be taught*: words taken from the children's next arithmetic assignment: size, space, figure, base, side, scale
- *Assumption*: The children know the consonant grapheme → phoneme relationships.
- *Step one*: The teacher tells the children that, "Usually when a word ends in single-vowel-(consonant)-e, the *e* signals that the vowel is long." Several word pair contrasts are presented to the children, e.g.,

| hat - hate | pet - Pete | bit - bite | hop - hope | cut - cute |
| pan - pane | let - complete | dim - dime | cop - cope | purr - pure |

Then the teacher writes the new words on the board and asks the children to pronounce them:

   size   space   figure*   base   side   scale

- *Step two*: The teacher asks the children if they know a meaning for each word. They are encouraged to use each word in a sentence. The teacher writes a sentence for each word on the board or on an overhead transparency, which could be kept for future use. E.g.:

1. My dog *sizes* everyone up.
2. I'm interested in *space* travel.
3. It was hard to *figure* out the answer.
4. Tim made a two *base* hit.
5. We were told to stay on the *side*walk.
6. I weigh myself on the *scale* once a week.

---

*"R modified" long vowel

- *Step three*: The children are given the following sentences and told that each of these words has another meaning in the new assignment, and that one of the words fits each sentence. They are asked to write the word they think fits *underneath* the line. If they don't know, they are to guess. (They may change singular to plural or plural to singular.)

1. You should know the following kinds of ___________: square, circle, triangle.
2. The ___________ is the bottom of a triangle.
3. The ___________ of the square was smaller than that of the circle because the square fits into the circle.
4. A square has four ___________.
5. Which ___________ are we using—inches or meters?
6. How do you find the ___________ within a square?

- *Step four*: The children read the assignment. One of their purposes is to learn the meanings of these words in the context of the assignment. After reading (or while reading) they fill in the correct word above the line. If they filled in the wrong word below the line and the right word above the line, they have shown themselves that they can learn meanings of words through reading.

☐ *Reinforcing Auditory-Visual Integration of Vowel Pairs*

- *Objectives*:   1) to reinforce auditory-visual integration for vowel pairs.
                  2) to reinforce meanings of words containing vowel pairs.
- *Materials*: Each child is given a blank WORDO (bingo) card and chips on which are written the vowel-pairs of the words used in the activity. Words selected might be from an arithmetic, science, language arts, social studies, music, etc., lesson or a combination of these. The words are written on the board or on a transparency, omitting the vowel pair. E.g.:

r__t	(root)	v_ce	(voice)
borr__	(borrow)	sp__ch	(speech)
r__	(row)	__ster	(oyster)
f__rth	(fourth)	r_ndeer	(reindeer)
p__nd	(pound)	s__l	(seal)

f__t	(feet, foot)	gr__n	(grain)
__ts	(oats)	y__ld	(yield)
wh__t	(wheat)	d__ry	(dairy)
c__l	(coal)	w__l	(wool)
l__d	(lead)	g__ds	(goods)
s__l	(soil)	highw__	(highway)
r__se	(raise)	pion__r	(pioneer)

- *Participants*: All children who need reinforcement in the above objectives.
- *Directions*:   1) The children are asked to write one of the above partial words in each square in their wordo card. Each card will have the words in a different order if the children are told to skip around on their cards when writing the words.

A card might look like this:

__ster	wh __t	p __nd	w __l	f __t
v __ce	c __l	d __ry	gr __n	__ts
sp __ch	highw __	WORDO	r __	s __ l
r __t	l __d	borr __	r __se	r __ndeer
g __ds	s __ l	pion __r	f __th	y __ ld

chips: oo   oo   oa   ai   ea
          oi   oa   oa   oi   etc.

2) The teacher reads a word, and the child covers it with a chip with the correct vowel pair. E.g. *root*

is covered with *oo*. This is played like Bingo. The child who wins calls "Wordo." The winner must name the words covered and give a definition for each. The winner can call the next time.

- *Variations*: The caller could give the definition, and the children would find the partial word and cover it with the proper vowel-pair. Or, the caller could give the vowel-pair and the children would have to find a word to use the pair with.

SYLLABICATION — CONTENT

Syllabication Generalizations: Two Types

There are two major types of syllabication generalizations in English. One is morphological, and the other is phonic.

- *The first step* in syllabicating a word is to separate one morpheme from another, if this is possible. This is called morphological syllabication.
- *The second step* (if necessary) is to phonically syllabicate a morpheme.

A morpheme is the smallest unit (*eme*) of meaning (*morph*). In English, as in other languages, there are *free* morphemes and *bound* morphemes. A free English morpheme is an uninflected English word, for example: dog, mouse, elephant, garden, rhinoceros. A bound morpheme is a unit of meaning which must be attached to another morpheme (either bound or free) to compose a word. Prefixes, suffixes, and some roots are bound morphemes.

According to morphological syllabication generalizations, we divide thus:

- prefix/root: un/pleasant, pre/school, in/formal
- root/root: basket/ball, air/port, bi/cycle
- root/suffix: thought/ful, go/ing, sly/ly

Then, if a morpheme is composed of more than one syllable, it is syllabicated according to phonic syllabication generalizations, e.g.:

morphological syllabication	*phonic syllabication*
un/pleasant	pleas/ant
in/formal	for/mal
basket/ball	bas/ket
bi/cycle	cy/cle

A major advantage for using morphological syllabication (rather than phonic syllabication) when both might apply, besides the fact that this is what speakers of English usually do, is that in morphological syllabication we are dealing with meaningful units (prefixes have meanings, roots have meanings, suffixes have meanings and/or are inflectional). In phonic syllabication, we are merely breaking words into units of sound to help the reader pronounce words which perhaps he or she knows orally.

Morphological syllabication generalizations are very simple: prefix/root/root/suffix. Phonic syllabication generalizations are also simple and easy to apply if the teacher is not unnecessarily rigid. The purpose for teaching these phonic generalizations is to help bring about oral and/or aural recognition of words, not to engage in busywork.

It seems to the present author that sometimes for pronunciation purposes it doesn't really matter exactly where a word is syllabicated. (Though it may matter in formal writing situations.) Does it matter—for pronunciation purposes—which one of these is "correct":

city:	ci/ty or cit/y* Which do *you* say?
hazard:	ha/zard or haz/ard* Which do *you* say?
lily:	li/ly or lil/y*
razor:	ra/zor* or raz/or
never:	ne/ver or nev/er*
feather:	fea/ther or feath/er*
magic:	ma/gic or mag/ic*
shadow:	sha/dow or shad/ow*
civil:	ci/vil or civ/il*
racy:	ra/cy[†] or rac/y
about:	a/bout* or ab/out

Although the pronunciation—or point of division—in these words may be debatable, this is not an argument in favor of throwing out phonic syllabication generalizations. It is an argument, though, in favor of flexibility—of not being picayunish.

---

* "Correct" for prounuciation and end of line break.
[†] "Correct" for pronunciation, incorrect for end of line break.

Phonic Syllabication Generalizations

In teaching phonic syllabication generalizations, there are three spelling situations that must be dealt with. First, it must be recognized that each syllable contains one—and only one—vowel grapheme (because it has one—and only one—vowel phoneme). So, if a word has one vowel grapheme, it is one syllable long. If it has two vowel graphemes, it is two syllables long. If it has three vowel graphemes, it is three syllables long, etc. We divide words into syllables between vowel graphemes. Our generalizations are:

- If two vowel graphemes are separated by one consonant, *divide either before or after the consonant* (usually it doesn't matter where, just so you do divide): ci/ty or cit/y, ne/ver or nev/er, ra/zor or raz/or, a/bout or ab/out.*
- If two vowel graphemes are separated by two consonants, divide between the consonants: gar/den, win/dow, pub/lic, tar/get.
- If a word ends in consonant + le, divide before the consonant: can/dle, fa/ble, poo/dle, ea/gle.

PHONIC SYLLABICATION — METHODOLOGY

□*Auditory Discrimination of Number of Syllables*

- *Objective*: to teach auditory discrimination of the number of syllables in a word.
- *Words to be taught*: words suggested by the children and/or any words selected by the teacher.
- *Step 1, Definition*: The teacher asks the children if they know what a syllable is (an unbroken unit of spoken language). The teacher may give examples orally:
  - These words are one syllable long: cat, dog, mouse, lamp, etc.

---

*The validity level of the commonly taught generalization: If two vowel graphemes are separated by one consonant, divide *before* the consonant is 43% for primary level words and 57% for more difficult words. The validity level for the generalization: If two vowel graphemes are separated by one consonant and the first vowel sound is long, divide before the consonant, but divide after the consonant if the vowel sound is short, is high if the vowel is e, o, u, and low if the vowel is a or i. Also, such a generalization is circular in nature: the assumption is that the reader knows the sound the vowel represents. He/she could only know the sound of the vowel if he or she knows the word. If he/she knows the word, there is no need to syllabicate it—for reading purposes.

• These words are two syllables long: apple, stocking, today, July, zebra, etc.
• These words are three syllables long: elephant, October, afternoon, mosquito, etc.

- *Step 2*: The teacher asks the children to give one syllable, two syllable, three syllable words.
- *Step 3, diagnosis*: The teacher gives each child three cards, one numbered 1, another 2, another 3 (or the teacher may just ask the children to use their fingers).

    The teacher says words of one, two, or three syllables, and each child shows the correct number card or the correct number of fingers. (Cards or fingers should be held so other children cannot see them.)

- *Step 4, diagnosis*: The children have a sheet numbered from 1–25. The teacher reads a number, followed by a word, and the children write the number of syllables after the number. Children do not see the words. E.g.:

1. farm	(1)	9. entry	(2)	17. important	(3)
2. raccoon	(2)	10. tobacco	(3)	18. ball	(1)
3. dog	(1)	11. Florida	(3)	19. Chicago	(3)
4. September	(3)	12. children	(2)	20. teacher	(2)
5. store	(1)	13. box	(1)	21. elephant	(3)
6. box	(1)	14. tomato	(3)	22. boy	(1)
7. apple	(2)	15. happy	(2)	23. girl	(1)
8. bridge	(1)	16. April	(2)	24. zebra	(2)
				25. Africa	(3)

The teacher can easily see which children need extra help.

□*Auditory and Visual Discrimination of Number of Syllables*

- *Objective*: to teach auditory-visual integration of number of syllables in words. In this, the child must recognize what a vowel grapheme is. In English, vowel graphemes are spelled with
  • single vowels (a, e, i, o, u, y)
  • vowel-pairs
  • final vowel-(consonant)-e
- ■*Plan one*—to teach that single vowels represent one vowel sound.
- *Words to be taught*: any words the teacher or children select that contain only single vowel graphemes.
- *Step 1*: Children are given books at random—or they may be given sections of newspapers. They are told to write down (or

circle) at least five words that contain only single vowels. (Assumption: they have already worked on single vowels, as in the previous section on vowels.)

- *Step 2*: Each child writes one or two of these words on the board and underlines the single vowel(s):

go	finger	children
apple	word	kettle
tiger	level	Dennis
elephant	my	tell
open	America	for

- *Step 3*: The teacher and children say each word and note that there are as many syllables as there are vowel graphemes.
- ■ *Plan two*—to teach that vowel pairs usually represent one sound. (Validity: 85 percent)
- *Words to be taught*: any words the teacher or children select that contain vowel-pairs.
- *Step 1*: Children may use the same materials they used in Plan one, above. This time they note words with vowel-pairs. (In polysyllabic words, the words may also have single vowels.)
- *Step 2*: Each child writes one or two of these words on the board and underlines the vowel pair(s) twice and the single vowel(s) once:

grows	roaring	blood
journey	coons	coax
heart	yellow	looking
coffee	country	sweaters
stood	money	discounting

- *Step 3*: The teacher and children say each word and note that there are as many syllables as there are single-vowel graphemes plus vowel-pair graphemes.
- ■ *Plan three*—to teach that final vowel-(consonant)-e usually represents one sound. (Here the "final vowel" may be single or a pair.)
- *Words to be taught*: any words the teacher or children select that contain final vowel-(consonant)-e.
- *Step 1*: Children may use the same materials they used in Plans one and two, above. This time they note words that end in vowel-(consonant)-e.

- *Step 2*: Each child writes one or two of these words on the board and underlines the v-c-e three times, vowel pairs twice, single vowels once:

mouse*	compete	dime
creature	lemonade	manlike
voice*	parole	beige*
cascade	trombone	globe
because*	perfume	failure

- *Step 3*: The teacher and children say each word and note that there are as many syllables as there are vowel graphemes of the three types.
- *Plan four-diagnosis*: The children are given a list of words. They are to tell the number of vowels they see and the number of vowel-sounds they hear and the number of syllables in each word. E.g.:

Words	Number of Vowels Seen	Number of Vowels Heard	Number of Syllables
cat	1	1	1
mouse	3	1	1
elephant	3	3	3
apple	2	2	2
breakfast	3	2	2
sound	2	1	1
tomato	3	3	3
Rascal	2	2	2
fisher	2	2	2
above	3	2	2
etc.			

The teacher can easily see which children need additional help. (For primary level children, these activities should be spaced over several weeks of time. For older youngsters, in most cases these can be completed in a week or less.)

---

*Note that a final e has no effect on the sound of a vowel-pair that precedes it (except: breath, breathe).

□ *Dividing Words into Syllables*

- *Objective*: to teach children that there is a syllabic division between vowel graphemes within words; that is, that there is only one vowel grapheme per syllable. Also, to teach them where that division is likely to be.
- ■ *Plan one*—to teach that, "When two vowel sounds are separated by a single consonant, the division may be before or after the consonant."
- *Words to be taught*: any words the teacher or children select. E.g.: words used in the previous activity. Words selected are those of this construction: vcv. Consonant digraphs (ch, sh, ph, th, -ng) are treated like single consonants. Some linguists suggest that two adjacent *like consonants* be treated as single consonants, since only one is pronounced.
- *Words for this lesson*: tiger, elephant, open, level, America, money, creature, lemon, parole. These are written on the board.
- *Step 1*: Each child writes these words on a piece of paper and underlines the vowel graphemes, thus:

tiger	elephant	open
level	America	money
creature	lemon	parole

- *Step 2*: The teacher shows a picture and asks the children to say the word (perhaps with help) and show where it is divided. E.g.:

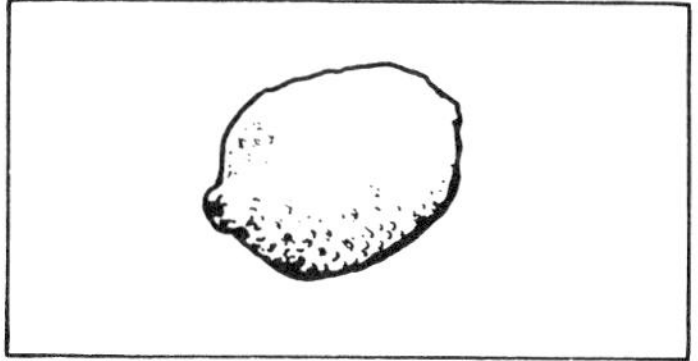

1. lem/on (or le/mon)

2. ti/ger

3. mon/ey (or mo/ney)

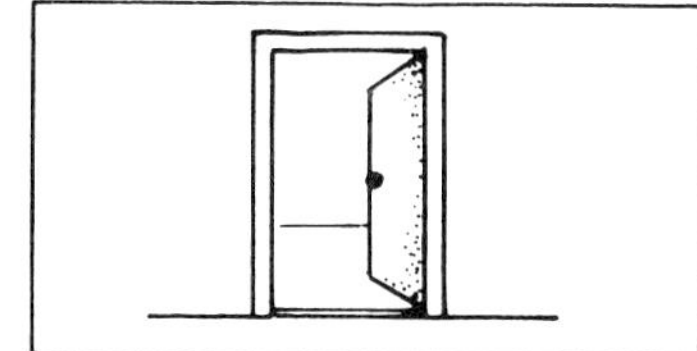

4. o/pen

5. crea/ture

6. par/ole (or pa/role)

7. el/e/phant (or e/le/phant)

8. A/mer/i/ca (or A/me/ri/ca)

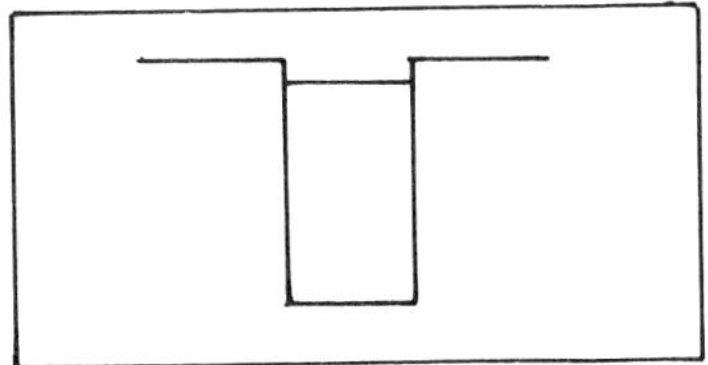

9. le/vel (or lev/el)

- *Step 3*: It is pointed out that the division may come before or after the consonant.
- *Plan two*—to teach that, "When two vowel sounds are separated by two consonants (not digraphs, though), the division comes between the consonants.

  Words for this lesson: finger, Dennis, cascade, trombone, perfume, journey, coffee, yellow. These are written on the board.
- *Step 1*: Each child writes these words on a piece of paper and underlines the vowel graphemes, thus:

fin<u>ge</u>r	D<u>e</u>nn<u>i</u>s	c<u>a</u>scade
tr<u>o</u>mb<u>o</u>ne	p<u>e</u>rf<u>u</u>me	j<u>ou</u>rn<u>ey</u>
c<u>o</u>ff<u>ee</u>	y<u>e</u>ll<u>ow</u>	

- *Step 2*: The teacher gives children copies of the following sentences and asks the children to write the correct word in each blank and show where the word is divided.

1. Tom shouted, "ouch," when he caught his _________ in the door. (fin/ger) (really: fiŋ/ger)
2. Maria got a bottle of _________ for her birthday. (per/fume)
3. Harry plays the _________ in our school band. (trom/bone)
4. The water fell in a beautiful _________. (cas/cade)
5. The Incredible _________ is the story of a voyage of a cat and two dogs. (Jour/ney)
6. I'm too young to drink _________. (cof/fee, or co/ffee or coff/ee)
7. Tom has a _________ shirt. (yel/low, or ye/llow or yell/ow)
8. _________ the Menace is a favorite cartoon character. (Den/nis, or De/nnis or Denn/is)

(The teacher may have to help the children read some of the words in these sentences.)

- *Step 3*: It is pointed out that the division comes between the two consonants, unless *perhaps* if the two consonants are alike and are treated as single consonants—since one is silent.
- *Plan three*—to teach that, "When a word ends in consonant + l + e, the division comes before the consonant." (The word is pronounced as though it ends in consonant + /əl/.)
- *Words for this lesson*: apple, kettle, noodle, eagle, turtle, bundle, maple, dimple. These are written on the board.
- *Step 1*: Each child writes these words on a piece of paper and underlines the vowel graphemes, thus:

apple	kettle	noodle
eagle	turtle	bundle
maple	dimple	

- *Step 2*: The teacher shows the children the real object or a picture of it and asks the children to write the word, telling where it is divided into syllables:

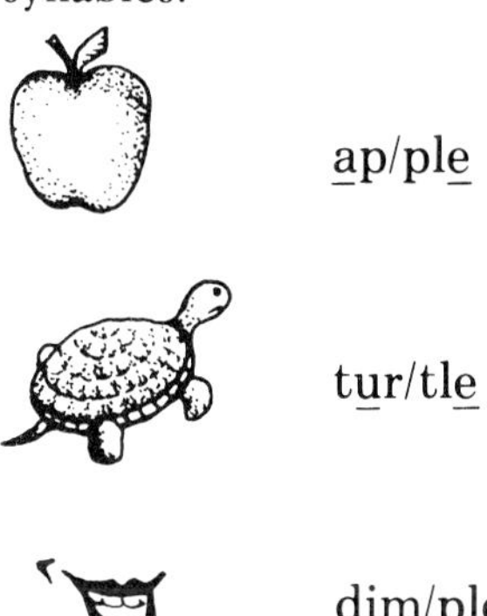

ap/ple

tur/tle

dim/ple

- *Step 3*: It is pointed out that the division comes before the consonant-l-e.
- *Plan 4, diagnosis*: All of the above activities can be used diagnostically. The following might also be used:
Each underlined word is also written in a blank to the left. Show where you would syllabicate the words at the left.

lizard turtle Bessie Rascal raccoon journey garden garbage along	The <u>lizard</u> and the <u>turtle</u> went out one day to play. They met <u>Bessie</u>, the cow, and <u>Rascal</u>, the <u>raccoon</u>. Do you think that Bessie or Rascal wanted to <u>journey</u> with them? Bessie said she had to stay in her <u>garden</u>. But Rascal wanted to search for <u>garbage</u>. He would go <u>along</u>. (Etc.)

The teacher might just thermofax a passage from the children's book and underline the polysyllabic words and ask the children to divide them into syllables.

□ *Reinforcing Phonic Syllabication in a Science Lesson*

- *Objectives*: 1) to reinforce phonic syllabication generalizations to help children pronounce words found in a reading assignment on parts of the body.
  2) to review meanings of words they already know to some degree and to set the stage for them to learn the meanings of other words through reading.
- *Words to be taught or reviewed*: thyroid, stomach, muscle, liver, tissue, kidney, intestine, colon, appendix, bladder, abdomen, tonsil, vertebra, larynx
- *Step one*: The teacher asks the children to write at the top of a piece of paper these headings:

| vcv | vccv | -cle |

Then the teacher asks the children to list each word in the appropriate column and underline each vowel grapheme. One paper might look like this:

vcv	vccv	-cle
thyroid	tissue	muscle
stomach	kidney	
liver	intestine	
colon	appendix	
abdomen	bladder	
larynx	abdomen	
	tonsil	
	vertebra	

- *Step two*: The teacher asks the children to show where the words would be syllabicated according to the rules they learned before. (These may have to be reviewed briefly.) E.g.:

vcv	vccv	-cle
thy/roid	tis/sue	mus/cle
(or thyr/oid)	kid/ney	
sto/mach	in/tes/tine	
(or stom/ach)	ap/pen/dix	
li/ver	blad/der	
(or liv/er)	ab/do/men)	

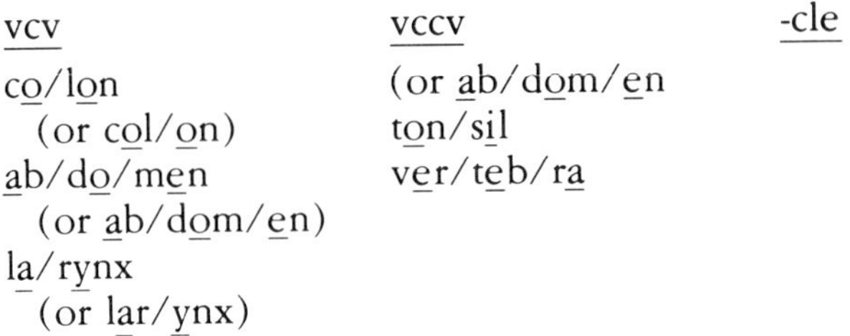

- *Step three*: The children are encouraged to try to pronounce each word. The teacher may supply a sentence to give them clues to help those who orally know the word to recall it. E.g.:

  1. This is my ____________ gland. (thy/roid)
  2. When I am hungry my ____________ growls. (sto/mach or stom/ach)
  3. You've heard of little ____________ pills. (li/ver or liv/er)
  4. Etc.

- *Step four*: Perhaps only four or five of the new words are in the next assignment. Children should be asked to look for the meanings of these words while they are reading. A picture of the body might be dittoed for each child, and the child might be asked to put the following labels where they belong after they have completed the reading:

      bladder   liver   colon   intestine   kidney

  The child might also be asked to write the functions of each of these organs.

□ *Syllable Blending*

- *Objectives*:   1) to teach, or reinforce, the ability to blend sylla-
                  bles into a word
                  2) to reinforce meanings of the words used
- *Materials*: Cards prepared for two and three syllable words—with one syllable on each card, e.g.:

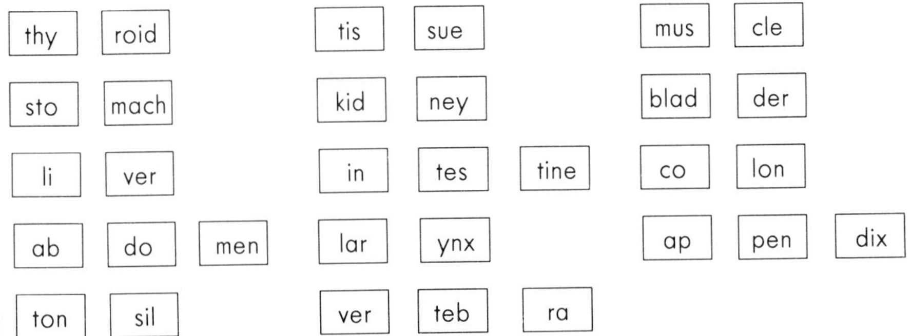

• *Participants*: Two teams, one to three persons per team.
• *Directions*: 1) Cards are mixed and placed face up.
           2) First player picks enough cards to compose a word. The player says the word (one point) and defines it (one point). Next player goes.
• *Variation*: 1) Cards are mixed and placed face down. Cards are numbered on back side.
           2) First player calls two numbers—or if after having two cards needs another (all of which can be used to compose a word) he or she may call another number. If player has a word and can pronounce it and define it, she or he keeps the cards and may play again. When player fails in any of the above, the next person goes.
• *Variation*: Write syllables at top of page and partially completed sentences underneath. Children complete the words by filling in the blanks. E.g.:

mach   ney   tis   ynx   lon   ton   blad   cle
 pen   kid   mus   co   men   sue   sto   der   ab
       do   dix   lar   sil   ap

1. A kid_____ is a bean shaped organ about 4½ inches long.
2. The _____lon is part of the large intestine.
3. Neither of these is necessary to people and are sometimes removed in operations: __________ and _____pen_____ .
4. Etc.

Syntactic Cues

Most children are familiar with the sentence patterns of English, and, therefore, syntactic cues can serve as powerful cues in helping children understand what they are reading. Syntactic cues help clarify meaning by showing how word or sentence elements relate.

To test the validity of this statement, you might give the children a sentence that contains several nonsense words, e.g.:

The merkle sogged a snarkle.

Ask the children what real words they could substitute for the nonsense words. Chances are that they will come up with a real sentence each time. For example, they might suggest sentences such as these:

The class played a game.
The bird warbled a song.

The boy shouted a warning.
The police stopped a robber.
The donkey kicked a ball.
The Senate passed a bill.

They sense that they are working with a noun-verb-noun sentence, and therefore, they supply the appropriate parts of speech for each element. If they had another pattern, e.g.:

The flump is mump.

they might suggest these sentences:
The grass is green.
The kitten is happy.
The cookie is delicious.
The water is cold.

Here they sense a noun-linking verb-adjective pattern and, therefore, again suggest appropriate parts of speech when they substitute words for the nonsense words.

If they were reading a real sentence (with no nonsense words) and they recognized most of the words, their "sentence sense" might tell them intuitively what part of speech each unknown word was, and if they know an appropriate word, they would supply it, e.g.:
The class played a ____________.
The donkey ____________ a ball.
The ____________ passed a bill.

Recognizing patterns and other syntactical elements described later helps narrow choices. The activities that follow help children become more conscious of this knowledge.

SENTENCE PATTERNS

Linguists tell us that English syntax is perhaps the simplest of all languages in the world. (It is the vocabulary of English that is complex.) A part of syntax is sentence patterns. Following are the sentence patterns found in English:

Pattern I:	NV	Peter swims.
	NVAd	Peter swims well.
Pattern II:	NVN	Peter likes music.
		Peter teaches swimming.
		Peter threw the ball.

Pattern III:	NVNN	Peter gave Susan a present.
	NVNA	Peter made Susan happy.
Pattern IV:	NLvN	Peter is my name.
	NLvA	Peter is sad.
	NLvAd	Peter is here.

To teach children to use the syntactic understandings that they already have, or to teach them about English syntax should they just be learning English, activities like the following might be used.

☐ *Sentence Patterns* If teaching children who are unfamiliar with English syntax, you may wish to slowly but systematically proceed through the patterns given above, starting with one pattern and teaching it well before going on to another. Use the cloze technique and word substitution, e.g.:

Noun-Verb Pattern:

Peter swims.	The boy is swimming.
Peter ______.	The boy is ________.
reads.	reading.
plays.	playing.
walks.	walking.

Peter swims.	The boy is swimming.
________ swims.	The ____ is swimming.
Johnna	girl
Mary Ann	frog
Hank	turtle

Peter and Hank swim.	Peter and Hank swim and skate.
_____ and _____ _____.	_____ and _____ _____ and _____.
Marty and Sue read.	Sam and Fred sing and dance.

After the children have learned to say the sentences and to read them as whole sentences, individual words might be printed on cards. The cards for each sentence would be scrambled. Then the children would learn to arrange the word cards in order.

☐ *Noun-Verb Pattern* After showing the children several examples of sentences of the N-V pattern, as above, write sentences about children in the class or from a story the children know. Delete one word, and ask the children to circle words that syntactically could fit in the blank. E.g.:

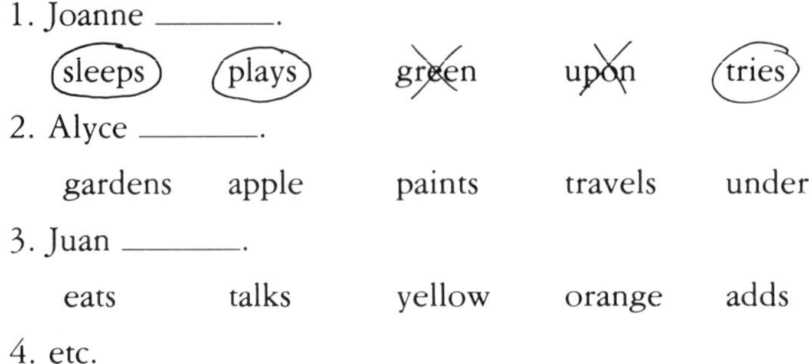

(Here inflectional endings signal words that are syntactically appropriate.) Then use the following form and have the children observe what each child is presently doing—or pantomiming. They circle only the correct verb or verbs.

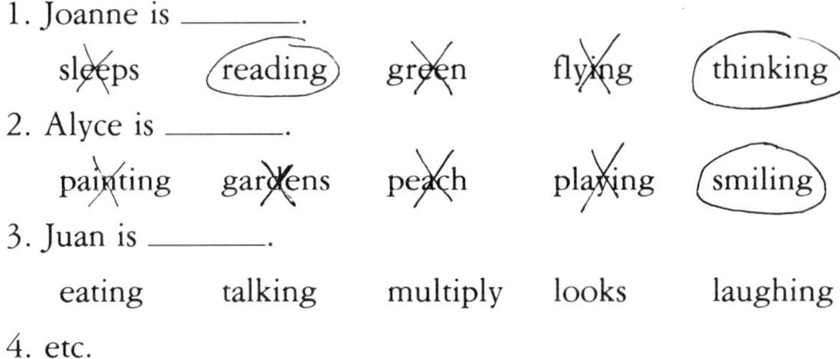

(Again, inflectional endings signal words that are syntactically appropriate. Experience signals those among these that may be correct.)

Other forms in the N-V pattern are:
Mary was swimming.
Mary will be swimming.
Mary has been swimming.

□ *Noun-Verb-Noun Pattern* Show the children examples of another pattern, e.g., the N-V-N pattern:
Juanita saw the mouse.
Freda made the homerun.
Robert caught the ball.
Again, delete one word. Ask children to circle words that syntactically could fit in the blank and X words that could not fit in the blank. Also, have children star words that reflect what each child has really done or seen:

1. Juanita saw the __________.

    (tarantula) ✶ (elephant)   not   ask   (movie)

2. Freda made the __________.

    base hit   homerun   from   cake   also

3. Robert caught the __________.

    ball   but   frisbie   swimming   are

4. etc.

(Here the child senses that only nouns are appropriate syntactically because "the" introduces a noun phrase.)

• *Variation*: Use any other sentence pattern. You may instead want to use sentences children have dictated or sentences from books the children are reading.

SYNTACTIC SIGNAL WORDS

Signal words, sometimes called markers, are terms that tell us a phrase or clause is coming. That is, they "signal" that a "string of words" is involved, and they introduce that string. Signal words tell us how parts of sentences are related. They aid in suggesting words that might follow them. Signal words otherwise are "empty" words usually: they serve a function but they usually have little meaning in themselves. Among the most common signal words are:

• *noun markers*: a, an, the; one, two, three . . . ; these, those, etc.
• *verb markers*: is, am, was, were, will be, has been, etc.
• *phrase markers*: in, of, above, under, with, into, from, for, etc.
• *clause markers*: however, nevertheless, since, consequently, if, etc.
• *question markers*: who, what, where, when, why, how

Each of these words usually signals the beginning of a phrase, dependent clause, or question. For example, a noun marker tells us a noun is coming, perhaps immediately or perhaps after an adjective or two. When we see *the*, for example, we can expect it to introduce a noun phrase:

the mouse   the big grey mouse
the elephant   the enormous elephant
the book   the fascinating book
the movie   the mysterious movie

The child who is aware of such relationships and who recognizes these words of a sentence: "The cat caught the ___________." knows that "the" introduces a noun phrase. Experience with cats might suggest the correct word for the blank. If, in addition, the initial consonant $<m> \rightarrow$ /m/ is known, the choice is narrowed.

□*Syntactical Signal Words* Children should be helped in reading strings of words rather than just single words. To help them do this, teachers might write signal words on the board, followed by a blank. Children are asked to fill in words that make sense, and even to compose sentences by connecting several strings, e.g.:

The ___________	was ___________	in ___________.
The moon	was shining	in the sky.
The dog	was barking	in the yard.
The bird	was chirping	in the tree.

□*Add Elaborations* Children should also be taught that words may come between a noun marker and its noun and that the complete string of words begins with the noun marker and ends with the noun, e.g.:

the ___________ tiger	one ___________ quail
hungry	baby
angry	mother
beautiful	bell

The same is true of any marker and its phrase completer.

□*Sight Words* Instead of teaching single words as sight words, as often as possible work with phrases or clauses. If children have begun to learn words of their own choice, these will be interesting words to them. In sentences these words are usually a part of a string of words. For example, if *baseball* is the child's word, it will probably be the final word in a string, e.g.:

| The boy | hit | the baseball | for a homerun. |

| The baseball | was hit | to centerfield. |

As soon as possible children should be taught strings of words—containing words of their choice, signal words, possibly words on high frequency word lists, and strings from the books they're reading.

NATURAL PHRASING

To help children read aloud using the natural rhythms of English, and also to lay foundations for silent reading in meaningful units, the following strategies are suggested:

□ *Read Alongs with Tapes or Records* Many tapes and records of books are available along with the scripts. Children who need help in pronunciation, phrasing, or intonation might read aloud along with these tapes or records. This can be done individually or in groups. If groups are used, it might be wise to have one good reader in each group to help keep the group together and to pay special attention to specific needs of any child. This good reader might be an older child from a higher grade level—a poor reader at that level, but good for the group he or she is working with. This would help build the self-concept of the older child. Several such groups could be reading simultaneously in a classroom.

□ *Echo Reading* Children who have problems in oral reading (as well as others) might enjoy "echoing" an excellent model. The teacher or another child reads a line or so, and the child or children repeat it. Then the teacher reads the next line, which is echoed, etc.

□ *Choral Reading* Choral reading is exciting to children. It is an art, a learning experience, and a joy. The class may read in unison. Groups may read in rounds or in parts when plays are read. They may read poetry, the lyrics of songs, plays, or other prose—even their own experience charts. They may alternate lines or verses or paragraphs or sentences. There's no end to the variety.

Poor oral readers and/or children for whom English is a second language may be grouped with one or more very competent oral readers to learn pronunciation, phrasing, and intonation as all children "perform" together. The good oral readers will lead the group, and all will learn and have fun.

□ *Intonation* To show children how the change in the intonation pattern of a sentence changes the meaning of the sentence, ask children to read sentences, each time stressing a different word. E.g.:

<u>Your</u> dog barked all last night.   (Your dog, not mine.)
Your <u>dog</u> barked all last night.   (Your dog, not your puppy.)
Your dog <u>barked</u> all last night.   (barked, not growled)
Your dog barked <u>all</u> last night.   (all, not part of)
Your dog barked all <u>last</u> night.   (last night, not another night)
Your dog barked all last <u>night</u>.   (night, not last week)

In a group, each child might hold a card with a word in the sentence, as above. First one child steps forward to stress the word that child is holding. The sentence is read with that word stressed. A group of children then act out the meaning of the sentence. Then another child steps forward, and a group acts out the new meaning, etc. The actions must be appropriate to the intonation.

□ *For Intonation and Phrasing Try Choral Reading of Sentences*

E.g.: "John didn't catch that big fish," thus:

Group 1:   <u>John</u> didn't catch that big fish.
   No, <u>he</u> didn't.
<u>John</u> didn't catch that big fish.
   No, <u>John</u> didn't.
<u>Who</u> caught that big fish, since <u>John</u> didn't?
JoAnn caught that big fish—That's why <u>John</u>
   didn't.

Group 2:   John <u>didn't</u> catch that big fish.
   No, he <u>didn't</u>.
John <u>didn't</u> catch that big fish.
   No, John <u>didn't</u>.
Why <u>didn't</u> John catch that big fish,
   since he <u>didn't</u>?
JoAnn caught that big fish.
   That's why John <u>didn't</u>.

Group 3:   John didn't <u>catch</u> that big fish.
   No, he didn't.
John didn't <u>catch</u> that big fish.
   No, John didn't.
John didn't <u>catch</u> that big fish.
   No, John didn't.
JoAnn gave it to him!

Group 4:   John didn't catch <u>that</u> big fish.
   No, he didn't.
John didn't catch <u>that</u> big fish.
   No, John didn't.

> John didn't catch _that_ big fish.
>   No, John didn't.
> John caught that big muskie,
>   over _there_.

Group 5:   John didn't catch that _big_ fish.
>   No, he didn't.
> John didn't catch that _big_ fish.
>   No, John didn't.
> John didn't catch that _big_ fish.
>   No, John didn't.
> But John did catch
>   that _little_ blowfish over there.

Group 6:   John didn't catch that big _fish_.
>   No, he didn't.
> John didn't catch that big _fish_.
>   No, John didn't.
> John didn't catch that big _fish_.
>   No, John didn't.
> But he did catch that great big _smile_.

(by L.B.)

Instead of using a different group for each stanza, you may wish to use two groups, alternating lines or pairs of lines, or any other variation. Here is another one to try:

Group 1:   _Mary_ had a little lamb -
Group 2:   _Mary_ did!
Group 1:   _Mary_ had a little lamb -
Group 2:   Yes, _she_ did!
Group 1:   _Mary_ had a little lamb -
Group 2:   _Mary_ did!
Group 1:   A little lamb had _Mary_-
>   Yes, _she_ did.

Group 2:   Mary _had_ a little lamb -
Group 1:   Mary _did_.
Group 2:   A little lamb _had_ Mary -
Group 1:   Yes, she _did_.
Group 2:   Mary _had_ a little lamb -
Group 1:   Mary _did_.
Group 2:   But she _doesn't_ anymore.

Group 1:   Mary had _a_ little lamb -
Group 2:   Mary did.

Group 1:   Mary had <u>a</u> little lamb -
Group 2:   Yes, she did.
Group 1:   <u>A</u> little lamb had Mary -
Group 2:   Mary did.
Group 1:   Mary had <u>one</u> little lamb -
            She did.

Group 2:   Mary had <u>little</u> lamb -
Group 1:   Mary did.
Group 2:   A <u>little</u> lamb had Mary -
Group 1:   Yes, she did.
Group 2:   Mary had a <u>little</u> lamb -
Group 1:   Mary did.
Group 2:   Mary had a <u>baby</u> lamb -
            She did.

Group 1:   Mary had a little <u>lamb</u> -
Group 2:   Mary <u>did</u>.
Group 1:   A little <u>lamb</u> had Mary -
Group 2:   Yes, she <u>did</u>.
Group 1:   Mary had a little <u>lamb</u>-
Group 2:   Mary <u>did</u>.
1 and 2:   But now she has a <u>sheep</u> -
            A great big <u>sheep</u>.

(by L.B.)

□ *Punctuation* Provide activities that demonstrate that punctuation does matter. For example, contrast:

1. Betty Jane and Bob went to the movie.
2. Betty, Jane and Bob went to the movie.

1. Harry said Patricia enjoys tacos.
2. "Harry," said Patricia, "enjoys tacos."

Children might practice writing descriptions of incidents to sense how writers do this. E.g., a woman with hands on her hips shouts, "Stop." The children might write: "The angry woman shouted, "Stop!"

□ *Impress Reading Method.*[13] For students who need special help in recoding and reading in natural rhythms, the Impress method has proved helpful.

The teacher and child hold the same book, with the teacher seated slightly behind the child. The teacher reads aloud into the child's ear, and the child reads along orally while also running a finger along the line, following the words being read, after learning how to do this by following the teacher's example. The same passage may be used several times to attain fluency.

Reading is done rapidly, for this is not an art. It is done to simulate silent reading. There is no preparation on the child's part before beginning—and reading progresses without interruption for teaching correct pronunciation. Reading continues, as the child is told simply to do the best he or she can.

No questions are asked after the reading is completed, but the child may comment about the passage if he or she wishes. Always, the teacher praises the fluidity of the child's reading.

Thad Trela[14] recommends that the child be allowed to select the material to be read but should be encouraged to begin with easy materials. "Concern is always with the flow of reading rather than with word accuracy." He also recommends that this method be used in 15-minute sessions and that a minimum of 12 hours work (48 sessions) be given over a period of three months.

Additional suggestions for using syntactic cues are given in other chapters of this book.

Semantic Cues

Semantic cues are those that can be used to build expectations concerning meanings among listeners or readers. A person talking or writing about a subject is expected to continue talking or writing about it, and is not expected to abruptly change to another topic unless some transitional warning device is used. Following are examples of ways of making readers aware of semantic cues. Additional suggestions for using semantic cues are given in several other chapters in this book.

□*Add to the Examples* Give children two or three starter words, and ask them to add to the list. To do this successfully, they must induce a category and then draw from their background of experiences to arrive at further examples that would fit the category. This relates to reading in this way: The child may have read part of a paragraph, story, or article and noted major points. He or she begins to classify these points and then forms expectations about what will follow. Categories may be broad (for young children) or narrow (for older ones). Some phonic cues may be added if deemed desirable.

    peach, apple, pear, b_______, o_______, _______
    spinach, cabbage, l_______, _______, _______, _______
    scream, howl, yell, sh____, _______, _______
    robin, blue jay, sparrow, wr_______, _______, _______
    daisy, rose, _______, _______, _______, _______
    cake, pie, cookies, _______, _______, _______
    red, blue, green, y_______, pur_______, _______
    violin, cello, harp, _______, _______, _______
    violin, flute, drum, _______, _______, _______
    lobster, shrimp, crab, _______, _______, _______

□ *Semantic Signal Words* Introduce semantic signal words that serve as cues to what might follow:

    peas, beans, **or** beets, **not** _______, _______, _______
    sundaes, sodas, **or** popsicles, **not** _______, _______, _______
    blueberry, raspberry, cherry, **and** o____, l____, l____
    beagles, dachshunds, collies, **and** _______, _______, _______

Compare final items added by different children and discuss. Ask children to compose sentences or paragraphs using the listings.

□ *Analogies* Use analogies to help children anticipate what is coming next.

    E.g.:
        black : white = night : _______
            (i.e., Black is to white as night is to day.)
        add : subtract = multiply : _______
        city : state = small : _______
        kitten : cat = _______ : dog
        sentence : paragraph = _______ : story
        line : stanza = _______ : poem
        fish : water = b_______ : sk____
        house : lot = _______ : _______
        book : _______ = song : _______
        cup : _______ = _______ : _______

Summary

In this chapter, proficient recoding and decoding together are viewed as the art of using a variety of cue systems. These cue systems begin with graphic, or surface structure, input of these types: sight vocabulary, grapho-phonic cues, syntactic cues, and semantic cues. Capable readers use most or all of these cues, synthesize the input, and move back and forth from deep structure, or meaning, to surface structure. Decoding involves this constant interaction between the mind of the reader and the language of the text. Techniques for building children's ability to use these cue systems were discussed.

First, strategies for building the sight vocabularies of young children were exemplified. The emphasis was placed on teaching children words of high interest to them. It was shown how these words can be used in introducing children to phonics and also to enriching their vocabularies in related areas. A later chapter in which the Language Experience Approach is discussed further elaborates this idea. In addition, a list of high frequency words was included.

Next, content and methodology for teaching children to use graphophonic cues were discussed. Included in the discussion of content were symbol-sound (grapheme-phoneme) relationships for consonants in these categories: single consonants, consonant blends, digraphs, and "silent" consonants. Five part lessons (involving auditory discrimination, visual discrimination, auditory-visual integration, blending, and contextual application), shorter lessons, and reinforcement activities were described to serve as models, or suggestions, for designing individual, group, or classwide activities.

Next, vowel sound-symbol relations were discussed. Grapheme-phoneme relationships for the three types of vowel patterns were given: single vowels, final single-vowel-(consonant)-e, and vowel pairs. Also sample lesson plans were included.

The final part of the grapho-phonic section included a discussion of syllabication. There are two types of syllabication generalizations: morphological and phonic. We use morphological syllabication generalizations in dividing between meaningful parts of words: prefix/root/ root/suffix. Within any of these meaningful units, we use phonic syllabication generalizations. These were explained. Next, ways of teaching phonic syllabication were exemplified.

The next major section of the chapter contained a discussion of syntactic cues, with suggestions of ways of teaching children to use such cues. Included were activities for teaching sentence patterns, signal words, sight words in phrases, and reading aloud to help children get the rhythm, or flow, of the language.

Finally, the use of semantic, or meaning, cues was discussed. Additional activities in the vocabulary and comprehension sections of this book include suggestions for using both syntactic and semantic cues.

Questions and Activities

After answering the questions at the beginning of this chapter, consider these questions and activities:

1. Which of the four cue systems is/are most appropriate for a bottom-up reading program? top-down? interactive? Under what circumstances is each cue system appropriate for a person who is reading?
2. In your opinion, what cue system(s) should be taught to a child first? Explain. Does the child's learning style and/or background of experience determine the order of cue systems taught to the child? Explain.
3. In your opinion, what sight words are most important for a child to learn in the first stages of reading—words of high interest to the child or words of high utility in reading materials? Why?
4. Is it necessary (or important) for children to be able to state phonic principles? Can children follow phonic principles without being able to state them?
5. For the child's reading success, weigh the relative importance of a child's ability to syllabicate words to bring about word recognition with her or his ability to syllabicate words precisely as the rules (or a dictionary) indicate they should be syllabicated. Might paying a great deal of attention to preciseness slow a child's word recognition ability and cause "evaporation" or "decay" of meaning when reading a passage?
6. Demonstrate how a reader might use multiple cues in reading a sentence or longer passage.
7. What cues are available for use when lists of single words are read? Why? How often in a normal reading situation are lists of single words read?
8. What cues are available for use when phrases are read? E.g.:

a boy	is playing	to the park
a cot	is running	in the lake
a rabbit	is swimming	at the movie
an apple	was laughing	with the dog

an elephant	has gone	by the box
the book	has read	upon a rock
the job	has been	over a bridge

9. What cues might be used when sentences are read?

NOTES

1. Constance Weaver, p. 153. See Selected References.
2. *Ibid.*, p. 30.
3. Sylvia Ashton-Warner, p. 32. See Selected References.
4. E.g.: Edward W. Dolch. "A Basic Sight Vocabulary." *Elementary School Journal*, 36 (1936): 456–460. Also: Henry Kucera and W. Nelson Frances. "Kucera-Francis Corpus," in *Computational Analysis of Present-Day American English*. Providence, Rhode Island: Brown University Press, 1967.
5. Shirley Hollingsworth, p. 180. See Selected References.
6. S. Jay Samuels, pp. 275, 278, 281. See Selected References.
7. A. Sterl Artley, pp. 124–125. See Selected References.
8. S. J. Samuels, *op. cit.*
9. Marilyn Jager Adams, *et al.*, p. 20. See Selected References.
10. Lou E. Burmeister, "The Effect of Syllabic Position. . ." See Selected References. See Appendix B for raw data.
11. Lou E. Burmeister, "Final Vowel-Consonant-e." See Selected References.
12. Lou E. Burmeister, "Vowel Pairs." See Selected References. See Appendix B for raw data.
13. Thaddeus M. Trela, "Fourteen . . ." pp. 6–8. See Selected References
14. *Ibid.*, p. 8.

SELECTED REFERENCES

Adams, Marilyn Jager and Richard C. Anderson and Dolores Durkin. "Beginning Reading: Theory and Practice." *Language Arts*, 55 (January 1978): 19–25.

Artley, A. Sterl. "Phonics Revisited." *Language Arts*, 54 (February 1977): 121–126.

——————. "Words, Words, Words." *Language Arts*, 52 (Nov./Dec. 1975): 1067–1072.

Bailey, Mildred Hart. "The Utility of Phonic Generalizations in Grades One through Six." *The Reading Teacher*, 20 (February 1967): 413–418.

Bloomfield, Leonard and C. Barnhart. *Let's Read: A Linguistic Approach.* Detroit: Wayne State University Press, 1961.

Burmeister, Lou E. "The Usefulness of Phonic Generalizations." *The Reading Teacher*, 21 (January 1968): 349–364.

——————————. "Vowel Pairs." *The Reading Teacher*, 21 (February 1968): 445–452.

——————————. "Selected Word Analysis Generalizations for a Group Approach to Corrective Reading in the Secondary School." *Reading Research Quarterly*, IV (Fall 1968): 71–95.

——————————. "Final Vowel-Consonant-e." *The Reading Teacher*, 24 (February 1971): 439–442.

——————————. "The Effect of Syllabic Position and Accent Pattern on the Phonemic Behavior of Single-Vowel Graphemes." *Reading and Realism.* Newark, Delaware: International Reading Association, 1969: 645–649.

——————————. "Content of a Phonics Program Based on Particularly Useful Generalizations." *Reading Methods and Teacher Improvement*, Nila B. Smith (editor). Newark, Delaware: International Reading Association, 1971.

——————————. *Words—from Print to Meaning (Classroom Activities: for Building Sight Vocabulary, for Using Context Clues, Morphology and Phonics)*. Reading, Mass.: Addison-Wesley, 1975.

Chomsky, Carol. "After Decoding: What?" *Language Arts*, 53 (March 1976): 288–296.

Clymer, Theodore L. "The Utility of Phonic Generalizations in the Primary Grades." *The Reading Teacher*, 16 (January 1963): 252–258.

Culyer, Richard C. III. "Guidelines for Skill Development: Word Attack." *The Reading Teacher*, 32 (January 1979): 425–432.

Dawson, Mildred (editor). *Teaching Word Recognition Skills*. Newark, Delaware: International Reading Association, 1971.

Durkin, Dolores. *Strategies for Identifying Words*. Boston: Allyn and Bacon, 1976.

Emans, Robert. "The Usefulness of Phonic Generalizations above the Primary Grades." *The Reading Teacher*, 20 (February 1967): 419–425.

Frenzel, Norman J. "Children Need a Multipronged Attack in Word Recognition." *The Reading Teacher*, 31 (March 1978): 627–631.

Fries, C.C. *Linguistics and Reading*. New York: Holt, Rinehart and Winston, 1963.

Froese, Victor. "How to Cause Word-by-Word Reading." *The Reading Teacher*, 30 (March 1977): 611–615.

Fusaro, Joseph A., Fobert G. Carroll, and Raymond L. Kimble. "More Support for the Value of Context in Reading Without Vowels." *Journal of Reading*, 21 (January 1978): 317–320.

Goodman, Kenneth. "Reading: A Psycholinguistic Guessing Game." *Journal of the Reading Specialist*, 4 (1967): 123–135.

Haddock, Maryann. "Teaching Blending in Beginning Reading Instruction *Is* Important." *The Reading Teacher*, 31 (March 1978): 654–658.

Hollingsworth, Shirley. "Tuck in a Poem or Two." *Language Arts*, 54 (February 1977): 180–181.

Lefevre, Carl. *Linguistics and the Teaching of Reading.* New York: McGraw-Hill Book Co., 1964.

————. "The Simplistic Standard Word-Perception Theory of Reading." *Elementary English*, 45 (1968): 349–353.

McCabe, Don. "220 Sight Words Are Too Many for Students with Memories Like Mine." *The Reading Teacher*, 31 (April 1978): 791–793.

McConaughy, Stephanie H. "Word Recognition and Word Meaning in the Total Reading Process." *Language Arts*, 55 (Nov./Dec. 1978): 946–956.

Miller, Robert. "The Mexican Approach to Developing Bilingual Materials and Teaching Literacy to Bilingual Students." *The Reading Teacher*, 35 (April 1982): 800–804.

Samuels, S. Jay. "Modes of Word Recognition," in *Theoretical Models and Processes of Reading*, Harry Singer and Robert B. Ruddell (eds.). Newark, Delaware: International Reading Association, 1976, pp. 270–282.

Singer, Harry. "Substrata-Factor Patterns Accompanying Development in Power of Reading, Elementary through College Level," in *Theoretical Models and Processes of Reading*, Harry Singer and Robert B. Ruddell (eds.). Newark, Delaware: International Reading Association, 1976, pp. 619–633.

Smith, Frank. "Learning to Read by Reading." *Language Arts*, 53 (March 1976): 297–299, 322.

————. *Understanding Reading: a Psycholinguistic Analysis of Reading and Learning to Read*, Second Edition. New York: Holt, Rinehart and Winston, 1978.

Spache, Evelyn. *Reading Activities for Child Involvement.* Boston: Allyn and Bacon, 1976.

Trela, Thaddeus. *Fourteen Remedial Reading Methods.* Belmont, California: Fearon Publishers, 1968.

————. *Sensible Phonics.* Belmont, California: Fearon Publishers, 1975.

Weaver, Constance. *Psycholinguistics and Reading: From Process to Practice.* Cambridge, Mass: Winthrop Publishers, Inc., 1980.

Wulz, S. Vanost and John H. Hollis. "Word Recognition: A Task-Based Definition for Testing and Teaching." *The Reading Teacher*, 32 (April 1979): 779–786.

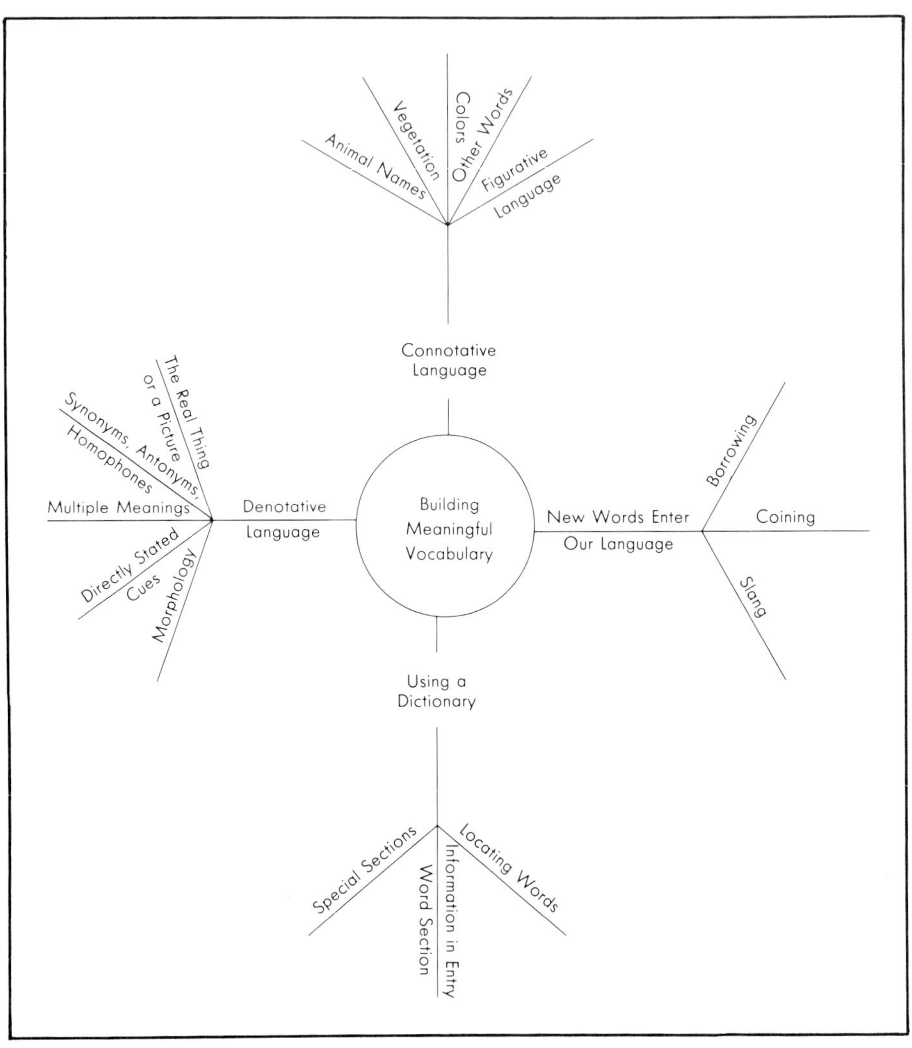

- What is meant by the "denotation" of a word? How can we help children learn denotations of words?

- What is meant by the "connotation" of a word? How can we help children understand word connotations and figurative language?

- Is the English language the same today as it was a few years ago? many years ago? How do we add new words to our language? How can we teach children about the changing nature of language?

- What should children know about using a dictionary? How can we teach children these essentials?

CHAPTER 7

Building Meaningful Vocabulary

Vocabulary study in the classroom can be pure joy because there are so many fascinating ways of working on building the vocabularies of children and young people. This chapter has been written to describe some of these ways.

Some of these activities can be presented to children in the form of handouts, or the teacher might use a chalkboard or transparency on an overhead projector. Many of the activities are designed as games because children enjoy games, are motivated by games, learn efficiently and effectively through playing games, and children can develop socially through playing games. Games and transparencies prepared by the teacher are quite inexpensive because they usually last for several years. Also, if a master copy of a handout is kept by a teacher, thermofax copies can be made from it for a long period of time if the original is not on erasable paper.

The best vocabulary activities are those designed by a teacher who knows the children who will be using them and also knows the content of the assignments these children are having. Thus some activities prepared for some children or classes may not be appropriate for others. However, many will be useful from year to year in the same school situation.

Activities might be designed to relate to children's interests or even to an individual child's interests. Activities might also be designed around chapters or units of books the children are reading—for reading class, science class, arithmetic, social studies, art, music, physical education classes, etc. Vocabulary activities can be designed around themes of general interest, e.g., national holidays, holidays around the world, travel, interesting local situations, timely occurrences—such as a national election, international peace conference, a special state's fair, or other celebration.

Words are usually not studied in isolation, but are best studied as they relate to an assignment, to an area of general interest, or to something vital in a person's life. Thus the activities that are suggested here serve as guides for designing activities you may wish to prepare using terms important in the classrooms in which you will be teaching. In most cases, they are not meant to be copied and used exactly as they are given here.

It is important for you to recognize the following: Words do not *have* meanings. Words *represent* meanings in the minds of readers and listeners. To understand a word, one must have had an experience—direct or vicarious—with the idea or concept behind the word. It's one thing to talk, talk, talk about dogs and another thing to know a few dogs and then talk about them. It's one thing to talk, talk, talk about communism and another thing to experience communism and then talk about it. The deeper and richer our experiences (direct or vicarious) can be, the more we will use words with deep feeling. The more impoverished our experiences are as they relate to the words we use, the more glib and superficial our speaking and reading will be.

With all people, but especially with the very young, it is highly important to supply direct experiences for word understandings to have depth. Thus field trips take on immense importance—to an airport, a farm, a zoo, a petting zoo, an art museum, etc. Also, bringing in to the classroom real objects—as in Show and Tell—is desirable. A teacher who travels may bring back slides and postcards, seashells, rocks, cones from trees, just as children may. The excitement that precedes, exists with, and follows a real experience is contagious. It engenders natural learning.[1] Examining a chambered nautilus and then reading a poem about one is far more exciting than just reading the poem. Playing baseball or tennis while learning the rules is far more effective than trying to learn the rules without the experience of playing. Active participation, when it is possible, promotes learning—and this includes learning of words in depth. So, one of the steps in every vocabulary lesson is to provide direct experience (or if that is not possible, vicarious experience) with the object or idea behind the word—when this is at all possible.

There are some words, however, that you might say do not represent objects or ideas. Perhaps. For example, syntactical signal words might be in this category (a, an, the, these, those, etc.; is, has, has been, was, were, etc.; of, by, from, to, etc.; since, if, however, consequently, etc.; who, what, where, when, why, how). Such words are probably best learned in context—as words that introduce meaningful phrases or clauses, rather than as individual words. One can hardly get excited about such words. Yet one or more of these are a vital part of many sentences.

This chapter is divided into four major sections, each dealing with a different aspect of vocabulary. The first section is about word denotations. Section two deals with word connotations and figurative language. Section three is about the changing nature of language and about the ways in which the English vocabulary has grown. The final section is about dictionary use.

Denotative Language

Denotations are literal meanings of words. If a word has a physical referent, that referent represents its denotation. Thus the fluffy four-legged
animal, usually with a tail, is the denotative referent for the word *cat*.
The bright color found in every other stripe of the United States flag is a
denotative referent for *red*, and the color of the other stripes is a denotative referent for *white*.

Denotations are scientific meanings of words. They are unemotional,
though perhaps highly interesting. They are different from connotations,
which are full of emotion—and thus may suggest different things to different people. Calling a person a cat is a connotative use of the word, as
is calling a person a *Red*. This section deals with teaching word denotations.

SEEING AND DISCUSSING THE REAL THING OR A PICTURE OF IT

Among the techniques you may use to teach word denotations is
showing children real objects or pictures of them by providing for:

□ *Field Trips* Children may be taken on field trips to learn many
things—among these things are new words and their meanings.
For example, some airports or airlines welcome groups of children
on field trips. Before going, children might be prepared to see a
specific type of plane, e.g., a DC-10 or a 727, or they might be
prepared to compare different types of planes. They might be prepared to be introduced to a pilot, a stewardess or steward. They
might be prepared to look for the control tower, the gates, the
runway, landing field, and hangars. You might talk about
enplaning, deplaning, taking-off, landing, climbing, soaring, zoom-
ing, etc. Then, when you're at the airport all of these in real life
could be pointed out to them. After you return from the field trip,
these words could be reviewed. Perhaps a Language Experience
story could be written.

Before a trip to a zoo, children could be shown pictures of animals that are found in the zoo. Children might be told a little
about habits of these animals. This will prepare them for observing
these animals in greater depth. They might be asked to find an animal they might like to feed for a day or a week or two if the local
zoo has a "feed the animals" policy or a "buy an animal a dinner"
program. When they return, they could vote to select the animal

and then contribute coins for the program. Before voting, children might give campaign speeches for their favorites.

□ *Show and Tell* Children should be encouraged to bring to class something of special interest to them. If it's a pet, they might just bring a picture. Here are some things children might bring: a blowfish, a plant or flower, an interesting rock, a travel folder, a book, a tool or kitchen utensil, a musical instrument—anything that catches their fancy. The class, then, has an opportunity to see something that is special to one of their classmates and to listen to the child talk about it and to ask questions about it.

□ *Viewing Slides, Pictures, Real Objects* The teacher might select slides, filmstrips, pictures from magazines, and real objects to show the children. Children enjoy travelogues. Travel folders are often obtainable from local travel agencies. Other materials might be obtained by writing to Chambers of Commerce. Children might plan an imaginary trip, read stories about people of other areas—learn their customs, which means learning new words, too.

Children might wish to learn more about a particular ethnic group in their own community. The teacher could gather pictures, borrow some interesting objects, or even invite a member of the group to talk with the class. Several recipes might be obtained, and the children might prepare some simple ethnic foods for the class to share. Names for foods are interesting to most people.

When the teacher sees that a child or a group of children are especially interested in a topic, the teacher might try to gather pictures and, if possible, objects and stories to enlarge this interest. These things might be placed in a special display in the room. When necessary, labels would be placed on them. For example, a child or several children might express an interest in skiing. The teacher might find magazine articles on skiing. Different kinds of skis might be pictured, several ski lodges, and some trails. Many words related to this sport could be learned. Short stories and books could be read about skiing, e.g., *Snow Treasure*, by Marie McSwigan, the true story of Norwegian children who skied past German troops to carry money to Americans behind the lines during World War II.

Enriched experiences mean enriched vocabulary—if the experiences are discussed. Such school experiences are especially valuable for culturally different and disadvantaged children, who may not have similar experiences at home.

SYNONYMS, ANTONYMS, AND HOMOPHONES

Children's vocabularies should be extended so that they learn to become more and more precise in their choice of words. Helping them choose from among synonyms the best word for a situation makes it possible for them to communicate both efficiently and interestingly.

Some techniques that might be used are:

□ *Play the Tired-Word Game* Some words are terribly tired because of overuse. *Said* is one such word. Ask the children to jot down words that could be used instead of *said*. Then put children in random groups by having them count-off: 1, 2, 3, 4, 5, 6; 1, 2, 3, 4, 5, 6; . . . All like numbers are grouped together.

Each group has a turn to give a word in a sentence along with a direct quote: e.g.,

Sue *cheered*, "Hurry, you'll win."

They *buzzed*, "I bet we'll have a test soon."

Mrs. Jones *laughed*, "You expected a test, but I won't give you one."

Harry *stuttered*, "I forgot to do my homework."

The first time around, the group receives one point for using a word not used before. The second time around, a group receives two points, then three, etc., until no one can go. Then points are added to see who has won. Some words that might be used are:

chuckled	croaked	slurred	objected
giggled	screamed	explained	concurred
pleaded	shouted	bragged	nagged
exclaimed	gurgled	asked	injected
hissed	babbled	pronounced	announced
inquired	whispered	yelled	barked
cried	coughed out	proclaimed	demanded
summarized	chewed out	sang out	repeated

Children should be encouraged to use these words when speaking and writing.

□ *Which Word Fits the Context?* Words, though synonymous, are not used interchangeably. People who are careful use the precise word for the setting. Children might be asked to choose the best word from column two for the blanks in column one.*

---

*You may wish to coordinate this activity with dictionary study activities given later in this chapter.

Context		Choose from:	
1. the ___aroma___ of coffee		fragrance	stench
2. the __________ of wine		whiff	redolence
3. the __________ of flowers		musk	spiceness
4. the __________ of oil		aroma	incense
5. the __________ of garbage		bouquet	scent
6. the __________ of roses		balminess	odor
7. the __________ of a criminal		attar	perfume
8. the __________ of spring		trail	
9. the __________ of cool air			
10. the __________ of a gardenia			
11. the __________ of a carnation			
12. the __________ of burning spices			

Antonyms are words that have opposite meanings. To teach children to make contrasts, it is helpful to work with antonyms. The following techniques might be used.

vertical		addition		difference		wide	
	profit		expand		divide		equal
credit		day		withdrawal		plus	
	owe		×		÷		gain
income		numerator		≠		symmetry	
	deposit		denominator		circumference		given
answer		horizontal		+		short	
	purchase		question		buy		sum

□*Antonym Checkers* Print a word on each square of a checker board for which there are antonyms you'd like the children to learn. In order to move, the child must give an antonym for the word on the square (or squares, in the case of jumping several times) upon which she or he lands. There are 32 squares that might be used, so the same word may be used several times, if you wish. A board might look like the one on page 234.

□*Seek and Find* Use a seek-and-find puzzle to reinforce specific antonyms previously studied. E.g.: Find the antonyms in the puzzle below for the clue words given. Write the antonym in the blank provided after each clue word, and circle the antonym in the puzzle. Words may run horizontally, vertically, or diagonally in any direction.

B	R	T	E	G	R	O	F	I	C
D	D	L	R	K	P	Q	U	F	D
U	Q	K	U	F	H	S	A	V	O
L	U	T	G	J	W	N	P	I	O
L	G	B	L	A	C	K	J	O	G
E	V	X	Y	Y	B	C	A	E	O
Y	Z	F	L	X	G	F	N	K	N
H	W	E	S	T	A	K	C	A	B
T	S	X	M	S	A	W	B	T	H
D	U	Z	T	Y	M	D	E	M	C

1. white   (black)   6. plain   __________
2. pretty   __________   7. east   __________
3. slow   __________   8. bad   __________
4. bright   __________   9. front   __________
5. give   __________   10. remember   __________

Homophones are words that sound alike but are spelled differently and have different meanings. *To, too,* and *two* are homophones. Try the following activities for working on homophones. Such activities are best done by using homophones from the children's reading assignments. For example, children may have known the word *by*, and just met the word *buy* in a reading assignment. They might have known the word *see* and just met the word *sea*, etc. Use those words that are important to children at a given time.

□ *Underline:* Use sentences, and have children select from the context the correct homophone. Ask them to underline it.

1. Maria went to the store to (by, buy) a gift.
2. Our team (won, one) by a score of 5-3.
3. Do you (no, know) the answer?
4. Mark (through, threw) the ball to Betty.
5. Joan wanted to go to the (see, sea) -shore to (see, sea) the (see, sea).
6. (Here, Hear) Ye, (here, hear) ye, the town crier called, shouting his message of joy.
7. Did you see that bumble (bee, be)?
8. Our class is to have a (soing, sewing) lesson.
9. I (to, too, two) wish (to, too, two) play baseball and make (to, too, two) runs for our team.
10. I'd like (meat, meet) in my sandwich today.

□ *Concentration* Play concentration, having the children match homophone cards. Cards that might be used are:

Cards are shuffled, numbered on the back and placed in order in rows on a table. The first player calls two numbers. If there is no match, the cards are returned to the table. If there is a match, the child must use each of the words in a sentence to keep the cards. The player continues until he or she fails to make a match and/or to use the words in a sentence.

WORDS WITH MULTIPLE MEANINGS

Many English words have several, or many, meanings. As some words (like *said*) are tired, others are so vigorous that we use them over and over—often with different meanings. Such words often confuse children because the children think they know the words, but the context suggests that the meaning they know is not the one the author intends. More sophisticated users of language frequently coin puns, which play upon these multiple meanings:

Confucious say, "Good baker make plenty *dough*." On a report to his parents, the teacher said, "John is *trying*." To show children how many meanings one word might have, try the following:

□ *Words of Many Meanings Run* is a word of many meanings. Ask the children to write as many sentences as they can using the word *run* (in any form), each time with a different meaning. Some examples are:

Sue has a *run* in her stocking.
George made a home*run*.
Senator Smith *ran* for office again.
My nose is *running*.

After a few minutes have passed, group the children randomly. Ask each group, in order, to give a sentence using the word run with a meaning not used before. As in the previous game for *said*, each successful group gets one point the first time around, two the second, three the third, etc. The children, themselves, are the judges and vote when a question arises about whether a meaning was used before. Right or wrong, the majority rules. Examples of sentences are:

I'll *run* around the block.
The peaches are *running* big this year.
The movie *ran* for a month.
She *ran* through her mail.
The clock is *running* fast.
The car stopped *running*.
My dad *runs* a store.

The dog *run* was too small.
He was *run* out of town.
The river *runs* through town.
There was a *run* on that book.
The snow on the ski *run* melted.
She gave him the *run* around.
He *ran* her ragged.
Etc.

To incorporate work on multiple meanings with children's reading assignments, the teacher must be alert to identify words that children may know in one way, but not with the meaning intended in a particular assignment. One of the things that makes content area reading difficult is that words frequently have unique meanings in specific areas. For example, compare the meanings of the following underlined words in different content areas, that is, in different contexts:

Language Arts	Arithmetic	Science	Social Studies
1. root of a word	square root	root of a plant	the root of evil, or of an idea
2. meaning of a word	the mean average		a mean person
3.	product of two numbers	agricultural product	
4. poetic feet	multiply 2 feet by 4 feet	a dog has four feet	He put his foot in his mouth
5.	raise 2 to the 4th power	electrical power, atomic power	a world power
6. a person of culture		microscopic culture, cultured pearls	Micronesian culture
7. punctuation marks, e.g., colon: semi-colon; period.		colon, as part of the intestine	Napoleonic period, Elizabethan period
8. first draft of a theme		a draft in the room	drafted for military service

The following techniques might be used to help children grasp the idea that many words have multiple meanings. These activities would also help them learn the unique meanings that are necessary for a particular reading assignment.

□ *Two Alike* Write three, four, or five sentences, each using a familiar word whose new meaning is being taught. Two of the sentences will use the word in the same way—with the new meaning. Children are to identify the two sentences in which the meaning is the same.

left

1. Sue left so she could go to the show.
2. Senator Brown voted to the left on all issues.
3. Our dog seemed afraid he'd be left alone when we traveled.
4. On energy matters, I lean slightly to the left of the middle.
5. Four children in our class are left handed.
   left means: _________________________ in (2, 4).

bill

1. I had to pay my bill at the candy store.
2. The bird's bill was one-half inch long.
3. I wonder if that bill will pass Congress.
4. The dog seemed to fill the bill.
5. The bill on air pollution was presented to the City Council for approval.
   bill means: _________________________ in (3, 5).

□ *Nonsense Words* Use nonsense words as substitutes for real words being taught. Ask children what real words the nonsense words represent. Ask them if they can define the word in the new context. (This might be done before a reading assignment to alert them to the fact that a word they already know has a new meaning. It should motivate them to look for that new meaning when they are reading.) E.g.:

trof

1. His smile was a sure trof that he wanted to go.
2. The sum of plus 3 and minus 9 has a negative trof.
3. You should trof your name at the end of a letter.
4. What is the trof of -3×6?
5. The trof at the corner said STOP.
   trof = (sign)

The new use of a familiar word is given in sentence 2. In what other sentence is <u>trof</u> used in the same way? ________. What do you think <u>trof</u> means in these sentences? _______________________

The chapter will explain the meaning more fully.

DIRECTLY STATED CUES

Authors frequently use specific kinds of syntactic patterns to help the reader along. These patterns tend to fall into the following categories: definition or explanation, restatement, examples, and contrasts. Each is exemplified in the following sections. Each pattern might be taught directly to children at the time that authors of their books begin using each pattern. This might be directly followed by examples from the children's books.

□ *Definition or Explanation Pattern* Teach children to notice words which may signal that a definition or explanation is to follow. The following steps may be used.

Step 1: Show children examples of the definition pattern: This is the N-Lv-N pattern and can be used in one of two ways: the definition might be found in the subject or predicate, and the word being defined is in the other part. Use first:

N_1-Lv-N_2, where N_1 = word being taught (single underlined)
$\qquad$ Lv = linking verb (circled)
$\qquad N_2$ = the definition or explanation (double under lined)

1. A <u>beetle</u> (is) <u>an insect with four wings</u>.

2. A <u>mouse</u> (is) <u>a rodent</u>.

3. <u>Prairie dogs</u> (are) <u>rodents</u>.

4. <u>Cats</u> (are) <u>members of the feline family</u>.

5. <u>Hurrying</u> (means) <u>going in haste, rapidly</u>.

6. <u>To prolong</u> (means) <u>to extend or lengthen in time</u>.

Step 2: Ask each child to write one or two words to be defined on a slip of paper and toss them in a box. On multiple slips write: <u>is</u>, <u>are</u>, <u>means</u>, and any other linking verbs you may wish to use. Put these in another box.

Children, in order, pick a slip from each box and must compose a definition type sentence using the key word and the linking verb selected. This may require changing a plural subject to singular or singular to plural. Play like a spelling bee, except that points are given for a correct response. No children are eliminated from the activity because of failure to respond correctly. (When children are eliminated from participating, the children who need the practice most get the least practice.)

Step 3: Follow this with examples taken from the children's books.

Step 4: N_2-Lv-N_1: Repeat the above, using transposed sentences, e.g.:

1. A person who keeps secret watch to obtain information (is known as) a spy.

2. A person who fails to pay due revenue (is known as) a tax-evader.

3. A written contract (is) a charter.

4. A government of, by, and for the people (is) a democracy or a republic.

5. A collected assessment (is called) a levy.

6. A plan of expenditures (is called) a budget.

□*Examples Pattern* Authors frequently use multiple examples to explain a "family name," or category. They may do this in two major ways, which should be explained to children. These are: The family name is given first, followed by examples. Arrows point to the beginnings and endings of apositives in which examples are listed.

1. Felines, including domestic cats, lions, tigers, and snow leopards, are fast afoot and see well at night.

2. Rodents, such as mice, rats, and beavers, are known to gnaw and bite.

3. Eyesight is well developed in primates—gorillas, chimpanzees, orangutans, gibbons, monkeys, marmosets, lemurs, and mankind.

Or the examples may be given first, followed by the family name:

1. People, seals, and porpoises are gregarious mammals.

2. <u>The cow, ox, bison, sheep, goat, antelope, camel, llama, giraffe, deer, elk, caribou, and moose</u> are all <u>ruminants</u>. These animals have four chambered stomachs.

After teaching these patterns at the time when the children are coming across them in their reading materials, an activity like the following could be designed:

Step 1: Cut 3 × 5″ cards into four pieces. Decide on about 4 to 6 groups or "families" you'd like children to classify, and write names of members of the families on the cards—one per card. The families might be taken from children's personal interests or from their reading assignments. Examples of *families* and *members* are:

   rodents: mice, rats, beavers, etc.
   felines: lions, tigers, leopards, etc.
   canines: poodles, German shepherds, collies, etc.
   whole numbers: 1, 2, 3, etc.
   fractions: 1/2, 1/4, 2/3, etc.
   even numbers: 2, 4, 6, etc.
   taxes: city, county, state, federal
   senators: state, national
   land formations: canyons, steppes, deserts, islands, etc.
   trees: oak, elm, ash, pine, etc.
   seashells: olives, angel wings, harps, etc.

Step 2: Place cards with names of members face up and family names face down but numbered on the back. Children are to pick from the family name cards first, then compose a sentence using the family name first, as, "Examples of *fractions* are:" and as they pick up the cards with fractions on them they continue, "1/2, 2/3, 1/4, etc." They must pick up *all* cards in the group to get a point. Then the next person goes.

Step 3: Return cards to their original positions. The children *first* pick up the cards of the *family members* and start their sentences, thus: "Poodles, German shepherds, collies, etc., are called. . ." Then they must pick up the correct family name card (which is face down) to finish the sentence: ". . .canines."

□*Apositive Pattern* Authors also frequently use a pattern in which they either give a definition within an apositive or else give the word being defined in a apositive: thus:

definition in the apositive:

1. <u>Deltas</u>, or <u>triangular deposits of soil</u>, are often found at mouths of rivers.

2. <u>Steppes,</u> or <u>vast treeless areas,</u> are found in southeastern Europe and Asia.

3. A large <u>desert,</u> an <u>arid and barren area,</u> is found in northern Africa.

4. An <u>island,</u> a <u>body of land surrounded by water,</u> is some people's idea of paradise.

5. <u>Peninsulas,</u> that is, <u>bodies of land surrounded on all but one side by water,</u> are found up and down the Atlantic coast.

6. A <u>meadow,</u> that is, a <u>low and level grassland,</u> is found east of our city.

word being defined is in the apositive:

1. A <u>bowl-shaped depression,</u> or <u>crater,</u> was found around the mouth of the volcano. .6

2. A <u>narrow strip of land,</u> called an <u>isthmus,</u> connects two large land areas.

3. This is the <u>line or ridge which marks the drainage of water to the east or west in North America,</u> known as the <u>continental divide</u>

After familiarizing children with this pattern, give them words from a reading assignment. Ask them to write definitions using this pattern. In class, compare sentences written by several children for each word being defined.

☐ *Contrast Patterns* Another frequently used pattern is the contrast pattern, telling what a word *does not* mean, not necessarily what it does mean. E.g.:

1. These are *whole numbers*, not fractions
2. We had a *hail storm*, not a rain storm.
3. The food is *decayed*, not fresh.
4. The report is of the *annual*, not monthly, rainfall.
5. Windows were covered with *frost*, but we could still see out.
6. Mountain goats look *clumsy*, but they are suprisingly *nimble*.

After showing this pattern to children, ask each child to think of one word that characterizes him or her. Have each child (or group of children) pantomime that word and its opposite and have the other children guess the two words and state them in a sentence, e.g.,

1. George is *tired*, not *wide awake*.
2. Christina is *happy*, not *sad*.
3. Jerome likes to *hit the baseball*, but he doesn't like to *strike out*.

MORPHOLOGY

As stated in the chapter on phonics, a *morpheme* is the smallest unit (*eme*) of meaning (*morph*) in a language. As in other languages, in English there are *free* morphemes and *bound* morphemes. A free English morpheme is an uninflected English word, such as *man, friend, grass, elephant,* and *giraffe.* Bound morphemes must be attached to other morphemes (either bound or free) to compose a word. Examples of bound morphemes in English are:

- prefixes: in-, sub-, pseudo-
- some roots: tri, quad, geo, thermo
- suffixes: -ing, -ful, -less, -est

When teaching children, we progress in stages from the easiest to the most difficult. A commonly followed sequence for introducing morphology to children is:

first: introduce free English morphemes

kindergarten and first grade: teach children to combine two free morphemes to compose a compound word, e.g.,

sand + box = sandbox   house + boat = houseboat
base + ball = baseball   oat + meal = oatmeal

late second grade: introduce bound morphemes by attaching them to free morphemes the children know, e.g.,

un + kind = unkind   in + field = infield
dis + honest = dishonest   re + open = reopen

(Inflectional suffixes are normally taught at all stages because children need these to speak in sentences. E.g.: runn*ing*, boy*s*, bigg*est*, etc. But they may be taught *directly* at this stage.)

fourth grade: introduce words composed of two bound morphemes, e.g.,

geo + graphy = geography   syn + onym = synonym
thermo + meter = thermometer   poly + theism = polytheism

Following are activities you might use in the classroom to teach morphology.

Easy Compounds

□ *Pairs of Pictures:* To teach children easy compound words, cut out pictures from magazines, and mount them on cards. Show the pictures in pairs that could be used to compose words. Ask the children to name both pictures and then put them together to form a word and draw (or find) a picture of that word.* E.g.:

---

*You may provide a stack of pictures for them to select from.

□ *Sentence Completion* Read sentences to the children, or have them read the sentences. Children suggest the compound word that completes each sentence. For example:

1. *Rain* that *falls* is ___________.
2. A *port* on the *sea* is a ___________.
3. A *bonnet* worn in the *sun* is a ___________.
4. A *skin* from a *sheep* is a ___________.
5. Something a *cat* likes to *nip* is ___________.
6. A *case* for *books* is a ___________.
7. *Water* that comes down in a great *fall* is a ___________.
8. A *room* where there is a *bed* is a ___________.
9. A *stick* with a *broom* at the end is a ___________.
10. A *knife* one keeps in a *pocket* is a ___________.

□ *Pair-Off Children* Give each child a card with a word printed on it that is one root of a compound word. Ask children to find their partner. Cards might have these words on them:

blue	bird	oat	meal	air	port
sea	port	sea	shore	air	plane
corn	field	grand	mother	sea	plane
ice	cream	grand	father	eye	brow
neck	lace	pan	cake	news	paper
steam	boat	after	noon	foot	step

This is a good place to begin teaching children about morphological syllabication. Ask the children to pronounce each word as they look at the two cards of the compound. Point out to them that there is a brief break in voice between the two words (*auditory discrimination*). Write the compound word on the board, and ask a child to draw a slash where the break occurs: blue/bird, sea/port, etc. (*visual discrimination*). Be sure children understand the meanings of the compounds.*

---

*Children may use words they do not understand. For example, in one study, children reported that breakfast was so-called because it was eaten fast, and Friday was so-named because it is the day when people eat fried fish. One child thought ice cream was so-named because he screamed for it once.

An example of compound words from a content area follows:

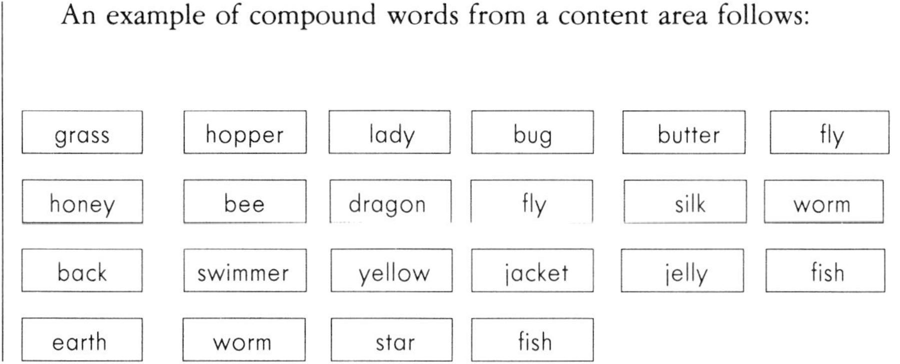

Easy Prefixes—Meaningful Units

In Thorndike's word list of the 20,000 most common English words, there are 5,000 words that have prefixes. Eighty-two percent of these 5,000 words use one of the following prefixes:

ab—away from
ad—to, toward
be—on all sides, overly
co, con, com—with, together
de—reverse, undo, downward
dis—not
dis—reverse
en—in, into, to cover
ex—out of, former

in   into
in—not
pre—before
pro—in favor of, for
re—again, restore
sub—under, beneath
un—not
un—do the opposite of

Because a prefix occurs frequently does not necessarily mean it is easy to teach. Some of the above prefixes are more difficult to teach than are the whole words that contain them. Such is the case with be-, as in bewitch, belittle, bemoan, befit, etc. The prefixes ab-, and ad-, and pro-, are also difficult to teach young children because they are only rarely attached to free morphemes. The other prefixes in this list are usually taught to young children. They are attached to free English morphemes. For example:

□ *Word Wheels* Make word wheels, with a prefix inside and free morphemes outside:

in = into   in = not

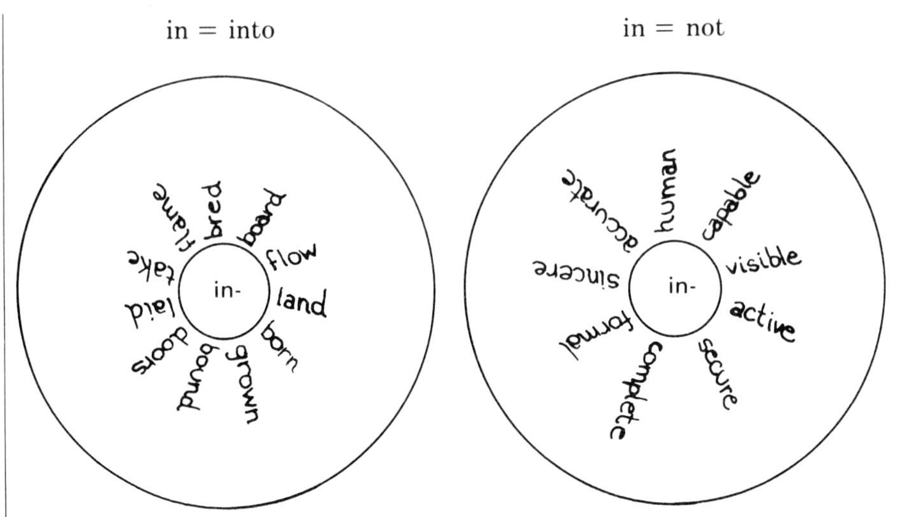

Compare meanings of "in-"

un = do the opposite of   un = not

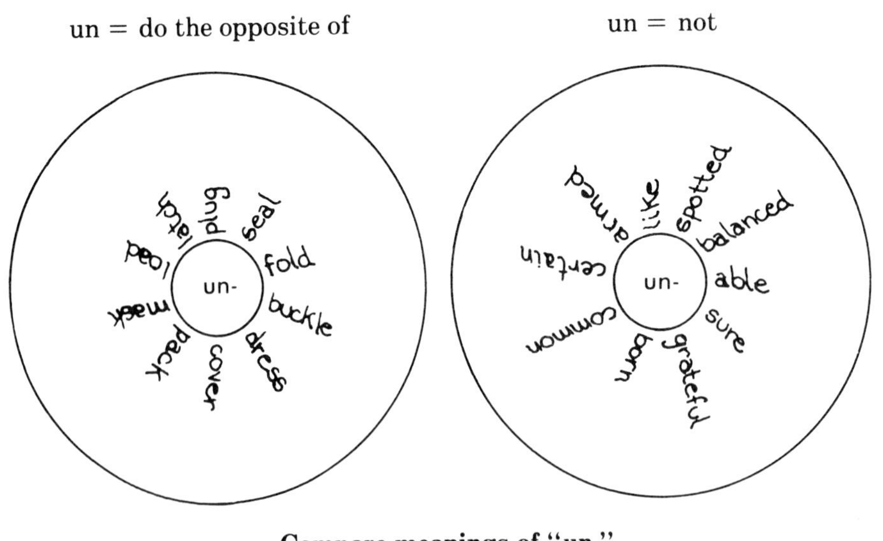

Compare meanings of "un-"

dis = reverse, do the opposite of   dis = not

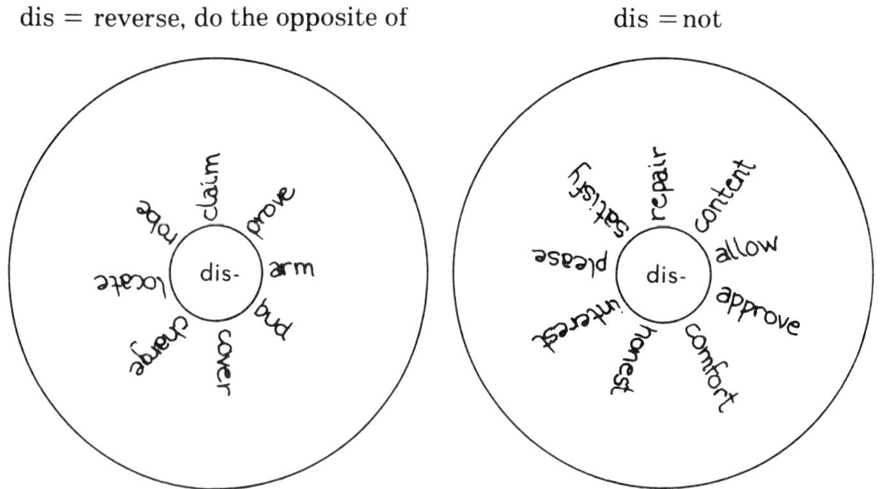

Compare meanings of "dis-"

Wheels could also be made for the following prefixes:

  sub-:   way, soil, station, marine, tropical, heading, normal, merge, set, point

  pre-:   dawn, date, historic, caution, fix, form, judge, mature, occupy

    co-:   author, pilot, exist, operate, educational

    re-:   do, set, unite, live, broadcast, cover, fresh, claim, assure, build, born, elect

    en-:   noble, close, act, case, courage, lace, fold, large, throne, twine, plane

    ex-:   wife, husband, student, prisoner, king, port

    de-:   throne, activate, brief, classify, face, form, frost, grade, mobilize, odorize, port, tour, plane

Children could use these wheels for reviewing words and for short written assignments: e.g., they might be asked to write sentences using each of the words on a wheel. Or they might play a game such as the following:

1. Wheels are turned upside down on a table. Each child or team picks one wheel.
2. Each child, or team, gets *one point* for each word correctly defined.
3. Each child, or team, gets *one point* for every word used in a meaningful sentence.

4. Each child, or team, gets *two points* for each additional word written down using the prefix with a word not on the wheel, and *one point* for defining it, and *one point* for using it in a sentence.

The teacher decides whether dictionaries may be used.

□ *Give an Example* Ask children to give an example to clarify the meanings of prefixed words:

1. Give an example of something that is:
   inborn   indoors   informal   insecure
   inactive   ingrown   inland   insincere
2. Give an example of someone who was:
   reborn   reunited   reelected   refreshed
3. Give an example of where one would find a:
   subway   substation subpoint   subsoil
   subtropical region   submarine
4. Give an example of someone or something that is:
   unsure   ungrateful unpacked   unmasked
5. Give an example of something that has been:
   defrosted degraded   declassified detoured

□ *Wordo* On the board, list about four prefixes, each followed by about ten free morphemes that can be attached to them to compose a word. Give children a blank Wordo (Bingo) card. Ask each child to write 24 free morphemes in the blanks. Ask each child, also, to write each prefix on about six small pieces of paper.

If the prefixes selected were *sub-*, *en-*, *de-*, and *in-*, one card might look like this:

land	throne	way	visible	port
noble	tropical	act	brief	soil
marine	formal	FREE	courage	grown
grade	large	classify	twine	heading
active	flow	station	point	capable

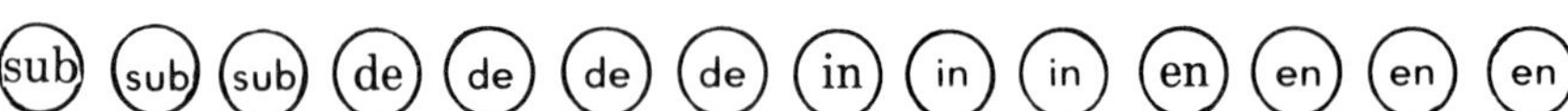

The game is played like Bingo.

The teacher reads sentences that give the clue to the word. The child covers the free morpheme with the correct prefix, thus:

1. A point under a main point is a (<u>subpoint</u>).

    Child covers <u>point</u> with (sub).

2. A city within the land is (<u>inland</u>).

    Child covers <u>land</u> with (in).

3. Dress that is not formal is (<u>informal</u>).

4. etc.

(If the child does not have the free morpheme on his or her card, he or she cannot go even though the word is known.)

The teacher may prefer not to give definitions, but rather to call free morphemes. Children who have the morpheme on their cards cover it with a slip that will make a real word. For example, if the teacher calls *marine*, children cover it with (sub) to make the word *submarine*. If the teacher calls *courage*, children cover it with (en) to compose the word *encourage*, etc. The child who wins must pronounce the words and use them in sentences. Using this technique, the winning child could be the next caller.

Easy Suffixes—Inflectional Endings

Prefixes are added to words to form new words with new meanings. (*Marine* means "of the sea," but *submarine* means underwater, as a submarine is capable of maneuvering in the depths. One can see something that is *visible*, but something *invisible* cannot be seen, etc.) Suffixes, on the other hand, are usually added to words to change the part of speech, and to a lesser extent the meaning of the word. (*Girl* is singular, but *girls* is plural. So, too, changes from *go* to *going*, *be* to *being*, *bake* to *baker*, *swim* to *swimmer*, etc., are basically changes in part of speech, though you might argue that changes in meaning accompany the changes in part of speech.) Two suffixes that function like prefixes are *-ful* and *-less*: thought*ful*, power*ful*, thought*less*, power*less*.

Since suffixes are usually used to change part of speech, and since part of speech is a function of syntax, suffixes are usually best taught by using sentences. For example:

☐ *The Suffix -s* Use sentences, such as the following, to teach the suffix -s. Ask children to circle the word that fits each blank.

1. The _____________ is going.   (boy)   boys
2. The _____________ are going.   boy   boys
3. The _____________ runs fast.   girl   girls
4. The _____________ run fast   girl   girls

□ *Blocks* Use foam-rubber blocks (for silence when tossing) like the following:

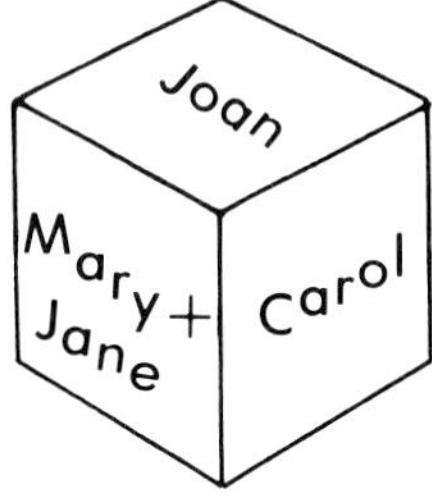

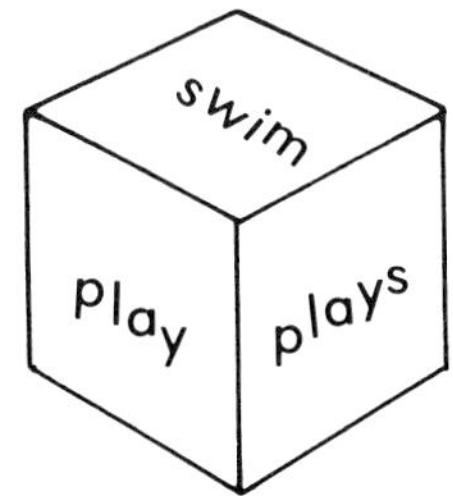

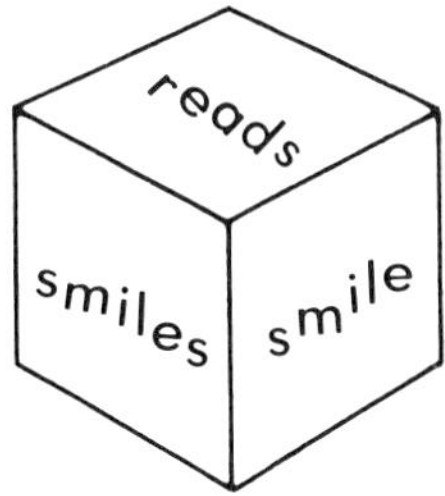

(also: Carol + Lorraine,   (also: swims,   (also: read, jump,
Joan + Alyce, Connie)   sew, sews)   jumps)

Children toss the three blocks. The subject block must be used with a verb that agrees with it to get a point. (A child may get 0, 1, or 2 points for a toss. E.g., if *Joan* is up, and also *swim* and *reads*, one point is possible: Joan reads. If *Joan* and *swim* and *smile* are up, no points are possible. If *Joan* and *swims* and *smiles* are up, two points are possible. Etc.)

□ *The Suffix -ed* Use sentences, also:

Today we will _____________ ball.   (play)   played
Yesterday we _____________ ball.   play   played
Tomorrow I will _____________ the plants   cover   covered
at night.
Yesterday I _____________ the plants.   cover   covered
Etc.

□ *Comparative Suffixes -er, -est* Pictures can be used to teach comparative suffixes. Ask children to illustrate on paper—in sets—the following words. If you prefer, ask them to play charades, illustrating these in sets:

loud - louder - loudest   dark - darker - darkest
proud - prouder - proudest   long - longer - longest
small - smaller - smallest   tall - taller - tallest
sad - sadder - saddest   good - better - best

□*Add an Ending* List common inflectional endings at the top of a paper:

-s	-ed	-ness	-ly	-er
-es	-ing	-ment		-est

Write sentences containing words that require the use of an end ing listed above. Leave space for the child to write in the proper ending. E.g.:

1. José is tall, but Mark is an inch tall _______.
   Fred is two inches tall _______, so he's the tall _______.
2. Carrie is a kind girl. she believes kind _______ is very important.
3. Frank left the house alone. But his two dog _______ followed him.
4. It takes ten bus(s)_______ to bring the boy _______ and girl _______ to our school.
5. The girls in the class are play _______ baseball now.
   The boys play_______ yesterday.
6. We are ready to leave, final _______.
7. Boat _______, swim(m) _______, and water ski _______ are favorite summer sports. Many people love walk _______, too.
8. A person who bakes is a bake _______. A person who teach _______ is a teach _______. But a person who sews is a seamstress, a seamster, or a tailor.
9. They were amazed and show _______ their amaze _______ by cheer _______.
10. Would you like to go into the entertain _______ business?

Bound + Bound Morphemes

By the fourth grade level, most children are ready for work on more difficult morphemes than those previously given, for they are ready to build and understand words that are composed of *two bound morphemes*. Vocabulary building of this type continues throughout high school and college.

When a person learns a new bound morpheme, this morpheme frequently becomes a clue to the meanings of dozens of words. If a person, for example, knows that *logy* means "science, or study of," as in zoology, he or she has strong clues as to the meanings of other words that include the morpheme *logy*: dialectology, phonology, criminology, ethnology, sociology, psychology, biology, astrology, etc. The person who knows *logy* from the word zoology (*the study of* animal life) and knows *anthropo* from anthropoid (*man*-like) will have little trouble figuring out that *anthropology* means the study of mankind. Also, the reader is likely to read or hear this word in context, and the contextual clues will help her or him refine the definition.

To help you on your way, the following list of commonly used bound morphemes is included. The time to teach them is when they begin appearing in the reading assignments of youngsters—or when they will be useful to youngsters.

morpheme	meaning	examples
uni (L)	one	unicycle, unilingual, unicorn, unilateral
mono (Gl)	one	monologue, monarchy, monotheism, monorail
bi (L)	two	bicycle, bilateral, bigamy, bicameral
di (Gk)	two	disect, dioxide, diatomic, digraph
tri	three	tricycle, triangle, trilogy, trio
quad, quar	four	quadruplet, quadrangle, quadruped
pent (Gk)	five	pentagon, pentad
quin (L)	five	quintuplet, quintessence
sex (L)	six	sextet, sextuplet
hex (Gk)	six	hexagon
sept	seven	September, septagenarian
oct	eight	October, octet, octogenarian
nov	nine	November
dec	ten	decimal, decade, decathlon, December
cent	hundred	century, cent, centennial, centipede
mil, mill	thousand	millennium, milligram, million
multi (L)	many	multiply, multilateral, multitude
semi (L)	half	semicircle, semicolon, semiconscious
hemi (L+Gk)	half	hemisphere, hemiparasite
omni (L)	all	omnibus, omnipotent, omnivorous, omnirange
pan (Gk)	all	Pan-American, pandemic, panchromatic
a-	not, without	atypical, asymmetric, amoral, asocial
ambi	both	ambiguous, ambivalent, ambidextrous
anim	life, mind, soul	animal, animate, magnanimous
ante	before	antebellum, antecedent, antedate
anthropo	mankind	anthropoid, anthropomorphic, misanthrope
anti	against	anticlimax, antihero, antibody
arch	chief, principal	monarch, oligarchy, patriarch
astro	star	astronaut, astroid, asterisk
auto	self	automobile, autograph, autocriticism
bene	well, good	benevolent, benign, benediction
biblio	book	bibliography, bibliophile, bibliotherapy
bio	life	biology, biography, biodegradable
capt	head, chief, seize	decapitate, capital, capture
chrom	color	achromatic, panchromatic, chromosome
chron	time	chronological, anachronism, chronic
cide	kill	genocide, suicide, regicide, insecticide
circum	around	circa, circumference, circumlocution

morpheme	meaning	examples
contra	against, opposite	contradict, contraband, counteract
cosmo, cosm	world, universe	cosmonaut, cosmopolitan, cosmic
crat, cracy	government, rule	democracy, autocracy, Dixiecrat
cred	believe, trust	incredible, discredit, credibility
cycle	circle	cyclotron, cyclone, epicycle
dem	people	democracy, endemic, epidemic
dia	across, through	dialogue, diagnose, diatribe
dic, dict	speak	contradict, dictate, predict
duc, duct	lead	introduce, inductive, deductive
epi	upon	epilogue, epithet, epitome
eu	well	eulogy, euphony, euphemism
fac, fic	do, make	factory, artifact, facilitate
fin	end, limit	define, finite, finale, finis
flex, flect	bend	inflection, reflect, reflection, flexible
flu	flow	fluent, superfluous, affluence, confluence
gamy	marriage	monogamy, misogamy, bigamy
gen, gene	produce, beget	genealogy, genesis, genocide
geo	earth	geology, geophysics, geometry
gnos	know, knowledge	prognosis, cognition, agnostic, ignorance
gogue, agogue	drive, lead	protagonist, demagogue, pedagogue
graph	write	grapheme, graphic, biography
hetero	other, different	heterogeneous, heterosexual, heterodox
hyper	above, excessive	hyperbole, hypercritical, hyperactive
inter	among	interject, interview, interbreed
intro, intra	inside, within	introduction, intrastate, intracoastal
logy	science of, study of	psychology, zoology, biology
logy, loc, loq	speech, to speak	trilogy, prologue, loquacious
luna	moon	lunar, lunatic
mal	bad, ill	malaprop, malnutrition, malign, malformed
mania	madness for	pyromania, monomania, dipsomania
meter, metr	measure	diameter, metrical, geometry
morph	form, meaning	morphology, anthropomorphic, amorphic
mov, mot	move	motive, emotion, automobile
naut	sailor	astronaut, cosmonaut, nautical
non	not	nondescript, nonlinear, nonsense
nym	name, word	pseudonym, synonym, antonym
oid	likeness, similarity	anthropoid, lithoid, planetoid
para	beside	parallel, parable, paraphrase
ped	foot	biped, tripod, pedal, moped
phil	loving	philosophy, philanthropy, bibliophile
phobia	fear	claustrophobia, aquaphobia
phon	sound, voice	phoneme, phonograph, telephone, symphony
photo	light	photograph, photosynthesis

morpheme	meaning	examples
post	after	postwar, posterior, postscript
pre	before	preface, prefix, prejudice, precipitate
pro	for, forward	pronoun, produce, project
proto	first, earliest form	prototype, protrude, protohistory
pseudo	false	pseudonym, pseudoclassic, pseudoscientific
psych	mind	psychology, psychiatry, psychic
retro	backward	retroactive, retrograde, retrorocket
rupt	break	rupture, abrupt, bankrupt, erupt
scrib, script	write	scribble, scribe, transcribe
sol	sun	solar, solarium, insolate, parasol
spect	look	inspect, retrospect, spectator
stat	stable	statue, state, resist, status
super	over	superlative, superabundant, superior
syn, sym	together	symbolic, synthesis, symphony
tact, tang	touch	tangible, contact, tactful
tele	far off	telephone, telegraph, teletype
terra	earth	terrestrial, terra firma, territory
the, theo	god, God	atheism, apotheosis, theology, theocracy
trans	across	transmit, transfer, transect
ultra	beyond	ultramodern, ultrasonic, ultraviolet
val	worth, strength	value, evaluate, ambivalence
vert, vers	turn	conversation, advertise, divergent
voc	voice, call	vocal, vocabulary, advocate

Words containing morphemes that are useful to youngsters at specific times should be taught as other words are taught, utilizing context. The activities that follow might serve as review, or reinforcement activities.

□ *Spiral-Bound Cards* Prepare spiral-bound cards for teaching and reviewing morphemes that are found in many words the children are reading. On the back of each card that flips, write the definition of the complete word. Also, use the word in at least one sentence. E.g.:

Other cards:

bio-	anthropo-		-plane	-lateral
geo-	eco-		-valve	-cameral
astro-	psycho-		-linqual	-centennial
physio-	crimino-		-sect	-annual
socio-	radio-		-polar	-ped

□*Fold-Ins* Make fold-ins for pictureable words. Let children study these when they wish. E.g.:

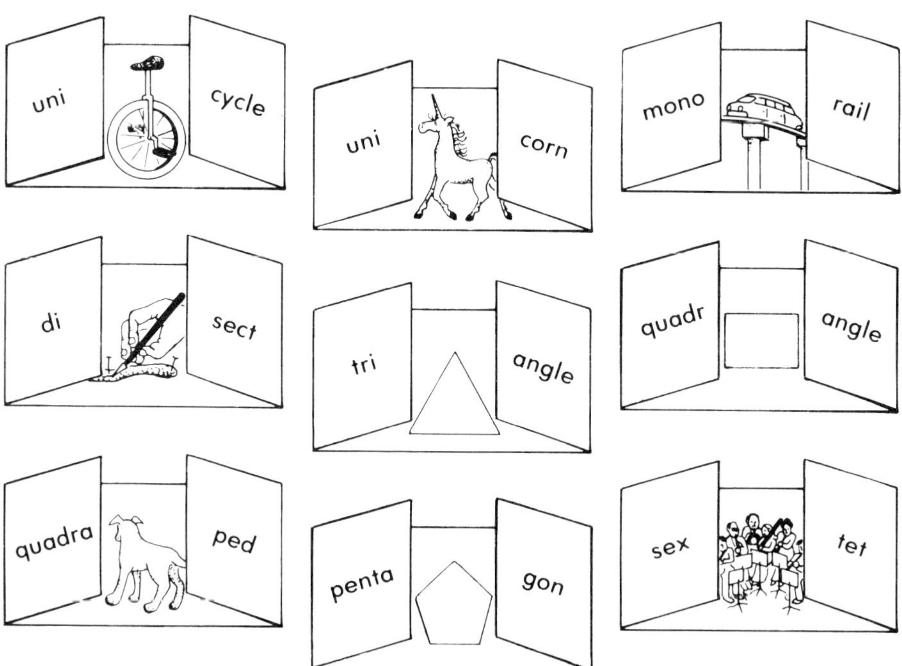

□*Concentration* Children can play concentration in small groups. For words composed of two morphemes, each morpheme would be written on a separate card. Cards are numbered at random on the back. Sets for number morphemes might be:

Easy: (*uni, mono, bi*)

uni	cycle	mono	gamy	bi	lateral
uni	lateral	mono	rail	bi	lingual
uni	corn	mono	theism	bi	gamy
		mono	logue	bi	partisan
				bi	ped

Harder: (tri, quad, quint, penta, sex, hex)

tri	pod	quadr(a)	lateral	quint	tet
tri	angle	quadr(u)	ped	penta	dactyl
tri	cycle	quadr	angle	sex	tet
tri	lateral	quint	essence	hexa	gon

Hardest: (sept, oct, dec, cent, mil, multi, poly)

sept	(a)genarian	centi	pede	multi	pede
oct	(a)genarian	mill	ennium	poly	theism
oct	(t)et	multi	lateral	poly	gon
dec	ade	multi	ply	poly	gamy

□*Dice Game** From two to six children may play this game. Each child plays individually if 2, 3, or 5 play. If 4 or 6 play, there should be two teams.

Use two dice. Children take turns—in clockwise order—tossing the dice. At one toss, the children can make 0, 1, 2, or 3 points for themselves or for their team, thus:

1 point for giving a word using a bound morpheme for the number of dots on one die

1 point for giving a word using a bound morpheme for the number of dots on the other die

1 point for giving a word using a bound morpheme for the total number of dots on the two dice. Since total point value could be 11 or 12, for these use:

    for 11: cent or mil, or else semi or hemi

    for 12: poly or multi, or else pan or omni

A word that has been given once during the game cannot count again.

---

*Lou E. Burmeister. *Words - From Print to Meaning*. Reading, Massachusetts: Addison-Wesley Publishing Co., 1975, pp. 42–43. Used by permission.

□ *Three Point Values* Print morphemes in three kinds of figures. Each figure has a different point value. Children write as many words as they can in a given amount of time by combining morphemes. The child with the highest point value wins. E.g.:

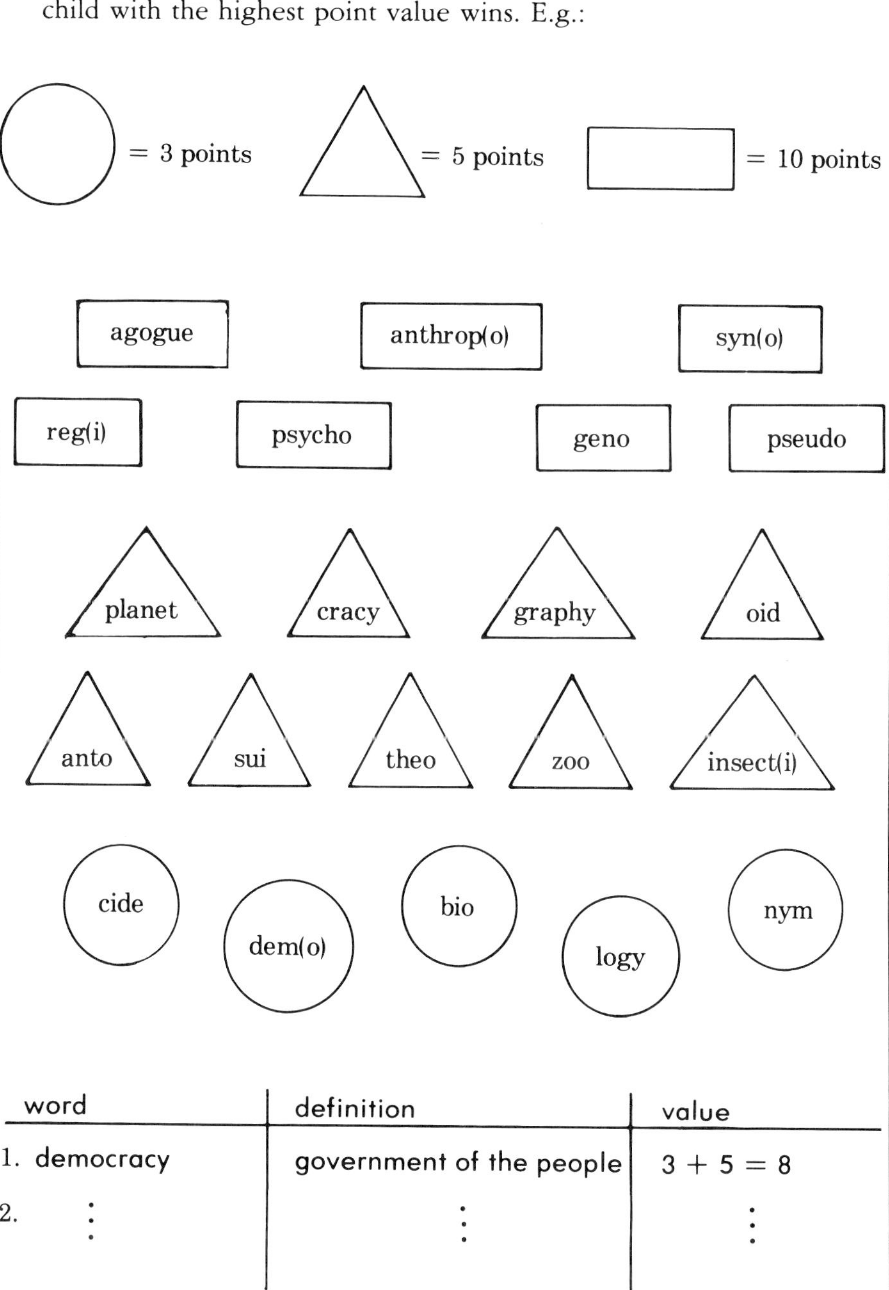

word	definition	value
1. democracy	government of the people	$3 + 5 = 8$
2. ⋮	⋮	⋮

□ *Morpheme Baseball* Put morphemes that have been studied on slips of paper. Put slips in a box. Form two teams for baseball. The pitcher holds the box, and the batter picks a slip, e.g., *ped, pod.* To get to first base, the batter must give a word using the morpheme, e.g., *biped.* To get to second base, the batter must use the word in a sentence, e.g., *I am a biped.* To get to third base another word must be given, e.g., *tripod.* To get home, the word must be used in a sentence, e.g., *I use a tripod when taking pictures.*

A batter is out if he or she cannot get to first base on the first try. But a player who makes it to first, second, or third base can be brought home by a teammate. Three outs and the other team is up to bat.

□ *Morpheme Tree* Make a morpheme tree or other illustration, with a "theme," for your bulletin board. For example, you may wish to have a three-dimensional tree and have the children hang words on it, like ornaments on a Christmas tree. See Figures 7.1–7.4 for ideas.

□ *The Earth and Heavens* Morphemes that relate to the earth and heavens are usually fascinating to children. Among the commonly used ones are:

| stella
astro | } star | | sol - sun
luna - moon | | |
| cosmo
cosm | } world, universe, order | | geo
terra | } earth |

Prepare an exercise, such as the following. Have the children fill in the blanks.

1. *Naut* means *navigator,* or *sailor.* Americans call their travelers in space *astronauts,* and Russians call theirs *cosmonauts.* Are both names appropriate? Why? _______________________________

2. Is the earth in *solar* or *lunar* orbit? _______________________________
3. Have our astronauts ever been in *solar* orbit? _______________ in *lunar* orbit? _______________________________
4. People once thought a person became a *lunatic,* or insane, because that person stared too long at the _______________________.

astronaut
astrology
astrometry
astronomy
asterisk
astrography
asteroid
astronavigation
disaster
astrophotograph
cosmopolitan
cosmopolite
cosmic
cosmonaut
cosmetic
Argonaut
nautical
nautilus
aquanaut
nausea
Cosmonaut
Astronaut
aster = star   naut = sail   cosm = order, universe

Figure 7.1

The METER Daisy
kilometer
decameter
thermometer
barometer
calorimeter
pyrometer
odometer
speedometer
hydrometer
geometer
optometer
photometer
micrometer
altimeter
radiometer
chronometer
centimeter
millimeter
decimeter
picometer
nanometer

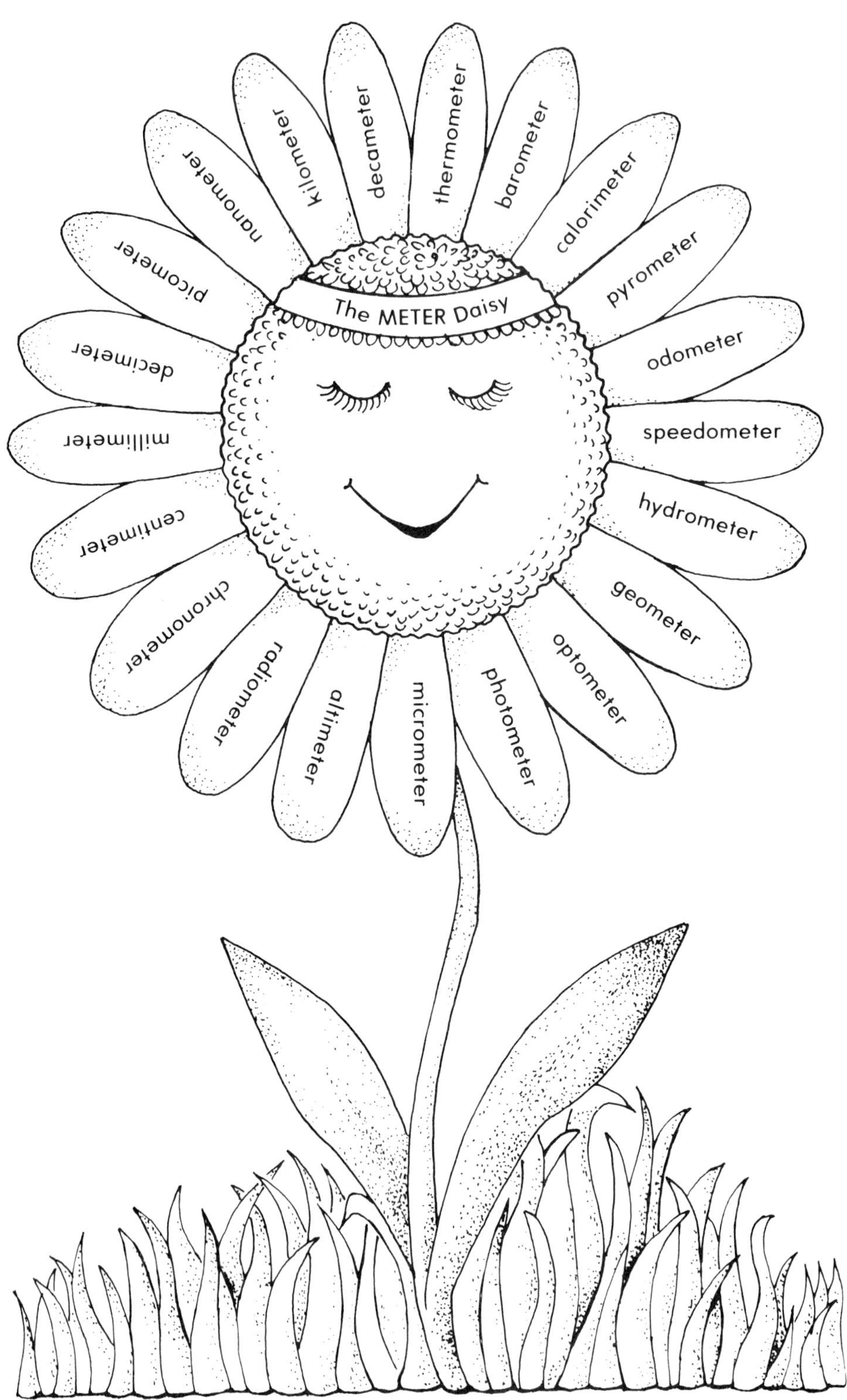

Figure 7.2

bio ecology
bio graph
bio acoustician
bio graphy
bio acoustic
bio magnetic
bio grapher
bio logist
bio electric
bio dynamics
bio filter
bio geny
bio energy
bio plasm
bio aeration
bio logy
bio lyctic
bio meter
bio genist
BIO Balloons

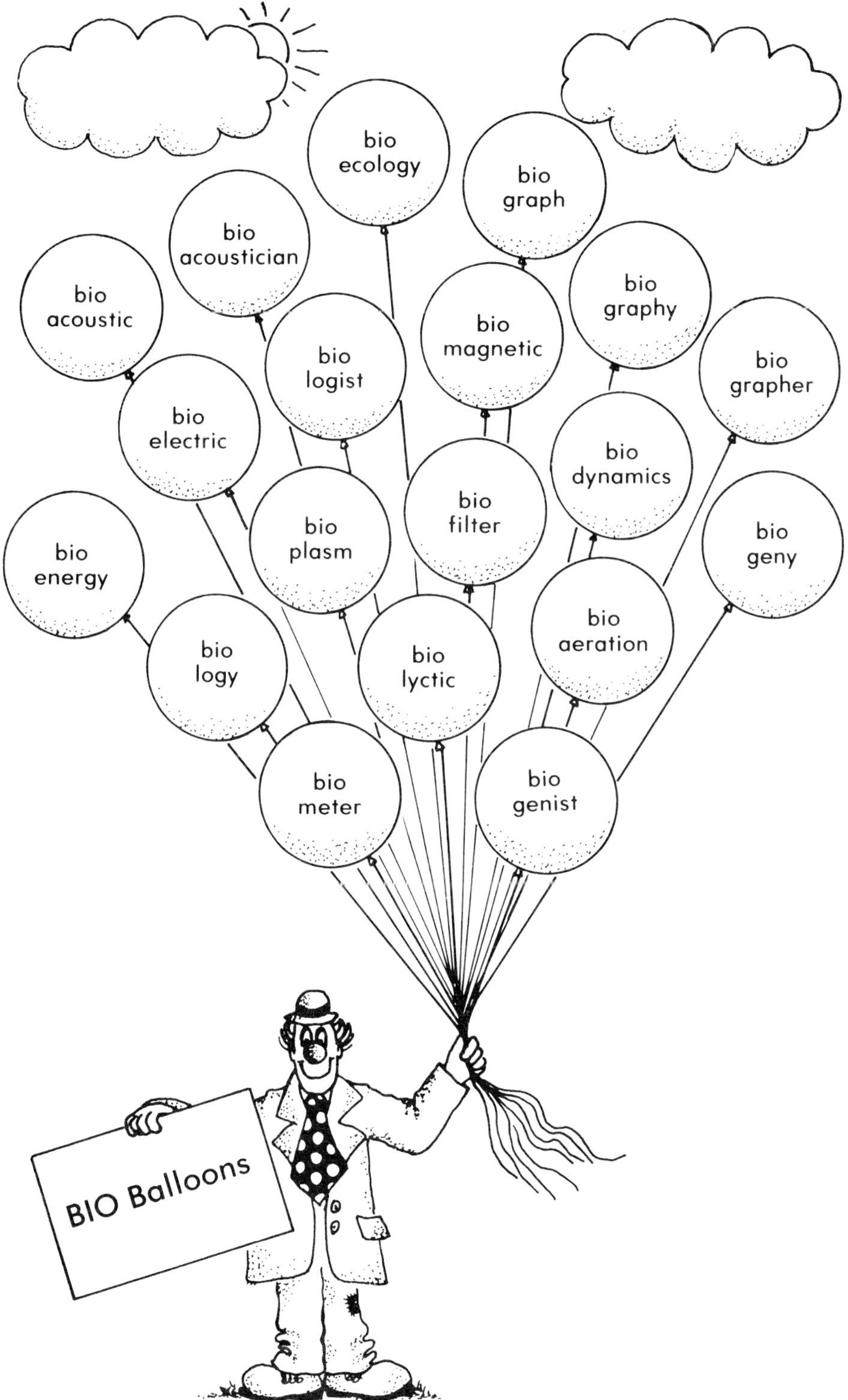

Figure 7.3

sea urchin
sea shore
sea side
sea food
sea weed
sea breeze
sea shell
sea way
sea foul
sea cow
sea lion
sea quake
sea level
sea gull
sea power
sea farer
sea man
sea scape
sea plane
sea squirt
sea otter
sea eagle
sea lily
sea legs
sea port
sea borne
sea horse

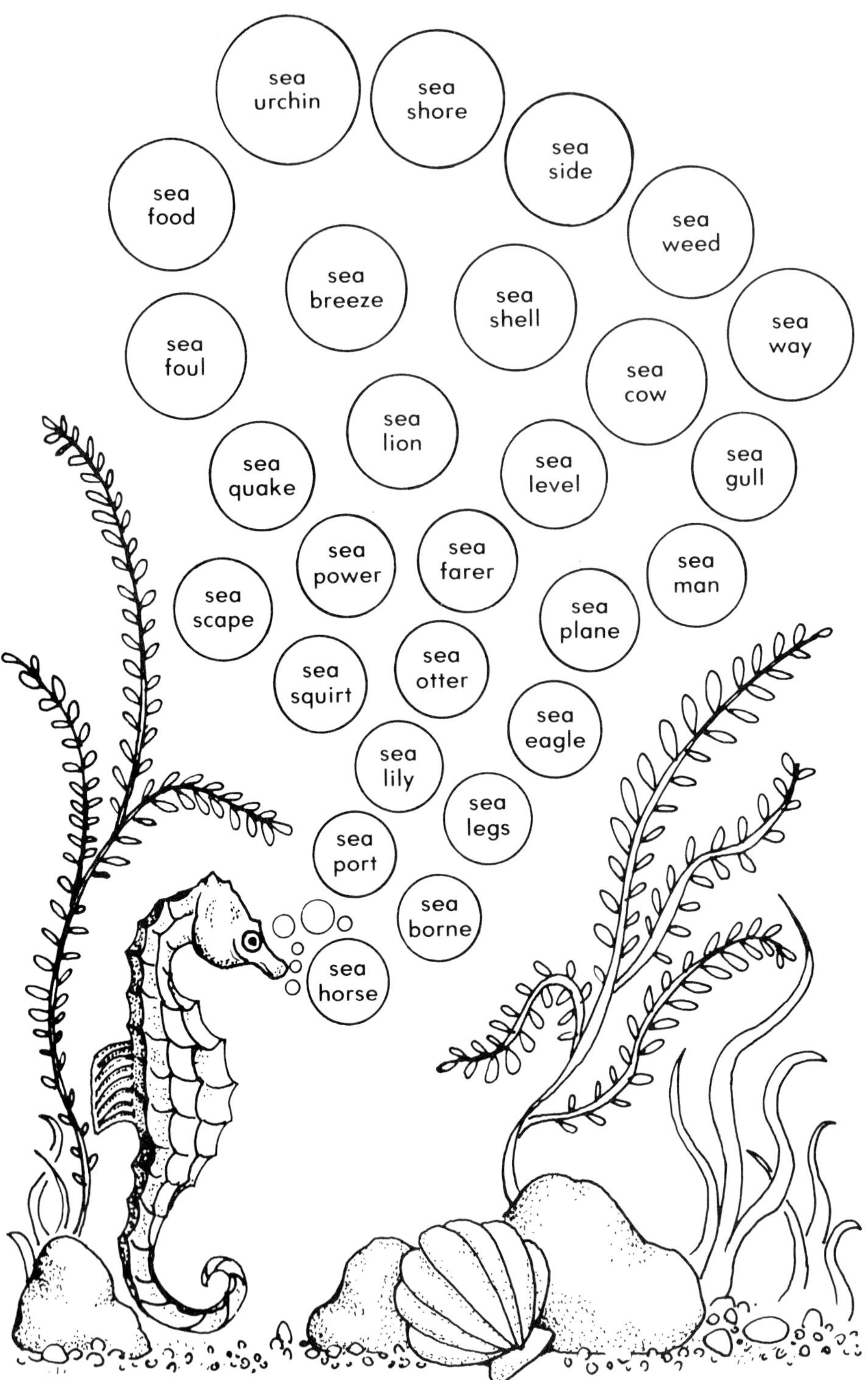

Figure 7.4

5. What does *celestial* mean if it means the opposite of *terrestrial?*

6. If *-oid* means like, as in *anthropoid* (*manlike*), would you expect a starfish to be a member of the Aster*oid*ea class or the Sol*oid*ea class? _______________ Why? _______________
7. What is a dis*aster*? _______________
8. "His success was *astro*nomical." What does *astronomical* mean? _______________ Name someone you would consider to be a *stellar* success: _______________
9. *Polis* means city. Do you think Paris is a *cosmopolitan* city? _______________ Why? _______________
What do you think a *cosmopolite* is? _______________
10. *Cosm* also means order. What do you think the literal meaning of *cosmetics* is? _______________

□*Crossword Puzzle* Use a crossword puzzle to "test" retention of words and their meanings. To make a crossword puzzle, begin with graph paper, and write the words in intersecting patterns:

					C															
					O			A										C		
					S			S	O	L	A	R						E		
					M			T						S	T	E	L	L	A	R
					O			R										E		
	A				P		C	O	S	M	O	N	A	U	T			S		
	S				O			N										T		
S	T	A	R		L	U	N	A	R			A	S	T	E	R	O	I	D	
	E				I			U										A		
	R				T			T	E	R	R	E	S	T	R	I	A	L		
	I				A															
A	S	T	R	O	N	O	M	Y												
	K																			

Next, clip this on a ditto master, pull out the insert sheet, and trace just the squares that have letters in them. Then number the first square for each word. Following this, write the clues.

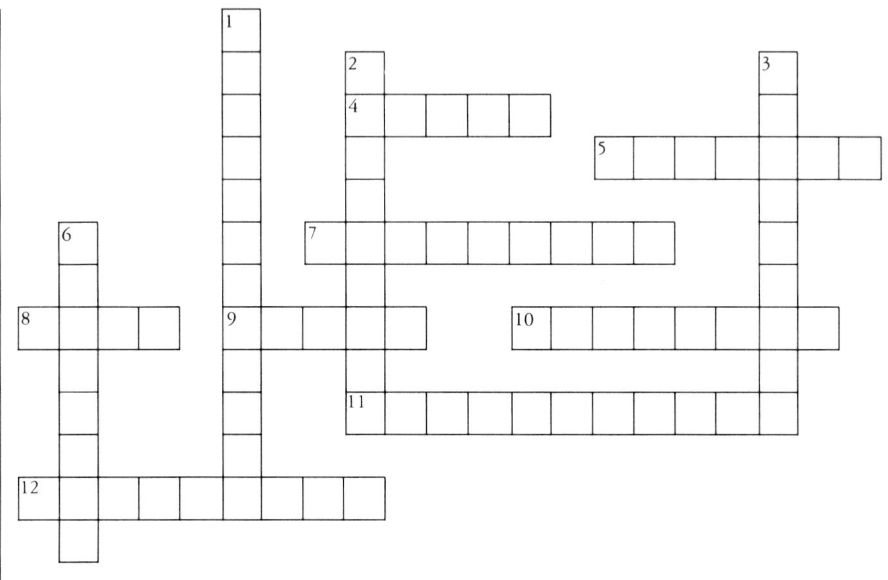

Across:
4. of the sun
5. relating to stars
7. a Russian space traveler
8. the meaning of "aster"
9. of the moon
10. star-like
11. of the earth
12. the study of heavenly bodies

Down:
1. "universal city"
2. an American traveler in space
3. of the heavens
6. a little star used as a reference mark

Connotative Language

Denotations of words are scientific, literal meanings of words. But many words also have connotations, or emotional, meanings. Connotations are meanings words suggest beyond the literal level. At times they are very imaginative.

Children should be taught that when connotative language is used to describe people and situations, such descriptions are not objective, for connotative language reflects the way its user "sees" (or interprets) what he or she is describing. Two different observers (or even the same observer at different times) may use very different descriptors for the same person or situation. Connotative language reflects opinion, not fact.

Many people are aware of optical illusions. For example, the railroad tracks appear to meet in the distance. On viewing the Necker Cube, almost everyone will notice that the face seen closest to the viewer changes while gazing at the cube:

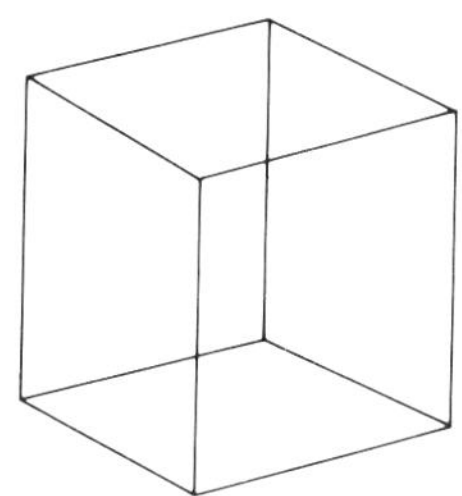
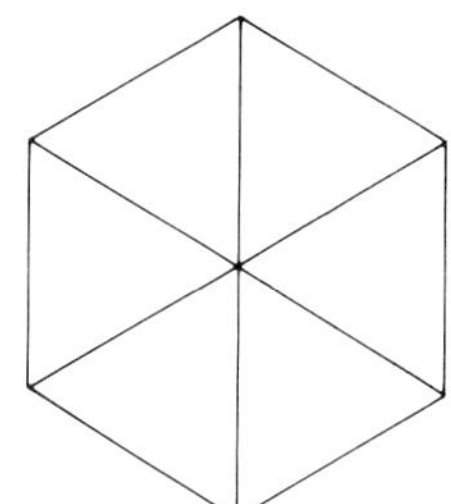

And, the shifting of perspective makes the cube appear to be a flat surface hexagon—at least at times.

One can also observe that one of these lines appears to be longer than the other, while in reality both are of the same length.

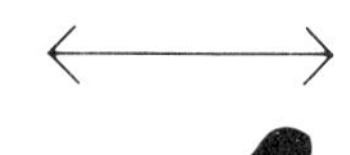

What do you see when you look at this figure—a man's face or a girl?

Since it can be demonstrated that what we think we see with our eyes may change as we look at the same object for some time, it might also be demonstrated that how we view people and situations may be equally variable—or at least debatable. Our connotative language reflects our perspective and reveals our feelings. Children should be taught this.

Children, though, should have fun using such language, and they can be taught—in the following ways.

ANIMAL NAMES

A simple way of introducing children to the concept that many words have connotations is to ask them to give animal names that are used to describe people. You may be surprised at the number even first and second graders will give you. Among them may be:

ox	pig	baboon	teddy bear
chameleon	honey bee	deer	moose
chicken	hen	peacock	fish

What we are doing when we describe a person by using an animal name is saying that to us that person appears to possess one or more characteristics that the animal is thought to possess. However, we are not necessarily clearly communicating because connotations for a particular word may vary greatly from one person to another, though some connotations become highly stereotyped.

Most of us would agree about what is meant when a person is called "catty" or is called "a dog"—though it may be a very rare cat or dog that possesses the characteristics said to be "catty" or "doglike." Nevertheless, connotative language of this type usually is fresh and alive—and fun—and probably not harmful. (However, if children begin using terms that relate to stereotypes of groups of people, a real danger arises. May such terms die, for they often incite hatred.)

Following are activities that could be used to reinforce the idea that animal names are often used connotatively.

Wordo Ask children to suggest animal names that can be used connotatively. Write the list on the board as they are volunteering (or write it on an overhead transparency so you can keep it).

Furnish children with magazines and loose pictures. Ask them to clip and mount pictures of each of the animals suggested. Ask them why the name is used as it is connotatively. E.g.: *chameleon.—* When a person is called a *chameleon*, it means that he or she changes his or her point of view to fit different situations. What does a *chameleon* do that is similar to this? Another example: What does a *beaver* do that inspires the use of the term *eager beaver*? What about a *wolf*? What does it mean when a person is called a *wolf*? How does this relate to the animal? Etc.

It might be pointed out that in most cases a connotation relates to only one characteristic of the animal, and that animals have many other characteristics. For example, when a person is called an *elephant*, it usually means that person is *huge*. On the other hand, we might say a person has an *elephant's memory*. This relates to another characteristic elephants are thought to have.

Next, supply children with duplicated blank wordo cards. Ask them to write 24 of the animal names on their cards. To play, the "caller" shows a picture, and the children cover the word. (Here we are working denotatively.) The child who wins (according to preannounced standards: columns, rows or diagonals; four corners; picture frame; T; L; J; blackout; etc.) calls "Wordo" and must use each word covered in a sentence connotatively. If the child can use one of the words with two different connotative meanings, he or she becomes the next "caller."

Connotative or Denotative Use? The children write sentences on separate 3 × 5" cards using animal names in sentences. There will be at least two cards for each animal name—one for its denotative use and the other for a connotative use. E.g.:

<table>
<tr><td>My cat loves to sleep in her tree house.</td><td>I was so pleased with my gift, I said, "Oh, that's the cat's pajamas."</td></tr>
</table>

Children draw a card, read the sentence, and tell if the word is used denotatively (they might say, *scientifically*) or connotatively (they might say, *emotionally*). Then they give an oral sentence using the word the other way.

VEGETATION

Names for things that grow in our gardens—or other people's gardens around the world—frequently inspire the use of connotative language. Again, start the children off, and they'll give you many examples. Ask them to put the words in phrases or sentences:

peach (He's a peach.)
peachy (Everything's peachy.)
apple (apple of my eye)
sour apple (what a sour apple)
nuts (They're nuts.)
egg (good egg, bad egg)
banana (top banana)
plum (plum of a job)
fruity (what fruity ideas)
olive branch (i.e., peace)
florid (florid show)

lemon (That TV's a lemon.)
sour lemon (She's a sour lemon.)
potato (hot potato)
pea (two peas in a pod)
violet (shrinking violet)
pansy (They're shrinking pansies.)
vegetable (He's a vegetable.)
vegetate (She's vegetating.)
daisy (fresh as a daisy)
rose (smelling like a rose)
flower (flowery language)

> *Charades or Puppetry* Children could play charades, characterizing the connotative use of one or more of these terms. (What's a car like that is a *lemon*? What's it like to be in a situation described as *hot potato*? What does a *shrinking violet* do? Etc.) Other children guess what the term is. Children might like to make hand puppets to use in their "act," or they may like to make little finger puppets, one person taking two or more roles.

COLORS

Color names are also frequently used connotatively. Some examples are:

green (with envy)
green (naive)
purple (regal)
purple (passion)
blue (sad)
blue (justice, loyalty, sincerety, as in U.S. flag, and "true blue")
white (with fear)
white (purity)*

pink (glowing)
pink (socialistic, mildly communistic)
red (communistic)
red (in the red—in debt)
red (valor, as in U.S. flag)
rosy (happy)
brown (brown nose)
yellow (cowardly)
black (in the black—not broke)*

---

*Avoid statements such as: "Things are never black or white," as such statements have taken on racial tones.

Connotative or Denotative Use? Give children a handout with a passage using color words denotatively and connotatively. Ask them to indicate which way the word is being used each time. When the words are used connotatively, ask them to give the meanings.

Mother turned white (fear - connotative) when she found that her pretty white (denotative) laundry had been torn to shreds by some wild animal. Would that fierce animal—a coyote!—return? Mother was blue ______________. Already the family budget, though still in the black ______________, was almost in the red ______________. Now she would have more to buy.

She thought how green ______________ she had been not to know what damage animals in the area could do. She felt what might be called a purple passion ______________ for that coyote.

There he was—coming again—acting like a rogue. She fetched a gun, and shot, but missed. She had meant only to frighten him away—to make him turn yellow ______________. As he dashed behind the green ______________ brush and brown ______________ rocks, she felt a rosy ______________ glow come over her. But she knew that was only temporary.

OTHER WORDS

Words other than animal names, vegetation names, and colors are also used connotatively. And the words authors and speakers use tell us just how they feel about their subjects. When they use words connotatively, readers and listeners must be alert to identify such clues, which are like signposts, cautioning us to realize that biases are being expressed. These biases, of course, can be positive or negative—friendly or unfriendly.

Which Word? A teacher might ask children to check the word, or words, in each group that they would choose to use if they liked the person or persons they were discussing:

1. He's a	colorful flashy neat	person.	2. She's	sensible conservative thoughtful	about spending money.
3. Their clothes look	slovenly. sloppy. comfortable.		4. They're a	well-informed talkative gossipy	group.
5. He joined the	club. flock. pack. group.		6. Joan has	ladybugs beetles bugs mantises	in her yard.

7. He's a	mousy quiet peaceful meek	person.	8. They enjoy	privacy. isolation. being aloof. solitude.
9. What a	brief cursory hurried concise	remark!	10. She's	clever. shrewd. wise. calculating.

FIGURATIVE LANGUAGE

"Figures of speech" are a form of connotative, nonliteral language. Some of the most commonly used figures of speech are similes, metaphors, hyperboles, personification, and allusions. Figurative language also includes the use of proverbs. Children will come across these frequently when they are reading. Figures of speech are used to make language more interesting and colorful and also to make difficult ideas easier to understand.

Similes

A simile is an analogy in which two different things are shown to be alike, at least in one respect. In a simile, the word *like* or *as* is used. For example:

> The bluejay shouted *like a noisy politician.*
> His sensitive fingers move so fast they blur *like hummingbird wings.*
> They're as slow *as molasses in January.*
> He grinned *like a Cheshire cat.*
> "A house without books is *like a room without windows.*" (Horace Mann)

Metaphors

Metaphors are like similes, but the word *like* or *as* is not used:

> She was in the *springtime* of her life.
> "All the world's a *stage*" (Shakespeare)
> "No man is an island." (John Donne)
> It was *a month of Sundays.*

"My books are *water*; those of great geniuses are *wine*. Everybody drinks water." (Mark Twain)
"Liberty, when it begins to take root, is *a plant of* rapid growth." (George Washington)

Hyperboles

Hyperboles are obvious exaggerations or extravagant statements that are not intended to be taken literally:

All the gold in Fort Knox couldn't buy that house.
I could sleep a month.
This paperback is light as a feather.
She'll weigh a ton when she grows up.
The sound was heard round the world.

Personification

Personification is the technique of representing a thing or an animal as a person:

The pages of my books *speak* to me with many voices.
The flames *devoured* the forest in one of the biggest fires of the year.
The flowers *smiled* and made our table *happy*.
"Said" is a *tired* word, but "run" is *vigorous*.

Allusions

An allusion is an indirect reference to a person—real or mythical—or to a place or a thing. For example, if we call someone "a modern *David*," we are referring to the Biblical story of David slaying the giant Goliath. If we say that someone "raised cain," we're referring to Cain as the murderer of Abel. If we say we "feel like Daniel," we mean we feel like someone in a lion's den.

Proverbs

Proverbs are commonly used short expressions that represent a truth or fact:

on exaggeration: You should have seen the fish that got away!
on pride: Every man thinks his geese are swans.
on using opportunities well: Make hay while the sun shines.
on worthiness of small efforts: Great oaks from little acorns grow.

To help children write and understand figurative language, the following types of activities might be used.

□*Similes* Ask children to write their own similes. Children can be remarkably creative, and they should be encouraged to make their own comparisons. After a few rather stereotyped comparisons are given, they probably will come up with some fresh ones. Ask them to complete statements like these:

as fresh as ___________   as soft as   ___________
             ___________   ___________
             ___________   ___________
             ___________   ___________
as careful as ___________   as happy as   ___________
             ___________   ___________
             ___________   ___________
             ___________   ___________
as fast as   ___________   as clever as ___________
             ___________   ___________
             ___________   ___________
             ___________   ___________

□*Metaphorical Language* List metaphors children have come across in their reading materials. Ask them to draw a picture, or to pantomime, showing the literal meaning of the metaphor. Also ask them to choose from the top of the page the interpretive meaning. E.g.:

a. always together and very   d. very busy
   much alike   e. partly finished and/or
b. deeply and completely or   nonsensical
   excitedly   f. felt proud
c. get lost

	literal meaning	figurative meaning
1. Dad *burst his buttons* when Sue won the contest.		___(felt proud)___
2. Jill and Jane are *two peas in a pod*.		___________
3. The nurse reported that the doctor was *tied up for the day*.		___________
4. "What a *half-baked* idea," Jim groaned.		___________

5. Connie fell *head over heels* in love with her new poppy.

6. "*Go fly a kite*," Tim shouted to Jerome.

____

Many other examples might be used:

Cat got your tongue?	Hold your horses.
She caught my eye.	The cat's out of the bag.
He was on pins and needles.	I don't give a hoot.
His face fell.	Fire away.
She dropped her eyes.	He took off.
Pipe down.	He blew his top.
Get off my back.	Her wings were clipped.

☐ *Compare Literal with Figurative Language Descriptions* Encourage children to write descriptions for the same object or event that are literal and figurative. Help them compare the effect of each on a reader or listener. E.g.:

⎡ literal: Thunder is the sound heard accompanying lightning.
⎣ metaphor: Thunder is a great dragon that lives in the water and
             flies in the air.

⎡ literal: Sue is a good swimmer.
⎢ simile: Sue swims liks a fish.
⎢ metaphor: Sue was a fish during the swim meet.
⎣ hyperbole: Sue is the finest and best swimmer in the world.

⎡ literal: I laughed so hard.
⎣ hyperbole: I nearly died laughing. I split my sides laughing.

⎡ literal: The old man died.
⎢ metaphor: The old man kicked the bucket. (U.S.)
⎣ metaphor: The old man hung up his tennis shoes. (Mexican)

⎡ literal: He's very smart in science.
⎣ allusion: He's the Aristotle of our class.

⎡ literal: For every effect there is a cause.
⎢ proverb: There's no smoke without a fire. (U.S.)
⎣ proverb: An old crow doesn't croak for nothing. (Russian)

Pictures might be drawn by children to illustrate each meaning.

□*Allusions* Children enjoy mythology, and as they grow older, they will notice that there are many allusions to mythology in their reading materials. To prepare them for this, you might show them how some of the more popular mythological characters and situations are used as points of reference. For example:

1. What do we mean when we say a person *tantalizes* someone? (Of course, we know that means he or she teases or torments by showing or promising something but keeping it out of reach. But who was *Tantalus*? He is always pictured in a pool of water, about chin deep. Around the pool grow trees that are full of ripe fruit. When he wants a drink of water, the pool recedes. When he has an appetite for fruit, the wind blows it beyond his reach. Why was he so punished? One version of the myth is that when he was invited to dine with the gods, he served them his own son Pelops to test their wisdom. Other versions are not that drastic: According to one, he stole food from the table of the gods and served it to mortals, and another is that he revealed the table-talk of the gods to mortals.)

2. What do we mean when we say something might open a *Pandora's Box*? (Of course, we mean if something happens, chaos will result. But who was *Pandora*? Pandora was the first woman. She was entrusted with a box in which were found all the ills of the world and was told not to open it. Her curiosity, however, won out, and she succumbed—and out flew all the ills to afflict mankind.)

3. What do we mean when we talk about an *Icarian* adventure. (We mean a *foolhardy* adventure. But who was Icarus? Icarus was the son of Daedalus. Both were imprisoned in Crete in the

Labyrinth. Daedalus built wax wings for himself and his son, and they escaped by flying. Daedalus warned his son not to fly too high, but Icarus ignored this advice. The sun melted his wings, and he drowned at sea. Daedalus, however, made it to shore, and *Daedalean* means *wise.*)

□ *Match Proverbs* Help children match proverbs that have approximately the same literal meanings. These may include proverbs from different countries and/or cultures. E.g.:

_______ The ripest fruit will not fall into your mouth. (Chinese)	a. Silence is golden
_______ You should have seen the fish that got away.	b. Be sure to keep an eye out for what you can swallow - and also for what can swallow you. (India)
_______ It's one thing to cackle and another to lay an egg. (Ecuadorian)	c. If you kick one walnut in the sack, all the rest clatter. (Hungarian)
_______ If the fish had not opened its mouth, it would not have been caught. (Mexican)	d. The cow that was stolen used to give four pails of milk. (Hungarian)
_______ One rooster awakens all the roosters in the village. (German)	e. God gives food to the birds, but they must look for it. (German)
_______ Don't bite off more than you can chew.	f. Handsome words don't butter cabbage. (German)

Children may wish to suggest proverbs they know to add to these.

New Words Enter Our Language

The English language is alive and well. One proof of this is that it is growing and changing. One important way in which a living language grows is by adding new words—enlarging the vocabulary. This is frequently done by borrowing and coining words. Another way is by using words already in the language in new and different ways. In the beginning stages, such uses of words may be considered slang. Both of these changes are evident in modern English, as they have been in English of all historical periods.

BORROWING

The English language borrows heavily from languages around the world. Here are some examples:

American Indian: moccasin, toboggan, raccoon, chipmunk, wampum, te-
            pee, yucca
Eskimo: kayak, igloo, mukluk
Spanish: patio, chocolate, potato, llama, maize
Italian: violin, piano, opera, volcano, cameo
French: camouflage, marionette, puppet, genie, calendar
German: dollar, otter, house, wiener, dachshund, glockenspiel
Greek: calypso, organ, alphabet, theater, circus, pumpkin
Scandinavian: sister, teeter totter, sky, ski
Russian: sputnik, babushka, balalaika
Arabic: algebra, giraffe, candy, sugar
Turkish: coffee, yogurt, turkey
Hindi: shampoo, pajamas, jungle, bungalow
Australian English: kangaroo, boomerang, koala
Japanese: kimono, teriyaki
Persian: caravan, kiosk, lemon, peach

What's *not* borrowed in English? Fortunately words, like ideas, can be "borrowed" without impoverishing the giver, for "borrowed" words are not returned. And it's fortunate we don't have to pay for borrowed words, because we'd owe almost every country in the world.

Let's look at words around a theme, say music. From what language did English borrow names of musical instruments?

□ *Borrowed Words* For an activity, you might just list the instruments and have the children find the sources by using a dictionary. Or, you may wish to give them the answers, as above, and ask them: (1) what this information tells them about each of the instruments that is listed, (2) what it tells them about Italy and France (and the other areas) as a source of musical culture for English speaking people. You may wish to ask them if they would like to add any instruments to the illustration.

An activity like this might be followed with names of composers of music they enjoy. Children might check their nationalities by using dictionaries and/or encyclopedias.

Such an activity can be done in relation to a classroom interest or content area. Animal names could be used, sea creatures and

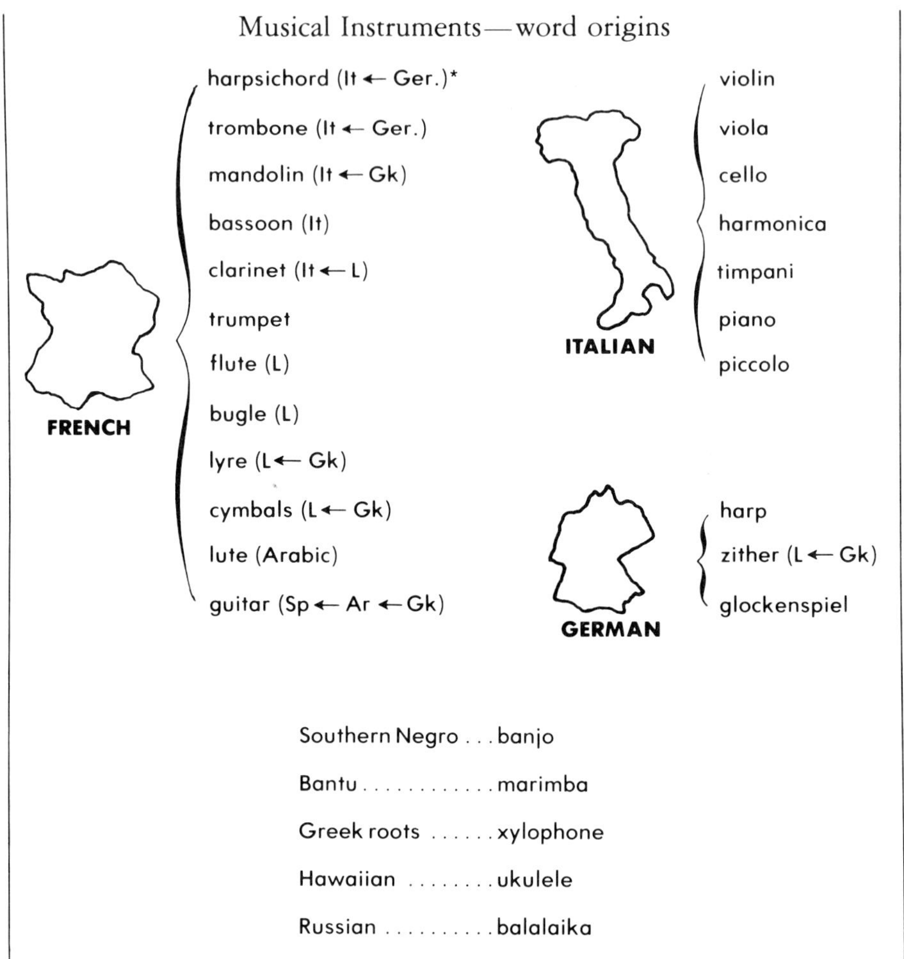

sea shells, plant life, arithmetic terms, government terms, stars, planets, galaxies, art terms—anything that sparks the interest of children. (A thesaurus in dictionary form will help them identify clusters of words.) Other themes and terms might include:*

*Languages listed here are the original language from which a form of the word, as it represented the object, came - according to *The American Heritage Dictionary of the English Language.* Boston: Houghton Mifflin Co., 1969. Some language listings may be slightly debatable because in some listings it was suggested that yet an earlier source might be credited. The word may have passed into one or more languages on its way to English.

clothing

babushka	(Russian)	parka	(Russian)
mantilla	(Spanish)	moccasin	(Algonquian)
poncho	(Araucanian)	sarong	(Malaysian)
sombrero	(Spanish)	sari	(Sanskrit)
chapeau	(Latin)	caftan	(Turkish)
camisole	(Latin)	helmet	(French)
kilt	(Old Norse)	derby	(Modern English)
kimono	(Japanese)	dress	(Latin)
mukluk	(Eskimo)	shoe	(German)
culotte	(Latin)	stocking	(Middle English)

housing

hogan	(Navaho)	kiosk	(Persian)
wigwam	(N. American Indian)	gazebo	(mock Latin)
		ranch (style)	(Spanish)
tepee	(N. American Indian)	cave	(Latin)
		tent	(Latin)
igloo	(Eskimo)	shack	(Aztec)
villa	(Latin)	cabin	(Latin)
palace	(Latin)	house	(German)
hut	(German)	hotel	(French)
pagoda	(Sanskrit)	inn	(Old English)
		apartment	(Italian)

fruit

pear	(Greek)	guava	(S. American Indian)
olive	(Greek)	orange	(Sanskrit)
pumpkin	(Greek)	apple	(Old English)
melon	(Greek)	fig	(Latin)
peach	(Persian)	lemon	(Persian)
pomegranate	(Latin)	lime	(Arabic)
cantaloupe	(Italian)	grape	(German)
papaya	(Cariban)	cherry	(Greek)
banana	(West African)	plum	(Latin)
mango	(Tamil)	apricot	(Latin)

animals

peacock	(Latin)	kangaroo	(Australian English)
impala	(Zulu)	koala	(Australian English)
orangutan	(Malay)	opossum	(Algonquian)
penguin	(Welsh)	caribou	(Algonquian)
eagle	(Latin)	bison	(German)

porcupine	(Latin)	zebra	(Spanish)
elephant	(Greek)	parakeet	(French)
armadillo	(Spanish)	platypus	(Greek)
burro	(Spanish)	giraffe	(Arabic)
horse	(German)	cat	(Latin)
		dog	(Old English)

COINING

English speaking people coin, or make-up, many words, principally in three ways:

- by *combining morphemes* to create new words.
- by *blending* the beginning of one word with the end of another. The resulting word is called a *blend.*
  smoke + fog = smog   strong + soft = stroft
  breakfast + lunch = brunch   motor + hotel = motel
- by composing words made up of the first letter (or letters) of words. The resulting word is called an *acronym.*
  SCUBA   RADAR   NATO   MOPED

Since morphology has already been discussed, activities in this section will involve only the other two processes: blending and creating acronyms.

  □*Blends* To teach children about blends, use an activity like the following. Ask them to try to figure out what goes in each blank. They might have to use a dictionary.

  1. smoke + (fog) = smog
  2. breakfast + _______ = brunch
  3. _______ + _______ = lupper*
  4. boat + _______ = botel
  5. motor(ize) + hotel = _______
  6. _______ + hotel = flotel
  7. home + hotel = _______
  8. skirt + short = _______
  9. slip + glide = _______
  10. twist + _______ = twirl
  11. flash + blush = _______**
  12. squeeze + _______ = squash
  13. cattle + buffalo = _______
  14. beef + _______ = beefalo
  15. strong + soft = _______
  16. picture + _______ = pictionary

---

* For fun
**As a "flush of pride"

□*Blending for Fun* Give children a set of cards on which are listed words related to a theme. For example, animal names. Have them turn cards over, draw two cards and create a new word by blending the initial part of one word with the final part of another. Pictures might be drawn to illustrate the new words, and stories might be written about them.

1. *ti*ger + kang*aroo* = tigaroo
2. *ele*phant + kang*aroo* = elegaroo
3. *pan*da + ant*elope* = pantelope
4. *go*rilla + hy*ena* = gorena
5. etc.

□*Acronym Search* Make a seek-and-find puzzle, using acronyms the children should learn. Give clues—either the acronym or the words—and have them fill in the missing part. Then have them find the acronym in the chart and draw a ring around it. E.g.:*

1. Very Important Person   (VIP)
2. (Very, Very Important Person)   VVIP
3. Strategic Arms Limitations Talks
4. ______________________   UNESCO
5. North, East, West, South
6. SOund NAvigation Ranging
8. ______________________   UFO
9. Self-Contained Underwater Breathing Apparatus

*Additional common acronyms are: RSVP, IOU, ZIP, COD, NASA, UFO, POW, MIA, AWOL, ASAP, TLC, SWAK, ESP, TGIF, KKK, MPH, NAACP, UNICEF, etc.

F	U	P	O	T	I	S	O	S	C	L
S	A	L	T	E	H	V	B	N	X	W
V	G	R	A	N	O	S	K	O	S	E
R	R	Q	D	S	M	N	J	C	D	M
A	N	D	C	G	E	O	U	S	P	Q
D	H	E	F	W	M	B	A	E	R	U
A	B	P	S	L	A	Z	S	N	K	F
R	I	O	K	P	Y	U	X	U	B	A
J	Y	M	T	I	Z	F	W	A	C	N
U	P	I	V	V	E	O	I	H	N	S
A	V	F	M	P	T	D	J	G	L	O

10. ________________________________   <u>SOS</u>
11. Situation Normal - All Fouled Up   ________
12. MOterized PEDals   ________

Slang

Slang expressions are new and often faddish. Most come and go, though some remain in the language and become a part of the regular vocabulary of English. When new, slang is fresh and appears to be spontaneous. It's alive (or so it seems). Clusters of slang expressions are used by specific groups or subgroups within a society and are very much in vogue in these groups. If these expressions spread to the major part of the society, they are no longer slang.

Some slang expressions are:

The library book was *ripped off.*

Let's *split* and go elsewhere.

He's *cool.* What a *sharp* guy!

How much *bread*'ll I get for an hour's labor?

Bug off. Scat.

Such *zazz* you want me to believe.

You'll see that these words are not new. Rather, they are old words with new meanings.

□ *C.B. Slang* C.B. radio operators are a prolific source of slang to-day. Many children are familiar with this slang and might like to share their knowledge with their classmates. For example, CB slang for city names would be interesting to study. Some examples arc:

Boston	- Bean Town	Los Angeles	- Shaky City
Chatanooga	- Choo Choo Town	Miami	- Bikini City
		Milwaukee	- Beer City
Dallas	- Big "D"	Nashville	- Guitar Town
Detroit	- Motor City	New Orleans	- Mardi Gras Town
Houston	- Astrodome City	Phoenix	- Cactus City
		St. Louis	- Big Arch
Las Vegas	- Dice City	San Francisco	- Hill Town

Try to match the C.B. term with its meaning:

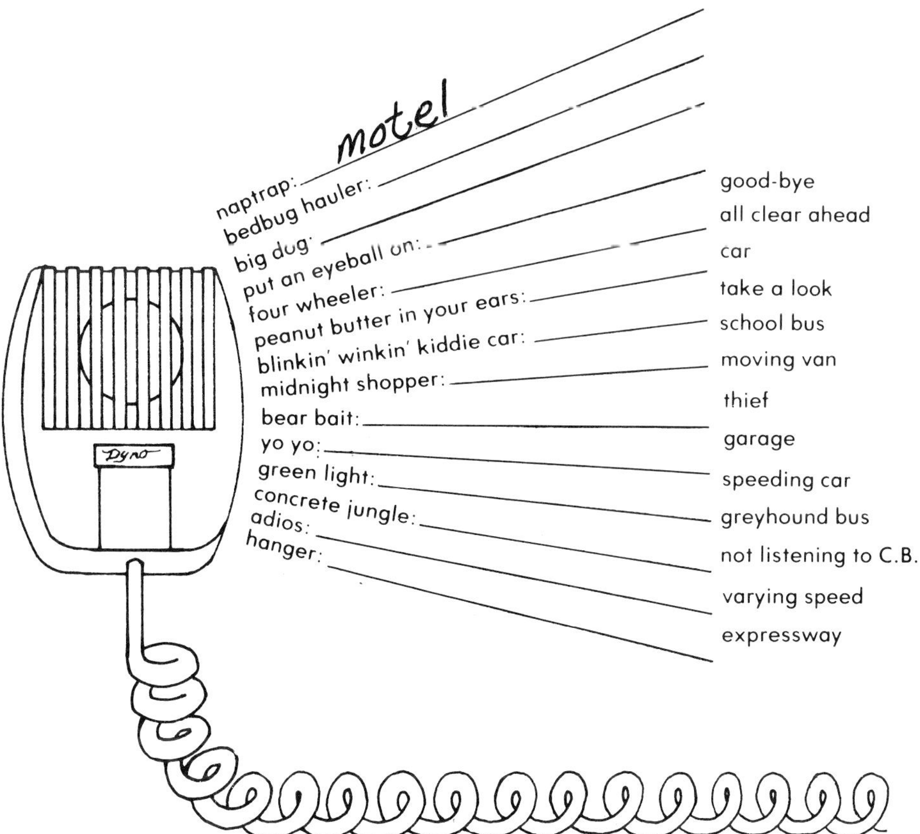

Children might not understand that the C.B. slang term names one characteristic of a city (a very stereotyped characteristic). They might not even know about that characteristic. It might be interesting for them to briefly study about that one characteristic of some of the cities. E.g., why is Boston called the "Bean Town"? Why is New Orleans the "Mardi Gras Town"? What is the Mardi Gras?

Using A Dictionary

Dictionaries contain a wealth of information for both children and adults. Anyone who wishes to be an independent reader must know how to use a dictionary. Very young children may learn some of the principles of using a dictionary by making a picture dictionary of their own.

In order to make a dictionary of their own (or a classroom dictionary) or to use a published dictionary, children will have to know or learn about some basics. These include:

- the alphabet
- guide words
- entry words
- homographs
- multiple meanings

As they progress, they should also learn about using

- a pronunciation key
- information given about etymology
- synonym discussions, which follow some definitions
- illustrations
- special sections of a dictionary

Techniques for teaching these skills follow. Within each section the activities are sequenced from easy to more difficult.

LOCATING WORDS

Alphabetical Order

Children must know that entry words are listed in alphabetical order in dictionaries. If they are making their own dictionaries, they must know this too. To teach alphabetical order, the following activities could be used.

□*Alphabetizing by First Letters* The teacher should have the letters of the alphabet posted in large print in alphabetical order somewhere in the room. Children can be taught to say the alphabet in sections, e.g.:

```
a - b - c - d - e        f - g - h - i - j        k - l - m - n - o
p - q - r - s - t        u - v - w                x - y - z
```

Then they increase this to larger units. Children may be given cards with letters on them and asked to arrange them in order. Then they could be given a handout with some letters omitted. They are asked to fill in the missing letters without looking at the posted alphabet.

```
a __ c __ e __ __ h __ j __ __ m __ __ p q __ s __ u __ __ x
__ z
```

Then they are asked to put words with different first letters into alphabetical order, e.g.:

apple	__(apple)__	house	_________
cake	__(book)__	king	_________
fox	_________	goat	_________
book	_________	lion	_________
dog	_________	ice	_________
elephant	_________	jack	_________

Now they could make a small dictionary with 26 words and pictures—one for each letter, and one page for each letter. The teacher might put guide words (in this case, letters) at the top of each page. It might be best if pictures were not put in permanently, but were moveable.

□*Alphabetizing by First Two Letters* Next, children are ready to alphabetize by the first two letters of words. Lists like the following could be given to them to alphabetize:

Atlantic	_________	box	_________
apple	_________	ball	_________
acorn	_________	big	_________
aunt	_________	blue	_________

Now they could add several words and pictures to each page of their dictionary. The teacher could write guide words at the top of each page—using the first and last words of each page.

□ *Alphabetizing by First Three Letters*   Next they could be given lists of words with the first two letters alike, but differing in the third letter. They would circle lists that are in alphabetical order and X lists that are not:

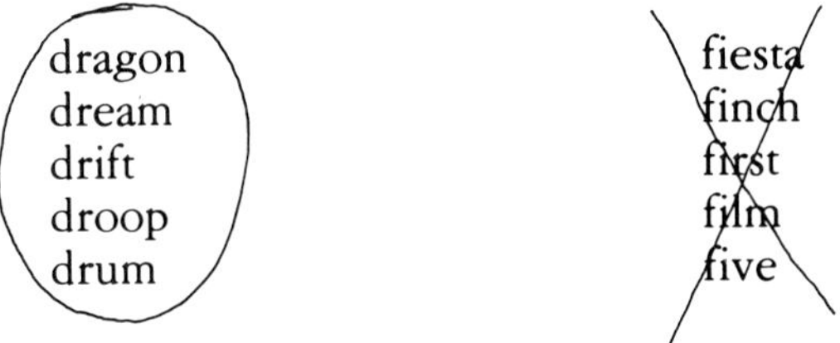

Guide Words

Guide words are the words at the top of a dictionary page that tell us the first and last words included on that page. The following activities could be used to teach children to use guide words:

□ *Dictionary Guide Letters and Words*   When putting several words and pictures on a dictionary page, the teacher and children should work together, putting the words in alphabetical order. Together, they decide which is first on the page and write that word on the top left corner of the page. The word for the final entry on the page is written on the top right corner. Only these words and those that are alphabetically between them can be put on that page.

□ *Handout Activities*   Children may be given handouts to complete of the following types:

Guide words are given at the top of each section. Children are asked to circle the words that will be found on a dictionary page with these guide words. They are to draw an X through words that will not be on that page.

finger — fisherman		needle — Nevada	
fireplace	fir	needy	nest
finch	flag	need	never
fiord	first	Neptune	neck
fix	fizz	noble	nation

Next, children may be asked to tell if the X'd words will be before or after the given page.

Finally, children may be given several lists of entry words and asked to write the guide words if all these words were on one page, e.g.:

Entry words: popular, poor, pompon, poppy, portal, port, porridge, porch, porpoise, poorly, pontoon, pond

Guide words: (pompon) (portal) Etc.

□ *Dictionary Activities* Have children use real dictionaries. If there aren't enough dictionaries to go around the class, children can work individually at different times. First, give them a list of words. Ask them to look up each word and write the guide words for the page on which each word is found. E.g.:

entry word	guide words	
moccasin	(misty)	(model)
disaster		
quote		
etc.		

Next, give them guide words and ask them to find the page and write one interesting word from the page, along with a definition:

guide words	entry word	definition
1. ribbon - right	riddle	a puzzling question
2. shadow - shark		
3. Oregon - ostrich		
4. etc.		

Entry Words, Including Homographs

Entry words are the words listed in alphabetical order in the major part of a dictionary. These are the words the children are putting in alphabetical order in their dictionaries. These are the words, including the guide words and all words between them, on a given page of a dictionary. There is probably only one area of difficulty here for children. That is the area of *homographs*.

Children are puzzled to find that for some entry words there may be many definitions. Then they find that some words (or same-spellings) are listed several times as entry words. These are homographs: words spelled alike (*homo* = same, *graph* = writing) but words of different origins. Many dictionaries list homographs with raised numbers following them, indicating that there is at least one more entry word with the same spelling. For example, one dictionary gives four listings for *duck*:

duck[1] (dŭk) n., a wild bird
duck[2] (dŭk) v., to lower quickly
duck[3] (dŭk) n., a durable cloth
duck[4] (dŭk) n., a military truck

The first two come from Middle English, but from different roots; the third comes from Dutch, and the fourth from the acronym DUKW, but *duck* is written in lower case letters.

When children are working on their dictionary, they might very likely think of the two homographs duck[1] and duck[2] (as given above). If the teacher recognizes them to be homographs, they could learn about this principle at an early age.

There are many such words in the English language, but it's sometimes difficult to know if we have one word with multiple meanings or if we have homographs. When there are two or more meanings for a word that are difficult to reconcile, it might be well to check a dictionary to see if the words are homographs.

> □ *Homographs* List words you know to be homographs. Ask children to look them up. Ask them if they can tell why these words are entered twice (or more often) in a dictionary. Ask them to give the pronunciation for each and the first definition for each. E.g.,
> wind[1] (wĭnd), air motion
> wind[2] (wīnd), move one way then another
>
> | will[1] | fuse[1] | close[1] | press[1] |
> |---------|---------|----------|----------|
> | will[2] | fuse[2] | close[2] | press[2] |
> | recount[1] | lumber[1] | present[1] | cue[1] |
> | recount[2] | lumber[2] | present[2] | cue[2] |

INFORMATION GIVEN WITHIN ENTRY WORDS AND/OR REFERENCED TO ENTRY WORDS

Multiple Meanings

Most words have more than one meaning. Children must learn to read the definitions given in a dictionary until they find the one that fits the context. To teach them to do this, you might design an activity like the following.

□*Multiple Meanings* Write groups of sentences that include a single word in contextual settings that suggest different meanings of the word. Ask children to write the number of the correct meaning and the definition, both as given in their dictionary. E.g.:

Freeze

1. I always *freeze* when I go ice skating.
   number (3), meaning (become very cold)
2. The water on the pond was *frozen.*
   number (1), meaning (turned into ice)
3. The cat *froze* when she saw the tarantula.
   number (10), meaning (became motionless)

Illustrations

Most dictionaries include illustrations of nouns and of famous people. This is an excellent source of visual aids. Children must be taught to look for these illustrations, which are almost always found on the same page as the entry word.

□*Illustrations* Consult the dictionaries the children have available to them to see which important words in a chapter just read—or about to be read—are illustrated. List about ten such words, and ask each child to pick five to draw pictures of. The words might be:

frigate	magnetic pole	junk (ship)
pontoon	longitude circles	jib
outrigger	latitude circles	galleon
catwalk		

Etymology

Most dictionaries for older children and adults list origins of words. They give the assumed original morpheme or morphemes that compose the word and the historical development of these bases. A major question may arise when using this section within an entry: when asking about the language from which English "borrowed" a word, children may be confused. Are you asking about the original language from which the word came or the language that fed the word to English? This must be clarified for children.

For example, if we look back to our section on borrowed words in this chapter (pp. 277–280), we see an illustration listing the languages from which English directly took words for musical instruments. We see, also, that the given words may not have originated in that language, but flowed to that language from another language, which may have taken the word from still another language. (E.g., *mandolin*: English took this word from French. But French took it from Italian, and Italian took it from Greek.) So these questions are different:

- From which language did English borrow the word *mandolin*? (French)
- In which language did the word *mandolin* originate? (Greek)
- Trace the history of the word *mandolin* as it relates to the English language. (Greek → Italian → French → English)

The Oxford English Dictionary supplies detailed information on etymology. Children who are especially interested in this phase of word study should be introduced to this set of books as soon as possible. Also, an excellent source is *The American Heritage Dictionary*. This is a desk dictionary which gives excellent detail on word histories in an appendix.

Synonyms

As part of the definition of a word, synonyms are often given. Dictionaries for older children and adults usually also include synonym sections within the entry word section after definitions are given. In these sections, synonyms are listed and differentiated so that the reader knows precisely how each synonym is used.

□ *Differentiating Synonyms* Ask older children to tell precisely how each synonym is used, e.g.:

1. joke, jest, witticism, quip, crack, wisecrack, gag
2. nullify, negate, abolish, annul, void, invalidate, cancel, repeal, revoke, rescind
3. form, figure, outline, shape, configuration, contour, profile
4. dishonest, lying, untruthful, deceitful, tricky, shady, underhanded
5. etc.

Pronunciation

Each dictionary uses its own pronunciation key, although there is a great deal of uniformity from one dictionary to another. Children are best advised to refer to the pronunciation key given in the dictionary they are using at a particular time. However, the use of a pronunciation key must be taught. It is hoped that knowing how to use a key in one dictionary will help a child use a slightly different key in another.

When teaching the use of a pronunciation key in one dictionary, the teacher should call attention to that key and show children exactly where it is found. Together, the teacher and children should read the key while the teacher explains it. After that, activities such as the following could be used:

□ *Key-Picture Associations* Write the respelling of words from the dictionary the children are using. Ask the children to match the pronunciation respellings with the correct picture and write the number in the box. (See pictures on page 292.)

1. kap	2. to͞o	3. rō
4. res′ · ə · pē	5. sinj	6. rek′ ərd
7. rou	8. kāp	9. toi
10. ri · kôrd′		

□ *Use Sentences* Use dictionary respellings and sentences, omitting the respelled word. Children indicate the correct respelled word and write the real word in the blank:

1. gon′ · də · lə	5	We stayed in a (chateau) in France.
2. dēp sē		We ___________ fished in the Mediterranean.
3. drēm		We set ___________ on Lake Lucerne.
4. sāl		In Venice we rode in a ___________.
5. sha · tō′		This trip was my ___________ last night.

Antonyms Match antonym respellings.

1. hwit	d	a. ji′ · ənt
2. lärj		b. rông
3. mij′it		c. smôl
4. rīt		d. blak
5. nēt		e. mes′ · ē

Capitol
Tigers
Chicken à la King
2

SPECIAL SECTIONS

Many dictionaries have special sections at the beginning and/or end. These sections usually supply valuable information. Dictionaries designed to be sold in the school market frequently include a comprehensive section which shows children exactly how to use the book. There frequently are exercises and activities keyed to the use of that dictionary. Some dictionaries make available the same kind of material in pamphlet form.

Many dictionaries include appendixes on rhyming words (for the budding poet), on etymology and/or the history of the English language, on common abbreviations, on weights and measures, on colleges and universities as well as other important things. The dictionary should not be overlooked as an invaluable source of some types of specialized information.

Summary

This chapter contains four major sections, each with important subsections. These sections dealt with:

- *denotative language*, that is, literal language in which words are used with their "scientific" and perhaps visible meanings. Many activities were included as suggestions for helping children learn word denotations. Among the most important of these is helping children have, discuss, and interpret many direct experiences. Also important is work with synonyms and antonyms, recognizing that words frequently have multiple meanings, and that directly stated clues help reveal meanings. A highly important section deals with morphology, for work in this area can rapidly multiply word power.
- *connotative language* is used to appeal to the emotions. Besides having denotations, many words have connotations. Three fruitful areas to work on with children in this respect include animal names, vegetation, and colors. Figurative language, including similes, metaphors, hyperboles, personification, allusions and proverbs, was also suggested as desirable for working with children.
- how *new words enter our language*. Included in this section is a brief discussion that includes some ways in which new words enter the English language. Major subsections dealt with "borrowing" words, coining words, and adding slang terms.
- *using a dictionary*. In this section, it was suggested that young children might enjoy making a dictionary and that by doing this they could learn much about locating words in published dictionaries. They could learn about entry words, about putting entry words in alpha-

betical order, about homographs and also guide words. Children should also learn about multiple meanings, illustrations which might be found in dictionaries, etymology, synonym explanations, and how to use a pronunciation key. Additionally, many dictionaries include special sections, perhaps even a section designed to teach children to use a dictionary. Other important reference aids are also included in many dictionaries.

Many activities were suggested for classroom use. In most cases these activities were presented to serve as guides to teachers who might wish to compose their own activities which would correlate with and reinforce areas of knowledge that relate to the interests and needs of children in a particular classroom. In most cases, these activities are not meant to be copied and used as given, for if they were used this way they probably would be isolated drills. It is hoped that they will suggest a variety of formats to make word study vital. The teacher studying or using these formats will soon discover many more to design independently.

Questions and Activities

After answering the questions at the beginning of this chapter, consider these questions and activities:

1. Look at each of these words separately. Explain to a friend what images they evoke in your thinking. Compare your images with his or hers.

   Fiji . . . Paris . . . Berlin . . . Taj Mahal . . . Tibet . . . San Francisco . . . Wild Safari . . . park . . . lagoon . . . Blue Lagoon . . . idol . . . lion . . . giraffe . . . cat . . . puppy . . . rattle snake . . . cobra . . . skyscraper . . . jazz . . . tango . . . waltz . . . New Orleans . . . Polish . . . Italian . . . British . . . Russian . . . Japanese . . . onofu . . . ennui . . . joie de vivre . . . good-bye . . . adios . . . chow . . . sayonara . . .

   • Do some of the words leave you blank (e.g., *onofu*—a nonsense word)? Do others excite you? Do some make you feel calm? happy? How do your previous experiences affect your knowledge of and feelings about these words and the images they bring to mind?

   • Do you think children's reading experiences when they meet words unknown to them evoke images similar to yours when you "read" *onofu*? Can reading an unknown word in context help a child understand the word? E.g.: "The little wiggly *onofu* tickled my arm as my kitten pulled it along when playing in my lap. She purred as the *onofu* sprang back and forth. I fear that this *onofu*, a special spring used for holding a small plant, will never hold another ivy in place." Can seeing a real *onofu* clarify the meaning even more?

• Explain the importance of understanding the statement: "Words do not *have* meanings. They *represent* meanings in the minds of readers and listeners—and speakers and writers."

2. Design a field trip you would like to take a group of children on. Where would you go? What would you—and they—see . . . feel . . . touch . . . smell . . . hear . . . taste? How would you prepare them for the trip? What would you—and they—do while on the trip? What would you have them do after the trip?

3. Ask a child—in your class or in your neighborhood—to show you something of real interest to her or him. Encourage the child to talk about it. You may help the child along, if necessary. Then read the child a little story to thank him or her.

4. Play the "Tired Word Game" (p. 233) with a group of children.

5. Make a synonym or antonym checkerboard (p. 234) for use with words in a chapter of a science, arithmetic, music, art, physical education, etc., story or chapter.

6. Make a concentration game using words to be matched with their definitions or pictures for a part of a book—basal or content area—children might be using at a grade level of your choice.

7. Search a textbook children might be reading at a grade level of your choice for sentences that use directly stated context cues (pp. 240–243). Classify these cues according to the patterns suggested in this section. Have you found any additional patterns?

8. Choose a basal reader or other textbook at the second or third grade level or above. Open it at random to any page and write the first 25 words (continuing to further pages if necessary) that are two or more syllables long (omit names). What proportion of these words are composed of two or more morphemes? Compare your results with your classmates' results. Draw a conclusion about the importance of teaching children about morphology—and perhaps about which morphemes are most important at specific grade levels.

9. Prepare a crossword puzzle for use in a special unit of study—or for a chapter in a textbook—for a vocabulary posttest.

10. Pantomime the denotative and connotative meanings of a word. Ask a friend to guess the word.

11. Make a list of as many proverbs as you can recall. Share them with your classmates.

12. Write a list of ten words that are synonymous. Show how each has a specific use in context by using each word in an appropriate sentence or by matching the each word with an appropriate picture.

NOTES

1. See Massialas and Zevin in Selected References.
2. The author wishes to recognize the following students for "The Meter Daisy"- Alidia Diane Ackerman, "Bio Balloons"- Susan Stapleton.

SELECTED REFERENCES

Askov, E.N. and K. Kamm. "Context Clues: Should We Teach Children to Use a Classification System?" *Journal of Educational Research*, 69 (May-June 1976): 341–344.

Burmeister, Lou E. *Words—From Print to Meaning (Classroom Activities: for Building Sight Vocabulary, for Using Context Clues, Morphology and Phonics)*. Reading, Mass: Addison-Wesley Publishing Co., 1975.

Burroughs, Robert S. "Vocabulary Study and Context, or How I Learned to Stop Worrying about Word Lists." *English Journal*, 71 (February 1982): 53–55.

Cole, Luella. *The Teacher's Handbook of Technical Vocabulary*. Bloomington, Illinois: Public School Publishing Co., 1940.

Culyer, Richard C. III. "Guidelines for Skill Development: Vocabulary." *The Reading Teacher*, 32 (December 1978): 316–322.

Dale, Edgar, Joseph O'Rourke and Henry A. Bamman. *Techniques of Teaching Vocabulary*. Palo Alto, Calif.: Field Educational Publications, Inc., 1971.

Evans, Bergen. *Dictionary of Mythology (Mainly Classical)*. New York: Dell Publishing Co., 1970.

Hargis, Charles H. and Edward E. Gickling. "The Function of Imagery in Word Recognition Development." *The Reading Teacher*, 31 (May 1978): 870–874.

Kaplan, Elaine M. and Anita Tuchman. "Vocabulary Strategies belong in the Hands of Learners." *Journal of Reading*, 24 (October 1980): 32–34.

Lacey, Patricia A. and Philip E. Weil. "Number - Reading - Language." *Language Arts*, 52 (September 1975): 776–782.

Lee, Joyce W. "Increasing Comprehension through Use of Context Clue Categories." *Journal of Reading*, 22 (December 1978): 259–262.

Lewis, Norman (ed.). *Roget's New Pocket Thesaurus in Dictionary Form*. New York: Pocket Books, 1961.

Massialas, Byron and Jack Zevin. *Creative Encounters in the Classroom*. New York: John Wiley, 1967.

Rivers, Susan New. "Puppets with a Purpose." *The Reading Teacher*, 32 (May 1979): 956–958.

Shuy, Roger W. "What Should the Language Strand in a Reading Program Contain?" *The Reading Teacher*, 35 (April 1982): 806–812.

Walker, Charles Monroe. "High Frequency Word List for Grades 3 through 9." *The Reading Teacher*, 32 (April 1979): 803–812.

Vaughan, Sally, Sharon Crawley and Lee Mountain. "A Multiple-Modality Approach to Word Study: Vocabulary Scavenger Hunts." *The Reading Teacher*, 32 (January 1979): 434–437.

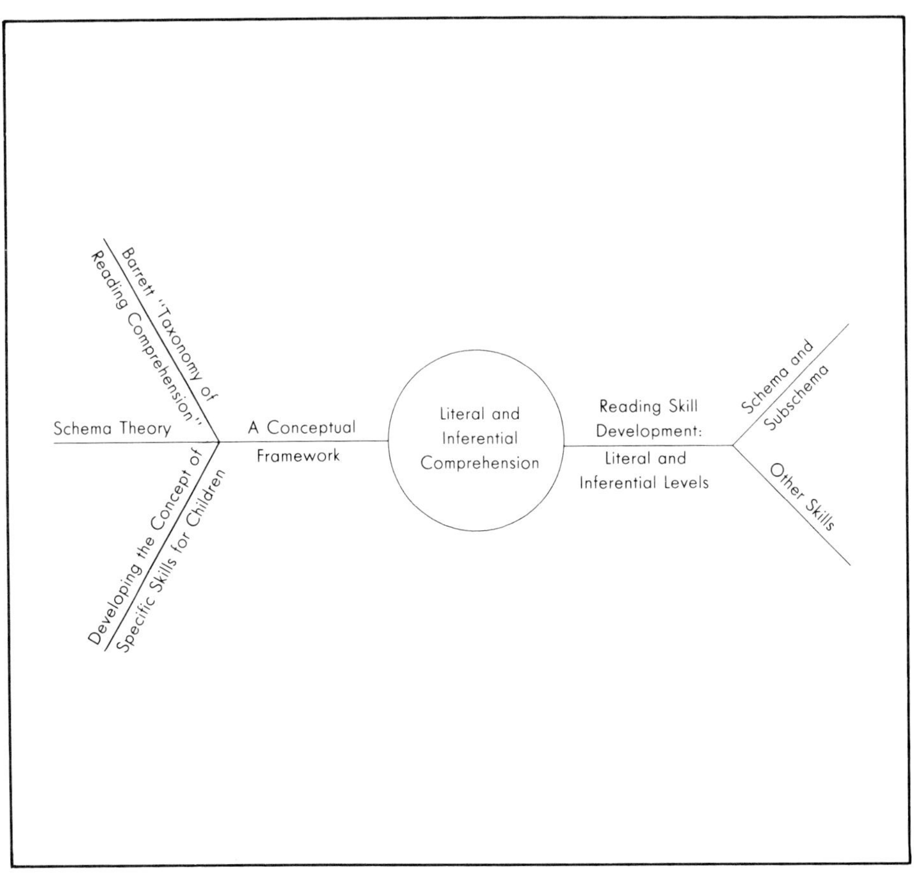

- What is meant by "literal" and "inferential" comprehension?

- Do you think it's important to have a conceptual framework for understanding and teaching comprehension? Why or why not? What are the essential levels and "tasks" in reading comprehension according to the Barrett "Taxonomy of Reading Comprehension"? What is "schema theory"? To what tasks in the Barrett taxonomy does schema theory relate? How can a teacher develop the concept of specific skills, such as those in the Barrett Taxonomy, for children?

- How can we help children develop additional reading skills at the literal and inferential levels?

CHAPTER 8

Literal and Inferential Comprehension

One of the more controversial topics in the teaching of reading today is whether comprehension should be viewed as a united whole (holistic approach) or a series of skills and subskills (skills, subskills approach). Those who favor a holistic approach believe that reading assignments—and the teaching of reading—should normally involve materials that focus on concepts of substance and interest to the reader and that these materials should be read as "wholes." They argue that the language of the printed page must unite with the reader's thought for reading to occur, and that there is a constant interaction between the reader's and the author's thoughts and language during the reading process (top-down/interactive model). There appears to be much logic to this philosophy. Capable readers interacting with reading materials that contain ideas, words, and syntax that are at least somewhat familiar may, indeed, read holistically, or primarily holistically.

The polar opposite of a holistic approach is a complex subskill approach (primarily a bottom-up model). Authors of some published programs have analyzed reading into dozens and even hundreds of subskills and have developed intricate diagnostic and management systems. Children are tested and placed at a level in each subskill (or the series of subskills designated for their grade level or reading achievement level) at which, according to this testing, they can achieve, and then they work to move ahead in each designated subskill. Some of these programs are so complex that they involve the use of a computer to feed in information for each child and to then identify activities or exercises to be used.[1]

While holistic advocates may be accused of being vague, subskills advocates are often accused of being too specific and atomistic. Opponents of subskills approaches wonder if the skills ever unite in the minds of children to help these children be in tune with an author. Such "readers" may be like swimmers who have learned how to breathe, how to move their arms and legs, but who never get anywhere in the water because they can't coordinate the act.

One might realistically argue that the amount of phonics subskill instruction a child needs is the least amount that enables him or her to recode and decode.[2] A similar argument might be forwarded for the direct development of any other reading skill, including vocabulary, comprehension, study skills, rate, etc. Some children need more subskill work than others to enable them to understand the materials they are assigned to read and choose to read.

The heart of reading involves the interaction of the reader with the author. Skill and subskill development might best be viewed as work toward enabling a reader to reach the heart of the act. Affective components must also be involved. These are discussed in Chapters 9 and 10. Chapter 12 deals with teaching reading holistically.

A Conceptual Framework

Teachers need a conceptual framework to help them understand what is meant by reading comprehension. They need such a framework for several reasons. Among these are:

- to help them judge teachers' guides, such as those that accompany basal readers, other textbooks, and other materials that might be available in the classroom.
- to help them design lessons and activities for the classroom.

Without a comprehensive framework, teachers may tend to stress certain types of reading tasks while forgetting about others. Guszak[3] has found that elementary teachers tend to stress literal comprehension skills, particularly those related to recalling minutae. It is not inconceivable that some teachers might stress another pet area—such as pure enjoyment of reading, finding symbolism in everything, "correct" word calling, interpretive oral reading, etc. With a framework, teachers will be more aware of a variety of areas and subareas and will be better able to achieve a balance in the types of assignments given.

Many frameworks, or taxonomies, are available in the literature of the reading field and in the area of education in general. One need only look at the reading (or comprehension) objectives of several reading programs designed for individual or classroom use to realize this.[4] The philosophies of the authors and publishing company determine the objectives of each program.

The Barrett "Taxonomy of Reading Comprehension"

Recently, however, several taxonomies have emerged that are accepted by many. One of these is the Barrett "Taxonomy of Reading Comprehension." In framing this taxonomy, Barrett used the work of Benjamin Bloom, et al, in their volume *Taxonomy of Educational Objectives: Handbook I, Cognitive Domain*, of J.P. Guilford's "The Faces of Intellect," of Norris Sander's *Classroom Questions - What Kinds*, and of Frank Guszak's "Teachers' Questions and Levels of Reading Comprehension."[5] Each of these is in itself a classic in educational literature.

Barrett's desire was to formulate a taxonomy that differentiated levels and, within each level, tasks. His idea was that the Taxonomy should be used as a "teaching tool and not as a complete classification of comprehension abilities and tasks."[6] It is this taxonomy that is being used as the framework for the next section of this chapter* and the first part of Chapter 9, with certain specific deviations, as explained at appropriate places. The taxonomy is being used as a framework to illustrate skill development.

Levels

Of primary importance is to note that the taxonomy is divided into four levels: literal reading, inferential reading, evaluation, and appreciation. Each of these is briefly explained below.

*Literal Level (Text-Bound)*** Literal level activities, according to Barrett, require "recognition or recall of ideas, information, and happenings that are explicitly stated in the materials read. *Recognition Tasks* . . . require the student to locate or identify explicit statements in the reading selection itself or in exercises that use the explicit content of the reading selection."[7] *Recall Tasks* require that the student produce from memory explicit statements from a selection.

According to Norris Sanders,[8] another sublevel exists between what Barrett calls recognition and recall (literal level) and inference. This sublevel is termed *translation*. This will be included in the present chapter as another sublevel in the literal category for some activities. At the translation level, "The student changes information into a different symbolic form or language . . . Translation thinking is quite literal and does not require students to discover intricate relationships, implications, or subtle

---

* Thomas C. Barrett. "Taxonomy of Reading Comprehension," *Reading 360 Monograph*, 1972. Used by permission of the publisher, Ginn and Company (Xerox Corporation).
**Terms in parentheses in titles have been added by the present author and are not a part of Barrett's description.

meanings. The student identifies one part of the original communication at a time and translates it into the new form."[9] Such activities might include paraphrasing, making syntactical transformations (sentence surfing), changing information given in a word passage into graph, map, or chart form, or vice versa, and even literally acting out parts of a story or producing a sociodrama.

At the literal level, the reader is working within the author's framework. The reader is recognizing, recalling, and/or structuring the author's ideas in the author's way.

Inferential Level (Interactive Model: Text-Driven and Concept-Driven) Inferential level activities, Barrett's second major level, require the reader to synthesize, or combine, "the literal content of a selection (with) his personal knowledge, his intuition and his imagination as a basis for conjectures or hypotheses."[10] Inferences are continuations and extensions; they are reconstructions and recombinations, and in reading they change or go beyond the author's statements. Such combinations or recombinations may proceed along what J.P. Guilford[11] calls convergent or divergent lines.

Convergent production, or convergent synthesis, occurs when ideas are combined in usual, or traditional, ways. Divergent production, or divergent synthesis, comes about through combining ideas in unique, or unusual, ways. E.g., given the necessary materials and equipment and the assignment to build a bookcase, many students are likely to build one very much like one they have seen (convergent production). A few students, however, might design a new type of bookcase (divergent production).

In synthesizing ideas, sometimes students combine them convergently. (Some students tend to be convergent thinkers; and, also, some situations call for convergent thinking. E.g., in answering the question, What is the thing to do when someone is drowning? A convergent response is, "Try to save the person.") Sometimes, however, ideas are synthesized in a divergent manner. (Some students tend to be divergent thinkers; and, also, some situations may call for divergent thinking. E.g., after realizing that a drowning person should be saved, the best way to do it might differ vastly from individual to individual especially if there are unusual problems involved.)

Commonly, divergent production, or divergent synthesis, is called creativity: the combining of ideas and/or materials in unusual or unique ways. E. Paul Torrance, in a pamphlet called *Creativity*, notes that the components of creativity are "sensitivity to problems, fluency (the ability to produce a large number of ideas), flexibility (the ability to produce a variety of ideas or use a variety of approaches), originality (the ability to produce ideas that are off the beaten track), elaboration (the ability to fill in the details), and redefinition (the ability to define or perceive in a way different from the usual, established, or intended way, etc.)." Torrance also states that, "Scores derived from measures of creative thinking have little relationship to performance on intelligence tests." Teachers might, therefore, find students on many I.Q. levels to be divergent thinkers.

The activities described in the inferential sections in the present chapter may, in some cases, be even higher level reading-thinking activities. Some other authors might classify some of these activities as critical-creative reading-thinking activities.

Evaluation Level (Interactive Model: Text-Driven and Concept-Driven) Evaluation level activities require the student to make judgments about the content of a reading selection by comparing it with external criteria or internal criteria. External criteria is that external to the student, e.g., "information provided by the teacher on the subject, by authorities on the subject, or by accredited written sources on the subject" (text-bound: bottom-up). Internal criteria is that within the student (concept-bound: top-down), e.g., "the reader's experiences, knowledge, or values related to the subject under consideration."[12] To comprehend on the evaluation level, a student obviously must previously have had and/or must develop experiences beyond the immediate reading assignment itself. A concern common to all tasks at this level is: How does what the author is saying compare with what I know and feel to be true about the subject, and how does it compare with what authorities say about the subject?

Appreciation Level Appreciation level activities relate to the student's awareness of techniques, as well as forms, styles, or structures authors use to stimulate emotional responses within readers. Such tasks "require varying degrees of inference and evaluation, but their primary focus must be," according to Smith and Barrett, "on heightening students' sensitivity to the ways authors achieve an emotional as well as an intellectual impact on their readers." Such appreciation involves the recognition of and response to the "artistry involved in developing stimulating plots, themes, settings, incidents, and characters," and also, "the artistry involved in selecting and using stimulating language. . . ."[13]

Tasks

What Barrett calls tasks might be called skills by others. Following is the outline of his Taxonomy:

1.0 Literal Recognition or Recall
    1.1 Recognition or Recall of Details

1.2 Recognition or Recall of Main Ideas
1.3 Recognition or Recall of Sequence
1.4 Recognition or Recall of Comparisons
1.5 Recognition or Recall of Cause and Effect Relationships
1.6 Recognition or Recall of Character Traits
2.0 Inference
    2.1 Inferring Supporting Details
    2.2 Inferring the Main Idea
    2.3 Inferring Sequence
    2.4 Inferring Comparisons
    2.5 Inferring Cause and Effect Relationships
    2.6 Inferring Character Traits
    2.7 Inferring Outcomes
    2.8 Inferring about Figurative Language
3.0 Evaluation
    3.1 Judgments of Reality or Fantasy
    3.2 Judgments of Fact or Opinion
    3.3 Judgments of Adequacy or Validity
    3.4 Judgments of Appropriateness
    3.5 Judgments of Worth, Desirability, or Acceptability
4.0 Appreciation
    4.1 Emotional Response to Plot or Theme
    4.2 Identification with Characters and Incidents
    4.3 Reactions to the Author's Use of Language
    4.4 Imagery

The first two levels will be discussed in the present chapter; however, they will be reorganized in the following way:

Literal followed by Inferential Level Activities related to:

- Details
- Main Ideas
- Sequence, including Outcomes
- Comparisons
- Cause and Effect Relationships
- Following Directions*

Chapter 9 includes a discussion of Evaluation Level activities. Appreciation level activities, as outlined by Barrett, are normally a major part of

---

*Following Directions has been added, while Character Traits has been omitted from this chapter. Character Traits is included, instead, in Chapter 9. Figurative language was discussed in Chapter 7.

a course in children's literature. The present author has included a discussion of some of these in various places in this book. Building appreciation and interest will be dealt with in a different manner in this book. (See Chapters 9 and 10.)

Schema Theory

Among several interdisciplinary attempts to explore how readers comprehend, schema theory has emerged as a possible partial explanation. A schema might be considered a main idea or theme, subschema are the essential elements within the schema, and schemata is the plural of schema. Thus, if we look at a three course meal schema, we might expect to find as course one—soup or salad, course two—entrée and vegetables, course three—dessert. Each course is a subschema of a three course meal schema and might be further analyzed, e.g., what are the components of the soup or salad, etc. (These would be sub-subschema.)

"A schema represents generic knowledge, that is, what is believed to be generally true of a class of things, events, or situations." The schema is the "top of the hierarchy and must be sufficiently general to capture the essential aspects of all members of the class."[14] Yet, surely, it must also be specific enough to eliminate irrelevant aspects.

The schema, or context, renders subschema understandable. (And sometimes subschema makes schema understandable.) Mary Monteith quotes research done by others[15] in which the following sentences were used: "The lock that held him was strong, but he thought he could break it. He knew, however, that his timing would have to be perfect." Those readers working with the schema of prison interpreted the passage one way. However, those working with the schema of a wrestling match interpreted it in another way.* Additionally, most subjects reported that they were unaware of alternative interpretations. A conclusion that was drawn was that readers interpret subschema in light of their own frame of reference. The above example might also serve to reinforce the contention that individual words are ambiguous or meaningless by themselves. Context helps reveal the meanings of words and sentences.

In the present chapter, schema theory relates particularly well to the development of the following subskills: details, main idea, and sequence at both the literal and inferential levels. These three subskills can best be understood as they interrelate, rather than as separate entities.

---

*Another example cited in the literature is: "The notes were sour because the seams were split." This is understandable when the reader recognizes the schema to be "bagpipes." Future text clarifies the schema of "House" in the following sentence: "A woman's place is in the House . . . or the Senate."

Another interesting term related to schema theory has also emerged: "story grammar" or "text grammar." Instead of thinking of grammar as it relates to parts of speech within syntax, here one would think of grammar as representing the essential elements of a story (e.g., setting, theme, plot, resolution) as in "story grammar," or as the essential elements in a chapter in a science text, or mathematics text, etc. (text grammar). Story grammars and text grammars relate to sequence as discussed in this chapter and later chapters.

DEVELOPING THE CONCEPT OF SPECIFIC SKILLS FOR CHILDREN BY RELATING READING SKILLS TO FAMILIAR NON-READING EXPERIENCES

In order that children may benefit from reading skill development activities, it is essential that they have a concept of the skill being studied before it is studied and developed when using reading materials. Such concepts may be developed by using their experiences, and by using films or pictures. For example, the teacher might discuss with the children a picture one of them has drawn—of a rabbit eating.

To develop the concept of literal level schema tasks, or skills, the teacher and class might discuss schema first. The schema is the one thing the picture is all about (the highest order main idea, the theme). The children might be asked what the picture is all about. They might title it: "The Rabbit Eating the Grass." (Then, when reading a story or section of a story or chapter, they are asked what it is all about or to title it.)

Next discussed would be subschema,* the next order of main ideas. These can just be listed, or they can be put in an order (sequence). The children might be asked to identify the major parts of the picture, e.g.: the rabbit, the grass, the sky. (Then, when reading a story or chapter, they are asked to title it or judge the appropriateness of the author's title, and they are asked to tell the major parts of it and to put them in order.)

Next discussed might be sub-subschema, that is the details about the main ideas. The children might be asked to describe the main ideas:

the rabbit	*the grass*	*the sky*
(two brown) eyes	short grass	blue
(a rounded) nose	tall grass	(white) clouds
(short & long) whiskers	green grass	(yellow) sun
(two big) ears	dry tan grass	etc.
(a fluffy white) tail	etc.	
(soft brown) fur		
(four) legs		
(four soft) feet		
etc.		

Here they might include details the child artist included plus details they might like to add. They might even wish to delete some details that were included. (Then when reading a story or a chapter, they are asked to identify important details that relate to the main ideas. The teacher might help the children identify details the author included—text-bound—and also ideas the children think should have been included—concept-bound. They might also discuss the effect of adding and/or deleting certain details.)

To help children understand other tasks, e.g., sequence,** comparisons, cause-effect, and inferential and higher level skills the teacher might proceed thus:

- After the children have seen a picture, cover a part of it, and ask them what was in that part (spatial sequence, recall).
- Before the children have seen a picture, cover a part, and ask them what might be in that part (spatial sequence, inference level).

* If the schema is a theme, the subschema are main ideas of the theme, and the sub-schema are details. If the schema is a main idea, the subschema are details.

**There is a section later in this chapter showing the children how to relate sequence to their experiences.

- After the children have seen a picture, ask them, e.g., if the above picture were used, what the rabbit might do next (time sequence, inference level).
- Ask the children how the rabbit will feel after eating the grass (cause-effect, inference level).
- Ask the children what will happen if the rabbit eats all of the grass in a spot (cause-effect, inference level).
- Ask the children if the rabbit in the picture looks like the rabbits they have seen in nature (comparisons: analogies and contrasts, inference level). (This may be a cottontail, and they may have seen only jack rabbits).
- Help them describe the rabbit (language development).
- Ask them what time of day it is (main idea or detail, inference level).
- Ask them if they want to add anything to the picture or take anything out of it (adequacy, validity, appropriateness, evaluation level).
- Ask them if it's a picture of reality or fantasy (reality or fantasy, evaluation level).
- Ask them if rabbits eat grass and if it's their favorite food (fact or opinion, evaluation level).
- Ask them if they like the picture and would like to see more similar to it (worth, desirability, acceptability, evaluation level).
- Ask them if they would like to be a part of the picture and how the picture makes them feel (emotional response to theme, appreciation level).
- Ask them if they want to act in a skit as the rabbit, the grass, or the sun (identification with characters or incidents, appreciation level).
- Ask them how they feel about the way the painter drew the picture (the author used language). Do they like the painter's (author's) style (reactions to author's use of language, painter's style, appreciation level).
- Ask them if they can—in their imagination—touch the rabbit—how does it feel? Can they "hear" the rabbit chomping on the grass—how does it sound? How does the sun feel on their skin? What music might accompany the picture? (imagery, appreciation level).

Before working on a skill, the analysis of a picture might be stressed, and especially in relationship to the type of task, or skill, that is to be taught at that time: The teacher should be specific in selecting the type of task so that it is appropriate to the skill being taught. The teacher should assure himself or herself that the child understands the concept of the skill before working on the skill when using reading materials. Often that concept may be taught by using repetitions and variations of the suggestions given above.* Stories and familiar content area concepts might also be used, or might be used instead.

COMMENT

The next section of this chapter is organized according to Barrett's taxonomy, with deviations as previously noted. The activities, however, are the work of the present author.

In examining the explanations and suggested activities in this section, the reader of this book must understand that it is impossible to deal with these topics and subtopics as completely discrete items, for there is a great deal of overlapping both among levels and among skills. Debate about discrete, or very specific, levels and skills is academic. The discussions and suggested activities are designed to help the reader of this book formulate a viewpoint related to the area of reading comprehension as it refers to levels and tasks. The activities are designed to show examples at various grade levels in the elementary school and are not meant to be exhaustive. Content can be varied to produce activities at other grade levels and also appropriate to content being taught in the classroom.

Reading Skill Development: Literal and Inferential Levels

This section is provided to explain and exemplify ways of teaching selected reading skills at the literal and inferential levels.

*1.0 and 2.0** Literal and Inferential Reading*

SCHEMA AND SUBSCHEMA (DETAILS, MAIN IDEAS, SEQUENCE)

Details

Details are items, specific points, fine points, perhaps trivia. They are subschema of a main point; that is, details are small component parts of a larger part or of a whole. Sometimes details are extremely important, es-

---

* The above example is spatial order. Time order might also be used, as in a baseball game, etc. Logical order might also be used, as in giving the important parts of a recipe, etc.

**Numbers refer to the Barrett taxonomy.

pecially as they function to give color, balance, and understanding to a main idea. Sometimes details are mere trivia and might best be passed over rapidly.

At the literal level, children are asked to do one of the following:

- recognize (identify), usually with the text visible,
- recall (remember), usually with the text covered,
- translate (change the form of), with the text visible or covered,

such things as the names of minor characters, the time of an occurrence or discussion, a minor setting, or a minor incident when such information has been given by the author. (These are details if, or when, they are not major components of the discussion.)

At the inferential level, children are asked to conjecture about additional details the author might have included that would have made the passage more informative, interesting, or appealing.

As explained later under evaluation, children might also judge the adequacy, validity, appropriateness, worth, etc., of the details included.

The following examples of questions and activities are meant to demonstrate different formats that might be used in working with details.

1.1.1 Recognition or Recall of Details

The children have just read a brochure on zoos and petting zoos.

□ *Examples of Questions Focusing on Details*

1. Name as many animals as you can remember that were discussed in the brochure you just read on zoos and petting zoos. (recall)
2. Page through your brochure on zoos and petting zoos, and write down the names of the animals that were discussed. (recognition)
3. Circle the names of the animals discussed, and cross out the names of those that were not discussed. (recall and recognition):
      giraffe   kangaroo   tiger   dachshund   (etc.)
4. How much does the average adult lion weigh?
      a. 300 pounds   b. 400 pounds   c. 250 pounds   d. _______
5. How tall is the average giraffe?
6. What colors are tigers?
7. Circle the names of animals that hibernate:
      woodchucks   porpoise   bears   (etc.)
8. When do lions sleep?

9. What is the temperature of the room in which the penguins are kept at the zoo?
10. Are elephants carnivorous? herbivorous? omnivorous?
11. How much per day would it cost this class to feed a giraffe? _____ a lion? _____ a tiger? _____
12. Where is the petting zoo that is discussed? _______________
13. When was this brochure written? _______________

For these to be recall or recognition questions, the author must have given the answers. All the reader must do to answer the questions is either recall the information (i.e., remember it from the passage), or recognize it (i.e., refer to the passage or the item for the answer).

1.1.2 Translation of Details Translation questions or activities require the reader to change the information to another form without altering the ideas of the author. The reader is still performing at the literal level. Translation activities that relate to detailed information might include: paraphrasing, literally defining terms and identifying an equivalent term in another language (especially useful for ESL children).

□*Examples of Translation Questions and Activities*

1. Define *carnivorous*: _______________________________
   herbivorous: _______________________________
   omnivorous: _______________________________
2. What does *carn* mean? (flesh)
   "   "   *herb*   "   (plant)
   "   "   *omni*   "   (all)
   "   "   *vorous* "   (eating, feeding on)
3. List additional words that use these roots:
   (carn: *carn*al, *carn*ival, in*carn*ate)
   (herb: *herb*icide, *herb*s)
   (omni: *omni*potent, *omni*directional, *omni*bus)
4. Many of the denotative vocabulary activities given in Chapter 7 (pages 231–266) would qualify here.
5. Give the Spanish (French, German, Polish, etc.) word for elephant _______________, lion _______________, tiger _______________, etc. (Children might use an English-Spanish, English-French, etc. dictionary to find equivalents. Or, they might ask if anyone knows the answers. Pictures might be used as a reference point, and children might name the animals the pictures depict.)

6. Match the name of the animal with a picture of it. E.g.:

A. lion   B. tiger   C. giraffe
D. kangaroo   E. lamb   F. elephant

( )   ( )   ( )

( )   ( )   ( )

□ *Rebus* The children may have read a passage in which the rebus technique was used. They are asked to name the intended words, e.g.: The petting zoo had [rabbits] in one corner and a young [kangaroo] in another. A baby [lamb] was asleep, while the [anteater] was moving from one end to another of the [cage].

□ *Adaptation of Rebus* An adaptation of the rebus technique is for the teacher to read a passage, and when he or she comes to a word (or idea), instead of pronouncing the word (or reading the subpoint), the teacher shows a picture of it. The children supply the term. This could also be done when a child is reading and is unable to recognize a term.

Variation. Flannel board characters, puppets, etc., might be used. Even short verbal or musical descriptions might be used.

□*Map* Children may be asked where the petting zoo is. They might respond that it's at the Downtown Shopping Center. Then they might be asked to locate it on a city map.

2.1 Inferring Supporting Details (What additional details might the author have included to make the passage more informative, interesting, or appealing?) Examples of activities are:

□*Characteristics* Ask the children to list as many characteristics (subschema) as they can for one or more of the main ideas or details (either of which now becomes the schema). At the literal level, they will list those subschema the author has given. At the inferential level, they will add to the author's statements, probably from their backgrounds of experience. (At the evaluation and appreciation levels, they may seek out library resources and research subtopics, or subschema, in which they are especially interested. At these higher levels they will also judge the adequacy, validity, worth, etc., of the author's and their own subschema.) E.g.:

level	Elephant Characteristics		
	physical	*behavioral*	*uses*
l i t e r a l	size: huge color: grey food: herbivorous ⋮	diurnal ⋮	beast of burden ivory ⋮
i n f e r e n t i a l	class: mammal order: proboscidian life span: _______ ⋮	% of time spent in activity: _______ in rest: _______ ⋮ behavior toward their young: _______ ⋮	circus performer provides rides ⋮

Variation. The teacher might supply subschema and ask the children to classify them.

□ *Related Ideas* The teacher may state the main idea, or schema, and list items or sentences that may or may not enhance or support it. Children circle letters for items that add to the main idea (or support or clarify the schema) and "X" items that are irrelevant or detract from the main idea. E.g.:

1. Petting or playing with some zoo animals would be fun for all.
   (a.) Children would enjoy petting a cat or kitten.
   (b.) Most would like to ride a llama.
   X. Children should be encouraged to make friends with a grown lion. (false statement)
   X. And baby birds should be held to comfort them. (false statement)
   (e.) A lamb would delight almost everyone.
   f, g, h, etc. (child adds ideas)
2. Unless they are pets, carnivorous animals other than humans must hunt for their food.
   (a.) Lions reign supreme, eating their choice of wild animals.
   X. Elephants eat large trees—branch by branch. (irrelevant, since elephants are not carnivorous)
   (c.) Owls are dependent on many types of insects for food.
   X. Deer chase wild animals such as coyotes and fox for food. (false statement)
   X. Cattle eat mice, rats, woodchucks and other small animals they find on a farm. (false statement)
   f, g, h, etc. (child adds ideas)

□ *Use Children's Reading Materials* Take paragraphs from children's materials, including newspaper articles if the children are old enough. Ask children to look at each sentence or statement to see if it is needed or if it adds to the completeness of the paragraph. Ask if any more detailed information is needed.
Variation. Show children a picture. Ask them to point out details and to tell if they belong. Why or why not? Ask if other items might have been included to make the picture more complete or interesting.

□ *Use the CLOZE* Technique* Take passages from the children's reading materials in which important details are given. Delete these

---

*CLOZE technique: a visual image (letter, word, phrase, etc.) is deleted, and an underscoring is substituted. The reader uses the contextual information provided and his or her background of information to fill in the blank.

items, and substitute an underscoring. Ask children to fill in the blanks. There are several variations that might be used:

- *List clues at top of page.* Children select from these:

1945	1941	Pearl Harbor	Atlantic
1968	1917	Iwo Gima	Pacific
1937	1943	Hiroshima	Australia

1. On December 7, ____________, Japanese planes flew over the ____________ toward ____________. The United States was soon to suffer its most devastating attack in history.
2. Early in August, ____________, an American plane sought its Japanese target, carrying the product of one of the best kept secrets in modern times—the atom bomb. Soon ____________ was to be destroyed.
3. Etc.

- *Give initial letter clues.* Children complete the rest.

1. O ____________ u ____________ a t ____________ there were three little bears—a m ____________ bear, a p ____________ bear, and a b ____________ bear. (Once, upon, time, mama, papa, baby)
2. . . . there was a f ____________ called Mr. Jeremy Fisher; he lived in a little damp h ____________ amongst the b ____________ at the edge of a p ____________ . (frog, hutch, bushes, pond)
3. One m ____________ a little rabbit sat on a b ____________ . . . a gig was coming along the r ____________ ; it was driven by Mr. McGregor, and b ____________ him sat Mrs. McGregor in her best b ____________ . (morning, bench, road, beside, bonnet)
4. Etc.

(These would be recall items if the children had already read the stories or passages. Any answer that makes sense might be accepted. . . The teacher may wish to read these sentences to the children and give the children the letters by name or written on the board.)

- *Give no clues.* Children fill in the blanks. (Sometimes more than one word could make sense in a blank.)

1. It was the last Thursday of November. The Pilgrims were preparing for their first ____________. They were a small band of Christians with an immense devotion to ____________.
2. It was the overpowering desire for the ____________ to practice their religious beliefs that sent the Pilgrims first to Holland, then to ____________.

3. In selecting _____________ for their new home, the Pilgrims chose the one site in all _____________ where there were no Indians to _____________ for the land.
4. Etc.

☐ *Related Syntactic Forms: Anaphoric Forms—Noun Forms and Pronoun Forms* Teach children to identify referents by using noun and pronoun forms. For example:

*noun form:** Michelle and Hank went swimming. Michelle enjoys swimming, but Hank doesn't like to swim.
Who enjoys swimming? _____________
Who doesn't enjoy swimming? _____________

*pronoun form:*** Michelle and Hank went swimming. She enjoys swimming, but he doesn't like to swim.
Who enjoys swimming? _____________
Who doesn't enjoy swimming? _____________

*pronoun form:*** Michelle and Hank went swimming. They enjoyed it.
They = _____________   it = _____________

☐ *Related Syntactic Forms: Anaphoric Forms—Noun, Pronoun, and Null Forms* Teach children to identify referents when the null form is used (that is, when the pronoun is not stated). For example:

*noun form:** Henrietta took Susan to the party. Henrietta enjoyed taking Susan.
Who took Susan? _____________
*pronoun form:**** Henrietta took Susan to the party. She enjoyed taking her.
She = _____________   her = _____________
*null form:**** Henrietta took Susan to the party and enjoyed taking her.
Who enjoyed taking her? _____________   (her = _____________)

*noun form:** Anna gave Rover a bone. Rover took the bone away.
Who took the bone away? _____________
*pronoun form:*** Anna gave Rover a bone, and he took it away.
he = _____________   it = _____________
*pronoun form:**** Timmy gave Rover a bone, and he took it away.
he = _____________ or _____________ (ambiguous) it = _____________
*null form:**** Timmy gave Rover a bone and took it away.
Who took it away? _____________   (it = _____________)

---

*   Recognition of details (literal).
**   Translation of details (literal).
*** Inferential level.

*pronoun form:*** President Reagan tried to get his tax bill passed, but he had much trouble.

his = _____________   he = _____________

*null form:**** President Reagan tried to get his tax bill passed, but had much trouble.

Who had much trouble? _____________   (his = _____________)

□ *Related Syntactic Forms: Anaphoric Forms—Forward and Backward Reference* Teach children to identify referents both when they follow and precede their references. For example:

*forward reference:*** The show was good. I really liked it.

it = _____________

I like to swim. It's fun.

it = _____________

John and Harry had a fight. They were angry.

They = _____________.

*backward reference:*** I really liked it. The show was good.

it = _____________

It's fun. I like to swim.

it = _____________

They were angry, so John and Harry had a fight.

They = _____________

□ *Anaphoric Chains** or **** Use longer passages in teaching children to "chain" (thus to identify) linkages. Use different colors in chaining different linkages. For example:

Susan and Gary sometimes played together, but she was most happy when fishing, and he preferred to play ball. She sometimes played on his team, and he occasionally put the worm on her hook. He didn't like catching fish, though.

□ *Use a Year for Schema* Subschema, then, may be important happenings during the year. (Subschema might also be weather, length of days, etc.) For young children, use pictures to suggest time of year. Ask children to match season with picture. E.g.:

** Translation of details (literal).
***Inferential level.

Spring   Summer   Fall   Winter

Fall

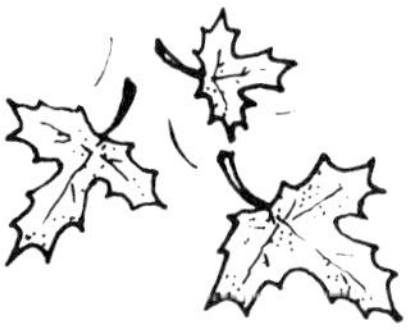

You may wish to ask children about other things that happen during these seasons.

□ *Subschema for Schema* Ask children what comes to mind when they think of:

the sun	a vacation	television
the moon	a picnic	making their bed
a garden	arithmetic class	doing the dishes
a woods	science class	a free afternoon

You may wish to help them map (or web) these. E.g.,

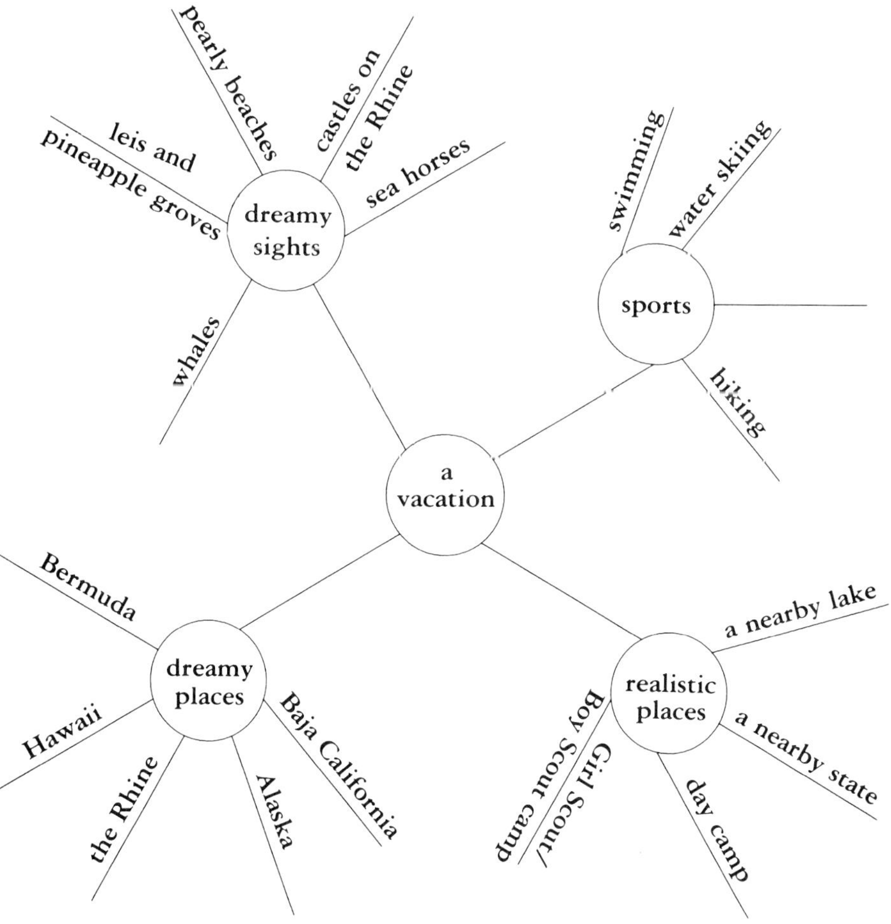

□*Nature: When and Where?* Give children written or picture clues. Ask them to supply time, place, and reason.* E.g.:

Clue	When?	Where?	Why?
1. The explorers found an immense polar bear hibernating for the season.			
2. The squirrels were seen collecting acorns and nuts for the season to come.			
3. On a high wire, a mother robin was observed teaching her young to fly. She became impatient, and pushed one off. We cheered, for it succeeded.			
4. Our yard was filled with robins and indigo buntings. What a marvelous sight. But they would stay only a week.			
5. Hundreds of Canada geese winged their way north.			
6. The mallards were grouping on the almost frozen waters. Soon they would depart for a warmer climate.			
7. Etc.			

Main Ideas

Main ideas are frequently called central thoughts. They're the ideas (schema) that are broad enough to encompass all the details (subschema) that relate to them. Yet they are specific enough to exclude irrelevant thoughts.

When developing main idea skills at the literal level, children are asked to do one of the following:

- recognize (locate or identify the main idea), usually with the text visible,
- recall (remember the main idea), usually with the text covered,
- translate (change the form of the main idea, perhaps by paraphrasing it.

At the inferential level, children are required to provide the main idea or theme, or general significance of a passage, when such is not given by the author.

Following are activities at the above levels. To provide background for understanding the main idea in reading materials, some simple examples

---

*These are probably not all questions of detail.

may be needed to show children what is meant by main idea. Such examples are included here also.

1.2.1 Recognition or Recall of Main Ideas

Examples of activities:

□*Family Names* To help children understand the concept of main idea, it might be well to begin by working with "family names," i.e., main ideas or schema, and relating these to details, or subschema. This can be done on several levels of difficulty. E.g.:

- *step 1*: Provide a list of "family names" (main ideas). Also group like items. Children match family name with group members (requires inductive or deductive recall), e.g.:
family names: processes, geometric figures, units of measurement

(units of measurement)

feet	add	triangles
inches	subtract	squares
yards	multiply	circles
acres	divide	rectangles
miles		

- *step 2*: Combine family name with subpoints. Children circle family name (requires inductive or deductive recall), e.g.:

addition	bu. gal.	+
subtraction	min. yd.	−
(processes)	pt.	×
multiplication	qt.	signs
division	abbreviations	÷

- *step 3*: Group like items, but do not supply family names. Children supply family names (requires inductive recall), e.g.:

(fractions)

numerator	bushel	cent
denominator	gallon	quarter
one-half	quart	dime
3/4	pint	nickel
	peck	penny

Variation: For younger children, content should be made easier, to relate directly to their interests and backgrounds. E.g., days of the week, months of the year, games they enjoy, characters from books they have read or heard read, etc., supply content.

□ *Multiple Choice* Ask children to read a paragraph or several consecutive paragraphs. Give them several multiple choice items, from which they select the one that is the main idea, as stated by the author (recognition). E.g.:

> Many birds are found in our aviary. Tiny ruby throated hummingbirds are in cages with cardinals, wrens, and yellow finches. Beside them is another cage with bell quail, robins, wild turkey and blue jays. A small pone supplies water for mallards and other wild ducks. Flying free and perching on the trees in the center are parrots—some of brilliant plume—and myna birds. Don't be surprised if one whistles at you!

The main idea of this paragraph is:
a.   Don't be surprised if a myna bird whistles at you.
b.   Cardinals, wrens, yellow finches and hummingbirds are together in one cage.
c.   Many birds are found in our aviary.

Instead, you might wish to ask the children to read a paragraph, cover it, and *state the main idea* (recall, if the main idea was given).

□ *Use Symbols* ▽ ⊠ △ ⬦ ◯   Ask children to underline main idea statements in paragraphs (recognition). Then ask them to use the correct symbol to show where the main idea was found. This is done to emphasize that main ideas may be found anywhere. (The horizontal line indicates the placement of the main idea.)

▽ = first sentence
⊠ = first and last sentences
△ = last sentence
⬦ = within the paragraph or section
◯ = not stated

1. <u>Many birds are found in our aviary.</u> Tiny ruby throated hummingbirds are in cages with cardinals, (etc., as above.)   <u>▽</u>
2. Adelie penguins love to dive into the frigid pool and swim and frolic with one another. Before you know it, they've jumped ashore—almost too fast for the eye to see. Then they'll dive in the water again. The larger emperor penguins appear more regal, but they love the water, too. They get

along well with the Adelies. Both are native to the Antarctic regions of the Southern hemisphere. <u>You will enjoy seeing our two species of penguins from Anarctica playing in the water.</u>   <u>Δ</u>

3. Giraffes, with very long necks and legs and tan coats with brown spots, are found in their own area, which is much like their African homeland. Elephants are just beyond them to the north. You'll notice their large trunks and curved tusks. Their zoo territory resembles that of south-central Asia, for these are Asian elephants.

   To the west you'll find mule deer, natives of western North America. They have long ears, two-pronged antlers and are brownish grey. Their area, too, is designed to be like their native land.   <u>O</u>

4. <u>In the petting zoo, you'll find small and friendly animals that children may touch and even play with.</u> There are three lambs that are very comfortable when people are around. There's a llama, a native of South America, that looks like a small camel without a hump. Children sometimes ride on llamas. There are piglets, too, a few kittens and puppies, and even a small goat. <u>Children will enjoy all of these animals.</u>   <u>X</u>

5. You may hear a chirp, a trill, and a tweet. Perhaps you'll note a whistle, a cackle or caw—or maybe a hoot, a tu-whoo, or tu-whit. <u>If you do, you'll know you're in the aviary; but if you hear these, you're elsewhere:</u> a bark or a cry, a howl or a yowl, a bleat, a hiss or a roar, a growl or a snarl . . . or even a rattle.   <u>⊕</u>

From multiple examples like these, children should conclude that main idea statements may be found anywhere in a paragraph or series of paragraphs.

1.2.2 Translation of Main Ideas Translation activities require the reader to do a little more than the preceding with the information. Children may state the main idea in their own words or match a paragraph (or several paragraphs) with its main idea.

Activities might be like these:

□ *Paraphrase the Main Idea Statement* Ask children to identify the author's main ideas and then to state them in their own words. E.g., take main idea statements like those above.

Restate in your own words:
1. "Many birds are found in our aviary." Children respond:

- Our bird house has lots of birds.
- There are lots of different birds in our big bird cage.
2. "You will enjoy seeing our two species of penguins from Antarctica playing in the water." Children respond:
- Visitors will like seeing two kinds of penguins playing in the water.
- Two different kinds of penguins from Antarctica can be seen playing in water.
3. Etc.

□ *Match Main Idea Statement with Text or Picture* Cut main idea or thesis statements or pictures off paragraphs or articles before the children read them. Ask children to match the main idea with the correct paragraph or article. This might best be done with photocopies or with newspaper or magazine articles. (See page 325.)

2.2 Inferring the Main Idea (The children provide the main idea or general significance of the passage. They may provide the main idea, i.e., schema, for the details, i.e., subschema, the author has given.) Examples of activities follow.

□ *Supply Titles for Pictures or Stories* Children are shown pictures, or use their own, and title them. Also they may supply titles for stories they read or that are read to them.

□ *Interpreting Subschema from Schema* Children may be shown that they interpret subschema according to the schema they have in mind. If they have incorrectly inferred the schema, perhaps because of limited experience or insufficient evidence, they will misinterpret the subschema. E.g.:

meaning?	schema (concept)
puppet	shows for children, governments
story	a house, t.v. programs, lies
Washington	cities, states, Presidents, money, monuments
wind	weather, clocks
spread	a bed, disease, food, gossip
pumpkin	Halloween, a child
pound	money, weight, ways of hitting things
horse	animals, woodworking
pupil	eyes, school

□ *Syntactical Synthesis* Sometimes when an author has not stated a main idea, students can decide what it is by synthesizing like sentence parts. For example, we might look at the paragraph

1 Trapped Couple Waiting For Hatching Of Eggs

2 Wolves to share in song royalties

3 Today I'm playing for the polar bears

4 Sea turtles: help swims into view

Early Bird Gets the Basket

5

By Sara Terry

Los Angeles

Most musicians would probably consider it pretty stiff criticism when dogs tilt back their heads and howl in accompaniment. But when Paul Winter plays his saxophone and coaxes timberwolves to bay in low, bittersweet reply, it's a response that is, quite literally, music to his ears.

Mr. Winter, a widely respected jazz musician and leader of the Paul Winter Consort has played tapes of timberwolves and humpback whales during his concert performances for the past several years. But it wasn't until "Common Ground," his latest album, that he put animal sounds on record.

Unlike albums that consist mainly of animal calls, Mr. Winter has integrated the cries of such endangered species as the humpback whale and the timberwolf into the mainstream of the Consort's music.

The results are fascinating, particularly in the case of "Wolf Eyes," a hauntingly lovely duet between the saxophonist and two timberwolves. Mr. Winter gave the wolves credits as co-authors and has pledged the royalties from the song to an organization that is trying to protect the last 300 timberwolves living in the continental United States.

I was sitting on a bench in the weekend sunshine, waiting for the bus. Next to me sat an old man in a pale-blue suit, a white, widebrimmed sun hat on his head.

"Lovely day," he said.

"Beautiful."

"You play that instrument there?" he asked, nodding at the banjo on my lap.

"I pluck away at it."

"It seems all the young people these days play something or other. I've got a grandson who plays the fiddle."

"Oh, yeah?"

"He taps his foot so hard he's wearing out his shoe."

I laughed. "I'm not that dedicated. I just play for myself, and my friends. And sometimes for the creatures in the zoo. That's where I'm headed today."

Usually when I tell people I play my banjo for the creatures in the zoo, something I've been doing ever since I taught myself to play five years ago, they look at me as if they think I might be putting them on. But my bench companion seemed delighted by this revelation.

"Hah," he exclaimed. "I like that."

"They're a great audience," I said, elaborating. "I go into the monkey house and play, 'Yes, We Have No Bananas,' and they clap their hands and their feet and do somersaults in midair, and I feel like I'm in Carnegie Hall."

"The zoo people, the ones who look after the animals, they let you do this?"

"Sure, why not? The animals love it, the kids love it. It kind of brings a little freedom to everybody."

"I'll have to tell my grandson."

"Maybe he and I could do duets."

"Well, they say that that's the way a lot of musicians have gotten started."

"Of course, you can't play for all the creatures," I said. "Some of them just don't appreciate music, or at least my music. They've got some exotic birds out there, you know, chartreuse and pink and lavender and scarlet, ones with those lobster-claw beaks and bloodshot eyes, man, they just glower at me like they'd love to see me sinking like a stone in the Amazon."

"Hah!" The old man slapped his knee.

"Today I'm going to play for the polar bears. They're beautiful. They just sit up there on their rocks, like overgrown kids with their tongues hanging out, and they drink it in. I give them a lot of razzmataz — 'Alexander's Ragtime Band,' 'The Darktown Strutters' Ball' — to help them take their minds off the heat. Can you imagine how hot they must get on a day like this? Those bears ought to be up there in the Yukon, having snowball fights with the Eskimos."

David Mann

6

Fern and Jim Miller watch a nesting robin on the propane tank of their trailer. Because the Millers are parked on state grounds, conservation measures prohibit them from moving the trailer until the birds are hatched and leave the nest. (AP Laserphoto)

By Chris Kemrick
Staff correspondent of The Christian Science Monitor
Washington

It is said Christopher Columbus never would have made it to the New World without being able to use then-plentiful sea turtles for sustenance.

But today the world population of sea turtles has so dwindled that the U.S. Government — after years of debate — is taking action to prevent their extinction.

Some environmentalists say it is already too late to save many of the turtle habitats. Even the federal official who is initiating the program to save the turtles admits "it should have been done years ago."

previously given (page 323), marked with O, indicating that no main idea was stated:

Giraffes, with very long necks and legs and tan coats with brown spots, are found in their own area, which is much like their African homeland. Elephants are just beyond them to the north. You'll notice their large trunks and curved tusks. Their zoo territory resembles that of south-central Asia, for these are Asian elephants.

To the west you'll find mule deer, natives of western North America. They have long ears, two-pronged antlers and are brownish grey. Their area, too, is designed to be like their native land.

Subjects of major sections:
  giraffes, elephants, mule deer   >   =   animals
Verbs of major sections:
  are found, are, (you)'ll find   >   = are found
Completers (where they are found):
  in their own area—like homeland   =   in areas
  to the north—resembles south-   resembling
    central Asia   their homelands
  to the west—like their native land,
  western North America

Main Idea: Animals are found in areas resembling their homelands.

To be able to do this, children must be able to recognize subjects and verbs. Often they must also be able to recognize complete kernels of sentences if the kernel goes beyond subject-verb. They might be taught to do this in the following steps:

- *first:* Teach them to recognize the subject (noun) of a sentence. Ask them to underline the noun (N) in each of a series of sentences:

1. Maria is singing a pretty song.
2. Dee went home.
3. The house is being painted white.
4. John threw the ball.

• *second*: Teach them to recognize the verb (V) of a sentence. Ask them to underline the verb with two underscorings.

1. Maria is singing a pretty song.
2. Dee went home.
3. The house is being painted white.
4. John threw the ball.

• *third*: Give them experience with a variety of patterns to help them recognize common kernels, (N = subject noun, N_2 = predicate noun, N_3 = second predicate noun, V = verb, Lv = linking verb, A = adjective, Ad = adverb).

1. Henry is singing.	(NV)
2. Henry is singing happily.	(NVAd)
3. John threw the ball.	(NVN_2)
4. Beth named her dog Bandit.	(NVN_2N_3)
5. Honey is a hamster.	$(NLvN_2)$
6. Honey is hungry.	(NLvA)
7. Honey is here.	(NLvAd)

• *finally*: Combine the two processes of underlining kernels of sentences and finding family names to induce the main idea of a paragraph. (This process will work with some, but not all paragraphs. It works best with paragraphs that are developed in logical order, simple listing.) E.g.:

1. Beth named her dog Bandit. Alyce called her cat Cinnamon. Jennifer named her pet hamster Honey. And Rosalee chose Suzie for the name of her poodle.

N_1 = Beth, Alyce, Jennifer, Rosalee   > =   my cousins
V = named, called, named, chose   > =   named
N_2 = dog, cat, hamster, poodle   > =   their pets
N_3 = Bandit, Cinnamon, Honey, Suzie   > =   differently?

Main idea: My cousins (or whatever the relationship of the girls is) named their pets differently (or however you wish to synthesize these names, e.g., by pretty names, names that characterize them, etc.)

2.

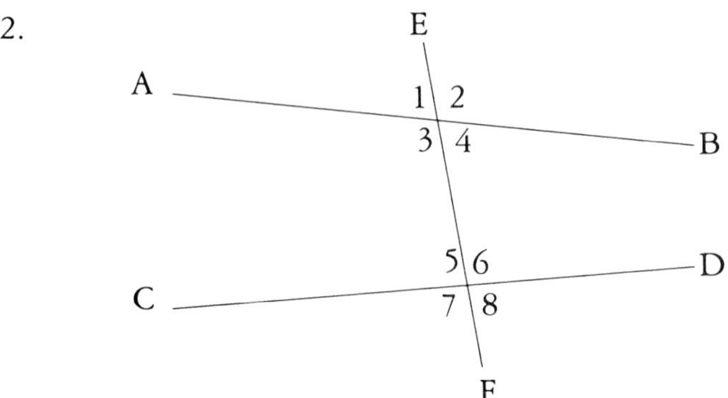

The angles 1, 2, 7, 8 are called exterior angles. Angles 3, 4, 5, 6 are interior angles. Angles 3 and 6 are alternate interior angles, as are 4 and 5. Pairs of corresponding angles are angles 1 and 5, 3 and 7, 2 and 6, 4 and 8.

[This is simple enough to hold the subjects (angles being described) in mind without underlining. The same is true of the verbs: (are called).]

N_2 = exterior angles, interior angles, alternate interior angles, corresponding angles ⟩ = by different names

Main idea: Angles are called by different names (according to their positions).

3. Sometimes it is necessary to make an inference in synthesizing similar grammatical elements, e.g.:

Yesterday Jane and Pam rode the roller coaster and the whip snap. Harry, Jack, and John threw bean bags at decoys to win prizes. Sue watched the man on the flying trapeze. Everyone had a good time.

N_1 = Jane and Pam, Harry, Jack, John, Sue, everyone ⟩ = We, the Jones family, i.e., whatever the relationship is

$V + N_2$ = rode the roller coaster and the whip-snap threw bean bags, watched the man on the flying trapeze, had a good time ⟩ Where are such things done?

Main idea by inference: Yesterday we went to a carnival.

Sequence

In schema theory, sequence is called "story grammar" or "text grammar." Sequence refers to the components of a whole arranged in some type of order. Sequence refers to a continuous connected series, the "chaining" of events or ideas.

The chaining of events or ideas may be accomplished by using the following patterns:

- time order, as is common in stories and history texts,
- space order, as on maps, in comparing people or events or land formations from country to country or area to area,
- logical order, as stories that fit into a theme (e.g., a trilogy), major classifications of animals, etc.
- affective order, or the order of preferences.

To help children understand these patterns and get a sense of what sequence (or order) means, it might be well first to relate them to the children's own experiences. Following this, children might recognize, recall, translate, and infer (and even react to) patterns used by authors.

Relating Sequential Patterns to Children's Experiences—Background for Reading Skill Development Each of the patterns listed above lends itself to specific types of "mapping, webbing, or charting" visual aids. Using such aids helps children understand relationships. Some of the major types of illustrations are exemplified here.

<u>Time Lines</u> To teach children about time order, you might ask them about major things they do during the day—in time order. You might put these in a time line.

Important Events in My Day		
	time	
Morning	6	
	7	breakfast
	8	go to school
	9	
	10	} classes
	11	
Afternoon	12	lunch
	1	
	2	} classes
	3	
	4	sports
	5	read/help with dinner

Important Events in My Day		
	time	
Evening	6	dinner
	7	watch TV
	8	visit
	9	go to bed
	10	

<u>Flow Charts</u> Some events in time order might be shown on flow charts. For example:

Seasons of the Year

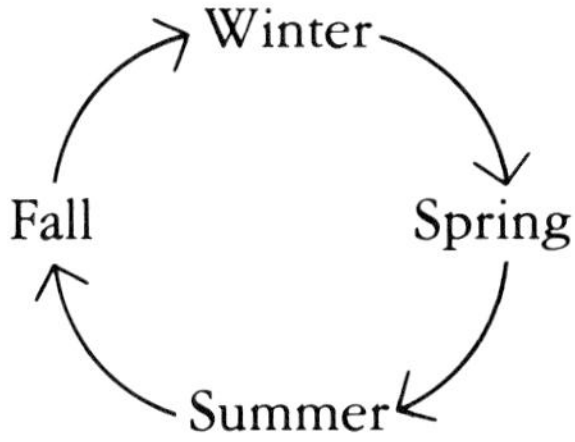

Steps in a Neighborhood Baseball Game

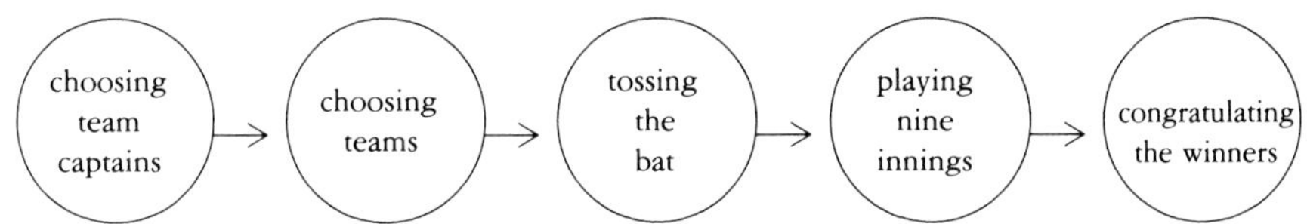

<u>Maps</u> Spatial order relationships can be shown on maps.

A Baseball Diamond

Map of Our School Neighborhood

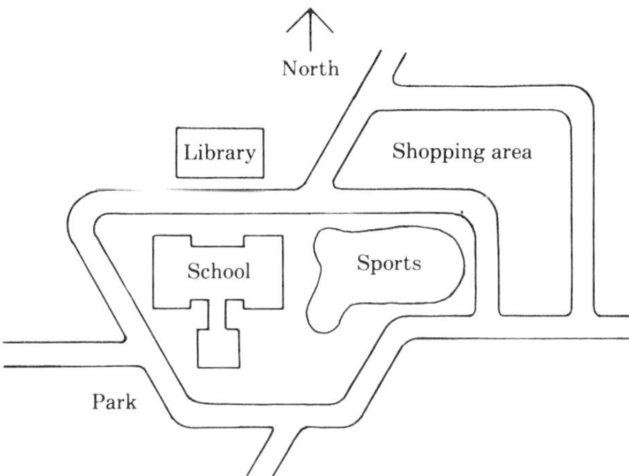

<u>Charts</u> Logical order and affective order relationships can be shown by using various charts, among them are the *spoke graph*, or webs, used for simple listings related to a main idea or theme:

My Favorite Pastimes

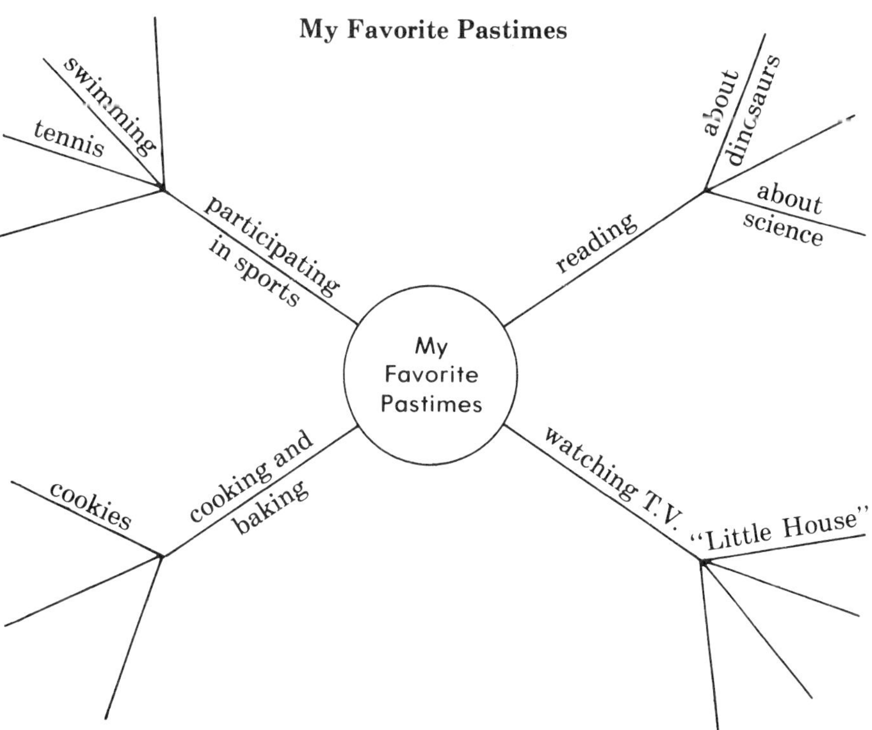

the *pie graph*, used to show proportional relationships within 100 percent of something:

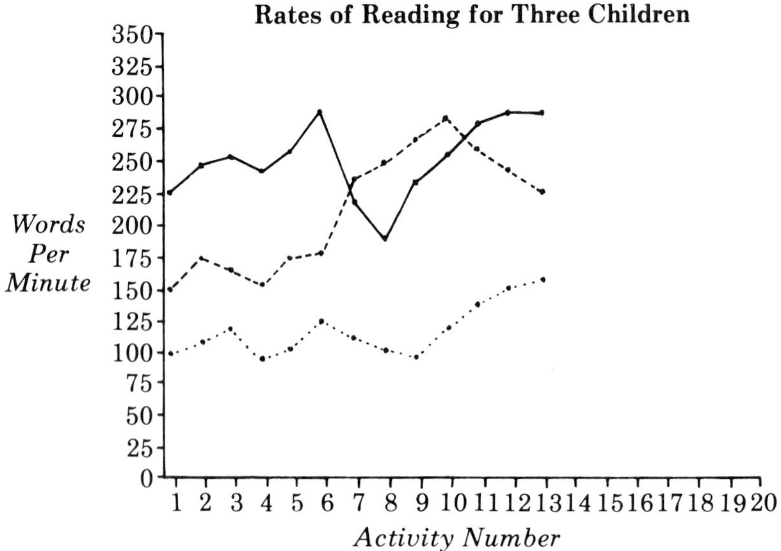

the *line graph*, used for making comparisons:

the *bar graph*, used for recording quantities:

Number of Books Read by Children in Our Class This Year

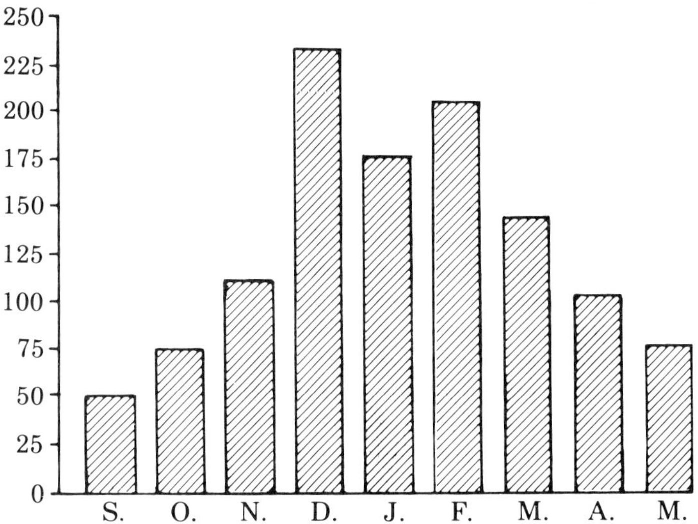

(Many of the illustrations given here can also be used for other purposes than those given.)

the *pictograph*, used for recording quantities:

**Our School's Contribution to Our Zoo's
"Buy an Animal a Dinner" Fund**

Sept. + Oct.	
Nov. + Dec.	
Jan. + Feb.	
March + April	
May + June	
July + Aug.	

key: = $5.00

the *chart*, used for classifying information:

	Characteristics of Holidays			
Holiday	Reason for Holiday	Characteristic Music	Typical Foods	(etc.)
Fourth of July	U.S. Declaration of Independence	"Stars and Stripes Forever" (etc.)	hot dogs, hamburgers, ice cream (etc.)	
Thanksgiving	Gratitude for good received USA/Canada	"We thank thee and we bless thee . . . " (etc.)	turkey, pumpkin pie, corn, yams (etc.)	
Christmas	Birth of Jesus	"White Christmas" "Silent Night" (etc.)	ham/turkey, cookies, plum pudding (etc.)	
(etc.)				

If your purpose in using such visual aids is to show organization, the illustrations should not be cluttered. A good principle to try to follow is to never (or only rarely) include more than four or five points at any level. If you include more than four or five points at one level, you're dealing with an excessive amount of nonsynthesized information—too many details to indicate organization, or sequence.

Thus if you are considering using an outline as a visual aid, you would not have more than five main points, nor more than five subpoints under any main point. If there seem to be more, some must be synthesized, or combined. Also, in outlining, if there is one point at any level, there must be at least two points at that level, since outlining is dividing, and nothing can be divided into one piece.

Outlining–Background for Reading Skill Development Today there are two commonly used outline formats: the Roman and Arabic forms. Children should be introduced to both of these.

□ *Teaching About Outlining (or Putting Main Ideas Together in an Outline Format)* To teach outlining, *per se*, you may wish to follow these steps (some of these are drawn from, or are closely related to, the two previous sections on details and main ideas).

   • *step 1*: Supply family names (main ideas) in outline form. List subpoints (details) ungrouped. Children fill in subpoints under appropriate headings (requires inductive or deductive recall). E.g. #1:

Sounds of Nature

---

meow	chirp	cock-a-doodle	low
moo	bark	neigh	whine
roar	trill	squeek	honk
coo	yowl	snarl	etc.

Roman Numeral Format
   I. Pet Sounds
      A. (meow)
      B.
      etc.
  II. Farm Animal Sounds
      A.
      B.
      etc.
 III. Wild Bird Sounds
      A.
      B.
      etc.
 IV. Wild Animal Sounds
      A.
      B.
      etc.

Arabic Numeral Format
  1.0 Pet Sounds
     1.1 (meow)
     1.2
     etc.
  2.0 Farm Animal Sounds
     2.1
     2.2
     etc.
  3.0 Wild Bird Sounds
     3.1
     3.2
     etc.
  4.0 Wild Animal Sounds
     4.1
     4.2
     etc.

You may see many other ways of classifying these sounds. Some of these classification systems may be unique, i.e., creative. Seeing unusual relationships may require what Torrance calls fluency, originality, redefinition, and even elaboration. This requires a much higher level of thinking than the literal level, now being discussed. It does exemplify how simple the priming of creativity may be.

Variation. With younger children, simpler terms and fewer main points should be used than those suggested in the following activities. E.g. #2:

Units of Measure

---

foot	bushel	quart	dime	acre
peck	inch	mile	hour	pint
square inch	century	week	yard	month
day	cent	rod	square mile	square foot
square yard	nickel	quarter	gallon	dollar

Roman Numeral Format
   I. Measures of
      Geographic Length
      A. (foot)
      B.
      etc.

Arabic Numeral Format
  1.0 Measures of
     Geographic Length
     1.1 (foot)
     1.2
     etc.

Units of Measure (*continued*)

foot	bushel	quart	dime	acre
peck	inch	mile	hour	pint
square inch	century	week	yard	month
day	cent	rod	square mile	square foot
square yard	nickel	quarter	gallon	dollar

Roman Numeral Format

    II. Measures of Area
        A.
        B.
        etc.
    III. Measures of Volume
        A.
        B.
        etc.
    IV. Measures of Time
        A.
        B.
        etc.
    V. Measures of U.S. Money
        A.
        B.
        etc.

Arabic Numeral Format

    2.0 Measures of Area
        2.1
        2.2
        etc.
    3.0 Measures of Volume
        3.1
        3.2
        etc.
    4.0 Measures of Time
        4.1
        4.2
        etc.
    5.0 Measures of U.S. Money
        5.1
        5.2
        etc.

• *step 2*: Supply family names. List no subpoints. Children supply subpoints (requires deductive recall). E.g.:

Abbreviations for Units of Measure
1.0 Measures of Volume
    1.1 (bu.)
    1.2
    etc.
2.0 Measures of Geographic Length
    2.1 (ft.)
    2.2
    etc.
3.0 Measures of Time
    3.1 (yr.)
    3.2
    etc.
Etc.

• *step 3*: Do not supply family names. List items ungrouped. Children form outline (requires inductive recall if convergent response is given; requires creative thinking if divergent categories are given). E.g.:

Measurement Terms

breadth	capacity	depth	height
space	volume	rate	enter
weight	dimensions	thick	angle
distance	diameter	width	altitude
triangle	square	diagonal	base
solid	degree	radius	perimeter
circumference	length	size	weight

Title: __________________

1.0 __________   2.0 __________   3.0 __________
    1.1   2.1   3.1
    1.2   2.2   3.2
    etc.   etc.   etc.

- *step 4*: Children move from outline form to another format, such as one of those illustrated previously in this section. (This is recommended because most children do not like outlines very much, and they seem to understand relationships better if they are "mapped" using a different visual format.) E.g.:

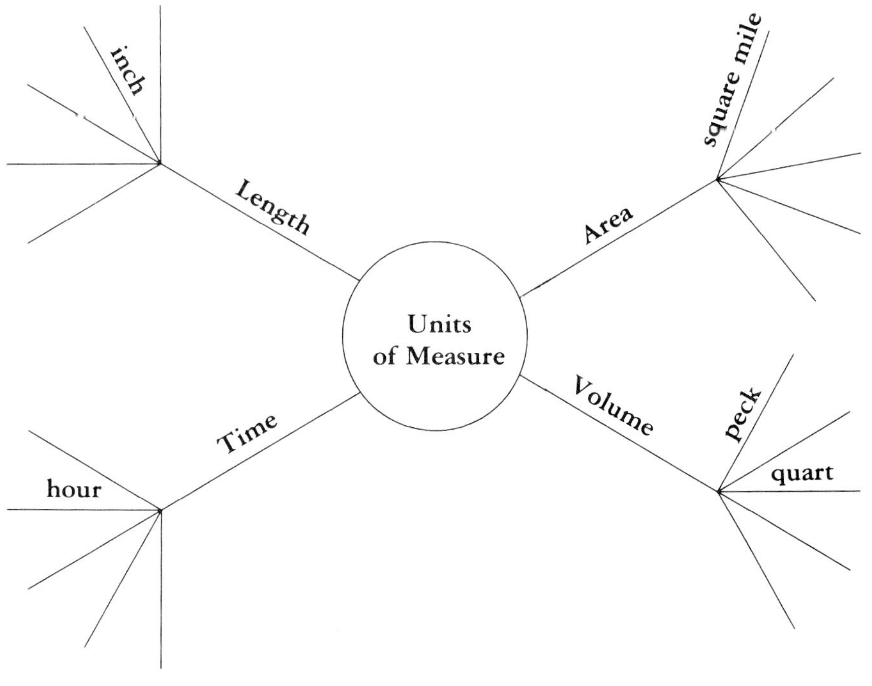

Relating Sequential Patterns to Children's Reading At the literal level, children are required to do one of the following:

- recognize (locate or identify), usually with the text open,
- recall (remember), usually with the text covered,
- translate (place the points into a form not given by the author, e.g., into an outline, map, graph, chart, etc.) the order of incidents or actions as reported by the author.

At the inferential level, children may be asked to hypothesize about incidents that may have taken place between incidents the author reported, or before or after incidents reported. Children may be asked to predict what may come next. At higher levels (evaluation and appreciation) they may be asked to reorganize, by putting the ideas into another order. Or they may be asked to add ideas, to judge the appropriateness of the author's ideas, and the worth and acceptability of the ideas.

1.3.1 Recognition or Recall of Sequence

Examples of activities:

□ *Supply Guideposts* Some children may be helped in following the story line if they are told some of the main points of the story before they read it. For example, they might be told: "This is a story about Louisa, a little girl who lost some money on the way to the store. She needed the money to buy some pet food for a little kitten who came to her family's door. Her mother was understanding, but Louisa wanted to find the money so she could get the food for the kitten . . . She was upset and began retracing her steps, looking everywhere she had been . . . Read the story to find out what happened to Louisa as she looked around the neighborhood. Try to remember three funny things . . . Draw a picture of each of them."

The teacher might wish to use flannel board characters, finger puppets, etc., to introduce the story line.

□ *Survey (Preview) Passages* Teach children to survey written material before they read the material thoroughly. Ask them to write down the main ideas. (These may be headings given in boldface print.) Frequently it is wise to give children a few minutes in class to do this. Often the teacher should page through the assignments with the children, pointing out the main headings. Later, the teacher might be able to expect the children to do this on their own. The headings usually should be written down and related to each other. (See next section on translation level activities.)

If they are to read a story, the children might look at pictures and try to make up a story to accompany the pictures. Then they could read the story and compare the versions (inferential level).

□ *Review or Reconstruct* Sometimes children will not be introduced to stories or chapters before they read them, for example, when they choose their own independent reading materials. After they complete their reading, they might write a short summary, draw pictures (like cartoons) telling the story in order, or just tell the teacher the main points.*

1.3.2 Translation of Sequence After surveying or reviewing, children may be helped to and finally may learn to independently illustrate the sequential pattern of the author by using an outline or other appropriate format. Such formats may be directly related to the ones on which they illustrated their own experiences, as in the previous section. Before they can do this, they may need an activity such as the following.

□ *Rhetorical Signal Words* Authors frequently use rhetorical signal words to indicate organizational patterns of clauses, sentences, groups of sentences, and even paragraphs or groups of paragraphs. Children should be alerted to pay special attention to such words. An activity such as the following might be used.

• *step 1*: Give children a cluster of rhetorical signal words that frequently are used together in specific kinds of organizational patterns, and ask them to indicate the pattern. At different times during a semester you might use one or two of the following clusters:

	Pattern
1. first, second, next, then, shortly after, finally . . .	(time)
2. furthermore, besides, also, and, . . .	(logical) simple listing
3. however, on the contrary, the other, . . .	(logical) contrast
4. ahead, behind, on the left, to the right, . . .	(space)
5. later, next, after an interval, . . .	(time)

---

*Young children tend to remember just the beginnings and endings of newly read stories. They usually must be helped in remembering other episodes. Older children remember more episodes.

<table>
<tr><td>6. because of that, consequently, so, . .</td><td>(logical) cause-effect</td></tr>
<tr><td>7. to the north, the east, the west, . . .</td><td>(space)</td></tr>
<tr><td>8. in addition, also, another, . . .</td><td>(logical) simple listing</td></tr>
<tr><td>9. at the coast, the shore, inland, . . .</td><td>(space)</td></tr>
<tr><td>10. on that account, hence, because, . . .</td><td>(logical) cause-effect</td></tr>
<tr><td>11. my first preference, next, then, the least, . . .</td><td>(preferences)</td></tr>
<tr><td>12. there is, there are, and there are, . .</td><td>(logical) simple listing</td></tr>
<tr><td>13. (other patterns you may wish to use or that you find their authors are using)</td><td></td></tr>
</table>

- *step 2*: Individually, or in groups, children may be asked to compose a paragraph, or a few paragraphs, using a set of these signal words in order—or in reverse order.
- *step 3*: Children may be asked if they know what organizational pattern they have used in their writing. They choose from:

1. time order, i.e., chronological order (which may be forward, backward, or flashback)
2. space order, i.e., spatial/visual order (which moves from area to area)
3. logical order, i.e., expository order (which could be a simple listing of related items, a listing moving from most important to least important, or vice versa, cause-effect, comparison, contrast, etc.)
4. preferential order, i.e., affective order (which is an order related to their likes or dislikes)

If they can't decide, they need help from other children or from the teacher.
- *step 4*: If possible, help the children locate something in their reading materials that uses these, or similar, signal words. Ask them to examine it to see if the organizational pattern is the same as theirs.

□ *Time Lines* A time line, like the one given on pages 329–330 can be used to show almost any three (or two, four, five) stage time order occurrence. Such charts could be drawn from content of reading assignments, and should also be explained if they are supplied by the author. Example of such a chart:

World War II Period		
Pre-War Period	1932 1933 1934 1935 1936 1937	
WW II	1938 1939 1940 1941 1942 1943 1944 1945	 Dec. 7 - Pearl Harbor/U.S. enters war V-E Day, V-J Day (end of war)
Post-War Period	1946 1947 1948 1949 1950	

Children could "flesh-in" major events.

□ *Circular Flow Charts* A *circular flow chart* could be used to show the flow of events that are continuous, e.g.:

Election Cycle of United States Politics

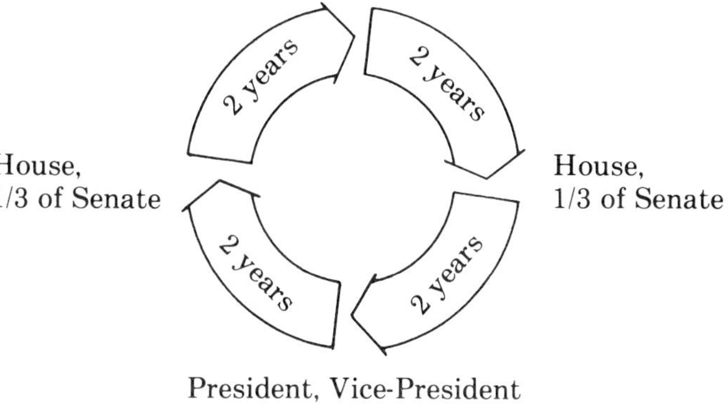

□ *Linear Flow Charts* A linearflow chart can be used to show steps that flow one from another, e.g.:

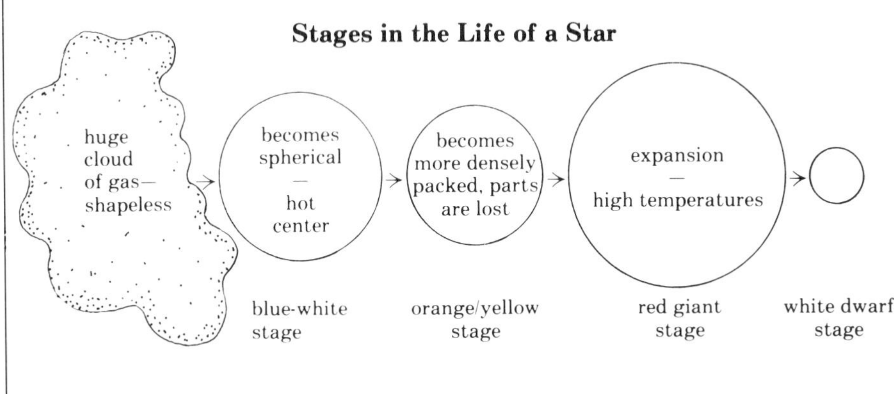

□ *Maps* A map can be used to show time flow across space, e.g.:

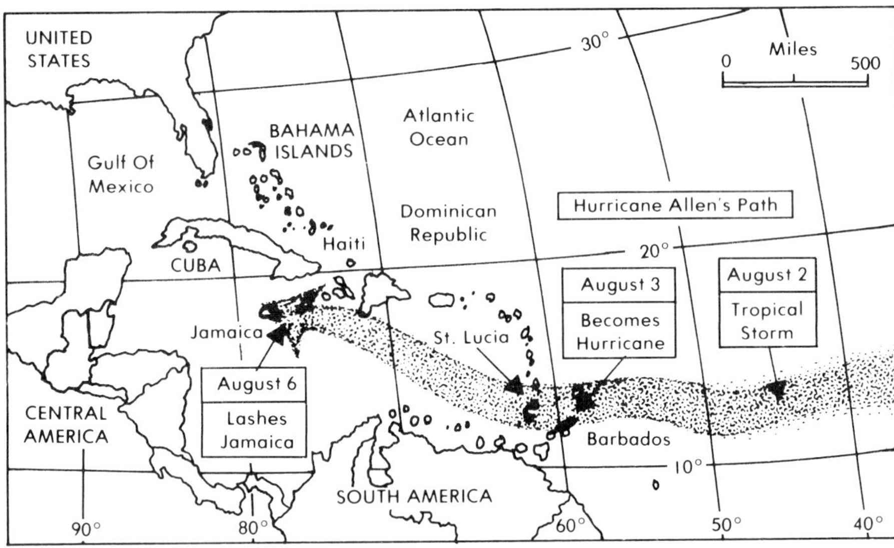

A map can also be used to show geographic divisions, to record elections, social characteristics of inhabitants, land forms, altitudes, etc., e.g.:

Time Zones of the Contiguous United States

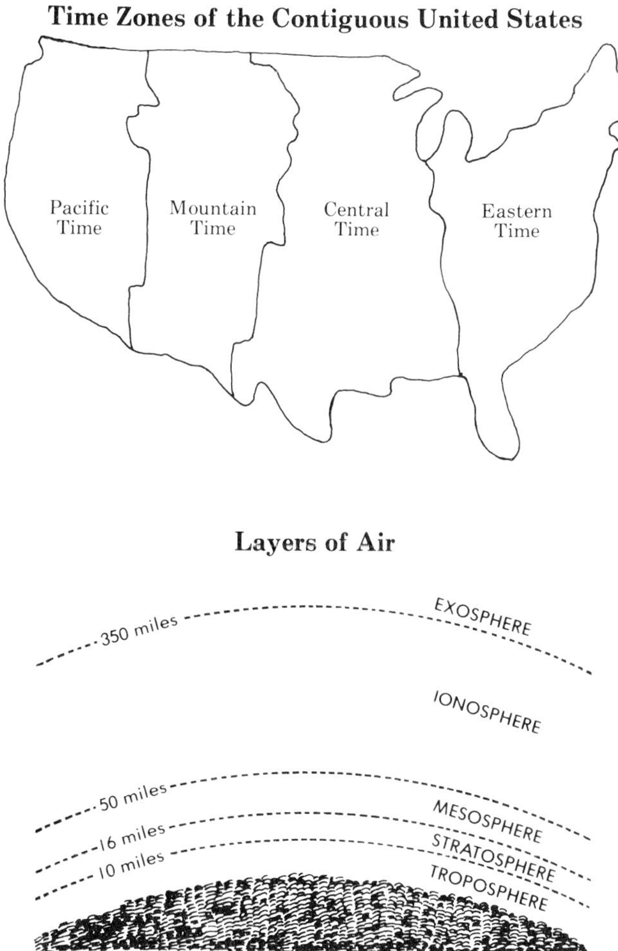

Layers of Air

□ *Spoke Graphs* A spoke graph, or web, can be used to show components of a theme, main ideas within it, and related details, e.g.:

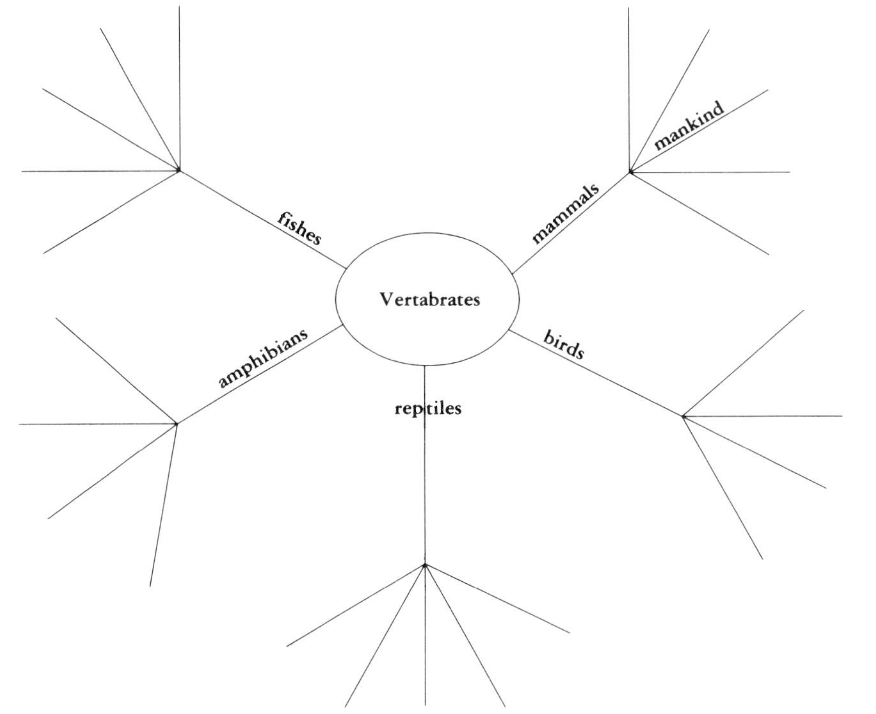

2.3 and 2.7 Inferring Sequence and Predicting Outcomes Inferential level activities require readers to add something to the ideas given by the author. This "something" comes from their background of experience or from extended related listening or reading at this point in time (e.g., of an encyclopedia entry, article, pamphlet, or program on T.V., etc.). The ideas that emerge at the inferential level, or higher level, go beyond the statements of the author, or may reorder or reorganize author's statements.

Activities follow:

□ *Arrange Sentences in Order* List sentences that could be used to compose a paragraph. Ask children to number them in an order that makes sense to them. Then ask them to write a main idea or title.

_____ "But I always look white," said the seal. "I'm a baby harp seal."

___ "I'll spray you in spots with permanent green paint," said the young man, and he did just that.*

(1) One day in spring a baby harp seal was not feeling well.

___ "I feel better now," said the baby harp seal. "Thank you."

___ A friendly young man said to it, "You are looking quite white."

___ "But today you look very white, even for a harp seal," said the friendly young man.

Variation. Items might be put on cards instead and the cards arranged in order.

□*Arrange Pictures or Paragraphs in Order* Cut up comic strips. Ask children to arrange the pictures in order to compose a story. Ask them to tell the story. Compare story lines for the same strip suggested by different children.

Variation. Use newspaper articles and/or photocopies from the children's books. Cut them up and ask children to rearrange them.

□*Anticipation* When children listen to or read a story or a chapter, they should be encouraged to actively anticipate the ideas that may follow. The teacher might read part of a story and ask the children to finish the story. This requires them to synthesize ideas to arrive at a logical and/or interesting conclusion. The same might be done with a chapter in a content area book.

Also, the teacher might give the class (or compose with the help of the children) a partial outline or other visual aid showing the structure of an assignment but omitting a part, e.g., the last important point. The children should be encouraged to anticipate what that point will be before they read the assignment. This requires them to synthesize main ideas to decide what logically will follow.

Later, children can compare their anticipations with the author's endings.

□*Reading Between the Lines and Retrospection* Instead, the teacher might omit the beginning of a story or chapter (or take a chapter out of context). The children should be encouraged to tell what might have preceded the discussion (retrospection). Or the teacher might omit an idea in the middle of the discussion. This would re-

---

*This is what some conservationists did one year, since the pelts would not be of value if they weren't white. Another year they sprayed them red, but this time they made the mistake of using water soluble paint.

quire the children to "read between the lines" to discover it. The same could be done with pictures.

Later the children should compare their answers with the author's discussion.

□*Analyze Titles, or Schema*   The teacher might write the title of a story or chapter or part of a chapter on the board. The children should be encouraged to hypothesize about main areas of discussion in the passage. These might be written on the board or on an overhead transparency (probably using one of the formats previously illustrated). Next, if it is a story, the children should read it (or the teacher may read the story to them) and the children can then compare their expectations with the story itself. If the passage is not a story, the children might preview it before reading it and may at this point compare expectations with the main ideas included by the author. The children may find that the author did not include all they expected and may wish to do further research.

□*Synthesize Subschema into Categories—Convergently and Divergently*   Give children a list of details (or use a list they have formulated in some way, e.g., by brainstorming about subschema of a schema), e.g., a list of animals. Ask children to classify terms convergently and divergently, e.g.:

bear	llama	fawn	frog	eft
calf	kitten	giraffe	kangaroo	iguana
camel	elk	puppy	ape	tiger
elephant	otter	piglet	orangutan	lamb
baboon	gorilla	turtle	chameleon	dolphin
toad	beaver	hamster	rabbit	siamese
seal	goat	porpoise	shepherd	beagle

classification	common characteristics	animals
1. pets	small, clean, fun, sociable	kitten, puppy, lamb, siamese, beagle, shepherd, hamster, piglet—(add others)
2. etc.		

Children probably will have to formulate *many groups* before they arrive at divergent classes. They will need time for this—and encouragement.

You might prefer to have the children write the names of the animals (or other items) on cards and have them classify and reclassify the cards. Encourage the children to think in terms of the four major types of classification patterns: time, space, logic, preference. For example, animals might be classified according to:

- *time patterns*: this includes those characteristics that relate to time in any form. In using this pattern, children might classify according to same or different, e.g.,
  - eras in which animals (etc.) lived and/or flourished on this earth (e.g.: prehistoric, present-time, endangered species, etc.)
  - life-span (of animals, etc.)
  - average time required to reach maturity
- *spatial/visual patterns*: this includes those characteristics that can be seen—large or small. In using this pattern, children might classify according to same or different, e.g.,
  - continents of the world (animals of Africa, Asia, North America, etc.)
  - altitudes of the world or a region (e.g., mountain animals, sea life found at the top level of the ocean, etc.)
  - physical features of surroundings (desert animals, grassland animals, etc.)
  - colors of animals
  - sizes of animals
  - other physical features of animals (number of feet, number of toes, length of neck, etc.)
- *logical patterns*: this relates to logical and/or functional relationships. In using this pattern, children might classify according to same or different, e.g.,
  - uses to which animals, etc., might be put (food, entertainment, pets, clothing, etc.)
  - classes/families, etc.
  - mental and behavioral characteristics (calm, placid, excitable, ferocious, etc.)
- *affective patterns*: this relates to personal and/or group preferences. In using this pattern, children might classify according to likes or dislikes, e.g.,
  - personal preferences (e.g., for a pet, for a zoo, for a carnival, for food, etc.)
  - preferences of specific groups of people or animals
  - compatability (e.g., animal-animal compatability or hostility)

You might want to make a game of this. E.g., form children into groups and go around the class—first, having each group suggest subschema (animal name) and second, having them suggest the classification. Points may be given for correct responses.

After demonstrating this technique to the children by using simple items, as above, use main ideas—either from their reading materials or from their experiences. Work along with the children in classifying these ideas into the four types of patterns, i.e., time order, space order, logical order, affective order. Children may at any time add subschema to complete a pattern.

□ *Mock Radio or T.V. Show* Children might put together a 30-minute show in which they schedule and perform using literary pieces or their own written materials. They might select their favorites and organize them in a way that is meaningful to them. The "show" might be taped. The same kind of thing could be done in content area classes also, using student dialogue and passages from written materials. Children might wish to borrow the tapes to take home to play to their parents.

□ *Chronological (Time) Approach* Children might be especially interested in a particular era or age—the age of knights, the crusades, prehistoric dinosaurs, ancient Egypt, the biblical period, the colonial period, civil war period, etc. Reading materials of these periods could be made available to them.

They might wish to study the historical development of a favorite concept, e.g., the evolution of tennis as a popular sport (in physical education class), the life of a favorite scientist (in science class), the development of different forms in interior decorating (in home economics class or woodworking), etc.

□ *Regional (Spatial) Approach* Children might also, or instead, be especially interested in reading materials about a special geographic region. Some might be interested in Alaska, or New England, or the prairies, or the Southwest, the Carribbean, England, Spain, France, Germany, Mexico, Canada, etc. (This could relate, also, to regional discussions in content areas: foods of Hawaii in home economics, Danish furniture in woodworking, Rugby in physical education, building adobes or geodesic domes in mathematics, turquoise in science and art, the battle of the Alamo in history, etc.)

□ *Thematic (Logical) Approach* Children could group together stories, plays, poetry, etc., that deal with a common theme of special interest to them. They could select additional materials that treat the same theme and share these in small groups. One group might be particularly interested in the sea, another in animals, still another in space travel, another in pioneer families, etc. They could read poetry, drama, short stories, books, pamphlets, etc. (This could relate, also, to subthemes within content areas: desserts in home economics, furniture in woodworking, baseball in physical education, architecture in mathematics, rock formations in science, noted spies in history, etc.)

OTHER SKILLS (COMPARISONS, CAUSE-EFFECT, FOLLOWING DIRECTIONS)

Comparisons

Comparisons consist of analogies and contrasts. Analogies are used to show how two or more things are alike. Contrasts stress differences.

At the literal level, children recognize or recall likenesses and differences among characters, times in history, places or anything else explicitly compared by an author. When inferring comparisons, the children formulate ways in which people, ideas, events, etc., are alike or different. Such comparisons may revolve around "here or there," "then and now," or two people, cultures, civilizations, etc. Certain figures of speech are used to make comparisons as are certain literary forms.

1.4 Recognition or Recall of Comparisons

Examples of activities are:

☐ *Figures of Speech and Connotations* Children are taught to recognize figures of speech, such as similes, metaphors, personification, allusions. They are also taught to recognize connotative language. At higher levels, they learn to write their own figures of speech and to use connotative language appropriately. (See Chapter 7.)

☐ *Signal Words* Children learn that certain signal words may be used to indicate comparisons. E.g., *like, as* suggest analogies (similes); *but, however, yet, on the other hand, nevertheless*, suggest contrasts. Ask children to circle signal words that suggest likenesses and to underline words that suggest differences (contrasts):

1. Frogs, like toads, live underwater during the early parts of their lives. Both are amphibians. But toads spend more of their adult lives on land than do frogs.
2. Mammals, birds, reptiles, amphibians, and fishes are alike since they are all vertebrates. Yet each subset of vertebrates has its own characteristics.
3. Mary seemed to be very happy; however, she constantly bit her fingernails.
4. It rained more than usual this spring and summer; nevertheless the farm did not produce well.
5. As was predicted, Henry ran well in the race. On the other hand, the other children did not do as well as expected.

☐ *The Suffixes -er, -est* The suffixes -er and -est indicate contrasts. Ask children to draw illustrations that show the meanings of the contrasting words:

big	bigger	biggest

others: small, smaller, smallest
      tall, taller, tallest
      smart, smarter, smartest
      etc.
Variation. They may wish to pantomime these contrasts.

2.4 Inferring Comparisons

Examples of activities are:

☐ *Literature* Children may be asked to show how two characters are alike and/or different—in personality, behavior, appearance. They may compare settings from one episode to another and from one story to another. They may be asked which character is most like themselves or least like themselves, etc. They may be asked to tell which characteristics they would like to emulate, which setting (time and/or place) they would like to be in, etc.

Children may read proverbs, allegories, parables, fables to find comparisons—sometimes unstated. They may be led to understand these comparisons. Examples of proverbs that might be used are: "Great oaks from little acorns grow." "A burnt child dreads the fire." "A drowning man will catch at a straw." The parable of the sower and the seed might be used (Matthew 13:3–23), the tale of the boy who called "wolf" too often, etc.

☐ *Arithmetic* In arithmetic class, comparisons are often used. E.g.:

1. Put $>$, $=$, or $<$ in each ◯

    $50 + 2$ ◯ 50 $50 + 0$ ◯ 50

    $50 - 1$ ◯ 50 $50 - 5$ ◯ 50

2. How are these alike? Which one is different? How is it different?

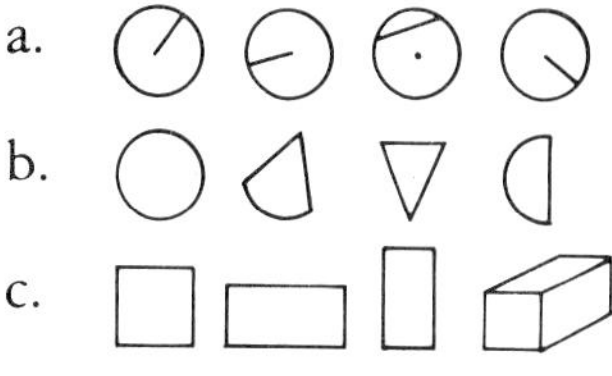

d. etc.

3. Susan has 12 upper teeth and 12 lower teeth. When she is an adult she will have 32 teeth. How many more teeth will she have as an adult than she has now?

□ *Science* Comparisons are frequently used in science. E.g.:

1. How are stars and planets alike? How are they different?
2. Compare the planets in terms of the number of moons each has.
3. Group the pictures of the following snakes into these categories: poisonous, nonpoisonous. (Pictures are supplied, or children find pictures.) What do you notice that is the same about the eyes of the poisonous snakes? How are the eyes of nonpoisonous snakes different?

□ *Social Studies*

1. Compare average yearly earnings of adults who have not graduated from high school with those of adults whose highest degree is a high school diploma.
2. Compare advantages and disadvantages of living in a city with those of living in a rural area.
3. Compare average annual costs of heating for families living in the sunbelt with those living in northern states.

□ *Use an Illustration* The following illustration might be used to clarify likenesses and differences:

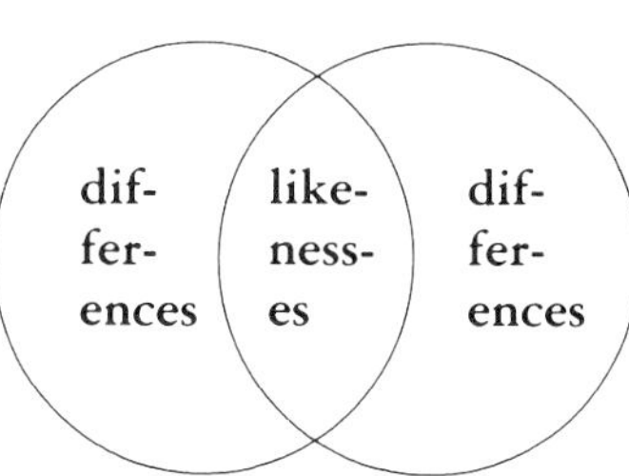

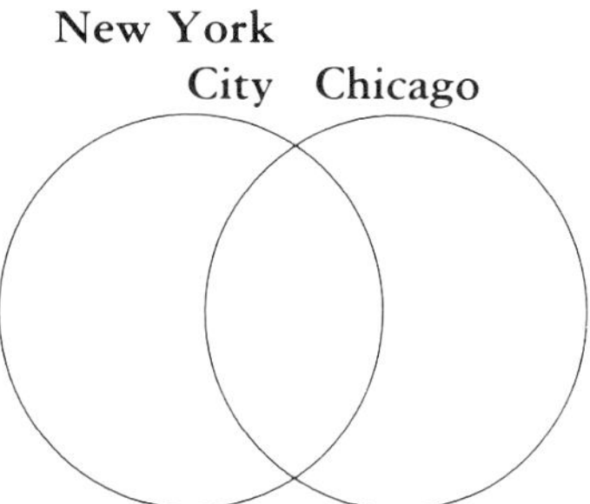

In addition, the following types of charts are appropriate for illustrating comparisons and are frequently used by authors to suggest comparisons: pie graphs, bar graphs, pictographs, line graphs, and charts.

□ *Compare Sources* Children might be led to compare articles, chapters, books on the same topic. These might be written by different authors or by the same author at different times. They might also compare speeches and visual illustrations.

They might compare the reporting of a political speech in a news column with an editorial about the speech. They might compare articles about one sports event as reported in several newspapers. They might compare a biography with an autobiography of the same person.

Cause and Effect Relationships

One event or action may trigger another—or may just appear to do so. Often it is very difficult to pinpoint a cause when an effect is observed.

At the literal level, the reader merely recalls or identifies a statement of cause and effect as given by an author. Authors frequently explicitly state why certain incidents or events occurred.

At the inferential level, the reader may question whether the author's statement is valid. Also, the reader may wonder about what caused an author to include certain statements. Sometimes an author gives an effect without a cause, or a cause without an effect. Supplying the missing part requires inferential (or higher level) reasoning.

1.5 Recognition or Recall of Cause and Effect Relationships

Examples of activities:

□ *Signal Words* Certain words may signal the statement of a cause-effect relationship. Recognizing such terms helps readers identify author's statements of cause and effect. The following words frequently signal that a cause is about to be stated: *because, since, if.* On the other hand, these words are used to signal effects: *therefore, so, and so, hence, consequently, thus.*

Ask children to complete the following sentences and to compare their answers. Then ask them if the underlined term suggests a cause or an effect is to follow the word.

Signals
Cause or Effect?

1. Because _______________________,
   I fell into the lake.   (cause) __________
2. I was tired! So _______________
   _______________________   __________
3. Since _______________________,
   Sue was smiling all day.   __________
4. "Yes," John repeated, "you did say you
   spent all of your money; therefore,
   _______________________.   __________
5. You failed your exam; hence _________
   _______________________.   __________
6. If _______________________,
   you'll win a trip to Paris.   __________
7. Two plus three equals five; thus
   _______________________   __________
8. Henry was very careless and stayed in
   the water too long; consequently, _______
   _______________________.   __________

Next, ask children to look in their books or at a newspaper to find
these words. Have them write the sentences on the board. Check to
see how often these words signal either a cause or an effect.

□*Baseball* Put words such as the above, plus other words or phrases,
  on slips of paper, and put the papers in a hat. Form two baseball
  teams, probably each with only a few members. The pitcher holds
  the hat while the batter draws one slip from the hat. To get to first
  base, the batter must use the term in a sentence signaling a cause-
  effect relationship. To get to second base the batter must tell
  whether the term signals the statement of a cause or of an effect.
  To get to third base he or she must make another statement using
  the same kind of signal word and must do this again to go home.

  A child gets only one chance to go to first base but may stop
there or at second or third base and be brought home by a teammate.

  Following are terms that might be used:

because	by-product	conclusion
so	reap	accordingly
if	harvest	is derived from
since	aftermath	blamed for
therefore	outgrowth	responsible for

hence	upshot	for that reason
thus	conclusion	the root of
consequently	spawned	the seeds of
result	create	produce

2.5 Inferring Cause and Effect Relationships

Examples of activities follow:

□ *Complete the Relationship* Help children identify in real life situations and in their reading materials statements of effect or of cause. Ask them to give the completing part. E.g.:

Cause	Effect
1. Alfonso was out in the rain.	1. (He got wet.)
2. (Since it wasn't raining, he may have fallen into a puddle or pool—or whatever is around that is wet. Maybe someone pushed him in.)	2. Alfonso got wet.
3.	3. Jerry's mother received a call from his principal.
4.	4. Mr. Jones is very poor.
5. Mr. Jones is very poor.	5.
6. The dog barked all night out in the back yard.	6.
7. The lights went out during the class play.	7.
8. etc.	8. etc.

□ *Chain Reaction* Sometimes one event causes another and that, in turn, causes another, and so on. So, the effect of one event becomes the cause of another. Give children one event, and ask them to supply a chain of cause-effect relationships. E.g.:

I didn't study   - so, I failed the test
              - so, I stayed for special help
              - so, I missed our baseball game
              - so, someone else became pitcher, and
                 she/he was very good
              - so, now our team has two pitchers

A statement in a history book is: "A thousand men died from the bite of one monkey."

Cause: a monkey bit a man
Effect: a thousand men died

Chain reaction:
A monkey bit a general during wartime -
                              - and, the general died
                              - so, a change in command occurred
                              - therefore, ___________________________

□ *Use Pictures* Choose pictures from magazines or from the children's books. Ask for cause-effect relationships. E.g.: There is a picture of a mother in a kitchen. The mother is holding a ruler while a child sits at the table . . . Ask children why the mother is holding the ruler. Some responses might be: "She's going to whip the child." "She's going to measure something." "She found the ruler elsewhere and is going to put it away." Etc. Do the responses reveal something about the children?

□ *Use Proverbs* In addition to using proverbs to teach comparisons, many proverbs can also be used in teaching cause-effect relationships. For example, in analyzing the proverb: "Don't buy a cat in a sack," the implied comparison is: "Don't buy something that may not pay off, or don't spend a lot of time or effort on something that may not pay off." The cause-effect relationship is: cause— avoid spending money, time, effort on something that may not have value to you; effect—you won't be disappointed. Help children understand the literal cause-effect relationships and the figurative cause-effect relationships in proverbs such as

- A stitch in time saves nine.
- Strike while the iron's hot.
- He who mixes with garbage ought not to be astonished if pigs devour him. (Serbian)
- He who ate the nuts must sweep away the shells. (German)
- When elephants battle, the ants perish. (Cambodian)
- One bell does not make a concert. (Italian)
- He jumped from the frying pan into the fire.
- Word by word great books are written. (Italian)
- If you want the hen's egg, you must put up with her cackling. (English)
- Unity among the small makes the lion lie down hungry. (Swahilian)
- The early bird catches the worm.
- He locked the barn door after the horse was stolen.

Ask children if they can relate these proverbs to their own experiences or experiences they have read about or heard about on T.V.

□*Author's or Artist's Choice* Have children read selections and comment about why authors included certain ideas or why they did not include others the children might think are important. The same might be done when examining pictures—in newspapers, magazines, books, etc.

□*Fallacies of Reasoning* Sometimes statements that appear to be cause-effect statements are not. Middle grade students might examine such statements in terms of fallacies of reasoning (critical reading-thinking). E.g.:

* *The "Correlation Suggests Causation" Fallacy* Because two characteristics or factors are frequently found together does not mean that one causes the other. To assume that it does often leads to the fallacy of "correlation suggesting causation." E.g., one science book contained the following statement: "Penguins live near water because they eat fish;" i.e., penguins eat fish, and, therefore they live near water.

  Cause: penguins eat fish

  Effect: they live near water

Simple enough—for those who believe everything an author says. Might it just as well be said that: "Because penguins live near the water, they eat fish." In this case we have:

  Cause: penguins live near water

  Effect: they eat fish

Does this make as much sense as the author's statement? It may be that *neither* statement is really true. Consider this: "Penguins happen to live near the water and eat fish because they evolved in the Antartic region, where it is cold enough for them to survive." (It just happens that there is water there and the only available food is fish.)

  Cause: penguins need cold temperatures and evolved in Antartica

  Effects: they live near water and eat fish

Here we have three possible cause-effect relationships. Which is true? Perhaps none, and an altogether different cause-effect relationship exists. It might be well frequently to question cause-effect relationship statements. Additional examples follow:

1. Children in a class may have observed that the students who get the best grades always seem to have the biggest vocabularies. They conclude:

     Cause: Having a big vocabulary causes

     Effect: high grades in school.

   Probably not a cause-effect relationship. Both are likely to be effects of other causes, e.g., broad experiences, a verbal home and/or neighborhood environment, intelligence, desire to learn, etc.

2. Children may have observed that, "Children who smile a lot are the most popular." They assume that:

    Cause: Smiling causes
    Effect: popularity

    Probably both are effects of some other causes: inner happiness and peace, enjoyment of others, etc.

3. In an old folk tale, Chanticleer thought he was a most impressive creature because every morning shortly after he crowed, the sun came up.

- *The "Either-Or" Fallacy* The either-or fallacy is the error of assuming that: one or the other statement must be true or valid, but not both; or possibly that one is valid when neither is. Analyze these, for example:

1. Either you're on a diet, or you can have a cookie. (That is, *if* you're on a diet, you cannot eat a cookie.)
2. Either your mother is boss, or your father is. (That is, *if* your mother is boss, your father can't be boss. Also one must be boss.)
3. Either you're a Republican and you vote for Hank Simmons, or you're not a Republican.
4. Either you come along and play ball with us, or you're not a good sport.
5. Either you break that window, or you're a sissy.
6. Either you help me cheat, or you're not my friend.
7. Etc.

- *Oversimplification* An oversimplification is a conclusion drawn that may be partly true but that doesn't account for all the causes. E.g.: "Mary Jo is an excellent student because she comes from a family of excellent students." It's probably partly true that coming from such a family causes success, but, no doubt, she also had to work hard. What might be some other causes for her success?
  What may be omitted in the following causal statements?

1. Martina has so many chores to do at home, so she doesn't ever have time to play with us.
2. Henry watches T.V. at least five hours a night because his folks have it on all the time.
3. Ken was asked why he bought Christmas presents for three of his close friends but not for the fourth. He said he ran out of money.

4. Consider these pairs of contradictory proverbs:
   He who hesitates is lost.
   Act in haste; repent in leisure.

   Out of sight, out of mind.
   Absence makes the heart grow fonder.

   Never leave till tomorrow what you can do today.
   Do it tomorrow. You've made enough mistakes today.
5. Jim said he couldn't go to Jerry's birthday party because he couldn't afford a gift.
   Cause: Jim can't afford a gift.
   Effect: Jim can't go to the party.

Probably. Jim's experience is limited. Among other things, he may not have heard the song, "The Little Drummer Boy." The Little Drummer Boy gave the greatest gift of all: he gave of himself. He played his drum as a gift to the Christ child. . . and this was the favorite gift.

* *Ignoring the Question* A question is ignored if the answer given is irrelevant. This may be done deliberately or through a misunder-

standing of the question. Ask children to analyze statements like the following:

1. The teacher asked Billy why he was late to school. He answered, "I left home late." (Why did he leave home late?)
2. The question on the exam was, "State three major reasons for the American Civil War." The child gave three outcomes of the war.
3. The senator was asked why he did not support a specific tax bill. He commented that he didn't feel it made sense. (Why didn't it make sense?)
4. The children on an elections committee were asked why they decided that there could be no more than three candidates for any one office. They answered, "We have to stop somewhere." (Why did they have to stop with three?)
5. Etc.

"The reason nothing has been done is because no one has made any effort to do anything about it," said one transportation official.

— Washington Post

Happens all the time, come to think of it. *— New Yorker*

Following Directions

There are obvious instances when children need to know how to follow directions, e.g., for their own safety, in order to learn how to do things successfully, and to actually do them well. To be unsuccessful in following instructions might be dangerous (e.g., in certain chemistry experiments) or might result in failure (e.g., when baking a cake, when constructing packaged materials like toys, when being taught to do many things in school, etc.). To literally follow some other instructions, however, might be dangerous (directions that are misleading, poorly written, tricky, etc.). Children need to learn how to follow directions, and they also need to know when not to follow directions.

At the literal level (recognition or recall), children need only recognize or recall directions, or instructions, given to them. At the literal level (translation), they carry out these instructions almost automatically, and without changing them. At the inferential (and higher levels) they may or may not carry out the instructions after having considered the consequences. They may also knowledgeably improvise at the inferential or higher levels.

1.7 Recognition, Recall, and Translation of Directions

Examples of activities follow:

□ *One Direction at a Time* When children are very young, they should be given just one direction to follow and be expected to follow it. The person giving the direction should be sure to have the child's attention and should be sure the direction is clearly given in a way that is understandable. The direction should be given only once. E.g., each child may have a set of blocks. Children should be positioned so that they cannot observe each other. Instructions may be:

1. Put a red block on the floor in front of you. (Wait for this to be done. Help those who have not been able to do this.)
2. Put a blue block on top of the red block. (Wait for this to be done. Again, help those who are unable to do this.)
3. Put a yellow block on top of the blue block. (Wait for this to be done. You may soon see that children might be grouped—those who are able to follow these instructions may move to more difficult activities soon. Those who cannot follow instructions may not do so because they don't understand the language —perhaps they don't know the colors. They might be taught the colors. Other children may know the words but may not be able to follow instructions.)
4. Etc.

□ *Two or Three Directions at a Time* Next, give children two, then three, directions to follow at a time. Do not repeat directions. E.g.:

1. Put a red block and a green block next to each other. (Wait for this to be done.)
2. Put a blue block next to the red block and a yellow block next to the green block. Be sure all four blocks are in a row. (Wait.)
3. Put an orange block on top of the red block, and put a purple block on top of the green block. (Wait.)
4. Etc.

Three:

1. Put a red block on the floor. Put a green block on one side of it, and put a yellow block on the opposite side. (Children do not begin following instructions until the teacher stops speaking. In some cases, the teacher may have to teach vocabulary first, e.g., "opposite.")

2. Put a purple block on top of the red block. Put an orange block on top of the green block, and put a blue block under the yellow block. (Wait.)
3. Etc.

□ *Use Letter Blocks* When children know letter names or are learning them, letter blocks might be used: e.g.:

1. Put an "L" in front of you. (Wait.)
2. Put an "O" to the right of the "L". (Wait.)
3. Put a "V" to the right of the "O". (Wait.)
4. Put an "E" to the right of the "V". (Wait.)
5. Ask them what word they have spelled. If they don't know, tell them.

Or:

1. Put an "H" down, and put an "O" to the right of it. (Wait.)
2. Add a "P" after the "O", and tell me the word. (Wait.)
3. Add an "E" after the "P", and tell me the word. (Wait.) You may wish to teach these words as sight words. Children should be taught what the words mean if they don't know the words.

Variation. Children may put sentences together using words from their word-banks. If they are using the Language Experience approach, they might be asked to take a word (or two) out and put in other words that would make sense in the sentence.

□ *Visual-Motor Skills* Children might be given a dittoed sheet with pictures outlined and asked to:

1. Color the bird blue. (Wait.)
2. Color the flower yellow. (Wait.)
3. Color the grass green. (Wait.)
4. Etc.

Also:

1. Connect the dots to form the letters:

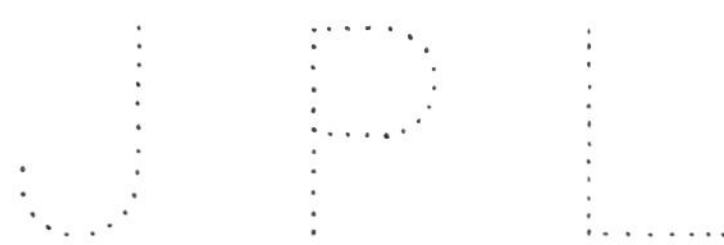

2. Etc.

Also:

Children might be given a piece of paper and asked to:

1. Fold the paper in half. (Wait.)
2. Open the paper. (Wait.)
3. Fold the paper in half the other way. (Wait.)
4. Open the paper. (Wait.)
5. Draw a picture in each section. (Wait.)
6. Etc.

□ *Simon Says* Children might play the game "Simon Says," in which they do only what Simon says. E.g.:

"Simon says, hop on your left foot." (They do it.)
"Now hop on your right foot." (They don't do it.)
Etc.

□ *Sports and Games* Children should be taught to play games. They can learn baseball one or two steps at a time. Hopscotch, card games, etc., could be taught one or two steps at a time. When possible, children should be asked to teach a game to other children. When children are able to read, they might learn to play games by reading about them.

□ *Scavenger Hunt* When children can read, they might be sent on a scavenger hunt with a list and asked to find:

1. a book about animals.
2. a definition for "horse," not meaning the animal.
3. a piece of chalk.
4. a recipe for chocolate fudge.
5. etc.

□ *Map Reading* Children might be given a map and asked to:

1. find the city in which they live.
2. draw a line following highway ___ 100 miles south of their city.
3. draw a line 200 miles due east.
4. etc.
5. Ask them where they would be if they followed that route.

□ *Following Written Instructions* Children should be given written directions and asked to follow them. They frequently have simple directions on work sheets and must be expected to follow them provided they understand them. They also have directions to follow in textbooks and for many activities.

2.9 Inferring and Judging Directions Children should know when they should follow directions and when they should not follow directions. When possible, they should know why they follow some instructions and why they do not follow others. E.g.:

□ *To Follow or Not to Follow* Children should be asked which of certain instructions they should follow and which they should not follow. They might be asked to circle "yes" if they should follow the direction and "no" if they should not.

(Yes) No 1. You are playing "Simon Says," and the instruction is: "Simon says, clap your hands."

Yes No 2. You are playing "Simon Says," and the instruction is: "Sit down."

Yes No 3. You are playing baseball, and you make three strikes. Do you surrender the bat?

Yes No 4. You are out for "Halloween Collection" and are given unwrapped candy at a stranger's house. Will you eat it?

Yes No 5. Your mother or father has told you not to go in the street in front of your house. Your basketball rolls into the street, and you don't see any cars around. Will you go into the street to get your ball?

Yes No 6. You are walking home from school and are very tired. A stranger offers to drive you home. Will you go?

Yes No 7. You're preparing yams for a fall dinner at home. The recipe calls for brown sugar and marshmallows. You run out of brown sugar, and you cannot borrow any or go to the store. Would you substitute honey or white sugar for the brown sugar?

A discussion should follow about answers and dilemmas.

□ *Which Sign?* Draw pictures of signs at the top of a page. Write sentences after them. Ask children to decide which sign the person or persons in each sentence probably saw and to write the number of the sign in the blank.

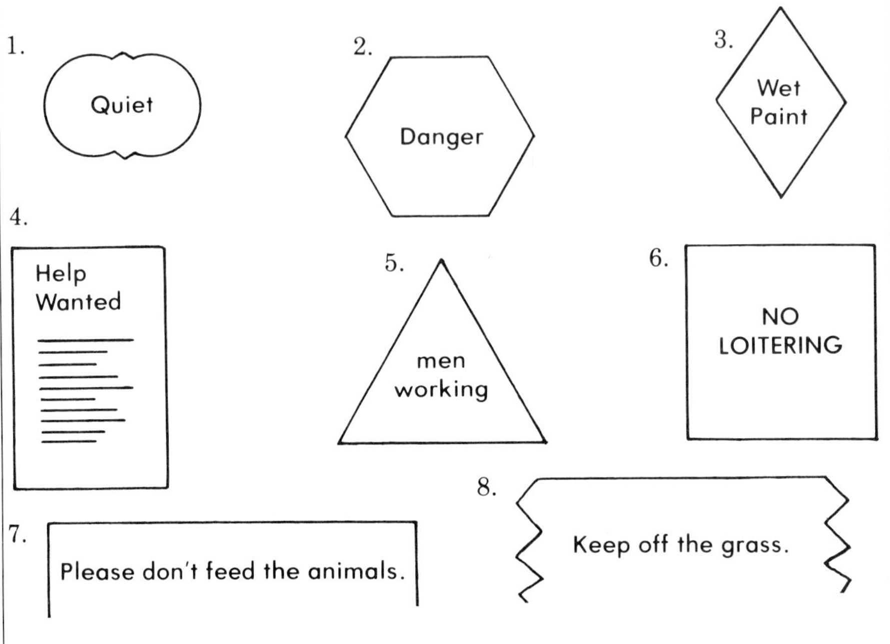

1. ____ Susan didn't sit on the bench after reading this sign.
2. ____ Bob didn't visit with his friends in the library.
3. ____ Jim applied for the job.
4. ____ Joanne and Jean threw their left-over bread away at the zoo.
5. ____ The children rode their bicycles on the sidewalk only.
6. ____ The group of teenagers moved on, rather than standing around to visit.
7. ____ Everyone walked carefully around a man-hole on the sidewalk.
8. ____ Everyone driving downtown found that a main street was closed to traffic.

□ *What Would Happen If* Children might be asked what would happen if:

1. they did not follow the instructions in a certain science experiment? Why?
2. too much chlorine was added to water in a swimming pool? Why?
3. they took a gold fish out of the water for a few minutes, against instructions given in their manual? Why?
4. they watered a certain cactus every second day after they had read that it should be watered only every second week? Why?

  5. they added rather than subtracted as told in their mathematics assignment? Why?
  6. they made a mobile as suggested by their teacher telling about a book they enjoyed reading? Why?
  7. etc.

A discussion should follow in which children compare answers.

Summary

This chapter has been written to explain and exemplify the teaching of selected comprehension tasks, or skills, at the literal and inferential levels. Literal level skills, as defined in this chapter, are those that require recognition, recall, or translation of content explicitly stated in materials read. Inferential level activities require the reader to use his or her personal knowledge, intuition, and imagination to hypothesize about, reconstruct, and extend an author's message. Inferential level responses may be convergent or divergent.

Tasks discussed are those detailed in Thomas C. Barrett's "Taxonomy of Reading Comprehension" literal and inferential levels. Added to Barrett's recognition and recall literal tasks were translation level activities, as defined by Norris Sanders.

The first three tasks discussed relate to literal and inferential activities in areas traditionally labeled details, main ideas, and sequence. These are components of what has been more recently called "Schema Theory." A schema is a main idea or theme, and subschema are the essential elements within the schema. The schema is the top of the hierarchy. Subschema are components of the schema—main ideas of a theme and details. Sequence is the arrangement of the subschema—usually in one of the following orders, or patterns: chronological, spatial, logical, or affective (or combinations of these). "Story grammar" and "text grammar" are terms frequently used to explain typical arrangements of subschema in stories and different content area textbooks, etc. (A continuation of this concept is included in Chapter 12 of this book.)

The final three tasks described and exemplified are called comparisons, cause-effect, and following directions.* Examples of activities for teaching these are given on the literal and inferential levels also.

---

*Barrett's "Character Traits" task has been omitted in this chapter as a main heading. "Figurative Language" was discussed in Chapter 6. "Following Directions" was added by the present author.

Questions and Activities

After answering the questions at the beginning of this chapter, consider these questions and activities:

1. Some medical doctors treat their patients holistically; i.e., they treat the whole person to alleviate a disease or malfunction. Other doctors treat their patients' specific ills only, in an attempt to cure them. Can you draw an analogy between holistic medical treatment and holistic teaching of reading? between treating specific ills and/or developing specific physical strengths and a subskill approach to the teaching of reading, including remedial reading?
   • Which do you prefer—a holistic or subskill approach to the teaching of reading? Do you think one approach might be effective at one time and the other at another time? Explain.
2. Explain by using schema terminology how a specific word (or concept) might be a schema at one time and a subschema at another. You may wish to draw an illustration to show the relationships.
3. How important is it to develop the concept of a specific skill for children before developing the specific skill? Give an example of how you might develop the concept of details, main ideas, and sequence and their relationship. How would you develop the concepts of
   • comparisons—literal, inferential levels
   • cause-effect relationships—literal, inferential levels
   • character traits—literal, inferential levels
   • reality or fantasy—literal, inferential, evaluation levels
   • fact or opinion—literal, inferential, evaluation levels
   • adequacy, validity, appropriateness—inferential, evaluation levels
   • worth, desirability, acceptability—inferential, evaluation levels
   • response to plot or theme—inferential, appreciation levels
   • reaction to author's use of language—inferential, appreciation levels
   • imagery—inferential, appreciation levels
4. Write a short passage using the rebus technique. When might it be appropriate to use the rebus technique?
5. Design a three-step activity like that under the title of "Family Names," (p. 321) using terms from a lesson children might be studying. You may wish to use cards instead of lists. (All members of one family should be on the same color of cards. Family names should be on another color.) Later, to encourage divergent classification, the color of cards can be ignored when reclassifying these same terms.

6. Demonstrate to a group in your classroom how you would supply guideposts (p. 338) for reading a specific short story or play.

7. Demonstrate to a group in your classroom how you would help children survey a chapter in a content area textbook (any level) before reading it. Show how you would illustrate the main points by using an appropriate "mapping" or "graphing" technique. Ask the members of your group to suggest questions and/or to hypothesize about the author's discussion.

8. Show how one general topic (e.g., vegetation) might be discussed in each of the following orders:
   * time—e.g., time of year when specific plants are at their height
   * space—e.g., location of plants, perhaps in a yard
   * logic—e.g., uses of plants: beauty, fruit, vegetables, etc.
   * affective—e.g., favorite plants

9. Read a chapter in a children's textbook at the level of your choice. In one column on a sheet of paper write words the author uses to signal analogies, and in another column write words the author uses to signal contrasts. Consider how knowledge of these words can be used in teaching children to recognize comparisons.

10. Using the same, or another chapter, write signal words that indicate cause or effect relationships.

11. How important is it in your opinion to teach children about fallacies of reasoning? Choose one or two fallacies and list statements under each that might be appropriate to that fallacy. Share these with your classmates.

12. Design an activity for following directions at the literal level. Design another one at the inferential level. What are the basic differences in activities at these two levels?

Notes

1. See Chapter 13 of this book.
2. Arthur Heilman in A. Sterl Artley, "Phonics Revisited," *Language Arts*, 52 (Nov./Dec. 1975):1068–1072.
3. See Frank J. Guszak in Selected References.
4. See, for example, the Pathfinder Program, Robert Ruddell, *et al.*, Boston: Allyn and Bacon, 1979. The Pathfinder Comprehension Taxonomy is shown in Fig. 8.1 on p. 368. Figure 8.2 (p. 369) shows the Addison-Wesley taxonomy, called "Processing Strands". In this program, detail, main ideas, and sequence activities are classified on just two levels.
5. See Benjamin Bloom, *et al*; J.P. Guilford; and Frank Guszak in Selected References.
6. Richard J. Smith and Thomas C. Barrett, p. 62. See Selected References

Pathfinder Comprehension Taxonomy

Skill Compentencies	Comprehension Levels		
	Factual	Interpretive	Applicative
Details			
Identifying	●	●	
Comparing	●	●	●
Classifying		●	●
Sequence	●	●	●
Cause and Effect	●	●	●
Main Idea	●	●	●
Predicting Outcomes		●	●
Valuing			
Personal judgment	●	●	●
Character trait identification	●	●	●
Author's motive identification		●	●
Problem Solving			●

Fig. 8.1: From Teacher's Editions by Robert B. Ruddell, et al. (Pathfinder—Allyn and Bacon Reading Program). Copyright 1978–81 by Allyn and Bacon, Inc. Reproduced by permission.

7. *Ibid.*, p. 63.
8. See Norris Sanders in Selected References.
9. *Ibid.*, pp. 3 and 32.
10. Smith and Barrett, 1974 edition, p. 54.
11. See J.P. Guilford in Selected References.
12. Smith and Barrett, 1978 edition, p. 65.
13. *Ibid.*, p. 66.
14. Mary Monteith, pp. 368–369. See Selected References.
15. *Ibid.*

Comprehension

	Comprehension	Study Skills
PROCESSING STRANDS — **LINGUISTIC**	Using punctuation clues	
	Using function word clues	
	Using sentence patterns	Study Skills
	Recognizing parts of speech	Locating
	Relating pronouns to antecedents	Following directions
LITERAL	Associating pictures and sentences	Classifying
	Identifying details, character traits, cause and effect, comparisons, and mood	Using parts of books
	Sequencing	Alphabetizing to 1st letter
	Identifying main idea	to 2nd letter
	Relating details to main idea	to 3rd letter
	Paraphrasing	Proofreading
INFERENTIAL	Inferring details, character traits, cause and effect, comparisons, and mood	Using reference materials maps and charts
	Inferring sequence	dictionaries
	Inferring main idea	encyclopedias
	Drawing conclusions and predicting outcomes	
	Interpreting expressive language	
EVALUATIVE	Making judgments or expressing opinions	
	Distinguishing real and make-believe	
	Distinguishing fiction and non-fiction	

In this program, classifying activities are included as study skills activities.

Fig. 8.2: From Scope and Sequence brochure of The Addison-Wesley Reading Program by Pleasant T. Rowland. Menlo Park: Addison-Wesley Publishing Co., 1979. Reprinted by permission.

SELECTED REFERENCES

Athey, Irene. "Syntax, Semantics, and Reading," in *Cognition, Curriculum, and Comprehension*, John T. Guthrie (ed.). Newark, Delaware: International Reading Association, 1977.

Barnitz, John G. "Syntatic Effects on the Reading Comprehension of Pronoun—Referent Structures by Children in Grades Two, Four and Six." *Reading Research Quarterly*, XV, no. 2 (1980–81): 268–289.

Barrett, Thomas C. "Taxonomy of Reading Comprehension" in *Teaching Reading in the Middle Grades, Second Edition*, by Richard J. Smith and Thomas C. Barrett. Reading, Massachusetts: Addison-Wesley Publishing Co., 1979, pp. 62–67.

Bloom, Benjamin, *et al. Taxonomy of Educational Objectives: Handbook I, Cognitive Domain.* New York: David McKay, 1956.

Burmeister, Lou E. *Reading Strategies for Middle and Secondary School Teachers, Second Edition.* Reading, Massachusetts: Addison-Wesley Publishing Co., 1978, Chapters 7 and 8.

Crowder, William W. "Using Content Materials to Sharpen Comprehension Skills," in *Reading Comprehension at Four Linguistic Levels*, Clifford Pennock (ed.). Newark, Delaware: International Reading Association, 1979, pp. 87–93.

Eeds, Maryann. "What To Do When They Don't Understand What They Read—Research-Based Strategies for Teaching Reading Comprehension." *The Reading Teacher*, 34 (February 1981): 565–571.

Frazier, Lynne and Edward Caldwell. "Testing Higher Cognitive Skills in Young Children." *The Reading Teacher*, 30 (February 1977): 475–478.

Gillet, Jean Wallace and M. Jane Kita. "Words, Kids and Categories." *The Reading Teacher*, 32 (February 1979): 538–542.

Guilford, J.P. "Frontiers in Thinking Teachers Should Know About." *The Reading Teacher*, 23 (February 1960): 176–182.

Guszak, Frank J. "Teacher Questioning in Reading." *The Reading Teacher*, 21 (December 1967): 227–234.

Guthrie, John T. "Research Views: Paragraph Structure." *The Reading Teacher*, 32 (April 1979): 880–881.

_______________. "Research Views: Purpose and Text Structure." *The Reading Teacher*, 32 (February 1979): 624–626.

Hansell, T. Stevenson. "Stepping Up to Outlining." *Journal of Reading*, 22 (December 1978): 248–252.

Haupt, Edward J. "Writing and Using Literal Comprehension Questions." *The Reading Teacher*, 31 (November 1977): 193–199.

Henry, George H. *Teaching Reading as Concept Development: Emphasis on Affective Thinking.* Newark, Delaware: International Reading Association, 1974.

Lamme, Linda Leonard and Frances Kane. "Children, Books, and Collage." *Language Arts*, 53 (Nov./Dec. 1976): 902–905.

Moberly, Peggy C. and Dianne L. Monson. "Effect of Instruction on Fifth Graders' Comprehension of Anaphoric Structures," paper delivered at national conference of the International Reading Association, Chicago, 1982. Seattle, Washington: University of Washington, unpublished paper.

Monteith, Mary K. "ERIC/RCS—Schemata: An Approach to Understanding Reading Comprehension." *Journal of Reading*, 22 (January 1979): 368–371.

Richek, Margaret Ann. "Reading Comprehension of Anaphoric Forms in Varying Linguistic Contexts." *Reading Research Quarterly*, XII, no. 2 (1976–77): 145–165.

Rystrom, R. "Reflections on Meanings." Paper presented at the Preconvention Institute on Reading Comprehension and Syntax, International Reading Assoc., 1975.

Salisbury, Rachel. *Better Work Habits*. Glenview, Ill.: Scott, Foresman, 1966.

Saltz, Eli and J. Johnson. "Training for Thematic-Fantasy Play in Culturally Disadvantaged Children: Preliminary Results." *Journal of Educational Psychology*, 66 (1974): 623–630.

Sanders, Norris. *Classroom Questions—What Kinds?* New York: Harper and Row, 1966, Chapters 1–4.

Smith, Richard J. and Thomas C. Barrett. *Teaching Reading in the Middle Grades, Second Edition*. Reading, Massachusetts: Addison-Wesley Pub. Co., 1979.

Strange, Michael and Richard L. Allington. "Considering Text Variables in Content Area Reading." *Journal of Reading*, 21 (November 1977): 149–152.

Sullivan, Joanna. "Comparing Strategies of Good and Poor Comprehenders." *Journal of Reading*, 21 (May 1978): 710–715.

——————————. "Liberating Children to Creative Reading." *The Reading Teacher*, 25 (April 1972): 639–642.

Torrance, E. Paul. *Creativity*. Washington, D.C.: National Education Association, 1963.

Vaughan, Sally and Sharon Crawley and Lee Mountain. "A Multiple-Modality Approach to Word Study: Vocabulary Scavenger Hunts." *The Reading Teacher*, 32 (January 1979): 434–437.

Whisler, Nancy G. "The Newspaper: Resource for Teaching Study Skills." *The Reading Teacher*, 25 (April 1972): 652–656.

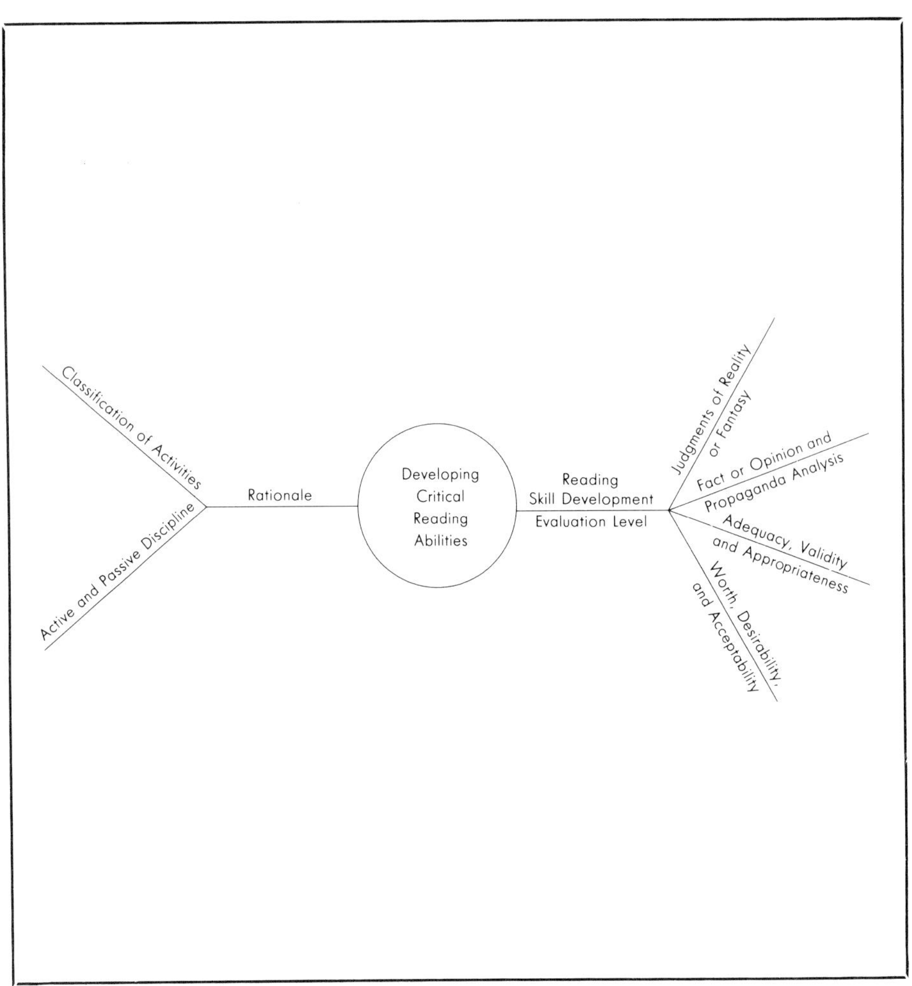

- What is critical reading? What skills or "tasks" are involved?

- Is it always possible to classify skills or activities at a specific level? Why or why not? What is meant by active and by passive discipline? How do these relate to critical reading?

- How can we teach children to read critically (or evaluatively)? What "tasks" or skills are involved, and what techniques or strategies can be used that are appropriate to each?

Developing Critical Reading Abilities

Children of all ages make judgments about the ideas in the materials that they read or that are read to them. Even the very youngest children do so. Children can name their favorite books and their favorite characters. And they can tell you the characters they don't like: the stepmother in *Cinderella* and the big bad wolf, and so on. In school they need to extend their ability to make judgments.

Barrett's third level in his taxonomy is titled "Evaluation."[1] It deals with making judgments of the following types:

- Judgments of Reality or Fantasy
- Judgments of Fact or Opinion
- Judgments of Adequacy or Validity
- Judgments of Appropriateness
- Judgments of Worth, Desirability, or Acceptability

The present chapter is structured using these components to explain ways in which children might be taught to read evaluatively. This is what is frequently called critical reading.

Rationale

CLASSIFICATION OF ACTIVITIES

According to Sanders,[2] an activity or thought process is always classified at its highest level, and all lower levels are subsumed under that. A reader must be able to recognize, recall, and infer before being able to evaluate or judge. In other words, when a person evaluates or judges logically, that person has carefully examined the input—literally and inferentially first. These lower level steps may have to be directly taught to read evaluatively.

It might be noted here, also, that some activities in previous chapters dealt with making judgments and evaluations. Tasks sometimes classified at lower levels may inspire or call for higher level responses. According to Sanders, it is not the task, itself, that indicates the level of thought involved, but rather it is the thought process that lead to the reader's response. Thus, for example, certain types of sequence activities are surely evaluation level activities. For example, if children are asked to finish a story and then to compare endings with each other and with the author's ending and then to judge which ending is most appropriate (or which ending they prefer) in terms of their experiences, they are thinking at a high level. Also, when children use connotative and figurative language effectively, they are thinking at a high level. When children decide that certain details are appropriate or inappropriate to an author's discussion and know why, they are thinking at a high level. Nevertheless, the fact that reading "tasks" may involve various levels of thought does not invalidate the use of a taxonomy. It may, however, lead to greater flexibility in its use.

ACTIVE AND PASSIVE DISCIPLINE

People who think critically—who make judgments and evaluate ideas—must be able to "listen" to another's point of view. Such people must learn to withhold personal judgments until they are able to grasp an author's message and consider it. This is very difficult for people who prefer to respond without "listening"—who are already sure they know the answer.

David Elkind[3] explains, "Good readers, like good listeners, have to be simultaneously passive (being receptive to the representations of others) and active (interpreting those representations within their own framework)." According to Elkind, some people lack a receptive discipline. "A young person demonstrates receptive discipline when he attends fully to the representations of others and resists following his own free associations and tangents."

Elkind suggests the following strategies as aids to building a receptive attitude: use text material that is at the level of the reader's competence and that is of interest to the reader, and set goals for reading when the materials are not being read purely for recreational purposes. (The reader should know he or she is responsible for learning a specific something.)

Holding difficulty of materials constant, those materials that express the reader's point of view are easiest for the reader to comprehend. Those that are diametrically opposed to the reader's point of view are more difficult. Those that in part agree and in part disagree are even more difficult, as they may confuse the reader.

Reading Skill Development: Evaluation Level

This section is provided to explain and exemplify ways of teaching selected reading skills at the evaluation level.

3.0 Evaluation Evaluation level activities require the reader to make judgments about content by comparing it to both external and internal criteria. External criteria is that information provided by others, e.g., the teacher or other authorities on the subject. Internal criteria includes the reader's own experiences, knowledge, and values related to the subject under consideration.[4]

3.1 Judgments of Reality or Fantasy Children "determine whether incidents, events, or characters in a selection could have existed or occurred in real life on the basis of their experience."

Suggested activities follow:

□ *Two Stories* Read two stories to children, one real and one fictional. Ask children which one could have happened in real life. Ask them to explain why. Also, when reading just one story, ask children to pick out parts that could be real and parts that are definitely fantasy.

□ *Truth or Fantasy?* Thermofax copies of a story or newspaper article that contains truth and fiction. Ask children to underline statements that are probably true and box in statements that are fictitious. E.g.:

Buzzard-crash pilots rehearsed emergency

MIAMI (AP)—Marine 2nd Lt. Steve Hoenie had just rehearsed what to do if a bird collided with his plane and was heading for base on the last flight with his instructor. Then a turkey buzzard came crashing through the canopy.

Both Hoenie and his instructor were knocked unconscious at 2,800 feet over southern Alabama. Hoenie's instructor, thinking his student had been killed, bailed out, leaving Hoenie to handle his first solo flight a day early.

"My instructor said one of the highest compliments I could have paid him was bringing the plane back," the 24-year-old Leonia, N.J., officer said Thursday. "He's one of the best instructors around and that's a reflection on him.

"The commander of the base just said he was glad I saved him a $500,000 airplane. He looks at it in slightly different terms."

Navy Capt. Kenneth Dickerson, the base commander, said Friday that he had recommended Hoenie for the Air Medal, which is awarded for "meritorious achievement in flight."

Hoenie and his instructor, Capt. Dean Lucas, spent two days in the hospital after the accident Monday.

"I just remember seeing two birds," Hoenie said of the collision. "I veered to miss one and slammed into the other. It knocked me right out. I woke up after about 20 or 30 seconds.

"My instructor came to and he couldn't see anything," he continued. "He said, 'Steve, get out.' When I didn't answer, he said it again. I came to at about 1,000 or 1,200 feet and there was no instructor."

> "My theory is that the buzzard came through the windshield, hit me, hit the instructor and took over the plane," Hoenie joked. "He flew it over the Brewton airport, had a heart attack and gave the plane to me and I landed it." *fictitious*

The buzzard was found dead in the back of the cabin. The plane is ready to fly again, but Hoenie isn't. His broken collarbone means he'll have to stick to flight simulators on the ground for five weeks.

Used with permission of the Associated Press.

Ask what they think the person is like who fictionalized part of this story. Does he have a good sense of humor? Ask them what would have happened if the turkey buzzard had flown the plane. (They might write a short story about it.)

▢ *Truth Is Stranger Than Fiction* Show children some things that have actually happened—that are almost unbelievable. Ask them questions before and after they read the descriptions.

• Example 1: Could someone be tried for espionage by a nation for trying to sell a recipe—a recipe for chocolate?

Apprentice arrested

Swiss fear candy coup

BERN, Switzerland (AP)—The Swiss, who guard their industrial secrets as closely as they do other people's money, have arrested a 20-year-old chocolate-maker's apprentice who tried to sell his employer's formulas to foreign powers, the Justice Ministry said Friday.

A ministry spokesman said the apprentice copied about 40 recipes from the firm's files, then offered them and knowledge of production methods to the Soviet Union, East Germany, China and Saudi Arabia.

Used with permission of the Associated Press.

The ministry did not name the firm or the apprentice, who will be charged with economic espionage.

Ask them if they have changed their minds after reading this. Ask them how they would describe the apprentice's character. Is he a traitor?

- Example 2: Would a nation ever fail to protect the welfare of its citizens for some reason, e.g., for economic advantage?

Japan accused of hiding dolphin meat poisoning

Ecologist says shoppers not told of mercury

By David Tharp
Special to
The Christian Science Monitor

Tokyo

Thousands of dolphins slaughtered for human consumption by Japanese fishermen contain massive overdoses of mercury poisoning.

This charge is leveled at the Japanese Government by American ecologist Dexter Cate, president of the Hawaii-based Earth Co-Existence Organization.

According to Mr. Cate, dangerous levels of mercury poisoning in the meat have been verified by a Japanese Government research center in Tokyo. But he claims the results have not been made public and that the center refuses to be identified.

Mr. Cate insists that despite the contamination, the meat continues to be sold to the public with the Japanese Government's knowledge.

In an interview, Mr. Cate said that dolphin meat sold commercially by Izu Peninsula fishermen near Tokyo contains 10 times the amount of mercury considered safe by Japan's own Ministry of Health. . . .

David Tharp is a veteran journalist. He has lived in Asia 17 years. He is currently writing in Tokyo and completing a Medical Doctor's (MD) degree.

(Ask the children if they know of any other examples of governments not protecting the interests of their citizens. Ask them if perhaps sometimes the interests of some are sacrificed for the interests of larger numbers of people, e.g., in the testing of atomic weapons.)

Ask the children to respond to the article they have read. Do they think the American ecologist is right, i.e., is he telling the truth, or is he exaggerating? How would they describe Dexter Cate? How would they describe Japan's Ministry of Health?

- Example 3: Do cats ever give presents to their human friends? (Perhaps some children can cite examples from their own experiences. I can! After I returned from a two-week vacation, my cat brought me a bird . . . perhaps one of the most generous gifts a cat could give a human, though I was far from thrilled with the gift.) Here is another example of feline generosity:

A feline fancy

Father's Day gifts come in all sizes and shapes, but this year the most unusual gift to my husband came from a stray cat.

For months, my husband has been feeding strays and when he realized one was going to have kittens he made special trips for extra food and milk.

At 11 a.m. Father's Day the stray cat scratched on the door. When I opened the door, there sat the cat with the most loving and grateful look.

Next to the stray sat the most beautiful fluffy kitten. I knew it was the pick of her litter she had given to my husband as a gift on his special day.

If I had not seen it, I would not have believed it possible.

The El Paso Times.

Is this account credible to the children? How would they describe the cat? . . . the cat's relationship to the man? . . . What is the man like?

□ *Real or Fictional?* Describe situations from stories the children have read. Ask children if they could have happened in real life or if such things are impossible. Ask children why authors use impossible situations.

R Ⓕ 1. The cow jumped over the moon.

R F 2. The mouse rode a motorcycle.

R F 3. Jerome was sent to the principal's office because he was naughty.

R F 4. The cat wore a hat.

R F 5. Etc.

□ *Make Up Stories* Ask children to make up two stories about people they know. One should be realistic and another fantasy. Let children compare their stories. (The stories might, instead, be about famous people, animals, etc.)

□ *Sexism and Racism* Ask the children if the following types of things could happen (or have happened) in real life.

H = has happened. C = could happen. N = could not happen.

H C N 1.   They find stories in their basal readers (or other books) showing girls doing exciting, adventuresome things.

H C N 2.   They find as many stories or episodes showing girls and women doing fascinating things as boys and men.

H C N 3.   Boys and men are shown cooking and cleaning at home.

H C N 4.   A father stays home to care for the children while the mother goes to work outside the home.

H C N 5.   Children and adults of minority groups are portrayed in their reading materials as positively as are middle and upper-class whites.

H C N 6.   A woman is Prime Minister of Great Britain.

H C N 7.   A woman is President of the United States.

H C N 8.   A man is President of the United States.

H C N 9.   A black is President of the United States.

H C N 10.   A white is President of the United States.

H C N 11.   Etc.

Variation.   Compose a similar list for ageism and another for "handicapped" people.

3.2 Judgments of Fact or Opinion, Propaganda Analysis The reader is "asked to decide whether the author is presenting information which can be supported with objective data or whether the author is attempting to sway the reader's thinking through the use of subjective content that has overtones of propaganda."[6]

FACT—OPINION

A statement of fact may be true or false. The important identifying feature of a factual statement is that it can be proved to be true or false. Opinions cannot be proved to be true or false. Though many people may agree with a stated opinion, objective evidence cannot be found to verify it or to disprove it. For example, the statement that a certain person is 5′ 6″ tall is a statement of fact (the person can be measured). It is, however, false if the person is shorter or taller than that. The statement that it is a beautiful day today is a statement of opinion, for objective evidence cannot verify or disprove the statement, even though most people may agree that it is beautiful.

Literal Level

These activities require recognition of statements as fact or opinion.

> □*Fact or Opinion?* List statements. Ask children to circle "F" for a statement of fact and "O" for a statement of opinion.
> F O 1. It is raining now.
> F O 2. I am 5'2" tall.
> F O 3. Yesterday was Monday.
> F O 4. Lincoln was the best president the U.S. has had.
> F O 5. Washington was the first president of the U.S.
> F O 6. The prettiest roses are yellow.
> F O 7. Cats make the best pets.
> F O 8. I weigh 92 pounds.
> F O 9. Our school colors are orange and white.
> F O 10. Chocolate bars are expensive.

> □*Circle and Underline* Give the children a passage from the newspaper or elsewhere. Ask them to underline all statements of fact and circle all statements of opinion. E.g.:

Cuddly is the only word for harp seals. The baby ones, especially, are so irresistable that one would think that sealskin coats would have disappeared as soon as the first possible buyer saw a picture of a live seal.

This book is about harp seals—and 75 percent of its pages have pictures on them. The text is pleasant and timely. Children will love this book.

> □*Children Supply Statements* Ask children to state a fact or opinion about themselves or about one of their class assignments. Have other children tell if it is a fact or opinion.

Inferential and Evaluation Levels

At the inferential and evaluation levels, children must think about, react to, compare, analyze, synthesize, extend information given to them. Following are some fact-opinion activities that would require children to respond to what an author has said.

> □*Change the Statement* Have children change statements they have identified as fact or opinion to the other kind. E.g.:

Fact	Opinion one	Opinion two
1. I am 5'2" tall.	1. (I'm of average height.)	1. (I'm tall.)
2. (Zingy Bars cost 25¢.)	2. Zingy bars are expensive.	2.
3.	3. It's warm outside today.	3. It's coolish today.
4. Our school has 500 children.	4.	4.
5.	5. I live far away from school.	5.
6.	6. Harp seals are beautiful.	6.
7.	7. Summer is the best time of the year.	7.
8. Beatrix Potter wrote 40 books.	8.	8.
9.	9. My grandmother is old.	9.
10.	10. Our house is big.	10.

□ *Prove or Disprove Factual Statements* Teach children the uses of various reference works.* Then ask children what source(s) they would use to prove or disprove a factual statement. E.g.:

From the list below, select a source you could use to prove or disprove the following statements.

almanac   encyclopedia   ruler
atlas   dictionary   scale   thesaurus   thermometer

1. One of the two commonly used pronunciations for word *family* is făm' - lē.   (dictionary)
2. The Mississippi River is 1500 miles long.   ______
3. Lou Gehrig is honored in the Baseball Hall of Fame in Cooperstown, N.Y.   ______
4. Our classroom measures 25 meters by 30 meters.   ______
5. Lincoln was the 16th president of the United States.   ______
6. The House of Tudor gave Britain ten monarchs.   ______

*Explained in Chapter 10.

7. Five wives of King Henry VIII were execut-
   ed. One was not.   _____________
8. There are at least 150 words in English for
   "supernatural beings." Some of them are:
                                                       ____
____

9. It's 52° in the sunshine now.   _____________
10. My cat weighs 9½ pounds.   _____________

□ *Who Is Likely to Believe This?* Take statements of opinion, and ask
children who is likely to believe the statement and who is unlikely
to believe the statement.

1. My grandmother is old. (Fact: She is 51.)
   a. an octogenarian
   b. my little brother
   c. my mother
   d. my grandfather
   e. my grandmother's best friend
   f. etc.
2. Summer is the best time of year.
   a. one whose favorite sport is swimming
   b. one whose favorite sport is skiing
   c. one who lives where there's a shortage of heating fuel
   d. one who loves to go to school
   e. one who hates school
   f. etc.

□ *Relate to Reading Materials* Help children identify and react to similar statements in their reading materials. You might also wish to
ask them to identify and react to statements they hear on T.V.

PROPAGANDA ANALYSIS

Frequently children are told—either directly or subtly—what they
should do. They might be told to buy something, do something, or believe in something. Often this is done for someone else's welfare and not
their own. Children are bombarded by T.V. ads that feature sugared
foods, like certain cereals that contain 70 percent sugar, and chocolate
bars, cookies, cola, etc. According to Jack Anderson,[7] ". . . corporations
are now shelling out more than $600 million a year to transform young
television viewers into what one advertiser calls 'highly successful nag-
gers.'" The average child watches about four hours of T.V. daily, seeing

20,000 commercials a year. Many children naïvely believe they need what the commercials tell them they need.

Newspaper and magazine articles, as well as books, are also frequently biased. One need only compare several newspaper articles or several books on the same subject to discover such biases. For example, compare articles in several newspapers about last week's big football or baseball game—in the hometown papers of each team. Compare editorials in several newspapers about a coming election. Compare chapters written about the Civil War in two different books—one written by a Northerner and one by a Southerner. One way of doing this is to give half of the class one selection and the other half a conflicting one without telling the children they have different selections. Before reading, state questions that they should answer using the information supplied by their author. After reading, have them discuss their findings. See how long it takes them to discover that they have read different passages.

When analyzing propaganda in school situations, it is often customary to begin with advertisements. Perhaps this is because the principles of propaganda can then be taught without strong emotional reactions from children. However important it may be for children to be alert to commercialism, it is also important for children to know that propaganda techniques are used in many other areas of their lives. Schools should be responsible for teaching children about biases in many areas.

Literal Level

Children should be able to identify seven propaganda techniques. These are: glad names (glittering generalities), sad names, plain folks, bandwagon (and bandwagon of the elite), card stacking, transfer, and testimonial. Each is briefly explained below.

Glad Names Glad names, often called "glittering generalities" or "purr words," are terms with pleasant connotations. They are expressions used to engender a glowing feeling—to make us happy—to make us feel good about something. E.g.:

yummy (chocolate)	freedom
crunchy (cereal)	democratic
snap-crackle-pop	All-American
delicious	liberal *or* conservative, but not
fantastic	both, depending on the
bubbly, effervescent	point of view of the person

Sad Names Sad names, sometimes called "bad names," have unpleasant connotations. They may be used to turn us away from a competitor's product or to incite hatred or fear. E.g.:

saggy   communist
dirty   un-American
itchy   totalitarian
cheap, expensive

Plain Folks Always popular, the plain folks technique is gaining in popularity today. Note the number of rather average looking people on T.V. today—both in programs and advertisements. One need no longer be ultraglamorous to advertise certain products. Politicians have long used the plain folks technique: they bring their families along on the campaign trail; they kiss babies. Now Presidents carry their own suitcases, wear sporty clothing, eat hot dogs, and prepare their own breakfasts.

Bandwagon Most people want to get on the bandwagon—that is, they want to be like other people. "Everybody's doing it" suggests that we should do it too—but is *everybody*? Do we wish to be one of those "everybodies"? Why or why not?

A new type of bandwagon technique has recently emerged—the "bandwagon of the elite." Only the elite do (or buy) certain things. If you want to be elite, you'll follow the small, but elite, group. E.g.: "Nine out of 10,000 Americans drink Campari." To my knowledge this technique hasn't caught on in children's ads as yet, but it probably will.

Card Stacking Card stacking has always been with us. It is the technique of presenting only one side of an argument. When criticized by his mother for listening to too many detective programs, a young friend of mine replied, "I'm learning that crime does not pay." What do you say after staying out too late at night, when not having your homework assignment, when forgetting to go to the store? Do you present all sides fairly?

Transfer In the transfer technique, a highly regarded person, symbol, or concept is related to the idea or product "being pushed." If a toothpaste contains *fluoride*, it must be good. If *research proves* something, it must be true. If Robert Young endorses a certain brand of coffee, his T.V. image suggests that doctors endorse it, which means it must be all right to consume it. If animals rush to devour a certain pet food on T.V., you are led to believe that your pet will do the same. Everybody likes eagles, and a picture of one on a dictionary will probably increase sales, as a picture of a baby on a magazine cover will sell the magazine to many people. You may feel patriotic if you purchase something wrapped in red, white, and blue. Many think that if they smoke the "right" brand of cigarettes, they'll be put in a scene like that shown in the ad.

Testimonial A testimony is an affirmation of gratitude (or value) and is often a recommendation that others do as the testifier has done. Unfortunately, in advertising many people testify to the value of products they rarely use. They are paid highly to do so. Paul Newman shocked many when he turned down a million dollar contract to advertise a product he personally could not endorse. Pets advertise pet foods: Cats ask for "Meow Mix" by name, and finicky Morris said he would eat anything— as long as it's "Nine Lives."

There's probably not a person in this world who doesn't use propaganda. The use of propaganda may be self-serving or altruistic—or a combination of both. Surely we all would have problems if there were no advertising—where would we go to buy products? Where would we get the best buy? How would we find out that a pound of choice pecans are $9.00 in one store, $6.50 in another, and $4.98 in still another? It would take a lot of time to run from store to store . . . and a lot of gasoline.

Honest advertising is a service to a community. Dishonest or misleading advertising is a disservice. "Let the buyer or consumer beware" unfortunately is a valid caution. Such is the case, also, when biased writing of any type is available.

The following activities are literal level activities in propaganda awareness.

□*Explain With Extra Care Some of the More Difficult to Identify Techniques to the Children* E.g.:

• *card stacking*:
  1. Smoke _____________s. They'll make you feel cool. (Nothing is said about the fact that cigarettes are dangerous to one's health.)
  2. "Spray _____________ in your kitty litter box. It'll destroy the cat odor." (It'll destroy the cat, since it is toxic to cats.*)
  3. "Eat _____________ cereal every day. It has all the vitamins you need for a balanced diet." (What about the minerals you also need? What about all the sugar that's bad for you?)

---

*One brand that advertises, or has advertised, thus is toxic to cats according to *Cats* magazine.

• *transfer*:
1. In a T.V. ad, a peddler is selling fresh fruit in a neighborhood. Elves appear, and he asks them if they would like to buy some fruit. Instead, the elves offer the peddler a cookie from their sack. The peddler finds it so good that he throws away his fruit and begins to sell the cookies. (*Moral*: Cookies should be eaten instead of fruit.)
2. A glamorous woman is pictured in a full-page ad wearing a beautiful fur coat. Nothing is said. (*Moral*: Glamorous women wear fur coats. If you want to be glamorous, buy a fur coat. Also, forget about ecology.) Children may decide they have such "needs" long before they are adults.
3. Pencils, notebooks, note paper, etc., are for sale at a store. These have boy scout or girl scout emblems on them. (Members of groups often like to identify themselves and be identified with their groups—not necessarily bad.)

• *bandwagon*:
1. "Men, women, children—*everyone* in this colony must commit suicide or, in the case of young children, be killed by an adult." (Peoples Temple, Guyana, fall 1978—more than 600 Americans perished—almost the whole colony.)
2. "*Everybody* smokes pot." (*Moral*: You should too.) Does everybody? Do you want to be like the people who do?
3. "We're *all* going out to trick-or-treat this Halloween. Be ready with some tricks." (*Moral*: If everybody is tricking, you should too.) Is everybody going to trick? Maybe you can offer an alternative—e.g., asking for money for UNESCO—but *no* tricks.

☐ *Children Supply Examples* Explain a technique, and give examples. Ask children to suggest examples from T.V. ads. These should be written on slips of paper and put in a container. Also ask children who are old enough to clip ads from newspapers and magazines, circle the specific technique being used, and bring it to share with the class. These also could be added to the container. Finally there will be seven such containers—one for each technique.

Older children could do the same, adding newspaper and magazine articles about specific controversial topics. They may also write down statements from T.V. Children could also write their own ads or statements.

☐ *Identifying the Technique* Mix slips from different containers as described above, and ask children to identify the technique being used. A spelldown could be used or other game. A form could be used instead such as the following:

In the blank provided, write the technique being used. (The techniques are listed at the top of this page.)

glad names   testimony   bandwagon   card stacking
sad names   transfer   plain folks

1. Our *cookie crisp* cereal looks like *chocolate chip* cookies.   (glad names)
2. Our chocolate is *milk* chocolate.   (transfer)
3. Avoid that *saggy, restless* feeling with just one ___________ before bed at night.   (sad names)
4. *Nine out of ten cats*, when given a choice, ask for "Meow" mix by name.   (bandwagon)
5. Your *school crest* is on a shirt for sale at the bookstore.   (transfer)
6. You tell your mother that you're late from school because you stayed to get extra help. (You also stopped at the corner drug store for a soda.)   (card stacking)
7. Buy *Mother's* Pies—they're just like *mother* used to make.   (transfer)
8. "Tennis is the *fastest growing* sport today. You should learn to play it."   (bandwagon)
9. "Jimmy likes it! Look at him eat that cereal. Jimmy says, "I like it."   (testimony)
10. *"All of us folks down on the farm* like this good hickory smoked bacon."   (plain folks)

(You might note that it is not always bad to use propaganda techniques.)

Inferential and Evaluative Levels

In analyzing and evaluating propaganda, children should be taught to ask the following questions:

* Who are the propagandists?
* Whom are they serving?
* What is their aim in writing (or speaking) about this topic?
* To what human needs, interests, desires, emotions do they appeal?
* What techniques do they use?

The following are suggested as possible activities for teaching these. (The "item" is the statement identified as propaganda. Remember, not all propaganda is bad, but it all is persuasive.)

□ *Use a Chart* Set up a chart, such as the following. The teacher or children may select the items, and the children fill in the blank spaces.
Variation. The teacher or children might fill in the final column, and then select an item that would be appropriate to it. Such items might be posted on a bulletin board.

Item	Who are the propagandists?	Whom are they serving?	What is their aim?	To what interests, desires, emotions do they appeal?
"_____ is a remarkable tale of exile and survival . . . the epic novel of a group of adventurers."	book publishers or book critic	themselves and/or the interests of proposed readers	increased sales and/or promoting information about the book	sense of adventure, excitement, desire to read interesting books
"Fabulous new game for kids . . . for you to get or give this Christmas."	manufacturer or seller	themselves _____ your knowledge of what is available	increased sales	love of games, fun
"Rhodesia, South-West Africa, Iran, Nicaragua —these areas abound in turmoil and anguish. Yet at the heart of the conflicts there are the welcome yearnings of people for freedom, basic human rights and greater human dignity . . ."	editorial writer	people around the world who might empathize with those who have such needs	increased information and empathy concerning these nations	feelings many have for people in deep trouble with needs for freedom

□ *Propaganda Bee* Ask each child to bring to class an item that could be classified as propaganda. Put these in a container. Group the children into two teams, as for a spelling bee. Proceed thus:

Team 1   — Child picks slip and reads it. The child answers the question: "Who is the propagandist?"
points: one logical answer—1 point
two logical answers—2 points

Team 2   — Child answers the question: "Whom are they serv-
           ing?"
           points: one logical answer—1 point
                   two logical answers—2 points
Team 1   — "What is their aim in writing (or speaking) about this
           topic?"
           points: up to 2 points, as above
Team 2   — To what human interests, desires, or emotions do
           they appeal?"
           points: up to 2 points, as above
Team 1   — "What techniques do they use?"
           points: one point for each technique correctly identi-
                   fied.

You may wish to allow teammates to form small groups for
responding to each question.

□ *Special Awards* Tell children they will receive a special award (like
a bookmark, but *never* food) each time they identify propaganda in
one of their textbooks. You may wish to add that they analyze the
item according to the above criteria. The child with the greatest
number of such awards in a given time may receive a bonus award
—like a paperback book of the child's choice. (The teacher should
keep track of each award given: otherwise the child may feel he or
she cannot immediately use the award for fear it may be lost.)

□ *Compare Information from Two or More Sources* As suggested earlier,
give part of the class one statement and another part a conflicting
statement without telling the children they have different passages.
State purposes for reading before the children read.

• Example 1: "Read to find out when America was discovered
and by whom."

In 1492, the Italian navigator Christopher Columbus discovered America. At the time, he was sailing under the Spanish flag . . . Etc.	In about 1000 A.D., the Scandinavian navigator Leif Erickson, sailed to Nova Scotia. He was the first European to set foot on North America and, thus, was its discoverer . . . Etc.

After they have finished reading, ask children questions such as:
When was America discovered? What was the name of the person who discovered America? What European nation should be

credited with the discovery of America? Wait to see how long it takes the children to discover they have read different articles. Ask them if often there might be conflicting statements about the same topic.

- Example 2: "Read to find out what kind of pet a dog would be."

<table>
<tr><td>Dogs are good pets, I had heard. So I talked my folks into letting me have one. Since then, it's been nothing but trouble with a capital T.

My dog's a finicky eater. And he messes up the back yard. Yesterday he chewed our best davenport. We scolded him, and he yelped all night . . .</td><td>Dogs are good pets, I had heard. So I talked my folks into letting me have one. He's now the best friend I've ever had!

We trained him well, and allow him in only certain parts of the house when we're not around. He's so cuddly and loves to sit on my lap while I pet him. I enjoy brushing him and having him sleep at the foot of my bed . . .</td></tr>
</table>

Ask literal level questions first, and wait for the discovery that the children have read different articles. They might finally conclude, in this case, that more is being said about the owners of the dogs than about the dogs themselves.

3.3 and 3.4 Judgments of Adequacy, Validity, and Appropriateness The reader is asked to judge whether the author's treatment of a subject is

- adequate, i.e., complete when compared to internal criteria (the reader's needs, i.e., top, reader's schemata) and external criteria (compared to other sources, i.e., bottom, schemata of this author and other authors);
- valid, i.e., true or accurate when compared to internal criteria (what the reader knows about the subject, i.e., top) and external criteria (compared to other sources, reference aids, i.e., bottom);
- appropriate, i.e., relevant in that it can contribute to resolving an issue, problem, need, or desire.

Relevant considerations in terms of internal criteria (i.e., top, reader's schemata) are the following:

- What motivates children to want to read?
- What materials will children choose to read in relation to each motive?
- How can the teacher help to satisfy the children's needs and desires?

Considerations in terms of external criteria (materials read or examined) relate directly to the reader's reason for reading (top) and the reader's background (top) in relation to the materials that are available.

Why Do Children Read? What Do They Read for Each Purpose?

After analyzing research on the subject, Grover Mathewson[8] concluded that the following may be reasons for reading:

- *curiosity and exploration*: A child may read because of being curious, of wishing to explore, to find out more about a subject. Perhaps a child becomes curious because he or she sees a book that stimulates curiosity. Or a child may be interested in a subject and seek reading materials to satisfy that interest.
- *achievement*: A child may read to achieve a goal, e.g., to learn about a school subject, to learn how to do something like playing tennis better, to pass a test, etc.
- *anxiety*: A child may read out of fear or because of pressure. A child may read because he or she fears failure in school or in future life. A child may read to escape the pressure of real life.
- *activity*: A child may read because reading is enjoyable and gives the reader something to do. A child may read to have a holiday.
- *self-actualization*: A child may read to help realize goals to satisfy himself or herself, perhaps to bring about a feeling of worth, a sense of accomplishment. A child may read to see himself or herself in literature—to see how another person deals with problems or aspirations similar to his or hers. A child may read to see what life is like for someone slightly older or slightly more mature than himself or herself. A child may read to find a model for his or her own life.
- *vicarious aesthetic experience*: Douglas Waples[9] would add that a child may read because a reading experience may offer beauty and insights beyond those normally achievable in real life—as music and art may also offer beauty and insights. An author may express ideas more clearly, more forcefully, more aesthetically than most readers can. Authors of classics—poetry and prose—portray characters by using uncommon insight. Such authors can transport readers into other ages—past and future—and other areas, and even help readers see what is at home more clearly. Such authors spark the imagination and make life much richer.

Each of these motivating forces suggests specifics in relationship to subject matter and quality of reading materials the child might be willing to read or desire to read. For example, when children read out of curiosity, they select materials that specifically satisfy the curiosity they have in terms of content. They may read voraciously almost anything they can lay their hands on—e.g., to know everything about their favorite T.V. star, their favorite baseball team, to know all there is to know about astronomy, about dinosaurs, about cars, or any other interest. The children will read as much or as little as is needed to satisfy that curiosity. Of course, reading may actually increase curiosity and lead to more and more reading and exploration.

When children read to achieve, they are goal oriented. They may read a textbook and other required materials to get a grade that satisfies them —and may even seek additional reading material to achieve the goal. In most cases children will look for material that is clear and specific in leading toward the goal. Materials read for this purpose are usually judged in terms of completeness and clarity and in terms of the child's background of understanding in relationship to the author's presentation. Frequently, almost total comprehension is desired—or the level and kind of comprehension tests measure.

For purposes of achievement, children will even read materials that may be unappealing to them—and may read them with good comprehension. A textbook may not really interest a child, but the reward for having read it—a satisfactory grade or learning something one "ought" to know—may be highly appealing.

In contrast, when children read for curiosity, they may often look for new vistas to spark their imagination. Often it may not really matter if there is only slight comprehension. At other times, the child's curiosity may demand total comprehension. All teachers have worked with children who find grade level textbooks hard to understand but who can read other materials way above grade level because these materials relate to their strong interests and to their well-developed experiences in these areas.

Children do read because of anxiety and fear. Usually the materials are those that are assigned to them and must be read to pass a test, etc. They may find that they like these materials and may then begin reading for other reasons—like curiosity, activity, or self-actualization. They may also choose to read "escape" literature because of anxiety—to escape from the real world, which may be terribly harsh. In such cases, the books they choose provide avenues for escape to the degree that the setting, story line, and characters are far removed from the realities of their own experiences and to the degree that they need not report to someone what the material was about. Required book reports may prevent a child from reading for escape and, therefore, from allaying anxiety.

When children read because of fear of failure, the anxiety and fear can promote reading disability. Anxiety tends to excite functions such as fluency and to depress word recognition, memory, and comprehension. Reading because of fear of failure may also promote negative attitudes toward reading in general.

Children sometimes read just to have something to do, or because they prefer reading to other pastimes. In such cases they may also read to escape—to have a holiday. Books selected for such purposes may be most appreciated also if they are far removed from the child's real experiences.

When children read for self-actualization, they choose materials that help them feel good about themselves and/or help them reach goals they set for themselves. When reading to promote self-concept, they frequently desire materials that are slanted to glorify their own position and may judge materials to be satisfactory if they do correspond with their point of view (cognitively) or their feelings (affectively). If materials are read that differ from the child's bent, such materials may be judged by the child to be unsatisfactory or may, if the child can read without prejudice, lead to tolerance, understanding, and possibly conversion.[10]

One of the most difficult things for a reader or listener to do is to suspend judgment—to read or listen with an open mind—in order to understand another's point of view. Teachers must help children learn to do this. One way is to have the child role-play a character quite different from himself or herself and in this role interact with others of various persuasions. A middle class white child might role-play as a lower-class black, and vice-versa. A litterbug might role-play as a conservationist or taxpayer who has to pay for cleaning up an area. A child whose pet is allowed to reproduce at will might read about humane societies and then role-play as an employee of one. Etc.

Children may decide that to satisfy themselves, they must accomplish something, perhaps in the distant future, and reading may help in doing this. For example a child may wish to become an expert skier, a highboard diver, a scientist, veterinarian, author, cartoonist, police officer, sky diver, etc. Having such a goal may motivate the child to select "how to do it" books as well as biographies and autobiographies of successful people in these fields. Such materials can be compared in terms of completeness (how to do it books and articles), validity (two biographies about the same person, or an autobiography and biography about the same person), and appropriateness (how helpful is the source?).

Sometimes children read to enjoy the beauty of fine poetry or to know characters in depth. Literature may feed the imagination of children and may help them find peace. Where else could children meet Charlotte of *Charlotte's Web?* . . . and poor Pig, who emerges after severe trials not too badly off? The paintbrush of authors adds rich hues to life.

Basic Considerations for Appropriateness of Choice

Mathewson hypothesizes that, ". . . it appears that all reading which is self-sustaining, not the result of external press, must be accompanied by a favorable attitude toward the reading materials."[11] When discussing attitude in relation to adequacy and appropriateness of reading materials,

Mathewson contends that three factors emerge: content, form, and format. "The content or meaning of a book is a primary attitude object because it may correspond with the reader's motivations and general background, or it may not correspond."[12] It may often be essential to find materials that do correspond. However, surely it is also essential to broaden the child's background—to extend and at times to modify her or his beliefs. Children must be exposed to a wide variety of topics and ideas, to various types of materials, and many types of writing.[13] Reading should open new vistas for children.

Another consideration is form: How appropriate are the syntax and the dialect to the reader? How appropriate is the vocabulary? How difficult is the writing style (or readability*) in terms of the child's reading achievement? Also important is format—the organization of the material, the presence or absence of pictures, the quality of the illustrations, the type of cover (paperback?), the size and style of print, etc.

The previous discussion supplied general ideas about motivation and materials. Following are some specific techniques that might be used in classroom situations to promote related goals.

To help provide an understanding that some sources are more valid than others and that some topics are highly controversial (related to motivation by curiosity and exploration, achievement, and self-actualization), the following types of activities might be helpful:

□*Authors' Qualifications* Children should know that writers' and speakers' qualifications in relation to topics vary. They might consider this through an activity such as the following:

Who is/are likely to be the best person(s) to make an accurate and unbiased statement about:

1. a balanced diet—
   - _X_ a school nurse
   - _____ a manager of a supermarket
   - _X_ a general science teacher
   - _____ a school aide
   - _X_ author of a textbook on nutrition
   - _____ author of TV or newspaper ads
2. animal ecology—
   - _____ person who hunts seals for a living
   - _____ owner of the local Fashionable Furs Shoppe
   - _____ Belton P. Mouras, president, Animal Protection Institute of America
   - _____ Sarah P. Hughes, professor of Zoology, State University
   - _____ Jake Spooner, sports hunter

*Discussed in Chapter 14.

3. Etc.
Children might brainstorm about people who might be authors of an article or book. Then they would decide who might be most accurate and unbiased.

□ *Detecting Biases* Statements from children's materials (T.V. ads, newspaper and magazine articles, books, etc.) could be analyzed in the following way:

1. Who said so? What are the person's qualifications for making such a statement?
2. Why does the person (or organization) want me to believe this?
3. What makes the person (or organization) think so? What evidence supports the statement?

□ *Controversial Topic* Ask children how they feel about a topic that is controversial, e.g., an upcoming election, a local or national issue in ecology, any issue in which there appear to be at least two popularly held points of view. Ask them to research the point of view that differs from theirs and to present the strongest case they can for that point of view. You may instead, wish to have them carefully explain exactly how proponents of that point of view feel and to answer questions as those people would. Helpful here might also be the kinds of activities suggested under fact versus opinion and propaganda analysis.

To help motivate children to read and to select materials that appeal to them in terms of their attitude in relation to adequacy and appropriateness, the following techniques might be used:

□ *Free Choice* Have many books available. Or take the children to the library. Children choose books they think they would like. Books might be displayed on a table, perhaps opened to interesting illustrations. Books that are displayed with their front jackets showing are far more likely to be selected than books lined up in a bookcase with just the binding showing.

□ *Book Talk* Give a "book talk," or have the school librarian or a child give a "book talk," telling the highlights of a favorite book —or telling an interesting episode or telling the story to its climax.

□ *Ring-a-Bell* Give each child in the class (or in a group) a different book. Allow the children five minutes to examine their books. Then ring a bell. At the sound of the bell, children pass books to another child. Repeat five times. At the end of 30 minutes, each child has examined six books. Now children may choose their favorites to read.

□ *Fish* Write the names of books on slips of paper. Each child picks a slip and then looks at the book. If the child doesn't like the book, let him or her fish again.

□ *Pocket Charts* Make one or more pocket charts, each of which has a theme, e.g., space travel, children from other lands, or any topic in which children show an interest. In each chart insert book jackets or cards—or even paperbacks—with brief descriptions of each book. You might prefer to use illustrated cards with descriptions written by children who have read the books.

□ *Make a Theme Exciting and Colorful* Use an illustrative pattern, e.g., a map of the world. As children read books about a world theme (e.g., travel around the world, music around the world, children of the world, animals of the world) have them stick pictures of characters from the book or the flag for the country read about on the map. (They may have to consult an encyclopedia or almanac to draw the flag.) If they read about different areas of one country, they may use pins to show the area, or they may use pictures of characters from the books. The same kind of thing could be done using a flow chart, a time line, a spoke graph or other pattern.

Illustrations such as these may promote a feeling of self-actualization among those children who have read the materials and may promote curiosity among others.

□ *Interest Centers* Build interest centers using pictures, possibly posters, tapes, and reading materials. Each center is based on a theme of interest to children. This might be done using a wide variety of themes, as in a reading class. Or it might be done using themes related to a unit in a content area class. Use books, magazines, and pamphlets of a wide range of difficulty—something to appeal to good and poor readers.

□ *Interest Inventories* Write interest inventories related to a topic. Include brief descriptions of books so that children can decide which books they wish to examine and perhaps read. The following format might be used:

Theme: Animals—Domestic and Wild
Would you like to read a book about (circle yes or no):

Yes No 1.   why fish live underwater, flies can walk on walls, birds fly, some animals sleep in wintertime, cats can see at night, turtles carry their houses, fireflies

Yes No   light up, and other things animals can do? (Jeanne Benedick: *Why Can't I?*)

Yes No 2.   the mysterious world of night-time animals? (Glenn Blough: *After the Sun Goes Down*)

Yes No 3.   where small animals—raccoon, fox, squirrel, chipmunk, rabbit and others—go during the season of cold and snow? (Charles Fox: *When Winter Comes*)

Yes No 4.   different baby animals and how they grow? (Millicent Selsam: *All Kinds of Babies*)

Yes No 5.   poems about small animals—cats, dogs, horses, cows, frogs, and others? (William Cole: *I Went to the Animal Fair*)

         .
         .
         .

Yes No 20.   small animals from Africa—such as a story about a hyena who lies, a lonely lioness, a tricky rabbit, and more? (Verna Aardema: *Tales for the Third Ear from Equatorial Africa*)

Theme: Indians
Would you like to read a book about (circle yes or no):

Yes No 1.   suspense and mystery as you discover the origins of the first Americans? (C.W. Ceram: *The First American*)

Yes No 2.   Indians telling their own history of when they roamed unchallenged in the wilderness of forests and plains? (Charles Hamilton: *Cry of the Thunderbird*)

Yes No 3.   the very early history of two unique Indian tribes? (John H. Seger: *Early Days among the Cheyennes and Arapaho Indians*)

Yes No 4.   Indians who were farmers of the Rio Grande and artisans of the Southwest? (Stanley A. Stubbs: *Bird's Eye View of the Pueblos*)

Yes No 5.   short biographies of some famous Indians? (Sidney E. Fletcher: *The American Indian from Prehistoric Times to the Present*)

         .
         .
         .

Yes No 20.   societies and cults of the Plains Indians, written by an Indian? (Thomas E. Mails: *Dog Soldiers, Bear Men and Buffalo Women*)

Theme: Children Around the World
Would you like to read a book about (circle yes or no):

Yes No 1.   the story of a Japanese fishing village when a tidal wave strikes? (Pearl Buck: *The Big Wave*)

Yes No 2.   Lu, a Hawaiian boy in ancient times, who prepares to succeed his grandfather as tribal chief? (William Lipkind: *Boy of the Islands*)

Yes No 3.   three children who find shelter with their mother under a Paris bridge and then win the affection of a hobo who shows them Christmas in the city and finds them a real home? (Natalie Savage Carlson: *The Family Under the Bridge*)

Yes No 4.   a small Chinese boy who was separated from his family in time of war and finds his way back to his pet pig? (Meindert De Jong: *The House of Sixty Fathers*)

Yes No 5.   the son of a great Spanish bullfighter, who is
    ·   expected to fight as his father did? (Maia
    ·   Wojciechowska: *Shadow of a Bull*)
    ·

Yes No 20.   a lonely boy on a Canadian farm who brings home a moose calf for a pet? (May McNeer and Lynd War: *The Story of Little Baptiste and the Moose*)

□ *Read to Children* Regularly—even every day—read aloud to children. You may wish to read an old favorite, but better still, read a book to them that would be a little hard for them to read to themselves—to stretch them a bit. Read something that introduces new ideas and vistas to them.

□ *Read with Children* Alternate in reading a story with an individual child. You read one page, the child reads the next.

□ *Field Trips* When possible, take children on a field trip—real or vicarious—to extend their backgrounds and interests. Select books related to the field trip, and make them available for children to read.

□ *Reading Wheel* To encourage wide reading, give each child a "Reading Wheel," a pie-shaped drawing with different designated areas in it. Each time a child reads a book, he or she puts a star in the appropriate wedge. (See Figs. 9.1 and 9.2).

□ *Book Train* To encourage in-depth reading about one topic, have a child build a book-train, naming the train after the topic and adding a car for each related book. On each car have the child write the name of the book and author. You may wish to do this as a class-wide project instead.

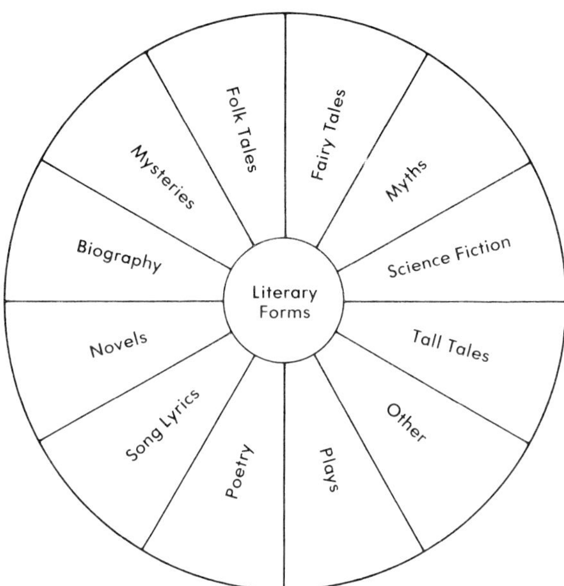

Fig. 9.1: A sample reading wheel for an English or language arts class.

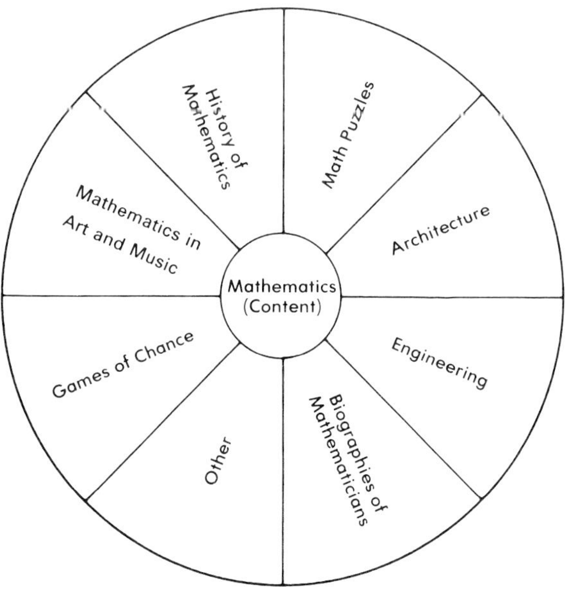

Fig. 9.2: A sample reading wheel for a mathematics class.

3.5 Judgments of Worth, Desirability, and Acceptability The reader passes judgment on the suitability of a character's (perhaps real person's) action in a particular incident or episode. Was the character right or wrong, good or bad, realistic or unrealistic—or somewhere in between? Barrett states, "Tasks of this nature call for opinions based on the values the reader has acquired through his personal experiences." The reader's stage of moral development is an important factor that affects the judgment made by the reader. In the opinion of the present writer, such judgments may be internalized and need not always be discussed.

Some children have been unable to accept or identify with stories like *The Yearling* and *Amigo* because of the tender child-parent relationships involved. To these children such stories have little value because the children cannot conceive of love in a household because it has never been a part of their personal experience. Yet such stories may be exactly what the child needs, for a child may learn vicariously what he or she cannot learn directly.

Bibliotherapy

Reading materials can be used to supply some experiences that may help children understand themselves and their environment better. When children read books that help solve personal problems and bolster self-image, according to some authors, bibliotherapy has taken place. "The main premise on which this process is based is that books are dynamic and have potential to change the attitudes, habits and skills of the people who read them. . . . Reading allows children to explore or realize various means of solving personal problems . . ."[14] On levels perhaps appropriate to the classroom, bibliotherapy can be thought of simply as "the process of helping children find books that will help them personally."[15]

According to Del Schubert,[16] bibliotherapy works this way:

- first is the shock of recognition, in which the reader realizes that he or she is not the first person to have such a problem. The reader may view the problem from a new perspective, which may help promote personality adjustment and growth;
- second, catharsis occurs, at which time there is release of tension and relaxation;
- third, there is insight through which the reader understands, modifies, and changes attitudes and behaviors.

According to Schubert, bibliotherapy in the classroom may help in solving—or giving perspective to—developmental problems of adjustment that all face.

Yet, bibliotherapy should not be conceived of as a panacea. There is potential for real problems if teachers attempt therapy in the classroom, and sometimes more harm can be done than good. Teachers are not therapists, and it is the wise person who knows his or her limitations.

The following guidelines are suggested by Terry Shepherd and Lynn Iles:[17]

1. Most children have only "minor" problems or questions (or as Schubert suggests, developmental problems). In these situations, children might be helped. Seriously disturbed children probably need professional help.
2. Try to avoid mentioning the problem to the child. For example, the teacher shouldn't say, "Why don't you read this book? It's about a fat person just like you." It is best if children choose the books to be read. They may do so when seeing an appropriate book displayed or because parts of it have been read aloud or discussed.
3. The book need not deal directly with the problem. E.g., as in the previous illustration, the book may simply show a fat child as a member of a group.
4. Books chosen should be believable enough so that the child can identify with both the character and the situation.

Bibliotherapy may be a term that is too strong to use for typical classroom situations. Yet essences of it may be appropriate. Through reading, children can learn what it's like to be a little older, a little more mature. They can also live many other lives (briefly) through reading, and this may help them become more understanding of people in other situations as well as of themselves.

On the other hand, reading materials can teach and reinforce unfavorable attitudes, too. Books filled with sexism, for example, show women and girls in subserviant roles, and girls may soon learn "their place" in society. And racist books show some racial groups in subserviant roles. Ageism[18] should also be considered: How are older people depicted in children's stories? Children should see models as active and intelligent senior citizens for several reasons. One reason is that this may help them in relating well to older people, and another reason is best summarized in the "self-fulfilling prophecy"—what seeds are they now sowing for their own futures? Another area of extreme importance relates to the handicapped. How are handicapped children and adults portrayed in the books children read? Careful selection of required reading materials for the classroom is essential. Also work on stereotyping and cardstacking* is appropriate.

---

*Cardstacking has been discussed under propaganda analysis.

Stereotyping is the process of overemphasizing characteristics that groups of people or objects are thought to have in common and underemphasizing the uniqueness of individuals. Women and girls do the cooking and cleaning in a household; men and boys live adventuresome lives. Blacks are uneducated. Culturally diverse groups are strange. Etc.

The importance of breaking the stereotype cannot be overemphasized if we are to progress in our democratic society.* People should be viewed as individuals, each with many facets, and perhaps today there is even a place for affirmative action in the selection of reading materials for the classroom: women and girls should be shown having a wide variety of experiences, and men and boys might be shown acting with tenderness and doing household chores. Members of a variety of ethnic groups should be shown in situations in the mainstream of American life as well as being proud of distinctive cultural traits. The elderly and the handicapped should be portrayed positively.

An activity that might be used is this: Select a newspaper article or passage from a book in which a man's or boy's activities are described. Substitute a woman's or girl's name for the masculine counterpart and analyze the effect. Do the same in relation to a middle- or upper-class white by substituting the name of a member of a minority group. Perhaps a better technique (i.e., one to be used more often) is to use actual experiences of women, girls, minorities, senior citizens and the handicapped.

Acceptability of Resolutions in Reading Materials

There is some evidence that children choose to read books that portray characters resolving issues at a level that is at or one step above their (the reader's) level of moral development. If children read books that resolve issues at a level two or more steps above their developmental stage, they either do not accept or do not understand the resolution. Also, although they understand resolutions that are at a lower level than they are at, they reject these.

Kohlberg[19] describes the stages of moral development that individuals pass through developmentally. Apparently the stages are universal—found in all societies—and they are progressive. Children begin at the lowest stage and progress one step at a time, never skipping a step, although most people stop before reaching the highest stages.

---

*Activities such as "Synthesizing Subschema into Categories—Convergently and Divergently" (pp. 346–349) are appropriate here. Names of real people or book characters might be used as subschema. Also appropriate are activities on "Oversimplification" (pp. 357-358).

These stages are:*

- preconventional level
  - *Stage 1: Punishment and Obedience Orientation* To people in this stage, physical consequences of an action determine its goodness or badness. If a child is rewarded with candy, a smile, etc., the action is thought to have been good. If a child is spanked, the action was bad. The child obeys rules to avoid being punished and understands this in characters in books and in articles in newspapers. (Some adults pay taxes only so they won't have to go to jail or obey speed limits so they won't get a ticket. At this stage a person is behaving in a certain way simply to *receive* a reward or to avoid a punishment.)
  - *Stage 2: Instrumental-Relativistic Orientation* To people in this stage, right action results in the satisfaction of one's needs and occasionally the needs of others. Elements of fairness, of reciprocity, and of equal sharing are present. Reciprocity is viewed in this context, "You scratch my back, and I'll scratch yours." People in this stage conform to rules or moral values in order to obtain rewards, but additionally there is a small desire to return some good for that received. Also they understand and accept resolutions of problems in reading materials—books, newspapers, magazines—at this level. (Some adults would do almost anything for money or would support political candidates only if they are assured a definite feedback.)
- conventional level
  - *Stage 3: Good Boy—Nice Girl Orientation* To people in this stage, good behavior is viewed as that which pleases or helps others and is approved by them. The person conforms to stereotyped images of what is thought to be the behavior of the majority or what is thought to be "natural" behavior. (They want to get on the bandwagon.) People in this stage conform to rules or moral values to avoid disapproval of others and to avoid being disliked. Also, they understand and accept the resolution of problems in reading materials based on such values.
  - *Stage 4: Law and Order Orientation* To people in this stage, right behavior is viewed as doing one's duty. Fixed rules are followed, as are the rules given by those in authority. There is an emphasis on maintaining social order. People in this stage obey rules, etc., to avoid censure by those in authority and to avoid feelings of guilt.

---

*Chapter 10 includes a discussion of the affective domain. Parallels might be drawn between Kohlberg's Stage 1 behavior and Level 1 of the affective domain (receiving). Also parallels might be drawn between Kohlberg's Stage 2 behavior and Level 2 of the affective domain (responding), especially the first two sublevels (acquiescence in responding, willingness to respond). Kohlberg's Stage 3 somewhat parallels sublevel 1 of Level 3 of the affective domain (acceptance of a value).

(People pay taxes because it is their duty. What would happen to the country if nobody paid? Young men register for the draft because they feel it is their duty, etc.)

- principled level (postconventional level)
  - *Stage 5: Social Contract, Legalistic Orientation* To people in this stage, right action is defined in terms of individual rights and standards that have been critically examined and agreed upon by the whole of society. This may bring about the changing of laws—or the Constitution—because of rational considerations and social fairness. People in this stage conform in order to receive and maintain respect *from others* in terms of community welfare. (People at this stage of development agree that women, minority groups, senior citizens, the handicapped, etc., deserve equal treatment by society and by them because *most* of society has decided that they do. People at this stage of development grant these people equality in order to gain the respect of others.)
  - *Stage 6: Universal—Ethical—Principle Orientation* To people in this stage, self-chosen ethical principles that appear to the individual to be logical, universal, and consistent determine, for that individual, what is right. The principles are those viewed as universally just, as promoting the equality and reciprocity of human rights, and as respecting the dignity of human beings—(and animals?)—as individuals. People in this stage conform to their own principles *to avoid self-condemnation.* (People at this stage of development grant others equal rights because they want to. To them, it would be wrong not to value the diversity of individuals and it is very satisfying to do so.)

Kohlberg also describes the six stages in terms of how children and young people value human life. The stages are the same as before:

- preconventional level
  - *Stage 1:* A human life is valuable in relation to the social status of the individual and in terms of the individual's possessions. (A child of the elite wealthy is more valuable than a child of the poor.)
  - *Stage 2:* A human life is valuable in relation to the value the individual himself or herself places on it, but even more so in relation to the needs it satisfies in others, e.g., mother-child relationship, husband-wife relationship. (Thus if the child is not important to the mother, or the husband is not important to the wife, the woman would not view the child's or husband's life as valuable.)
- conventional level
  - *Stage 3:* A human life is valuable in relation to the degree of attachment other people (e.g., the person's family, the boss) place on it.

- *Stage 4:* All life is valuable because it is sacred to God (or other ideal).
- principled level (postconventional level)
  - *Stage 5:* Life is a human right and is, therefore, valuable. Everyone has a life and is at the center of his or her own life, and that is valuable to the person.
  - *Stage 6:* All human life is valuable, and the individual is of extreme importance. Each human life is more valuable than anything other than human life.

To help put these stages in perspective for teachers, it might be well for teachers to have some idea of percentages of children's responses at each stage. Kohlberg supplies a small bit of information from a long-term study of 75 middle class boys in the United States. In this study, Kohlbert found that the boys' responses to questions posed as moral dilemmas were in approximately the following percentages by stages and ages:

Age	Grade	Stages					
		1	2	3	4	5	6
10	4.8	38%	29%	22%	10%	1%	
13	7.8	12%	19%	30%	24%	9%	3%
16	10.8	10%	12%	21%	26%	27%	6%

Teachers who are aware of these stages and who can analyze children's discussions are in a position to identify the stage at which the child is operating. The next step may well be to ask further questions, promote a discussion, (for children learn from other children who are a step above them) and make materials available at the next higher level. Thus the child who views the following action as right:

Senator J. M. Twiddledee decided to support candidate M. P. Newselwich for President because the candidate promised that if he became President, he would divert federal monies to Twiddledee's district. (stage 2)

might be asked if such behavior would be viewed as fair or good by the majority of Americans (stage 3). Though such action might be viewed as a common occurrence, it might not be judged as "good" (stage 3). At stage 4, the question might be, "Is the President doing his duty as a President of all the people if he diverts such monies?" Etc.

Summary

Critical reading, called "Evaluation" by Barrett, was discussed in this chapter. According to Barrett's taxonomy, reading at the evaluation level involves making judgments of the following types:

- Judgments of Reality or Fantasy
- Judgments of Fact or Opinion (Including Propaganda Analysis)
- Judgments of Adequacy or Validity
- Judgments of Appropriateness
- Judgments of Worth, Desirability, or Acceptability

Each of these was discussed in this chapter, along with suggested activities in each category. Introducing this discussion was a brief explanation of the need for receptive discipline—that is, the need of the reader to be passive enough to receive the ideas of others and active enough to interpret these ideas in his or her own framework.

Judgments of reality or fantasy include determining whether incidents, events, or characters in a selection could have existed or occurred or are likely to exist or occur in real life in the future. Judgments of fact or opinion require the reader to decide whether the author is presenting information that can be supported by objective evidence or whether the author is attempting to sway the reader's thinking. Included in this is the analysis of propaganda using the following techniques: glad names, sad names, plain folks, bandwagon, card stacking, transfer, testimonial. It was suggested that the following questions be asked when analyzing propaganda: Who are the propagandists? Whom are they serving? What is their aim in writing (or speaking) about this topic? To what human interests, desires, emotions do they appeal? What techniques do they use? It was stressed that the use of propaganda is not necessarily bad—(it is often good)—but propaganda is used to persuade, and the reader and listener should be aware that he or she may be manipulated.

Judgments of adequacy, validity, and appropriateness were next discussed, and activities were suggested. Of major concern were

- What motivates children to want to read?
- What materials will children choose to read in relation to each motive?
- How can the teacher help to satisfy the children's needs and desires?

Finally, judgments of worth, desirability, and acceptability were discussed. Included was a discussion of using "bibliotherapy" for developmental reasons, to show that books might be used to help readers understand themselves and others better and a discussion of the concept that books can teach and reinforce unfavorable attitudes also. A brief discussion followed concerning Kohlberg's description of the stages of moral development and the relationship of moral development of an individual to his or her ability to accept specific types of resolutions to problems.

Questions and Activities

After answering the questions at the beginning of this chapter, consider these questions and activities:

1. Might one call "internal criteria" the reader's own schemata and "external criteria" the author's (speakers, etc.) schemata? Explain. Name as many types of "external criteria" as you can. Under what conditions do these affect the child's internal criteria? Explain.
2. Begin a collection of articles that show that reality can be as strange as fantasy and truth can be stranger than fiction. How could these be used in the classroom in teaching children to reason evaluatively?
3. Compare a list of opinion statements that relate to topics of interest to children. Ask the question: "Who is likely to believe this?"
4. Begin a collection of advertisements and other passages written to influence children for each of the propaganda techniques. Circle and name the technique in each. You may wish to include T.V. ads in written form.
5. Begin a collection of passages from different sources that deal with a common topic of interest to children. These should represent different points of view and/or some should be more complete than others. Analyze how these might be used when teaching children about an author's perspective and purpose.
6. Analyze the reasons for reading given in this chapter. Do they all make sense to you? Is the discussion complete? Consider a group of children of a specific age. What reading materials might they select to read for each reason?
7. What is the role of the teacher in adding depth and breadth to a child's interest in reading? Should the teacher follow a "hands-off" policy, or should the teacher attempt to strengthen and/or broaden interests? Explain. Should a teacher ever discourage the reading of certain materials? Explain.
8. Write a short interest inventory related to a theme, such as those suggested on pages 396–398. Consider the age and the reading levels of the children who are to use it.
9. Consider the value of using a "reading wheel" (p. 399).

Does the use of such a wheel encourage broad or in-depth reading?

10. Are there any dangers that might be related to using bibliotherapy in a classroom? What special cautions should a teacher observe? What might be some positive effects of using bibliotherapy?
11. Begin collecting articles and stories from newspapers and magazines in which moral issues are resolved. Try to classify the level of resolution of the issue. Do you see a value in analyzing these resolutions with children or young people? Explain.

NOTES

1. Thomas C. Barrett, pp. 65–66. See Selected References.
2. Norris Sanders, p. 10. See Selected References.
3. David Elkind, pp. 338–339. See Selected References.
4. Barrett, *op. cit.*, p. 65.
5. *Ibid.*
6. *Ibid.*
7. Jack Anderson. "T.V. Ads Selling Sweet Things Are Bitter Trap for Children," a syndicated column appearing the week of April 15, 1978.
8. Grover Mathewson, pp. 658–659. See Selected References.
9. Douglas Waples. See Selected References.
10. *Ibid.*
11. Mathewson, *op. cit.*, p. 658.
12. *Ibid.*
13. Thomas C. Barrett, "Goals . . . ," p. 24. See Selected References.
14. Terry Shepherd and Lynn Iles, p. 569. See Selected References.
15. *Ibid.*
16. Delwyn Schubert, pp. 497–499. See Selected References.
17. Shepherd and Iles, *op. cit.*, pp. 570–571.
18. See Jerry J. Watson in Selected References. Watson includes a list of recommended books about the elderly for children in grades 4–6.
19. Lawrence Kohlberg, "The Child as a Moral Philosopher" and "Stages and Sequence . . ." See Selected References.

SELECTED REFERENCES

Atkin, Charles and Gary Heald. "The Content of Children's Toy and Food Commercials." *Journal of Communication,* 27 (Winter 1977): 107–114.

Baldwin, R. Scott and John E. Readence. "Critical Reading and Perceived Authority." *Journal of Reading,* 22 (April 1979): 617–622.

Barrett, Thomas C. "Goals of the Reading Program: The Basis for Evaluation," in *Perspectives in Reading #8, The Evaluation of Children's Reading Achievement,* T. C. Barrett (ed.). Newark, Delaware: International Reading Association, 1967, pp. 13–26.

__________. "Taxonomy of Reading Comprehension," in *Teaching Reading in the Middle Grades, Second Edition.* Reading, Mass.: Addison-Wesley Pub. Co., 1980, pp. 61–67.

Boyan, Catherine S. "Critical Reading: What Is It? Where Is It?" *The Reading Teacher*, 25 (March 1972): 517–522.

Burlando, Andrew A. and Nannette L. Farrar. "Teaching Primary Children to Read Critically." *Language Arts*, 54 (February 1977): 187–188.

Burmeister, Lou E. *Reading Strategies for Middle and Secondary School Teachers, Second Edition.* Reading, Mass.: Addison-Wesley Publishing Co., 1978, Chapter 9.

Cassidy, Jack. "Grey Power in the Reading Program—a Direction for the Eighties." *The Reading Teacher*, 35 (December 1981): 287–291.

__________. "Inquiry Reading for the Gifted." *The Reading Teacher*, 35 (October 1981): 17–21.

Chall, Jeanne S., Eugene Radwin, Valarie W. French, and Cynthia R. Hall. "Blacks in the World of Children's Books." *The Reading Teacher*, 32 (February 1979): 527–533.

Clary, Linda Mixon. "How Well Do You Teach Critical Reading?" *The Reading Teacher*, 31 (November 1977): 142–146.

Dieterich, Daniel (ed.). *Teaching about Doublespeak.* Urbana, Illinois: National Council of Teachers of English, 1976.

Elkind, David. "Cognitive Development and Reading," in *Theoretical Models and Processes of Reading, Second Edition*, Harry Singer and Robert Ruddell (eds.). Newark, Delaware: International Reading Association, 1976, pp. 331–340.

Eller, William and Judith Wolf. *Critical Reading: A Broader View.* Newark, Delaware: International Reading Association, 1969.

Engel, Rosalind E. "Is Unequal Treatment of Females Diminishing in Children's Picture Books?" *The Reading Teacher*, 34 (March 1981): 647–652.

Fein, Ruth L. and Adrienne H. Ginsberg. "Realistic Literature about the Handicapped." *The Reading Teacher*, 31 (April 1978): 802–805.

Feitelson, D. and G. S. Ross. "The Neglected Factor—Play." *Human Development*, 16 (1973): 202–223.

Fraenkel, Jack R. "The Kohlberg Bandwagon: Some Reservations." *Social Education* (April 1976): 216–222.

Gilliland, Hap. "The New View of Native Americans in Children's Books." *The Reading Teacher*, 35 (May 1982): 912–916.

Guilford, J. P. "Frontiers in Thinking Teachers Should Know About." *The Reading Teacher*, 23 (February 1960): 176–182.

Hersh, Richard H., Diana Pritchard Paolitto, and Joseph Reimer. *Promoting Moral Growth: From Piaget to Kohlberg.* New York: Longman, Inc., 1979.

Hoffman, James V. "The Intra-Act Procedure for Critical Reading." *Journal of Reading*, 22 (April 1979): 605–608.

King, Martha, Bernice Ellinger and Willavene Wolf (eds.). *Critical Reading.* Philadelphia: J. B. Lippincott, 1967.

Kohlberg, Lawrence. "The Child as a Moral Philosopher," *Psychology Today* (1968): 25–30.

——————————. "Stage and Sequence: the Cognitive-Developmental Approach to Socialization," in *Handbook of Socialization Theory and Research.* Chicago: Rand-McNally, 1968, pp. 347–480.

Lehr, Fran. "Bibliotherapy: ERIC/RCS." *Journal of Reading,* 25 (October 1981): 76–79.

Liebert, Diane E., Joyce N., Sprafkin, Robert M. Liebert and Eli A. Rubenstein. "Effects of Television Commercial Disclaimers on the Product Expectations of Children." *Journal of Communication,* 27 (Winter 1972): 118–124.

Martin, Charles E., Bonnie Cramond, and Tammy Safter. "Developing Creativity through the Reading Program." *The Reading Teacher,* 35 (February 1982): 568–573.

Massialas, Byron and Jack Zevin. *Creative Encounters in the Classroom.* New York: John Wiley, 1967.

Mathewson, Grover C. "The Function of Attitude in the Reading Process," in *Theoretical Models and Processes of Reading, Second Edition,* Harry Singer and Robert Ruddell (eds.). Newark, Delaware: International Reading Association, 1976, pp. 655–676.

Mavrogenes, Nancy A. "Positive Images of Grandparents in Children's Picture Books." *The Reading Teacher,* 35 (May 1982): 896–901. Includes bibliography of picture books for children, grades K–3.

May, Jill P. "The American Literary Fairy Tale and Its Classroom Uses." *Journal of Reading,* 22 (November 1978): 153–160.

Mize, John M. "A Directed Strategy for Teaching Critical Reading and Decision Making." *Journal of Reading,* 22 (November 1978): 144–148.

Peters, F. J. J. "Printed Messages in American Commercial Television and the Reading Teacher." *Journal of Reading,* 22 (February 1979): 408–415.

Purpel, David and Kevin Ryan. *Moral Education . . . It Comes with the Territory,* a Phi Delta Kappa Publication. Berkeley, Calif: McCutchan Publishing Corp., 1976.

Sanders, Norris. *Classroom Questions—What Kinds?* New York: Harper and Row, 1966, Chapters 4–9.

Schoof, Robert N. "Four-color Words: Comic Books in the Classroom." *Language Arts,* 55 (October 1978): 821–827.

Schubert, Delwyn. "The Role of Bibliotherapy in Reading Instruction." *Exceptional Children,* 41 (April 1975): 497–499.

Shepherd, Terry and Lynn Iles. "What Is Bibliotherapy?" *Language Arts,* 53 (May 1976): 569–571.

Stauffer, Russell G. "Cognitive Processes Fundamental to Reading Instruction," in *Cognition, Curriculum, and Comprehension,* J. T. Guthrie (ed.). Newark, Delaware: International Reading Association, 1977.

Storey, Dee C. "Reading in the Content Areas: Fictionalized Biographies and Diaries for Social Studies." *The Reading Teacher,* 35 (April 1982): 796–798.

Swineford, Edwin J. "The Perils of Reading." *Language Arts,* 52 (September 1975): 816–819, 851.

Turner, Thomas N. and J. Estill Alexander. "Fostering Early Creative Reading." *Language Arts,* 52 (September 1975): 786–789.

Tutolo, Daniel. "Teaching Critical Listening." *Language Arts,* 52 (Nov./Dec. 1975): 1108–1112.

Waples, Douglas. *What Reading Does to People.* Chicago: University of Chicago Press, 1967

Watson, Jerry J. "A Positive Image of the Elderly in Literature for Children." *The Reading Teacher,* 34 (April 1981): 792–798.

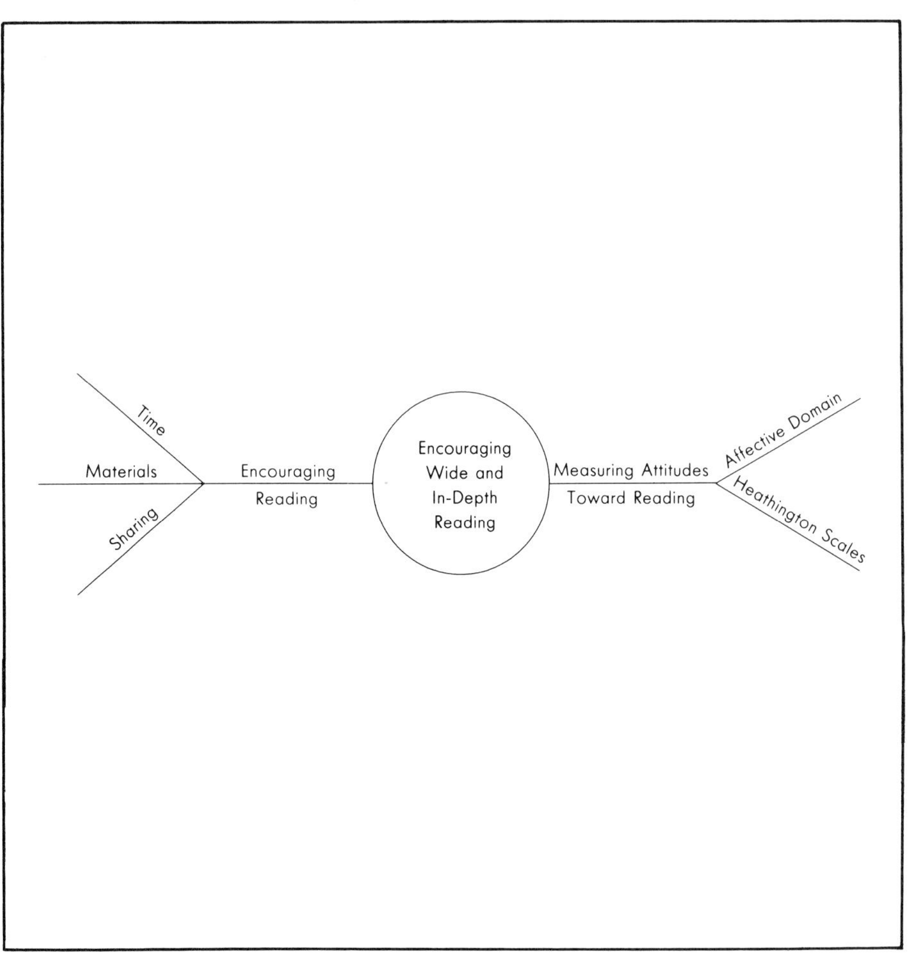

- How can we encourage children to read widely and in-depth?

- Why is time in school for free reading an essential element in developing interest in reading? When can such time be found? How should it be used? How can teachers provide materials for reading? What kinds of sharing experiences might children engage in?

- What is the affective domain? What are its levels? Of what value is it to the teacher to use knowledge of the affective domain in the classroom? What are the Heathington Scales? What is their value for use in the classroom?

Encouraging Wide and In-Depth Reading

If children are going to read in-depth, as well as widely, in order to be able to make inferences, as discussed in Chapter 8, and evaluations that require comparing internal and external criteria, as discussed in Chapter 9, certain provisions must be made for them in the school situation. Such provisions promote their desire to read for these reasons: for curiosity and exploration, for achievement, for activity, self-actualization, and vicarious aesthetic experiences. These provisions are discussed under the following headings: time, materials, and sharing.

Teachers may wish to measure the degree of interest children display toward reading, or toward reading about specific topics. The taxonomy of the affective domain is a useful hierarchal description which enables teachers to informally make such measurements in regular classroom situations. This is discussed in the second section of this chapter. Also included in that section are two instruments designed to help children reveal their feelings about reading in different situations—free reading in the classroom, organized reading in the classroom, reading at the library, at home, other recreational reading, and general reading.

Encouraging Reading

TIME

Giving children time in which to read (and to read what they like) is an integral part of a reading program. Such time should not be thought of in terms of a reward, e.g., for having finished an assignment early or having done an especially good job of something. Time for reading must be available to all children, even those who didn't do their homework, etc. Otherwise it will be just the most able students who have time to read widely and develop an interest in reading. Some ways of providing time are:

□ *Informal Times* An individual child, group of children, or whole class might just decide that at a certain time they wish to read. The teacher might allow those children who wish to read to do so when they ask. They may read in the classroom or in the library.

□ *Specified Times* The teacher might decide that a certain specific time should be set aside for reading each day. Content area teachers might wish to devote the class period on Friday (or some other day) to free reading about their subject. A schedule might be set up; e.g., on Monday, there is free reading in science class—about science topics; on Tuesday there is free reading in social studies class—about social studies topics; on Wednesday—arithmetic; on Thursday—art and music; on Friday—physical education. Appropriate materials* would be readily available.

□ *Sustained Silent Reading* Many schools provide for periods of Sustained Silent Reading (SSR), which are school-wide. At a certain time during the day, e.g., first thing in the morning, just before or after lunch, fifteen to thirty minutes are set aside for free reading. Everyone reads something of his or her choice: the children read, the teachers read, the principal reads, the janitors read, etc.—wherever they happen to be. (The janitors, principal, nurse, etc., might sit in different classrooms during this time.) All adults read adult books of their choice: this may be the only time a child sees an adult read for pleasure. So the adult serves as a model. Some schools call this U.S.S.R.: Uninterrupted Sustained Silent Reading.
Certain principles have been found to be essential:

- everyone reads—no interruptions are allowed, and no teaching is allowed;
- reading materials have been selected before the period begins and are not exchanged during the period;

---

*Outstanding science trade book titles are available in a yearly list published in the March issue of *Science and Children* magazine. Included is a short review of each book and the appropriate grade level for each book. The April issue of *Social Education* has a similar list for social studies trade books. Each is also available from The Children's Book Council, 67 Irving Pl., New York, N.Y. 10003. Enclose a stamped self-addressed business size envelope for each order.

- teachers do not ask questions about the content of the materials—thus all may read for escape, if they wish;
- sharing of ideas may take place.

It has been found to be helpful to prepare children and the community for S.S.R. Parents should be informed so that they understand the purpose. Suspense might be built up for children before the program begins. There might be public address announcements. Two weeks before S.S.R. begins the following announcement might be made: "S.S.R. is coming . . . Are you ready? . . . Are you ready for S.S.R.?" Posters might be placed around the building also. A week before S.S.R. starts, the following announcement might be made: "Next week S.S.R. will be here . . . at 8:45 Monday morning and every morning after that . . . You'll love it! . . . Are you ready?" Without telling the children what it is, teachers might help children find books and leave them on their desks Friday before they go home.*

Special provisions will have to be made for nonreaders and beginning readers in kindergarten and first grade. Such children might be taught to tell themselves stories from picture books. Time spent doing this might be just a few minutes. Also, such children might listen to tapes or records that accompany some books.

MATERIALS

Obviously, if all children are expected to read widely and in-depth, a wide variety of books and other materials must be available—in the classroom and in the school library.

Classroom Resources

If the teacher is to encourage and help children choose their own books, a classroom library is almost essential, although surely the children will also use the school and public libraries. Estimates are that a classroom library should have at least three to ten books per child at levels corresponding to the reading levels of the children. For a classroom of 25 children this would mean at least 75 books to at least 250 books. If the books are paperbacks, this would not be very expensive. From this beginning point, the classroom library can expand.

---

* See Appendix C for "Children's Choices for 1981."

The following are offered as suggestions for continued growth of the library:

□ *Library Books* The teacher might borrow books from the school or public library for a specified period of time—perhaps a few weeks or a whole semester.

□ *Buy Books Periodically* The teacher may wish to make an arrangement with the principal that would allow the teacher to purchase books every few weeks from a local bookstore. The teacher would note interests of children and attempt to buy books that would satisfy these interests. The books would be charged to the school.

□ *Book Swap* Children may wish to bring in their paperbacks and trade them for other children's paperbacks.

□ *Book Fair* The school might sponsor a book fair once a month or once a year. Used paperbacks and hardbacks could be sold there.

□ *Book Clubs* Children might join commercial book clubs from which they purchase books periodically. Bonus books are usually given to members after purchasing a certain number of books.

□ *Bind Stories Separately* Teachers might cut magazines, paperbacks and old books into separate stories or articles. One magazine might have ten stories, each of which could be stapled with its own cover. Some teachers separate stories of basal readers and cover each one. Thus children can progress from story to story rather then from book to book. (Psychologically, a paperback or separately bound story seems easier than the same story in hardback.) When there is a common page for two stories, a photocopy might be made of it.

□ *R.I.F.*[1] R.I.F. stands for Reading Is Fundamental, or Reading Is Fun. R.I.F. is a national organization that has as its purpose helping groups buy books. R.I.F. will pay 75 percent of the purchase price of books and postage for those groups that are given a grant. Books must be purchased for all children in a specified group (e.g., for all third graders in a school, for all third graders of a particular classroom, for all Scouts in a troop, etc.), not just for some children in the group. Also, books purchased must be given to the children to keep.

□ *Listening Centers* Listening centers might be provided in which children can listen to recordings of books, perhaps while following along in the book itself. Recorded interviews with authors might also be provided. Visual tapes, if available, would also provide motivation.

Library Use

Children must know how to use a library. There are many things they should know about a library. Among these are: how to use the card catalog, how to use the Dewey Decimal System (or other system the library uses), and how to use the *Readers' Guide to Periodical Literature*. These will be explained briefly here.

Card Catalog The card catalog of a school library is an index to the entire collection of resources housed in the library. Besides containing the usual subject, author, and title cards for books in the library, the catalog also contains cards for the school's filmstrips, films, records, tapes, pictures, and information found in vertical and picture files. These cards guide the user to the desired sources of information.

Since there are so many ways of classifying nonprint materials, no attempt is made here to explain any one scheme. However, catalog cards for printed materials all follow a general pattern, as shown in Fig. 10.1. An explanation of the various items is given in Fig. 10.2. For example, variations of the author card are indicated in the "tracings." They are *subject cards* and *title cards*—and possibly joint-author cards and illustrator cards.

Frequently, the librarian types his or her own cards, using an abbreviated form, such as that shown in Fig. 10.3. Abbreviated subject and title cards are shown in Figs. 10.4 and 10.5, respectively.

All such cards are filed alphabetically in the card catalog by the first line. The Dewey decimal system classification number indicates the sec-

```
Call
Number    Author, Surname first
             Title  . . . . . . . . . . . . . . . . . . . . . . . . . . . . . . . . . . . .
             . . . . .  Publisher, date.
             paging illustrations
             Notes  . . . . . . . . . . . . . . . . . . . . . . . . . . . . . . . . . . .


             contents  . . . . . . . . . . . . . . . . . . . . . . . . . . . . . .



             training
```

Fig. 10.1: Skeleton author card, showing location of items.

Call Number:

 Dewey decimal no. →

 Author's name in code →

     tracings: →

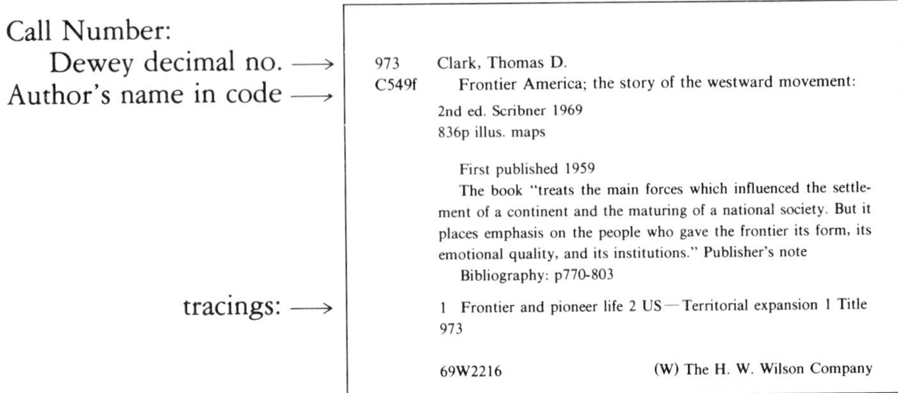

Arabic numerals indicate subject cards;
Roman numerals indicate title card and
all cards other than subject cards, e.g.,
joint author card, illustrator card, etc.

Fig. 10.2: Completed author card, with explanation of items.

tion of the library in which the book is located. For the book shown in Fig. 10.2, for example, that section is 973—United States history. Within this section, all books are classified according to the authors' last names. Thus, a book by Borrowman would be found before this book by Clark, and a book by Curti would be found after it. Alphabetizing by author within a Dewey number is the rule, except for individual biography (combined with autobiography), where the subclassification is by subject (the person written about).

973
C549f   Clark, Thomas D
Frontier America; the story of the
westward movement. 2nd ed. Scribner,
1969.
836p. illus. maps

1. Frontier and pioneer life. 2.
U.S.-Territorial expansion. I. Title.

Fig. 10.3: Librarian's abbreviated author card.

Media cards usually are similar to book cards. they are often color-banded, a different color being used for each media: filmstrips, records, tapes, etc.

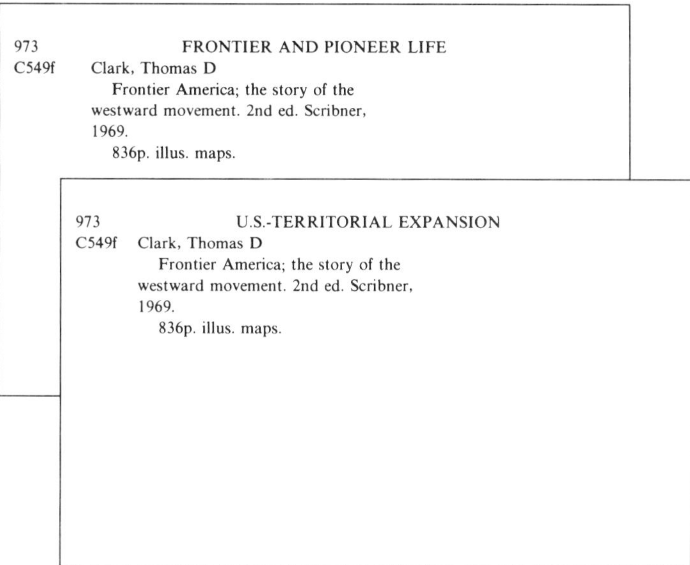

Fig. 10.4: In abbreviated subject cards, the subject may be typed in either color or capital letters, to distinguish it from a title card.

Fig. 10.5: Librarian's abbreviated title card.

Dewey Decimal System Most school libraries in the United States use the Dewey Decimal System to classify all of their nonfiction books. The system is simple for children and young people to understand and should be explained, as needed, to students of all ages.

Libraries that use this system normally shelve their books consecutively, beginning with the series number 100–199, followed by the 200s, the 300s, and so on. The only books usually omitted from this sequence are the 000–099 books (Generalities, or Reference Works), partly because many of them are oversize, and fiction, which is usually located in the most accessible spot in the library.

The major divisions of the new Dewey Decimal System are as follows:[2]

000–099: Generalities
100–199: Philosophy and Psychology
200–299: Religion
300–399: The Social Sciences
400–499: Language
500–599: Pure Sciences
600–699: Technology (Applied Sciences)
700–799: The Arts
800–899: Literature
900–999: General History and Geography

Some of the more useful and interesting subdivisions within these major divisions are:

000–099: Generalities
    010: Bibliographies
    020: Library Science
       028: Reading Aids
    030: Encyclopedias
    050: Periodicals and Their Indexes
100–199: Philosophy and Psychology
200–299: Religion
    220: Bible
    290: Religions other than Christian
       292: Classical Mythology
300–399: The Social Sciences
    390: Customs
       398: Folklore
400–499: Language
    410: Linguistics
    420: English Languages
       421: Written and Spoken English
       422: English Etymology
       423: English Dictionaries
    430: Germanic Languages (with same subdivisions as given under English above)
    440: French Languages (same subdivisions)
    450: Italian Languages (same subdivisions)
    460: Spanish Languages (same subdivisions)

500–599: Pure Sciences
        510: Mathematics
        520: Astronomy
        530: Physics
        540: Chemistry
        550: Geology (Earth Sciences)
        560: Paleontology
        570: Life Sciences (Anthropology, Biology)
        580: Botany
        590: Zoology

600–699: Technology (Applied Sciences)
        620: Engineering
        630: Agriculture
        640: Home Economics
        650: Business

700–799: The Arts
        710: Civil and Landscape Art
        720: Architecture
        730: Sculpture
        740: Drawing and Decorative Arts
        750: Painting
        760: Graphic Arts (Prints)
        770: Photography
        780: Music
        790: Recreation and Performing Arts
            792: Theater (Stage Presentations)
            793: Indoor Games and Parties
            796: Outdoor Sports and Games

800–899: Literature
        810: American Literature in English
        820: English Literature
        830: German Literature
        840: French Literature
        850: Italian Literature
        860: Spanish Literature

900–999: General History and Geography
        910: General Geography and Travel
            912: Atlases
        920: General Biography and Genealogy
        930: History of the Ancient World
        940: History of Europe
        950: History of Asia
        960: History of Africa

970: History of North America
980: History of South America
990: History of Other Areas
999: Extraterrestrial Worlds
Variations: B, 92, or 921: Biography (Individual)
F . . . . : Fiction
SC . . . . : Story Collection

The teacher who knows this system, or who has it accessible for reference, can easily guide children to sections in the library that will be most helpful to them for specific assignments. For example, if José wishes to find books on outer space, he would be guided to the section numbered 999. Catherine, who enjoys golf and swimming, would go to the 796's. Alyce, a painter, would look for books on painting in the section numbered 750, but Charles, a photographer, would go to the 770's. Etc.

More detailed information about the Dewey decimal classification is available through many sources. Most common is the abridged edition of the current *Dewey Decimal Classification and Relative Index* (see note 2 at the end of the chapter). The subject cards found in the card catalog also lead the user to the classification number.

Readers' Guide to Periodical Literature A school library will probably subscribe to either *The Readers' Guide to Periodical Literature* or to *The Abridged Readers' Guide to Periodical Literature*. These are briefly described here.

1. *The Readers' Guide to Periodical Literature*, 1900– . New York: H. H. Wilson. An index to the contents of about 160 popular magazines, published twice monthly, September to June, and monthly in July and August. Cumulated volumes, which include all information from a number of issues combined into one alphabet, are available periodically.

   Each magazine article in the 160 magazines indexed is entered under both the author's name and the subject, and sometimes also under the title.

2. *The Abridged Readers' Guide to Periodical Literature*, permanent volumes available from 1948– . New York: H. W. Wilson. An index to the contents of about 44 magazines of general interest, especially suitable for use in elementary and junior high school and other small libraries. It uses the same format as the *Readers' Guide* and is published monthly except in June, July, and August. The September issue includes indexing for these summer months. Cumulated volumes are available yearly.

Teachers who wish to teach children to use the above indexes may wish to send for *The Readers' Guide to Periodical Literature (or the Abridged Readers' Guide): How to Use the Readers' Guide to Periodical Literature*, revised edition, 16 pages. New York: H. W. Wilson, 1973. This pamphlet is designed for teaching the use of the *Readers' Guide* to elementary and secondary school students. Class-size sets are free.

Choosing Sources of Information

Often young children need or wish to read principally the sources suggested to them by teachers, parents, and friends. But sometimes, especially as they grow older, they must begin to recognize that they must make some important decisions in the selection of reading materials. The following sections describe some concepts children should have for the selection of materials.

Literal level activities for book and magazine selection relate to the recognition of available sources of reading materials and knowing how to use these sources. Children should know how to use the school and public libraries and bookmobiles, if they are available in the community. They should be taught how to use the card catalog, the Dewey decimal system, and available reference aids, such as the *Readers' Guide to Periodical Literature.*

When and how to use dictionaries*, encyclopedias, atlases, a thesaurus in dictionary form, etc., should be taught in the classroom as soon as children are able to benefit from such instruction. These resources, then, should continue to serve as aids for selecting materials or as sources for information and enjoyment themselves. Teachers should provide opportunities for their use in regular assignments.

> To teach the use of these references, the following types of activities are appropriate (subskill approach):
>
> □ *Thesaurus in Dictionary Form* Ask children to use a paperback thesaurus to find information like the following:
>
> 1. List as many animal sounds as you can. E.g.: howl, yowl, wail, blat, moo, low, squeal, hiss, rattle, bark, yap, bay, neigh, whinny, snort, bray, purr, meow, roar, growl, chirp, twitter, cock-a-doodle, cluck, quack, caw, hum, drone, etc. (This is about 25

---

*Dictionary use was explained in Chapter 5.

percent of those suggested in one thesaurus. There are also cross references suggested.)
2. List as many animal names as you can (or as many reptiles, rodents, bear, bovines, deer, frogs, monkeys, sheep, whales, etc. These are all listed and grouped under "animal".)
3. What words can be used for *merriment?* for *confusion?* etc.
4. Etc.

□*Almanac* Ask children to use an almanac to find information like the following:

1. List the seven aircraft accidents that resulted in the greatest number of deaths world-wide since 1937.
2. List 12 major tornadoes since 1957.
3. Draw a picture of the flags of the following nations:

Canada	New Zealand
Denmark	Malaysia
Bangladesh	Togo
Sierra Leone	Uruguay
Panama	

4. Compare the total net income per farm in Utah with that per farm in Pennsylvania in 1970, 1974, 1978, 1982.
5. List winners of the "Most Valuable Player Awards" in baseball since 1960.
6. Etc.

□*Atlas* Ask children to find information such as the following in an atlas:

1. What are the major dairy farming regions in the world?
2. In what parts of Europe is the Ukranian language spoken?
3. Name three languages widely spoken in the British Isles. Show on a map where each is spoken.
4. How far is Cairo, Egypt, from Kaduna, Nigeria?
5. What is the approximate altitude of Santiago, Chili?
6. What is the average date of the first killing frost in New Orleans?
7. Etc.

□*Encyclopedia** Children must be taught to use the Index volume of an encyclopedia to locate some information because not all information can be located in the alphabetical volume in which they might expect to find it. For example, you might ask children to tell where they would find information about:

1. Burmese cats—under "cats," in one encyclopedia
2. Maurice Herzog (mountain climber)—under "Anapurna"
3. Lord Haw-Haw—(British traitor)—under Warfare, Psychological
4. "The Love for Three Oranges" (opera)—under Prokofiev, Sergei (composer)
5. Prisoner of war—under Prisoner of War, but also Geneva Conventions, International Law, Korean War (Truce Talks) and (Prisoner Exchange)
6. Etc.

When given an assignment, children should be taught to make their own decisions about sources to be used for information and/or enjoyment. For example (holistic approach):

□*Research a Topic* A group of children in a class may be very much interested in a special topic. You might wish to give them an opportunity to study it. For example, they might be fascinated with *dinosaurs and their relatives.* What materials might they use?
   • *thesaurus*—Under reptiles in one thesaurus we find· "saurian, dragon, dinosaur (extinct), icthyosaur (extinct); snake, ophidian, serpent, viper; crocodile, alligator; turtle, tortoise, terrapin; lizard, chameleon, dragon, eft, gecko, Gila monster, horned toad, iguana, newt."**
   • *dictionary*—Short descriptions of most, perhaps all, of these can be found in a good college level dictionary.†
   • *encyclopedia*—Longer descriptions, place of present or former habitats, behaviors, etc., could be found in many encyclopedias.
   • *atlas*—Children could use a map to locate these areas. A copy of a world map could be supplied to them. By using information

---

* Many encyclopedias have reading and study guides for classroom use.
**Norman Lewis, editor. *Roget's New Pocket Thesaurus in Dictionary Form.* N.Y.: Pocket Books, 1961, p. 19.
† E.g., *The American Heritage Dictionary of the English Language.* Boston: Houghton Mifflin Co.

> from an encyclopedia and atlas, they might mark areas indicat-
> ing locations (present/former) of the reptiles they are most in-
> terested in.
> - *Dewey decimal system*—Several numbers are used in libraries to
>   classify materials about reptiles, depending on the point of view
>   of the material—
>   598—living birds and reptiles
>   568—fossils/ extinct animals (e.g., dinosaurs)
>   636—animals as pets (e.g., snakes, turtles)
> - *card catalog*—Under "reptiles" and/or specific types of reptiles,
>   children would find cards for all of the books the library con-
>   tains about the topic. Fiction books will also be listed in the card
>   catalog, though not in the Dewey Decimal System.
> - *Readers' Guide to Periodical Literature*—Under "reptiles" and/or
>   specific types of reptiles, children would find listings of maga-
>   zine articles that have been published relating to the topic.

Although children should be encouraged to select their own reading materials, they should be made aware of the fact that when their topic is on
a controversial subject, they (like most people) are likely to seek sources
that agree with their point of view. They should be encouraged, perhaps
required, to broaden that point of view by reading and reporting on materials that differ from their persuasions. They should also be taught that
some authors are more knowledgeable about a subject than are others.

SHARING

Freedom to share what one wishes to share is an important part of learning and of building interest—both for the child who wishes to share and
the child or children with whom he or she shares. Also, freedom not to
share is sometimes important, for sometimes a child may wish to keep a
book or an idea all to himself or herself—and the child should be free to
do so. (Writing a required book report may be the punishment one sus-
tains for having read a book.) Following are suggestions of provisions
that might be made for the sharing of ideas from books and other experiences.

> Children may benefit from oral reading experiences of the fol-
> lowing types:
>
> □ *Language Experience* Children dictate to the teacher, who in turn
>   writes what the child or children have said. Then children learn to
>   orally read what the teacher has written down. (See Chapter 13 of

this book.) Children learn that what they say can be written down and then read.

□ *Play Reading* Children may be assigned parts in a play comparable to their reading achievement levels. Most plays have parts that vary in difficulty—or at least some parts are shorter than others. Children prepare their own parts (perhaps with the help of the teacher), and then the play is read or produced. In some cases, parts may be assigned and read without preparation, e.g., if no child would be embarrassed by the inability to successfully read an assigned part. Also, basal reader stories may be read as plays.

□ *Prepared Reading* Children may be asked to prepare a poem or story or part of a book they especially liked to read to the class or to a group of children. Some children will benefit from "trying out" their reading on the teacher first.

□ *Oral Reading after Silent Reading* In a regular lesson, perhaps a basal reader lesson or lesson in a content area subject, children may read orally to prove a point after they have read the passage silently.

□ *Sharing Information* Children may bring in an interesting newspaper or magazine article to read to the class. Perhaps every day one or two or more children could do this.

□ *Older Child Reading to a Younger Child* Older children, perhaps 4th, 5th, or 6th graders, who read poorly for their own grade levels often enjoy reading easier materials which they can read well to younger children. And they learn from doing this, too. In fact, they may learn to read well enough orally—and enjoy it—that when they become parents, they will read to their own children.

Other ways of sharing include:

□ *Book Visits* Often children desire an informal means of sharing what they have read. A child may simply wish to talk with another child about a book. Children are usually not noisy or bothersome about this. If they are not, they might be allowed to "book visit" almost anytime they wish.

□ *Mobiles* Artistic, semiartistic, or even nonartistic children might wish to make a mobile showing major characters and/or settings of a favorite book. Such a mobile might be hung in the classroom to call attention to the book.

□ *Bulletin Board Displays* Children might wish to post dust jackets they have made for a favorite book on a bulletin board. A short description of the book might be included—or a brief episode from the book.

Children might post dust jackets around the border of the board and write the authors' names to the center. They might use colored yarn to connect the book jacket with the author's name.

□ *Puppetry* Children might make puppets of characters of a book. A child might role-play. Several children might act out a scene or several scenes. Or characters in the form of puppets from different stories might interact. (Peter Rabbit and Mrs. Tiddywinkle might enjoy a visit with Alice of *Alice in Wonderland*.)

□ *Marionettes* Children may also wish to produce a marionette show —using characters on strings and perhaps a stage setting.

□ *Skits* Children might like to write and perform a skit using an episode or episodes from a book. Or they might combine episodes (or characters) from several books. For example, the spider Charlotte of *Charlotte's Web* could share her wisdom with Francisco of *Amigo* while Francisco is trying to attract a prairie dog to be his special friend. Frog and Toad could visit with Mouse of *The Mouse and the Motorcycle*. The skits could be presented to the class or to a group of children. And children could make puppets if they wished. Also, poetry could be pantomimed. (This could relate, also, to content area subjects: Einstein and Frank Lloyd Wright might visit in mathematics classes, Buckminster Fuller might also be included in a science class; Julia Childs might visit with Richard Simmons and a Japanese chef in a home economics class; Arthur Fiedler might visit with Elvis Presley in music class, etc.)

□ *Feelings Unlimited Box*[3] Children might write short descriptions about how a character felt at a critical time in a story. Children may include as many clues as they wish but not the character's name or the title of the book. Children may also include their feelings about the character. They put these descriptions in the "Feelings Unlimited" box. Other children draw cards from the box and try to identify the book or story.

□ *Armchair Travelers*[4] When children read books or stories about unfamiliar locales, the teacher or child may contact a travel agency for posters and brochures about the area. Children might wish to prepare an illustrated talk about the area using these materials, plus others that they might find in magazines.

If a large map is available, a pin can mark the locale, and colored yarn can lead to illustrations or a synopsis of the book.

□ *Book Talk* Children might prepare brief talks about a favorite book. They could present these to a group or to the whole class.

□ *Crossword Puzzle* Children might prepare a crossword puzzle for their classmates about books discussed or displayed in class. For example, see Fig. 10.6.

Fig. 10.6: A crossword puzzle featuring books in a classroom.

□ *Twenty Questions* Children might play Twenty Questions to identify a book, author, character, or setting. Or they might play some other popular game.

□ *Class Book* Children might make a class book, or several books, each with a theme or literary genre (e.g., travel, fairy tales, animals, space travel, music, etc.) in which they put illustrations of books read and comments about the books.

□ *Card File* Instead of making class books, children might like to file information about books in one large file or several smaller thematic files.

□ *Most Valuable Idea* Each child, or each group of children, could be asked to contribute to the class the most valuable idea gleaned from their reading materials each week. They could tell how they might use this idea.

□ *Most Fascinating Idea* Each child, or each group of children, could also contribute the most interesting (to them) idea they have come across during the week. The idea may be purely enjoyable, might be frivolous, and might or might not be useful in any practical sense.

□ *Favorite Book, Story, Poem* At regular intervals, children might share an episode from a favorite book or story. They might read a favorite poem to the class.

□ *Best Radio or T.V. Show* Children might tape radio and videotape T.V. shows of their own. Using standards the children have agreed upon, the class might decide which of their taped radio or T.V. shows was the best. They could share this show with another class in the school.

Some noncompetitive and enjoyable ways of showing how much has been read in a classroom are:

□ *Bookworm* Have a classroom bookworm. Every time a child finishes a book, a hump is added with the name and an illustration of the book completed. Instead, a train might be used, with a car added for each book.

□ *Book Wheel* Have a classroom book wheel. A star or other illustration is added to the correct area each time a book is completed.

Measuring Attitudes Toward Reading

To help teachers measure how much children value reading, or the degree of enjoyment received through reading or through reading certain types of materials, a discussion of the affective domain is included in this section. Along with this, suggestions are included that would help both the teacher and the child recognize the degree of involvement of children in reading. Following this are two scales—one a primary scale and the other an intermediate scale—that teachers might use to measure children's feelings, or attitudes, toward specific reading situations.

The Affective Domain

David Krathwohl is the senior author of the book *Taxonomy of Educational Objectives: Handbook II, Affective Domain.* An article titled "Evaluating the Affective Dimension of Reading," by David W. Darling, delineates this domain and gives excellent suggestions of ways to develop interests of children through the use of printed materials.

Affective Levels

The taxonomy gives us a "hierarchical continuum" of the affective domain. The affective domain is the realm within people that deals with their value systems, their enjoyments, their aspirations. By using this taxonomy and observing the behavior of children, we can approximate the affective level of each child as it relates to our classroom activities. Such recognition may, when necessary, encourage us to provide more appealing materials and ideas. Thus we may raise the level of involvement of some children. According to Krathwohl, et al., there are five major levels of affective involvement, and these form the basis of the present author's elaboration in the sections that follow. The lowest level is the receiving level.

Receiving: Awareness→ Willingness to Receive→ Controlled Attention If children are not receiving information or ideas, they are not affectively involved, even at the lowest level. One can spot such children easily: they may be reticent, daydreaming, or highly aggressive. To know the reason for their noninvolvement, however, may be more difficult. They may display several of these characteristics: they may be hard of hearing; their vision might be inadequate; they may read English poorly; they may already know the ideas being imparted or may lack the background to understand them; they may be uninterested in the subject; their friends or family may discourage them from learning; or their family may push them too much. Some of these factors can be remedied more easily than others. Perhaps the help of a specialist may be required.

Children who are at the lowest end of the affective continuum—in the *receiving* category—will be seen to listen and observe, but not to respond. Their eyes and ears follow the teacher and the class discussion, but they may be only mildly involved. They may be merely *aware* of what is going on; or better, they may be *willing to receive* ideas; or better still, they may exhibit *controlled attention.* It is sometimes difficult to know the degree of their reception or even their sincerity.

Responding (Sharing): Acquiescence in Responding→ Willingness to Respond→ Satisfaction in Response However, when a stimulus is given, we usually look for more than simple receiving. We hope for some type of response. In fact, the stimulus-response theory of learning is widely respected. Children who progress beyond the receiving category can be further classified by the type of responding (or sharing) behavior they display—those who *acquiesce in responding*, those who are *willing to respond*, and those who display *satisfaction in responding*, replying, or reacting.

It is simple to observe which children must be strongly encouraged to share with others and/or to openly react in class. They must always be invited or called upon, and their answers, or means of sharing, are usually brief and half-hearted. Some may, however, be interested but insecure, and this may account for their *acquiescence* in responding.

Other children know they should respond (or share) in class, so they do—but with little satisfaction. Their projects are worked on and their hands are up because they want a better grade or because they want to fill in a time gap, not because they feel they have a fascinating idea or because they love to share their thoughts with others. These students are *willing* to respond.

Others, however, are enthusiastic about a book they read or an idea that just flashed through their mind—or they may find that they learn by sharing ideas. They volunteer and are *satisfied* by sharing.

Valuing: Acceptance of a Value → Preference for a Value → Commitment to a Value A level above responding, or simple sharing, is valuing. Some children may value the act of reading, and thus they will be readers (provided that they have time and that satisfactory materials are available), and/or some children may value subject matter (perhaps in a specific area) enough to pursue this interest. In other words, they may be devoted to reading, *per se*, or they may be devoted to specific ideas they get through reading.

Again there are three sublevels in this category of behavior. The lowest level is *acceptance of a value*—the child approves of reading or of what he or she learns through reading. A higher level is *preference for a value*—when given time and choices of things to do, often the child chooses to read or to read certain things. An even higher level is *commitment to a value*. To evaluate commitment by observing external behavior characteristics, "the teacher should look for (a) constant reading, (b) depth reading in special areas, and (c) a dependence on reading as a means of recreation as well as a means of becoming informed."[5]

Children can be helped to recognize their own value system if the teacher asks them such questions as: "What books (or activities) did you try before settling on this one?" Or, "Why did you decide you like to read so many stories about dinosaurs (or space travel, or adventures at sea, or children of other countries, etc.) rather than about mysteries, etc.?" (*preference level*). Or, "Are you willing to recommend that book to a friend?" (*commitment level*).

Photo courtesy of Frank Ainsa.

Retrospective-introspective* questions might be utilized to help children recognize their degree of valuing. Such questions as the following might help them recognize their own value system.

Retrospective Questions

- How long have you enjoyed reading about children of other countries (about dinosaurs, etc.)?
- During your free time, have you frequently thought of the children you read about?
- Have you used what you learned about the children when talking with your friends? Have you used any of their ideas in drawing a picture? . . . in planning a skit or a puppet show? Etc.
- Have you ever found yourself dreaming about these children?

Introspective Questions

- Why do you enjoy knowing about these children (dinosaurs, etc.)?
- Do you think you will continue to enjoy reading about them?
- Have you noticed that you find time to read about and/or study about these children (dinosaurs, etc.) when there are other things you might be doing?

---

*Retrospective questions request children to look into their past to find answers. Introspective questions request children to seek internal answers—answers within themselves.

When such retrospective and introspective questions are answered by children, they may move into the organizing level, the level at which they display a conscious awareness of their value system and see a value as part of their life structure.

Organizing: Conceptualization of a Value→Organization of a Value System If children have a well-organized value system, they are aware of what they value, and there is a degree of consistency in their value system. The two areas within the organizing category, thus, are *conceptualization of a value* and *organization of a value system.*

Retrospective and introspective questions help children become aware of, and thereby conceptualize, their values. Questions that will lead students to analyze whether this value is consistent with the way they feel and with their immediate and future goals are important here. For example, children might be asked how long they have felt the way they do about reading or about the content of what they are reading. Those who recognize reading—or the kinds of ideas they get from reading certain things—to be of value to them may begin to organize themselves (a bit, since they are very young) so that they will have time for reading, or for reading certain things. In other words, this kind of reading will become an integral part of their lives (for a long or short time). They are then taking steps toward *organizing a value system.*

Characterization by Value or a Value Complex People who reach the very highest level—characterization—are completely devoted to a value or group of values. They embody the value in an internally consistent way (though this may last only for a brief time). Actors and actresses sometimes temporarily become the person they are portraying. Children may in time become scientists, mathematicians, musicians, poets, or lovers of poetry. These people have reached the highest level of affective involvement. Unfortunately, sometimes youngsters become delinquents or dropouts because they have not learned to love anything the school offers and, therefore, they must look elsewhere.

<u>Discussion</u> Judging children's interests by using the affective domain may be highly subjective. Children do not always reveal their true selves, and teachers cannot be completely accurate in making evaluations. Yet, teachers may find the basic idea helpful and may even wish to use a chart like the one shown in Fig. 10.7 in recording their observations.

The teacher would use a different symbol or color for each successive recording. If such a chart is used in a content area course, it seems reasonable to assume that as a unit progresses and children become more familiar with the ideas of the unit they will move up the affective ladder. If this does not happen, teachers might ask questions such as:

1. Why is interest not growing?
2. Am I using materials appropriate to the reading achievement levels of individual children?
3. Am I diversifying materials enough?
4. Am I building skills necessary for understanding the concepts of the materials (or of the unit)?
5. Am I varying my approaches to teaching?
6. Am I allowing children free time to read materials of their choice, or unit-related materials?
7. Am I allowing children to share their ideas with one another if they wish?
8. Etc.

AFFECTIVE CHART

Unit Title: *The American Civil War*   Dates: *Oct. & Nov.*

Affective Levels

Names	Receiving			Responding			Valuing			Organization		Characterization
	awareness	*willingness*	*controlled attention*	*acquiescence*	*willingness*	*satisfaction*	*acceptance*	*preference*	*commitment*	*conceptualization*	*organization*	*characterization*
1. Adams, Sue	1		2									
2. Borchart, Betty			1				2					
3. Cadillo, Juan		1	2									
4. Dolpher, Jim	1					2						
5. Finch, Joan								1	2			
6. King, Carl	2		1									
7. Lock, Irv						1			2			
8.												
9.												
10.												

Figure 10.7

By reading this chart, we can see by looking at the first observation (marked "1") that most children were in the receiving category at the beginning of the unit. This is to be expected because at the beginning of the unit most children would know very little about the topic: they could just listen, or accept ideas. However, Joan Finch was already at the valuing level. Undoubtedly previously she had read or heard much about the Civil War. She was strongly interested in it. The "2's" indicate the teacher's judgment of the level of involvement of the children sometime later. Most children moved up the scale. However, Carl King displayed "controlled attention" at the beginning and then seemed to lose some interest. The teacher might find that reading materials are too difficult for Carl . . . or too boring.

Heathington Scales*

Another type of information a teacher might wish to have concerns the way individual children view different kinds of reading situations. The Heathington Scales may help children reveal their feelings to a teacher.

Primary Scale

The Primary Scale consists of 20 questions which are read to the children. After listening to a question, each child marks one of five faces (very unhappy, unhappy, neutral, happy, very happy), which shows how he or she feels about the situation. A score of five is given for each very happy face, four for each happy face, three for a neutral face, two for an unhappy face, and one for each very unhappy face. Thus the range of scores would be 5 × 20 (100) to 1 × 20 (20). See Fig. 10.8 for a sample of an answer sheet.

The following directions should be followed in administering the primary scale:

Your answer booklet is made up of two pages. Page one goes from number 1 to number 10, and page two goes from number 11 to number 20. Beside each number are five faces: a very unhappy face, an unhappy face, a face that's neither happy nor unhappy, a happy face, and a very happy face. I will ask you how you feel about certain things and you will put an X on the face that shows how you feel. Suppose I said, "How do you feel when you eat chocolate candy? Which face shows how you feel?" Someone may have chosen an unhappy face

---

*Betty S. Heathington. "Heathington Primary Scale" and "Heathington Intermediate Scale," in *Attitudes and Reading*, (eds.) J.E. Alexander and R.C. Filler. Newark, Delaware: International Reading Association, 1976, pp. 27–32. Reprinted with permission of the author and the International Reading Association.

Sample of Partial Answer Sheet

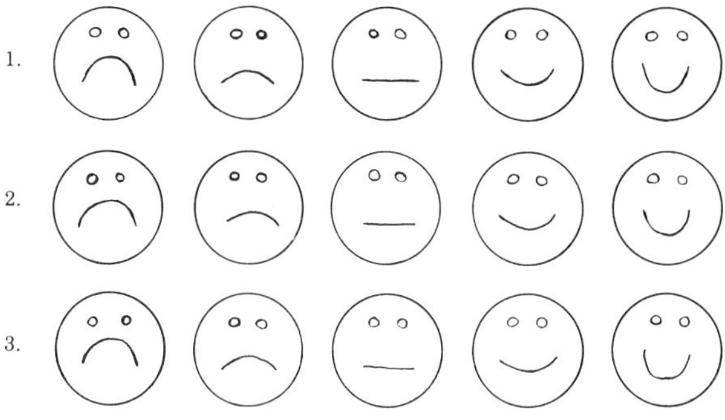

Figure 10.8

because he doesn't like chocolate candy; someone else may have chosen a happy face because he likes chocolate candy. Now, I'll read some questions to you and you mark the face that shows how you feel about what I read. Remember to mark how *you* feel because everyone does not feel the same about certain things. I'll read each question two times. Mark only one face for each number. Are there any questions? Now listen carefully. "Number 1. . . ."

PRIMARY SCALE

How do you feel . . .

1. when you go to the library?
2. when you read instead of playing outside?
3. when you read a book in free time?
4. when you are in reading group?
5. when you read instead of watching TV?
6. when you read to someone at home?
7. about the stories in your reading book?
8. when you read out loud in class?
9. when you read with a friend after school?
10. when you read stories in books?
11. when you read in a quiet place?
12. when you read a story at bedtime?
13. when it's time for reading circle (group)?
14. when you read on a trip?
15. when you have lots of books at home?
16. when you read outside when it's warm?
17. when you read at your desk at school?
18. when you find a book at the library?
19. when you read in your room at home?
20. when you read instead of coloring?

Certain groupings of questions can be considered diagnostic. That is, they indicate specific areas of a child's reading environment toward which he may feel positively or negatively. The following groupings are suggested:

1. Free reading in the classroom (items 3, 17)
2. Organized reading in the classroom (items 4, 7, 8, 13)
3. Reading at the library (items 1, 18)
4. Reading at home (items 6, 12, 15, 19)
5. Other recreational reading (items 2, 5, 9, 16)
6. General reading (items 10, 11, 14, 20).

Intermediate Scale

The Intermediate Scale is designed to be used with older children. It is composed of 24 statements about reading and is given to the children to read to themselves:

Heathington Intermediate Scale

Name ___________________

Blacken the box for each number to indicate how you feel about each statement, using this system:

SA = strongly agree   U = undecided   D = disagree
 A = agree   SD = strongly disagree

SA A U D SD

☐ ☐ ☐ ☐ ☐ ____ 1. You feel uncomfortable when you're asked to read in class.

☐ ☐ ☐ ☐ ☐ ____ 2. You feel happy when you're reading.

☐ ☐ ☐ ☐ ☐ ____ 3. Sometimes you forget about library books that you have in your desk.

☐ ☐ ☐ ☐ ☐ ____ 4. You don't check out many library books.

☐ ☐ ☐ ☐ ☐ ____ 5. You don't read much in the classroom.

☐ ☐ ☐ ☐ ☐ ____ 6. When you have free time at school, you usually read a book.

☐ ☐ ☐ ☐ ☐ ____ 7. You seldom have a book in your room at home.

☐ ☐ ☐ ☐ ☐ ____ 8. You would rather look at the pictures in a book than read the book.

☐ ☐ ☐ ☐ ☐ ____ 9. You check out books at the library but never have time to read them.

☐ ☐ ☐ ☐ ☐ ____ 10. You wish you had a library full of books at home.

☐ ☐ ☐ ☐ ☐ ____ 11. You seldom read in your room at home.

☐	☐	☐	☐	☐	___	12. You would rather watch TV than read.
☐	☐	☐	☐	☐	___	13. You would rather play after school than read.
☐	☐	☐	☐	☐	___	14. You talk to friends about books that you have read.
☐	☐	☐	☐	☐	___	15. You like the room to be quiet so you can read in your free time.
☐	☐	☐	☐	☐	___	16. You read several books each week.
☐	☐	☐	☐	☐	___	17. Most of the books you choose are not interesting.
☐	☐	☐	☐	☐	___	18. You don't read very often.
☐	☐	☐	☐	☐	___	19. You think reading is work.
☐	☐	☐	☐	☐	___	20. You enjoy reading at home.
☐	☐	☐	☐	☐	___	21. You enjoy going to the library.
☐	☐	☐	☐	☐	___	22. Often you start a book, but never finish it.
☐	☐	☐	☐	☐	___	23. You think that adventures in a book are more exciting than TV.
☐	☐	☐	☐	☐	___	24. You wish you could answer the questions at the end of the chapter without reading it.

Scoring of each item can be done in the blanks just before the numbers. Five points are given for a very positive response, four for a positive response, three for an undecided response, two for a negative response, and one for a very negative response.

On nine of the items (items 2, 6, 10, 14, 15, 16, 20, 21, 23) a response of "strongly agree" is very positive and receives 5 points. On all of the other items, a response of "strongly disagree" indicates a very positive attitude and receives 5 points. the possible range of scores is 5×24 (120) to 1×24 (24).

The Intermediate Scale also has groups of questions which can be used by classroom teachers to diagnose specific areas of reading attitudes. They are as follows:

1. free reading in the classroom (items 5, 6, 15)
2. organized reading in the classroom (items 1, 24)
3. reading in the library (items 3, 4, 9, 17, 21)
4. reading at home (items 7, 10, 11, 20)
5. other recreational reading (items 12, 13, 23)
6. general reading (items 2, 8, 14, 16, 18, 19, 22)

Summary

Encouraging wide and in-depth reading is essential if schools are to develop readers who can reason inferentially and evaluatively and who enjoy reading. Provisions must be made to encourage such reading.

Providing children with time for reading in the school setting is essential. All children need to enjoy and learn from reading, and giving children time to read should not be thought of as a reward for having done something well or rapidly, lest only good students have time to develop interest in reading.

Providing a wide range of reading materials is also necessary. Each classroom should have a library, and books, pamphlets, and magazine articles should be added to it regularly—in response to the present interests of children and to encourage expanding interest. Care should be taken that books and other reading materials are on levels appropriate to the children. Children must also be taught to use the school library and local libraries. They should be taught to use the card catalog, the Dewey decimal system (or other classification system that is used), the *Readers' Guide to Periodical Literature*, as well as a thesaurus, almanac, atlas, encyclopedia and other available aids.

Providing opportunities for sharing helps strengthen the interest of the child who gives, and it builds interest in the child who receives. Sharing is a mutually rewarding experience. Many ways of sharing both by individuals and groups were described.

Teachers may wish to measure the intensity of interest that children feel toward reading and/or toward reading about specific topics. The Taxonomy of the Affective Domain, as described by David Krathwohl, is a helpful instrument to use for such a purpose. There are five major gradients included: receiving, responding, valuing, organizing, characterization. Each level was described. A chart was supplied to show teachers how to plot interests as time progresses in the study of a unit.

The Heathington Scales—a primary scale and an intermediate scale—were also described. These scales have been designed to help children reveal how they feel about reading in various situations.

Questions and Activities

After answering the questions at the beginning of this chapter, consider these questions and activities:

1. Design a program for S.S.R. for a school in your area. Tell specifically how you would introduce the program. Consider discussions with the school administrators, and ways of introducing the program to children and to the community. Consider scheduling the program. For how long would each session run and for how many days a week? How would reading materials be made available?

2. Write to Reading Is Fundamental for a proposal form and guidelines (see Note 1, following). Discuss and share the materials with your classmates.

3. Design an activity that would require children to use the library. Provide for their use of the card catalog, of the *Reader's Guide*, and of other reference aids such as an almanac, atlas, thesaurus, encyclopedias, etc.

4. Design an activity for "armchair travelers," (pp. 428–429). Visit a travel bureau to collect brochures and pictures. Compose an interest inventory or reference list suggesting reading materials that relate to the area chosen.

5. Using the chart for the affective domain (p. 435) attempt to grade yourself and five or six of your classmates indicating their degree of involvement in this course. You may wish to grade them several times—until the end of the semester. After completing this, consider the possibility of a lack of objectivity on your part, and weigh this against the values of increased awareness on your part of affective dimensions related to learning.

6. How will the information gained from administering the Heathington scales help you understand and make provisions for improving the reading climate for a child? Explain.

Notes

1. R.I.F., i.e., Reading Is Fundamental, Inc., Smithsonian Institute, L'Enfant 2500, Washington, D.C. 20560.
2. Melvil Dewey. *Dewey Decimal Classification and Relative Index.* Lake Placid Club, New York: Forest Press, 1971.
3. Nicholas P. Criscuolo, "Effective . . ." p. 544. See Selected References.
4. *Ibid.*, p. 545.
5. David Darling, p. 137. See Selected References.

Selected References

Arthur, Anthony. "The Uses of Bettelheim's *The Uses of Enchantment.*" *Language Arts*, 55 (April 1978): 455–459, 533.

Alexander, J.E. and R.C. Filler. *Attitudes and Reading.* Newark, Delaware: International Reading Association, 1976.

Allen, Virginia Garibaldi. "Books to Lead the Non-English Speaking Elementary Student into Literacy." *The Reading Teacher*, 32 (May 1979): 940–946.

Bennett, John E. and Priscilla Bennett. "What's So Funny? Action Research and Bibliography of Humorous Children's Books—1975–80." *The Reading Teacher*, 35 (May 1982): 924–927.

Bettelheim, Bruno. *The Uses of Enchantment: The Meaning and Importance of Fairy Tales*. New York: A. Knopf, Inc., 1976.

Carbo, Marie. "Teaching Reading with Talking Books." *The Reading Teacher*, 32 (December 1978): 267–273.

Carlsen, G. Robert. *Books and the Teen-Age Reader* (for teachers of children in 4th grade and above). New York: Bantam, 1980.

Carlson, Ruth Kearney. *Enrichment Ideas, Second Edition*. Dubuque, Iowa: Wm. C. Brown Co., 1976.

Chall, Jeanne S., Eugene Radwin, Valarie W. French, and Cynthia R. Hall. "Blacks in the World of Children's Books." *The Reading Teacher*, 32 (February 1979): 527–533.

"Classroom Choices for 19xx: Books Chosen by Children." *The Reading Teacher*-October each year.

Criscuolo, Nicholas P. "Book Reports: Twelve Creative Alternatives." *The Reading Teacher*, 30 (May 1977): 893–895.

————. "Effective Approaches for Motivating Children to Read." *The Reading Teacher*, 32 (February 1979): 543–546.

Darling, David. "Evaluating the Affective Dimensions of Reading," in *The Evaluation of Children's Reading Achievement*, Thomas C. Barrett (ed.). Newark, Delaware: International Reading Association, 1967, pp. 127–141.

Fein, Ruth L. and Adrienne H. Ginsberg. "Realistic Literature about the Handicapped." *The Reading Teacher*, 31 (April 1978): 802–805.

Henderson, Mary Ann. "Reading While Becoming: Affective Approaches." *Journal of Reading*, 20 (January 1977): 317–326.

Krathwohl, David. *Taxonomy of Educational Objectives: Handbook II, Affective Domain*. New York: David McKay, 1964.

Larrick, Nancy. *A Parent's Guide to Children's Reading* (for parents and teachers of children under 13). New York: Pocket Books, Inc.

Macklin, Michael D. "Content Area Reading Is a Process for Finding Personal Meaning." *Journal of Reading*, 22 (December 1978): 212–215.

Maring, Gerald H. "Books to Counter TV Violence." *The Reading Teacher*, 32 (May 1979): 916–920.

Mathias, Sandra L. Ess and Mary E. Massa Fanyo. "Blending Reading Instruction with Music and Art." *The Reading Teacher*, 30 (February 1977): 497–500.

Mikkelsen, Nina. "Celebrating Children's Books throughout the Year." *The Reading Teacher*, 35 (April 1982): 790–795.

Monson, Dianne L. and Betty J. Peltola. *Research in Children's Literature—an Annotated Bibliography*. Newark, Delaware: International Reading Association, 1976.

Nist, Joan Stidham. "The Mildred L. Batchelder Award: Around the World with Forty-Two Books." *Language Arts*, 56 (April 1979): 368–374.

Noyce, Ruth M. "Team Up and Teach with Trade Books." *The Reading Teacher*, 32 (January 1979): 442–448.

Olson, Willard C. "Seeking, Self-Selection, and Pacing in the Use of Books by Children," in *The Packet*. Boston: D.C. Heath, Spring 1952.

Painter, Helen W. *Reaching Children and Young People Through Literature*. Newark, Delaware: International Reading Association, 1971.

Povenmire, E. Kingsley. "Advantages of Verse Choir for Reading." *The Reading Teacher*, 30 (April 1977): 761–765.

Ransburg, Molly Kayes. "An Assessment of Reading Attitude." *Journal of Reading*, 17 (October 1973): 25–28.

Reid, Virginia M. (ed.). *Reading Ladders for Human Relations*. Washington, D.C.: American Council on Education, 1972.

Rowell, C. Glennon. "An Attitude Scale for Reading." *Reading Teacher*, 25 (February 1972): 442–447.

Sargent, Eileen E., Helen Huus, and Oliver Andresen. *How to Read a Book*. Newark, Delaware: International Reading Association, 1970.

Shuy, Roger W. "What Should the Language Strand in a Reading Program Contain?" *The Reading Teacher*, 35 (April 1982): 806–812.

Small, Robert C., Jr. and Donald J. Kenney. "Reading Interests and Library Organization." *Language Arts*, 52 (Nov./Dec. 1975): 1127–1129.

Spache, George D. *Good Reading for Poor Readers*. Champaign, Illinois: Garrard Publishing Co., 1974, pp. 195–207.

Troy, Anne. "Literature for Content Area Learning." *The Reading Teacher*, 30 (February 1977): 470–474.

Witucke, Virginia. "The Book Talk: A Technique for Bringing Together Children and Books." *Language Arts*, 56 (April 1979): 413–421.

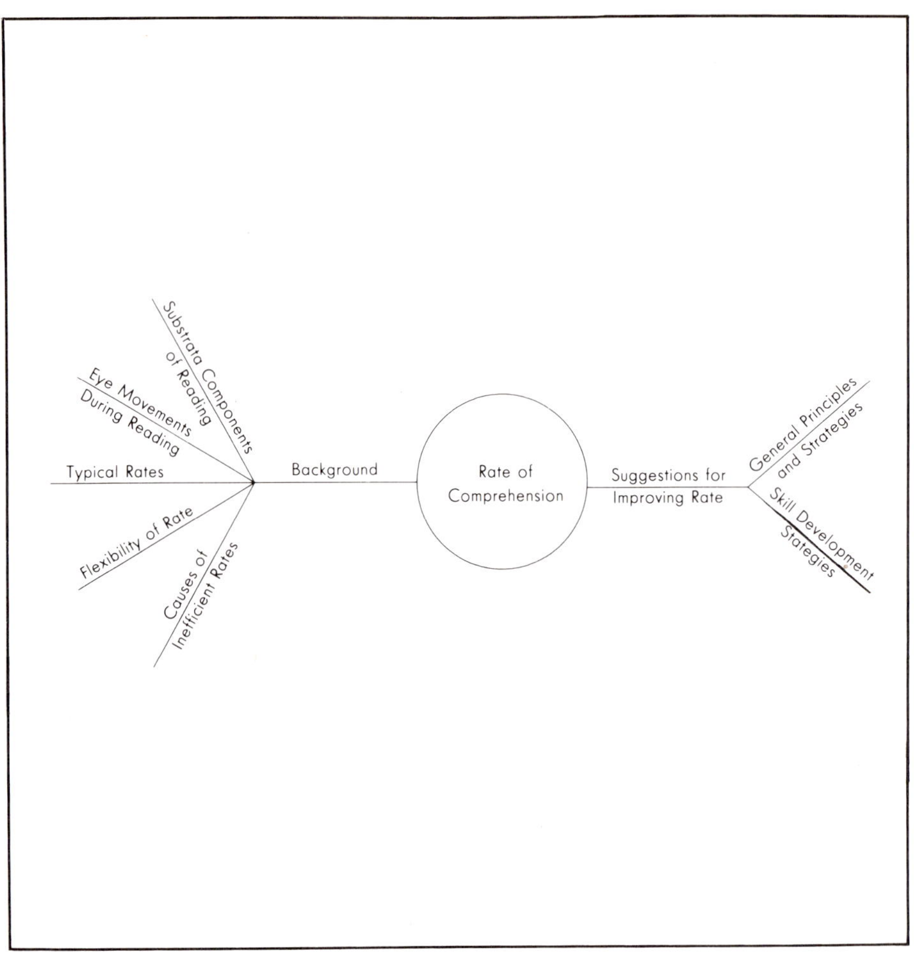

- Is working on improvement of rate of reading important in the elementary school? Why or why not?

- What are the substrata components of reading that relate to the bottom-up model of reading? How do these relate to rate of reading? How do the eyes move when a person is reading—smoothly or in jumps? Why? What are typical rates of reading at each grade level? What is the average improvement in rate each year? Should children vary their reading rates when reading different materials and/or when reading for different purposes? Explain. Why do some children read at inefficient rates?

- What are some important principles and strategies that should be used with all children in building appropriate rates of comprehension? What are some skill developmental strategies that might be used with some (or all) children? Which strategies would you like to use?

CHAPTER 11

Rate of Comprehension

Advertised promises that rate of reading can be doubled in one session, then soon after tripled, quadrupled, quintupled, and so on, have intrigued adults for two decades. So fascinated have they been that thousands have been willing to spend some effort, more time, and much money hoping that they will be able to devour volumes at a speed approaching that of light and far surpassing that of their own "thought waves" and ability to turn pages.

At the present time it appears that those who have attained such speeds—with accompanying comprehension—must be superhuman. In the future, perhaps we'll all be superhuman by today's standards. We can hope, but it'll take more than hope to get us there.

Background

Substrata Components of Reading—Their Relation to Rate

Chapter 1 of this book included a brief discussion concerning "assimilation of information." Within this was a discussion of the short-term memory system and the "chunking" of information. Apparently, the short-term memory system is able to hold only about 5 ± 2 or 7 ± 2 chunks —and these only for a few seconds before they either decay or are synthesized and transferred to a more permanent memory system. A beginning reader, no doubt, will put only a small bit of information into a chunk, while an advanced reader's chunk may contain much more—and even a different type of information than is found in the beginning reader's chunk.*

According to Harry Singer,[1] modern instructional reading programs include word-recognition-substrata, word-meaning-substrata, and reasoning-in-context substrata, which, according to Singer, are developed simultaneously. As discussed in the present book, word-recognition-substrata includes the use of at least some of the cue systems discussed in Chapter 6, "Recoding and Decoding: the Art of Using a Variety of Cue Systems." Word-meaning-substrata includes the act of decoding (large or small units), and includes the semantic component as discussed in Chapters 6 and 7. Reasoning-in-context substrata includes comprehension and, perhaps, the affective components of reading.

Singer summarizes research done by Brownell and Hendrickson[2] thus: "As an individual develops word-recognition-substrata to overcome the barrier presented by words in the form of printed symbols, he becomes increasingly able to use reading as a means of acquiring facts, forming concepts, and relating them as generalizations." Singer concludes that, "as a result of mental capability, training, and practice, the time and mental energy required for word-recognition-substrata in the process of reading gradually decrease while the time and energy employed for word-meaning-substrata and reasoning-in-context substrata gradually increase. This development eventually reaches a point where the mature and competent reader is relatively unconscious of the organization and dynamics of his word-recognition-substrata as he reads."[3] That is, recoding and decoding become automatic. The competent reader, thus, is able to focus attention and energy on comprehension and enjoyment and is limited only by his or her word-meaning-substrata and his or her ability to reason-in-context.

The following chart illustrates the process:

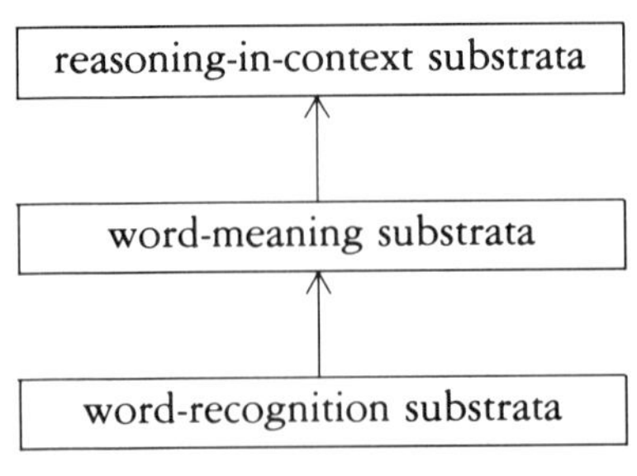

As readers become more competent, less and less time is spent on this substrata, leaving more and more time for higher substrata (bottom-up model).

---

*A beginning reader's chunk may contain a letter or perhaps a word. An advanced reader's chunk may be a phrase and/or a semantic unit.

Eye Movements During Reading

Visual perceptual ability for most of us is a marvelous thing. For although we see in circles, we have learned to perceive only one line of this circle in print. During one fixation, we perceive as much as we (individually) are able to, and then we have a saccadic sweep, which stops in another fixation, during which time we read again, and then we move on again. The breadth of what we visually "take in" in one fixation is called our *eye span*. Fig. 11.1 illustrates the principle:

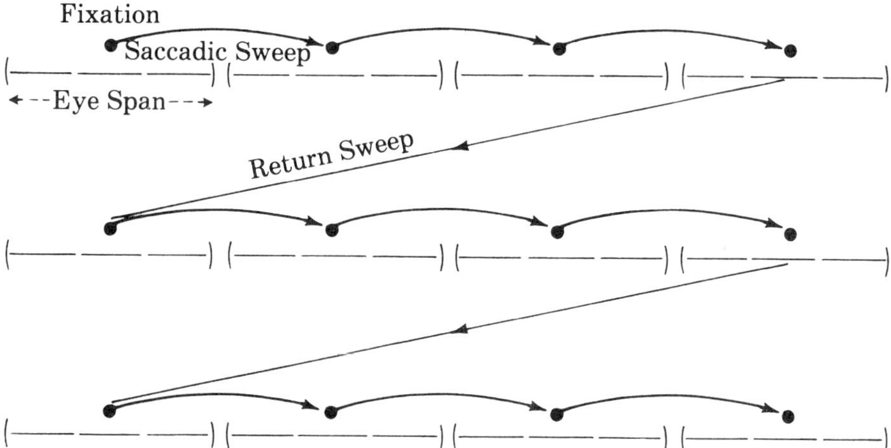

Fig. 11.1: Eye movements in reading.

The eye span, or span of recognition, is the range of what is perceived at one fixation. For the best mature readers, this might be up to three words on the average—during continuous reading. The fixation takes 1/6 second or more. The saccadic sweep to the next fixation point takes 1/30 second or more. Thus, according to research findings reported by George Spache,[4] our fastest readers can read three words and move on to the next fixation in 1/5 of a second (1/30 + 1/6). Thus in a second, 15 words can be read, and in a minute 900 words can be read by our fastest readers at the present time.

Sanford Taylor,[5] however, reports that the average college student has a "span of recognition," i.e., eye span, of 1.11 words, a fixation that takes about 1/4 second (.24 of a second), and a "rate of comprehension" of 280 words per minute. He also reports that it is not until eleventh grade that the average student has fewer fixations (including regressions) than there are words in a passage (96 fixations per 100 words). Eighteen of these fixations are regressions.

According to Taylor's findings, the average first grader fixates 224 times (including 52 regressions) per 100 words, and has a "rate with comprehension" of 80 words per minute. The average second grader fixates 174 times (including 40 regressions) per 100 words, and has a rate with comprehension of 115 words per minute. By sixth grade the average reader fixates 120 times (including 25 regressions) per 100 words, and has a rate of 185 words per minute. (Taylor reports that the average eleventh grader's rate is 237 words per minute, and the average twelfth grader's rate is 250 words per minute.)

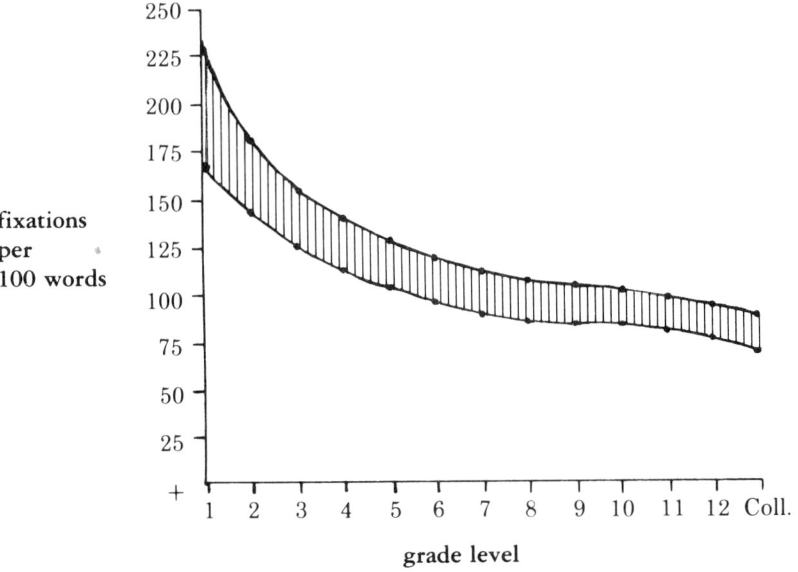

Fig. 11.2: Average number of fixations per 100 words, by grade level (darkened areas designate regressions).

TYPICAL RATES

According to Taylor's report, there is an average increase in rate each year between grades one and five of 20 words per minute. Beyond grade five, the average gain per year is about 10–12 words per minute. Taylor commented that skilled readers make fewer fixations per line, indicating that they have a wider perceptual span. More recently, Hochberg has argued that "this difference in number of fixations is not the result of differences in what readers can actually see, but it reflects differences in cognitive activities during each fixation."[6] In other words, the wider eye span is not the result of visual training or visual perception, per se, so much as the increased ability of the child to assimilate ideas.

As reading materials become more difficult, the average number of syllables per word increases (see Fry Graph, p. 610, and the research of Rudolf Flesch[7]). The average number of syllables per 100 words in grade one materials is 120 (1.2 per word). By grade seven it is 131 syllables per 100 words (1.31 per word), and by grade 16, it is 180 per 100 words (1.8 per word). Using such information, we can compare the average increases in words read per minute with that of syllables read per minute from grades one to sixteen, thus:

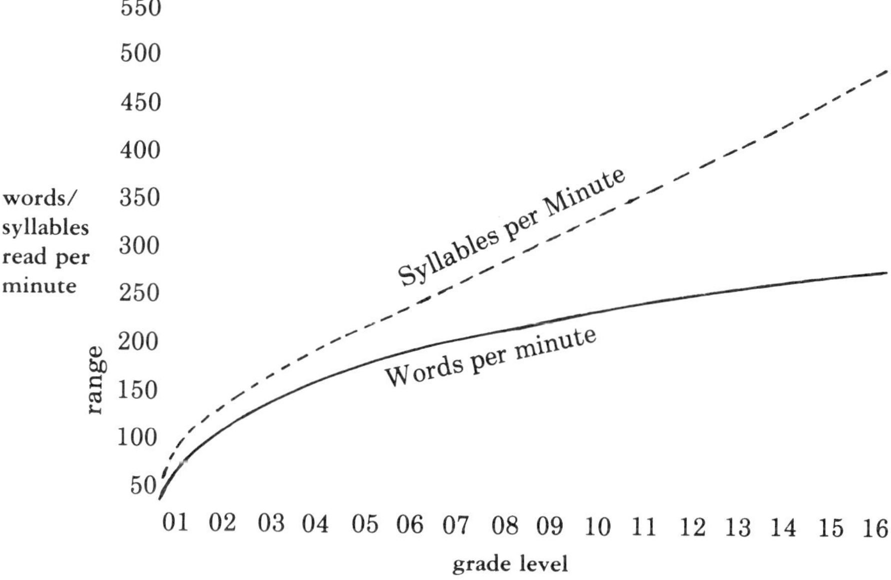

Fig. 11.3: Average number of words read per minute and syllables read per minute, by grade level.

Sentence length, syntactical complexity, and concept load also increase as materials become more difficult.

Such findings are of interest to most teachers, but they probably pose as many questions as they answer. Research dealing with rate of reading is extremely difficult to interpret. Some questions that might be asked in relation to most studies are:

- What is meant by rate of reading? What is rate without comprehension?
- What is meant by rate with comprehension? What kind of compre-

hension are we talking about? What kinds of questions are asked? What percentage of correct responses is necessary to qualify for rate with comprehension?

- What rate of reading is being discussed, or is it assumed that each reader has but one rate?

These are questions a teacher must ponder when reading research and when designing activities to help children increase their reading speed.

FLEXIBILITY OF RATE

For many years teachers have talked about flexibility of reading rate, of teaching children and adults to read at several rates, that is, at rates appropriate to the reader's purpose and to the nature of the material. (The Gray-Robinson model, given in Chapter 1, includes this description of rate.) Thus teachers have felt it was desirable for children to have rates such as those shown in Table 11.1.

TABLE 11.1   Possible explanation for use of various rates.

Rate	Difficulty of material	Purpose for reading (examples)
fast	easier	to get general idea, main points, for pure enjoyment, especially of plot, escape
	more difficult	to thoroughly preview, get main headings, main ideas, sequence, to review (when main headings are given)
medium	easier	to read to remember sequence for later recall, to appreciate style of writing, for greater depth of understanding than would be possible at a faster rate
	more difficult	to note important details, to formulate main ideas, to interpret, to classify
slow	easier	to mull over ideas, to absorb and analyze thoughts, to anticipate uses for ideas, to promote tangential thinking
	more difficult	to examine thoroughly, to analyze, criticize, react to ideas, evaluate ideas, to solve problems, to follow directions

Research reports on the subject of rauding[8] (an acronym composed of *r*ead*ing* and *auding*)* suggest that perhaps the reason that easier materials are read more rapidly than are more difficult materials by an individual

---

*That is, rauding is silently pronouncing words to oneself when reading.

reader in terms of words per minute is that easier materials have fewer syllables for a given number of words than do more difficult materials. Such research suggests that perhaps reading rate (rauding rate) for an individual in terms of syllables read per minute may be constant across materials of varying difficulty. Readers who vocalize or subvocalize may be limited in the processing of vocalizations to a maximum number (for them) in a given amount of time. Until they are able to reduce or eliminate vocal or subvocal (auditory) clues used, their rates may defy growth beyond a given number of syllables per minute. This is just one of the factors that may restrict rate of reading.

It appears that some oral component—inner speech or subvocalization—normally accompanies the process of reading,[9] although advanced readers may at times be able to "suppress or not activate part of it." Singer suggests that perhaps, "For slow, analytical or study type of reading, oral reconstruction may be part of the process, but for rapid, skimming type of reading, oral reconstruction may be suppressed or not mobilized."[10] Top-down theorists, of course, deny the need for, or presence of, oral/aural components in silent reading.

In addition to the rates suggested above, which are used for total coverage of reading materials, there are two rates that good readers use for partial coverage of materials. These are called scanning and skimming.

Scanning is used when the reader wishes to locate a word, item, name, date, etc., quickly. The scanner's eyes glance rapidly over a page or pages, searching for the one detail or idea she or he is seeking. Readers may scan chapters of books, columns in a telephone book, a page of an index or dictionary, a table of contents, etc. When the reader finds the idea or detail she or he is seeking, the reader may begin to read more thoroughly. Scanning is a very useful skill, which children should be taught, though probably not during the earliest stages of reading.

Skimming is more thorough than scanning, for in skimming the reader quickly views an entire section of printed material. The reader skims to get an overall view of the material—to grasp the sequence, to write an outline or other visual "map," to get the author's point of view, if it is obvious, to see if topics included suggest complete coverage or card stacking, and to see if the material is worth reading in its entirety. Readers may skim material in order to preview it so that they can begin with a framework. Or a reader may skim in review, as an aid toward reconstructing what has been read.

In discussing various speeds, T.L. Harris states, "I would particularly stress the point that reading speed is relative to what you are reading and what you want to get out of it. Furthermore, the key to the efficient use of reading speed is flexibility in its application."[11]

Dr. Harris cites research evidence that flexibility in reading speed can be taught, in this case to nine-year-olds. In a research study, he and his colleagues worked with three specified purposes for reading. They were

- reading to find a specific detail,
- reading for the main idea,
- reading for the sequence of ideas.

Seventy-two fourth grade pupils who were reading at or above grade level composed the experimental group. The rate of comprehension score was defined as the amount of time it took a reader to achieve 100 percent comprehension, including rereading time, when necessary, to achieve a perfect score.

Short daily training sessions were held for two weeks, and in that time the "nine-year-olds learned to vary their speed of reading significantly according to reading purpose."[12] They read faster for details than for main ideas, and faster for main ideas than for sequence. Retention tests given three weeks later verified that further gains were evident. Harris cautions, however, that "The development of flexible readers is not a stop and go proposition; it is a matter of continued application."[13]

CAUSES OF INEFFICIENT RATES

The eye span information given previously is worthy of scrutiny. It tells us that most children and young people do not read in phrases. Indeed, it tells us that until eleventh grade they usually read less than one word at a time. However, we are not told why this is true.

Findings such as those reported by Taylor are not new. In fact, teachers have been peeping through holes torn in pages to observe eye movements since the 1930's, and as early as the 1920's eye movement photographs were made by researchers. Conclusions were drawn by some that perceptual inefficiency needed treatment. This gave rise to the production and sale of numerous mechanical devices designed to broaden eye span and "lead" the eyes to move more rapidly. Many of these machines, purchased in the 1950's and 1960's, can now be found stashed away in school closets.

Although there are some children and young people who might benefit from direct treatment of perceptual inefficiency, it seems to many reading experts that perceptual inefficiency is not in itself a major cause of slow reading. Instead, it usually is a symptom.

Causes of slow reading may be related to

- the child's ability to assimilate information (to add to what is known) and/or to accomodate to new ideas (to alter a point of view)
- the child's desire to assimilate and/or to accomodate to the information, i.e., the child's interest in the ideas expressed and willingness to consider various viewpoints

- the child's background as it relates to the ideas expressed
- the difficulty level of the material in relation to the child's reading achievement level
- the child's alertness and/or attitude toward reading or toward a particular kind of reading
- the child's vocabulary as it relates to the assignment
- the child's recoding and/or decoding skills—does the child analyze words excessively? dawdle over letters and syllables? Or does the child take a more global approach?
- the way the child has been taught and is being taught.

Suggestions for Improving Rate

To read at any level of understanding, the reader must activate at least a minimum amount of each of the following systems:

- word-recognition-substrata
- word-meaning-substrata
- reasoning-in-context substrata.

GENERAL PRINCIPLES AND STRATEGIES

The more automatic word recognition becomes, the more effort can be extended to the other systems. David La Berge and S. Jay Samuels[14] suggest principles that may lead to automaticity of decoding. These include: practice at the letter and word level, reorganizing material into higher order units even before lower order units are recognized at a high level of automaticity (e.g., moving from words to phrases to encourage chunking), also working from levels of meaning to perceptual levels, i.e., working in a top-down fashion:

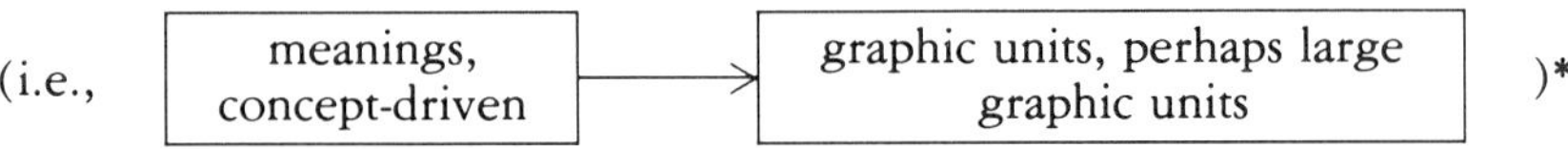

rather than the reverse to encourage semantic chunking.

David Elkind[15] suggests the following considerations for the promotion of rapid silent reading:

---

*E.g., using the Language Experience Approach; brainstorming and discussing before reading; anticipating and hypothesizing before and while reading.

- *visual independence:* After the age of about eight or nine rapid reading requires independence from tactile motor skills, such as using a finger as a marker (which may be helpful for younger children).
- *meaning construction:* Meaning is not in the printed page, but rather, it is in the mind of the reader, who interprets what is read within his or her own storehouse of knowledge. "Satisfaction in reading derives, in part at least, from the degree of fit between the material being read and the conceptual level of the subject who is reading it."[16] (I.e., select material, that is suitable to the child.)
- *receptive discipline:* Many children are not only poor readers but also poor listeners—and for the same reason. They are more interested in their own thoughts than in other people's thoughts. Their problem is not basically with rate of reading but rather with the desire to listen to others. (I.e., select material that is of vital interest to the child—that he or she will wish to listen to. State purposes for reading so the child is responsible for something.)

Added to this might be the findings of Anne McKillop[17] that reading in many cases requires the child not only to conceptualize what the author is saying (literal level), but also requires the child to change, modify, and reorganize ideas he or she already has. Those children who lack the flexibility to change (i.e., to accommodate) may become slow readers and primarily literal readers.

Strategies helpful in building rate of comprehension should be designed to alleviate (when possible) the causes of slow reading when slow reading is undesirable. Such strategies require much more than just training sessions. They require adherence to classwide practices of

- adjusting materials to each child's reading level in all classes, to avoid frustration or boredom
- allowing children to read materials of their own choice when possible
- building and increasing interest in concepts and materials that are read or are to be read
- building background through direct and vicarious experiences and relating background to reading assignments, stressing imagery (E.g., Can you see in your mind what the author is discussing? Can you hear the sounds? . . . taste? . . . smell? . . . touch?)
- previewing and stating purposes for reading before assignments are read in full
- teaching children to hypothesize and anticipate meanings while reading
- avoiding classroom practices that are detrimental to increasing rate, e.g., round robin reading, teaching words in isolation when other ways can be used.

Skill Development Strategies

If desirable classroom practices are followed, rate of reading should increase. However, direct attention to increasing rate in addition to the above might prove helpful. Suggestions for improving rate are divided into two levels, those especially appropriate for all children and those appropriate for more advanced readers.

The following types of activities are recommended for primary level children and older children:

□ *For Extremely Slow Readers* Some activities are especially appropriate for extremely slow readers:

- The teacher may sit with a child and run his or her finger under the words at a rate a bit faster than the child's. Individual words are not pointed to. The child may read silently or orally.
- The impress method discussed in Chapter 6 of this book (pp. 220–221) is helpful for use with children who are very slow readers.
- In teaching all children to phrase and to pay attention to punctuation, echo reading and choral reading are helpful. These are particularly helpful to slow readers in improving rate.

□ *Emphasize Thinking, Comprehension, and Enjoyment* Teachers who wish to improve rate of reading may have to relax requirements for "perfection" in oral reading. And, in both oral and silent reading, children should be encouraged to think about the author's ideas and enjoy reading. Allowing time for free reading is likely to improve rate of reading for most children.

for more advanced readers:

□ *Eye Movement Activities* The activities given in this section may or may not be valuable in themselves, but they can be used profitably to set the stage for activities that follow. They wake children up, get them going, and take little time. They should be followed directly by other activities designed to improve rate.

The teacher prepares mimeographed copies of activities like the following. Each page should be double spaced and must have the same number of lines so that rate scores are comparable. The teacher hands out only one page at a time, but about three or four pages per session. Children underline the numbers, letters or words that match the key in each line. Children are timed on each column or page singly and can compare their scores with scores they made during previous sessions.

(The teacher might write times on the board every two seconds or might use an overhead transparency and a covering sheet with a slot. The slot could be moved every two seconds to reveal the amount of elapsed time since the timing began. Children copy the time that is posted when they finish the activity.)

For example

1	7	6	9	1	3	6	5	3	2
5	6	1	5	2	7	9	1	4	7
8	4	8	1	7	2	8	2	1	9
3	2	1	3	4	6	4	9	5	6

(etc., to bottom of page)   (etc.)

time________   time________

12	14	21	12	35	82	16	29	82	79
25	22	95	42	25	71	85	71	17	65
91	82	76	91	31	54	69	25	54	97

(etc.)   (etc.)

time________   time________

a	f	g	a	h	b	c	f	g	b
p	m	l	d	p	t	q	j	t	r
s	r	k	s	n	v	w	v	h	c

(etc.)   (etc.)

time________   time________

cat	fin	till	miss	cat	far
sin	win	dirt	sin	tar	slip
dog	rag	tan	hog	lamp	dog

(etc.)

time________

□*Scanning* Groups of children can use any books they have in common. The teacher tells the children to open their books to a certain page and then tells them exactly what detail to look for. Just to add zip, the teacher might write times on the board for children to record when they finish. Several activities like this could be done in one session.

□*Skimming* Skimming is like previewing and should be done regularly preceding textbook assignments. As a timed activity, the teacher might announce that the children are to preview a chapter or a section of a chapter and that they will be timed when doing so. (Or the teacher may decide to give them a specified amount of time, e.g., three minutes or five minutes.) The teacher might give them a blank chart form, like a time line, flow chart, spoke graph, that would be appropriate for the relationships of the chapter and ask the children to complete the chart in the amount of time given.)

The teacher might wish, also, to prepare special materials for this by using periodical items that lend themselves to this type of comprehension activity.

□ *Periodical Items* The teacher might wish to prepare materials from magazines and newspapers. (If one article is selected every day, the teacher would have 30 in a month.) Items selected should be highly interesting to children, e.g., sports items, human interest items, science, etc.

The items could be photocopied or pasted on cards and laminated so they could be used frequently. At the top of each, the teacher states a few (1-5) questions the reader should answer. The number and types of questions will depend on the teacher's purpose. Is the teacher testing for details, main idea, sequence, or what? Perhaps in each set of activities the questions should relate to the same purposes and should be standard in number. Answers to these questions can be written on the reverse side. The teacher should write the number of words in the passage somewhere on the card.

Children should be timed when reading these. To figure out their *words per minute,* they divide the time it took them to finish into the number of words, e.g.:

time: 2 min., 15 sec. = 2.25 minutes
words : 340

$$2.25 \overline{)340.00} \quad \frac{151.}{} = words/minute$$

$$
\begin{array}{r}
151. \\
2.25\,\overline{)\,340.00} \\
\underline{225} \\
1150 \\
\underline{1125} \\
250
\end{array}
$$

To figure out *reading efficiency,* they multiply the words per minute score by their comprehension score, e.g.:

words per minute: 151   comprehension: 68%

$$
\begin{array}{r}
151 \\
\underline{.68} \\
1208 \\
\underline{906} \\
102.68 = reading\ efficiency
\end{array}
$$

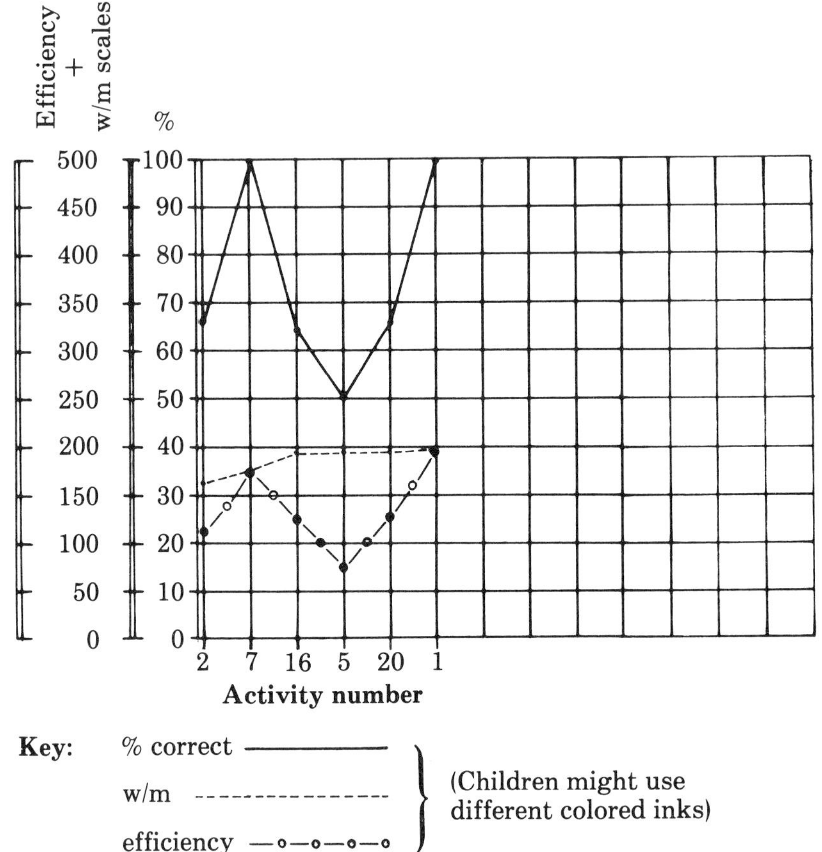

Fig. 11.4: Charting a student's words per minute rate, comprehension, and reading efficiency

They could chart their rate, comprehension, and reading efficiency scores for each article, as shown, for example, in Fig. 11.4.

Children must understand that all articles and questions are not of comparable difficulty. They should be most interested in general trends in the graph.

□ *Commercially Prepared Timed Exercises* Some commercially prepared timed reading lessons are available. Among these are the McCall-Crabbs *Standard Test Lessons in Reading,*[18] published in booklets at different difficulty levels. Groups of children can work together on these while the teacher times them. Each lesson can be discussed, since the children in each group read the same lesson. Also available are *Rate Builders*, a part of SRA Reading Labs.[19] These are individual multilevel exercises. Both of these are educational and highly interesting to most children.

□ *Encourage Easy Reading* Encourage children to do much easy and interesting reading by providing such material and giving them class time in which to read. You may wish to teach them to use a card or envelope which they slide down over the print, from the top of the page going down. They read the line under the card. They push the card at a rate that is just slightly uncomfortable for them. As soon as that rate becomes comfortable, they push a little faster.

□ *Irrelevant Item* The teacher might select short paragraphs from the children's textbooks and alter one detail in each paragraph. These paragraphs could be mimeographed on one page hand-outs. Children are timed as they read them. They have completed the page when they have underlined the irrelevant statement in each passage. E.g.:*

1. The Communist party is the only political party allowed in the Soviet Union. Though it is a Communist nation, not all Soviet citizens are members of the Communist party. A person can join the party when he or she becomes 18 years old and brings chips, dips or drinks.

2. One complete trip of a planet around the sun is called one revolution. Each year, the earth revolves around the sun once, like a dog chasing a cat. The path which a planet follows through space around the sun is called an orbit.

3. With the discovery of seed planting, early man lessened his need to search for food. With a food supply they could depend on, people had more time to come together and watch T.V.

4. Most Russian farmers live in villages. Many have their own backyard farms. Farmers can grow many types of vegetables, fruit trees, coffins, headstones or whatever they wish on their small plots.

5. The earth's magnetism is very weak. Even though a compass needle is attracted by the earth's magnetic poles, it can be pulled away from them by other magnetic fields. You may be surprised to discover some unusual kinds of magnets that love each other in your classroom.

6. Perhaps the strangest of the

*The author is indebted to the following students in her classes for writing these: Carolina Casillas, Kay Ruhl, Cathy Worsham, Marge Martin, Carolyn Clemmer, Sheri Ramsey, Maria Castillo, Virginia Casper, Margaret Struckman, and Esther Fleshman.

earth's neighbors are the comets. These rare members of the solar system look like glowing balls with long fiery tails. Comets travel around the sun, stopping only to eat and sleep, but their orbits are long and narrow rather than almost round like those of the planets.

Time______

1. The kings of Europe were fighting each other for wealth and power. When two countries were at war, each tried to take the other's jelly beans.
2. The amount of dirt that falls on you each day depends on where you live. In some parts of some cities, as much as one hundred tons of vanilla wafers fall on each square mile every month.
3. Words that tell when, where, and how are called adverbs. Adverbs that tell when are called adverbs of time. Adverbs that tell where are called adverbs of place. Adverbs that tell how are called American Indians.
4. About this time, the first theaters were built. Wealthy or noble persons were provided with seats, but common people stood and watched the play from space satellites.
5. A person can survive for a few weeks without food, and get along for three or four days without water. But it is impossible to survive for more than five minutes without a new pair of sox.
6. English has thousands of words that are made by adding prefixes and suffixes to roots. Prefixes and suffixes are different from roots because they usually grow above the ground and often have flowers.

Time______

1. The Pilgrims reached Massachusetts Bay late in the fall of 1620. After exploring Death Valley for a time, they found the site that was to become their home.
2. West from Cincinnati and beyond the Mississippi River was another kind of country. It was a land of Indians and buffalo, astronauts, of great mountains, of desert and open prairie.
3. Newton was sitting under an apple tree at his home in England. A bowling ball fell from the tree to the earth. This simple event set off a

chain of thoughts in Newton's mind. Putting together the facts he knew, and thinking beyond these facts, he developed the theory of gravity.

4. There were many different Indian tribes scattered across the eastern part of the country. These eastern Indians lived in villages of 50 to 200 people. They located each village next to a water faucet so they would have water.

5. Visitors from other countries did not always find what they wanted in the West.

One of them, an Englishwoman name Mrs. Trollope, was looking for a reducing spa and couldn't locate one.

6. When people talk about literature, they usually mean stories or poems or folk tales or myths. Most of the time people are thinking of things that have lots of imagination in them. But literature can be almost anything that somebody has written and somebody else wants to serve at a dinner party.

time______

After finishing these, it might be interesting to ask the children what should have been stated where the irrelevant statement was found. This is a form of critical reading.

□ *Hand Tachistoscopes* Children who spend an excessive amount of time analyzing words might benefit from using a hand tachistoscope. These can be made by the teacher or perhaps by the children themselves. All that is needed is an interesting form, like a bowling pin, a football, a doll, an ice cream soda, etc. A slit is cut in the form, through which words or phrases can be exposed rapidly. E.g.:

in the park	is going
at the lodge	was running
in a school	is swimming
at a dance	was singing
in the book	was hoping
at the library	is acting
at a zoo	is playing
in an alley	was reading
at the circus	is jumping

Mechanical Devices

Since there is a great deal of curiosity about mechanical devices, the following section is included. However, it is recommended that great caution be exerted when making decisions about purchasing equipment. The machines are expensive. Many of them cost as much as a good classroom library of paperbacks. After summarizing research related to the use of mechanical devices in reading programs, Robert Karlin concluded that, "It appears that gains in rate of reading can be achieved through programs which include mechanical instruments . . . It is apparent that instruction which does not favor machines not only can bring about these same gains but also . . . surpass them. Dependence upon expensive equipment to achieve suitable outcomes in reading rates cannot be recommended in view of present knowledge."[20]

There are three types of machines: tachistoscopes, pacers, and film or filmstrip machines.

Tachistoscopes, like the hand tachistoscope discussed above, are designed to broaden eye span and lessen fixation time. Mechanical tachistoscopes are designed to flash a single exposure on a screen at a rapid rate—usually between one second and 1/100 of a second. Anything might be included in this exposure, from pictures used in visual discrimination to digits, words, phrases, or sentences. The exposure might look like any of these:

$\triangle$ O $\square$ O X O $\square$ O $\triangle$

A

5

4   9   7   6   5   3   1

are

are going

Jane is swimming today.

Groups of children can work together for short periods of time using this machine. The teacher usually flashes the exposures using the 1/100-second setting, and the children write what they have seen. After about eight or ten exposures, children check their papers. Then the teacher flashes another series. About 20 to 30 exposures are seen at one sitting.

The object is to increase eye span and to minimize the time for each exposure, or fixation. Single words, then two-, three-, or four-word phrases can be flashed. Accompanying these can be digits—three- or four- or five-digit numbers. Sometimes the teacher starts flashing the tachistoscope at 1/25 of a second and works up to 1/100 of a second.

Pacers usually incorporate a shade, metal bar, or light beam that moves down a page to cover successive lines of print at a rate set by the reader. The child reads below the shade or bar or within the light beam. Almost any kind of reading material can be used, including paperbacks, magazines, and textbooks.

Children set the device so that it is comfortable for them, and then they set it slightly faster to push themselves a bit. As soon as that rate becomes comfortable, they set the machine to go faster, etc. Some reading experts recommend that children alternate pages, reading one page on the machine, the next without it, etc. Or, children might read one on the machine and two or three without it—to help eliminate their dependence on the machine for increased rate.

Filmstrip machines are available with accompanying workbooks and filmstrips on all levels, from reading readiness through college levels. The workbooks that accompany some of these are well planned and use a survey technique, programmed vocabulary development, and statements of purpose which should be read before the film is read.

The purpose of these machines is to increase children's reading rates by improving their left-to-right eye movements and by increasing eye span. Such machines are best used by individual children, rather than by groups, for few children read at the same rate and few are likely to progress at the same rate.

Summary

Reading normally involves the simultaneous use, or almost simultaneous use, of the following substrata:

- word-recognition-substrata
- word-meaning-substrata
- reasoning-in-context substrata

Beginning readers and inefficient readers frequently spend much time and energy on word-recognition. As readers move toward automaticity of word recognition, they are able to expend more energy on word-meaning-substrata and reasoning-in-context substrata, and thus they are better able to assimilate thoughts.

During reading the eyes fixate on a graphic image, during which time the image is perceived; then the eyes make a saccadic sweep to end in another fixation, and move on again. The range of what a person perceives at one fixation is called his or her eye span. Reports of research concerning the number of fixations per 100 words made by average readers of different grade levels were summarized, and typical rates of reading were given. A discussion followed concerning flexibility of rate —and of teaching children to adjust rate according to the nature of the reading material and the purpose for reading. Following this, causes of inefficient reading were discussed.

In the 1950's and 1960's perceptual inefficiency was often directly treated as though it were the cause of slow reading. More recently most reading experts consider perceptual inefficiency to be the result of other factors which tend to slow down reading rate. These are factors that deserve most attention in reading programs.

Programs that promote a better rate of comprehension include those that adjust materials used in all classes to the reading achievement levels of all children and to the interests of children, when possible. They provide for improving the conceptual level of children through direct and vicarious experiences and through introducing lessons to children in meaningful ways.

Activities designed specifically for improving rate of comprehension are often extremely helpful also, especially for older children. Strategies for designing such activities were included in this chapter.

Because of the broad interest in mechanical devices designed to help students improve their rate of reading, a brief description of some of these devices was included, along with the warning that caution be exerted when making decisions about purchasing such equipment.

Questions and Activities

After answering the questions at the beginning of this chapter, consider these questions and activities:

1. Pair-off with one of your classmates. While one of you reads silently, the other should observe his or her eye movements. Do the eyes move smoothly or in jumps while a person is reading? When are the eyes "reading"?
2. Do you say words in your mind when you are reading . . . one after another, as in the text? Do you think you are a "bottom-up," "top-down," or "interactive" reader?
3. Two terms frequently found in the literature today are *assimilation* and *accommodation*. When ideas an author is discussing are in harmony with the reader's ideas, the reader may *assimilate* the author's concepts. When ideas an author is discussing are divergent in light of the reader's experiences (reader's schemata), the reader must

make *accommodations* in order to synthesize text schemata with his or her own schemata. Which process do you think takes more time: assimilation or accommodation? Why? Why would an inflexible person have difficulty with accommodation? How can we help children read at appropriate rates under each of these circumstances?

4. What do you think are more important in building appropriate rates of reading—bottom-up (perceptual) strategies or top-down (concept) strategies? Why? Is there a place for both in a reading program? Explain. Consider the "interactive" process.

NOTES

1. Harry Singer, p. 314. See Selected References.
2. *Ibid.* Reference: W.A. Brownell and G. Hendrickson, "How Children Learn Information, Concepts, and Generalizations." *Yearbook of the National Society for the Study of Education*, 49, Part I, 1950.
3. *Ibid.*
4. George D. Spache. See Selected References.
5. From Albert J. Harris and Edward R. Sipay, p. 560, as they report findings of Sanford E. Taylor, Helen Frankenpohl, and James L. Pettee. See Selected References.
6. According to George McConkie and Keith Rayner, p. 138. See Selected References.
7. Rudolf Flesch. *How to Test Readability.* New York: Harper and Brothers, 1951.
8. Ronald P. Carver, pp. 8–63. See Selected References.
9. Harry Singer, p. 647. References: Robert B. Ruddell. "Psycholinguistic Implications for a Systems of Communication Model," in *Psycholinguistics and the Teaching of Reading*, Kenneth S. Goodman (ed.). Newark, Delaware: International Reading Association, 1969, pp. 61–78. Also Ake W. Edfeldt. *Silent Speech and Silent Reading.* Chicago: University of Chicago Press, 1960.
10. Harry Singer, *op. cit.*, p. 648.
11. T.L. Harris, p. 29. See Selected References.
12. *Ibid.*, p. 32.
13. *Ibid.*, p. 34.
14. David La Berge and S. Jay Samuels, pp. 570–71. See Selected References.
15. David Elkind, pp. 336–338. See Selected References.
16. *Ibid.*, p. 337.
17. See Anne S. McKillop in Selected References.
18. McCall-Crabbs. *Standard Test Lessons in Reading.* New York: Bureau of Publications, Teachers College Press, Columbia University.
19. Rate Builders, a part of the SRA Reading Laboratories. Chicago: Science Research Associates, Inc.
20. Robert Karlin, p. 183. See Selected References.

Mechanical Devices

Tachistoscopes

1. *EDL Tach-X Tachistoscope*
   Educational Developmental Laboratories, Huntington, New York
   Shutter Speed: 1/100 to 1 1/2 second
   Levels: k–adult

2. *Keystone Standard Tachistoscope*
   Keystone View Company, Meadville, Pennsylvania
   Shutter Speed: 1/100, 1/50, 1/25, 1/10, 1/5, 1/2, 1 second
   Levels: k–adult

3. *Rheem-Califone Percepta-matic Tachistoscope*
   Carlton Films, Beloit, Wisconsin
   Shutter Speed: 1/100 to 1/10 second
   Levels: 1–8 grades

4. *T-ap All-Purpose Tachistoscope Attachment*
   Lafayette Instrument Co., Lafayette, Indiana
   Shutter Speed: 1/100, 1/50, 1/25, 1/10, 1/5, 1/2, 1 second
   Comments: converts any brand of projector to a tachistoscope

5. *SVE Speed-I-O-Scope*
   Society for Visual Education, Inc., Chicago, Illinois
   Shutter Speed: 1/100 to 1 second
   Levels: 1–6 grades

6. *Electro-Tach*
   Lafayette Instrument Co., Lafayette, Indiana
   Shutter Speed: 1/100, 1/50, 1/25, 1/10, 1 second
   Levels: 1–college
   Comments: near-point for individual use

7. *Tachist-O-Viewer, Tachist-O-Flasher*
   Learning Through Seeing, Inc., Sunland, California
   Shutter Speed: 1/40, 1/20, 1/10, 1/5 second
   Levels: 1–12 grades
   Comments: near-point for individual use; programs mainly phonics and vocabulary; series available for remedial classes

8. *AVR Eye-Span Trainer*
   Audio-Visual Research, Waseca, Minnesota
   Levels: 4–13 grades
   Comments: manually operated

9. *Phrase Flasher*
   The Reading Laboratories, Inc., New York
   Comments: manually operated; designed for individual use

Pacers

1. *Shadowscope*
   Psychotechnics, Inc., Glenview, Illinois
   Comments: uses a light beam

2. *Prep-Pacer*
   The Reading Laboratories, Inc., New York
   Comments: electrical pacer using disk

3. *AVR Reading Rateometer*
   Audio-Visual Research, Waseca, Minnesota
   Comments: three models: (a) above forth grade level, (b) elementary and remedial, (c) advanced

4. *SRA Reading Accelerator*
   Science Research Associates, Chicago, Illinois

5. *Reading Pacer*
   Genco Educational Aids, Chicago, Illinois
   Comments: lesson rolls inserted like film in a box camera

Films or Filmstrips

1. *Controlled Reader, Controlled Reader, jr.*
   Educational Developmental Laboratories, Huntington, New York
   Level: k–adult

2. *Tachomatic 500 Reading Projector*
   Psychotechnics, Inc., Glenview, Illinois
   Levels: k–adult

3. *Craig Reader*
   Craig Research Inc., Los Angeles, California

Selected References

Berger, Allen and James D. Peebles (eds.). *Rates of Comprehension* (an annotated bibliography). Newark, Delaware: International Reading Association, 1976.

Carver, Ronald P. "Toward a Theory of Reading Comprehension and Rauding." *Reading Research Quarterly*, 13, No. 1 (1977–1978): 8–63.

Elkind, David. "Cognitive Development in Reading," in *Theoretical Models and Processes of Reading, Second Edition*, Harry Singer and Robert B. Ruddell (eds.). Newark, Delaware: International Reading Association, 1976, pp. 331–340.

Hafner, Lawrence E. (ed.). *Improving Reading in Middle and Secondary Schools-Selected Readings, Second Edition*. New York: Macmillan, 1974, Section 9.

Harris, Albert J. and Edward R. Sipay. *How to Increase Reading Ability, Seventh Edition*. New York: David McKay, 1980, Chapter 19.

Harris, Theodore L. "Reading Flexibility: a Neglected Aspect of Reading Instruction" in *New Horizons in Reading*, John E. Merritt (ed.). Newark, Delaware: International Reading Association, 1976.

Jensen, Poul Erik. "Theories of Reading Speed and Comprehension." *Journal of Reading*, 21 (April 1978): 593–600.

Karlin, Robert. "Machines and Reading: A Review of Research." *The Clearing House*, 32 (February 1958): 349–352.

——————————. "Research in Reading." *Elementary English*, 37 (March 1960): 183.

La Berge, David and S. Jay Samuels. "Toward a Theory of Automatic Information Processing in Reading," in *Theoretical Models and Processes of Reading, Second Edition*, Harry Singer and Robert B. Ruddell (eds.). Newark, Delaware, International Reading Association, 1976, pp. 548–579.

McConkie, George W. and Keith Rayner. "Identifying the Span of the Effective Stimulus in Reading: Literature Review and Theories of Reading," in *Theoretical Models and Processes of Reading, Second Edition*, Harry Singer and Robert B. Ruddell (eds.). Newark, Delaware: International Reading Association, 1976, pp. 137–162.

McKillop, Anne S. *The Relationship Between the Reader's Attitude and Certain Types of Reading Responses*. New York: Bureau of Publications, Teachers College, Columbia University, 1956.

Schacter, Sumner W. "Developing Flexible Reading Habits." *Journal of Reading*, 22 (November 1978): 149–152.

Schubert, Delwyn and Theodore L. Torgerson (eds.). *Readings in Reading-Practice, Theory and Research*. New York: Thomas Y. Crowell, 1968, Section 5.

Singer, Harry. "Conceptualization in Learning to Read," in *Theoretical Models and Processes of Reading, Second Edition*, Harry Singer and Robert B. Ruddell (eds.). Newark, Delaware: International Reading Association, 1976, pp. 302–319.

——————————. "Theoretical Models of Reading," in *Theoretical Models and Processes of Reading, Second Edition*, Harry Singer and Robert B. Ruddell (eds.). Newark, Delaware: International Reading Association, 1976, pp. 634–654.

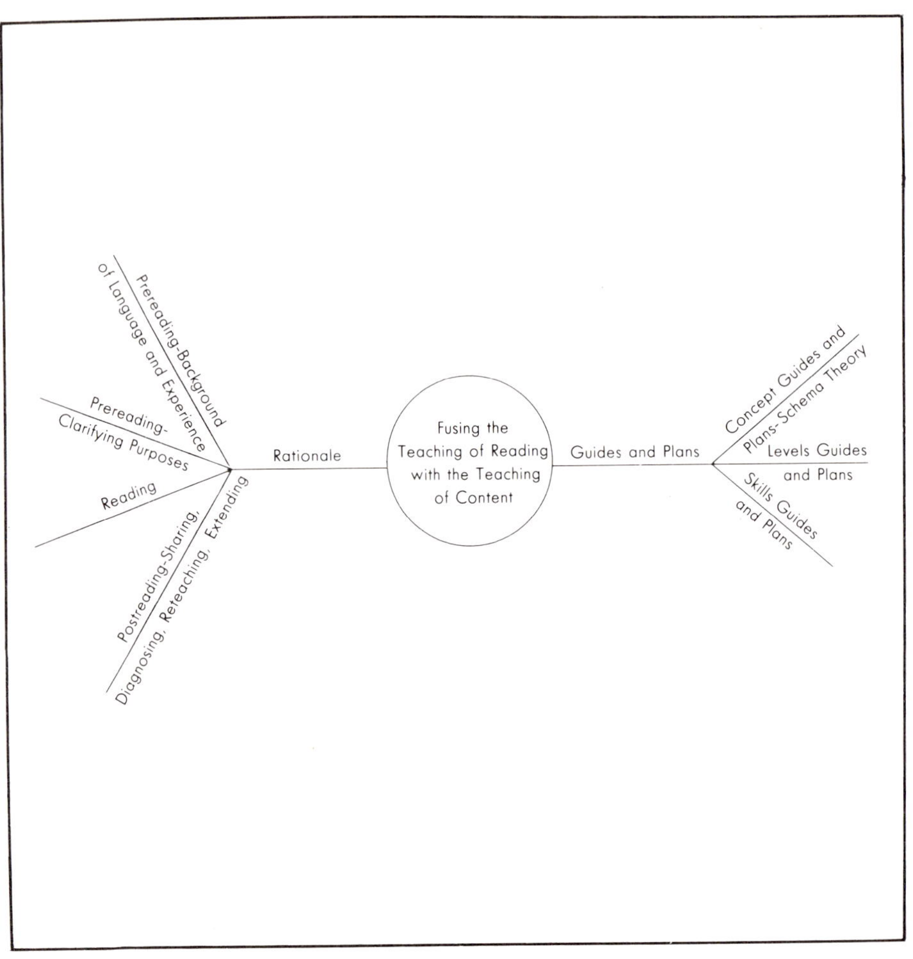

- How can we teach content and at the same time utilize the best or most appropriate principles of the teaching of reading? How does the use of appropriate reading strategies enhance content area learning?

- What should be done to prepare children for a reading assignment in terms of building and/or relating the child's language and experiences to the assignment? in terms of clarifying purposes for reading? Should children read silently or orally? What should they be doing while reading? What should be done after the children complete their reading? Relate these steps to the definition of reading as a matrixing event.

- What three different types of lesson guides or plans are explained in this chapter? What are the steps in each? How do they differ one from another? Explain when each might be appropriate.

CHAPTER 12

Fusing the Teaching of Reading with the Teaching of Content

Although reading skill development in itself may be important, provisions for teaching skills may be made while content is also taught. Sometimes the teacher's primary aim may be to teach a reading skill. This can hardly be done without including content of some sort, and there is no reason that this content should not be important, interesting, and appropriate to the children being taught. Thus in a skill lesson, children may progress in their ability to use the skill and may also learn ideas of interest and value to them.

Sometimes the teacher's principal aim is to teach content, as is usually true in a science, arithmetic, social studies, literature, art, etc., class. If reading is involved, such content can hardly be learned without the utilization of reading skills.

In the first instance, when skill development is the focus of the lesson, as it normally is in reading class, content is selected that will enable the teacher to teach the skill and the children to understand it. In the second instance, when the focus of the lesson is on learning content, as it normally is in content area classes, reading skills are selected that will help the teacher teach the content and the children to understand it. The present chapter includes guides and sample lesson plan suggestions for both of these instances.

Rationale

In Chapter 1 of this book, there is a brief discussion of reading as a matrixing event. The matrix for a complete passage or reading skill might be imagined to look like the illustration in Fig. 12.1.

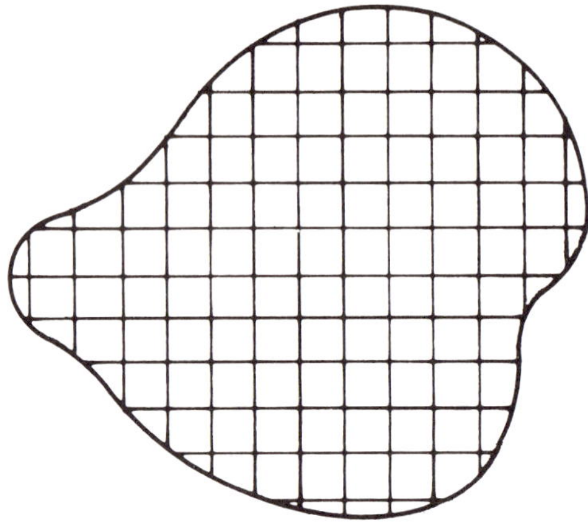

Figure 12.1

Each square might be thought of as an idea, or integral part of the passage, or a reading skill.

PREREADING—BACKGROUND OF LANGUAGE AND EXPERIENCE

Next, we might think of the teacher's job to be one of introducing the lesson. The introduction would involve relating the lesson to each child's background of language and experience and building these when necessary. This might be done through

- reviewing previous lessons (vocabulary and concepts) that relate to this lesson,
- previewing and discussing the main points of the present lesson, putting them into a graphic format, and hypothesizing about what might be discussed,
- discussing the children's personal language and experiences that relate to the lesson,
- building experiences, including language experiences, e.g., by taking a field trip, looking at objects, pictures, or other illustrations, and discussing these as they relate to the lesson, etc.

Figure 12.2 shows the matrix as it might appear after this step has been completed.

The blackened squares represent the ideas the reader recognizes from previous or newly developed experiences (the reader's schemata) and

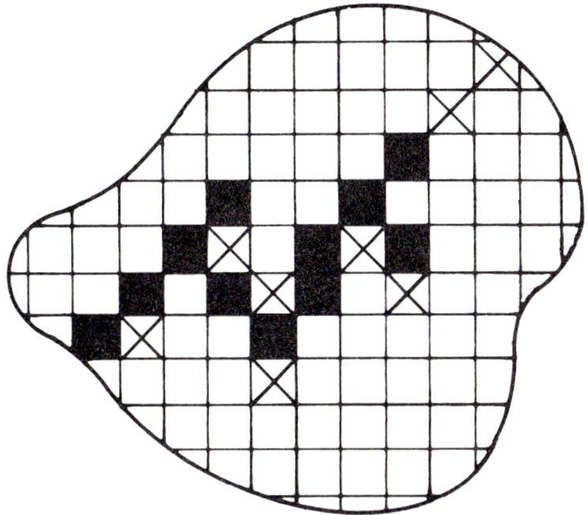

Figure 12.2

that the reader is consciously aware of before reading the assignment in its entirety. The "X'd" squares represent the ideas the reader is familiar with but has not consciously related to the lesson at this point.

PREREADING—CLARIFYING PURPOSES FOR READING

Statements of purpose for doing the assignment should also be made at this point. Consider, for example, that the assignment is about space travel and that the children are going to read for just one of the purposes below. Note how they would approach the assignment differently for each of the following purposes:

1. Read to identify the first three flights into space. By whom were they made, where did they go, and what were the purposes of each flight?
2. Read to compare the flights made by the Russians with those made by Americans. When were they made? Compare the basic objectives of the Russian flights with those of the American flights.
3. Who were the American astronauts? What was their training like? Are there any common features in their backgrounds? Looking at their lives, do you think you might become qualified to be an astronaut in the future?
4. What were the educational and scientific values of the American trips into space? What do you think will be future educational and scientific values?

5. Is the space program worth the cost? How much has it cost Americans so far? Do you think the money should have been spent in other ways? Explain.
6. Etc.

Sometimes statements of purpose are made by the teacher. Sometimes children can formulate such statements themselves. If it is feasible to differentiate assignments, statements of purpose might vary from child to child or group to group according to the strengths and weaknesses of different materials being used by different children and/or according to the varied interests of the children.

After statements of purpose are made, children might supply more information from their backgrounds, and they might also hypothesize about answers.

READING (AND INTERNALLY ANSWERING QUESTIONS IN RELATION TO PURPOSES)

Next, the passage is read silently. For very young children the passage may be very short—maybe a page or less.* For older children the passage is usually longer—perhaps a whole story or chapter. During this time a constant interchange should occur between the written message and the reader's language and thoughts.

> Sometimes (perhaps frequently) round robin reading is used in classrooms. Round robin reading, sometimes called circle reading, involves children reading aloud one after another in order. Each child has his or her book open while either reading aloud or supposedly listening to another child read aloud. It is difficult to discover a reason for round robin reading, yet it persists in many classrooms at all levels. Perhaps teachers teach as they have been taught, but that doesn't lead to progress. During round robin reading, an excessive amount of emphasis is usually given to precise oral reading. Little opportunity may exist for thinking . . . for either good or poor readers.
>
> Let's look at what happens to children during round robin reading. First, what happens to poor readers? As they wait (horrified) for their turn to come, they read ahead, hoping that by doing this

---

*See the sample lesson from a basal reader, pp. 551–558.

they will make fewer errors than they would otherwise. So they haven't heard what the present reader is reading. When called upon, they nervously twitch, lose their place, and embarrass themselves and others. They mispronounce words that they may know, and they learn to hate reading. Surely they have neither the time nor the opportunity to think about what they are reading. They are so concerned with oral reading that they don't listen—even to themselves.

Good readers may feel sympathetic or empathetic toward poor readers, but in time their patience is exhausted. And why not? Why should they be slowed down by weak efforts? Why should they be required to pace themselves by poor or even good oral reading rates? Good readers, even in the primary grades, may be able to read more rapidly silently than orally and may extend energies to thinking rather than to recoding. So round robin reading—if engaged in regularly—may ruin them.

Figure 12.3 shows what the child's matrix may look like after reading, and before discussing the lesson.

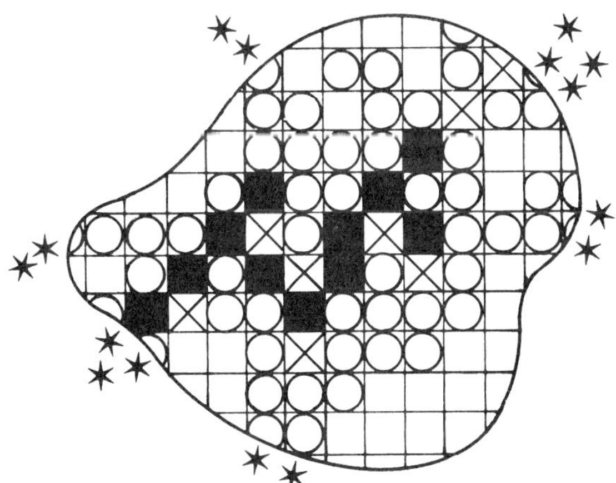

Figure 12.3

The "O's" and "*'s" represent ideas gained by the child while reading. Since the "O's" are in the grid, they are literal level thoughts—thoughts the author explicitly expressed. The "*'s" are beyond the grid and represent higher level understandings—related ideas, but ideas not directly stated by the author. The stars might be imagined to be in color—representing not only cognitive but also affective understandings. (Red stars might represent anger, a realization one may be in debt, etc. Blue stars may represent feelings of sadness as an outgrowth of reading the passage or doing the skill lesson. Green stars might represent feelings of naïvity or envy. Yellow might mean that what the character did was an act of valor, but the reader fears he or she couldn't do such a thing; or, it might suggest that the reader judges the character to be a coward. Etc.)

POSTREADING—SHARING, DIAGNOSING, RETEACHING, EXTENDING

In a teacher led lesson, usually after reading occurs, there is a sharing of ideas. Perhaps there is a quiz or a discussion. Responses or interchanges should help the teacher discover what each child has learned and where he or she needs additional help. The children can learn from each other and from the teacher by sharing in some way. Perhaps reinforcement activities—formal or informal will be used at this point. Also further reading may be done—reviewing what has been read or reading additional materials. Figure 12.4 illustrates what a child's grid may look like following this step.

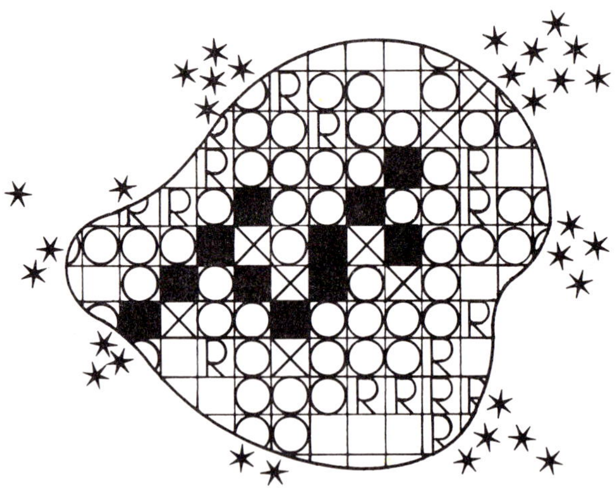

Figure 12.4

Here "R" means review, or ideas gained after the initial reading by rereading, sharing, discussing, through extended activities, etc.

Guides and Plans

The remainder of this chapter includes explanations and discussions of various types of plans and/or guides to serve as examples of ways of implementing the rationale just stated. These are given in three major sections:

- concept guides and plans
  - textbook schemas/textbook grammars
  - story schemas/story grammars
- levels guides and plans
- skills guides and plans

CONCEPT GUIDES AND PLANS—SCHEMA THEORY

Concept guides and plans emphasize organizational patterns (sequence), including vital major components (subschema, main ideas) of passages. They are of two general types: those that relate to the organization of textbook passages, and those that relate to the organization of narrative materials. Each is discussed separately in this section.

Textbook Schemas/Textbook Grammars

Text schema relates to major components (main ideas) of a chapter and the way they are sequenced, or organized. For example, in history books major ideas are often organized in time order. Science books are frequently organized in logical order, as are arithmetic books. Literature books are frequently organized in chronological (time) periods, although they may be organized in space (American literature, British literature, etc.) or in logical order (e.g., by literary form—poetry, drama, short stories, etc., or by theme—selections about courage, children around the world, growing up, etc.).

The term "texbook grammar" is a variation of "textbook schema." As a parallel term to the grammar of a sentence, textbook grammar suggests vital components and the order of the components. As most sentences include a noun and a verb (and perhaps more, e.g.: NV, NVAd, NVN, NVNN, NVNA, NLvN, NLvA, NLvAd, refer to pp. 212–215 of this text), so most textbook chapters include specific components (subschema of schema) and, perhaps, in specific relational orders.

Sentence orders may be transformed (e.g., NVA: "John is happy" may be transformed to VNA: "Is John happy?" in which case the transform results in a change of meaning; or it may be transformed to AVN: "Happy is John," in which case the transform results in a change of style). So, too, textbook grammars, as they are found in specific books may be grasped by the reader exactly as the author supplies them (bottom-up: text-bound). On the other hand, the text grammar may be transformed while the reader is reading, for the reader may fit the author's ideas into his or her own mental framework while reading (top-down: concept-bound). The reader who initially grasps the organizational pattern in a bottom-up fashion may, after reading, transform it to another pattern (i.e., the reader gets the author's literal meaning while reading, but later uses it as a thread for creating something new—bottom-up/interactive model).

As demonstrated earlier in the present book (page 329ff.), concepts are usually organized into one of the following patterns, or a combination of these patterns: time order, space order, logical order, affective order. Ideas organized by an author using one type of organizational pattern might be reorganized into another pattern by a reader and thus spur the reorganizer to other thoughts or concepts beyond the author's (perhaps creative) and certainly to other styles.

Familiarity with an author's pattern helps readers understand the author's message, just as seeing the framework of a building helps the viewer understand much about the building to be. Proficient readers have frequently internalized patterns to the extent that they can correctly hypothesize about major concepts as they approach them in reading. Children and teenagers usually can benefit from having these patterns shown to them before they read. One model that is frequently used for this purpose is called SQ3R. To this should be added the vocabulary component to complete a lesson.

Vocabulary + SQ3R Model The Vocabulary + SQ3R model has six steps:

1. *Vocabulary* New words, or terms, to be learned through reading the assignment are introduced before the children read. Thus, children are alerted to the fact that these words are important, and they know they should search for their meanings while reading. Meanings of words that are too difficult for the children and words that the author does not clarify should be taught in a prereading activity and reinforced after the reading is completed. If other language factors might interfere with comprehension (e.g., if the author's syntax or dialect differ from the children's) these should be clarified before the lesson.

2. *S Means Survey* Before children read, the lesson is surveyed. A visual "pattern" is developed ("mapped") to help the children understand the organization of the lesson. (Patterns were exemplified in Chapter 8.) Ideas should then be related to what the child already knows about the subject. Perhaps background will have to be built.

3. *Q Means Question (Purposes for Reading)* Questions related to the main points are formulated before children read. Levels guides, explained later, may be of help here.

4. *R₁ Means Silent Reading* Children read the lesson silently. They may read it section by section, asking questions before each section and discussing them after each section. Or they may ask all questions first, read the complete lesson, and then discuss the whole lesson.

5. *R₂ Means Recite (or Discuss, Share)* Children recite, or discuss, the answers to the questions they have asked. Now meanings of words may be reinforced and understandings may be further developed by using the content of the assignment.

6. *R₃ Means Review or Reconstruct* Children may review the complete assignment using the survey technique. They may wish to add to, or modify, the ideas of the author. They may wish to demonstrate alternative ways of organizing the ideas (i.e., subschema may be reorganized into other patterns: text grammars may be transformed).

Rationale for the Use of the Vocabulary + SQ3R Model You might question the reason for using Vocabulary + SQ3R as a guide for presenting lessons. There are clear reasons for doing so.

1. Children are introduced to important vocabulary terms before reading so that they are alerted to look for meanings and round-out their understandings of specific important terms when reading. If the meanings are not clarified in the passage, it is probably desirable for the teacher to directly teach the meanings before reading begins—perhaps by showing a real object, a picture, demonstrating an action, etc. However, if the meanings are supplied by the author, it is often not thought to be desirable to teach the meanings before reading. Such teaching is considered by many to be "spoon feeding," by others to be an "atomistic approach," i.e., the words are not seen in full context. The teacher who explains all meanings—in prereading—helps to make reading unnecessary. Making explanations, encouraging the use of a dictionary, and re-

inforcing meanings, however, are thought to be very suitable as post-reading activities for children who need additional help.

2. It is well for children to get an over-all view of what they are going to read before they read it. This gives them a framework into which they can fit finer points. First they see the forest. Next they group similar trees together. Then they note characteristics of individual trees. Ausubel[1] has used the term "advance organizer" for this procedure. Utilizing such an organizer appears to be helpful to some children of all ages, and to most older children.

Frequently it is argued that an advance organizer *per se* is not enough. That is, simply noting the title and main points and relating them, is not sufficient to prepare a child for an assignment. This is no doubt true. The teacher should also promote a discussion and fill in background when necessary so that children have something to cling to—i.e., so that part of the matrix is filled. The next step, during which questions are asked and purposes for reading are stated may provide the testing ground for the teacher to judge if enough background has been provided. During this step, the teacher should be able to identify children who are ready to read and those who need more background.

3. Asking questions whose answers will be sought, or stating the purpose for reading before reading begins or at intervals during reading, appears to be well justified by research.[2] It is most helpful if children themselves generate the questions, for they will do this using their own mental storehouse and thus will prepare their processing systems to retrieve and receive information.[3]

4. The previous steps promote active involvement in reading itself. Much information already known in relation to the topic has been retrieved. Utilizing graphic input retrieves more. The synthesis occurs as appropriate to the reader's needs and the author's ideas.

5. Recitation, internal or external, promotes active involvement in the thought and feeling processes, with concentration placed on focal points previously or newly discernable. Recitation should promote reorganization and synthesis of information and the transfer of information and feelings to long-term memory.

6. Reviewing results in more complete retention by emphasizing the most important points again. Reconstruction of ideas into other major relationship patterns (transformations, as described earlier and later) facilitates the examination of a variety of aspects of the ideas and is related to components of creativity (fluency, flexibility,

originality, elaboration, redefinition, even sensitivity to problems.
See pp. 302–303 of this book).

Reading involves:

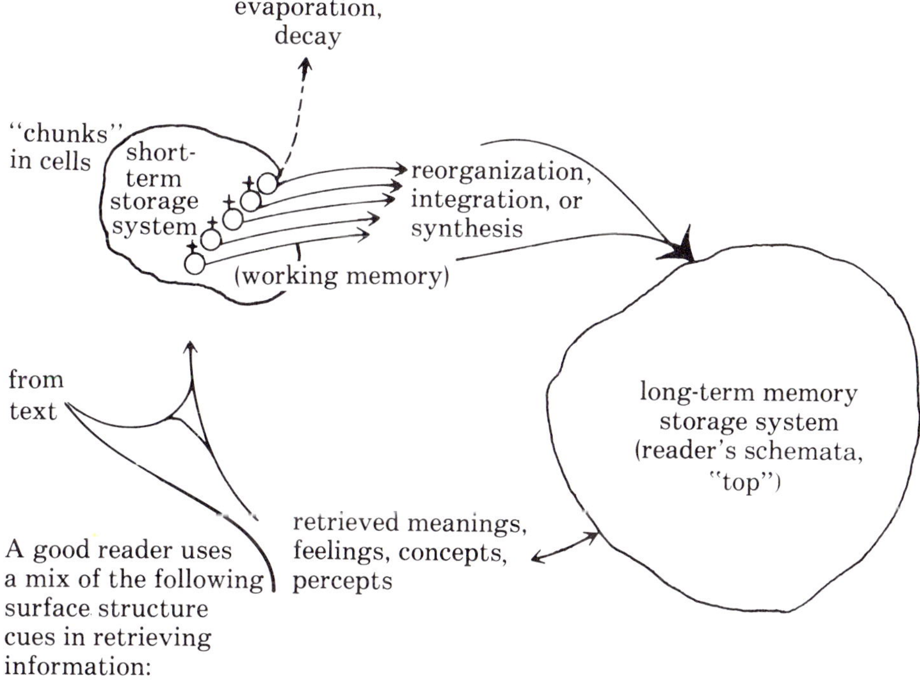

Example

Prereading

In a second grade science book there is a discussion about what animals do during different seasons of the year. One chapter is titled "The Winter Season." The lesson plan format is suitable for any grade level.

Children might be asked if they know what animals do in the wintertime in cold climates. Specific examples might be given:

- Do they know what snakes do? fish? frogs? bear? whales? birds? etc. Any information they have might be discussed. Many children who are unable to observe animals in nature may have learned about some animals by watching T.V. Children probably should be encouraged to watch specific animal programs on T.V.
- They might be asked if they've ever heard of animals hibernating. A few examples might be given about animals that remain in cold areas and that hibernate.
- Children who live in the South might have to be introduced to the concept of a Northern winter.

Survey Next children might be helped in surveying the chapter. The first two pages contain a picture of snow-covered terrain with a yawning raccoon in a hole in a tree, a skunk asleep underground, as well as the following: a wood frog, snails, snapping turtle, salamander, chipmunk, woodchuck, black snake, jumping mouse, and a bee. A big black bear is shown above ground. These might be noted as well as the verse that tells that these animals are warm in their homes and that they are all fat because they ate and ate all fall. The following chart might be drawn on the board:

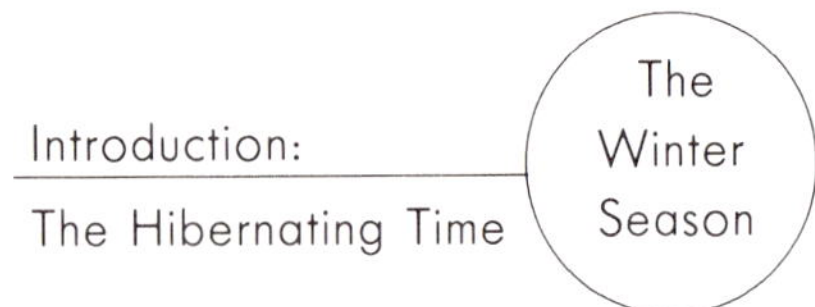

The survey step might continue in this way: The children are asked to turn the page. The heading is "Mammals." Pictured are bats, woodchucks, a skunk, a bear with her cubs. Some are already hibernating.

The children preview the next page, titled "Reptiles." On this page are pictures of turtles, snakes, lizards, and a skunk. All are underground hibernating.

Following this are pages titled "Amphibians" with pictures and "Fish" with pictures.

The chart might now be extended:

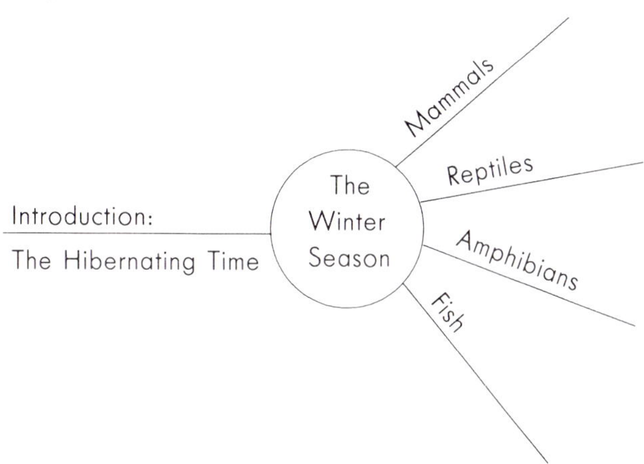

Vocabulary Words that are clearly defined and illustrated by the author are: *hibernate, mammals, reptiles, amphibians,* and *fish.* Understanding the meanings of these words is essential if the child is to understand the passage. The following procedure might be used as a prereading activity: The key words might be listed on the board or on a sheet of paper each child receives along with matching items. The teacher would help them in reading this and could make further explanations. But the teacher should refrain from "giving it all away."

	prereading	postreading	
1. mammals	(d)	______	a. They do not have warm bodies. They have scales. They live on the land.
2. fish	______	______	b. They do not have warm bodies. They have scales. They live in the water.
3. hibernates	______	______	c. Sleeps or rests during the winter
4. reptiles	______	______	d. They have warm bodies. They have fur or hair, and their mothers make milk for their babies.
5. amphibians	______	______	e. They live on land and in the water. They have smooth skin and cold bodies.

Children are asked to try to match words with definitions. They are told to look in their books for the answers while they are reading. They are told that after they read they may come back to this and make corrections.

Questions Next, the teacher might ask the children to name animals in which they are interested. Two sets of cards are then made out. One set (green cards) contains names of animals discussed in the book. The other set (yellow cards) contains names of animals suggested by the children, but not discussed by the author. Duplicate cards may be included. Each child selects cards of both colors, some choosing more than others. Some names might be:

Green Cards (bottom-up/text-bound)		Yellow Cards (top-down/concept-driven)	
bullhead	bear	cat	mouse
beaver	lizard	dog	camel
leopard frog	rattler	dinosaur	kangaroo
bullfrog	woodchuck	elephant	centipede
turtle	spotted turtle	goat	baboon
water snake	brook trout	caribou	gorilla
copperhead	toad	pig	dragon
bat	salamander	moose	eft
skunk	sunfish	crocodile	squirrel
race runner		rabbit	

Children might be asked to pay particular attention to the animals on their cards. They should try to classify each as a mammal, reptile, amphibian, or fish.* (Literal level if animal is pictured, inferential level if it is not pictured.) And they should (literally) see which of their animals are pictured as hibernators. If they cannot find a picture of their animal (yellow cards) they should try to guess (inferential level) if their animal hibernates (by comparing their animal with those not pictured).

Children may be asked to volunteer to come to the board before reading to list their animals in the correct category (class) and to star the animals they think hibernate. The chart might now look like this:

---

*Or other, e.g., if children also suggest bird names or non-vertebrates. If birds are included by children, they might conclude that most birds that summer in the North migrate to the South in the wintertime, where weather is warmer and their food is more readily available. Children in the North might learn that if they continue to feed birds beyond their normal migrating time in the fall, they must continue to feed them until spring or the birds may starve, as they do not hibernate. Also, they may freeze.

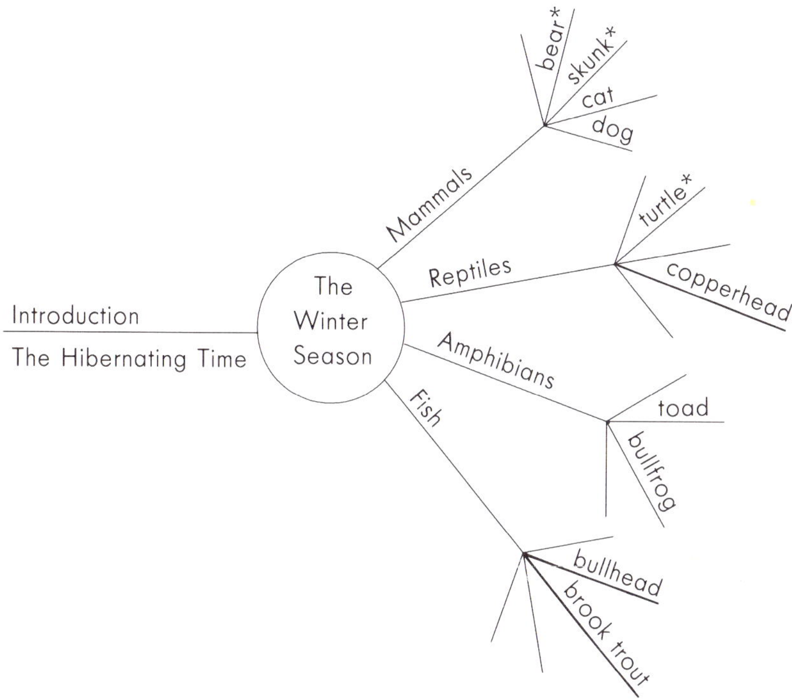

Reading

Now the children are ready to read. While they are reading, they may be classifying their cards. They will be looking for the answers to their vocabulary questions also. The children may read one section at a time and then proceed to postreading activities for that section and then return to read the next section, etc. Or they may read the complete lesson before proceeding to postreading. The teacher will make that choice.

Postreading

Recite The children now return to their vocabulary sheets and answer the vocabulary items in the postreading column. The children who missed an item before reading and got it correct after reading will know that they taught themselves the meaning of a word. The teacher may have to help some of the children better understand these terms through discussion and the use of pictures.

Next, the children are asked to classify their cards in the following categories either by using the original spoke graph or the following, which allows more room, and to star those animals that hibernate. Some children may have to use library resources to find answers related to animals on their yellow cards. The teacher may have to help the children locate and use these additional resources.

Mammals	Reptiles	Amphibians	Fish

A discussion will follow. The teacher may ask how the children decided upon the categories for the animals listed on the yellow cards.

Review/Reconstruct The items (details) have now been structured using the pattern supplied by the author (convergent synthesis).

The teacher may help the children understand that other organizational patterns (transformations) are possible. (Or children may even suggest these.) The teacher and children may suggest concept patterns such as:

- designating animals on a map (spatial pattern), showing where they live. This may be done by geographical regions and/or by land including altitudes or water including depth, etc. Does area have anything to do with hibernation?
- grouping animals according to living or extinct, expected life span, etc. (time pattern). Does length of life relate to hibernation? Are animals that hibernate more or less likely to become extinct than nonhibernating animals?
- grouping animals by those they would and would not like for pets (affective pattern). They might research an animal to see if it would be a good pet for them to have.
- selecting animals they would like to do other research on or read a story about (affective pattern).
- deciding which animal they would most like to be and why (affective pattern).
- etc.

Children may decide to work on projects in selected areas.

Skill Development Perhaps certain children need help in phonics (a skill lesson). This help might be given by the content area teacher who may also be the children's reading teacher or by the reading teacher in a team teaching situation. These children are second graders. Some may need work in an initial consonant sound—usually taught in first grade. This may be particularly appropriate in situations in which only one textbook is used and children are "reading" materials too difficult for them. (These children might also be taught some sight words with picture clues.)

Words that could be used from this lesson if the consonant to be taught is <b> are:

bullhead	beaver	bullfrog
bat	bear	baboon

(See lessons in Chapter 5.)

Other children may need help in the sounds <c> represents. Words that might be used are:

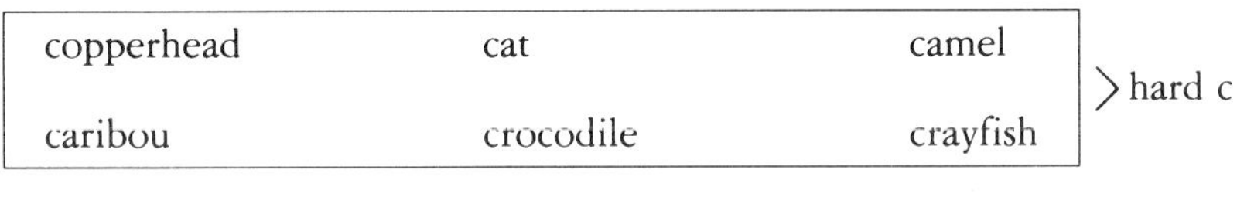

copperhead	cat	camel
caribou	crocodile	crayfish

> hard c

race runner	ice	centipede

> soft c

(See lessons in Chapter 5.)

Children who are a little advanced might benefit from work on morphological and phonic syllabication. The following words might be used:

vcv		vccv	
beaver	caribou	centipede	runner
leopard	camel	salamander	
water	crocodile		copperhead
lizard	salamander		
dinosaur	baboon		

(See lessons in Chapter 5.)

	Compounds
bullhead	sunfish
bullfrog	centipede
copperhead	woodchuck

(See Chapters 5 and 6.)

Class Constructed Schema/Grammar

Another guide or plan that might be used is particularly appropriate when the teacher is using multiple texts or other resources and/or when the teacher wishes to differentiate assignments (within a theme) to meet individual interests. The lesson is composed of the following steps: brainstorming, classifying, student assignment to, or selection of, specific area to work in, vocabulary (prereading), vocabulary (postreading), sharing. This is a concept guide because children's brainstorming ideas are classified (patterned), and children choose a specific pattern in which to work.

EXAMPLE

The theme used here is government, suitable for the intermediate grades, but the format is suitable for any grade level.

Prereading

Step 1: Brainstorming Brainstorming consists of suggesting as many terms as possible on a specified level of schema/subschema. Because it is probably easiest to understand, for this lesson the lowest level of subschema (or details) will be used: words. (However, any level may be used in a classroom situation, e.g., main ideas, themes of stories, books, etc.)

The teacher asks the children to suggest all of the terms they can think of that relate to government. These are written on the board or on an overhead transparency, e.g.:

state	city	representative	theocracy
president	despotism	emperor	self-rule
dictator	prime minister	autocratic	king

matriarchy	county	communism	nazi
patriarchy	democracy	independent	queen
oligarchy	freedom	mayor	senator
autonomy	governor	shah	federal
domestic	fascist	floor leader	parliament
legislature	executive	alderman	whip
house	nazi	congress	senate
bicameral	congressman	international	judicial
Supreme Court	congresswoman	despotic	judge

(Children may have been told a week before to make lists of terms from listening to T.V., reading the newspaper, etc.)

Step 2: Classifying Next, the teacher helps children to classify these into groups or categories, e.g.:

Types of Government	Levels of Government	Self-Government Terms
democracy	federal	freedom
theocracy	state	democracy
autocracy	county	self-rule
matriarchy	city	autonomy
oligarchy	domestic	independent
despotism	international	republic
communism		
patriarchy		

Leaders of Governments	Legislative Terms	Judiciary Terms	Autocratic Terms
president	congress	Supreme Court	fascist
prime minister	senate	judge	nazi
dictator	house		communist
shah	congressman		despotic
queen	congresswoman		absolutist
king	alderman		
governor	alderwoman		
mayor	floor leader		
senator	whip		
representative	parliament		
executive	bicameral		

(It might be noted that these are all expository, or logical, ways of classifying these terms. Other classification patterns are also useful, e.g.,

Time Order	Space Order
old forms of government newer forms of government modern governments	governments of Asia of Africa of Europe of North America of South America etc.

Classifying the terms in these ways might require more information than the children have at this time. However, the teacher might point out that these possibilities do exist.)

Step 3: Student Assignment to or Selection of Specific Area in Which to Work Next, either, or both, of these strategies might be used:

1. The teacher realizes that one of the available textbooks carefully discusses one of these major categories, e.g., types of government around the world. The children who are reading this book are told to expect to find information on this subject, which they will share with the class later. Other books may deal principally with other topics (e.g., The United States national government, levels of government in the United States. For these, classifications already given will have to be altered slightly). Children reading these books will also be told what to expect from their books, and they will later share their ideas with the class. In this case the three groups will be studying the topics indicated in the next web, and the terms might be classified as shown in Fig. 12.5.
2. And/or children may be asked to choose a category they are especially interested in (or to find another category) and research the topic by using tradebooks easily available to them, perhaps in interest centers in the classroom, or to read parts of their textbooks, and/or to find sources in the library. They are told that later they will share their findings with the class.

Step 4: Introduction to Assignment The introduction to one group might proceed thus: (The group has selected spatial order—governments around the world. They may decide to concentrate on the locations of democracies, communistic countries, socialistic countries, monarchies, and autocracies.)

government
types of governments in the world
dictatorship
monarchy
autocracy
theocracy
democracy
patriarchy
socialism
communism
despotism
oligarchy
matriarchy
U.S. government
Secretary of State
Secretary of Defence
Diplomatic Corps
Supreme Court
President
Vice-president
Cabinet
Congress
House
representative
Senate
senator
floor leader
whip
levels of government United States
Congress
representative
House
senator
Senate
city council
alderman, alderwoman
mayor
governor
President
city
county
state
federal
city attorney

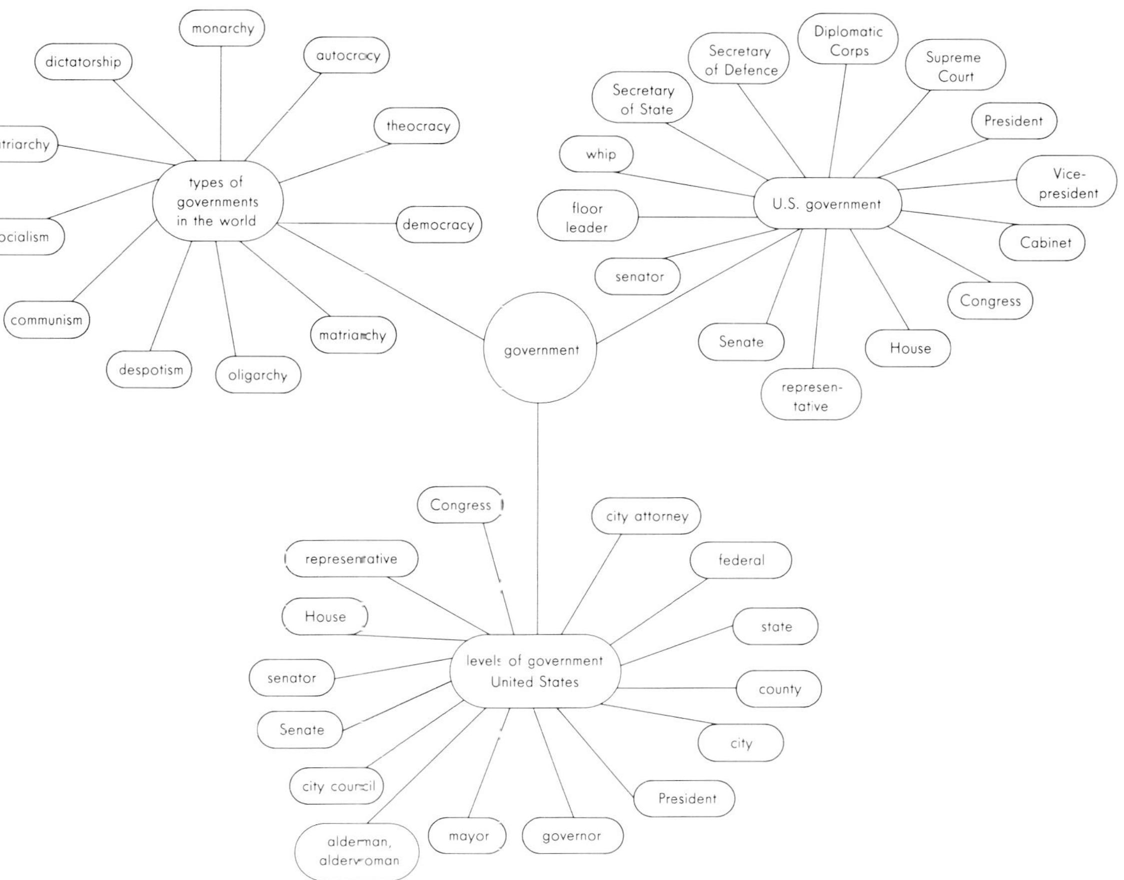

Figure 12.5

Questions, purposes. The children are given an outline map of the world. They are told to color the nations that they study according to the type of government. First they are to decide why a particular color might be used for each type of government. (In the following chart, in the connotation column, they are to underline the appropriate connotation of the color as it refers to the type of government.)

Type of Government	Color	Connotation (underline)
democracy	blue	sadness, <u>justice</u>, <u>loyalty</u> (as in the U.S. flag)
communism	red	anger, valor, blood bath
socialism	pink	happy, almost red, glowing
monarchy	purple	royalty, passion
autocracy	yellow	?

Questions. Children may be asked to examine the map after it is colored to see if countries of the same color (type of government) are usually in close geographic proximity. They may be asked why what they have observed is true. They may also be asked to note exceptions and seek the reasons for these exceptions.

Vocabulary (prereading). At an appropriate time, but before reading the assignment, vocabulary may be introduced to this group. The important words are: democracy, monarchy, autocracy, communism, socialism. At this time, students might simply be introduced to the literal meanings of these terms through the use of morphemes, e.g.:

arch = chief, ruler	ism = doctrine, system
cracy = government	auto = self
mono = one	commun = common (common ownership)
demo = people	social = communal living

They are asked to combine the morpheme meanings to arrive at the literal meanings of these words.

democracy	<u>government of the people</u>
monarchy	______________________
autocracy	______________________
communism	______________________
socialism	______________________

While reading they should get a more complete understanding of these terms.

READING—SILENT READING

Postreading

Vocabulary As a postreading vocabulary activity, the children in this group might play concentration. (See pp. 236–237.) The following cards might be used:

democracy	blue	royalty
rule by one, by royalty	pink	monarchy
autocracy	anger, blood bath	almost red
believes in common ownership of means of production	justice, loyalty	purple
socialism	red	producers possess political power and production of goods
yellow	self-appointed ruler—(govt. of)	rule by the people
communism	cowardice	

Each card has three cards that could match with it. E.g.:

<table>
<tr><td>democracy</td><td>rule by
the people</td><td>blue</td></tr>
</table>

<table>
<tr><td>justice, loyalty</td></tr>
</table>

Only two cards are needed for a book. Cards are turned with blank (or numbered) side up. The child selects two cards. If there's a match and the child can explain the relationship, the child keeps the book and continues to play until there is no match. Then the next child goes. The child with the most books wins.

Sharing Children then can share their findings with each other—through classwide discussions, panels, or in any other way, perhaps as suggested in Chapter 10, pp. 426–430.

They may learn vocabulary terms also from each other. For example, each child should be expected to know a certain percentage (80 percent? 100 percent?) of the words for the group he or she is in, plus some of the words from the other groups. All of the important words from all of the groups might be listed on the board. Each child is given a blank Wordo card. (See pp. 198–199). Each child lists on this card all of the words of his or her group plus enough other words to fill the card.

The definition then is given, and children who recognize the word being defined and have it on their cards cover it. The game proceeds as explained in Chapter 6.

Story Schema/Story Grammar

Story schema has emerged as a term used to describe the way in which a typical story is organized, or is thought to be organized. This is different from the ways textbooks are organized. Story grammars have been developed to describe how a story schema is organized into subschemas, or categories of information. "In general, the [story] grammar defines a story as a series of problem solving episodes centering on the main character's (or characters') efforts to achieve a major goal."

John Guthrie states, "Comprehension of a story is not comprehension of haphazard facts or a main idea, but it is comprehension of the structure . . . it is comprehension of the setting, theme, plot, and resolution, their components and interrelationships."[4]

Guthrie uses the illustration[5] in Fig. 12.6 to show the elements of story schema.

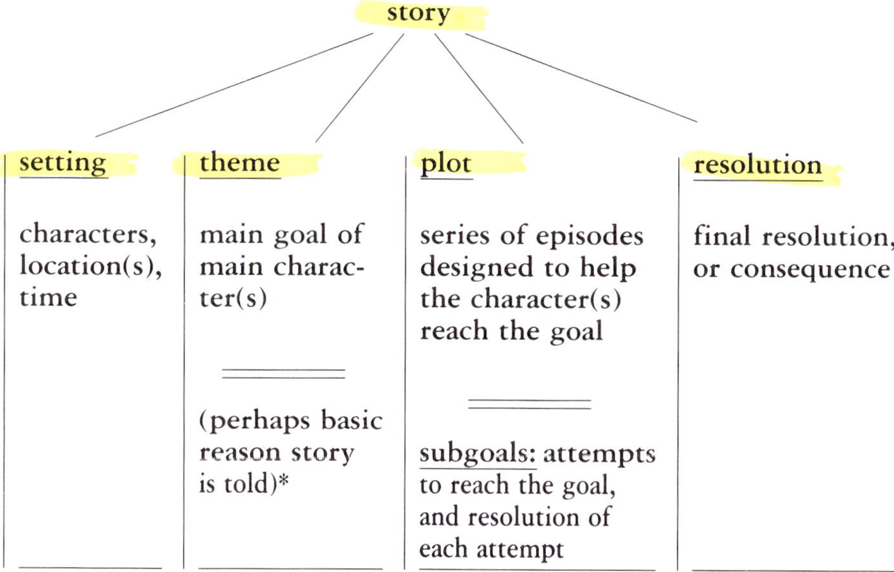

Figure 12.6

For example, the goal of a main character may be to rescue a beautiful girl from a dreadful dragon. The plot may be a series of episodes—each episode is a subgoal, an attempt to reach the goal. Guthrie emphasizes that questions should focus on story structure. Teachers might ask about the setting, theme, plot, resolution. Questions at different levels—literal, inferential, evaluative, and affective may be important.

In an article by Stephanie H. McConaughy,[6] components of plot are elaborated thus:

• the initiating event: this leads the main character to formulate a major goal and starts the sequence of actions and events (cause → effect)
• a number of attempts: these are the [major] actions of the characters,

*Added by present author

the series of episodes designed to help the character(s) reach the major goal. (effect of initiating event, and/or previous attempt)
- a series of outcomes: these are events or states produced by the characters' [major] actions. (effects)
- internal responses: these are the subgoals, thoughts and feelings of a character leading to his or her actions. (causes, motives)
- reactions: these are the thoughts or feelings produced by the outcomes of the actions. (effects)*

Any of these may suggest worthy questions to ask about the plot of a story.

Episodes of plot may be illustrated by use of the diagram in Fig. 12.7 showing rising and falling suspense.

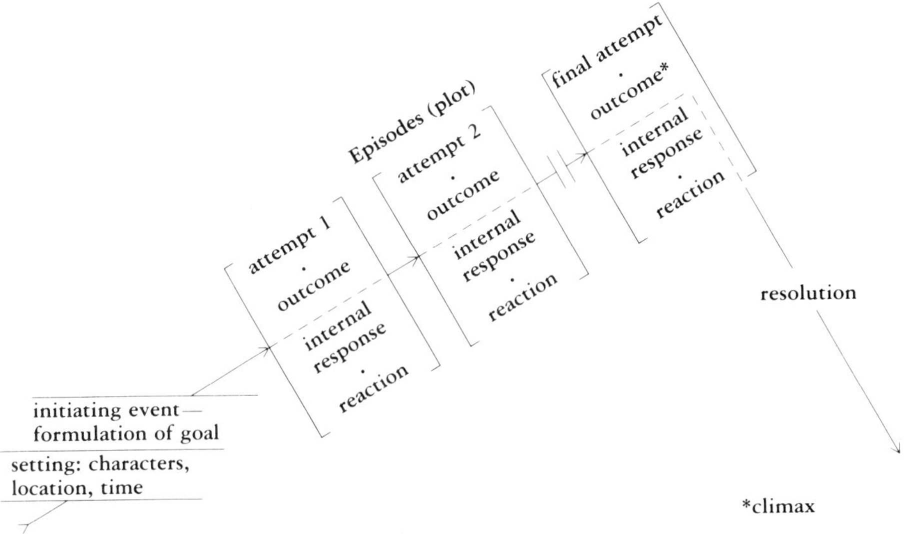

Figure 12.7

Suspense builds as attempt follows attempt until the climax is reached. The suspense falls as the resolution becomes apparent.

Questions The following question formats are suggested to help children relate to story schema:

About characters:

- Who are the characters?
- What are they like? . . . Are they make believe? . . . realistic?

---

*All terms in parentheses added by the present author.

- Do you like the characters? . . . Would you like to know any of them? . . . Would you like to be one of them?

About locations:

- Where did the story take place?
- Does the location make a difference to the story? . . . Could the story have taken place elsewhere? . . . here?
- Would you like to be where the story took place? . . . Why?

About time:

- When did the story take place?
- Does the time make a difference to the story? . . . Could the story have taken place today? . . . in the distant past? . . . Could it take place in the future?
- Would you like to be (have been) alive when the story took place? . . . Why?

About theme:

- What problem does the main character face?
- How did we learn about the problem?
- Is the problem an important one? . . . Would you like to have such a problem? . . . Would you like to solve such a problem?

About plot:

- What attempts were made to solve the problem?
- What was the outcome of each attempt?
- How did the character feel about the outcome?
- What did the outcome of each event lead the character to do?
- Which attempt was most interesting to you? . . . most tragic? . . . most humorous? . . . most important to the story?
- Would you have liked being a part of any attempt? . . . which attempt? . . . what part would you like to have played?

About the resolution:

- How was the problem finally solved?
- Did the ending satisfy you? . . . If you could have written the ending, how would the story have ended? Could you write a humorous ending? . . . a tragic ending? . . . Why not try? . . . You may then share your ending with others in the class.

Macro-cloze technique.[7] An alternative, or perhaps introductory approach, is the following: the teacher blocks out (clozes) a major part of the story, e.g., episode one (attempt 1) and its consequences. The children write or discuss their ideas. Better still, the teacher divides the class into groups, and each group is given the complete story except for one major component. They supply that component. E.g.:

group 1—whole story, except setting

group 2—whole story, except initiating event

group 3—whole story, except attempt 1, its outcome, the internal response and reaction

etc.

Before reading the complete story as written by the author, the children piece together the story, each group reading its contribution in order. Following this the author's story is read. Comparisons then can be made, and questions such as those in the previous section can be answered.

LEVELS GUIDES AND PLANS

Levels guides and plans outline ways of guiding children to read materials at different cognitive (comprehension) levels and perhaps with affective dimensions. The same "task" is dealt with at different levels—perhaps only one task per lesson. The major purpose is to get teachers and children used to asking and answering questions about the same basic idea(s) on different levels. Goals may include responding to questions of the following types:

1. *literal level.* What did the author say? Children are asked to pick out one or more ideas the author has explicitly stated. One day these may be important details, another day main ideas, another day sequence, comparisons, cause-effect, following directions, etc.

2. *inferential level.* How do these ideas relate to what I already know about the subject? Can I expand on these ideas? How do these ideas relate to the whole assignment? (Inferential level questions are directly related to the type of literal level questions given for the same assignment.)

3. *evaluation level.* What judgments can I make concerning the ideas? Are they facts, opinions? Is this real? Fantasy? Are the author's ideas adequate? Valid? Appropriate? Worthy, desirable, acceptable? Do I need to seek other sources before I can make a judgment? (These activities relate directly to lower level activities for the same assignment.)

4. *appreciation level and affective dimensions.* How do I feel about what the author has said? What is my response to the passage? Do I

want to read more about the subject? . . . by this author? . . . by another author?

The examples that follow show the integration of a levels guide with a content lesson.

EXAMPLE 1

Let's imagine that a class party is being planned and that reading assignments (or choices) relate to the party.

Prereading

The prereading discussion might include a decision about the kind of party the class would like, what foods, games, activities should be included, and what each child would like to contribute. Each child, or each group of children, is asked to select something to read that will help in making a contribution. The four levels of questions are then written on the board or distributed on paper, and each child or group of children is asked to respond to each question. Before the children read, there is a discussion about these questions.

Reading (and Answering the Questions, Perhaps Internally)

Each child, or group of children, reads the material selected. One child has decided to make fudge brownies and has a box with directions on it. The child silently reads the directions and responds to the questions thus:

1. *literal level.* What did the author say?

   • First I am to heat the oven to 350°.
   • Then I am to grease a pan $13 \times 9 \times 2$ inches.
   • Then I am to blend with a spoon the ingredients in the box with ¼ cup water and one egg. Then spread this in the pan.
   • Then I am to bake the mixture for 25 minutes.
   • After brownies cool, I am to cut them into squares.

2. *inferential level.* How do these ideas relate to what I already know about the subject? Can I expand on these ideas? How do these ideas relate to the whole assignment?

- Generally, the directions sound good, but I think I must make an adjustment for altitude, since I live at 4,500 feet.
- I would like to add nuts.
- I think square brownies are nice, but I'd prefer to make triangular ones for a party.
- These brownies should be good at the party.

3. *evaluation level.* What judgments can I make concerning the ideas? Do I need to seek other sources before I can make a judgment?

- This looks like its a good package to use. It has extra syrup in it. I think it might be better than some I've made before.
- When I go to the store, I'll compare ingredients with other brands. Then I'll select the best package to make at home for my brother's birthday.

4. *appreciation level and affective dimensions.* How do I feel about what the author has said? What is my response to the passage? Do I want to read more about the subject?

- I feel excited about making the brownies. The directions are clear, and I'm sure the brownies will be good.

Postreading

The teacher checks the answers given by the child (through discussion or by reading the answers if they have been written) and may respond by giving added suggestions. If the child has misunderstood anything, the teacher can help the child. If the child has additional questions to ask, the teacher can serve as a resource. Other resources might also be used.

EXAMPLE 2

Something as simple as a short advertisement can be discussed on several levels. Advertisements usually are interesting and often are written simply. They, therefore, might be used with older children who are poor readers. The ad in Fig. 12.8 has a readability level of grade two.*

---

*Using the Fry criteria. See pp. 611–614. Its grade level is 2.7 according to the New Spache Readability Formula.

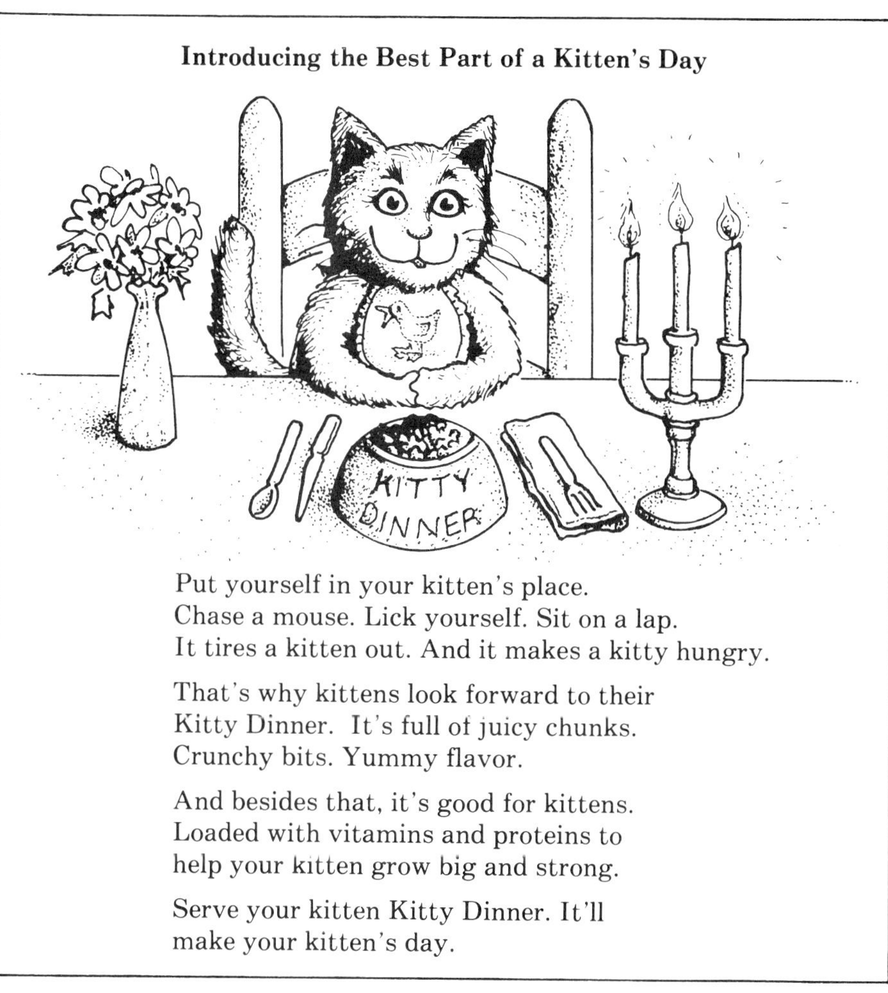

Figure 12.8

Questions

- set 1:   relating details to the main idea of paragraph 1
  literal level. What does a kitten do that tires it and makes it hungry?
      (chases mice; licks itself; sits on laps.)
  inferential level. What else might kittens do that might tire them?

- set 2:   relating details to main idea of paragraphs 2 and 3
  literal level. What's Kitty Dinner full of?

> (juicy chunks, crunchy bits, yummy flavor, vitamins and proteins)

evaluation level. Is that all kittens need? What else do they need in their diets?

> (Someone might check with a veterinarian. Perhaps there is a library reference. Then comparisons could be made with the ingredients on a package.)

• set 3: examining the use of propaganda

literal level. What propaganda techniques are used? Give examples.

> (*glad names*: juicy chunks, crunchy bits, yummy flavor, grow big, strong . . .
>
> *transfer*: vitamins, proteins
>
> *cardstacking*: Nothing is said about the fact that vitamins—which ones?—and proteins are not all a kitten needs for a balanced diet, though no claim is made that the diet is balanced. There is no suggestion of minerals.) (Analysis as given here is evaluation level; naming the techniques and giving the examples is literal level.)

evaluation level. The following questions are appropriate:

> Who is the propagandist?
>
> Whom is he/she serving?
>
> What is the propagandist's aim?
>
> To what emotions does the advertisement appeal?

appreciation level and affective dimensions. The child might be asked how he or she feels about the advertisement now that it has been analyzed. Would the child buy the product if she or he had a kitten?

EXAMPLE 3

5W + H levels guide. Teachers frequently ask *who, what, where, when, why,* and *how* questions and accept answers on the literal level, not having the children respond at higher levels. The 5W + H levels guide provides a framework, suggesting kinds of questions that might be asked and answered on several levels for each of these questions.

• Who: 1. *literally.* Who did the author say was involved? (A "mapping" or charting technique might be used to illustrate this.)

2. *inferentially.** Do you think it was a good choice of persons?

---

*The questions labeled "inferentially" are at that level if the child answers them by using his or her "common sense." They're at a higher level if the child uses formal logic, additional resources, etc. This is true in all sections of this guide.

Who played the most important role(s)? What other persons (or animals) might have been selected? What would the effects have been had others been selected?

3. *evaluatively.* Are the people (animals) involved real, or is this fantasy? Has the author given us all the people (animals) involved, or is the account incomplete? Research to find out if more appropriate choices of people (animals) might have been made.

4. *appreciatively* and affectively.* What is your response to the idea of involving these people (or animals) in such a venture? Can you identify with anyone in the episode? Are the author's descriptions of the people (animals) clear? valid? interesting? exciting? Explain. Can you see and hear (touch, smell) through your imagination—these people (animals)? What do they look like? What do you hear?

• What: 1. *literally.* What happened? (This may be illustrated by "mapping" or charting.) Does the author give cause-effect relationships? What are they?

2. *inferentially.* Do these things make sense to you? What will the effects be? What was the cause of each? Do you agree with the author's cause-effect statements?

3. *evaluatively.* Are any of these events real? fantasy? Which are facts? opinions? Were enough things done to bring about the results? Should any have been omitted? Which? Are the things done acceptable to society? to you? Are they desirable? Do they have worth?

4. *appreciatively and affectively.* How do you feel about what was done? Would you have done anything differently? If so, what and how? Have you experienced any incidents like these—or have you seen them on T.V.? Could you have been a participant in any of these? Can you visualize yourself in any of these incidents? How would you feel being a part of them?

• Where: 1. *literally.* Where did these things happen? (This might be shown on a map.)

2. *inferentially.* Why do you think they happened there? What are the causes and effects of their happening there? Compare what happened in one area with what happened in another.

3. *evaluatively.* Did these things really happen where the author said, or are any of the places made up? Which are factual places? Where else might these things have happened?

---

*These questions correspond to Barrett's Level 4: Appreciation. This is true in all sections of this guide.

Where might they happen in the future? Are these the best places for these events to have occurred?

4. *appreciatively and affectively.* What is your personal feeling about where these events occurred? Where they might occur? If you were in one of these places, how would you feel about such things occurring there? How does the author describe the areas? Do you think the descriptions are valid? interesting? Can you see (feel, hear, touch, smell)—in your imagination—any of these places? Explain.

- When:
  1. *literally.* When did these things happen? (This might be shown on a time-line, or a flow chart.)
  2. *inferentially.* Why do you think they happened then? Can you compare these events with similar ones that happened in the past? That may happen in the future?
  3. *evaluatively.* Did these things really happen when the author says they did? Which times are factual? Which are opinions or fantasies? Are all the important times given? Do the events seem appropriate to the times? Are there any anachronisms? Did these things happen at the best possible times? Explain.
  4. *appreciatively and affectively.* How do you feel about the times in which these things occurred? Did they take too much time? too little time? Explain. Would you wish to be involved in such things considering the time involved? How does the author describe the time involved? Does the author use terms such as *plodding, snail's pace, leisurely, by degrees, moderately, rapidly, rushing,* etc.? Do these seem appropriate to the events? Can you feel the time moving slowly or rapidly? Explain. Can you imagine yourself in the setting at the time (past, present, future) when the events occurred or will occur? Explain.

- Why?
  1. *literally.* Why did the author say these things happened? (This might be "mapped" on a "cause-effect" chart.)
  2. *inferentially.* Do the author's cause-effect relationships seem to be valid to you? When causes or effects are not given, can you supply them?
  3. *evaluatively.* Why does one of the causes result in one effect and another in a different effect? Are the causes or (effects) appropriate to the situation? Explain. Are they acceptable? adequate? Are any of the causes or effects real? fantasy? facts? opinions? Explain.
  4. *appreciatively and affectively.* How do you feel about the reasons for these things happening? Would you have caused such things to happen? Would you have done it in the same

ways? Would you have been affected in the same ways? Is it reasonable to think that others would be affected as the author says? Explain. Do the author's descriptions seem to be valid? interesting? Explain. Can you imagine yourself motivated or affected as any of the people (or animals) were in these episodes?

- How:
  1. *literally*. What does the author say about how these things happened? (A chart might be used giving events in one column and in another column brief explanations of how each event occurred. If the author explained how things were done by one group in comparision with another, these might be noted.)
  2. *inferentially*. Do the author's statements make sense? Did the characters (real people) do things in the best ways? Explain. Could or should they have done things differently? What would the results have been? Did the characters (real people) follow directions?
  3. *evaluatively*. Were these things really done the way the author explains? Is this fantasy? Which are facts? opinions? How adequate and valid were the actions of those involved? Were they appropriate? desirable? acceptable? worthy?
  4. *appreciatively and affectively*. What is your response to how these things were done? Do you accept the need for these things to be done but not the means? Could you or would you have done these things in the same ways? Explain. Does the author's language allow or help you to feel a part of the action or reject the action?

To answer all of these questions on all levels would be too time-consuming for a regular assignment. What the teacher might do is ask all children to answer the 5W + H questions on the literal level and then ask each child to pick one or two to answer on all levels.

Let's imagine that the children are about to read a chapter describing the translocation of wild animals in Africa, presumably engaged in to help preserve a species. A section of the chapter focuses on Grévy's zebras, a majestic breed of zebra with narrow stripes and large bat ears.

Prereading

Prereading activities proceed as explained previously. The passage is related to the children's background, vocabulary is introduced, and purposes for reading are given.

Relating Passage to Children's Backgrounds Children might be encouraged to discuss the translocation of animals, e.g.: moving wild animals to a zoo, airlifting burros from the Grand Canyon area to private properties or public properties in the West, moving deer that were starving in the Everglades, moving a variety of other species as seen on T.V. They might briefly discuss why such translocations have occurred and how they proceed.

Introduction of Vocabulary To understand the selection, readers will have to know the meanings of these words that may be new to them:

translocation   foal(s)
vulnerable   subadult(s)
poacher(s)   stallion(s)
antipoacher(s)

The teacher might ask the children if they know the meanings of any of these words. A discussion might ensue, and a dictionary might be used to check meanings and pronunciations, if necessary.

Then the children might be asked to try to fill in the blanks in the following sentences, taken from the chapter.

1. The stated reason for moving the Grévy's is to save them from ________, who have been killing them.
2. Certain members of the Grévy's population are especially ________ to attack.
3. These members are females, ________, and ________.
4. Except during the breeding season, mature ________ locate so that they are hard to capture or kill.
5. Kenya's ________ efforts have not been strong enough to protect the zebras.
6. Poaching is just as serious in the ________ areas as it is in the natural habitats of the Grévy's.

After this introduction to the new words, children will probably be able to learn the meanings more completely when reading the assignment. Each of these words is used several times in the passage.

It might be wise to ask the children to write the word they think fits the context below the line (for prereading). For postreading, they will write the word above the line. If they are wrong during prereading and right at postreading time, they have proven to themselves that they can learn meanings through reading.

Purpose for Reading The 5W + H guide might be posted in the room, and the children might be asked to answer each of the 5W + H questions at the literal level, plus one or two of the 5W + H elements at all levels. (*Variation*: The teacher might assign groups to each type of question.) If this guide is used regularly, children will become familiar with it and may automatically think at all of these levels when reading.

Reading (and Answering Questions Perhaps Internally)

The passage begins thus

Beginning in 1977 and still continuing, an American named Don Hunt has been leading a group of ten men in translocating Grévy's zebras from one area to another in Kenya. According to Hunt, this is being done to help preserve the species, especially to save them from poachers. Hunt and his men lasso the zebras. Following this, they crate them. Then they truck them off to a penned-in area for rest. After the animals rest, they are recrated and sent to a new location, where they are freed.

Hunt's critics contend that Hunt is rough on the Grévy's. They say that the zebras stampede at the sight of any vehicle. According to them, pregnant females frequently abort after being caught Many of the zebras die. They argue that the Grévy's cannot maintain their unique social order in the new location.

(The passage continues for several pages.) Following are possible answers to what and how questions on four levels. These may be written out by the reader or just answered in his or her mind. E.g.:

How:

1. *literally: What does the author say about how it happened?* The author said that violence is being used in capturing the zebras. Also, he says that as a result of crating and trucking, the animals are often wounded. Also, he says that the penning is cruel because lions have attacked the zebras in the pens (and several lions have been

shot to protect the zebras). Also, lions drawn to the zebras are killing horses at homes nearby.

How are things done?	Effect
1. Violence is used in capturing the zebras—lassos are used and Hunt is rough, according to his critics.	Many zebras are wounded, and zebras stampede at the sight of a vehicle. Pregnant famales frequently abort.
2. Zebras are crated and trucked off to a rest area.	Many zebras are wounded in the crates which are not padded. Some die in transit.
3. Zebras are placed in a penned in area "for rest."	Lions have attacked the zebras in the pens. Several lions have been shot to protect the zebras. Lions attracted to the zebras sometimes kill horses at homes nearby.
4. Zebras are recrated and sent to a new location where they are freed.	Hunt's critics say the zebras are not able to maintain their social order in the new location. Hunt says they can.

2. *inferentially: Do the author's statements make sense? Did the characters (real people) do things in the best ways? Explain. Etc.* No—capturing of animals, if done, should be humane. Crates should be padded. Penning, if done, should be done away from homes where horses are kept. In fact, the lions could even threaten humans. It's fine to send the zebras to a new location, but only if they can adjust.

3. *evaluatively: Were these things really done the way the author explains? Is this fantasy? Which are facts? opinions? How adequate and valid were the actions of those involved? Were they appropriate? desirable? acceptable? worthy?* A program I saw on T.V. agreed with this account. Also there were pictures of lions attacking the zebras in their pens. The lions were shot. The program also said many zebras were killed in the crates. I also found an article in another magazine that stated the same things.

4. *appreciatively and affectively: What is your response to how things were done? Etc.* I am only for translocation if it preserves the lives of animals. If it is done, it should be done humanely so the animals involved as well as other animals are not injured or killed in the process.

I think that laws should be enforced against poaching, if possible, so that the animals can be preserved in their natural settings. Is there any reason this is not possible?

I can see the animals being caught and trucked in unpadded crates over bumpy, rugged roads in Africa. I can feel their pain—

the author says "excrutiating pain. Their skin is often torn." I can visualize a zebra being attacked by a lion. To me this is terrible.

Postreading

Discussion The class as a whole might discuss the answers. They might debate their answers, one group taking Hunt's side and the other taking the side of his opponents. They might write letters to each other and look for other sources that discuss the topic.

Kohlberg's scale (as given in Chapter 9) might be used by the teacher for observation of children's reactions. Children might role play according to their feelings and thus attain involvement. The teacher might direct questions to the children to identify and attempt to raise their level.

Vocabulary A review of the vocabulary terms is in order also. A "sock-toss" game might be used. The group reading the passage (perhaps the whole class) is divided in two. A pitcher is selected for each group, and all other children are given numbers: a one in each group, a two in each group, etc.

The teacher (or a child) says a word (or a definition) and a number. The pitcher for each team tosses a sock to the child with that number. When the child catches the sock, he or she can give the definition (or word). The first to do so correctly scores a point for his or her team. Review words may also be used from previous lessons.

EXAMPLE 4

Example 4 integrates the use of both a levels guide and story schema in teaching a story. It is an explication of one lesson taken from an article by Joy F. Moss that contains many lessons in a unit on bears used with six and seven year olds.* Moss explains the questioning process thus:

The questions introduced by the teacher during each dialogue were intended to highlight particular ideas and concepts, to focus on basic elements of narrative,

---

*Joy F. Moss. "Using the 'Focus Unit' to Enhance Children's Response to Literature." *Language Arts*, 55 (April 1978): 482–488. Copyright 1978 by the National Council of Teachers of English. Reprinted by permission of the publisher and the author.

and to stimulate creative thinking. Some of the types of questions which accompanied particular books read aloud during storytime sessions are included below to clarify this critical feature of the Focus Unit experience.

The Biggest Bear by Lynd Ward (1952) was read aloud to the children. ". . . the children were then asked to discuss the characters and setting in terms of specific details used by the author/illustrator to develop these basic story elements." (character and setting, i.e., location—details, *literal level*)

"The children were encouraged to become detectives, to search for hidden or implied clues in order to extract meaning and enrich their understanding of the story. They were asked to consider cause-effect relationships in the narrative: 'Why did Johnny change his mind about wanting to shoot a bear?'" (cause-effect relationship, *inferential level*)
"Focus on the plot was stimulated by questions such as, 'How was his problem solved for him?' Questions such as 'How do you think Johnny felt when he had to take the Biggest Bear into the woods?' and 'What do you imagine his thoughts were as he walked into the woods?' were intended to foster inferential thinking." (plot, one episode: attempt → outcome → internal response → reaction, *inferential level*)
"The question 'Do you think this story could really have happened?' led to a discussion of the differences between 'make believe,' 'real,' and 'true' stories. The children continued to explore this issue during subsequent discussions as they reflected on each new story introduced during storytime." (judgment of reality or fantasy, *evaluation level*)
"The questioning process was also used as a vehicle for expanding vocabulary and studying word meanings. For example, the children were asked to discuss meanings of the words *wild* and *tame* since *The Biggest Bear* is about a wild animal that grows up as a child's pet. Various uses of the words were examined such as 'wild flowers' and 'wild behavior.' The children thought of *Where the Wild Things Are* and *Born Free* as well as the phrase from the commercial, 'tame unruly hair,' as they free-associated and explored the various connotations of these words." (vocabulary: background of experience, denotations and connotations, semantic webbing.)
"A final question was designed to bring the story close to their own lives: 'Did any of you ever have a pet that grew too big to keep? What happened?' The children shared their personal experiences with cute baby chicks or bunnies which eventually grew to adult size and could no longer be confined in a bedroom, apartment, or home. They related events and emotions similar to those described by Ward in *The Biggest*

Bear." (background of experience, *appreciation level and affective dimensions, sharing*)

"The questions used to guide each dialogue served to help the children discover how authors build plot, develop character, and use language to create a good story. With each successive dialogue session, the children showed a growing capacity to explore and discuss the various elements of narrative structure."

SKILLS GUIDES AND PLANS

A skills guide is appropriate to use if the focal point (or one of the focal points) of a lesson is the teaching of a skill (possibly on a long-time basis) when the skill is one necessary for understanding content.* The skill is taught to enable children to get ideas from their reading. In other words, teaching the skill is done to attain transfer. (A child doesn't study how to select important details, how to get main ideas, how to follow direction, etc., just to develop the skill, *per se*. The child develops these skills to use them in obtaining or selecting ideas in reading materials.) The lessons exemplified in this section stress both skill development and the attainment of content related to that skill.

As a prereading activity, a review of some of the skill steps already taught is appropriate, followed by setting the stage for the next step, that is the focus of the lesson.

As a postreading activity, the teacher checks to see which children need more help in applying the skill as taught in the focal point of this lesson and gives these children additional help. Then even another level of the skill may be introduced as an extension activity.

EXAMPLE 1

The first plan is a framework suggesting how main idea might be taught. Content selected relates to a chapter the children are reading about growing crops. Objectives are to develop and refine a skill and to use it in teaching content. The lesson begins with two review steps. The pur-

---

*Such lessons could be used just for developing a skill itself. However, they are more valuable if interesting or important content is included. Using the content as explained in Example 1 shows how transfer of the skill to a content area subject can be achieved.

pose is to review techniques already taught to the children to help them identify the main idea.

Prereading (I.E., Introduction)

Review Step 1 Children are reminded that they have learned to select the main idea of a group of words by circling the main idea thus:

flowers   trees   shrubs   (plants)   vegetables   cereals

They are then asked to complete these, perhaps as a group:

oak   apricot   elm   tree   peach   mimosa
daisy   flower   rose   hibiscus   geranium   aster
peas   beans   asparagus beets   vegetables onions
apple   orange   fruit   peach   strawberry pineapple
orange   lemon   lime   grapefruit citrus fruit   cumquat

Review Step 2 Next, they are reminded that they have learned to select a main idea of a paragraph from a list of choices, e.g.:

Farmers in our valley grow a variety of crops. Among the most popular ones are pecans and pima cotton. Many onions are also grown, as well as lettuce and alfalfa. You may be surprised to find that flowering plants, especially chrysanthemums and roses, are also grown for the market.

1. Among the most popular ones are pecans and pima cotton.
2. Many onions are grown, as well as lettuce and alfalfa.
(3.) Farmers in our valley grow a variety of crops.
4. None of the above.

A few additional similar examples of paragraphs might be given here, perhaps from their books.

Reading (I.E., Focus of Lesson)

This Lesson's Focal Point Next, children are told that in today's geography lesson (perhaps a chapter or part of a chapter in their book) they are to underline the main idea in certain paragraphs (or series of shorter paragraphs). These are paragraphs in the book selected by the teacher as especially appropriate to the assignment. The selection should be one in which main ideas are usually stated by the author. The above example, plus the few additional examples, could be used, and the teacher may demonstrate by underlining the main idea:*

<u>Farmers in our valley grow a variety of crops</u>. Among the most popular ones are pecans and pima cotton. Many onions are also grown, as well as lettuce and alfalfa. You may be surprised to find that flowering plants, especially chrysanthemums and roses, are also grown for the market.

Postreading (I.E., Follow-up, Extension)

Diagnosis A discussion and analysis of the children's books or papers reveals that some children need more help in this skill at this time. The teacher may give these children additional help by using another reading assignment and/or worksheets. (It probably will take some time to teach most of the children this skill. Continued assignments like the above probably need to be given for a month or more until most children will develop this skill. Then it becomes a review activity for the next step.)

Extension Following this, the teacher may teach the children the use of these symbols:

    ∇ = main idea at beginning of paragraph
    ∆ = main idea at end of paragraph
    ⋈ = main idea at beginning and end of paragraph
    ⬦ = main idea within paragraph
    O = main idea not stated

Then the children are asked to use these symbols to show the location of the main idea in each paragraph in the original selections (and/or in later selections). Then the children are asked to draw a conclusion about where this author usually places the main idea statement.

---

*Teachers may not want children to write in books. In this case, children write out the main ideas on a piece of paper.

Enrichment activities, if deemed desirable, might also

* involve children in matching newspaper headings with their articles
* involve the beginning stages of teaching children to infer main ideas from paragraphs in which the main ideas are not stated
* involve children in writing their own paragraphs appropriate for each of the symbols: ∇ Δ Ⴟ ⬦ ○
* involve the children in adding appropriate details to any of the paragraphs and critiquing the appropriateness of the details included by the author.

EXAMPLE 2

The second plan describes a way of teaching a skill by using whole class, group, and individual activities. The plan extends over a period of time.

Prereading (I.E., Introduction)

The activity might have developed because children displayed curiosity about something they first became aware of through reading. This lesson is on word connotations.

Several children have asked about words such as *dog, monkey, peach, blue,* being used in describing people. The whole class might display an interest in this and then begin working on word connotations. This might progress to the consideration of figurative language.

The whole class might be led to an understanding of what is meant by "connotative language, or word connotations." (*Connotations* are figurative, imaginative, emotional meanings of words, as opposed to *denotations,* which are literal meanings.) A few classwide examples might be given:

She's *blue.*	They're *monkeys.*
He's a *nut.*	Santa Claus is a *peach.*
She's a *mouse.*	We're in the *red.*

Focal Point of Lesson

Group Activity Children then could group themselves. One group might name colors that have connotations. Another group might list growing things (vegetation) whose names have connotations. Still another group might list animal names that have connotations. The teacher might circulate to help each group in its work. Their findings (briefly) might be:

Group One	Group Two	Group Three
Colors	*Vegetation*	*Animals*
red	peach	cat
blue	nut	mouse
green	apple	dog
black	lemon	elephant
purple	fruit (fruity)	monkey
.	.	.
.	.	.
.	.	.
pink	plum	turkey

Whole Class Activity To share and extend this work, a whole class activity might follow. To prepare for it, each group would write each word they listed on a separate slip of paper. The children would then come together and count off: 1, 2, 3, 4, 5 1, 2, 3, 4, 5,-etc. All with the same number would group together.

The teacher would draw a slip, read it aloud, and each group would write as many figurative uses of the word as they could. E.g., for the word *cat*:

He approached *on cat's feet.*
That's the *cat's pajamas.*
Cat got your tongue?
He's a *cool cat.*

Possibly the following might also be allowed:

They always *pussy foot* around.
He's got a *tiger* by the tail.
After being fixed, the engine *purred.*
That's a *lion*-hearted act.

After a specified amount of time, the group with the greatest number of examples wins the round. Then another round begins, and so on.

Extending the Activity

Next, the teacher might ask the children to watch their reading materials and also to note expressions heard when listening in order to find words used connotatively. The class might continue work on this by preparing a bulletin board display, making a mobile or mobiles, making a booklet, or by working on some other project. Such work might continue for several weeks or more and be in addition to other work in which the children are engaged.

Summary

Often the teaching of reading skills and content can, and should, be fused. This can be done when the teacher's principal aim is to teach content or when it is to teach skills. Lesson guides that demonstrate how both of these can be achieved were included in this chapter.

The discussion of rationale included an elaboration of reading as a "matrixing event." This was followed by guides and plans designed to utilize this process.

Concept guides and plans were explained first. These include the utilization of textbook schemas and textbook grammars and also story (narrative) schemas and story (narrative) grammars. The vocabulary + SQ3R model was explained first, with the final R (R_3) representing both a review stage and reconstruction (transformation) stage. Animal hibernation was the content. Following this was a lesson utilizing a class constructed schema/grammar with "government" as the content. Finally, story schema and story grammar were explained, and questions related to story grammar were given.

Next, levels guides and plans were explained. These relate to asking questions—or designing activities—on the literal, inferential, evaluation, and appreciation levels for one lesson. Examples consisted of lessons related to giving a party in school, analyzing an advertisement, using a 5W + H guide in responding to a lesson on the translocation of animals, and eliciting children's responses to a story read to them about a bear, which included questions on story schema, or story grammar.

The third type of guide was designed to teach skills to help children understand content. The first guide related to teaching main ideas in geography lessons. It began with review steps, a focal step, diagnosis, and suggested extension activities—all for teaching main idea and content. The second example demonstrated how skills can be taught using whole class, group, and individual activities to teach connotative uses of language.

Questions and Activities

After answering the questions at the beginning of this chapter, consider these questions and activities:

1. Chapters 8 and 9 of this book explained comprehension in terms of subskill development. Would you consider Chapter 12 to be closer to a holistic approach to reading? Explain.
2. Design a concept guide for teaching a chapter in a book (similar to "The Winter Season," p. 480 ff.) or for organizing a unit by using the brainstorming technique (similar to the government guide, p. 486 ff.). Share this with your classmates.
3. Using the ideas suggested in the section on story schema/story grammar (p. 492 ff.) design a plan for teaching a short story of your choice. Share this plan with your classmates.
4. Select one passage and write a levels guide (other than the 5W + H Guide) for use with it. Share this with your classmates.
5. Design part of a 5W + H guide for use with an article or chapter from a book. You may wish to select two of these basic questions: who, what, where, when, why, how and ask questions in these two areas at the following levels: literal, inferential, evaluation, appreciation/affective. Share this with your classmates.
6. Design a skills guide for teaching one subskill. Include these steps: review, focal point, diagnosis, extension. Content of the plan should include only one subject area. Share this with your classmates.

NOTES

1. See David Ausubel (1961 and 1963) in Selected References.
2. See Frances P. Robinson in Selected References.
3. Dolores Fadness Tadlock, p. 111. See Selected References.
4. See John Guthrie in Selected References.
5. *Ibid.*
6. See Stephanie H. McConaughy in Selected References.
7. Jill Fitzgerald Whaley, p. 769. See Selected References.

SELECTED REFERENCES

Applebee, Arthur N. *The Child's Concept of Story: Ages Two to Seventeen.* Chicago: University of Chicago Press, 1978.

Ausubel, David. "Learning by Discovery: Rationale and Mystique," *Bulletin of the National Association of Secondary School Principals,* 1961, pp. 18–58.

______________. *The Psychology of Meaningful Verbal Learning.* New York: Greene and Stratton, 1963, pp. 85–87.

Billig, Edith. "Children's Literature as a Springboard to Content Areas." *The Reading Teacher,* 30 (May 1977): 855–859.

Bruce, Bertram. "What Makes a Good Story?" *Language Arts,* 55 (April 1978): 460–466.

Burmeister, Lou E. *Reading Strategies for Middle and Secondary School Teachers, Second Edition.* Reading, Massachusetts: Addison-Wesley, 1978, Chapter 5.

Cleland, Craig J. "Highlighting Issues in Children's Literature through Semantic Webbing." *The Reading Teacher,* 34 (March 1981): 642–647.

Eeds, Maryann. "What To Do When They Don't Understand What They Read— Research-Based Strategies for Teaching Reading Comprehension." *The Reading Teacher,* 34 (February 1981): 565–571.

Estes, Thomas H. and Joseph L. Vaughan, Jr. *Reading and Learning in the Content Classroom.* Boston: Allyn and Bacon, 1978.

Guszak, Frank J. *Diagnostic Reading Instruction in the Elementary School, Second Edition.* New York: Harper and Row, 1978.

______________. "Teacher Questioning in Reading." *The Reading Teacher,* 21 (December 1967): 227–234.

Guthrie, John T. "Research Views: Purpose and Text Structure." *The Reading Teacher,* 32 (February 1979): 624–626.

Hafner, Lawrence E. (ed.). *Improving Reading in Middle and Secondary Schools.* New York: Macmillan, 1974.

Harris, Theodore L. "Making Reading an Effective Instrument of Learning in the Content Fields," in *Reading in High School and College,* N.S.S.E. 47th Yearbook, Part II, Chicago: University of Chicago Press, 1949, Chapter 7.

Hennings, Dorothy Grant. *Communication in Action: Teaching the Language Arts, Second Edition.* Boston: Houghton-Mifflin, 1982, pp. 95, 102–107, 112, and 265.

Jones, Linda L. "An Interactive View of Reading: Implications for the Classroom." *The Reading Teacher,* 35 (April 1982): 772–777.

Langer, Judith A. and M. Trika Smith-Burke (eds.) *Reader Meets Author/Bridging the Gap.* Newark, Delaware: International Reading Association, 1982.

Lapp, Diane, James Flood, and Gary Gleckman. "Classroom Practices Can Make

Use of What Researchers Learn." *The Reading Teacher*, 35 (February 1982): 578–585.

Macklin, Michael D. "Content Area Reading Is a Process for Finding Personal Meaning." *Journal of Reading*, 22 (December 1978): 212–215.

Mandler, Jean and Nancy Johnson. "Remembrance of Things Parsed: Story Structure and Recall." *Cognitive Psychology*, 9 (January 1977): 111–151.

Mathias, Sandra L. Ess and Mary E. Massa Fanyo. "Blending Reading Instruction with Music and Art." *The Reading Teacher*, 30 (February 1977): 497–500.

McConaughy, Stephanie H. "Using Story Structure in the Classroom." *Language Arts*, 57 (February 1980): 157–165.

Monteith, Mary K. "Schemata: An Approach to Understanding Reading Comprehension." *Journal of Reading*, 22 (January 1979): 368–371.

Moss, Joy F. "Using the 'Focus Unit' to Enhance Children's Response to Literature." *Language Arts*, 55 (April 1978): 482–488.

Noyce, Ruth M. "Team Up and Teach with Trade Books." *The Reading Teacher*, 32 (January 1979): 442–448.

Ortiz, Rose Katz. "Using Questioning as a Tool in Reading." *Journal of Reading*, 21 (November 1977): 109–114.

Patberg, Judythe P. "Validation of Reading Strategies in Secondary Content Areas." *Journal of Reading*, 22 (January 1979): 332–336.

Piercey, Dorothy. *Duplicate Masters for Reading Activities in Content Areas*. Rockleigh, New Jersey: Longwood Division of Allyn and Bacon, Inc., 1979.

——————————. *Reading Activities in Content Areas: An Ideabook for Middle and Secondary Schools*. Rockleigh, New Jersey: Longwood Division of Allyn and Bacon, Inc., 1976.

Pillar, Arlene M. "Revolutionary Reading: an Annotated Bibliography." *Language Arts*, 52 (September 1975): 902–912.

Robinson, Francis P. "Study Skills for Superior Students in Secondary School." *The Reading Teacher*, 25 (September 1961): 29–33ff.

Rupley, William J. "ERIC/RCS Report: Content Reading in the Elementary Grades." *Language Arts*, 52 (September 1975): 802–807.

Sadow, Marilyn W. "The Use of Story Grammar in the Design of Questions." *The Reading Teacher*, 35 (February 1982): 518–521.

Sebesta, Sam, James Calder, and Lynn Cleland, "Story Structures in Children's Book Choices." *The Reading Teacher*, 34 (May 1981): 946–947.

Stauffer, Russell G. and Max M. Harrell. "Individualized Reading-Thinking Activities." *The Reading Teacher*, 28 (May 1975): 765–769.

Tadlock, Dolores Fadness. "SQ3R—Why It Works, Based on an Information Processing Theory of Learning." *Journal of Reading*, 22 (November 1978): 110–112.

Thomas, Ellen Lamar and H. Alan Robinson. *Improving Reading in Every Class.* Boston: Allyn and Bacon, 1972.

Thomas, Keith. "Instructional Procedures for Content Reading." *Reading Improvement*, 15 (Summer 1978): 138–140.

Vacca, Richard T. "Readiness to Read Content Area Assignments." *Journal of Reading*, 20 (February 1977): 387–392.

Whaley, Jill Fitzgerald. "Story Grammars and Reading Instruction." *The Reading Teacher*, 34 (April 1981): 762–771.

APPROACHES, PROGRAMS, AND EVALUATION

Unit Three consists of two chapters:

Chapter 13 Approaches and Programs Used in the Teaching of Reading

Chapter 14 Evaluation of Reading Performance

Unit Three provides a discussion of approaches and programs commonly used in the teaching of reading in elementary school classrooms. It concludes with a discussion of techniques used in evaluating materials and student progress in reading achievement, sometimes with implications for diagnostic teaching.

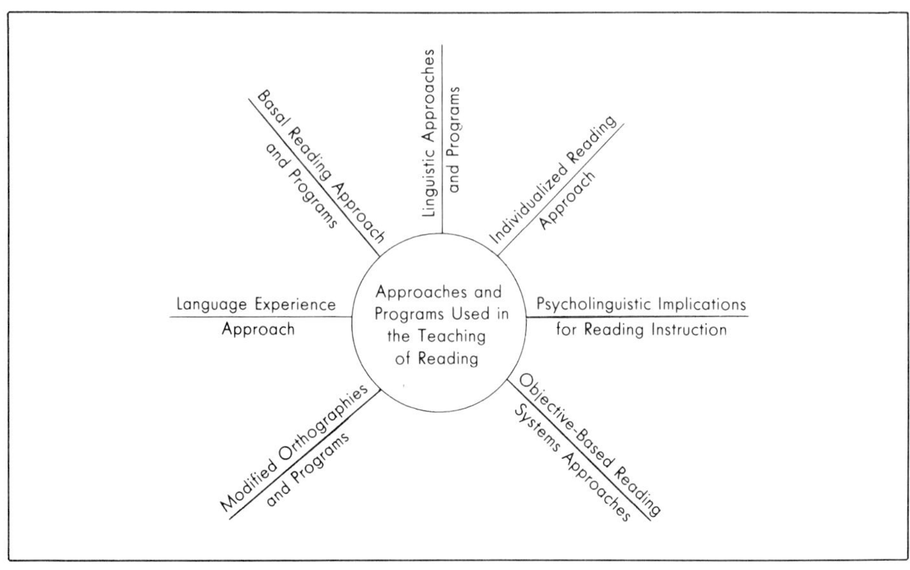

- Seven different approaches (and/or programs) are explained in this chapter. While reading, think about the rationale for each, the process used when teaching or using the approach, and the materials that are used in each. Consider the possible strengths and weaknesses of each approach. Then try to decide which approach or approaches you would like to use when teaching children.

- Is the Language Experience Approach a bottom-up or top-down approach to the teaching of reading? Explain how the LEA integrates the use of the language arts of listening, speaking, writing, and reading. What are the basic steps, and in what order are these steps followed in a typical LEA lesson? Why is it essential that the teacher respect each child's language? What language and reading skills can be learned using the LEA and how can they be taught?

- How can we characterize the basal reading approach? What is a "scope and sequence" chart? How is a typical lesson organized? What materials are available? How might you group children for basal reading lessons? How would you decide what group each child should be in?

- What are two basic types of linguistic programs? Compare these in terms of the unit of language that is stressed in the lessons. Might each be appropriately used with different types of children? Explain.

- How can we describe Individualized Reading? What are the usual teaching components in IR? Might IR be used to supplement other approaches? Explain.

- What is meant by "psycholinguistics"? What is the basic theory of a psycholinguistic reading process? What are some possible implications of this theory for classroom practice?

- How can we describe objective-based reading systems approaches? Explain why you think such a system could or could not be used together with another approach. If you think it could be so used, explain how.

- What is meant by a "modified orthography"? What do all modified orthographies and their uses in a reading program have in common?

Approaches and Programs Used in the Teaching of Reading

Among the diverse programs, materials, and/or approaches* used in the teaching of reading in today's schools are those briefly described in this chapter. Included are:

- the Language Experience Approach (LEA)
- basal reading approach and programs
- linguistic approaches (and programs)
- individualized reading (IR) approach
- psycholinguistic implications for reading instruction
- objective-based reading systems approaches (and programs)
- modified orthographies (and programs)

The purpose of this chapter is to introduce the reader of this book to a variety of concepts related to commonly discussed and used programs, materials, and approaches directed toward the teaching of reading. It is impossible to be complete in such a discussion, for volumes could be written on the subject. It is hoped that the discussion will serve as an introduction to those of you who may wish some general guidance before examining materials that may be available in college reading centers, and materials and teaching techniques that may be observed in schoolrooms.

---

*Approaches here-in refers to philosophies and techniques used in teaching reading. Programs refers to specific types, or sets, of materials available from publishers.

Language Experience Approach

RATIONALE

Children enter our schools with diverse background experiences, language experiences, and interests. Usually they come to us wanting to learn, but available published materials may not appeal to them, as they may not be culturally or linguistically ready or able to understand these materials. The content of these materials may be foreign or dull to them, and the language may seem strange or stilted. Even if the ideas and language are appropriate, the children may not be mature enough to profit from the use of such materials. They may, however, be ready for initial stages of reading instruction if we use a Language Experience Approach.

We can use their backgrounds, their interests, and their language in building a reading program for them. Such a program might be used as part of a reading readiness program* and for the beginning stages of reading instruction, perhaps for all children. In addition, it might be used as an ongoing supplementary program (used along with another program later) or as a complete reading-language-arts program throughout the primary or elementary grades.

The Language Experience Approach stresses the development and unity of all the communications skills—listening, speaking, reading, and writing. Its content is the children's own experiences—past and present. It provides for the development, understanding, and use of on-going experiences.

PROCESS

A Language Experience lesson usually is composed of these steps:

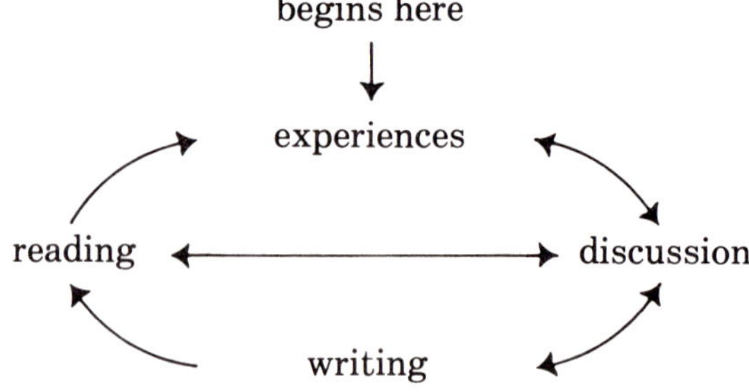

---

*The Language Experience Approach can be used to develop the concept that reading material represents meaning. Also, through its use children learn about left to right progression, and they learn concepts of what sentences, phrases, words, and letters are in meaningful printed language.

All children have had experiences, and these may serve as a foundation for discussion, which the teacher may record in writing, then teach the child or children to read, and then continue the circle by extending the experiences and introducing new experiences, which serve as a basis for discussion, writing, and reading, etc.

The teacher may ask the children what they want to learn to read, then write it for them and teach them to read it. The teacher may listen while the children visit with each other, and when hearing an interesting word, phrase, or sentence may write it for them and teach them to read it. The teacher may provide for field trips and other activities, e.g.:

- a visit to the zoo, a farm, an airport, a museum, a ball game, a library, etc.
- the viewing of a film or filmstrip, interesting pictures from magazines and books, the child's own pictures, a school play, etc.
- the observance of plant growth, of fish in an aquarium, of a gerbil, a T.V. program, etc.
- participation in a show-and-tell, etc.
- a visit from a librarian, the school principal, a parent, a community personality, etc.
- the reading of a story or part of a story, newspaper or magazine article, picture books about which they can write their own stories,[1]
- play acting, puppetry, music, dancing, games, etc.

Such experiences may engender a discussion, which could lead to the writing of part of it and, in turn, the reading of this, which may lead to further discussion and further experiences and activities. In Roach Van Allen's words, each child will soon learn that:

"• What I think about, I can talk about.
- What I say, I can write (or someone can write for me).
- What I can write, I can read (and others can read, too).
- I can read what I have written, and I can also read what other people have written for me to read."[2]

The children may have gone out to the school playground for recess and then returned to the classroom to talk about what they did. Individuals, groups of children, or the whole class might then dictate a story, and the teacher would record it. E.g.:

RECESS TIME

Today we played outside. We had fun.
John and Liz and Maria played hopscotch.
Suzie and Mike played on the monkey bars.
A bunch of us jumped rope: Tina, Jerry, Henry, Tony,
Jennifer, Carol, Ralph, and Sammy.
Connie and Joan watched a squirrel pick up
nuts. Mr. Lowrance said the squirrel would store them
for winter.
Tomorrow we will go out again.

Now that the experience chart has been written, the children can learn to read it. This may be accomplished in the following way:

- The teacher may begin by reading the story to the children. While doing this, he or she smoothly runs a pointer from left to right under the line being read. The reading is done using natural phrasing—not word-by-word, which would distort language.
- Next, the teacher begins reading the story again running the pointer again from left to right. The children join in as they are able to. Children may recognize their names in print, and they may remember what they did on the playground. This step may be repeated several times.
- The teacher may make a duplicate copy of the story and cut this into strings of words and/or single words. The teacher may give each child one or more of these pieces to be responsible for reciting as the story is read again.
- The teacher may point to each word or string of words on the chart in order while the child who has the copy reads it aloud. Finally most or all of the children may be able to read the chart.
- The teacher may make duplicate copies of the chart for each child to keep. The children may wish to take these home to read to their parents.
- The children may compose new sentences using the words they have learned in print.

Paramount to using such an approach is respect for each child's language. The teacher must understand that one language, or dialect, is not more correct than another. Dialects offer alternatives in pronunciation and syntax and other language variables. Yet it is likely* that such a program should, while building on the linguistic competence a child brings to school, provide a "basis for elaboration and modification of further language learnings through instruction."[3] This would facilitate social, cultural, and economic mobility for each child. And it would help the child build a linguistic and cultural background for reading a variety of printed materials that are normally available.

It is usually recommended that the teacher use the learner's exact vocabulary (but with traditional spelling, e.g., "go'en" is spelled going), sentence structure, and word order in the beginning stages. As time moves on, suggestions may be made for the use of middle class English.

As soon as the children are able, they should begin writing their own stories with the help of the teacher. They should be encouraged to use a variety of formats and to illustrate their experience charts. Among the formats they may wish to use are: posters, bumper stickers, postcards and letters to friends and relatives, birthday, Halloween, Thanksgiving Day cards, newspaper accounts, short stories, poetry—even Haiku, skits for the class, plays for puppet shows, radiocasts, classroom announcements, etc. The teacher may wish to take photographs of the children, and the children may later write about these experiences—using past tense.

> For beginning readers, very simple and short "charts" might be used. E.g.:
>
> □ *Child's Sentence* The teacher writes a sentence, recording child language, for a child or a group of children to learn to read. Such a sentence may be selected in many different ways:
>
> - the child may dictate a sentence he or she would like to learn to read.
> - the teacher may listen to informal conversations and select a sentence a child has spoken.
> - the teacher may provide motivation for discussion and from this discussion select a sentence.
>
> 1. Once the sentence is selected, it is printed, e.g.:
>
> Mark find a spider in his pocket.
>
> (As noted before, the child's grammar is used.)

---

*The following statement is controversial. Consider, for example, parents and cultures that do not wish their children to be mobile in such ways.

2. The teacher points to the sentence from left-to-right while reading it along with the child (or children). This is repeated several times.
3. The teacher makes a copy of this sentence on a piece of paper and cuts this sentence into word groups, e.g.:

| a spider | Mark find | in his pocket. |

4. The child arranges the papers in left-to-right sequence. If the child is unable to do so without looking at the original complete sentence, he or she may refer to the original.

| Mark find | a spider | in his pocket. |

5. Next, the teacher cuts the phrase slips into individual word slips:

| pocket. | spider | his | Mark | in | a | find |

and the child arranges these in order:

| Mark | find | a | spider | in | his | pocket. |

(Now the child is reading individual words.)
6. The teacher may now show that there is another way to say this sentence:

| Mark find a spider in his pocket. |

7. Several sentences may be put together to compose a story.
8. The teacher may make a copy of the sentence or sentences for the child to take home to read to his/her family. Also copies may be kept for an individual or class book. Children may wish to illustrate their sentences and stories.

□ *Extending Reading Vocabulary through Word Substitution* The children and/or teacher may suggest words that might be substituted for those in the sentence. The children may use words from their word-banks or orally suggest words. The teacher writes them down if a child cannot. E.g.:

Mark found a spider in his pocket.

___________ found a spider in his pocket.

Harry

Jimmy

Billy

___________ found a spider in her pocket.

Lily

Joan

Sally

Mark ___________ a spider in his pocket.

saw

felt

stuck

put

squashed

Mark found a ___________ in his pocket.

worm

bug

dollar

dime

marble

Mark found a spider in his ___________.

room

box

yard

shoe

desk

The teacher might write these words on cards—one word or string of words per card. Then the children might arrange them in a pocket chart to come up with a variety of sentences: (see p. 528, bottom)

□ *Introducing Phonic Elements* As the children progress, they might be asked to suggest words that have a common sound pattern, e.g., that sound alike at the beginning. The teacher would write these words and stress the sound-symbol relationships:

Mark found a spider in his (her) pocket.
M______
Milton
Monica
Mary
Monica found a spider in her pocket.

s______   p______
spoon   purse
sponge   pillow
spook   pajamas

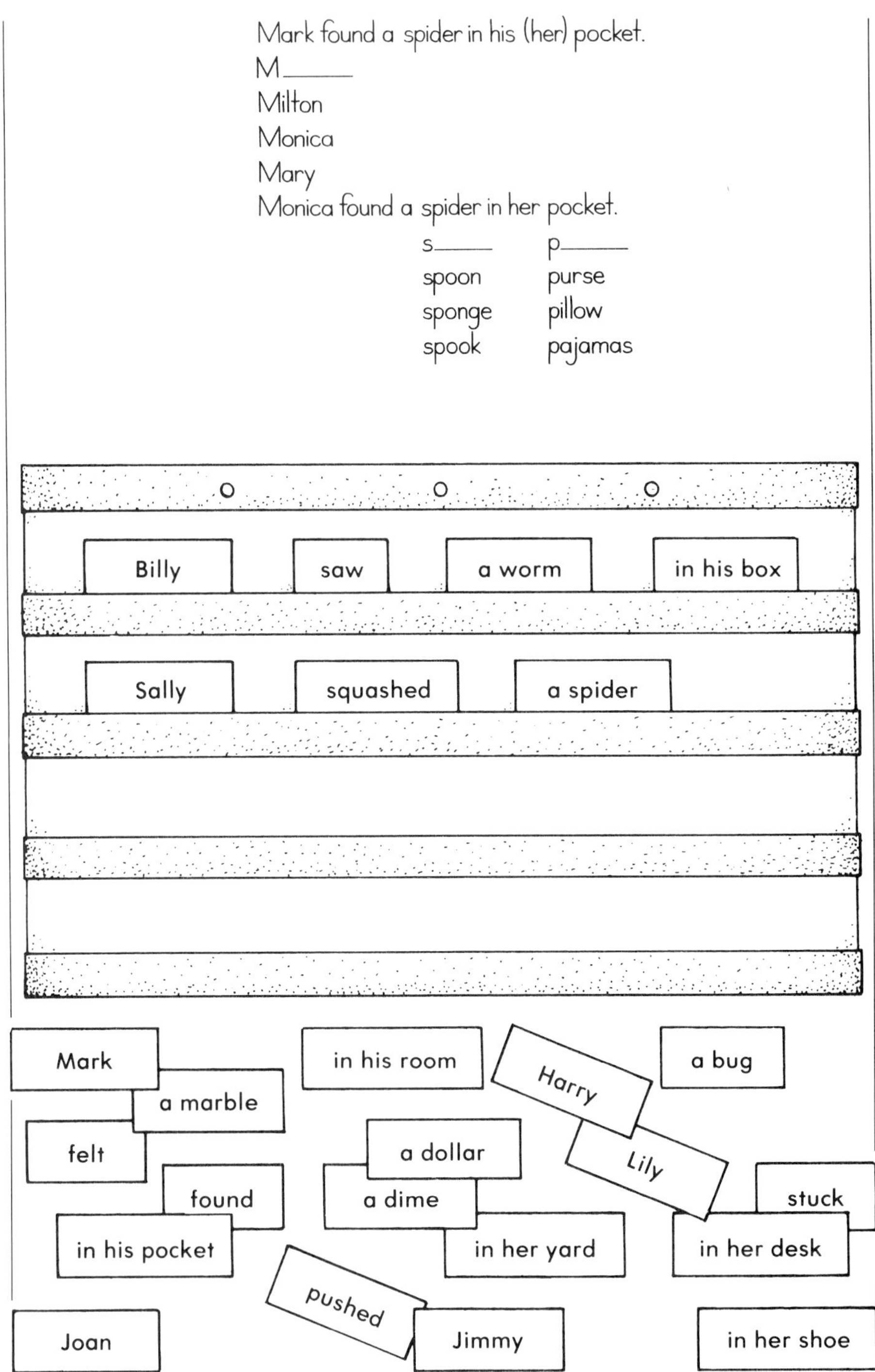

□ *Extending Children's Experiences* To build a child's concepts and oral and reading vocabulary, the teacher should provide for extended experiences—both real and vicarious. Some suggestions for doing this were given at the beginning of this section on Language Experience. There are numerous opportunities for building concepts and word power among young people.

In many of these, preparation for the experience is important. What are the children to listen to? . . . to look for? . . . to pay special attention to? For example, if the class is to visit a dairy farm, or to watch a movie about a dairy farm, the teacher and children might discuss what will probably be seen. While discussing this, the teacher might ask questions, and the children's responses might be written in an experience chart, which some of the children will learn to read. Those children who are less advanced may "read along" and may learn valuable language concepts without being responsible for having to read the chart, or the whole chart.

One teacher led her class with the following result:

Teacher's questions	OUR TRIP TO A FARM
Where will we go tomorrow?	Tomorrow we will go to a dairy farm.
How will we get there?	We will go on the school bus.
What will we see?	We will see a barn and a chicken coop
	and a pasture for the cows.
What does the farmer work for?	From the cows, the farmer gets warm milk.
	From the chickens he gets warm eggs.
What's another meaning for the names of the animals?	We are to look at a cow to see just why
	a person who is a cow is quite big.
	And we are to watch some chickens to
	see what it means to call a person a
	chicken, a chick, or a hen.
What will we do when we return?	When we come back to our class again,
	we will have many ideas to write (or to
	pen).

Notice the words the children are learning to read. Some of these words are already familiar to them in writing, and some, it seems, have been suggested by the teacher (or by rather precocious children). Notice the associations: warm milk and warm eggs (not just milk and eggs). Notice that the figurative use of some words is being taught: of cow, chicken, chick, and hen. There is much more that could follow the trip—to be written in another chart. For example, children might note the sounds of the animals: moo, cackle, and perhaps cock-a-doodle-doo. They might note products of milk: cheese and butter. They might learn how eggs are used. They might notice the personality of the farmer, his helpers, and his family. They might find that other animals are also on the farm, etc.

After the field trip (or film) each child might dictate an individual short story. The following schedule describes activities that might be used when working with these stories.

□ *Child's Story* Dorothy Garman,[4] in an article titled "So They've Dictated a Story . . . Now What?" suggests an interesting "five day cycle of activities." She explains that some of these activities are teacher-directed, while others can be completed independently by each child. The following description, in part, is taken from her article.

- *First Day—Familiarization.* On the first day, each child (or group of children) dictates a story. (Some of the stories may be very short.) The teacher writes it for the child. The child reads the story to the teacher, if possible. Otherwise, the teacher reads it to the child. If the child reads the story, the teacher quickly pronounces words the child doesn't immediately know so the story is read smoothly. Then the child illustrates the story.

  The teacher makes duplicate copies of the story to be used later.

- *Second Day—Reinforcement.* First, the child is asked to underline all of the words he or she knows. The child then pronounces the words. Next, the child reads the story aloud, and again the teacher quickly pronounces any unknown words. Then the teacher or child makes a word-bank card for each known word, and the child arranges the cards in alphabetical order.

  Finally, working with each child individually, the teacher selects three underlined words that begin with different sounds. Each of these is printed on the top of a different column on a three-column sheet of paper. The children then cut out pictures from old magazines, etc., that begin with each of these sounds and paste the pictures in the appropriate columns. As a variation, the teacher may, instead, paste a picture at the top of the column and ask the child to cut out all the words from his or her story that have a corresponding initial sound and paste them in the appropriate columns. If the child has word-bank words from previous stories, these may also be used. (The same procedure may be followed at later dates for final consonants, vowel sounds, etc.)

• *Third Day—Context.* The child reads the story again and puts a second underlining on words recalled this day that were also recalled the previous day. The teacher then isolates each of these words by framing it with his or her hands, and the child pronounces it. If the child is unable to pronounce it, the teacher removes her or his hands to let the child read the word in context.

Finally the child is given a paper folded in half. On one side the child pastes words that can be illustrated and draws pictures of them, e.g., chicken, milk, eggs. On the other side the child pastes words that cannot be illustrated, e.g., at, on, hot.

• *Fourth Day—High-Frequency Words.* The teacher cuts out several high-frequency words from a copy of each child's story and staples the story on another sheet of paper. The children take turns reading their stories aloud, and either they or a listener supply a word that would fit the context for each blank. (These need not be the original words.) Then the teacher returns the cut-out words to the child, and the child pastes the words in the appropriate places.

Finally, the teacher takes each child's set of word-bank words from this story and asks the child to pronounce them. If a child cannot pronounce a word, he or she locates it in the story and uses the context of the story to help recognize the word.

• *Fifth Day—Reconstruction.* The teacher has cut each child's story into phrases, or strings of words, and gives each child his or her phrases. Each child combines these into sentences to reconstruct the story, though the story need not be a duplicate of the original story.

If the child seems unsure of how to progress, the teacher tells the child to select a phrase that begins with a capital letter because usually that will begin a sentence. The child then is encouraged to look for a phrase or several phrases that might be used to complete the sentence. The child then reads the sentence to the teacher or a classmate.

Finally, if this is the first story the child has worked with, the teacher supplies him or her with a homemade booklet made by putting together sheets of construction paper with metal paper fasteners or staples. The child pastes his or her story in the booklet and illustrates the cover. The child will complete the booklet by adding future stories or perhaps stories of other children. These stories and additional ones may be used in building a classroom library which may be shared with the whole school.* Later, the children may wish to take their books home.

□ *Word-Banks* The use of "Word Banks" is often associated with the Language Experience Approach. An article by Sharon Garton, Paula Schoenfelder, and Patricia Skriba titled "Activities for Young Word Bankers"[5] elaborates the idea. These authors suggest that not only should words the children have learned by reading and rereading their Language Experience charts be printed on cards and placed in their individual word banks, but also additional words should be printed on cards—words from daily experiences of many types. These might be used in the following ways:

- For building *self-concept*, words that are "intimately linked with the child's identity are particularly helpful in developing a positive self-image." The following activities may be used to promote self-image:
  for exploring feelings—the child
  - writes a word describing present feelings, personal feelings about school, family, friends. The child puts these in her or his word bank.
  - selects an exciting word, a frightening word, a happy word and puts these in the word-bank and/or takes them from the word-bank to use in activities.
  for exploring one's identity—the child writes for and/or selects from word-bank
  - names of pets, favorite toys, books, colors, T.V. programs, movies
  - names of places of interest, places recently visited, places that would be exciting to explore
  - self-descriptive words for each letter in the child's name
  - a word describing something that is fun to do
  - names of special people, like parents, friends, teachers and attaches a photograph or picture the child has drawn to the name
  - words to be used in writing a brief autobiography
  - self-descriptive words for writing riddles, e.g.: "Who am I?" (e.g., "I like dogs. I have a sister named Vickie." Etc.)
  The child shares these with other children and the teacher.

---

*Anne Powers discusses how she taught first graders to build a classroom library using their experience stories. In doing this, they also learned how to use a library, and they shared their library with children in other grades. See Selected References (LEA).

- For *reading* purposes, these cards may be used
  for word analysis skills thus:
  - Children may label items in the room with words from their word banks. Then the children use the words in phrases or sentences.
  - After reading or listening to a poem or song, the children find words that rhyme with words in the selection.
  - Children select two words from their word banks and ask others: Do they rhyme? Do they end the same? Do they begin the same?
  - Children select words that begin the same as a picture they are shown.
  - Children select as many words as possible from a particular word family. The teacher may suggest a word, and children come up with as many derivatives as possible (e.g., rain, rains, rained, raining, raincoat, etc.)
  - Children arrange words according to the number of syllables in them, or similar vowels, consonants, etc.
  - Children find more than one name for the same thing (e.g., lady, mom, mother, wife, aunt, etc.).
  - Children pick any word. Then they find one that comes before it and after it in alphabetical order.
  - Children find a word for each letter of the alphabet.
  - Children find synonyms, antonyms, homophones, etc. They draw pictures and write sentences for each.
  - Children construct a long train or worm using synonyms or antonyms of the first word.

  for building comprehension, proceed thus
  - Children select a "naming word" or "string of words" and a "doing word" or "string of words." They combine them into a sentence, e.g.: The peacock is dancing.
  - Children cut out a picture from a magazine and write a title using word-bank words.
  - Children complete a sentence by using a word bank word, e.g.: "This is a ______ dog."
  - Children make a crossword puzzle using words from a friend's word bank. They give it to the friend to complete.
  - The teacher prepares a story omitting all nouns (or verbs, or adjectives). Children select words from their word banks to fill in the blanks.
  - Children select a word to be their "Word for the Day." They use it whenever possible that day.
  - Children make a shopping list using word bank words.
  - Children find words for things found in an ocean, a woods,

etc., or words used in playing ball, etc. They may write these on a chart and illustrate it.

- Children play "Scavenger Hunt" with words. The teacher gives each child a list of statements such as "Find a color word. Find the name of a farm animal. Find the name of a food." Children request words from particular classmates to fit each category.
- The teacher draws a "pet shop," "toy shop," etc., on the board. Children write words for things they could find in such a shop.

- For developing *language arts* abilities, these are suggested:

for developing oral language

- Children copy words onto paper "stones" and arrange them across a "river." They have a friend "cross the river" by saying each word and using it in a sentence when stepping on it.
- The teacher supplies a phrase like, "I'm going to Grandma's house, and I'm going to take . . ." Children supply nouns in alphabetical order, creating a list.
- A child selects a card and asks other children, "Guess what card I have?" The children respond by questioning the cardholder to discover the word. The cardholder responds "yes" or "no" until a player guesses the word.
- Several children put one word each into a paper sack. The first child draws a word and begins to tell a story using it. Children draw words successively and add to the story using these words.
- Children pantomime word-bank words.

for developing written language

- Children write a poem or story using one or more of their words.
- After participating in an activity, such as popping popcorn, children choose words related to the activity to enter into their word banks.
- The teacher adds punctuation marks to some of the cards. Children choose a card and use it in a sentence. Punctuation must fit the sentence.
- The teacher puts up a chart or begins a mobile. Children copy appropriate cards from their word banks and attach them.

□ *Providing for the Development of Thinking-Reading Abilities* The LEA provides excellent opportunities for the development of literal, inferential, evaluative, and appreciative level skills and abilities. Such abilities can be developed during all of the stages—experience, discussion, dictation (or writing), reading. Children can share their experience stories, critique the stories, respond to the stories, etc.

Children can make decisions when dictating or writing their own stories or when critiquing the stories of others about:

- Which details are appropriate? Are the important main ideas given and developed well? Does the sequence make sense? Would another ending be better? More interesting? Are directions clearly stated? Complete? Are cause-effect statements logical? Etc.
- Which statements are statements of reality? fantasy? Which are facts? opinions? Are statements valid? appropriate? acceptable? Etc.
- What is my emotional response to the given ideas? to the theme? Am I like any of the characters? Would I like to be? Would I like to be part of the account? What are my feelings about the language used? Can I vary my word choice? Can I help my classmates vary theirs? Can I see, feel, hear, smell, and/or touch (in my imagination) what has been described?

After reading this section you can, no doubt, see that the Language Experience Approach is a concept-bound, or concept-driven (top-down), approach to the teaching of reading. The passages that the children read originate in their own thinking: they come from the children's concepts, many of which are developed, enriched, and extended in the school setting. Because of the nature of the written material that the children are reading (their own dictated experiences) it is quite natural that their graphophonic, syntactic, and semantic cue systems will operate simultaneously,[6] provided they are taught to use these systems. Some suggestions for the use of these systems were given in this chapter. Others have been explained in Chapter 6 of this book. Also through the discussions, classroom interaction, and enriched experiences, children of all ages can learn to think and reason—to listen, speak, write, and read on all cognitive levels if the teacher makes provisions for this.

STRENGTHS AND WEAKNESSES

In considering the use of the Language Experience Approach in the teaching of reading, it might be well to consider its possible strengths and weaknesses. The following chart lists some of these.

TABLE 13.1   **Strengths and weaknesses of the Language Experience Approach**

Strengths	Weaknesses
• shows children that "talk can be written down" • encourages free talk and discussions and sharing and learning from others, higher level thinking skills and creativity • makes reading personal, concept-driven • helps children understand an author's position—and that authors are not infallible • encourages the expansion of experiences, the building of images in long-term storage • provides for the understanding of the concepts of sentence, phrase, word, letter (readiness) • provides for the understanding of punctuation marks • provides for the use of natural intonation, stress, and pitch as the child reads his or her own language • provides opportunities for bridging the gap between the child's dialect and the classroom dialect • provides for a means of acquiring a sight vocabulary, basic recoding skills, use of syntactic cues, and semantic cues • can be used prior to and concurrently with a basal or other approach and may even be integrated with that approach, e.g., basal stories may serve as experiences; children may complete stories after reading just to their climax; etc. • can be used to enrich content area learning	• requires much preparation by the teacher • requires a versatile, highly capable teacher who is knowledgeable in reading • may require the use of a teacher aide, especially for a large class • some skills may be neglected, but this is not inherent in the approach, nor is it necessarily a weakness • although children may make important gains in reading, these may not be evident on standardized reading tests. (Unfortunately, teachers are often judged by scores their children make on skills tests, *per se*, and/or on standardized tests.)

Basal Reading Approach and Programs

Basal reading programs are highly comprehensive in nature. Although individual programs differ a great deal—one from another—they are all concerned with the development of most aspects of reading—word recognition, vocabulary development, comprehension skill development on several levels of the cognitive domain, and presumably also with the enjoyment of reading.

Basal programs can be characterized by these terms: scope, sequence, and organization.

- *Scope* refers to the range of reading skills the program focuses on developing as well as the range of content included in lessons.
- *Sequence* relates to the order of the development of the skills and the order of the inclusion of specific topics or themes and literary forms.
- *Organization* involves harmoniously relating the following three components to each other: teaching style, children's capacities and interests, and instructional materials.*

SCOPE AND SEQUENCE

Levels

Each program component in a basal reading set, or series, is specifically graded to indicate its placement in the whole program. Each program has a series of readers that range in difficulty from the reading readiness stage up to sixth or eighth grade. Each of these readers is labeled to show its difficulty level in relation to the whole program.

Today most programs have several reading readiness books (or booklets), several soft cover preprimers, one or two primers, followed by a book usually appropriate (by the publisher's standards) for first grade, two books for second grade, two for third grade, and one for each of the middle grades. For example, one series is leveled and graded thus:

level number		grade	level number		grade
1	—	readiness 1	9		grade 2-2
2	—	readiness 2	10	—	grade 3-1
3	—	preprimer 1	11	—	grade 3-2
4	—	preprimer 2	12	—	grade 4
5	—	preprimer 3	13	—	grade 5
6	—	primer 1	14	—	grade 6
7	—	first grade	15	—	grade 7
8	—	grade 2-1	16	—	grade 8

Series differ in the number of readiness, preprimer, and primer books they include. Therefore, the above level-grade match is not appropriate for all series. Publishers who use level numbers rather than grade labels do so believing that this may promote individual or group (or even classwide) progression through the series at a pace related to the learn-

---

*The Informal Reading Inventory (IRI), designed to facilitate this relationship is described in Chapter 14. The IRI may be used to promote such a relationship with any type of materials. Also, test materials often accompany basal programs. These may be used for placement purposes and for testing mastery of skills, etc.

er's abilities, rather than as designated by grade level labels. Almost all of the newer programs use the level number labeling system.

Controls—Vocabulary and Syntax

Basal programs have always used controlled vocabularies. That is, the number of new words introduced at each level is controlled, and the characteristics of the words are controlled (e.g., regular letter-sound patterns, high frequency words, words thought to be of interest to children). In theory, introducing a limited number and type of new words per page or per book facilitates systematic teaching of word recognition skills and comprehension and provides for the number of repetitions necessary for learning each word. In practice, controlled vocabularies have often led to stilted stories. Authors of most newer basals have relaxed vocabulary control somewhat.

Some newer programs have built within them syntactic controls. There is an attempt to use sentence patterns that are in length and structure similar to those sentence patterns children who may be reading them use.

Skills and Interests

Basal program producers systematically and sequentially provide for the development of specific skills and often of appreciations. Programs differ in relationships to the timing of the teaching of subskills as well as the methodology used in teaching these subskills. Each publisher provides a "scope and sequence" chart that indicates which skills are provided for in the complete program as well as the level or levels at which each is taught.

Figure 13.1 shows a chart for levels 8 (2-1 reader), 9 (2-2 reader), and 10 (3-1 reader) from one publishing company* and is included to show the range (scope) and specificity of objectives for its program at these levels.

LESSON PLAN FORMAT

The lesson plan format used in most basal programs approximates what is commonly called a Directed Reading Activity (DRA). It typically has four steps:

(*continued on p. 541*)

---

*Economy Company, Oklahoma City, Oklahoma. Used by permission.

Comprehension Skills	**Lazy Circles** LEVEL 8	**The Livelong Day** LEVEL 9	**A Painted Ocean** LEVEL 10
LITERAL MEANING/INFERENCE	C1 Using context clues 　C1c synonyms 　C1d antonyms C2 Using aids to word meaning 　C2c abbreviations C3 Recognizing whole-part 　　relationships ＊ **C3c main idea** ＊ **C3d details** C4 Recognizing sequential 　　relationships 　C4a time and place 　**C4b ideas and events** C5 Recognizing causal 　　relationships ＊ **C5a cause and effect** 　**C5b predicting outcomes** C6 Recognizing comparative 　　relationships 　C6a similarities and differences C7 Using text signals of meaning 　C7c paragraphing **C15 Making inferences**	C1 Using context clues 　**C1a definitions** 　**C1b familiar experience** 　**C1c synonyms** 　**C1d antonyms** 　C1e homophones 　C1f homographs C2 Using aids to word meaning 　C2a technical words 　C2c abbreviations C3 Recognizing whole-part 　　relationships ＊ **C3c main idea** ＊ **C3d details** C4 Recognizing sequential 　　relationships 　**C4b ideas and events** C5 Recognizing causal 　　relationships ＊ **C5a cause and effect** 　**C5b predicting outcomes** C6 Recognizing comparative 　　relationships 　**C6a similarities and differences** 　**C6b classifying**	C1 Using context clues 　C1c synonyms 　C1d antonyms 　C1e homophones 　**C1f homographs** C3 Recognizing whole-part 　　relationships 　**C3c main idea** 　C3d details C4 Recognizing sequential 　　relationships 　**C4a time and place** C5 Recognizing causal 　　relationships 　C5a cause and effect 　C5b predicting outcomes C6 Recognizing comparative 　　relationships 　C6a similarities and differences
INTERPRETATION/ CRITICAL EVALUATION	C8 Recognizing forms of literature 　C8c poetry 　C8d play C9 Recognizing types of fiction 　C9a realistic fiction 　C9b fantasy C10 Recognizing elements of fiction 　**C10b characterization** C12 Developing oral reading 　　competence C13 Recognizing author's intent 　C13a entertain 　**C13b inform** C14 Recognizing stylistic devices 　**C14g imagery** 　**C14l mood** 　C14n humor	C8 Recognizing forms of literature 　C8c poetry 　C8d play C9 Recognizing types of fiction 　C9a realistic fiction 　**C9b fantasy** ＊ **C9c folklore** — fable, fairy tale, 　　legend C10 Recognizing elements of fiction 　**C10b characterization** 　**C10c setting** C11 Recognizing forms of nonfiction 　**C11a article** 　C11e written interview 　C11f biography C12 Developing oral reading 　　competence C13 Recognizing author's intent 　C13a entertain 　**C13b inform** 　C13d teach a lesson C14 Recognizing stylistic devices 　C14a figurative language — simile 　C14d rhythm 　C14e repetition 　C14g imagery 　C14l mood ＊ C14n humor	C8 Recognizing forms of literature 　C8c poetry 　C8d play C9 Recognizing types of fiction 　C9a realistic fiction 　C9b fantasy 　C9c folklore 　C9d historical fiction 　C9e science fiction C10 Recognizing elements of fiction 　**C10b characterization** 　**C10c setting** C11 Recognizing forms of nonfiction 　**C11a article** 　C11f biography C12 Developing oral reading 　　competence C13 Recognizing author's intent 　C13a entertain 　**C13b inform** C14 Recognizing stylistic devices 　C14a figurative language 　C14c onomatopoeia 　**C14g imagery** 　**C14l mood** 　C14n humor
	Increasing reading enjoyment	Increasing reading enjoyment	Increasing reading enjoyment

Note: Skills to be evaluated are indicated by boldface type.

*Indicates specific objectives for the lesson that is included in this chapter. The letter and number symbols used on this chart refer to the explanations in the *keys*, which set the skill being taught in a general perspective for the complete program. "C" preceding a number indicates the skill is a "comprehension skill," "S" indicates "study skill," and "W" means "word-analysis."

Figure 13.1

Skills		Column 1	Column 2	Column 3
Word-Analysis Skills	PHONETIC	**W15 Recognizing *eau* — /ū/, /ô/** W16 Recognizing *eigh* — /ā/ W20b Recognizing *ar* after *w* — /ôr/ **W20c Recognizing *ar* preceding *e* — /âr/** **W24 Recognizing *air* — /âr/** W27 Recognizing *ou, ow* — /ô/ W28d Recognizing *i* — /ē/ **W28e Recognizing *u* — /oo/** W28g Recognizing *ou* — /ô/, /oo/ **W28i Recognizing *ie* — /ē/** W30b Reviewing *c* — /s/ **W32b Recognizing *g* — /i/** W40 Recognizing consonant blends: *gl* — /gl/ **W43b Recognizing consonant digraphs: *gh* — /f/, silent** W45 Recognizing consonant digraphs: *ph* — /f/ **W53 Recognizing *gu* — /g/** W55 Recognizing *sc* before *e, i, y* — /s/	W3 Reviewing two or more vowel letters separated by more than one consonant letter W7 Reviewing *a* before *ll, lk, lt* — /ô/ W24 Reviewing *air* — /âr/ **W25 Reviewing *ear* — /ir/, /âr/, /ûr/** W28a Recognizing *o* — /oo/, /ū/ **W28g Recognizing *ou* — /ū/** W28k Reviewing *ew* — /ū/, /oo/ W34d Recognizing *s* before *ure* — /sh/, /zh/ **W40 Recognizing consonant blends: *tw* — /tw/; *spl* — /spl/, *sc* — /sk/, *scr* — /skr/** W48b Recognizing consonant digraphs: *wh* before *o* — /h/	W13 Reviewing *au, aw* — /ô/ W14 Reviewing *ay* — /ā/ W19a Reviewing *or* — /ôr/ **W20a Reviewing *ar* — /âr/** W21c Reviewing *ur* before *e* — /yoor/, /er/ W23 Reviewing a short vowel sound represented by *a, o, e, i,* preceding *rr* W27 Reviewing *ou, ow* — /ô/ **W28f Reviewing *oo* — /oo/, /oo/** **W28g Reviewing *ou* — /oo/, /oo/, /ô/, /ū/** W28i Reviewing *ea* — /ē/ W28k Reviewing *ew* — /ū/, /oo/ W30b Reviewing *c* — /s/ W35b Reviewing *t* before *u* — /ch/ W40 Reviewing *tch* — /ch/, *str* — /str/ W47 Reviewing *th* — /th/, /th/ W53 Reviewing *gu* — /g/ W54 Reviewing *qu* — /kw/
	STRUCTURAL	W10a Recognizing *ey* — /ā/ at the end of a monosyllable **W22 Reviewing *or, ar, er, ur* at the end of a plurisyllable — /ər/** **W58a Reviewing word division between double consonant letters** **W58b Reviewing word division between unlike consonant letters** W58c Reviewing word division between vowel letters and consonant letters **W67a Recognizing *tion* — /shen/** W67b Recognizing *tion* — /chen/ W72 Analyzing hyphenated compound words W73 Reviewing contractions **W74 Recognizing prefixes: *un, al*** **W75 Recognizing suffixes: *est*, *ed, ing*** W82a Reviewing the substitution of *i* for a final *y*	W22 Reviewing *or, ar, er, ur* at the end of a plurisyllable — /ər/ **W58d Dividing words between two vowel letters** W64b Recognizing *a* in syllables such as *ate, age, ace* — /ī/ **W68a Recognizing *sion* — /shen/** **W68b *sion* — /shen/** **W69,a,b Recognizing *tain*, stressed — /tan/; tain, unstressed — /ten/, /tn/** **W70a Recognizing *ex*, stressed — /ĕks/** **W70b Recognizing *ex*, unstressed before a consonant letter — /ĭks/, /ĕks/** **W70c Recognizing *ex*, unstressed before a vowel sound — /ĕgz/, /ĭgz/** ✾ **W72 Reviewing compound words** W73 Reviewing contractions **W74 Recognizing prefixes: *re*** W74 Reviewing *be* **W75 Recognizing suffixes: *less, or, ful, ed, ness*** W75 Reviewing *ment, en* W80a Reviewing the deletion of final *e* before an initial vowel suffix **W81 Recognizing the retention of final *e* preceded by *c* or *g*** **W82a Reviewing the substitution of *i* for a final *y***	W4 Recognizing a long vowel sound in a stressed syllable ending in a vowel letter W58a,b Reviewing word division between consonant letters **W58d Reviewing word division between two vowel letters** W62 Recognizing *o* at the end of a syllable — /e/, /ô/ W66 Reviewing *y* at the end of a syllable — /ī/, /ē/ W67a Reviewing *tion* — /shen/ **W70b Reviewing *ex*, unstressed before a consonant letter — /ĭks/, /ĕks/** ✱ **W72 Reviewing compound words** W74 Recognizing prefixes: *dis* **W75 Recognizing suffixes: *ish*, *ty*** **W75 Reviewing *ness*, *ment*** W77c Recognizing suffixes: *s* — /ĕz/, /iz/ W78b Reviewing *es* — /iz/, /ĕz/, /əz/

Study Skills		S18 Following directions
		S19 Locating information in books
		    S19a title page
		    S19c table of contents
		    S19f glossary
		S20 Using library sources
		    S20b dictionary — alphabetical order
		S21 Using graphic aids
		    S21a maps
		    S21f pictures
			S18 Following directions
			S19 Locating information in books
			    S19a title page
			    S19c table of contents
			    S19f glossary
			S20 Using library sources
			    S20b reference materials — alphabetical order
			    S20b reference materials — dictionary guide words
			S21 Using graphic aids
			  ● S21a maps
			    S21f pictures
			    S21g cartoons
				S18 Following directions
				S19 Locating information in books
				    S19b copyright page
				    S19f glossary
				S20 Using library sources
				    S20b dictionary
				    S20b encyclopedia
				S21 Using graphic aids
				    S21f pictures

Note: Skills to be evaluated are indicated by boldface type.

*Indicates specific objectives for the lesson that is included in this chapter. The letter and number symbols used on this chart refer to the explanations in the *keys*, which set the skill being taught in a general perspective for the complete program. "C" preceding a number indicates the skill is a "comprehension skill," "S" indicates "study skill," and "W" means "word-analysis."

Figure 13.1

- preparation for reading
- guided reading
- skill development and practice (prereading and/or postreading)
- extension activities

The lesson is thoroughly discussed and outlined in the teacher's manual which accompanies each level of reader. Frequently, additional materials (discussed later) are also available and referenced for use in attaining the objectives of each lesson. A lesson from one program is provided here.*

Overview Chart from Teacher's Manual

The following chart outlines the major objectives of the lesson, as well as the materials the teacher is to supply, and it references the related activity book and duplicating masters that relate to the lesson and are available from the publisher.

THUNDER IN THE MOUNTAINS: THE TRUE STORY OF KID COLORADO

Plan 25   Text Pages 157–166

Objectives	Materials	Activity Book	Duplicating Masters	Symbol and Word Cards
Comprehension Skills The pupil will **C9c** demonstrate the ability to recognize given tall tales as a type of fiction;		59	78	
C14n demonstrate the ability to identify humor as a stylistic device.		61	80	
Word-Analysis Skills The pupil will **W72*** demonstrate the ability to recognize and pronounce given compound words.	Chalkboard: birthday, birdhouse, summertime	58	77	
Study Skills The pupil will **S21a** demonstrate the ability to locate given points on a map.	U.S. map	60	79	
Glossary Words: earthquake, Wyoming				

*Louise Matteoni, *et al.* *The Livelong Day* (Level 9) pp. 157–166 and accompanying *Teacher's Manual*, pp. 129–133, 233, 235–36, 238–39, 240, 256, and *Activity Book*, pp. 58–61. Copyright © 1980, 1975, 1972 by The Economy Company. Used by permission of the publisher.

Preparation for Reading and Prereading Skill Development

The teachers' manual and accompanying materials provide for five activities before the guided reading of the lesson. The teacher may select from these—or may do none or all of them, according to the needs and interests of the children.

All of the suggested activities from the teacher's manual and the children's activity book are included here.

first: for enjoyment

INCREASING READING ENJOYMENT

Have the pupils bring magazines with many pictures in them to school. Instruct the pupils to make an imaginary animal by using parts of two or more pictures. Have each pupil write a tall tale telling the origin of his or her animal. Have volunteers put their stories with the pictures in the interest center of the fantasy world.

(This is a creative writing activity for the children. It may stretch the imagination and help the children relate to tall tales.)

second: word analysis skills (compounds)

Key:

PROCEDURE

WORD-ANALYSIS SKILLS

 **W72***

Skill Review   Recognizing compound words

Write the words **birthday, birdhouse,** and **summertime** on the chalkboard. Have individuals pronounce the words.

How are these words alike? (all are made of two words) What is a word called that is a combination of two or more words? (a compound word)

Have individuals go to the chalkboard and divide each word into two words with a vertical line.

Use Activity Book page 58 for further practice in recognizing compound words.

Use Duplicating Master 77 for further practice in recognizing compound words.

(This is a chalkboard activity directed by the teacher to help children recognize and then syllabicate compound words.)

COMPOUND WORDS

A compound word is a combination of two or more words.

snowman, scarecrow, upon, ice cream

The meaning of a compound word can often be determined by thinking of the meaning of the words that form it.

birdhouse, house for birds; cowhide, hide of a cow; towrope, rope used for towing

Words in a compound sometimes have a hyphen (-) between them.

shell-like, twenty-four, merry-go-round, man-of-war

A hyphen often joins two words that describe a noun if they precede the noun, but not if they follow it.

dark-gray rocks, rocks that are dark gray; well-known fact, fact that is well known

 **72**

In pronouncing a compound word, sound its syllables as in pronouncing any other word of more than one syllable.

(All "KEYS" are explanations for teachers.)

CHILDREN'S ACTIVITY BOOK—(RECOGNIZING COMPOUND WORDS)

Read the story and underline the compound words.

"We can't hide here until nighttime," said Burt. "My mom and dad will start to worry if I don't get home before dark."

"Tiptoe over here," said Yolanda, "and listen to my idea."

Yolanda whispered something to Burt.

Burt said, "That's a great idea!"

As they neared the place where Burt and Yolanda had been hiding, Curt and Natasha heard footsteps.

"Did you hear anything, Natasha?" said Curt.

Just then Burt walked from behind a garbage can to Curt and Natasha's car. He was holding a broomstick.

"Hi," said Burt cheerfully.

"Why, Burt," said Natasha, "whatever are you doing here?"

"Oh," said Burt, "I have a summertime job as caretaker for this place."

Just then Yolanda came by carrying a garbage can.

"This is my classmate Yolanda," said Burt. "She has a job here, too."

"Oh, Burt," said Yolanda, "it's almost dinnertime, and we have no way to get back to town."

"Perhaps we may be of service," said Curt.

"It would be nice if you could give us a ride to the nearest bus stop," answered Yolanda.

"We'll take you anyplace you wish to go," said Curt, "as long as I can find it."

"Well," said Burt, "downtown would be even nicer than the bus stop."

"Well, off we go," said Curt, and off they went.

Plan 25
W 72   Recognizing compound words

Directions: Help pupils read and follow the directions.

Exploration: Have pupils name things found in homes, the names of which are compound words, such as **bathtub** and **coffeepot.**

58

third: comprehension (recognizing tall tales)

COMPREHENSION SKILLS

O— C9c

Skill Development   Recognizing types of fiction: tall tales

Have you ever gone fishing and told somebody you caught a great big fish when you really caught a little one? Did you ever tell someone you climbed to the top of a very tall tree when you only climbed to the second branch?

What is a story called that is humorous and that makes the main character bigger, better, or braver than anyone else? (a tall tale)

Have pupils tell what they did after school one day. Then have them retell the story by exaggerating the events so much that it could not possibly have happened.

Use Activity Book page 59 for further practice in recognizing tall tales.

Use Duplicating Master 78 for further practice in recognizing tall tales.

(This is an additional activity to help children understand what a tall tale is.)

Key:

O— C9

Recognizing types of fiction

Fiction is imaginative narrative writing, usually in prose style. (See Key C8c Narrative poetry.) Learning to recognize the major types of fiction and the specific imaginative effects or qualities of each type can aid in the understanding and appreciation of literature. Some of the major types of fiction follow.

a. *Realistic fiction:* A story with believable characters and events, found most often in short stories and novels.
Examples: *Strawberry Girl*—Lois Lenski
To Kill a Mockingbird—Harper Lee
b. *Fantasy:* A highly fanciful story about characters, places, and events that are believable but that do not exist.
Examples: *Winnie-the-Pooh*—A. A. Milne
The Lord of the Rings—J. R. R. Tolkien
c. *Folklore:* Traditions, beliefs, and experiences of a people expressed in story and song. Some types of folklore follow.

Key:

Myth: A story designed to explain the mysteries of life and nature with bigger-than-life characters. Example: The Greek myth about Persephone, whose return from the underworld each year signaled the return of the spring season.

> *Tall tale:* A boastful story about impossible or exaggerated deeds performed by the central character but related in a realistic, matter-of-fact manner intended to be humorous.
> Examples: Tall tales about the deeds of legendary figures like Pecos Bill, Annie Oakley, or John Henry.

Fable: A story that teaches a moral lesson, frequently by means of animals with human characteristics.
Example: "The Hare and the Tortoise"—Aesop
Fairy tale: A folk story about real-life problems but usually involving imaginary characters and magical events.
Examples: "The Three Wishes"
"Rumpelstiltskin"
Legend: A folk story, handed down from generation to generation, about regional, national, or racial beliefs and concerns, usually a mixture of fact and imagination. In American Indian literature, legend is often closely related to myth.
Examples: "The Legend of Sleepy Hollow"—Washington Irving
"How the People Caught the Sun"—Kiowa legend
d. *Historical fiction:* A story of past events and characters, based in part on historical data.
Examples: *The Light in the Forest*—Conrad Richter
Gone With the Wind—Margaret Mitchell
e. *Science fiction:* A story of real or imagined scientific developments, often using elements of fantasy in a futuristic setting.
Examples: *A Wrinkle in Time*—Madeline L'Engle
A Trip To The Moon—Jules Verne

(This key is an explanation for the teacher, and includes the explanation of a tall tale, which is one type of fiction.)

CHILDREN'S ACTIVITY BOOK—(RECOGNIZING A TALL TALE)

Both of the selections below are from Reginald's book about dogs. Underline the title of the story that is a tall tale.

Big Dogs

Anyone who wants a dog as a pet must decide about the size of the dog.

Some people decide that they want small dogs.

Some people decide that they want big dogs.

A big dog eats more than a small dog, so the big dog costs more to feed.

A big dog that is not gentle can be trouble without meaning to be.

A big dog needs lots of room in which to move around.

A big dog should be exercised each day.

If a person can feed it and give it lots of room, a big dog can be a fine pet.

A big dog can be one of the best friends that a person has.

A Big Dog

Once there was a man who had a big dog.

Now, that dog was so big that it would not fit into the man's home.

So the man built a big barn in his yard.

The barn was bigger than the house, and the dog just fit into it.

When the dog was thirsty, it could drink a pond.

When it was hungry, it could eat a meal that was so big that it took five people just to carry it.

When the dog barked, people from Texas to Ohio covered their ears.

The dog was so big that it would not fit into the man's car.

Instead, the man would ride on the dog's back.

Plan 25
C9c Recognizing types of fiction: tall tale

Directions: Help pupils read and follow the directions.

Exploration: Have pupils illustrate the tall tale.

59

fourth: study skills (using maps)

STUDY SKILLS

 **S21a**

Skill Maintenance Using graphic aids: maps

Display a map of the United States and have pupils locate the state in which they live. Then have them locate the Rocky Mountains, Colorado, and Wyoming. Direct pupils to notice the length of the mountains as compared with the distance between two towns that are familiar to all the pupils.

Use Activity Book page 60 for further practice in using maps.

Use Duplicating Master 79 for further practice in using maps.

(This is a teacher directed activity designed to show the children the geographical setting of the tall tale they are about to read in their basal reader.

By comparing the distance between two towns with which they are familiar with the length of the Rocky Mountains, they will have some idea of the size of the area involved in the story.)

Key:

S21

Using graphic aids

Relating available graphic aids to what is read can help clarify meaning. Special care is needed with the more abstract aids to be sure that the symbols and relationships expressed are clear. Some of the most useful graphic aids follow.

a. *Map:* A representation of geographic regions, usually on two-dimensional surfaces.

CHILDREN'S ACTIVITY BOOK—(USING GRAPHIC AIDS)

Study the map and then read the story. Write in each blank **N, S, E,** or **W** to correctly complete the sentence.

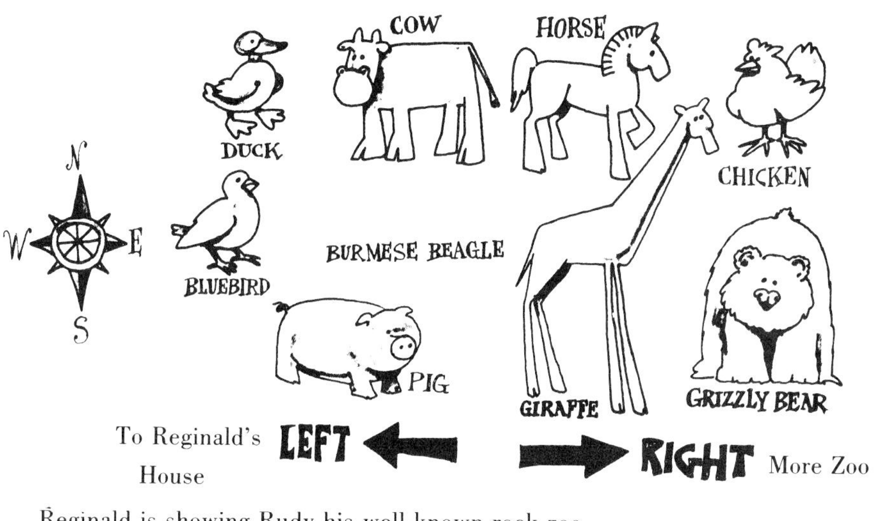

Reginald is showing Rudy his well-known rock zoo.

Rudy likes bears, so the men start their visit by looking at the grizzly bear.

Then they walk _______ to see the chicken and _______ to see the cow.

They go _______ from the cow to see the duck, and Rudy says that it is a beautiful duck.

"So, you like my duck, do you?" says Reginald, as he takes Rudy

_______ to see the bluebird.

While they are looking at the bluebird, Rudy asks about the place for the Burmese Beagle.

"Oh," says Reginald, "that's just _______ of here."

They go to see the place for the Burmese Beagle. Then they leave

the zoo and go _______ to get to Reginald's house.

Plan 25
S21a   Using graphic aids: maps

Directions: Help pupils read and follow the directions.

Exploration: Have each pupil draw a star at the place where the two men began their walk and a dotted line that shows their route through the zoo.

fifth: comprehension skills (recognizing humor)

COMPREHENSION SKILLS	Key:

 **C14n**

Skill Review   Recognizing stylistic devices: humor

If someone said that they had eaten fifty hot dogs in five minutes, would you laugh because that's too many hot dogs for a person to eat or would you be angry that they lied to you?

Why do you think the truth is sometimes exaggerated? (to make people laugh) Writers can sometimes make readers laugh by having the characters do something that most people don't usually do. Do you usually eat fifty hot dogs?

Listen to these sentences and decide which ones are funny:

1. Mary walked to school. <u>Mary's lamb skipped to school.</u>
2. The cow jumped over the small ditch. <u>The cow jumped over the moon.</u>
3. <u>Michael caught a whale.</u> Michael caught three fish.
4. Miguel rode his bike to town. <u>Miguel flew his bike to town.</u>

Use Activity Book page 61 for further practice in recognizing humor.

Use Duplicating Master 80 for further practice in recognizing humor.

(This is a teacher directed activity to help children understand exaggeration as a form of humor.)

 **C14**

Recognizing stylistic devices

Comprehension of meaning and appreciation of an author's effects often depend on the ability to recognize certain stylistic devices. Some major stylistic devices follow.

a. *Figurative language:* Use of words in ways to suggest other than the literal meaning—to say one thing in terms of something else.

Simile: A comparison between essentially unlike things, using the word *like* or *as*.

Example: He ran like a deer.

Metaphor: A comparison that is implied but not stated as in a simile.

Example: Angered by the remark, the young woman tossed her flowing red mane and pranced out of the office.

Hyperbole: Overstatement or exaggeration. The stating of something in terms greater than the situation requires, often used for the purpose of emphasis or for irony or satire. (See Irony and Satire below.)

Example: He ate a carload of groceries at one meal.

Personification: Giving human characteristics to animals or lifelike characteristics to inanimate objects.

Examples: The owl lectured.

The stone wept.

Idiom: A word combination with an accepted meaning that cannot be easily understood from the literal meanings of the individual words.

Examples: Rex was on pins and needles.

Cool it, Sally.

Pun: The use of a word or phrase to suggest more than one meaning, often humorous.

Example: "Stop, or I'll pull out all *stops* to *stop* you!"

Irony: A subtle form of ridicule or sarcasm in which words are used to mean the opposite of their literal meaning. Ironic statements are often based on overstatement. (See Hyperbole above.)

Example: "I can't imagine a more elegant suite," said the convict as he was pushed into the windowless cell.

Irony can also characterize entire passages or works when the author's tone (or attitude) is opposite to what the characters say and do, or when in a play (dramatic irony) the audience knows more about the situation than the characters do.

Some stylistic devices suggest meaning through different types of emphasis:

b. *Alliteration:* The repetition of the initial sounds, usually consonants, in two or more closely positioned words, reinforcing rhythm and rhyme.
Examples: living likeness
musical murmurs

c. *Onomatopoeia:* The use of words whose sounds suggest or emphasize their meaning.
Example: The bees buzzed busily.

d. *Rhythm:* A recurring pattern of sound, emphasis, or pulse.
Example: "Yó-ho-hó, and a bóttle of rúm!"

e. *Repetition:* The repeated use of words or ideas for emphasis or special effect.
Example: "I say, and I say again, that I will not I repeat will not—run again."

f. *Rhyme:* The repetition of similar or identical stressed sounds, occurring usually at the ends of lines of verse. (Lake-fate are similar rhymes; lake-fake are identical rhymes.) Rhyme provides pleasure through the recognition of like sounds being repeated, adds emphasis to the author's meaning and tone, and establishes the stanza form, or verse paragraph.

g. *Imagery:* The use of language to create sensory impressions, used to emphasize concrete sensory experience suggested by words rather than by concepts or ideas. Simile or metaphor are often present.
Examples: blood red
icy cold

h. *Allusion:* An indirect reference to well-known people, ideas, events, or places, used to emphasize and expand the author's meaning.

Examples: This is one time when a thumb in the dike won't be enough.
Well, this time he met his Waterloo.

Other stylistic devices that aid comprehension and appreciation follow.

i. *Foreshadowing:* Hints or clues of something important that will happen later in a narrative or play, usually given in a speech by a character or by special attention focused on an object or some aspect of nature. For example, a storm might foreshadow an intense conflict or disaster that will occur later in the story.

j. *Flashback:* A departure from the chronological events of a narrative or play in order to present scenes and incidents that occurred before the beginning of the story. Flashbacks fill in necessary background and explanatory material to help explain the characters' motives and actions.

k. *Tone:* The attitude taken by the author toward the subject or situation of a selection. Tone is inferred by the choice of words and the stylistic devices used. A narrative which uses numerous devices of irony would have an ironic tone, but a poem that contains pleasant images and a lilting rhythm would have a light or happy tone.

l. *Mood:* The emotional atmosphere of a narrative, poem, or play. Mood is suggested by the tone, the descriptive details used, the tempo of the action, the degree or type of suspense set up, and especially by the setting. An old deserted house on a dark and stormy night usually suggests a mood of mystery.

m. *Satire:* The use of wit, sarcasm, or irony to ridicule something the author thinks is foolish or evil. Satire is humorous criticism that may characterize various forms of expression, such as narratives, poems, plays, articles, informal essays, editorials, and cartoons.

---

n. *Humor:* Any manner of writing or form of expression, as a cartoon, that evokes laughter, often involving a failure of characters or incidents to conform to reasonable expectations. Humor also may use puns, satire, irony, and overstatement to achieve its effects.

(This key is an explanation for the teacher, including the explanation of "humor" for this lesson.)

CHILDREN'S ACTIVITY BOOK—(RECOGNIZING HUMOR)

Suzie needs material for the part of her magazine called "Funny Talk." Draw rings around the items below that are meant to be funny.

What is black and white and red all over?
A skunk that has been in the sun too long.

Rabbits like to eat carrots and green vegetables.

What is the longest word?
Smiles—because there is a mile between the first and the last letters.

A bike can't stand up by itself because it is two-tired.

The cost of clothes is going up and up.
Buy well-made things that will last a long time.

Television shows change with the seasons.

Child 1: Did you take a bath?
Child 2: No, is one lost?

Person A: I just saw something that had no legs run across the floor!
Person B: What was it?
Person A: The glass of milk that I dropped by mistake.

Plan 25
C14n Recognizing stylistic devices: humor

Directions: Help pupils read and follow the directions.

Exploration: Have pupils create humorous items for Suzie to include in "Funny Talk."

Guided Reading and Skill Development

The teacher guides the reading of the selection by introducing the lesson, providing motivation, and by stating general and/or specific purposes for reading.

> This lesson has an overall section that includes the introduction and motivation suggestions. It also includes suggestions for questioning and discussing the lesson section by section, here in three sections.

first: introduction and motivation

GUIDED READING

Introduction   Open your books to the table of contents. What story comes after "Jack and the Beanstalk"? ("Thunder in the Mountains") On what page does it begin? (157) Open your books to page 157.

Look at the first row of words under "We work with words." How are the words alike? (all begin with **kn**) What are the words?

Continue sounding words until the list is completed.

Look at the words listed under "Sound the words."

Have the words read aloud.

Call attention to the sentence under "Sight word."

Have pupils try to identify the underlined word by using clues from the context of the sentence and familiar sound-symbol relationships. Supply whatever help is needed.

Challenge words: Algonquin, cowboy, kid, roped, shot, shout, smile, tallest

Motivation   What is a mountain? How old do you think a mountain might be? How do you think mountains are made? "Thunder in the Mountains" is a humorous tall tale about the mighty deeds of Kid Colorado. Part of the title says this is a "true story." As you read the story, decide if you think the events could really happen.

> (The story begins on page 553 of this book.)

second: section-by-section reading (cause-effect, pp. 158–161 of the story; main idea, pp. 162–163 of the story; details, pp. 164–166 of the story.)

READING THE SELECTION

 **C5a**

Recognizing causal relationships: cause and effect

Turn to page 158. Read pages 158–161 silently to discover how the Rockies were made.

1. How were the Rockies made? (The Kid dug a sandpile for himself.)

2. Do you think anything in this story is exaggerated? What? (size of the Kid, amount of land he could dig up)

C3c

Recognizing whole-part relationships: main idea

Turn to page 162. Read pages 162 and 163 silently and decide on the main idea of each page.

3. What caused the land to shake? (the Kid riding Molly)

4. What do you think is the main idea of page 162? (The ground shook when the Kid rode his horse.)

5. What is the main idea of page 163? (Because of his size, the Kid could be a big help to people.)

6. How did the Kid help the people? (He pulled some mountains over to the other end of the Rockies to make pasture land for the ranchers.)

C3d

Recognizing whole-part relationships: details

Turn to page 164. Read pages 164–166 silently to find out what happened to Kid Colorado.

Key:

 **C5**

Recognizing causal relationships

To comprehend logical processes requires the ability to recognize causal relationships.

> a. *Cause and effect:* The association between an event and what brought it about, important for understanding a story, following an argument, or tracing the course of an experiment.
> Examples: He tired quickly because he had been sick.
> I hadn't realized how sleepy I was until my car ran off the road and I woke up in the hospital.

b. *Predicting outcomes:* The ability to make logical predictions from a series of facts or incidents.
Example: Ted's father makes him come home every night before dark, so I'm sure he won't let Ted go to a rock concert this weekend.

 **C3**

Recognizing whole-part relationships

Comprehension of a complete passage, which may range from a paragraph or a chapter to an entire book, can be aided by recognition of the following passage parts.

a. *Title:* A name, sometimes more specific than a topic, that indicates what a given passage is about.

b. *Topic:* The general category or class of ideas, often stated in a word or phrase, to which the ideas of the passage as a whole belong.

> c. *Main idea:* The major idea or proposition that is broad enough to cover the scope of the entire passage and that tells either directly or indirectly what the passage is about more adequately than the topic does.

> d. *Details:* Ideas, explanations, and events subordinate to the larger "whole" meaning of a passage but essentially contributing to an understanding of the larger meaning.
> Examples:
> *Topic:* Stage jitters
> *Title:* "Before the Curtain Rises"
> *Significant details:*
> John *pulled his ear* and *laughed nervously* as he took a last look at the script. Meg *paced up and down mumbling* to herself. George *cleared his throat* and *wiped his hands* across his shirt to remove the perspiration. Jane *peeked through the curtains* to see who was in the audience. Tom *arranged the props with trembling hands.* This was his first time to be in a play, and he wanted everything to be perfect. Everyone was tense. Would it never be time for the curtain to go up?
> *Main idea:* Each performer showed different nervous symptoms before the play began.

Thunder in the Mountains: The True Story of Kid Colorado

We work with words.

(51) know   knock   knife

(72) birthday   beanstalk   grandfather

(58d) Viola   fuel   create

Sound the words.

knees

earthquake

Rockies

wahoo

sandpile

Wyoming

Sight word.

My <u>ma</u> told me to stay home.

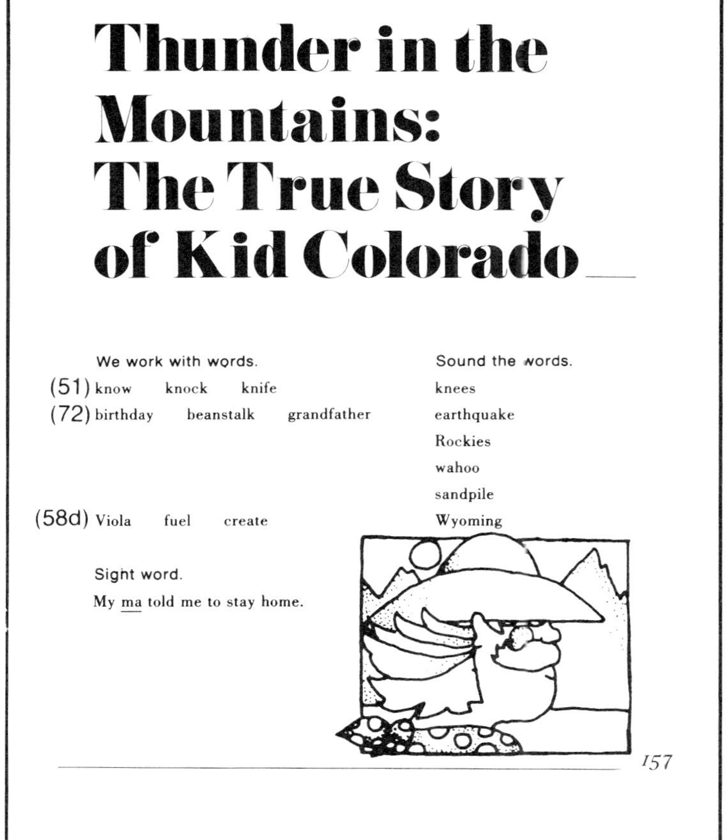

They called him Kid Colorado—the biggest, longest cowboy who ever rode a horse. The West will never see his equal.

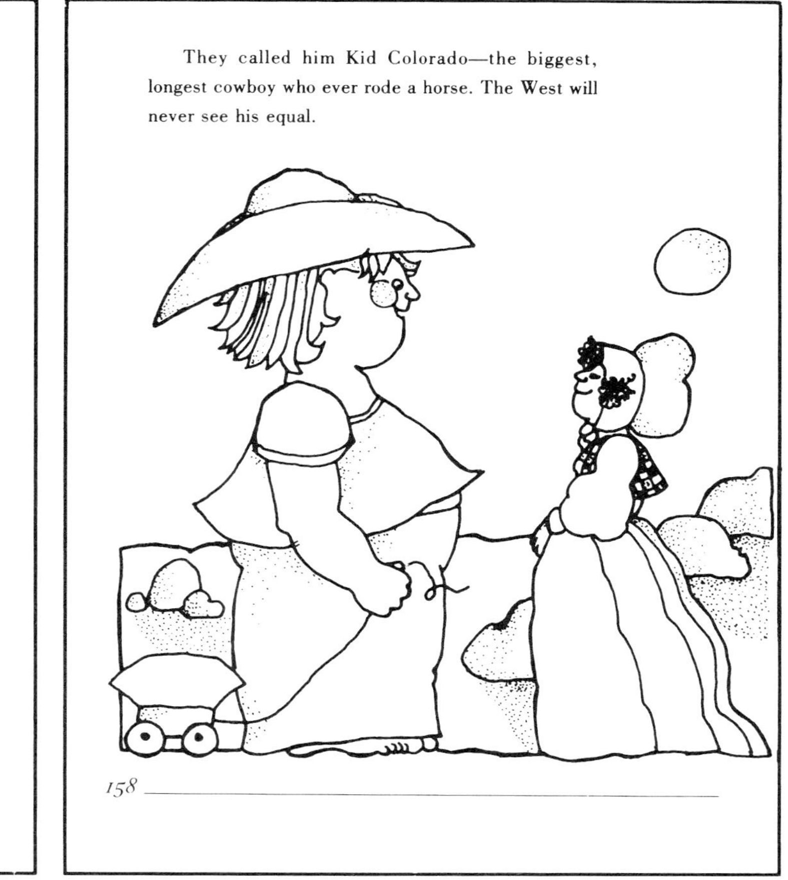

If it hadn't been for the Kid, Colorado wouldn't even have mountains, but more about that later on.

Kid Colorado was . . . Big. Why, even his baby shoes could have fit the Jolly Green Giant, almost. His ma never bounced him on her knees because, if she had, well, good-by knees, Ma.

Kid Colorado was big, yes. But he got bigger and bigger.

Came the day when he asked his ma for a sandpile.

She looked up at him . . . way up at him. And he could see her, way down there, shake her head.

"Sorry, my little boy," she called up to him, "but there's no sand around here. Just miles and miles of rocks and field, rocks and field, so you can't have a sandpile."

Now that might stop other children, but not Kid Colorado. He just went out into the field and dug up a pile of land, and another, and another. He dug all day and the next day and the next. Days ran into weeks, and weeks ran into a year. Still Kid Colorado dug. Then suddenly one day he was all through.

"Ma," he called, "come see my sandpile!"

But she had seen it by then. Who hadn't? Pile after pile of land and more land — the biggest "sandpile" the West had ever seen. True, there wasn't much sand in it, and true, there were a lot of rocks in it. Still, to Kid Colorado it was a sandpile. But after that the West was never the same, for Kid Colorado had put together the Rockies.

Well, Kid Colorado grew up . . . and up . . . and up. Next to him the Jolly Green Giant would just be small potatoes. He grew clean through the clouds, he did. And when he'd go galloping over the mountains on his great good horse, Molly, the land would shake all the way to Wyoming. All the way to Wyoming people would stop and look up.

"It's an earthquake," they said.

"It's thunder in the mountains," they said.

Then from far away they would hear a shout: "WA-HOOOOOOOOOOOO!!!!"

"It's Kid Colorado," they said. "Kid Colorado is at it again. Kid Colorado and his great good horse, Molly."

Being big (BIG!!!) Kid Colorado could be a big help to people, and he was. When the ranch hands had to have more pasture for their cattle, the Kid just jumped on Molly and roped a clump of mountains at the tail end of the Rockies. He said, "Get up, Molly!" and she got up.

Then he and Molly pulled those roped mountains clean over to the other end of the Rockies. That left a big space for pasture. And that's how Colorado got all that nice pasture land.

163

Kid Colorado would be there still, out in Colorado, galloping around on his great good horse, Molly. But something happened to Kid Colorado, and her name was Morning Sun. She was an Algonquin. It happened like this:

One day the Kid was galloping over the mountains, going "WA-HOOOOOOOOOOOO!!!" Suddenly the land under him began to shake more than ever before.

"It's an earthquake!" said Kid Colorado. "It's thunder in the mountains!" said Kid Colorado. Then from somewhere came "WA-HOOOOOOO!!!"

164

She came galloping around the mountains when she came. "Whoa, Goldenrod!" she said to her great gold horse. "Why, hello there," she said to Kid Colorado.

And the Kid almost fell off his great good horse, Molly, for there before him was the tallest, longest girl he had ever seen.

The West will never see her equal.

"I'm Morning Sun," she said and she shot Kid Colorado a smile like . . . guess what. Well, that did it. The Kid was done for. Love had hit him like pie in the face.

"WA-HOOOOOOOOOOOOOOOOOOOO! !" he said. Then he could feel his face get red, and he forgot his name, and he couldn't think of what to say. So he said, "Come on! I'll race you!"

People in the West remember that day well, because that day the land shook all the way to Japan. After that, Kid Colorado and Morning Sun were never seen again.

Still, sometimes, when you're in the mountains, you can feel the land begin to shake under you, and you look up.

"It's an earthquake!" you say.

"It's thunder in the mountains!" you say.

But — what was that? Did you just hear something? It seemed to come from far and far and far away, didn't it? It sounded like "WA-HOOOOOOOOO!!!" — now, didn't it?

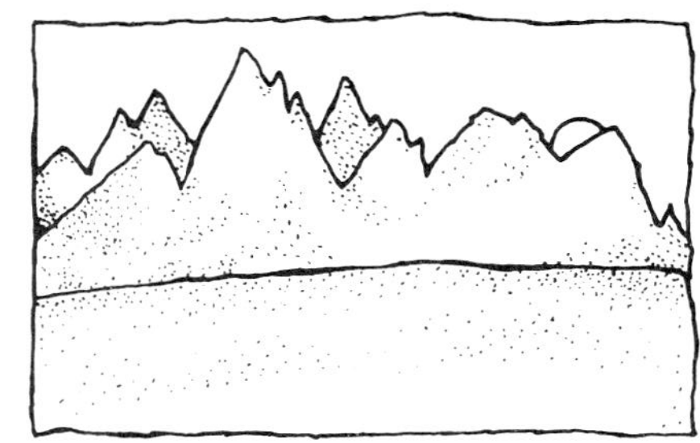

557

third: postreading guided reading

7. Whom did Kid Colorado meet? (Morning Sun)

8. How big was Morning Sun? (the tallest, longest girl the Kid had ever seen)

9. What did the Kid say to Morning Sun? ("Come on! I'll race you!")

10. How many times were the Kid and Morning Sun seen after they raced? (never)

Unit Theme

11. Why do you think things about the Kid were exaggered so much? Does this help to make a story humorous?

REREADING

C9c

Recognizing types of fiction: tall tales

Have the pupils read aloud passages from the story that have been exaggerated so much that they could not possibly be true.

Extension Activities (Postreading Skill Development and Enjoyment)

INDIVIDUALIZING INSTRUCTION

 **C14n**

Recognizing stylistic devices: humor

1. Have individuals read aloud passages from books that they found funny. Have them tell why they thought the passages were funny.

2. Have each pupil write a joke or riddle. Collect the jokes and riddles and combine them to make a class joke book to be kept in the library.

 **W72**

Recognizing compound words

1. Have each pupil describe a compound word through a picture. For example, a birdhouse could be shown by drawing a bird and a house. Have the rest of the group decide the compound word each picture depicts.

2. Write the words **birdhouse, doghouse, bookstore, seafood,** and **earthquake** on poster board worms. Cut the worms in half between the words within each compound word. Have individuals match the halves to make compound words.

KEYS were shown accompanying guides and materials used before guided reading.

Note: This has been one lesson from one basal series. It can't be assumed that this lesson is representative of all lessons in the series or of lessons in other series. It does, however, use the commonly found four-step lesson plan—preparation for reading, guided reading, skill development and practice (prereading and/or postreading), and extension activities.

AVAILABLE SUPPLEMENTARY MATERIALS

In addition to the children's books, the following types of materials are often available from publishers of basal programs.

Teacher's manual. A teacher's manual is always available. It almost always includes very specific suggestions for teaching each lesson, usually in four steps as shown in the previous lesson: preparation, guided reading, skill development and practice (prereading and/or postreading), and extension activities.

Children's workbooks are also available. In them activities are included for the development of skills and perhaps reading enjoyment. The teacher's manual usually cross-references these to specific lessons included in the children's readers. Variations are: boxes and kits of materials.

Teacher's editions of the workbooks are also available, showing how activities may be used and supplying correct answers.

Test materials are usually available. These include placement tests and mastery tests as they relate to the specific level of basal to use with each child and specific skills needed and mastered by each child.

Duplicating masters are frequently available. These may be designed for skill development and for the development of enjoyment. These may replace the children's workbooks.

Tapes may be available to introduce and reinforce skills. Also read-along tapes may be available. Sometimes tapes of an author reading stories are available. Children may follow along, reading from their books. Sometimes read-along tapes are for use with supplementary books.

Supplementary paperbacks may be available that relate to the content of the reading materials of the basals.

Picture and word cards may also be available for use in teaching meanings and word recognition.

Pocket charts may also be available with word, phrase, sentence, and picture cards correlated with basal passages.

ORGANIZATION FOR INSTRUCTION

As stated previously, organization involves harmoniously relating the following components to each other: teaching style, children's capacities and interests, and instructional materials. Since it should be expected that children in an individual class are reading on many different levels, both grouping for instruction and individualizing instruction are appropriate when using basal materials.

Some school systems use a tribasal program—that is, three different basals are used in a classroom, one for each of three groups of children. Often these basals are from different companies so that the average group and slower group of children do not hear discussions of lessons they will have at a later time. Children are placed into a set of materials most appropriate for their reading achievement levels, perhaps by using the placement test materials that accompany the basals or perhaps by using Informal Reading Inventories* designed by the classroom teacher. To assume that all children in a classroom can be taught by using only

---

*Explained in Chapter 14.

three different levels of basals would require the stretching of reality. Those children who are unusually accelerated or slow in achievement very likely will need other appropriate levels of materials if they are using basal materials, or they may be taught using another approach. With many children, the Language Experience Approach can be used along with the basal lesson to provide for the introduction and review of vocabulary, for the expansion of concepts, etc. This latter was exemplified in the manual suggestion accompanying the lesson given in this section: the first step was a suggestion that children write a tall tale.

Correlated supplementary materials, both for skill and interest development, are vast. The teacher should choose for each child those activities that the child particularly needs and/or will enjoy. And, although specific lesson guides are provided in teacher's manuals, there seems to be no reason that teachers must follow them specifically as outlined. Each teacher should modify the lesson guides to make them appropriate for the children being taught.

The teacher will have to spend his or her time with each group during the guided reading part of a lesson, but each group may work with little teacher-contact time during the other parts of a lesson. You may wish to review the chart (Table 3.2) given in Chapter 3 of this book which shows one way in which three different groups of children might be engaged in reading activities simultaneously for about an hour each day.

Discussion

As can be seen, basal reader programs provide highly comprehensive plans and a wide variety of materials on many levels to help make the teaching of reading systematic and successful. Many publishing companies produce basal materials, and each company has a distinctive philosophy which governs the skills taught, the content included, and the organization of these. States and/or school districts, thus, have a wide range from which to choose in terms of skills that are emphasized and content. More than 90 percent of American elementary school teachers who teach reading use one or more basal programs.

Strengths and Weaknesses

Table 13.2 lists possible strengths and weaknesses of basal programs.

TABLE 13.2   Strengths and weaknesses of basal reading programs

Strengths	Weaknesses
• skills are presented sequentially, and a scope-and-sequence chart identifies exactly what is taught at each level • there is a gradual, or paced, introduction of vocabulary and word analysis skills • programs provide for a continuity of skill development through the grades—introduction, teaching, reinforcement, testing • many activities are provided for the teaching of skills; children who need much reinforcement may do many activities, whereas other children may do a minimum amount of skill work • the teaching of skills is coordinated with the teaching of reading selections: skill work is not drill in isolation • most teachers are able to follow manual directions successfully • the basal program can be combined with other approaches, but a strong attempt should be made to coordinate multiple programs.	• skills are introduced and taught at a time prescribed by the program, rather than when needed by the child. (What may be a strength may also be weakness.) • many critics believe there is too much vocabulary control • sentences are frequently unnatural—not child language • stories are frequently not interesting to children and/or are not related by the teacher to the children's interests • multiple levels must be used in a classroom, making classroom management a problem for some teachers, but this is true in any teaching situation • teachers frequently over-rely or under-rely on the use of manuals and frequently do not utilize the child's related schemata enough. (This is not the fault of the programs, but of the teacher's naïveté about them.)

Linguistic Approaches

Linguists study language scientifically. Some of them have applied their knowledge to the development of reading programs. Two distinctly different types of programs have evolved: those based on the phonology of English and those based on sentence structure (syntax).

PHONOLOGICAL PROGRAMS: CODE EMPHASIS

Two well-known phonological programs are the Bloomfield-Barnhart *Let's Read*[7] series and C.C. Fries' Merrill *Linguistic Readers*.[8] Neither of these programs uses phonics. Instead they use a spelling approach to recoding or decoding. Both programs carefully control words that are introduced according to spelling patterns. The initial unit of instruction is the word.

In the *Let's Read* series, each word (or syllable) after the first word is a minimal contrast of the preceding word: e.g., cat → fat → rat. The program is strictly a recoding program, and no pictures are used in it. Words are first spelled and then pronounced—one at a time.

The Merrill series was designed to teach children to recognize in print "those words that they already know orally or aurally." Another objective was to teach children to read in a normal speaking way - using normal intonation and phrasing. The program is famous for the use of "spelling patterns" and a careful control of words using these patterns. Patterns used are, first: consonant-vowel-consonant, second: consonant-vowel-consonant-e, third: vowel pairs. The program was designed in an attempt to produce readers who would automatically recognize visual patterns and, therefore, could direct their attention to meaning and to relating the author's message to their own past experiences.

Following are two pages from *Book 1*, pages 6 and 7, of the *Merrill Linguistic Readers.**

A Cat	**Nat**
Nat is a cat.	Is Nat a cat?
Nat is fat.	Nat is a cat.
Nat is a fat cat.	Nat is a fat cat.

It can be seen that the pattern being taught in this lesson is the "consonant-a-consonant" pattern. Words not fitting this pattern have been taught as "sight words": *a, is*. The commonly taught phonic generalization is never taught. Instead, the "c-a-c" words are orally spelled after they are pronounced. It is assumed that after saying and then orally spelling many words of a single pattern, children will recognize the visual pattern-sound pattern relationships and that this will enable them to recognize previously taught words when they are seen again and also will transfer to untaught words and syllables of the same pattern.

---

*Charles C. Fries, Agnes C. Fries, Resemary G. Wilson, and Mildred K. Rudolph. *Merrill Linguistic Readers, Book 1*, pages 6–7. Columbus, Ohio: Chas. E. Merrill Publishing Co., 1966. Used by permission of the publishing company.

STRUCTURAL PROGRAMS

Two well-known linguistic programs that stress sentence reading from the beginning are the *Miami Linguistic Readers*[9] and the *Sounds of Language*[10] program. Both of these programs have been designed to integrate the language arts of reading, listening, speaking, and writing.

The *Miami Linguistic Readers* were designed to teach English to Cuban-Spanish speakers. Robert C. Aukerman[11] states that the rationale for developing these readers was twofold: "(1) to develop books which were 'culture-free,' and which would have themes with which children of any background could relate; (2) to develop books which would provide an approach to American English with the least amount of phonemic irregularity . . . " The initial emphasis of the program is on speaking and listening because the children for whom the program was designed did not speak English.

Differing from the phonological programs, the *Miami Linguistic Readers* included these objectives: interest, the use of natural language forms, the necessity for the child to have aural-oral control of the material he or she is expected to read, the control of grammatical structure and the emphasis in teaching on phrase and sentence length structures, the correlation of all the language arts including writing experiences that reinforce listening, speaking, and reading, and learner success. Every lesson includes listening, speaking, writing, spelling, and reading.[12]

The *Sounds of Language* readers were designed with the principal objective of making reading a joyous experience. The program is based on the premise that[13]

- language is learned first in the ear, then in the eye,
- sentence sounds are more important than individual word sounds
- a reading selection should be taught as a total linguistic experience from which children can analyze language and literature, and verbalize their understanding of how they work.

Cassette recordings are available of Bill Martin, an author along with Peggy Brogan, reading to a musical background supplied by a guitarist. Children are encouraged to listen first and then to join in choral reading of the passages. Two lessons from the teacher's edition of the preprimer and first primer are included here.*

---

*Bill Martin, Jr., and Peggy Brogan. *Sounds I Remember* (Preprimer 1) 1974, pp. 12–15, and *Sounds of Numbers* (Primer 1) 1972, p. 56. Also *Teacher's Edition*, Preprimer 1, pp. 74–77, 84–85. Used by permission of Bill Martin, Jr., and of Holt, Rinehart and Winston, Publishers.

(Teacher's manual includes the comments and the boxing of the word *hare* with suggested word substitutions.)

From the preprimer:

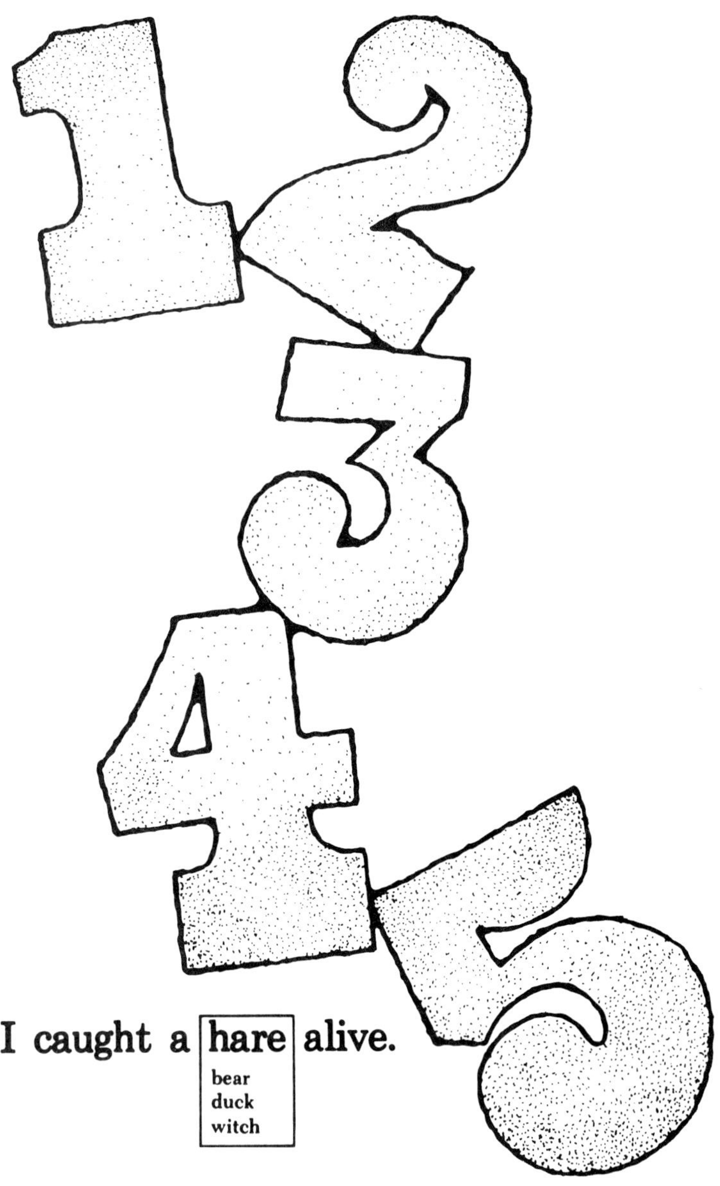

After children are familiar with this jingle and are chanting it fluently, you may want to use this sentence for transforming: 1) write the sentence on the board, 2) "Children, suppose we didn't want to say the word *hare*, what other words could we use?"

12

Most children recognize numbers in their printed forms before they recognize words. In this pre-primer, therefore, we have made broad use of number forms to help children know that they can figure out what they find on the printed page. The various number shapes also help them know that print has a dependable system and that once they recognize these shapes, they are engaged in the reading of words. The numbers in this and other selections invite sequence reading and an awareness of the one-to-one relationship of sound and printed symbol. Your oral use of this jingle from time to time ("1, 2, 3, 4, 5, I caught Janet alive, etc.") will help children know that all of the new language they are learning from day to day is theirs to use in personal situations. In other words, their natural way of learning oral language before they came to school is still available to them now that they're using books.

an old rhyme, pictures by Cornelio Martinez   **13**

14

Plan to come back to this jingle at various times during the year, using it for different purposes and enjoyment. This is germane to the SOUNDS OF LANGUAGE program which, first, attunes children's ears, then their tongues, then their eyes to print, and, finally, makes multiple use of the selections in the children's linguistic repertoire.

You may wish to

1) transform a sentence as shown on the preceding
spread;
2) offer the children word cards
from the jingle or the transformed sentence;
3) use the numbers as a stimulus
for counting to 10;
4) talk about the shape of a letter
or a word or a number;
5) talk about the artist
and his way of picturing the jingle;
6) use the jingle as a choral reading
with the boys chanting the numbers,
the girls chanting the words;
7) engage in an open-ended discussion
of whether or not you can
catch a hare alive,
and if so, would you let him go.

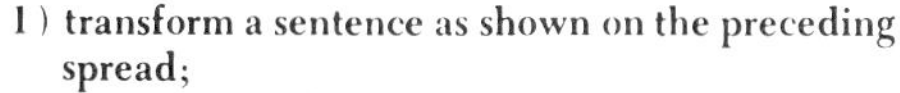

15

From the primer:

The Purple Cow

by Gelett Burgess

I never saw a Purple Cow,

I never hope to see one;

But I can tell you, anyhow,

I'd rather see than be one.

Learning sequence: a) listening, b) picture reading and speculating, c) reading aloud, d) choral speaking. See also on pages following "Transforming Sentences."

Additional pages from the back of the teacher's edition of the Primer 1 give suggestions for "Innovating on Sentence Patterns," first using the verse from the children's edition of that level, and on "Transforming and Expanding Sentences" beginning with a sentence from Reader 4. Such suggestions have direct applications for use with the Language Experience Approach also.

7 INNOVATING ON SENTENCE PATTERNS

By now you know
that when you read aloud to children
you are depositing various sentence patterns
in the children's linguistic storehouses
for a lifetime of use.
You probably are also aware
that when the children chime in on the reading,
especially in alive and dramatic ways
that include bodily movement,
they are themselves claiming and depositing these patterns.
One further activity
to help make these basic sentence structures
easily available to children for word-unlocking
in their reading and for writing and speaking,
is to invite them into systematic
and at the same time creative and lively experimenting
with the various patterns.
Here are four sentence manipulations
which have proved especially useful
for this kind of experimentation.

74 TE Innovating on Sentence Patterns

A) Transforming Sentences

Transforming a sentence
is the act of using the exact structure of a sentence
as the basis for creating a semantically new sentence
through either word-by-word substitution
or substitution of whole clusters of words.

> I never saw a purple cow.
>
> —from *Sounds of Numbers*

Your first step in helping children transform this sentence,
after all of you have enjoyed reading the whole poem
from which it came,
is to copy the model sentence on the chalkboard,
leaving space between each word.
Then your conversation goes something like this:

> *Children, I'm going to draw a line*
> *to the word* cow.
> *Now, supposing we didn't want*
> *to use the word* cow.
> *What other words could we use*
> *instead of* cow?

Suggestions will begin to flow.

> I never saw a purple cow.
> horse
> pig
> rabbit

Children, all of our naming words are animals.
Supposing we wanted another kind of naming word—
one that would make a spooky sentence.

> I never saw a purple cow.
> horse
> pig
> rabbit
> spook
> vampire

Now, children, supposing we didn't want
to use the word purple?
Who else has a describing word?

Again the suggestions will flow.

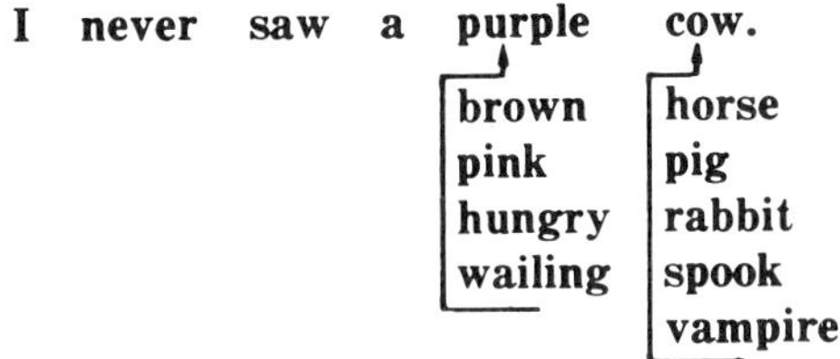

And so it goes until the children have suggested
vocabulary substitutions for all of the words.
You may wish to enter the game,
especially if the children are not having fun
with the substitutions they suggest.

Children, does anyone in this class
like silly sentences?
Well, I'm going to give you a new action word
that will really make a silly sentence.

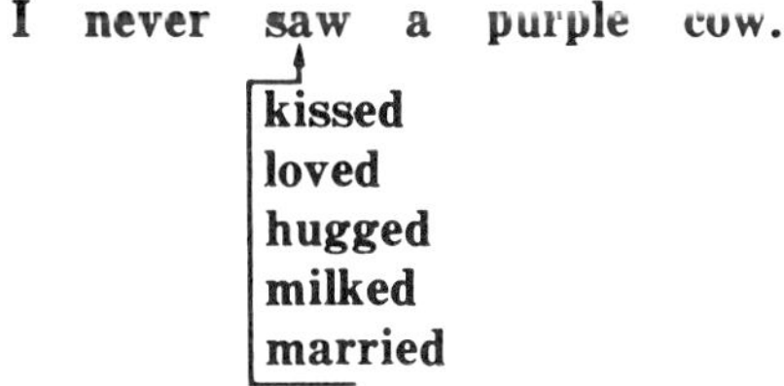

Now the lid is off and the children's merriment
knows no bounds as they contemplate kissing purple vampires
and marrying pink spooks.
You may wish to invite the children

76 TE Transforming Sentences

to go back to their tables
to write sentences of their choice.
At some point you may wish
to begin gentle conversation
about the word order in the sentence.

> *Isn't it interesting, children,*
> *that we don't say:*

> **I never saw a cow purple.**

> *I wonder why not.*

The children will probably suggest
that it just doesn't sound good—
meaning that their ears have already picked up
the usual word order in English sentences.
Gradually these kinds of conversations
help children add information
to their growing notions about how sentences work.
The *Sounds of Language* readers abound
in useful sentence patterns for the children to transform.
We have annotated a few of these sentences
to get you and the children started.
No attempt has been made to annotate every sentence
that lends itself to this kind of language analysis.
The peak value of the activity will come
when you and the children learn to go over a story
after enjoying it in its wholeness,
perusing it for *model sentences* rich in analysis potential.
It is your and the children's own selection
and manipulation of *model sentences*
that firmly connects the language learnings
with a child's personal use of language.
This is a qualitatively different learning experience
from that of filling in little blanks
in typical language workbooks.

Transforming Sentences TE 77

C) Transforming and Expanding Sentences

As children gain skill in sentence manipulations,
they will undoubtedly want to combine
two or more of the methods suggested here.
For example, colorful sentence possibilities emerge
when a model sentence is both transformed and expanded.
Consider the wide range of sentences
that is inherent in this diagram:

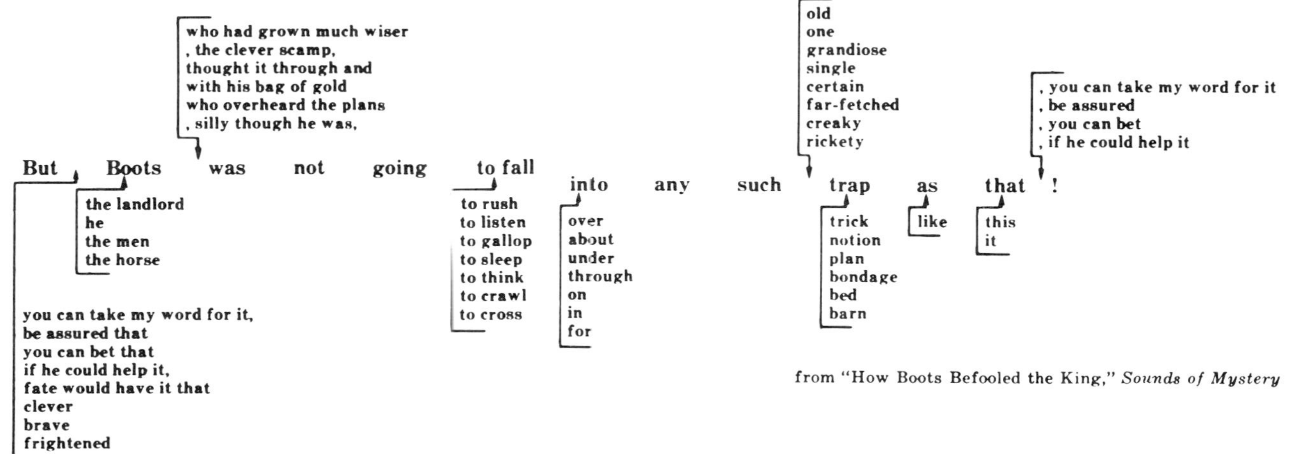

from "How Boots Befooled the King," *Sounds of Mystery*

DISCUSSION

Linguistic programs within each type are very different—one from another. Similarities among those programs classified as phonological are that all stress a spelling approach, rather than a phonic approach, to recoding and there is extremely careful control of words introduced so that all words fit the pattern being taught. (However, C.C. Fries' series does introduce some "sight words" that do not fit the pattern.) Programs differ in the amount of emphasis they give to the importance of meaning.

Structural programs, on the other hand, do stress meaning and often enjoyment, and are designed to teach oral English as well as reading. Sentences (or longer passages) are the initial units of instruction. These are manipulated by using word or phrase substitution and elaboration techniques.

STRENGTHS AND WEAKNESSES

TABLE 13.3   Strengths and weaknesses of linguistic phonological programs

Strengths	Weaknesses
• regular and paced introduction of spelling patterns. This may be a strength, especially for a person having extreme difficulty learning sound-symbol relationships.	• controls on introduction of vocabulary are extremely stringent • in some programs, sentences are almost always artificial • it is often assumed that children will learn symbol-sound relationships without being taught—simply through repetition of similar spelling patterns • little or no context (meaning) in some programs

TABLE 13.4   Strengths and weaknesses of linguistic structural programs

Strengths	Weaknesses
• sentence patterns and vocabulary are designed for use by specific children at a pace for those children and are appropriate for use with those children • an imaginative program (e.g., *The Sounds of Language*) with strong verse is interesting to children, helps children develop language power, and can be used to encourage creativity. It also lends itself to use as a supplementary reader in some programs and to choral reading	• some programs (e.g., *Miami Linguistic Readers*) may be appropriate for regional use only, though one of its major objectives was that it be "culture-free"

Single points given in the preceding evaluations may be appropriate for some, but not all, of the programs in the given categories. Individual programs will have to be reviewed by the reader of this book to make appropriate evaluations for each program.

Individualized Reading

RATIONALE

Individualized reading can be defined in many ways. For example, skill development might be individualized, as might recreational reading and research reading. People who talk about Individualized Reading as a core program, however, are likely to define it by using Willard C. Olson's[14] descriptive terms: seeking, self-selection, and pacing. These terms can be defined thus:

- *seeking* - the child seeks her or his own interests; that is, the child decides upon the content of the material that will be read.
- *self-selection* - the child selects the materials that will be read.-
- *pacing* - the child reads as much or as little as he or she desires.

Seeking. Although some children may be able to define their own interests, most reading experts would contend that reading programs - and teachers - should have as a major aim the broadening of interests. This is true of any reading program, including Individualized Reading. Tom Barrett suggests that, "an active effort should be made to make students aware of the variety of subjects and ideas about which people write. . . . Even more important is the act of involving pupils in reading materials that they would not pursue if they were left to their own devices."[15]

Barrett suggests that systematic oral reading by the teacher provides one avenue for broadening interests. This means daily reading of carefully selected materials that would expose children to a variety of topics, types of materials, and styles of writing. If children are given the time and opportunity to share materials and ideas obtained from reading, further extension of interests is likely.

Self-selection. The child, of course, selects materials from those that are available. The school's responsibility is to provide materials on a wide range of topics as well as a wide range of forms—books, magazines, newspapers, travel folders, etc. Poetry, stories, biographies, how-to-do-it passages, etc., should be available. Children must also be encouraged and taught to select materials at school and local libraries.

Self-pacing. Implicit in this program is that some children will read more than others, and all children will read at levels appropriate to them. Children keep an on-going record of books they have read and usually, also, of activities they have done. Building classwide bookworms, pie charts, or reading trains might be appropriate to show the amount and range of reading done by all children together.

TEACHING COMPONENT

Since children select their own materials to read, and since the reading of a variety of materials may require the use of a variety of skills, the identification of skills to be taught must be individualized. Such identification, or diagnosis, requires the use of student-teacher conferences.

Individual Conferences

Individual conferences need to be scheduled regularly. During each conference, the child will probably read to the teacher from the book or other material he or she has selected. During this conference, the teacher listens, takes notes, and asks questions to see if the child understands what is being read. The teacher observes the degree of interest the child has in the material and may offer suggestions about future reading materials.

The teacher will listen to determine the child's oral reading achievement and needs.* For example:

- are phrasing and intonation patterns appropriate? Does the child need help in this area? What kind of help?
- does the child omit words? regress and repeat words?
- does the child hesitate often?
- does the child use context (syntactic, semantic, etc.) in recoding words and in arriving at meanings of words and larger units?
- does the child have adequate phonic skills to recode words that he or she cannot otherwise recognize by using contextual clues?
- does the child need help in the application of syntactic cues, semantic cues, *specific* phonic cues? If so, what specific kinds of help are needed?
- etc.

---

*Diagnostic techniques are explained in more detail in Chapter 14.

Additionally, the teacher will ask questions to determine the degree to which the child understands the ideas being read. The teacher may ask himself or herself:

- does the child relate what is being read to what she or he already knows about the subject? Does the child need help in doing this?
- does the child recognize important details? grasp main ideas? sequential patterns? Does the child need help in any of these areas? If so, what kind of help?
- if the topic is controversial, does the child recognize that there are various points of view about it? Is the child willing and able to read these other ideas?
- is the child able to use the information gained through reading in practical—or other—situations (if the material lends itself to this)? Does the child need help in doing this?
- etc.

The teacher will also wish to know, when appropriate, if the child empathizes with the characters and/or whether the child is able to live vicariously through reading, also whether the child enjoys the reading material. The teacher may discuss with the child whether

- he or she imagines himself or herself to be living along with the story.
- which character the child would most (or least) like to be and why.
- the child reads rapidly enough to lose herself or himself in the book, or if the child is plodding along—reading word by word. Is the material too difficult? Does the child need help in selecting material at an appropriate level?
- the child enjoys the material being read.
- the child needs help in broadening and/or intensifying interests. The teacher may simply recognize that such help is needed and may supply it, but should refrain from "pushing."
- etc.

Also, the teacher may seek answers to other questions.

Once a teacher finds the answers to such questions as the above (or when finding the answers), teaching should begin. Ideally such teaching would be a part of the conference, or would be initiated during the conference. However, time may be too short for this to occur. This is where teachers may run into serious problems.

Ideally there should be several conferences each week with each child. Let us imagine that we have two hours per day to spend on an Individualized Reading program. Two hours per day, five days a week gives us

600 minutes per week. Let us imagine that we have 25 children in the class and that all we do during this time is conduct conferences for diagnostic and teaching reasons. This gives us 24 minutes per week for each child. It seems obvious that some compromises are necessary. Such compromises are an integral part of most "Individualized Reading" programs.

Skill Development

During the conference, the teacher may identify one or more skills the child needs to work toward developing. The teacher then needs to make available to the child materials that will be useful in the development of these skills and may have to explain to the child how to use these materials. If the teacher recognizes that two or more children need help in the same skill, a group might be formed to work on this skill. The teacher might have prepared a skill center in which materials are available to children for learning this skill.

Skill centers have frequently been available in many classes. For example, they may be used in a science class when some children have to learn to use a microscope or a Bunsen burner, or in a mathematics class when some need to learn to use a compass or ruler, or in a language arts class when some have to learn more about subject - verb agreement, or in any other class when certain specifics need to be learned. So, too, in reading class, when a specific skill (e.g., how to read and sketch time lines) has to be learned, those who need to learn it can be grouped together for that purpose. Such grouping would be only temporary, and continue only until the skill is learned. The children can be re-grouped to learn other skills necessary for understanding their materials.

Interest Development

Teachers might also develop interest centers that include a variety of materials dealing with topics of interest to children. Children who wish to explore materials together and share ideas should be provided time to do so.

Record Keeping

Teachers keep intricate records for each child indicating goals and proficiencies appropriate to the philosophy that governs the program. Usually, skills thought to be desirable for each child are outlined on a chart. The child's progress in the development of each skill is then recorded on the chart. New skills or higher levels of skills can be added at any time. The teacher may also keep a running commentary of each child's progress.

STRENGTHS AND WEAKNESSES

The following chart suggests strengths and weaknesses of Individualized Reading.

TABLE 13.5   **Strengths and weaknesses of Individualized Reading**

Strengths	Weaknesses
• seeking and self-selection are strong components of interest • self-pacing—working at one's own rate and level—provides for ease in acceleration, and makes those who learn slowly less obvious • provides easy opportunities for student interaction, sharing • children may read in breadth or depth, as they wish • classroom atmosphere is free and flexible • instruction is geared to the individual (perhaps in a group situation, though) and satisfies the needs of each individual • reading is life-like, and, therefore, may carry over to situations beyond the school • can be combined and integrated with other approaches	• requires a very competent, well-organized teacher who is able to diagnose and develop teaching strategies appropriate to a meaningful philosophy of reading • requires articulation among teachers of different grade levels to promote continuous growth from year to year. This is true of any program, but may be difficult to achieve in an Individualized Reading (core) program. • requires detailed record keeping • requires almost more time than is available for individual conferences

Psycholinguistic Implications for Reading Instruction

RATIONALE

According to Frank Smith,[16] the findings of research of major psycholinguists into the reading process indicate that:

> • only a small part of the information necessary for reading comprehension comes from the printed page.

- comprehension can precede the identification of individual words.
- fluent reading is not recoding to spoken language.

Smith[17] says there are two sources of information in reading. One of these sources is visual information (e.g., the printed page) and the other is non-visual information (knowledge of language, of subject matter, and of how to read).

The basis of comprehension is prediction, which is "the prior elimination of unlikely alternatives." The reader constantly asks questions, hypothesizes, and seeks answers to these questions. Comprehension, then, is a relative quality which cannot be measured by standardized reading tests because it depends upon the questions the reader asks himself or herself. When the questions are answered, comprehension is present. Smith states, "If we cannot predict, we are confused. If our predictions fail, we are surprised. And if we have nothing to predict because we have no uncertainty, we are bored."[18]

To Kenneth Goodman,[19] "Reading is a psycholinguistic guessing game." Psycholinguistics is the combination of two sciences: the science of cognitive psychology and the science of linguistics. The reader draws learnings from his or her long-term storage system and uses them together with information from the text while reading. To Goodman, reading is sampling from the text, predicting, confirming, and correcting. The reader uses minimal cues from the text together with his or her psycholinguistic understandings to construct meaning, or schema. "Effective reading can only be defined in terms of comprehension."

According to Goodman, the strategies of sampling, predicting, confirming, and correcting "depend on the use of graphophonic, syntactic, and semantic cues as they are found in natural language texts . . . (and) they function always in the context of the readers' striving to make sense of the text." Goodman argues that the "difference between readers of different levels of proficiency is not in how this process works but in how well it works." He suggests that poor readers may be too cautious. They may use too many cues or overuse strategies. They may have been taught to use nonproductive strategies, which may conflict with their own more natural productive strategies.

Smith[20] adds that "Reading must be fast and not over cautious." To Smith, slow reading interferes with comprehension and learning because it overloads the visual system and memory. "Nonvisual information permits fast reading . . ." Further, Smith contends that "Language is intrinsically ambiguous" (i.e., the surface structure is). "Nonvisual information ensures that meaning is brought to text at the deep structure level and that the reader does not become enmeshed in the pointless detail of surface structure."

METHODOLOGY

Smith suggests the following implications for the teaching of reading:

- children must have access to interesting and meaningful material (ideally of the child's own choice).
- children should have assistance where needed (and only to the extent that it is required).
- children need a willingness to take the necessary risks. (Anxiety increases the proportion of visual information a reader needs.)
- children must have the freedom to make mistakes.

Smith contends that children should learn to read by reading. To the question, how can children be expected "to read by reading, before they have learned to read?" Smith responds, "At the beginning . . . the reading has to be done for the children. Before children acquire any competence in reading, everything will have to be read to them, but as their ability expands they just need help. When reading, children will generate hypotheses on their own and if the child is not sure about the likely meaning context can provide clues." He draws an analogy with riding a bicycle: ". . . children do not need to be told when they are falling off."

Smith[21] does, however, discuss "mediated word identification," which he contends is a temporary expedient for identifying unfamiliar words which will later be recognized immediately. These strategies include: asking someone, using contextual clues, drawing an analogy with known words, and the use of phonics (spelling-sound correspondences). He adds that "spelling-sound correspondences are not easily or usefully learned before children acquire some familiarity with reading." At this stage they will be able to combine phonics with the use of context.

Kenneth Kavale and Robert Schreiner,[22] after analyzing the research of some major psycholinguists, contend that "a variety of visual, auditory, and cognitive activities must intervene before meaning is achieved." They suggest that three additional components are necessary for beginning readers when compared with skilled readers. They are:

- decoding of individual words to achieve recognition,
- processing of these words through an individualized oral language code to achieve identification, and
- combining individual words so they resemble connected discourse, since this is the form necessary for interpretation.

They refer to the research of Bond and Dykstra and of Jeanne Chall[23] that indicates that beginning readers benefit from a code emphasis form of instruction.

The Kavale and Schreiner article, titled "Psycholinguistic Implications for Beginning Reading Instruction" includes ten suggestions that "afford clear directions for instruction" for beginning reading. These are briefly noted here. It should be clear that not all psycholinguists agree with all of these points.

1. The primary focus of reading readiness should be on language activities. Psycholinguists, as well as many other researchers in reading, strongly contend that far too much time is spent on perceptual and discrimination activities that are only minimally related to the reading process.
2. Before reading instruction begins, the beginning reader should understand the nature of reading. This can be achieved by reading to the child while the child reads along.
3. From the beginning, the reader must understand that the purpose of reading is "to obtain meaning from the printed page. . . There must be safeguards to insure that the child does not establish a response set for word perfect reading, but rather for comprehension-centered reading." Children should feel the need to read for their own purposes.
4. Instruction should build upon the language and cognitive skills the individual reader possesses.
5. The Language Experience Approach is best. The authors caution that the teacher is not to edit the stories dictated by the child. Research done by Robert Ruddell and Susan Tatham[24] is cited that indicates that "children's reading performance improves when materials are written following the child's own syntactic patterns."
6. Because of the emphasis on meaning, reading materials must have something to say. "While reading series are a necessary part of instruction, they should not constitute the total program. An individualized reading program should be a component within the total reading program."
7. A large stock of sight words must be developed. "It is suggested that these be primarily structure or function words since they act as 'glue' words of language and are usually the most frequent but least regular."
8. Although teachers should guard against "overskilling," it is necessary for children to learn basic decoding skills. "Once the distinctive features* have been learned, a code emphasis program should

---

*Distinctive features are "rules" that allocate an object to a category, e.g., children must be aware that there is a visual category for a spoken word and that each word has its own visual representation. They might also learn that many words fit into a pattern, e.g., consonant-vowel-consonant, consonant-vowel-consonant-<u>e</u>, vowel-vowel, etc.

be initiated which stresses sound-symbol correspondences and blending."

9. Paralleling the code emphasis program should be a program teaching the use of context, which should be initiated through oral exercises and then reading. An appropriate question to ask is: "Does the sentence make sense with that word?"

10. It is essential that teachers "guard against the reading process being fractionated into a series of skills rather than a unified whole." The skills taught should be those that are essential for the beginning reader to gain information from the printed page. "Reading proficiency becomes the use of skills in comprehending the printed page." This is achieved through practice in reading, rather than through drill on isolated skills. The major part of instructional time should be spent in reading, not in isolated drill.

Constance Weaver[25] begins her chapter titled "How Can We Design a Psycholinguistically Based Reading Program" with this quotation:

"Students learn to read most successfully within the context of a total language arts experience, which includes speaking and listening activities, writing, leisure reading, and reading within a variety of content areas, such as the sciences, vocational education, social studies, mathematics, and so on." *Michigan Department of Education*

Her suggestions of components of a reading program include:

* creating reading materials: using a Language Experience Approach
* being immersed in reading: Some children have learned to read naturally: they read road signs, names of popular restaurants, words on T.V. ads; they have been read to, and words have been pointed out to them. In schools, teachers can read aloud to children while the children follow in their books. Choral reading, echo reading, etc., could be used.
* using sustained silent reading (SSR)
* sharing and experiencing reading
* reading for a specific purpose: Among ideas suggested are using SQ3R and the Directed Reading-Thinking Activity (DRTA) advocated by Russell Stauffer.[26] (This approach includes predicting what will come next and citing evidence to justify the predictions; reading to confirm, reject, or modify predictions; making and justifying new predictions; etc.) Weaver believes "A comprehensive reading program should help students learn to adjust their approach to the materials read and to their immediate and ultimate purposes for reading." This includes reading in all content areas.

In the same book, titled *Psycholinguistics and Reading: From Process to Practice*, Weaver includes a chapter in which she details specific strategies she suggests for use in a psycholinguistic approach to reading. The following headings are used: practicing reading strategies, helping readers learn their strengths, helping readers predict, helping readers sample, helping readers confirm or correct, helping readers integrate the cue systems, and helping readers comprehend.

STRENGTHS AND WEAKNESSES

Although psycholinguistics may not be considered an approach to the teaching of reading, its theory suggests possible implications for a reading program. On p. 585 are some possible strengths and weaknesses of the theory and implications.

Objective-Based Reading Systems Approaches

GENERAL DESCRIPTION

Recently a wide variety of materials has appeared with the objective of providing for individual progress in reading development. These have taken the form of programmed books, teaching machines, and management systems that utilize workbooks, boxed materials, modules, machines, computers, etc. They stress skills and subskills and break the teaching of reading into small, or minute, steps that are carefully sequenced. When one step is successfully completed, the child moves to the next step or perhaps to another skill. The teacher using such materials often conceives of the materials as the reading program, though this need not be so. The teacher frequently views his or her function as a diagnostician whose job is to identify the area or areas of subskills in which the child needs help, and to program him or her into materials designed to teach these skills.

These programs usually are designed around behavioral objectives and include criterion-referenced tests. Children who do not pass defined objectives are programmed into materials designed to teach those objectives, and they continue until they are able to pass the criterion-referenced tests at the level stipulated.

In some programs and/or some school systems, each child is tested, taught, then retested in the knowledge of or use of individual skills and moved up the ladder in each skill as the individual child is able to progress. In other situations, each child is tested in a broad range of skills and

TABLE 13.6   Strengths and weaknesses of psycholinguistic philosophies as they may relate to the teaching of reading

Strengths	Weaknesses
• stresses importance of background of experiences, linguistic ability, and cognitive skills • is "holistic" in nature, always stressing the integration of learnings in long-term memory, i.e., in the individual's own schemata • stresses total involvement in reading, building upon interests of the reader • may utilize several approaches: Language Experience, basal, individualized reading, especially for beginning reading • defines the fluent reader as an active participant in the reading process	• procedures for teaching and the coordination of them are vague at the present time • there appear to be major controversies about the value of teaching phonics as well as the approach to be used if phonics is taught • there is some question about the reliability of context cues in suggesting appropriate meanings • assumes readers are vitally interested in what they are reading (or should only read things they are vitally interested in) and that they have the experiences that enable them to ask questions and to hypothesize (some may consider a strength). Such experiences, of course, may be built. • assumes teachers are able to supply a language rich environment and that they know content area subjects well enough so that they can use texts principally as resources. This is not a weakness of psycholinguistic implications for teaching, but it may make teaching impractical, especially when teachers are in self-contained classrooms and must teach many subjects.

individual children are moved up only after passing all skills in the range. For example, in the test that follows, if a child passes all items but number 8, in some schools the child will be moved up in skill development in all areas but that and will be given additional help in skill number 8. In other school situations the child will remain "frozen" at the present level until able to pass that item. Some schools have reported "freezing" children at a level because of one item for several months' time—or even longer. Such "freezing" is not implicit in the use of criterion-referenced tests, but, instead is a result of a policy decision made by a school or school district.

An example of academic objectives for a partial test using criterion-referenced items that include behavioral objectives (acceptable levels of student performance) follows. Mastery of these objectives (individually—or en toto) is an indicator of readiness to progress into the next set of objectives. Failure in the mastery of any objective indicates that additional work is needed in that area until mastery is achieved.

EXAMPLE

alphabet: The learner will

1. ＿＿ write in manuscript form each capital and its corresponding lower case letter with 90% accuracy.

phonics (consonants): The learner will

2. ＿＿ write the letter that stands for the beginning consonant sound heard in words with 90% accuracy. (A list of words is read by the examiner.)

3. ＿＿ write the letter that stands for the ending consonant sound heard in words with 90% accuracy. (A list of words is read by the examiner.)

4. ＿＿ write the letter that stands for the middle consonant sound heard in words with 90% accuracy. (A list of words is read by the examiner.)

phonics (vowels): The learner will

5. ＿＿ read words containing vowel sounds in the cvc spelling pattern with 90% accuracy. (Student is given a list of words with the cvc spelling pattern.)

6. ＿＿ etc.

structural analysis: The learner will

7. ＿＿ read words having -ing and -s endings with 90% accuracy.

8. ＿＿ identify the two words used to form a compound word with 90% accuracy.

application of word attack skills: The learner will

9. ＿＿ apply word attack skills by reading a given list of words with 90% accuracy.

sight vocabulary: The learner will

10. ＿＿ recognize at least 90% of a sample of words most frequently used at the preprimer, primer, and first grade reading levels in the series used in the child's group (or class).

comprehension: The learner will

11. ＿＿ identify the one picture, from three shown, that best illustrates the theme of a story with 90% accuracy. (A story is read to the student, or class.)

12. ＿＿ etc.

Such a set of objectives need not be unique to a systems approach, for it may be utilized (and often is) in a basal reader approach. In a basal reader approach, fulfilling such a list of objectives may be used to indicate readiness to move into the next level of the basal series. This, of course, would be appropriate only if the school, or teacher, subscribed to a subskill approach to the teaching of reading. It would be inconsistent with a holistic philosophy.

OBJECTIVE-BASED READING SYSTEMS

A few of the better known diagnostic-prescriptive reading systems are briefly described here. The *Fountain Valley Teacher Support System*[27] includes assessment in phonics, structural analysis, vocabulary, comprehension, and study skills for grades one to six. There are 367 skills and objectives, which are assessed in 77 tests. Teachers are encouraged to compare records of each child and to group children who have common needs for instructional purposes. For each program objective, activities and materials are suggested to help in the teaching of the skill.

The *Wisconsin Design for Reading Skill Development*[28] provides for assessment in word attack, study skills, comprehension, self-directed reading, interpretive reading, and creative reading, covering levels K–6. Student "Profile Cards" are used for recording the performance of individual children. Instructional components are keyed to each skill. Such components include a listing of published materials and, within these, the page number of appropriate activities for teaching the skill. Also included are "teacher ideas" which might be used in teaching each skill.

The *Prescriptive Reading Inventory*[29] is an assessment system for evaluating achievement of children in the recognition of sounds and symbols, visual discrimination, phonic analysis, structural analysis, translation, literal-interpretive-critical comprehension, and study skills. Grade levels included are 1.5 to 6.5. Computer scoring is available, and printouts are made for individual children and for each class. The class printouts indicate how children can be grouped for instruction. "Program Reference Guides" list published materials, including page numbers, that may be used for teaching each skill.

STRENGTHS AND WEAKNESSES

In these programs, teaching is highly specific, is often impersonal, is usually isolated from the general language development of the child, and tends to be self-paced.

Following are possible strengths and weaknesses of this approach.

TABLE 13.7   Strengths and weaknesses of objective-based reading systems approaches

Strengths	Weaknesses
• breaks the teaching of reading into minute components, and strategies for teaching each component can be developed and sequenced according to difficulty • testing procedures provide for the placement of individual children at an appropriate level for each skill component. The children, then, should be able to progress satisfactorily in the program • skills taught frequently correlate well with test items on standardized reading tests. Thus children who work well in the program may score well on tests that are commonly used in schools today	• atomizes the teaching of reading • is frequently impersonal, as the teacher is usually not a vital part of the teaching situation • skills thus taught rarely transfer to the actual reading for meaning situation of the content area classroom or the everyday world • high scores on standardized tests may delude the student, school, and public until it is too late to make reparations, at least for some individuals

Modified Orthographies

GENERAL DESCRIPTION

Several modified orthographical "approaches" were popularly discussed and used in various areas of the United States—and the English speaking world—especially in the 1960's.[30] Since the sixties, their popularity seems to have waned, however.

More properly, these "approaches" might, instead, be termed simply "modified orthographies" or "modified alphabets," since inherent in each of them is simply a new alphabet which could be used with any approach—basal, individualized, Language Experience, etc. However, since each alphabet was commonly used with specific published materials utilizing that alphabet, the materials and the alphabet became almost synonymous in the minds of most people who used or discussed each program.

All of these had in common the following characteristics:

• they used approximately a one-to-one sound-symbol relationship, rather than the traditional English alphabet (t.o.)* of 26 letters.
• they were approaches used in the beginning stages of reading. The purpose was to make initial recoding from symbol to sound or from sound to symbol easier for the child by eliminating most of the inconsistencies in sound-symbol relationships of the English alphabet.
• inherent in the use of these alphabets was the need to finally transfer to t.o., for almost everything to be read is written in t.o. Children

*I.e., traditional orthography.

transferred to t.o. as soon as possible—toward the end of first grade for some, during second and third grade for others.

Among the most popular of these m.o. (modified orthographical) approaches are: the Initial Teaching Alphabet, Unifon, and Words-in-Color.

THE INITIAL TEACHING ALPHABET

I.T.A., commonly known as i/t/a, is an alphabet of 44 letters, or symbols, each one representing one of the phonemes of English. The Englishman, Sir James Pitman publicized the alphabet in the 1960's. John Downing, Albert Mazurkiewicz, Harold Tanyzer and others developed materials and conducted research to evaluate the use of i/t/a. Additional research was conducted nationally.

The alphabet is reproduced in Fig. 13.2, along with a short passage from a book that uses it (Fig. 13.3).

Upper case letters are enlargements of lower case letters. They are never a different symbol (as in t.o.. e.g.: G g g, B b, A a a, etc.)

UNIFON

UNIFON is a 40 letter alphabet, utilizing upper case letters only. John R. Malone designed this alphabet, and Margaret S. Ratz conducted research using the system. Both of these worked in the Chicago area. Additional research was conducted nationally.

WORDS-IN-COLOR

Caleb Gattegno originated "Words-in-Color." Words-in-Color uses t.o., but assigns a different color to each vowel sound and to most consonant sounds. For example, a long a sound, no matter how spelled would be assigned the same color, as in:

able	main	cafe	steak	eight
mate	they	neighbor	pay	etc.

Since Words-in-Color uses t.o., it has the advantage of possible use with children and adults who already know t.o. but who are having problems with symbol-sound relationships.

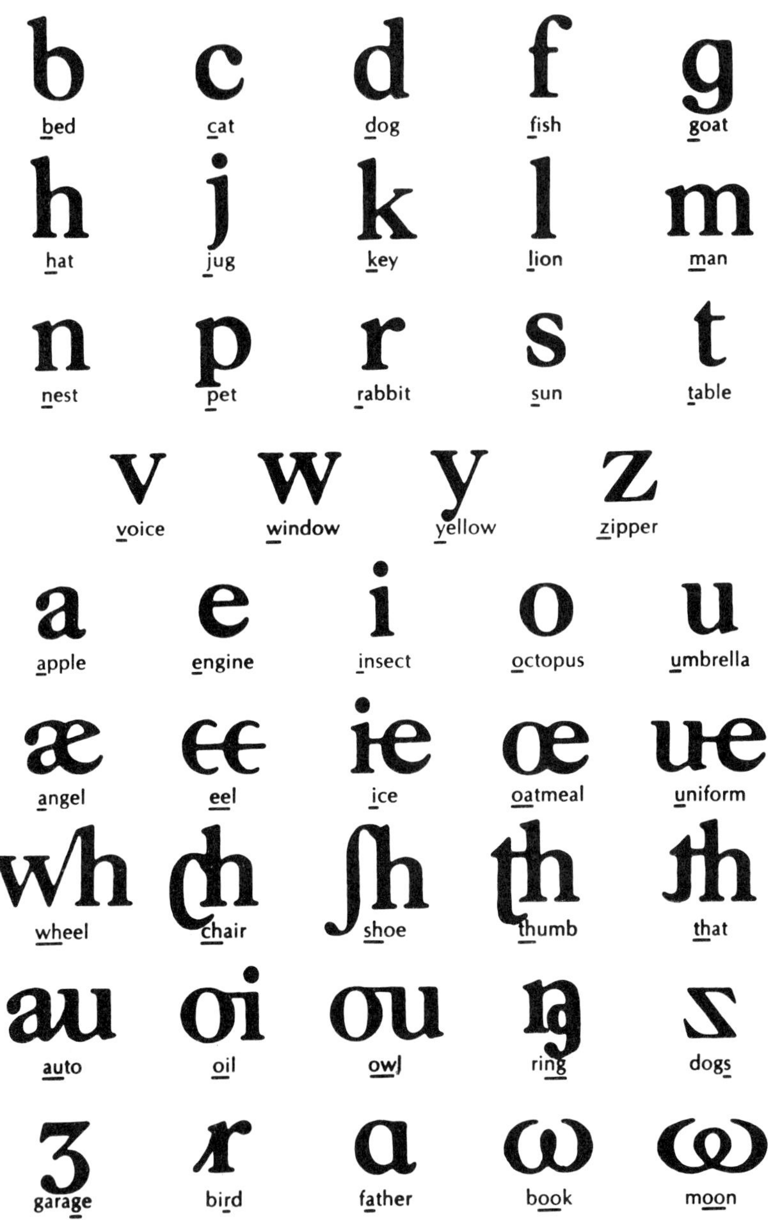

THE INITIAL TEACHING ALPHABET

Fig. 13.2: Reproduced with the permission of Initial Teaching Alphabet Foundation, 19 W. 34th St., New York, N.Y.

Fig. 13.3: *From The Trick (Book 5 in the Early-to-Read i/t/a Program) by Albert J. Mazurkiewicz and Harold J. Tanyzer, Copyright © 1966 by Initial Teaching Alphabet Publications, Inc. Reprinted by permission of Pitman Learning, Inc., Belmont, California.*

STRENGTHS AND WEAKNESSES

Following are possible strengths and weaknesses of the use of modified orthographies.

TABLE 13.8   Strengths and weaknesses of the use of modified orthographies

Strengths	Weaknesses
• promotes ease in beginning reading and writing because recoding is simple in comparison to recoding in t.o. • provides an alternate alphabet/approach for children who have failed when using t.o. Once these students have successful experiences with m.o., they may be able to transfer to t.o.	• children must learn two orthographic systems: m.o. first and t.o. second. If they come to school already knowing t.o., m.o.'s (except words-in-color) would be inappropriate for use. • materials are limited. Books, etc., in t.o. could not be used until transfer to t.o. occurs.

Summary

Six major approaches and/or programs for the teaching of reading were briefly explained. These included

- the Language Experience Approach (LEA)
- basal reading approach and programs
- linguistic approaches (and programs)
- linguistic approaches (and programs)
- individualized reading (IR) approach
- psycholinguistic implications for reading instruction
- objective-based reading systems approaches (and programs)
- modified orthographies (and programs)

The Language Experience Approach stresses the development and unity of all of the communications skills—listening, speaking, reading, and writing. Its content is the children's own experiences—past and present. It stresses the development and expansion of experiences, which are discussed, written about, and then read by the children. Children's experiences, words and syntax serve as a base for developing self-concept, reading skills, and oral and written language.

Basal reading programs are concerned with the development of most aspects of a traditional reading program—word recognition, vocabulary development, comprehension and study skill development on several levels of the cognitive domain, and the enjoyment of reading. They are characterized by the terms scope, sequence, and organization. Scope refers to the range of skills and content included in programs. Sequence relates to the order of the development of skills and the inclusion of topics or themes and literary forms. Organization involves relating teaching style, children's capacities and interests, and instructional materials to each other in an optimal manner.

Linguistic approaches have been of two major types: phonological and structural. Phonological programs stress the teaching of symbol-sound relationships, usually by using an alphabetic, or spelling, approach to recoding. Structural programs stress the teaching of larger units of language—sentences and complete works from the beginning.

Psycholinguistic theory and possible implications for reading instruction were also briefly discussed. Psycholinguists believe that both visual and nonvisual information are used in reading and that the basis for comprehension is prediction. Reading is sampling from the text, predicting, confirming, and correcting. The fluent reader constantly hypothesizes, seeking answers to his or her own questions. Implications for reading instruction were suggested.

Individualized reading has many definitions. The program discussed in this chapter (IR) can be described with three terms: seeking, self-selection, and pacing. Children seek their own interests, select their own materials, and individually read as little or as much as they wish—at their own levels. Such a program requires the use of teacher-student conferences for diagnostic and teaching purposes but also provides for the use of group work for developing needed skills and interests.

Objective-based reading systems approaches usually stress development of numerous reading skills and subskills and break the teaching of reading into small steps that are carefully sequenced. Most of them are designed around behavioral objectives and include criterion-referenced tests.

A discussion of modified orthographies was also included, principally for historical interest. I.T.A. (i/t/a), UNIFON, and Words-in-Color were briefly described.

Questions and Activities

After answering the questions at the beginning of this chapter, consider these questions and activities:

1. Work with a group of students in your college classroom in designing a Language Experience unit. Design activities to develop experiences and interests and to carry on a discussion. Have one person serve as the teacher in recording the episode and in teaching the "children" to read the passage. Discuss exactly how you might then follow the five day plan (p. 530 ff), or design an alternate five day plan, and show how you would use it. Then discuss other activities that might in incorporated in the unit.
2. If possible, visit a local classroom and work with a child or group of children using ideas from the unit. If you are already a teacher, you may wish to work with your own children.
3. Discuss with your classmates ways in which word bank words can be used. Make a list—with descriptions—for future reference.
4. If basal readers and supplementary materials are available, examine several lessons in one series. What format is used for lesson plans? What levels of questions are asked? How is comprehension taught (as distinguished from just tested)? What suggestions are given for developing vocabulary? What recoding-decoding cue systems are stressed? Do the passages seem to be interesting considering the target audience?
5. If possible, compare basals from two or more companies in terms of the questions stated above. Compare scope and sequence charts also.

6. After studying Chapter 14 of this book, design a chart for use in Individualized Reading for a hypothetical one or two children showing each individual's skill development needs for oral reading (using IRI or miscue analysis techniques) and also for comprehension (noting suggestions given in the section on "miscomprehension"). Also include a section on affect, including each child's level of affective involvement and suggestions for improvement (if necessary) in interest.

7. Consider the possible strengths and weaknesses of a psycholinguistic definition of reading. (You may wish to modify those given in this chapter.) To what extent do you think suggestions and implications for teaching as given in the present chapter and in current literature offer promise for a new era in the teaching of reading? What, in your opinion, are the strongest points in favor of psycholinguistics as it might be applied to the teaching of reading?

8. Under what circumstances (if any) might you favor using an objective-based reading systems approach to the teaching of reading? Weigh the strong points of such an approach. Compare the likelihood of the transfer of skill learning to content area reading when using this approach with the likelihood of transfer when using one or several other approaches.

NOTES

1. See Lois Sauer Degler in Selected References (LEA).
2. See Roach Van Allen and Gladys C. Halverson in Selected References (LEA).
3. See Vivian E. Cox in Selected References (LEA).
4. See Dorothy Garman in Selected References (LEA). Also see Russell Stauffer in Selected References (LEA).
5. See Sharon Garton, *et al.*, in Selected References (LEA).
6. Mary Ann Hall, "Language Centered Reading . . . ," p. 666. See Selected References (LEA).
7. Leonard Bloomfield and Clarence Barnhart. *Let's Read.* See Selected References (Linguistic Approaches).
8. C.C. Fries and Rosemary Wilson. *Merrill Linguistic Readers.* Columbus, Ohio: Merrill Publishing Co., 1967.
9. Ralph F. Robinett. *Miami Linguistic Readers.* Boston: D.C. Heath and Co., 1971.
10. Bill Martin and Peggy Brogan. *Sounds of Language Readers, Revised.* New York: Holt, Rinehart and Winston, 1970–1974.
11. Robert C. Aukerman, p. 209. See Selected References (General).
12. *Ibid.*, pp. 210–211.
13. "Sounds of Language Readers, Revised: K-8, 1970–74," in *Catalog of In-*

structional Materials, K-8. New York: Holt, Rinehart and Winston, 1979, p. 29.

14. See Willard C. Olson in Selected References (IR).
15. Thomas C. Barrett, p. 24. See Selected References (IR).
16. Frank Smith, *Psycholinguistics and Reading*. See Selected References (Psycholinguistics).
17. Frank Smith, *Understanding Reading*, p. 5. See Selected References (Psycholinguistics).
18. *Ibid.*, pp. 66–67.
19. Kenneth Goodman, "The Know More and the . . . ," pp. 658–659. See Selected References (Psycholinguistics).
20. Frank Smith, *Understanding Reading*, pp. 179–181, *op.cit.*
21. *Ibid.*, p. 150.
22. Kenneth Kavale and Robert Schreiner. See Selected References (Psycholinguistics).
23. See Guy L. Bond and Robert Dykstra. "The Cooperative Research Program in First Grade Reading Instruction." *Reading Research Quarterly*, 2 (1967): 5–142. And Jeanne Chall. *Learning to Read: The Great Debate*. New York: McGraw-Hill Book Co., 1967.
24. See Robert Ruddell. "The Effect of the Similarity of Oral and Written Patterns of Language Structure on Reading Comprehension." *Elementary English*, 42 (1965): 403–410. And Susan Tatham. "Reading Comprehension of Materials Written with Select Oral Language Patterns: A Study of Grades Two and Four." *Reading Research Quarterly*, 3 (Spring 1970). 402–426.
25. See Constance Weaver in Selected References (Psycholinguistics).
26. See Russell Stauffer in Selected References (Psycholinguistics).
27. *Fountain Valley Teacher Support System*. Huntington Beach, Calif.: Richard L. Zweig Associates, Inc., 1971.
28. *Wisconsin Design for Reading Skill Development*. Minneapolis, Minn.: Interpretive Scoring Systems/National Computer Systems.
29. *Prescriptive Reading Inventory*. Monterey, Calif.: California Test Bureau, McGraw-Hill, 1972.
30. For a description of i/t/a, UNIFON, Words-in-Color, and other one-to-one sound-symbol approaches, see Robert C. Aukerman (in Selected References, General) pp. 329–382.

SELECTED REFERENCES

General

Aukerman, Robert C. *Approaches to Beginning Reading*. New York: John Wiley & Sons, Inc., 1971.

Bean, Rita M. "Role of the Reading Specialist: A Multifaceted Dilemma." *The Reading Teacher*, 32 (January 1979): 409–413.

Cohen, Sandra B. and Stephen P. Plaskon. "Selecting a Reading Approach for the Mainstreamed Child." *Language Arts*, 55 (Nov./Dec. 1978): 966–970.

Darling, David. *"Evaluating the Affective Dimensions of Reading,"* in *The Evaluation of Children's Reading Achievement*, Thomas C. Barrett (ed.). Newark, Delaware: International Reading Association, 1967, pp. 127–141.

Graves, Donald H. "Research Update - What's New May Not Be Good." *Language Arts*, 54 (September 1977): 708–713.

Guszak, Frank J. *Diagnostic Reading Instruction in the Elementary School, Second Edition*, Chapters 17 and 18. New York: Harper and Row, 1978.

Guthrie, John T. "Research Views: Grouping for Reading." *The Reading Teacher*, 32 (January 1979): 500–501.

——————. "Research Views: Recreating Successful Reading Programs." *The Reading Teacher*, 30 (May 1977): 952–953.

Rupley, William H. "ERIC/RCS: Using Newspapers to Teach Reading." *The Reading Teacher*, 30 (December 1976): 346–349.

Sartain, Harry W. "Organizational Patterns of Schools and Classrooms for Reading Instruction," in *Innovation and Change in Reading Instruction*, Helen M. Robinson (ed.). N.S.S.E. Yearbook, Part II. Chicago, University of Chicago Press, 1968, pp. 195–236.

Scofield, Sandra J. "The Language-Delayed Child in the Mainstreamed Primary Classroom." *Language Arts*, 55 (September 1978): 719–723, 732.

Singer, Harry. "Resolving Curricular Conflicts in the 1970's: Modifying the Hypothesis, It's the Teacher Who Makes the Difference in Reading Achievement." *Language Arts*, 54 (February 1977): 158–163.

Stauffer, Russell G. (ed.). *The First Grade Reading Studies: Findings of Individualized Investigations*. Newark, Delaware: International Reading Association, 1967. (Reprinted from *The Reading Teacher*)

Vilscek, Elaine (ed.). *A Decade of Innovations: Approaches to Beginning Reading*. Newark, Delaware: International Reading Association, 1968.

Language Experience Approach

Allen, Elizabeth G. and Lester L. Laminack. "Language Experience Reading—It's a Natural." *The Reading Teacher,* 35 (March 1982): 708–714.

Allen, Roach Van. *Language Experience in Communication*. Boston: Houghton Mifflin Co., 1976.

——————— and Claryce Allen. *Language Experience Activities*. Boston: Houghton Mifflin Co., 1976.

——————. *Language Experience in Reading*. Chicago: Encyclopaedia Britannica Educational Corporation, 1970.

Allen, Roach Van and Gladys C. Halvarsen. "The Language Experience Approach to Reading Instruction." *Contributions in Reading.* Boston: Ginn and Co., 1961.

Aukerman, Robert C. *Approaches to Beginning Reading.* New York: John Wiley and Sons, 1971, pp. 299–328.

Ashton-Warner, Sylvia. *Teacher.* New York: Simon and Schuster, 1963.

Baratta-Lorton, Mary. *Math Their Way.* Menlo Park, California: Addison-Wesley Publishing Co., 1976.

Boorman, J. *Dance and Language Experiences with Children.* Don Mills, Ontario: Longman, 1973.

Braun, C. and V. Froese. *An Experience-Based Approach to Language and Reading.* Baltimore: University Park Press, 1977.

Buckley, Marilyn Hanf. "A Guide for Developing an Oral Language Curriculum." *Language Arts,* 53 (September 1976): 621–627.

Buescher, Thomas M. "Language As Play: A Case for Playfulness in Language Arts for Gifted Children." *Language Arts,* 56 (January 1979): 16–20.

Burmeister, Lou E. *Words- from Print to Meaning: Classroom Activities for Building Sight Vocabulary, for Using Context Clues, Morphology and Phonics.* Reading, Mass.: Addison-Wesley, 1975, Chapter 1.

Corcoran, Gertrude B. *Language Experience for Nursery and Kindergarten Years.* Itasca, Illinois: F.E. Peacock Publications, Inc., 1976.

Cox, Vivian E. *Reciprocal Oracy/Literacy Recognition Skills in the Language Production of Language Experience Approach Students* (Ed.D. dissertation). Tucson: University of Arizona, 1971.

Degler, Lois Sauer. "Putting Words into Wordless Books." *The Reading Teacher,* 32 (January 1979): 399–402.

Fries, C.C. *Linguistics and Reading.* New York: Holt, Rinehart, and Winston, 1963.

Garman, Dorothy. "So They've Dictated a Story . . . Now What?" *Teacher,* 96 (December 1978): 53–54.

Garton, Sharon and Paula Schoenfelder and Patricia Skriba. "Activities for Young Word Bankers." *The Reading Teacher,* 32 (January 1979): 453–457.

Gilbert, A.G. *Teaching the Three Rs: Through Movement Experiences.* Minneapolis: Burgess Publishing Co., 1977.

Gillet, Jean Wallace and M. Jane Kita. "Words, Kids and Categories." *The Reading Teacher,* 32 (February 1979): 533–542.

Goddard, N. *Literacy: Language-Experience Approaches.* London: Macmillan Publishing Co., 1974.

Hall, Mary Ann. "Language Centered Reading: Premises and Recommendations." *Language Arts,* 56 (September 1979): 644–670.

————————. *Teaching Reading as a Language Experience.* Columbus, Ohio: Chas. E. Merrill Publishing Co., 1976.

Hart, N.W.M. and B.N. Gray. *The Mount Gravatt Developmental Reading Program, Teacher's Manual, Level I.* Sydney, Australia: Addison-Wesley Publishing Co., 1977.

______________ and R.F. Walker and B. Gray. *The Language of Children- A Key to Literacy.* Menlo Park, Calif.: Addison-Wesley Publishing Co., 1977.

Laffey, James L. and Roger Shuy (eds.). *Language Differences: Do They Interfere?* Newark, Delaware: International Reading Association, 1973.

Lefevre, Carl. *Linguistics and the Teaching of Reading.* New York: McGraw-Hill, 1964.

McCracken, Robert A. and J. Marlene. *Reading Is Only the Tiger's Tail - A Language Arts Program.* San Rafael, Calif.: Leswing Press, 1972.

Pienaar, Peter T. "Breakthrough in Beginning Reading: Language Experience Approach." *The Reading Teacher*, 30 (February 1977): 489–496.

Pikulski, John. "Readiness for Reading: A Practical Approach." *Language Arts*, 55 (February 1978): 192–197.

Powers, Anne. "Sharing a Language Experience Library with the Whole School." *The Reading Teacher*, 34 (May 1981): 892–895.

Quisenberry, Nancy and Margo Welles. "Puppets as a Learning Tool." *Language Arts*, 52 (September 1975): 883–885.

Shuy, Roger W. "What Should the Language Strand in a Reading Program Contain?" *The Reading Teacher*, 35 (April 1982): 806–812.

Stauffer, Russell. *The Language Experience Approach to the Teaching of Reading, Second Edition.* New York: Harper and Row, 1980.

Stewig, John Warren. "Nonverbal Communication: I *See* What You Say." *Language Arts*, 56 (February 1979): 150–155.

Veatch, Jeannette. *How to Teach Reading with Children's Books.* New York: Scholastic Citation Press, 1978.

______________. *Key Words to Reading: The Language Experience Program Begins.* Columbus, Ohio: Chas. E. Merrill Publishing Co., 1973.

White, David E. "Language Experience: Sources of Information." *Language Arts*, 57 (Nov./Dec. 1980): 888–889.

Wiesendanger, Katherine Davis and Ellen Davis Birlem. "Adapting Language Experience to Reading for Bilingual Pupils." *The Reading Teacher*, 32 (March 1979): 671–673.

Basal Reader Approach

Barnard, Douglas P. and James DeGracie. "Vocabulary Analysis of New Primary Reading Series." *The Reading Teacher*, 30 (November 1976): 177–180.

Garman, Dorothy. "Language Patterns and Beginning Readers." *The Reading Teacher*, 31 (January 1978): 393–396.

Gourley, Judith W. "This Basal Is Easy to Read - or Is It?" *The Reading Teacher*, 32 (November 1978): 174–181.

Guszak, Frank J. "Reading Achievement Levels," in *Diagnostic Reading Instruction in the Elementary School, Second Edition*. New York: Harper and Row, 1978.

Hare, Victoria Choy. "Beginning Reading Theory and Comprehension Questions in Teachers' Manuals." *The Reading Teacher*, 35 (May 1982): 918–923.

Kress, Roy and Marjorie S. Johnson. *Informal Reading Inventories*. Newark, Delaware: International Reading Association, 1965.

Rosecky, Marion. "Are Teachers Selective When Using Basal Guidebooks?" *The Reading Teacher*, 31 (January 1978): 381–384.

Ruddell, Robert. "The Effect of the Similarity of Oral and Written Patterns of Language Structure on Reading Comprehension." *Elementary English*, 42 (1965): 403–410.

Smith, Nila B. *American Reading Instruction*. Newark, Delaware: International Reading Association, 1965, pp. 324–364.

Swaby, Barbara. "Varying the Ways You Teach Reading with Basal Stories." *The Reading Teacher*, 35 (March 1982): 676–680.

Tatham, Susan. "Reading Comprehension of Materials Written with Select Oral Language Patterns: A Study of Grades Two and Four." *Reading Research Quarterly*, 3 (Spring 1970): 402–426.

Linguistic Approaches

Bloomfield, Leonard and Clarence Barnhart. *Let's Read: a Linguistic Approach*. Detroit: Wayne State University Press, 1961.

Fries, C.C. *Linguistics and Reading*. New York: Holt, Rinehart and Winston, 1963.

Lefevre, Carl. *Linguistics and the Teaching of Reading*. New York: McGraw-Hill, 1964.

Miami Linguistic Readers. Lexington, Mass.: D.C. Heath and Company, 1960.

Individualized Reading

Barrett, Thomas C. "Goals of a Reading Program: The Basis for Evaluation," in *Perspectives in Reading #8: The Evaluation of Children's Reading Achievement*, T.C. Barrett (ed.). Newark, Delaware: International Reading Association, 1967, pp. 13–26.

Carlsen, G. Robert. *Books and the Teen-Age Reader* (for teachers of children in 4th grade and above). New York: Bantam, 1972.

Carlson, Ruth Kearney. *Enrichment Ideas, Second Edition*. Dubuque, Iowa: Wm. C. Brown Co., 1976.

Harris, Lary A., and Carl B. Smith. *Individualizing Reading Instruction: a Reader.* New York: Holt, Rinehart and Winston, 1972.

Groff, Patrick. "Individualized Reading," in *Perspectives in Reading - #5: First Grade Reading Programs*, James F. Kerfoot (ed.). Newark, Delaware: International Reading Association, 1965.

Macdonald, James B. and T.L. Harris and J.S. Mann. "Individual Versus Group Instruction in First Grade Reading." *The Reading Teacher*, 19 (May 1966): 643–647.

Miel, Alice (ed.). *Individualizing Reading Practices.* New York: Bureau of Publications, Teachers College, Columbia University, 1958.

Monson, Dianne L. and Betty J. Peltola. *Research in Children's Literature - an Annotated Bibliography.* Newark, Delaware: International Reading Association, 1976.

Musgrave, Ray. *Individualized Instruction: Teaching Strategies Focusing on the Learner.* Boston: Allyn and Bacon, 1975.

Noyce, Ruth M. "Team Up and Teach with Trade Books." *The Reading Teacher*, 32 (January 1979): 442–448.

Olson, Willard C. "Seeking, Self-Selection, and Pacing in the Use of Books by Children," in *The Packet.* Boston: D.C. Heath, Spring 1952.

Painter, Helen W. *Reaching Children and Young People through Literature.* Newark, Delaware: International Reading Association, 1971.

Sartain, Harry W. "What are the Advantages and Disadvantages of Individualized Instruction?" in *Current Issues in Reading*, Nila B. Smith (ed.), Newark, Delaware: International Reading Association, 1969, pp. 328–343.

Stauffer, Russell and Max M. Harrell. "Individualizing Reading-Thinking Activities." *The Reading Teacher*, 28 (May 1975): 765–769.

Waples, Douglas. *What Reading Does to People.* Chicago: University of Chicago Press, 1967.

Psycholinguistics and Reading

Cooper, Charles R. and Anthony R. Petrosky. "Psycholinguistic View of the Fluent Reading Process." *Journal of Reading*, 20 (December 1976): 184–207.

Goodman, Kenneth S. "The Know More and the Know Nothing Movements in Reading: A Personal Response." *Language Arts,* 56 (September 1979): 657–663.

_______________ and James T. Flemming (eds.). *Psycholinguistics and the Teaching of Reading.* Newark, Delaware: International Reading Association, 1968.

Goodman, Yetta M. and Kenneth Goodman. *Linguistics Psycholinguistics, and the Teaching of Reading.* Newark, Delaware: International Reading Association, 1980. An Annotated Bibliography.

Hittleman, Daniel R. *Developmental Reading: A Psycholinguistic Perspective.* Chicago: Rand McNally College Publishing Co., 1978.

Kavale, Kenneth and Robert Schreiner. "Psycholinguistic Implications for Beginning Reading Instruction." *Language Arts,* 55 (January 1978): 34–40.

Pearson, P. David. "A Psycholinguistic Model of Reading." *Language Arts,* 53 (March 1976): 309–314.

Smith, Frank (ed.). *Psycholinguistics and Reading.* New York, N.Y.: Holt, Rinehart and Winston, 1973.

——————————. *Understanding Reading: A Psycholinguistic Analysis of Reading and Learning to Read, Second Edition.* New York: Holt, Rinehart and Winston, 1978.

Stauffer, Russell G. and Ronald Cramer. *Teaching Critical Reading at the Primary Level.* Newark, Delaware: International Reading Assoc., 1968.

Weaver, Constance. *Psycholinguistics and Reading: From Process to Practice.* Cambridge, Mass.: Winthrop Publishers, Inc., 1980.

Objective-Based Reading Systems Approaches

Johnson, Dale D. and P. David Pearson. "Skills Management Systems: Critique." *The Reading Teacher,* 23 (May 1975): 757–764.

Lawrence, Paula Smith and Barbara Mathews Simmons. "Criteria for Reading Management Systems." *The Reading Teacher,* 32 (December 1978): 332–336.

Rude, Robert T. "Objective-Based Reading Systems: an Evaluation." *The Reading Teacher,* 28 (November 1974): 169–175.

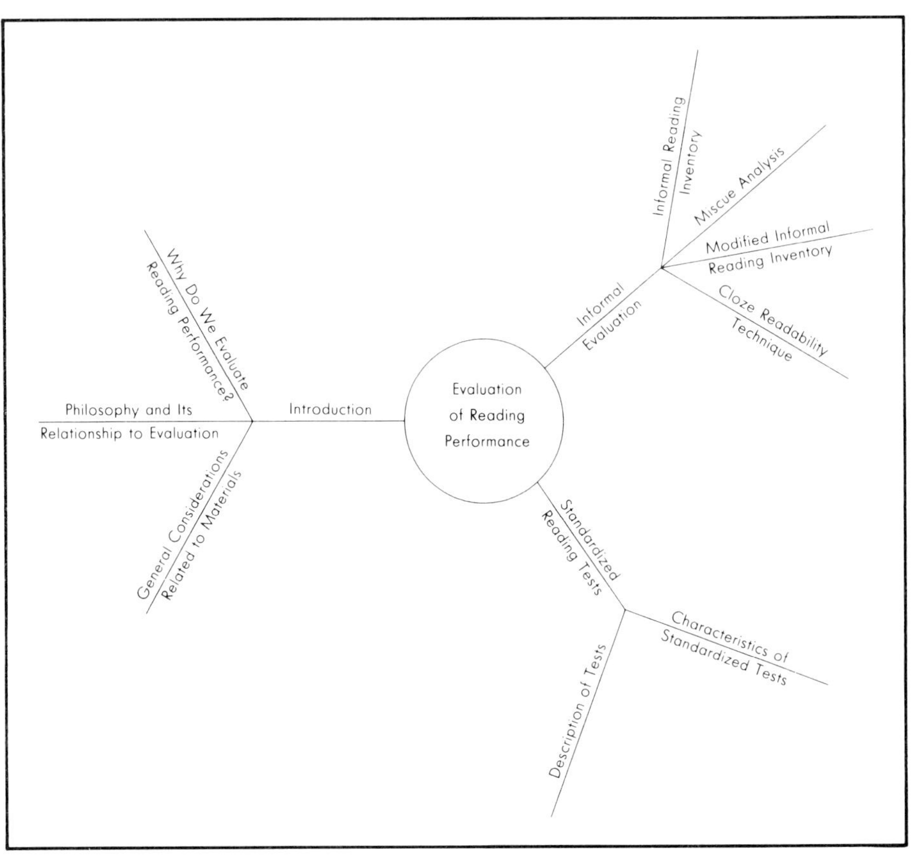

- What are some major valid reasons for evaluating reading performance? How does a teacher's or school's philosophy about reading affect the ways in which children's reading and reading materials are evaluated?

- What is meant by "informal evaluation"? What are the purposes of each of the following instruments: Informal Reading Inventory, Reading Miscue Inventory, Modified Informal Reading Inventory, Cloze Readability Inventory? How is each constructed? What diagnostic information can be gained from each? How can this information be used to improve reading comprehension?

- What is meant by "standardized" reading tests? How can such tests be characterized, or described? What are the basic uses and values of such tests?

CHAPTER 14

Evaluation of Reading Performance

Introduction

In school situations, the opportunity for the evaluation of student performance—and even teacher performance—seems to be ever-present. It can go on daily and even hourly. Yet, the important evaluation of student performance is frequently viewed as an annual occurrence—something that is done when children are given standardized and/or criterion referenced tests. And the evaluation of teacher competence is often viewed in relation to the results of these tests. Certainly these may constitute important evaluations. Yet, for the promotion of the goals of education—both in the cognitive and affective domains—these may be far less important than day-by-day informal observations and evaluations and other structured informal (nonstandardized) observations.

Why Do We Evaluate Reading Performance?

One may justly wonder just why students are or should be evaluated. What are the purposes for evaluation? If we can define worthwhile purposes for evaluation, we may be able to determine valid processes (techniques) and instruments (if needed) to use.

It seems that there are several valid reasons for evaluating the reading performance of children. Among these reasons are:

- to determine the level of materials a child can read, and thus to provide the child with appropriate levels of books and other reading materials for all situations in which the child reads. It is especially important that all materials basic to success in a given subject—reading, and all content area subjects—be selected at an appropriate level for each child in order to promote optimal growth for each child.

- to determine the specific needs of each child and to provide for these needs. Diagnostic procedures are necessary to satisfy this purpose. Diagnosis may occur daily in the regular teaching-learning situation, through the use of "structured," but nonstandardized, procedures, and perhaps through the use of some standardized tests.
- to identify special interests of children and to help satisfy these interests. Diagnostic procedures related to interests and ways of fulfilling interests were discussed in previous chapters.
- to compare groups, or classes, of children, perhaps nationwide. Standardized reading tests may be appropriate for this purpose.

PHILOSOPHY AND ITS RELATIONSHIP TO EVALUATION

Evaluation procedures must be appropriate to the philosophy of reading followed in the school and classroom, and to the materials used in the classroom. For example, if the teacher is looking for the best level of materials to use with the children, and the philosophy of the school is

- "bottom-up," behaviors that would be carefully examined are the child's ability to recode—to read orally in an accurate fashion. Perhaps literal comprehension would be considered important, with lesser or no importance given to higher level comprehension and interest, at least in the beginning stages of reading.
- "top-down/interactive," behaviors that would be carefully examined are the child's ability to relate to the reading materials and to interact with the materials. Accuracy in oral reading would be relatively unimportant, while higher level meanings and interest would be stressed.
- "top-down," as in the Language Experience Approach, there would be a lesser problem with level because the child learns to read what she or he dictates. The major level problem would be associated with the development of experiences and the discussion of these experiences at a level appropriate to the child.

When we look simply at materials, rather than at philosophy, we might note that if materials used are

- basal readers, these are leveled in a continuum. When a child finishes one level satisfactorily, he or she is probably ready to use the next level. However, it may be appropriate to change some children from one group to another. One's philosophy, as discussed above, enters into the decision of whether or not a child should be moved and into which group he or she should be moved.

- objective-based reading systems, the activities or exercises used are arranged in a sequence from easy to difficult, and as a child finishes one activity in a subskill, he or she would be ready to progress to the next. There, of course, is a temporary limit on the child's altitude in specific subskills.

The philosophy of the school and teacher will also enter into the types of diagnostic procedures that will be used. For example, if the philosophy is

- "bottom-up," grapho-phonic analysis will be stressed (see Chapter 6), and there may be much subskill analysis in areas of comprehension.
- "top-down/interactive," analysis of the use of all the cue systems may be important, as in miscue analysis, and analysis of the child's comprehension based on the child's retelling ability may be stressed. (See the section in this chapter on miscue analysis, including the section on miscomprehension.)

If teachers depend heavily on materials for teaching, diagnosis may proceed along the lines prescribed in these materials and in the teacher's manuals that accompany the materials. If such is the case, it is extremely important that materials selected for use, including the teacher's manuals, reflect the philosophy of the school and teacher who uses them.

Obviously, in any one chapter or book it would be impossible to come to terms with the sweeping scope of various types of evaluation. Yet, it is possible to briefly describe some evaluation procedures and perhaps to help make teachers and preservice teachers aware of their importance and of some ways of implementing them.

GENERAL CONSIDERATIONS RELATED TO MATERIALS

Materials used in schools should be selected to promote the advancement of children in curricular areas, including reading, determined to be important by schools and in additional areas important to individual children. Such materials should promote each child's learning and enjoyment. Basic to both learning and enjoyment is the promotion of each child's self-concept in a democratic society.

Content of Materials

In selecting materials to be used by children, a basic consideration relates to whether the materials promote academic and social goals of the school. Basic questions asked might be:

- Are the materials appropriate to the school's philosophy of teaching reading?
- Are the materials complete (or relatively complete in comparison to competing materials) in presenting the skills and/or subject matter to be taught?
- Are the materials well-organized?
- Are the materials free of stereotypes?
- Are the materials written in an interesting and readable style for the children who are to use them?

A teacher, or committee, selecting materials for children might formulate a check list against which they would evaluate the materials considered. A list such as the following might be used with additions and/or deletions appropriate to the school situation. Some items might be weighted more than others.

Check list for evaluating content of materials

Mark thus: 1-almost never   2-sometimes   3-usually

1	2	3	
☐	☐	☐	1. Are the materials relatively complete in presenting the subject matter and/or skills to be taught?
☐	☐	☐	2. Is the content appropriate for the social class of the children who will be using these materials?
☐	☐	☐	3. Do materials reflect the reading interests of the children who will be using them?
☐	☐	☐	4. Are the settings of activities related to a wide range of experiences and/or areas? (if important)
☐	☐	☐	5. Does the content foster the development of realistic and desirable attitudes and values?
☐	☐	☐	6. Are the materials well-organized, and is the organization apparent?
☐	☐	☐	7. Are illustrations appropriate to the children who will be using the materials?
☐	☐	☐	8. Are materials free of sex role stereotyping, and do they present both sexes in a wide variety of roles?
☐	☐	☐	9. Are the materials free of racial or ethnic stereotyping, and do they present members of minority groups in a wide variety of roles?
☐	☐	☐	10. Are the materials free of family size and/or family relationship stereotyping?
☐	☐	☐	11. Are a wide range of occupations represented, and represented without overt or hidden value judgments? (if appropriate to curriculum)
☐	☐	☐	12. Are children and/or adults dressed in nonstereotyped ways?

☐ ☐ ☐   13. Do story characters associate with a fair variety of people different from them?
☐ ☐ ☐   14. Are models of behavior appropriate?
☐ ☐ ☐   15. Is the reading level of the materials appropriate to the children who will be using the materials?
☐ ☐ ☐   16. Is the language (syntax and vocabulary) appropriate to the children who will be using the materials?
☐ ☐ ☐   17. Are the guidebook (manual) activities appropriate to the philosophy of the school-wide reading program? (if appropriate)
☐ ☐ ☐   18. Is vocabulary introduced in a logical and consistent way and in harmony with the other materials used in the school? (E.g., according to the phonic and linguistic principles being taught.)
☐ ☐ ☐   19. Do the materials present syntactic, semantic, and picture clues to word meanings?
☐ ☐ ☐   20. Do the materials include guidelines for the development of higher level thinking skills? (E.g., in guidebook or manual)
☐ ☐ ☐   21. Do the materials supplement and/or harmonize with and/or add to the curriculum?
☐ ☐ ☐   22. Etc.

Earlier in the present book, interest inventories were discussed as well as other ways of selecting books of interest to individual children.

Readability of Materials

General Considerations There are many factors that make printed materials easy or difficult to read. Among those that should be considered are:

- *size of print* - Is it appropriate for the reader?
- *kinds of illustrations* - Some illustrations help a reader; some are ignored by most readers; others add to the difficulty level of the book.
- *organization of material* - Clearly organized paragraphs, appropriate headings and subheadings aid understanding.
- *syntactical patterns* that are familiar to readers aid ease of reading. Syntactical patterns unfamiliar to readers add to the difficulty level of materials.*

---

*The teacher who knows the type of children she or he will be working with
decisions concerning these factors when examining reading materials. If de
materials are made during the school year, the materials can be "tried out"

- *words used* influence readability. Are words familiar to the reader orally? in print? Are meanings of these words, as used in context, familiar to the readers?*
- *experiential background* of the reader in relation to the topic is important.*
- *reader interest* in the topic discussed is important.*

Other factors may seem to make a difference in the difficulty level of materials. For example, a heavy book usually seems to be more difficult than a light book, and a paperback seems easier than the same book in hardcover. No doubt, you can add other factors that help determine the difficulty level of a book. Even the reader's mood at the time of reading makes a difference as to whether or not the book will be easy or difficult for her or him at that time.

Readability Formulas Many of these factors are difficult or impossible to measure objectively, or to measure when the children who are to use the materials are not known or are not available, as in the summertime, when materials may be selected for the following year or years. Because of this, readability formulas or graphs are commonly used to identify an approximate level of difficulty of printed materials.

The use of readability formulas and graphs has come under strong criticism recently among some people in the reading field, for these procedures use only two characteristics of printed materials for estimating difficulty. These are characteristics that can easily be measured objectively, although different formulas measure these factors differently.

The two factors commonly used are

1. word difficulty, and
2. sentence length.

The difficulty level of a word can be measured in a variety of ways: How many letters does it contain? How many syllables? Is it a high frequency word? Is it on a list of common words? Can you think of other ways of judging the difficulty of a word? Sentence length can also be measured in a variety of ways: Some authors of formulas indicate that a period, ex-

---

*The teacher who knows the type of children she or he will be working with can make decisions concerning these factors when examining reading materials. If decisions about materials are made during the school year, the materials can be "tried out" on children.

clamation point, and question mark indicate ends of sentences. Others say that a semicolon may also indicate the end of a sentence if the semicolon separates two independent clauses. How does one deal with quotes within a sentence? or with statements like: "Look, look, look"? When using a formula you must be sure that you understand the author's explanation of these points (if such an explanation is given).

Because these two factors—word difficulty and sentence length—are measured in different ways by different formulas, it is very possible that if you use two or more different formulas on the same passage, you may get two or more different grade level scores for the passage. Because of this, if you wish to use a formula, you may wish to make a decision as to which formula you prefer to use. You may even wish to use one formula on science materials and another on social studies materials, for example. Or you may wish to average the scores from two or more formulas.

However, it is important to understand the readability formulas, in general, are not intended to pinpoint the precise grade level of materials. Instead, they are meant to give you the range in difficulty of different printed materials. In other words, a readability formula will tell you which of a number of books is easiest, next in difficulty, next, next, and most difficult. This is the information most needed by a teacher. For, after all, a teacher doesn't really know the precise grade level of material specific children can read.*

So, if a teacher knows which materials are easiest, average, and hardest, and if that teacher knows which children are the poorest readers, average readers, and best readers, a step can be taken toward identifying the best level of materials for individual children. However, usually more steps than this one must be taken. These steps are explained later in this chapter.

Fry Readability Graph Because of its ease of application and wide use, the Fry Readability graph is given here in Fig. 14.1. Please see Appendix A of this book for an explanation of two other readability formulas you may wish to consider using—the New Spache Readability formula and the Dale-Chall Readability formula. You may wish to refer to an article by George Klare[1] in which most formulas in use today are explained and evaluated, including formulas for use with foreign language materials.

---

*The score a person gets on a standardized silent reading test usually indicates the frustrational reading level, i.e., the point at which a student cannot succeed with materials. Readability formulas also usually give the frustrational level. Both standardized tests and readability formulas, however, are probably best used in giving range scores.

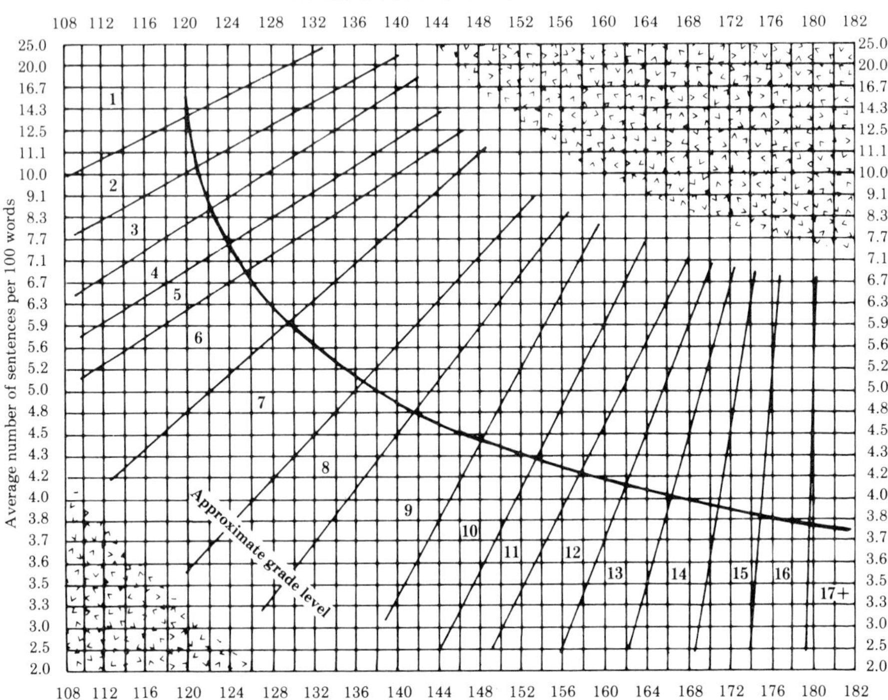

Fig. 14.1 "Fry's Readability Graph: Clarifications, Validity, and Extension to Level 17," by Edward Fry. Journal of Reading, 21, No. 3 (December 1977), p. 249, used by permission of the author and the International Reading Association.

To use the Fry graph on a given passage, proceed thus:

1. *Count 100 words.* Put a bracket before and after this passage.
2. *Count the number of syllables in this 100 word passage.* To do this easily, write above each word the number of syllables it contains in addition to one. Thus above "eight," "ten," "cat," "dog," nothing would be written. Above "rabbit," "table," "apple," "1" would be written. Above "elephant," "2" would be written, etc. Count syllables the way you pronounce the words. There is no need to use a dictionary. Each symbol receives a syllable count of one: 1945 is 4 syllables, USA is 3 syllables, "&" is one syllable. To find the total number of syllables, add these numbers together, and add 100 to that. This will give you the number of syllables in the 100 word passage.
3. *Count the number of sentences in the 100 word passage.* This will probably be a number plus a fraction. Since Fry does not give specific

criteria defining a sentence, none is included here. We would proceed thus in applying the criteria to the following passage:

["Help, help," the young boy shouted from the river. It was obvious that the undertow was tugging and grasping him. He was a good swimmer, but this was too much for him—alone. He needed someone—or something—to save him.

Just then his neighbor's German shepherd answered the call. A strong swimmer, Goldie lashed at the waves and soon grabbed the boy by the back of his shirt. She was slowed by his weight, but kept his head up. That was all she could do for awhile. The boy gained some strength from this help. Finally the two of] them made it back to shore together.

1. The brackets enclose the 100 word passage being evaluated.
2. There are 21–22, plus 100 syllables, or 121–122 syllables in this passage.
3. There are 9 and 4/11 sentences in this passage, i.e., 9.36, or 9.4 sentences.

Reading the Fry graph to the intersection point for 9.4 sentences and 121–122 syllables, we see that the level of difficulty is third grade, according to Fry.

To find the readability level of a whole book, Fry suggests that you sample three or more passages, average the number of syllables and average the number of sentences found in each passage and use the graph only once.

It seems that three passages are enough to use for very short books. But about ten passages would give you a better estimate of readability for longer books. The passages that you use should be taken at equal intervals throughout the book.

Let's say that we have a book that is 300 pages long and that we are going to sample ten passages. We would plan to take a sample passage about every 30 pages. We might start on page 8, next use page 38, then page 68, etc. The following chart might show our findings:

Page	Syllable/ 100 words	Sentences/ 100 words	Total readability	Readability of each passage
8	128	4.8	↑	7
38	140	5.9		7
68	116	6.3		4
98	150	4.3		10
128	142	6.1		7
161*	125	8.2		4
188	134	5.0		7
218	121	6.1		6
248	139	4.5		8
278	148	3.0	↓	11
sum	1343	54.2		
average	134.3 ——	5.42 ——→ 7th grade		

*First useable passage including and following designated page (158)

Knowing the approximate readability level of a book or of several books should help us make wise decisions about ordering books. In addition to knowing the readability levels of materials, we would also need to consider the other factors listed at the beginning of this section to estimate the difficulty of books.

Compatibility of Materials Each of several sets of materials may be well developed and yet be incompatible or insufficient for a well-developed reading program or other curriculum. Two sets of phonics materials that are sequenced differently may add a great deal to the burden of a child who may be expected to use both. (Such may be the case when a basal reading program is used along with a differently sequenced phonics workbook—unless the teacher resequences the phonics materials in line with the basal—or when a reading teacher uses one set of materials and the classroom teacher uses another.) The same is true when several sets of comprehension materials are used. Expecting a box of materials to do one job, a workbook to do another, paperbacks to do another, and a machine to do yet another may provide an atomistic approach to the teaching of reading. Materials must be selected in a balanced manner and advantageously synthesized and sequenced to produce optimal results. The teaching of reading should follow a philosophy, and materials should be selected, balanced, and sequenced in accord with that philosophy.

Informal Techniques for Evaluating Reading Performance

Having available what seem to be appropriate and compatible materials is necessary. Knowing for whom they are appropriate is also necessary, as the same materials are probably not appropriate for all children in class. Questions that must be answered when selecting materials for individual children are:

- Is the level of the material appropriate for the child?
- What kind of help does the child need in order to succeed with the material?

In answering the first question, we are looking for what is commonly called *survey* (level) information. In answering the second, we are looking for *diagnostic* information, perhaps in relationship to subskill activities needed and also in relationship to the needed development of the reader's schemata in both language and experiences. We can find answers to one or both of these questions by giving an Informal Reading Inventory (IRI), by using miscue analysis techniques, by using a modified IRI, and/or by using the cloze readability technique.

INFORMAL READING INVENTORY (IRI)

By giving an Informal Reading Inventory, we are able to determine whether reading material is at the child's independent reading level, instructional reading level, or frustrational reading level. If material is at the child's independent reading level, the child is able to satisfactorily read it without help from the teacher. If reading material is at the child's instructional reading level, the child should be able to understand it satisfactorily with the help of the teacher. If material is at the child's frustrational reading level, the child will probably find it too difficult to comprehend even with a teacher's help—although the child may be able to get some ideas from it, as, for example, when a child just wishes to peruse a very difficult (for the child) book even if she or he just understands a little of it.

All IRI's are not alike, and as a preliminary step in designing an Informal Reading Inventory, teachers should ask themselves why they are designing such an inventory. Just what is it that they wish to find out? An individual teacher's objectives in relation to a child or children are what determine the kind of IRI that is designed and given.

For example, if a teacher wishes to find out if a trade book an individual child has decided to read without help from the teacher is at the right level for the child, the teacher might simply sit next to the child while the child orally reads to the teacher. If the teacher finds that the child makes no more than about one oral reading error in 100 words, the book is probably at the right level for the child to read independently. The teacher may also wish to ask a few questions to check comprehension. The child should have 90–100 percent comprehension (if the questions are child-like) if the book is at the child's independent reading level.

Structured IRI's are normally given to children to determine which basal reader and/or content area textbook is at the instructional level for each child; that is, an IRI may be given to a child when the teacher wishes to identify the best book(s) to use with the child when the child is being instructed. Since the teacher is doing the instructing, it is important that the teacher compose the IRI. Additionally, the IRI should be presented to the child or children by the teacher in a manner typical of the teacher's teaching style. If these guidelines are followed, the teacher will be able to determine the "goodness of fit" that exists among these important classroom factors: the child, the teacher, and the materials.

The teacher usually seeks two types of information when giving an IRI: that which can be gained from analyzing the oral reading performance of the child, and that which can be gained from the child's answers to comprehension questions.

Children are asked to read orally because of the information oral reading yields. This relates to how well children use cue systems (sight vocabulary, graphophonic cues, semantic and syntactic cues), how they phrase, and whether they omit words, substitute words, repeat phrases, etc. The goal of this is twofold:

- to determine if such behaviors are dysfunctional to comprehension and "remedial" help is needed, and
- to determine the next steps to be taken developmentally in teaching reading. (To determine this, normally the child will have to read material at a level above the instructional level. The next section in this chapter on "Miscue Analysis" is most helpful in this respect. To gain meaningful diagnostic information, passages must normally be longer than those used in a typical IRI.)

In an IRI, children are asked comprehension questions of the type the teacher considers important principally to obtain a "level" score. (Passages are usually short, and only a few questions are asked, so reliable diagnostic information is normally not gained from this procedure.)

Oral Reading

Since oral reading IRI's must be given individually, passages used to evaluate oral reading skills are usually short. Because of this brevity, it is essential that passages be highly typical of the books from which they are taken, for if an unusually difficult or easy passage (for the book) is selected, the wrong kind of placement (level) information will be found.

The following technique is suggested to help the teacher find a "typical" passage:

1. *Select five passages*, each beginning with a new paragraph close to the beginning of the book. (It may be well to avoid the very beginning of the book, since the first few pages may be atypical of the book.) Each passage should be 100 or more words long, except in first grade books, where passages may be shorter. Passages may be one or more paragraphs long.

2. *Compute the readability level* of each of the 100 word passages (or shorter ones in first grade). Use only the passage, not the additional words needed to complete the sentence of the 100 word passage.

3. *Average the readability scores* of the five passages, and select for use the passage that comes closest to the average. E.g.: the readability levels of the five passages might be 3.2, 3.9, 3.4, 4.1, 3.6. The arithmetic average is 3.65. The passage closest to that is the last one (3.6). This is the passage that will be used for this book.*

This procedure is followed for each book that might be used.

Next, the oral passage is marked off in the book. The child reads from the book while the teacher scores deviations on a form such as the one that follows in Figure 14.2. Errors, or deviations from the expected response, are marked on the teacher's sheet as the child reads orally.

The following are usually considered to be errors,** and they are marked in the ways indicated.

1. *mispronunciations* and/or *substitutions*—the teacher records the way the child says the word (dialectal variations in pronunciation are not errors).

   E.g.: The elephant danced and blew water.

2. *omissions*—the teacher circles the word, or words, omitted.

   E.g: The elephant danced and blew water.

3. *insertions*—the teacher uses a caret (∧) and writes the added word or words.

E.g.: The elephant danced and blew *bubbles and* water.

4. *regressions* (or repetitions of *more than* one word)—the teacher draws a wavy line under the repeated words. A single word may be repeated without being counted an error if it is finally pronounced correctly.

E.g.: The elephant danced and blew water.

5. *hesitations*—if there is a hesitation of five or more seconds, the teacher writes "H" and supplies the word.

E.g.: The elephant danced and blew *H* water.

After the child completes the oral reading, the teacher fills in the grid, which may help in the diagnosis of the errors (Figure 14.2).

The following chart gives scoring guidelines for the oral reading of a 100 word passage:

Levels	Errors	Percentage
Independent	0–1	99–100
Borderline	2	98
Instructional	3–5	95–97
Borderline	6–9	94–91
Frustrational	10+	90–0

(The passage on page 619 was at Susanna's Borderline Level, between the Instructional Level and the Frustrational Level, since Susanna had seven errors.)

Diagnostic Information

The following are offered as suggestions for remediating specific difficulties observed when children read orally, or for deciding upon instruction the child would profit from developmentally. (Since the IRI is a test, the teacher does not interrupt while administering it.) The type of diagnostic information normally gained from miscue analysis is given in the next major section of this chapter.

□ *If the child substitutes words* and

- the substitutions make sense in the passage, this suggests that the child is using semantic and syntactic cues but not phonic cues.

Name *Susanna Brown*
Date *Sept. 16*

	Misp/ Sub.	Om.	Ins.	Regr.	Hes.
				1	
	1				
			1		
		1			
	1				
		1			
	1				
Subtotals	**3**	**2**	**1**	**1**	

Total errors: **7**

[No group of birds has made more of an

imp→ok
impact on mankind than pheasants have.

tame
For years they have been game birds. They

all over
have been hunted since the eleventh centu-

ry. Perhaps they were (hunted) before this

*per**
time. Many laws have been written to pro-

tect them.

By 1150 pheasant meat was served at

restaurants. By 1550 the pheasant was

established as a wild bird.

park
You may see pheasants in your yard to-

day. Perhaps you will see one on a (country)

specials
road. There are many species, and most

are large and strong. They are beautiful

birds and often bright in color.

*100 words * **
They] eat insects and roots.***

*   Not an error—child's dialect
**   Do not score beyond 100th word.
*** If the teacher wishes, she or he may indicate phrasing by using slashes, e.g.: No group/ of
birds/ has/ made/ more/ of an impact/ on mankind./ etc.

Figure 14.2

The child is thinking along with the author. Perhaps no corrective measures are necessary.

- the substitutions change the meaning, first compare the meanings of the two words (i.e., does the substitution make sense? does the substitution change the author's meaning?), and then compare the phonic elements of the two words. If the child consistently misses specific grapheme to phoneme relationships, these should be identified and taught. For example, the child might have problems with the *final vowel-consonant-e* construction. In such a case, contrast the pronunciation of words with and without a final e, and have the child use them in sentences. (See Chapter 6 for strategies.) Possible contrasts are:

| hat-hate | pet-Pete | bit-bite | hop-hope | cut-cute |
| pan-pane | | dim-dime | cod-code | cub-cube |

☐ *If the child hesitates for long periods of time,* or *omits words,* this may suggest that materials may be too difficult and/or the child is unwilling to make a mistake. You may encourage the child by:

- helping him or her use context cues. Ask the child what word makes sense in the passage. Ask the child to read on and then return. Perhaps the later context will be of help. Context may help the child come up with the author's word or with a synonym.
- helping him or her use semantic and phonic cues. Ask the child to think of a word that makes sense in the sentence that begins with the initial letter sound of the word, e.g.: "The black and white r_______ knocked over the garbage pail." Ask the child if he or she knows any animals that might do this. Perhaps stress added phonic cues (r_cc__n). Perhaps the child doesn't know the word orally. Then phonics will not help. The word will have to be taught.
- giving the child easier materials to read.

☐ *If the child inserts words that are not in the text and which change the meaning,* prepare activities to help the child compare the meanings of two sentences, one with an insertion and the other without: E.g., compare these:

1. Yesterday Dan went to the movie.
2. Yesterday Dan and Joan went to the movie.

1. Harry likes to swim.
2. Harry likes to eat and swim.

If the child repeats words or phrases, this may suggest that:

- materials may be too difficult. You may wish to suggest easier materials.
- the child has fallen into a bad habit. Tape the child while reading, and allow the child to listen.
- the child is stalling. This gives the child time to "work-out" an unfamiliar word or idea. If this happens frequently, materials may be too difficult.

If the child ignores punctuation, phrases poorly, or uses improper intonation,

- provide activities that demonstrate that punctuation does matter. For example, contrast

  1. Betty Jane and Bob went to the movie.
  2. Betty, Jane and Bob went to the movie.

  1. Harry said Patricia enjoys tacos.
  2. "Harry," said Patricia, "enjoys tacos."

- use choral reading, echo reading, and impress reading.

Comprehension

Some teachers may wish to ask questions on the oral passage. Other teachers may wish to ask children to read a longer passage that follows this and ask questions on the longer passage. If the shorter passage is used, the following questions might be asked:

1. What does the author say pheasants look like? (literal level: vocabulary, details)
2. In what ways have pheasants made an impact on mankind? (literal level: random order sequence)
3. The author says that pheasants have been established as wild birds and that they are game birds. What is the difference between calling a bird a wild bird and calling it a game bird? Are all wild birds game birds? Explain. (inferential level: comparison - contrast)*
4. How have pheasants been protected by mankind? (literal level: detail)

---

*Those who believe that reading tests must be "text-bound," i.e., the answers must be in the reading passage, would object to these questions. Their questions would all be at the literal level (textually explicit) or inferential level of the textually implicit type—all information is in the text, but the reader must "put it together."

5. Do you think it is important to protect pheasants? Why or why not? (affective)*

(Full or partial credit can be given for answers.) The following chart gives scoring guidelines for five questions:

Levels	Errors	Percentage
Independent	0–½	90–100
Instructional	1–1½	70–80
Borderline	2–2½	50–60
Frustrational	3–5	below 50

Obviously, a 100 word passage is rather brief to test comprehension. Therefore it probably would be better to use a longer passage (300 to 1500 or more words, depending on the level of the children) for the comprehension part of the IRI. This passage would be read silently by the children, and more questions could be asked. The teacher would, thus, gain information that is more reliable. This information might also be helpful in giving the teacher some clues, as to what to observe more carefully in the regular on-going diagnosis that should occur in every classroom.

Survey (Level) Guidelines

The following guidelines are commonly used in scoring an IRI:

	Oral Reading*	Comprehension*
Independent level	99–100%	95–100%
borderline	98%	90%
Instructional level	97–95%	70–85%
borderline	94–91%	55–65%
Frustrational level	90–0%	50–0%
Capacity level**	does not apply	70–75%

* These were first recommended by Emmett Betts,[2] without the borderline categories. Independent level: oral 99–100%, comprehension 90–100%; Instructional level: oral 95–98%, comprehension 70–90%; Frustrational level: oral 94–0%, comprehension 50–0%.
These are guidelines only. Teachers will have to decide themselves what percentages work best for them and for their children.
** If the teacher goes through the process of identifying the frustrational level for a child, the teacher can begin reading aloud comprehension passages at that level and higher levels until the comprehension score for the child is 70–75%. This is said to be the child's capacity (reading expectancy) level. It is the child's listening comprehension level.

---

*Those who believe that reading tests must be "text-bound," i.e., the answers must be in the reading passage, would object to these questions. Their questions would all be at the literal level (textually explicit) or inferential level of the textually implicit type—all information is in the text, but the reader must "put it together."

When giving an IRI, the teacher continues to test by using easier or harder materials until each child's instructional level is identified. Thus, if the teacher tests each child using the book of average difficulty, she or he will proceed to use books of a lower level for children who frustrate when taking this IRI, and will use books of a higher level for children who read this IRI at the independent level.

Caution   Although the guideline percentages given above have been widely used, Albert J. Harris[3] suggests that Instructional Level materials should be easier than these guidelines indicate. In making this recommendation he cites two important studies. One of these studies was made by J. Louis Cooper, who found that the easier a reader is for a child, the more progress the child made during the year. Cooper found that this "held for both boys and girls, and for above average, average, and below average children. The best average gains were made by children who made fewer than 3 errors per 100 words" (oral reading). "Primary children making 5% or more errors and intermediate children making 10% or more errors tended to make very small gains." The other study was done by Gerald Jorgenson, who found that "the easier the material was in relation to the child's reading ability, the better her/his classroom behavior tended to be."

Harris comments, "Some teachers do not seem to realize how few unknown words it takes to make a selection difficult for a child and, with the best of intentions, keep many children struggling with material that is unsuitably hard for them."[4] Everett Davis and Eldon Ekwall[5] cite polygraph evidence that most third through fifth graders tested by them show definite signs of frustration when oral reading errors reached 6% or more.

Miscue Analysis

Some teachers may prefer to use "miscue analysis" techniques to examine a child's oral reading. This is a psycholinguistic diagnostic technique designed to help teachers recognize the cueing system(s) the child is using—and is not using. These cueing systems were discussed in Chapter 6 of the present book. They include graphophonic cues, semantic cues, and syntactic cues, also sight and/or whole word cues. In most passages, all of these are normally available for use, but different children may use different cues, and the same child may use different cues according to the difficulty level of the material being read and her or his background in relation to the material.

For example, a child may be able to rapidly assimilate large graphic sequences by using his or her sight vocabulary, plus syntactic and semantic cues, when she or he is very much interested in the material and also is "in tune" with it. The child, then, would be reading in a "top-down" fashion. However, if parts of the material are more challenging and unfamiliar and contain words and/or ideas never seen or considered before, that same child may resort to "bottom-up" reading, using phonic cues. Or, the opposite may be true for different types of readers.*

According to Yetta Goodman and Carolyn Burke,[6] "When a person reads, there are times when what he thinks is printed on the page and what is actually there differ. The resulting deviation from the printed page is called a *miscue*." Their *Reading Miscue Inventory* (RMI) "provides a series of questions which the teacher uses to determine the quality and variety of the reader's miscues. These questions focus on the effect each miscue has on the meaning of what is being read. They also enable the teacher to analyze the reader's use of available language cues and background of information." The reader of this book is referred to the *Manual* for a thorough description of the technique. However, the following brief overview is offered here.

Marking Miscues

As in the oral part of the IRI, the teacher records deviations from the text (miscues) in a manner similar to the IRI. The following is a partial list of miscues and ways of marking them:

1. *substitutions.*

    E.g.: The elephant danced and blew water.

2. *omissions.*

    E.g.: The elephant danced and blew water.

3. *insertions.*

    E.g.: The elephant danced and blew water.

4. *reversals.*

    E.g.: "The elephant danced and blew water," Joanne said.

---

*See Chapter 1, pp. 16–19.

5. *repetitions.*
   - *correcting a miscue.*

     E.g.: The elephant danced (and) blew water.

   - *unsuccessfully attempting to correct.*

     E.g.: The elephant danced and blew water.

   - *anticipating difficulty with a subsequent word.*

     E.g.: The elephant danced and blew water.

6. *additional markings.*
   - *nonword substitution.*

     E.g.: The elephant danced and blew water.

   - *dialect difference.*

     E.g.: The elephant danced and blew water.

     The boy went to the show.

   - *intonation shifts internal to the word.*

     E.g.: The elephant danced and blew water.

Analyzing Miscues

The teacher analyzes the miscues according to the following categories:*

- The *graphic proximity* category represents the child's ability to analyze an unknown word by sight. If the word has a high graphic proximity, at least two out of three parts of the miscue and the text are alike: miscue: /c/ + /o͝o/ + /k/   text: <c> + <oo> + <l> **
- The *phonic proximity* category represents the child's ability to attack an unknown word by sounding out the various letters (graphemes). For

---

* From Donna Norton. *The Effective Teaching of Language Arts.* Columbus, Ohio: Chas. E. Merrill Publishing Co., 1980, pages 354–355, as these authors modified the procedure. Used by permission.
** The grapheme <oo> can be assumed for both pronunciations, since <oo>'s two common phonemes are /o͝o/, as in cook, and /o͞o/, as in cool.

a high phonic proximity, at least two out of three parts of an error and the text word are alike:
miscue: /sh/ + /ā/ + /p/
text: <shade>, i.e., <sh> + <a–e> + <d>

- The *grammatical function* category represents the child's ability to produce errors that are the same part of speech as the text word:
miscue: He had tomato juice, goldfish, and biscuits.
text: He had tomato juice, codfish, and biscuits.
Goldfish and codfish are both nouns. An example of an error that performs a different grammatical function from the text word is:
miscue: Yours was ready fire.
text: Yours was ready first.

- The *syntactic acceptability* category represents the child's ability to use syntactic constraints. To determine acceptability the whole sentence is analyzed:
miscue: Yes, the ship was heading this way.
text: Yes, the ship was heading his way.
Here we have high syntactic acceptability since the miscue is syntactically similar to the text.

- The *semantic acceptability* category represents the child's ability to use the meaning of the sentence when producing a word in context. An example of an error that is totally understandable is:
miscue: Harley saw a little box floating by.
text: Harley saw some little boxes floating by.

- The *meaning change* category represents the degree to which an error alters the message of the text. Some errors result in almost no meaning change:
miscue: My best friends would not believe it.
text: My best friends could not believe it.
Other errors cause extensive meaning change:
miscue: Harley was some little boxes floating by.
text: Harley saw some little boxes floating by.

- The *self-correction* category represents the reader's ability to correct miscues without prompting. Such corrections are made immediately following the error, or shortly thereafter. The error may be in one of the above categories. The child may have made an unacceptable response in that category and by himself or herself recognized that it was unacceptable and, therefore, made the correction.

By analyzing a pupil's ability to score high in a category—or not to score high in a category—the teacher may be able to determine the kind of instructional help a child needs. For example, the child who makes many errors that represent high phonic proximity but low semantic acceptability probably needs much work in using context cues of the semantic type. These readers probably would also benefit from being taught phonics in the context of sentences, while being taught and encouraged to use both semantic and syntactic cues. This might be accomplished by using a Language Experience Approach, by using sentences from the children's books, and/or by using workbook activities that combine the use of these cueing systems.

The oral passage to be used in miscue analysis should be considerably longer than that suggested for use in an IRI. It should require 15 to 20 minutes of reading time. The passage should be difficult reading for the child. Normally, the teacher will begin with material that is one grade level above what the child usually reads in class. This is done because the child must miscue to give the teacher a source of information from which to work in identifying needs of the child. The passage must be new to the child.

Using just the 100 word passage from the previous IRI section (Fig. 14.2) and analyzing it by using only some of the categories given in the miscue section, our recording and analysis would look like the following:

Name _Susanna Brown_

Date _Sept. 16_

No group of birds has made more of an impact on mankind than pheasants have. For years they have been game birds. They have been hunted since the eleventh century. Perhaps they were hunted before this time. Many laws have been written to protect them.

By 1150 pheasant meat was served at restaurants. By 1550 the pheasant was established as a wild bird.

You may see pheasants in your yard today. Perhaps you will see one on a country road. There are many species, and most are large and strong. They are beautiful birds and often bright in color. They eat insects and roots.

Name: _Susanna Brown_ Date: _Sept. 16_ Book: _______

	text	child	grapho/phonic similarity yes	no	syntactic acceptability yes	no	semantic acceptability yes	no	no meaning change yes	no	was miscues either acceptable or corrected yes	no
1.	of an impact	of an imp→impact									✓	
2.	game	tame	✓		✓		✓			✓		✓
3.	—	all over			✓		✓			✓		✓
4.	hunted	—			✓		✓		✓		✓	
5.	yard	park		✓	✓		✓			✓		✓
6.	country	—			✓		✓			✓		✓
7.	species	specials		✓	✓			✓		✓		✓
8.												
9.												
Analysis of miscues Σ			1	2	6	0	5	1	1	5	2	5
%			33%	67%	100%	0%	83%	17%	17%	83%	(29%)	71%

Score: 60–100: Highly Effective | 40–79: Moderately Effective | (15–45: Somewhat Effective) | 0–14: Ineffective

*This chart is a shortened form, using only some of the analysis categories given earlier in this secion.

626

From the final paired column, we get the "Comprehending Score": 29%. Using the following chart,[7] we can get an effectiveness level. We see Susanna is "somewhat effective." Looking at the analysis chart, we can see that Susanna is strong in using syntactic cues, strong in semantic acceptability, but she is weak in the "meaning change" category—i.e., she frequently altered the message of the text.

Effectiveness levels	Miscues showing no loss of comprehension (final columns)
Highly Effective	60–100%
Moderately Effective	40–79%
Somewhat Effective	15–45%
Ineffective	0–14%

Analyzing Comprehension

The following guidelines are used to analyze the comprehension of the child:

- First, the child is asked to retell the story or article. The child closes the book and tells all that he or she can remember. The teacher listens carefully but does not interrupt.
- Next, the teacher asks questions, building only upon what the child has volunteered or continues to volunteer. The teacher must be well prepared for this, having carefully studied the passage and having decided before-time about important points to stress. Some cautions are:
  - The teacher retains all of the child's mispronunciations in questions asked the child. If, for example, a character's name is Carl and the child has pronounced the name "Carol," the teacher uses "Carol" when referring to the character.
  - The teacher avoids simple questions that might have only a "yes" or "no" answer. Normally the questions probe for important information.
- The teacher asks questions that are basic to understanding the passage. E.g., if the passage is a short story, appropriate questions would relate to the setting, theme, plot, and final resolution. Questions are based only upon what the child has volunteered and continues to volunteer, e.g.:
    "What else can you tell me about . . . ?"
    "Who else was involved?"
    "Why do you think . . . ?"
    "Where did . . . happen?"
    "How did you feel when . . . ?"

The teacher does not react to answers given, except to encourage the child to talk.

- Finally, the teacher asks about key words that were mispronounced. E.g.: "You said the name was 'Carol.' Let's look at it. It's really . . . Carl. Does that matter in the story? Explain." Etc. In the passage in this section, Susanna talked about "tame" birds. But the author said pheasants are . . . (game) . . . birds. Does that make a difference? Explain . . . Also Susanna said that "you may see pheasants in your park today, but the author said "in your . . . (yard) . . . today." Is there a difference? Explain.

Analyzing Miscomprehension

"Miscomprehension" has been suggested as a term analogous to "miscue" by Michael Strange. In an article titled "Instructional Implications of a Conceptual Theory of Reading Comprehension," Strange[8] discusses some possible explanations for some responses children give when discussing a selection they have read, as follows:

1. *no existing schema*: The child lacks the schema (schemata) that would enable him or her to understand the passage. The child may lack the background of experience (in long-term storage) necessary for understanding the passage, or may have a different set of experiences (in long-term storage) that would interfere with understanding the author. An example given earlier in the present book was that many New York City children reject *The Yearling* because they are unable to conceive of loving family associations.
2. *naive schema*: The child's schema (schemata) may be at a different level (probably at a lower level) than is necessary for understanding the author. For example, the child may have schemata for fast food restaurants but will find it difficult to understand an article about an exclusive French restaurant. Earlier in the present book there was a discussion of Kohlberg's levels of moral reasoning. It was explained that people prefer to read stories (or articles) in which dilemmas are solved at one level above their present level, but that they cannot understand passages in which dilemmas are solved two or more levels above theirs. (They may be unable to understand concepts other than dilemmas at higher levels also.)
3. *no new information*: If no new information is given, the child is likely to be bored and probably will not pay attention to content.
4. *poor story/passage*: If the selection is poorly written, the schemata the reader possesses may not be cued to assist the child in integrating new information with old information to achieve full understanding.

5. *many schemata appropriate*: The passage may be nonspecific, or the reader may find it nonspecific, and may, therefore, find it open to various interpretations. Sometimes a variety of interpretations are appropriate considering various backgrounds of readers.
6. *schema intrusion*: Sometimes the response to a question comes from the child's head with no plausible line of reasoning connecting it to the story.
7. *textual intrusion*: Here the child's response is based on the text, but no plausible line of reasoning connects the question with the response. The child overresponds to one or more words or ideas of the text.

Identifying miscomprehension strategies a child uses may help the teacher plan instruction appropriate to the child's needs. The teacher then will help the children acquire appropriate schemata for comprehending the reading materials they encounter, according to Strange.

MODIFIED INFORMAL READING INVENTORY FOR THE MIDDLE GRADES

Although it seems important to evaluate the oral reading capacity of primary level children, the value of doing so for higher level children, particularly those children who read at the fifth grade level or above, is questionable. Also the task is time-consuming. Teachers may wish to use a standard IRI or RMI with children who read at the fourth grade level or below and a modified IRI with better readers. The modified IRI, as described here, omits oral reading. It is particularly appropriate for selecting books for content area reading.

Procedure for Writing the Modified IRI

Ideally, the teacher will have at his or her disposal several books at various levels of readability. These would probably be textbooks that are possible choices for using in a content area subject at a specific grade level. (Basic principles in all texts may be the same, but elaborations and examples may differ from text to text. In fact, it would be well if elaborations and examples differed so that all groups of children, including the slow group, would have something unique to add to a class discussion. Besides adding variety to a discussion, such variations in texts could be used to promote critical-creative thinking and reading.) From each of these books, the teacher will select a passage of about 1500 to 3000 words (shorter passages for lower level books, longer ones for more difficult books) that appears to be fairly representative of the book or at least the beginning of it.

The teacher carefully reads each passage to determine what kinds of reading skills are necessary for a student to have in order to understand it. The teacher then selects about four of these skills. For example, one teacher might select these skills:

1. ability to use context to arrive at meanings of words
2. ability to grasp and remember important details
3. ability to recall main ideas and sequences
4. ability to make inferences about what is read

Next, the teacher composes five questions in each of these categories. A modified IRI on a passage from a social studies textbook might look like this:

Book: *Nations Across the Oceans* Name: _______________________

Vocabulary:
1. A Swiss *canton* is similar to an American
   a. city
   b. state
   c. legislature
   d. Senate
2. A *plateau* is
   a. a level surface of land raised above adjacent land
   b. rough land, often quite hilly
   c. land surrounded by mountains
3. Describe an *avalanche*, such as one might see high up in the Alps.

4. The author discusses *radial drainage*. In what direction or directions does water flow if there is radial drainage?

5. Switzerland has many great mountain *ramparts*. Ramparts are used for:
   a. manufacturing of small articles
   b. military protection
   c. attracting tourist trade
   d. meeting places for U.N. decision making

Details (circle answer):

6. Switzerland has not been invaded for more than
   150 years.   T   F
7. Switzerland is about the size of Maine, USA.   T   F
8. Switzerland has about ___________ people.

      3 million   5 million   8 million

9. Swiss manufacturing began in ___________.

      homes   small factories   large buildings

10. The President of Switzerland serves a term of ___________
    year(s).

      1   4   7

Main Idea and Sequence

11. Before we read this chapter, we listed the bold-faced points (as
    given in the book) on the board. These points are still on the
    board. Do one of the following, using *all* of these points.

    a. Classify them into two, three, four, or five main points of your
       choice using the following chart. You will have to formulate
       the main ideas yourself.

Main Ideas					
Subpoints					

    b. classify them as we did before reading. Reproduce the chart
       (as closely as possible) that was on the board before we read
       the chapter:

12. Number in time order the nations that conquered Switzerland,
    starting with the first.

    _____ Austria
    _____ Germany
    _____ France
    _____ Roman Empire

13. Switzerland is an important industrial nation, but it has no coal.
    How does it generate power?

14. Switzerland has many industries. From which one does it derive
    the largest income?

15. Switzerland has two rivers which are its major outlets to the sea. Name these two rivers, and tell which sea each leads to.

    a. ____

    b. ____

Inferences

16. The author states that Switzerland is a republic. He also states that the government in some localities is a "true democracy." Explain what he means by a "true democracy." How does a democracy differ from a republic?

17. Explain why Switzerland has not joined the United Nations.

18. Why do most Swiss people live in valleys or on plateaus? Give as many reasons as you can.

19. Why has Switzerland not been attacked for such a long period of time? Explain.

20. Why is Switzerland so attractive to tourists? Would you like to travel to Switzerland? If so, what would you want to do there?

Procedure for Introducing the Modified IRI

The IRI should be thought of as part of a sample lesson. Thus the IRI should be introduced to children in a manner similar to one a teacher would use when instructing. The validity of an IRI is determined by the extent to which it approximates an actual teaching-learning experience. Its purpose is to find an optimal three-way match between teacher, child, and material. Therefore, it should be introduced to children by the teacher who will be teaching them, and in the normal way in which the teacher instructs.

The previous IRI might be introduced this way:

First, the teacher might call attention to the vocabulary terms in the inventory. This might be done in several ways, among which are:

• the words might be written on the board:

    canton   plateau   avalanche   radial drainage   rampart

Then, they might be pronounced, and the teacher might ask if any-one could suggest a meaning. (Such definitions are not verified by the teacher, though. The suggestion is that children verify or disqual-ify the definitions themselves when reading.)

• A preliminary—and not to be graded—activity might be given to the children to complete before they read. This is done, not to teach the meanings, but, rather, to arouse curiosity about the words.* The activity might be a duplicate of the vocabulary section of the IRI, or it might be quite different. For example, it might look like this:

Insert in the blank in each sentence the word you think best fits that sentence:

    plateau   radial drainage   canton   rampart   avalanche

1. Masses of a snow cap may break away and crash down the moun-tain in a(an) ____________.
2. A high and wide level area of land is a(an) ____________.
3. In Switzerland, a mountain ____________ is designed to be used by the military in protecting the country.
4. A(An) ____________ is like a state in the United States or a prov-ince in Canada.
5. When glaciers melt and form streams, these flow in every direc-tion. This is described as ____________.

This activity may be done by individual children or by the whole group taking the IRI. Again, the teacher does not indicate the correct answer for any item. Children are to search the chapter for the correct answers. (It would be a very positive occurrence if a child did the items incorrect-ly during the prereading activity and did them correctly in the postreading activity. This would mean that the child taught himself/herself the meanings through reading.)

Next, the teacher might lead the children in paging through the as-signment and noting the title and main headings and subheadings of sec-tions if they are given. The teacher might ask the children for these headings and write them on the board. For example, the title and head-ings in this chapter are:

---

*The rationale is that this will encourage children to use context clues. Teachers who teach everything before reading begins make reading unnecessary. If, however, the au-thor did not supply context clues, meanings probably should be taught before reading be-gins.

SWITZERLAND

Size and Shape   Manufacturing Industries
Surface   Tourist Trade
Climate   Transportation
History   Cities
Agriculture   Cantons
Forests   National Government

Since the author has not indicated major points, but rather subpoints of main points, the teacher might help the children classify these points into major areas. For example, the teacher might put the title of the chapter in a circle, put major points the children and/or teacher suggest on "spokes," and the above listed points on lines radiating from these spokes, e.g.,

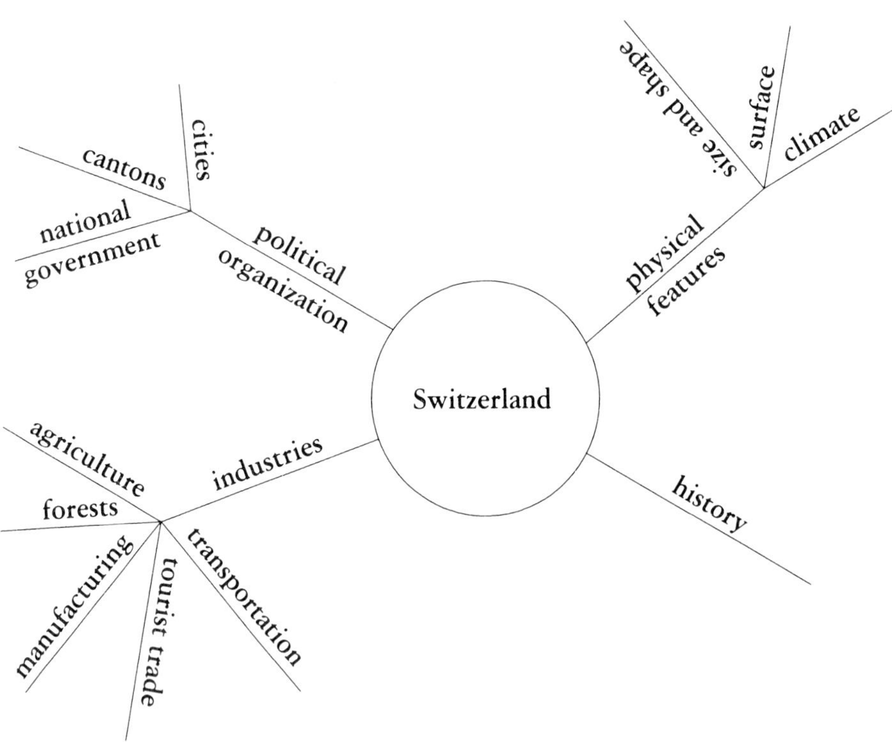

Finally, the teacher might elicit from the class some questions that might be answered in the author's discussion. For example, the children might ask:

1. How large is Switzerland?
2. What is Switzerland's climate like?
3. What is the history of Switzerland? To whom did it belong through history? Who conquered it, if anyone?
4. Switzerland seems to have five major industries. Which is the most important financially?
5. What agricultural products are important?
6. What does Switzerland manufacture?
7. How is Switzerland organized for political reasons? Into cities? Are there larger units like our states?
8. What kind of national government does Switzerland have?

Children might hypothesize about answers and then read. They read silently. When they finish reading, they close their books and answer the questions given in the IRI.

Interpretation of Results

Both survey and limited diagnostic information can be gained from this IRI. The following reading levels can be identified:

independent level	95–100% correct
borderline (high)	90% correct
instructional level	70–85% correct
borderline (low)	55–65% correct
frustrational level	0–50% correct.

Thus, students who score 95–100% correct probably need a more difficult and challenging book for instructional purposes. This book (or at least this part of the book) is at their *independent level*; that is, it is easy enough for them to read without the help of a teacher.

This book is at the *instructional level* for students who scored 70–85 or 90% on this IRI. The book is at the proper level for these students if the teacher introduces other lessons in a way similar to the way in which this lesson was introduced. Additionally, these students are in need of follow-up activities after the reading is completed.

Students who scored 50% or below will probably be frustrated if required to read this book. It is too difficult for them to use even with a teacher's help.

If an additional book is available on an easier level, those students who scored on the frustrational level should be similarly tested with it. If they score 70%–90% correct on this second book, it is on their instructional level and is the book they should use—with teacher guidance.

If an additional book is available on a higher level, those students who scored on the independent level should be similarly tested with it. If they score 70%–90% correct on it, it is on their instructional level.

Thus, it is suggested that if multilevel materials are available, the initial test be given using the materials of middle level in difficulty. Those who score below 70% on this test should be given a test on easier materials. Those who score 90% or better should be given a test on the more difficult materials.

Capacity level can also be determined if the teacher orally reads a passage and the questions to the student or to a group of students. If a student scores 70%–80% correct using such a procedure, the material is said to be on his or her capacity (reading expectancy) level. Teachers who wish to use this technique normally read passages from a book that was found to be at a student's frustrational reading level. Students whose instructional level is found to be considerably below their capacity level should be referred to a remedial reading teacher for further diagnosis and help.

Besides looking at the total percentage score, it is often interesting to look at patterns of both errors and correct responses, but this can be done only if there is a sufficient number of questions of the types analyzed. Students might be considered deficient in a skill if they miss two or more out of five items in a category. They might be considered strong in a skill if they score 100 percent in a category. From such an analysis, a teacher might get *clues* as to what types of items need emphasis among certain groups of students and might check out these clues through further observations.

The teacher might wish to compose a chart for each student for each IRI taken. For one student, the teacher might complete the chart thus:

Book ***Nations Across the Seas***   Student ***John Malone***
Readability of Passage ___**5**___
Survey Information

Independent level	Borderline	Instructional level	Borderline	Frustrational level
100-95	90	85-(80)-75-70	65-60-55	50-45-40—

Diagnostic information:

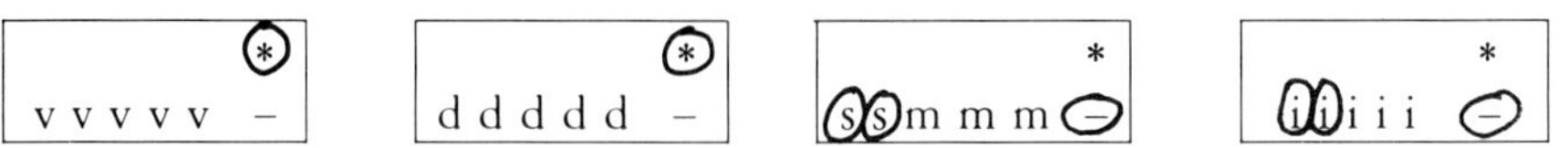

By reading this chart, we can see that this student scored 80% on this IRI. Therefore, this book is on his *instructional level*—the level at which he can learn with teacher help. Had he scored 65% or lower, he should be tested using an easier book. Or had he scored 90% or higher, he should be tested using a more difficult text. We can also see that this student had difficulty with sequence and inference type questions but that he did well on vocabulary and detail type questions.

After identifying the instructional level for each student, the teacher might compose a chart for either the entire class or for the group of children who are using a particular book. Below is a hypothetical chart for social studies classroom in which three books are being used.

Other comprehension skills, such as critical-creative reading skills, could be added to the chart later—after the children have used the books and the teacher has had the opportunity to observe each child's strengths and weaknesses in these areas of reading—or thinking— achievement. In addition, the teacher might time children when they read passages from the book. These rate scores could also be recorded on the master sheet, e.g.:

Classwide diagnostic information from IRI's

Book/Readability	Instructional Level for:	vocabulary	details	main idea and sequence	inferences	(add others later)
European and	Anderson, Betty	*	*		−	
Asian Nations	Calaton, James	−		*	−	
	DeVitt, Harry	*	−	*		
(7th grade)	Farnsworth, Joan		−	−	*	
	etc.					
Nations Across	Alvarez, Juan	−	−	*	*	
the Seas	Bronte, Mary	*			−	
	Ellison, Sue	−	*	*		
(5th grade)	Gomez, Tomas	−	*	−		
	etc.					
Europe and	Brighton, Julie	*	*	−	−	
Africa in	Eaton, Margaret	−	−	*	*	
Transition	Fisher, Paul		*	−		
	Hughes, Aaron	*	−		−	
(3rd grade)	etc.					

(The second section of each cell is provided for the second observation, or for the posttest.)

The chart shown above can be very useful. By reading across a line, the teacher can identify relative strengths and weaknesses of each child. If each child is placed in a book at his or her instructional level, he or she will have missed from two or three to six or nine questions. Thus, each child will have a profile of strengths and weaknesses—though for some it may be a fairly even profile (an equal number of errors may be made in all areas). Therefore, by giving an IRI of this type, a teacher might be able to get a limited amount of diagnostic information. Since diagnosis should be continuous, the teacher can constantly add to his or her understanding of a child's needs through daily observations in the classroom. The IRI is just the beginning.

Also, by reading down the columns, the teacher is able to identify those children who are most in need of help in a particular skill area. The teacher can also identify those who are strong and might serve as peer leaders in teaching in a specific skill area. Thus, by reading this chart, we can see that the following children probably need help in vocabulary development as it relates to the unit on Switzerland: James Calafon, Juan Alvarez, Sue Ellison, Tomas Gomez, and Margaret Eaton. We can also see that the following might be good peer leaders: Betty Anderson, Harry DeVitt, Mary Bronte, Julie Brighton, and Aaron Hughes.

Thus a teacher might design a skill center for teaching the vocabulary of this unit. (Chapters 6 and 7 of this book will give you ideas about how to design such a center.) Those who need vocabulary development most would be given time to work in this center. A skill center should also be designed to teach the important details of this unit, and other centers would be designed to reinforce main ideas and sequence, and inferences related to this unit. Unit Two in this book is designed to show you how to develop such skill centers.

Other centers, of course, should be added also, such as a center to develop critical-creative skills, in which materials are available from a variety of sources. Students would be taught how to select appropriate sources, how to compare ideas from various authors, how to identify biases, how to synthesize ideas from many sources, and how to evaluate ideas.

CLOZE READABILITY TECHNIQUE

The Cloze Readability Technique may be used as a substitute, or partial substitute, for the previously explained Informal Reading Inventory. The Cloze technique is elegant in its simplicity. Once a passage is selected that is representative of the book upon which the student is to be tested, the procedure is simple to use. However, selection of the passage is more complex. This will be explained last.

Let us say that we have the representative passage. It will be 250 words of continuous writing, and *every fifth word* will be "CLOZED." That is, every fifth word will be omitted, and in its place will be an underscoring. Each underscoring must be of uniform length (about 12 typewriter spaces). All students in a class can be given the same passage at the same time. They are asked to write in the *exact* word that has been omitted. There is no time limit.

In a 250-word passage, there are 50 clozures since every fifth word is deleted. Each correct response counts for two percentage points. To be correct, the student must supply the author's *exact* word, though it might be misspelled. That is the way the procedure has been standardized, and that is the way the passage must be scored. Credit is *not* given for synonyms—what one person may consider a synonym, another may not.

The percentage score a student receives is used to determine his or her reading level for the passage:

> 58%–100% correct—independent level
> 44%– 57% correct—instructional level
> 0%– 43% correct—frustrational level.

As with the modified IRI, several books may be needed to identify each child's instructional level. And, even if only one textbook is available to a classroom, it would be well for the teacher to identify children who may have a very hard time with it and other children for whom the book is too easy.

For the logic behind the "CLOZE" procedure, see John Bormuth's article.[9] This procedure is becoming increasingly popular with reading experts, for hidden in the correct response is an understanding of the author's style and technique as well as a revelation of the background of information and syntactic and semantic ability of the student being tested.

Selection of a Passage that is Representative of the Book

Obviously, the passage which is selected is of utmost importance. It must come very close to being representative of the book of which it is a part. Bormuth instructs that originally 12 passages should be selected from a book. If the book appears to be of uniform difficulty throughout, the passages are selected at equal page intervals throughout, e.g., every 50 pages. If the book becomes progressively more difficult, the 12 passages are selected from the beginning of the book, again at equal intervals, perhaps every eighth page.

Each passage is 250 words long and need not end with the last word of a sentence. The passage is the first 250-word passage of continuous writing that is found on or after the designated page number. Each *fifth* word is clozed to the end of the sentence in which the 250th word occurs. Only the first 50 clozures are scored.

The passage is typed on a single sheet of paper and should look something like the following: (You may wish to keep the first sentence intact, as suggested here.)

No group of birds has made more of an impact on mankind than pheasants have. For years they have _____________ game birds. They have _____________ hunted since the eleventh _____________. Perhaps they were hunted _____________ this time. Many laws _____________ been written to protect _____________.

    By 1150 pheasant meat _____________ served at restaurants. By _____________ the pheasant was established _____________ a game bird.

    You _____________ see pheasants in your _____________ today. Perhaps you will _____________ one on a country _____________. There are many species, _____________ most are large and _____________. They are beautiful birds _____________ often bright in color. _____________ eat insects and roots, _____________ for roots with their _____________ bills and never scratching _____________ their feet.

    (Etc., to 50 clozures.)

The clozed passage is reproduced so that all students have their own copy, and they fill in the blanks. Numbers and answer sheets cannot be used, for this would invalidate the results. (Each blank filled in serves as a clue to another blank. An answer sheet would make these clues more difficult to recognize.) Each of the 12 passages is given to at least 30 students. If six classes of 30 students each were being used, each student would be given only two passages.

    To ensure a random distribution of passages, teachers should refer to the alphabetical listing of students in their grade book. They divide the list into six equal parts, or count off students 1, 2, 3, 4, 5, 6 / 1, 2, 3, 4, 5, 6, etc., and designate the groups as 1, 2, 3, 4, 5, 6. Each of 12 passages is also numbered. The chart that follows can be used for the distribution of passages to students:

Student groups	Passages
1	4 and 7
2	3 and 12
3	6 and 11
4	1 and 8
5	5 and 10
6	2 and 9

After each passage has been scored, the mean average (arithmetic average) for the passage is computed by adding all of the percentage scores and dividing by the number of students who were tested on the passage. Thus, we might have the following average scores for the passage:

Passage	Mean average	Passage	Mean average
1	40	7	40
2	26	8	65
3	70	9	43
4	36	10	48
5	52	11	36
6	58	12	54

Next, the mean of the means is computed. For these passages it would be:

$$\frac{40 + 26 + 70 + 36 + 52 + 58 + 40 + 65 + 43 + 48 + 36 + 54}{12} =$$

$$\frac{568}{12} = 47.3.$$

The passage whose mean is closest to the mean of the mean is selected as representative of the book. In this case, it would be *passage 10*, whose mean is 48.

Now, all students (except those in group 5, who have already had it) are given this passage. Also, whenever testing is done on this book in the future, this passage should be used. Therefore, the "selection of passage" procedure is no longer necessary for this book.

Comment

The main type of information gained from using the Cloze Readability Technique is placement information: Is the book at the child's independent level, instructional level, or frustrational level? Through using a technique similar to the Miscue Analysis Technique, the teacher might be able also to determine whether the child uses semantic and syntactic cue systems well. Such an analysis might be far too much to expect a content area teacher to perform. However, in some instances, the reading teacher may be able to help the content area teacher in such a diagnosis. The reading teacher who works along with classroom teachers, rather than just with children in a reading center situation, may be able to design helpful activities to be used in the content area classroom.

All of the percentages given for use with the IRI, the modified IRI, and the Cloze technique are meant as guidelines only. They are not meant to serve as rigid cutting-off points. Teachers must carefully observe their students in other ways to be certain that the books they are using are appropriate.

Students vary greatly in their ability and desire to cope with easy and/or difficult materials. A student with a great deal of interest in a subject may not mind being frustrated a bit. Another who lacks interest may find material which is considered to be on the appropriate instructional level too difficult to be worth the effort. Indeed, the affective dimensions of reading must also be considered.

Standardized Reading Tests

Children should be tested in reading, as in other areas, with instruments that relate to the goals of the program in which they are working. Not all reading tests measure the same kinds of reading skills. Few, if any, standardized tests measure interest in reading. And no standardized tests measure achievement of the child's own goals for comprehension. Informal instruments, such as those described earlier in this chapter and the interest inventories described in a previous chapter may better measure achievement of the specific and general goals of a teacher's or a school's reading program. However, standardized tests do provide helpful information also, and different types of information. The following section is provided to describe some characteristics of standardized tests. Anyone interested in selecting and evaluating specific tests is advised to consult Buros' *Mental Measurements Yearbook*[10] for test descriptions and critiques.

Characteristics of Standardized Tests

Standardized tests are norm-referenced. That is, they provide information that allows the teacher to compare his or her students to large groups of students, usually selected nationally. If a test is given exactly as stated in the test manual, scores children make in one school or area can be compared with those made by other children around the country who served in the norming group.

Scores: Grade-Equivalent Scores, Percentile Scores, and Stanine Scores

The following types of scores may be provided: grade-equivalent scores, percentile scores, stanine scores, plus perhaps other types. All of these are based on the raw score (the number of correct responses usually). The *grade-equivalent score* indicates the grade level for which the raw score was the average score obtained by the students in the norming group. Half of the students at that grade level fall below this score, and half above it. Thus, if a raw score of 65 is the average (or midpoint) score for beginning fifth graders in the norming group, all other children who score 65 would be said to have a grade-equivalent score of 5.0. If a fifth grade class of children read like the children in the norming group, half of them would score below 5.0, and half would score above 5.0.

Percentile scores are used to compare a child's performance with other children of the same grade or age. The percentile tells how many students in one-hundred (or what percentage of students) in the norming group scored below the child. Thus a percentile of 99 indicates that 99% of the norming group (of the child's age or grade level) scored below him or her. A percentile of 50 indicates that the child is at the midpoint of the group. (50% scored below him or her.)

Stanine scores are single digit scores that range from 1 to 9. Except for numbers one and nine, each stanine represents the same number of raw score points in the test. Their relation to percentile scores can be seen in the following table.

stanine	1	2	3	4	5	6	7	8	9
% of scores in stanine	4%	7%	12%	17%	20%	17%	12%	7%	4%
percentiles	0 4	11	23	40	60	77	89	96	99
raw scores (e.g.)	20	25	30	35	40	45	50	55	

The middle stanine, number 5, includes the 40th to 60th percentile scores. Stanines 6, 7, 8, 9 represent increasingly better performance, while stanines 4, 3, 2, 1 represent decreasing performance.

It is important to recognize that age-equivalent scores, percentile scores and stanine scores are status scores. That is, they indicate the state of the art—how well individuals and large groups of students do read. They do not indicate how well they should read. They are not "ideal" scores.

Validity, Reliability, and Usability

Test manuals usually supply information about the validity, reliability, and usability of the tests. *Validity* means truthfulness, or accuracy. The validity of the test is a measure of the degree to which it measures what it is intended to measure. *Content validity* refers to the accuracy of its content in relationship to the purpose or objective of the test. (If it is a test of arithmetic vocabulary in grades 4–6, does it measure knowledge of arithmetic terms used in these grades? If so, to what degree? If it is a reading readiness test of visual discrimination, to what degree does it measure what experts think is important in visual discrimination at this level? Etc.) *Predictive validity* is a measure of the degree to which the test predicts future success in the area of the test. A test may have content validity but lack predictive validity.

Reliability relates to the degree to which the test renders consistent results. If a child were to take an equivalent test the same day or the next day, would the score be the same? The higher the reliability coefficient, the more consistent the test scores.

A standard error of measurement score is used to indicate the range of scores to be expected if the same student would retake the test several or many times without learning occurring between tests. The smaller the standard error of measurement, the more reliable the test.

A standard error of measurement of 0.3 means that there is a 67% probability that the true score of the student taking the test is within three-tenths of a year of the score obtained. Thus, if a child scores grade 5.0 on a test with a standard error measurement of 0.3, there is a 67% probability that his or her true score is 5.0 ± .3 (4.7 to 5.3). Also, there is a 95% probability that the true score is 5.0 ± .6 (twice the standard error of measurement). That is, there is a 95% probability that the true score is between 4.4 and 5.6. There is a 5% probability that the true score is either below 4.4 or above 5.6.

Usability of a test refers to the ease with which it can be given and scored, and the amount of time it takes to give and score the test. By reading the manual the examiner can determine these.

Survey versus Diagnostic Tests

Survey tests are designed to give a measure of the general level of achievement of a child. Survey tests usually have subtests, but a survey test is intended principally to give one over-all score.

Diagnostic tests, on the other hand, are designed to indicate strengths and weaknesses in subareas, or skills. Caution should be exerted in interpreting subtest scores because frequently subtest scores are low in reliability because of the brevity of the subtest. Also, most subtests lack "discriminant validity"; i.e., they do not measure distinct skills or abilities.[11]

Level of Tests

Thomas G. Gunning[12] cautions, "If the test doesn't fit, don't give it. The information yielded could be erroneous and, in some instances, injurious." Just as teachers are cautioned to give children the right level of books to read, they should also be cautioned to give children the right level tests. For a reading test to be at the appropriate level for the child, it must be in the range of the child's reading achievement level. If a test is too difficult for a child, the child will receive a "chance score," what Edward Fry once called an "orangutan score": the score a cooperative orangutan would receive for pushing buttons an appropriate number of times. If the test is too easy for a child, the child will not be able to demonstrate her or his strength.

Many publishers supply brief "locator tests," that help identify the correct level of test for a student. Most publishers supply tests at different levels but with the same timing and same instructions so that all children in a class can be tested simultaneously—each with an appropriate level of test. When out-of-level testing is done, care must be taken in interpreting percentile and stanine scores.

Limitations of Standardized Tests

Although standardized tests do have definite values, they also have some serious limitations. Some of these they have in common with informal tests. Thomas Newkirk* lists some of these:

- Any standardized test is only a measure of performance at one time.
- A standardized reading test purports to measure the student's reading ability by having him read passages which may be of no interest to him or her.
- The type of reading comprehension measured on reading tests is not the type of comprehension needed for most kinds of reading. (Passages are very short, and many questions may be asked on these passages.)
- The rigid time restrictions create an unrealistic environment for the testing of reading.

---

*Thomas Newkirk. "The Limitations of the Standardized Reading Test." *The English Journal*, 64 (March 1975): 50–52. Used by permission.

- Tests of reading comprehension tend to over-emphasize factual recall of relatively insignificant details.
- Because of standardizing procedures, many standardized tests may be inappropriate for low socio-economic and minority groups.
- Reading tests may actually test pre-existing knowledge as much as they test reading comprehension.[13]

Despite these limitations, standardized tests give us information it would be impossible to get without them. Standardized silent reading tests are especially helpful in providing a means for the comparison of groups, perhaps classes, of children.

Brief Descriptions of Some Available Standardized Reading Tests

Some of the tests a school might wish to consider for use are:

Silent Reading Tests-Group Tests

California Reading Tests Level 1, grades 1–2; Level 2, grades 2–4; Level 3, grades 4–6; Level 4, grades 6–9. (Vocabulary and comprehension subtests at all levels.) Levels 1 and 2 also include word-attack subtests. (California Test Bureau, Monterey, Calif. 93940)

Diagnostic Reading Tests This is a series of survey and diagnostic tests from first grade to college. (Committee on Diagnostic Reading Tests, Mountain Home, N.C. 28758)

Gates-MacGinitie Reading Tests Primary A, grade 1; Primary B, grade 2; Primary C, grade 3 (Vocabulary and comprehension subtests at these levels). Primary CS, speed and accuracy for grades 2–3. Survey D, grades 4–6; Survey E, grades 7–9 (vocabulary, comprehension, and speed-accuracy subtests at these levels). (Teachers College Press, Columbia Univ., N.Y. 10027)

Iowa Silent Reading Test Level 1, grades 6–9 (vocabulary, comprehension, study skills, speed-accuracy subtests). (Harcourt Brace Jovanovich, N.Y. 10017)

Iowa Tests of Basic Skills Primary Battery: Level 7, grades 1.7–2.5; Level 8, grades 2.6–3.5 (comprehension, word analysis, vocabulary). Levels Edition: Levels 9–14, grades 3–8 (vocabulary, comprehension, word-study skills). (Houghton Mifflin Co., Hopewell, N.J. 08525)

Metropolitan Achievement Tests Grades K–12.9 (combines norm-referenced and criterion-referenced components/also yields instructional reading level scores). (Psychological Corporation, N.Y. 10017)

Stanford Diagnostic Reading Tests Level I, grades 2.5–4.5; Level II, grades 4.5–8.5 (comprehension, vocabulary, syllabication, auditory skills, phonic analysis, and rate subtests). (Harcourt Brace Jovanovich, N.Y. 10017)

Stanford Reading Tests Primary I, grades 1.5–2.4; Primary II, grades 2.5–3.4; Primary III, grades 3.5–4.4, Intermediate I, grades 4.5–5.4; Intermediate II, grades 5.5–6.9 (vocabulary, comprehension, word-study, listening-comprehension subtests). Advanced, grades 7–9.5 (vocabulary and comprehension). (Harcourt Brace Jovanovich, N.Y. 10017)

Oral Reading Tests

Gates-McKillop Reading Diagnostic Test (Teachers College, Columbia University, N.Y. 10027)

Gilmore Oral Reading Test Grades 1–8. (Harcourt Brace Jovanovich, N.Y. 10017)

Gray Oral Reading Tests Grades 1–12. (Bobbs-Merrill Co., Indianapolis 46268)

Gray Standardized Oral Reading Paragraphs Grades 1–8. (Bobbs-Merrill Co., Indianapolis 46268)

Spache Diagnostic Reading Scales Grades 1–8. (California Test Bureau, Monterey, Calif. 93940)

Tests of Words in Isolation/Word Analysis

Slosson Oral Reading Test Grades 1–12. (Slosson Educational Publications, East Aurora, N.Y. 14052)

Sipay Word Analysis Tests (SWAT) (Educators Publishing Service, Cambridge, Mass. 02138)

Wide Range Achievement Test Age 5–adult. (Psychological Corporation, N.Y. 10017)

Criterion Referenced Tests

Criterion referenced tests were discussed in Chapter 13, pages 584–588. Teachers interested in examining published criterion-referenced tests may wish to see these:

Cooper-McGuire Diagnostic Word-Analysis Tests These are group tests in these areas: readiness for word-analysis, phonic analysis, and structural analysis. (Croft Educational Services, New London, Conn. 06320)

Fountain Valley Reading Skills Tests Grades 1–6. This is a series of 77 one-page tests covering 277 behavioral objectives in these areas: phonics, structural analysis, vocabulary, comprehension, study skills. (Richard Zweig Associates, Huntington Beach, Calif. 92648)

Metropolitan Achievement Tests (see norm-referenced entry).

Wisconsin Tests of Reading Skills Improvement Word Attack: grades K–3. This is a series of tests measuring 38 word analysis skills at four levels of difficulty. Study Skills: grades K–6. This is a series of tests measuring 77 study skills in these areas-maps, graphs, tables, and references. (Interpretive Scoring Systems, Minneapolis, Minn. 55435)

Summary

Opportunities for the evaluation of student performance are ever-present in school situations, and the most important evaluations occur day-by-day. Perhaps the most valid reasons for assessing student performance are to identify the level of materials a student can read and thus to supply the student with materials at an appropriate level, and to identify the specific needs and interests of the student and from this identification to help fill these needs and interests. This should be done to promote optimal learning and enjoyment for each child. Another reason for evaluation may be to compare groups of students, perhaps nation-wide.

Evaluation procedures used must be appropriate to the philosophy of reading followed in a school. Different types of reading skills—or at least different emphases—are evident in various philosophies, ranging from "bottom-up" to "top-down." Additionally, materials used in schools should be evaluated in terms of their usefulness in relation to the school's philosophy, in terms of completeness, organization, freedom from stereotypes, style of writing, and difficulty level.

Materials usually are not appropriate in and of themselves, but, instead, are appropriate for some children, and probably are not appropriate for others. Techniques for assessing appropriateness of materials in relation to individual children were next explained. Among the techniques, or instruments, explained were the Informal Reading Inventory, Miscue Analysis, a modification of the Informal Reading Inventory for the Middle Grades, and the Cloze Readability Technique. In addition to these, the use of interest inventories (as explained in a previous chapter) was also recommended.

Standardized (norm-referenced) tests were next discussed. Briefly explained were:

- scores: grade-equivalent scores, percentile scores, and stanine scores
- validity, reliability, usability of tests
- survey vs. diagnostic tests
- level of tests

Next discussed were limitations of standardized tests. Then the following types of standardized reading tests were briefly described: silent reading tests, oral reading tests, tests of words in isolation. Several published criterion-referenced tests were also listed.

Questions and Activities

After answering the questions at the beginning of this chapter, consider these questions and activities:

1. Consider the reasons given in this chapter for evaluating reading performance. Do they all make sense to you? Can you add to the list?

2. What is your philosophy of reading? List in some detail what skills or abilities and other characteristics you would diagnose in accord with this philosophy. Tell how you would diagnose each. Would the list differ according to the grade level of the children? Explain. You might wish to organize by using these broad areas:

Sociological factors	Physical factors	Educational factors

Psychological factors:

cognitive	affective	psycho-motor

3. Consider the relative importance of the interest factor in "bottom-up" vs. "top-down" and/or "top-down/interactive" programs. Would you evaluate materials differently (in terms of interest) for each of these programs? Explain.

4. Compose a list of the important factors to be considered in evaluating reading materials in accord with your philosophy of reading.

5. What are the strengths and weaknesses of readability formulas? What other considerations must be given to materials in determining whether they are "right" for a child to use?

6. Informal Reading Inventories are used to judge whether materials are appropriate for a child to use. Would the questions in such inventories vary according to the teacher's philosophy of reading? Explain. Would the materials used in the inventories vary?

7. What do you consider the major values of miscue analysis to be in terms of analyzing oral reading? comprehension? What are the values of analyzing "miscomprehension"?

8. Much has been written lately about the changing role of special reading personnel in schools. There appears to be a trend toward using reading personnel in "resource" roles, having them work with teachers, perhaps in team teaching, rather than in special reading classes. (This is referred to as the "multiplying effect": a

reading teacher may work with 30 students in remedial reading and thus affect 30 children, but by working with ten teachers, each of whom has 30 students, the reading teacher would affect 300 children.)[14] Do you think that one of the things a resource teacher should do is help teachers in evaluating the progress of children both in reading and in content area classes by helping in designing, giving, and gaining diagnostic information from IRI's, RMI's, and Modified Informal Reading Inventories? Explain.

9. Why is it of vital importance that the materials of the classroom be used as the materials of the informal tests? Why is it also of vital importance that the classroom teacher be directly involved in designing and giving these informal tests and in making the evaluations?

10. Consider this statement: "Informal Reading Inventories (and other structured informal assessment instruments) serve to give clues to the teacher about diagnostic teaching. However, daily evaluations are of even greater importance." Compare the importance of both of these types of observations.

11. Compare the uses and values of informal assessment instruments with those of standardized tests. Do each have a special place in the school situation? Explain.

Notes

1. See George Klare in Selected References.
2. See Emmett Betts in Selected References.
3. Albert J. Harris, p. 137. See Selected References.
4. *Ibid.*
5. See Everett Davis and Eldon E. Ekwall in Selected References.
6. Yetta Goodman and Carolyn Burke, p. 6. See Selected References.
7. *Ibid.*, pp. 116–119.
8. See Michael Strange in Selected References.
9. See John Bormuth in Selected References.
10. See Oscar Buros in Selected References.
11. See Roger Farr. *Reading: What Can Be Measured?* Newark, Delaware: International Reading Association, 1969.
12. See Thomas G. Gunning in Selected References.
13. See J. Jaap Tuinman in Selected References.
14. Rita M. Bean and Robert M. Wilson. *Effecting Change in School Reading Programs*, Newark, Delaware: International Reading Association, 1981.

Selected References

Allington, Richard L. and Anne McGill-Franzen. "Word Identification Errors in Isolation and in Context: Apples vs. Oranges." *The Reading Teacher*, 33 (April 1980): 795–800.

Baumann, James F. and Jennifer A. Stevenson. "Understanding Standardized Reading Achievement Test Scores." *The Reading Teacher*, 35 (March 1982): 648–654.

——————————————. "Using Scores from Standardized Reading Achievement Tests." *The Reading Teacher*, 35 (February, 1982): 528–532.

Bean, Rita M. "Roles of the Reading Specialist: A Multifaceted Dilemma." *The Reading Teacher*, 32 (January 1979): 409–413.

Betts, Emmett. *Foundations of Reading Instruction*. New York: American Book Co., 1957.

Bormuth, John. "The Cloze Readability Procedure." *Elementary English*, 45 (April 1968): 429–436.

Burmeister, Lou E. *Reading Strategies for Middle and Secondary School Teachers, Second Edition*. Reading, Massachusetts: Addison-Wesley, 1978, Chs. 2 and 3.

——————————————. *Words—from Print to Meaning (Classroom Activities: for Building Sight Vocabulary, for Using Context Clues, Morphology, and Phonics)*. Reading, Mass.: Addison-Wesley, 1975.

Buros, Oscar K. (Ed.). *The Seventh Mental Measurements Yearbook*, Vols. I and II. Highland Park, New Jersey: Gryphon Press, 1972.

——————————————. *Reading Tests and Reviews II*. Highland Park, New Jersey: Gryphon Press, 1975.

Cohen, Elizabeth G., Jo-Anne K. Intili, and Susan Hurevitz Robbins. "Teachers and Reading Specialists: Cooperation or Isolation?" *The Reading Teacher*, 32 (December 1978): 281–287.

Cooper, J. Louis. *The Effect of Adjustment of Basal Reading Materials on Reading Achievement*. Unpublished doctoral dissertation, Boston University, 1952.

Dale, Edgar and Jeanne Chall. "A Formula for Predicting Readability." *Educational Research Bulletin* (January 21, 1948): 11–20, 28.

—————————— and Barbara Seels. *Readability and Reading: An Annotated Bibliography*. Newark, Delaware: International Reading Association, 1966.

Davis, Everett and Eldon E. Ekwall. "Mode of Perception and Frustration in Reading." *Journal of Learning Disabilities*, 9 (August/September 1976): 448–454.

D'Angelo, Karen and Robert M. Wilson. "How Helpful Is Insertion and Omission Miscue Analysis?" *The Reading Teacher*, 32 (February 1979): 519–520.

Dillner, Martha H. and Joanne P. Olson. *Personalizing Reading Instruction in Middle, Junior, and Senior High Schools*. New York: Macmillan, 1977.

Ebel, Robert L. "The Case for Norm-Referenced Measurements." *Educational Researcher*, 7 (December 1978): 3–5.

Englert, Carol Sue and Melvyn I. Semmel. "The Relationship of Oral Reading Substitution Miscues to Comprehension." *The Reading Teacher*, 35 (December 1981): 273–279.

Farr, Roger. *Measurement of Reading Achievement: An Annotated Bibliography.* Newark, Delaware: International Reading Assoc., 1971.

Finkelstein, Miriam G. "What I Do (and What I Used to Do) as a Reading Specialist." *The Reading Teacher*, 32 (December 1978): 288–291.

Fry, Edward. "Fry's Readability Graph: Clarifications, Validity, and Extension to Level 17." *Journal of Reading*, 21 (Dec. 1977): 242–252.

Goodman, Kenneth S. (ed.). *Miscue Analysis-Applications to Reading Instruction.* Champaign, Illinois: National Council of Teachers of English, 1973.

Goodman, Yetta. "Developing Reading Proficiency" in *Findings of Research in Miscue Analysis: Classroom Implications*, P. David Allen and Dorothy J. Watson (eds.). Urbana, Illinois: National Council of Teachers of English, 1976.

_________________. "Test Review: Concepts About Print Test" (by Marie M. Clay). *The Reading Teacher*, 34 (January 1981): 445–448.

_________________. "Using Children's Reading Miscues for New Teaching Strategies." *The Reading Teacher*, 23 (February 1970): 455–459.

_________________ and Carolyn Burke. *Reading Miscue Inventory: Manual-Procedure for Diagnosis and Evaluation.* New York: Macmillan, 1972.

Gunning, Thomas G. "Wrong Level Test Information." *The Reading Teacher*, 35 (May, 1982): 902–905.

Guszak, Frank J. *Diagnostic Reading Instruction in the Elementary School. Second Edition.* New York: Harper and Row, 1978.

Harris, Albert J. "The Effective Teacher of Reading, Revisited." *The Reading Teacher*, 33 (November 1979): 135–140.

Hoffman, James V. "Characterizing Teacher Feedback to Student Miscues During Oral Reading Instruction." *The Reading Teacher*, 34 (May 1981): 907–913.

Hood, Joyce. "Is Miscue Analysis Practical for Teachers?" *The Reading Teacher*, 32 (December 1978): 260–266.

Jenkins, Barbara L., William H. Longmaid, Susanne F. O'Brien, and Cynthia N. Sheldon. "Children's Use of Hypothesis Testing When Decoding Words." *The Reading Teacher*, 33 (March 1980): 664–667.

Johns, Jerry L. "Strategies for Oral Reading Behavior." *Language Arts*, 52 (November/December 1975): 1104–1107.

Johnson, Marjorie S. and Roy Kress. *Informal Reading Inventories.* Newark, Delaware: International Reading Association, 1965.

Jorgensen, Gerald W. "Relationship of Classroom Behavior to the Accuracy of the Match Between Material Difficulty and Student Ability." *Journal of Educational Psychology*, 69 (February 1977): 24–32.

Klare, George. "Assessing Readability." *Reading Research Quarterly*, Vol. 10, No. 1 (1974–75): 62–102.

Lamberg, Walter J. "Assessment of Oral Reading Which Exhibits Dialect and Language Differences." *Journal of Reading*, 22 (April 1979): 609–616.

Leu, Donald J., Jr. "Oral Reading Error Analysis: A Critical Review of Research and Application." *Reading Research Quarterly*, XVII, No. 3 (1982): 420–437.

Maring, Gerald H. "Matching Remediation to Miscues." *The Reading Teacher*, 31 (May 1978): 887–891.

Micklos, John, Jr. "Commentary: Clouds and Silver Linings: A Realistic Look at Reading Achievement." *The Reading Teacher*, 35 (Mqrch 1982): 644–646.

Newkirk, Thomas. "The Limitations of Standardized Reading Tests." *The English Journal*, 64 (March 1975): 50–52.

Newman, Harold. "Oral Reading Miscue Analysis Is Good But Not Complete." *The Reading Teacher*, 31 (May 1978): 883–886.

Schell, Lee M. and Gerald S. Hanna. "Can Informal Reading Inventories Reveal Strengths and Weaknesses in Comprehension Subskills?" *The Reading Teacher*, 35 (December 1981): 263–268.

Schubert, Delwyn and Theodore Torgerson. *Improving the Reading Program. Fifth Edition.* Dubuque, Iowa: Wm. C. Brown Co. Publishers, 1980.

Spache, George D. "The New Spache Readability Formula," in *Good Reading for Poor Readers.* Champaign, Illinois: Garrard Publishing Co., 1974, pp. 195–207.

Strange, Michael. "Instructional Implications of a Conceptual Theory of Reading Comprehension." *The Reading Teacher*, 33 (January 1980): 391–397.

Trela, Thaddeus M. "Impress Reading Method," in *Fourteen Remedial Reading Methods.* Belmont, California: Fearon Publishers, 1968.

Tuinman, J. Jaap. "Determining the Passage Dependency on Comprehension Questions in Five Major Tests." *Reading Research Quarterly*, Vol. 9, No. 2 (1973–74): 206–223.

Weaver, Constance. *Psycholinguistics and Reading: From Process to Practice.* Cambridge, Mass.: Winthrop Publishers, Inc., 1980.

Zintz, Miles V. *Corrective Reading. Third Edition.* Dubuque, Iowa: Wm. C. Brown Co. Publishers, 1977.

Readability: New Spache Readability Formula and Dale-Chall Formula

The New Spache Readability Formula

The Spache readability formula is widely used for estimating the reading difficulty of printed materials below the fourth grade level.[1] Like the Dale-Chall formula, the Spache formula uses two factors to arrive at the score: average sentence length and difficulty of words (as indicated by presence or absence of each word on a word list).

One must refer to the original exposition of the new formula for directions and the word list. After the reader computes the *average sentence length* (by counting the number of sentences in a passage and dividing that number into the number of words) and the *percentage of difficult words* (as instructed by Spache), one need not do the computations. Instead, the reader can simply consult the following chart[2] and read to the point of intersection of the two figures to get the approximate grade level of the passage. For example, if the average sentence length were 12 words, and the percentage of difficult words were 10, the difficulty of the passage is 2.9.

The Dale-Chall Readability Formula

The Dale-Chall readability formula is widely used for estimating the reading difficulty of printed materials at the fourth grade level and above.[3] Two factors are used to arrive at the score—*sentence length* and *word difficulty.*

It is necessary to refer to the original article for the list of easy words. With certain stipulations, as explained in the article, all other words are hard.

When the reader knows the number of hard words within a 100-word passage (i.e., the percentage of hard words) and the number of sentences totally within the 100-word passage, he or she can use the "Computation Ease" chart on the following page to find the grade level score.[4]

If we wanted to find the average readability level of two or more passages, we would average the raw scores, and from that average, we would find the grade score.

654

A Chart for the New Spache Formula *(From "A Chart for the New Spache Formula," by Lou E. Burmeister,* **The Reading Teacher**, *29, January 1976, p. 385. Used by permission of the International Reading Association.)*

Percentage of Hard Words

Sentence length	0	1	2	3	4	5	6	7	8	9	10	11	12	13	14	15	16	17	18	19	20	21
5	1.2	1.3	1.4	1.5	1.6	1.7	1.8	1.8	1.9	2.0	2.1	2.2	2.2	2.3	2.4	2.5	2.6	2.7	2.7	2.8	2.9	3.0
6	1.4	1.5	1.5	1.6	1.7	1.8	1.9	2.0	2.0	2.1	2.2	2.3	2.4	2.5	2.5	2.6	2.7	2.8	2.9	2.9	3.0	3.1
7	1.5	1.6	1.7	1.8	1.8	1.9	2.0	2.1	2.2	2.2	2.3	2.4	2.5	2.6	2.7	2.7	2.8	2.9	3.0	3.1	3.1	3.2
8	1.6	1.7	1.8	1.9	2.0	2.0	2.1	2.2	2.3	2.4	2.4	2.5	2.6	2.7	2.8	2.9	2.9	3.0	3.1	3.2	3.3	3.3
9	1.7	1.8	1.9	2.0	2.1	2.2	2.2	2.3	2.4	2.5	2.6	2.7	2.7	2.8	2.9	3.0	3.1	3.1	3.2	3.3	3.4	3.5
10	1.9	2.0	2.0	2.1	2.2	2.3	2.4	2.4	2.5	2.6	2.7	2.8	2.9	2.9	3.0	3.1	3.2	3.3	3.3	3.4	3.5	3.6
11	2.0	2.1	2.2	2.2	2.3	2.4	2.5	2.6	2.6	2.7	2.8	2.9	3.0	3.1	3.1	3.2	3.3	3.4	3.5	3.5	3.6	3.7
12	2.1	2.2	2.3	2.4	2.4	2.5	2.6	2.7	2.8	2.8	2.9	3.0	3.1	3.2	3.3	3.3	3.4	3.5	3.6	3.7	3.8	3.8
13	2.2	2.3	2.4	2.5	2.6	2.6	2.7	2.8	2.9	3.0	3.1	3.1	3.2	3.3	3.4	3.5	3.5	3.6	3.7	3.8	3.9	4.0
14	2.3	2.4	2.5	2.6	2.7	2.8	2.8	2.9	3.0	3.1	3.2	3.3	3.3	3.4	3.5	3.6	3.7	3.7	3.8	3.9	4.0	
15	2.5	2.6	2.6	2.7	2.8	2.9	3.0	3.0	3.1	3.2	3.3	3.4	3.5	3.5	3.6	3.7	3.8	3.9	4.0	4.0		
16	2.6	2.7	2.8	2.8	2.9	3.0	3.1	3.2	3.3	3.3	3.4	3.5	3.6	3.7	3.7	3.8	3.9	4.0				
17	2.7	2.8	2.9	3.0	3.0	3.1	3.2	3.3	3.4	3.5	3.5	3.6	3.7	3.8	3.9	3.9	4.0					
18	2.8	2.9	3.0	3.1	3.2	3.2	3.3	3.4	3.5	3.6	3.7	3.7	3.8	3.9	4.0							
19	2.9	3.0	3.1	3.2	3.3	3.4	3.5	3.5	3.6	3.7	3.8	3.9	3.9	4.0								
20	3.1	3.2	3.2	3.3	3.4	3.5	3.6	3.7	3.7	3.8	3.9	4.0										
21	3.2	3.3	3.4	3.4	3.5	3.6	3.7	3.8	3.9	3.9	4.0											
22	3.3	3.4	3.5	3.6	3.6	3.7	3.8	3.9	4.0													

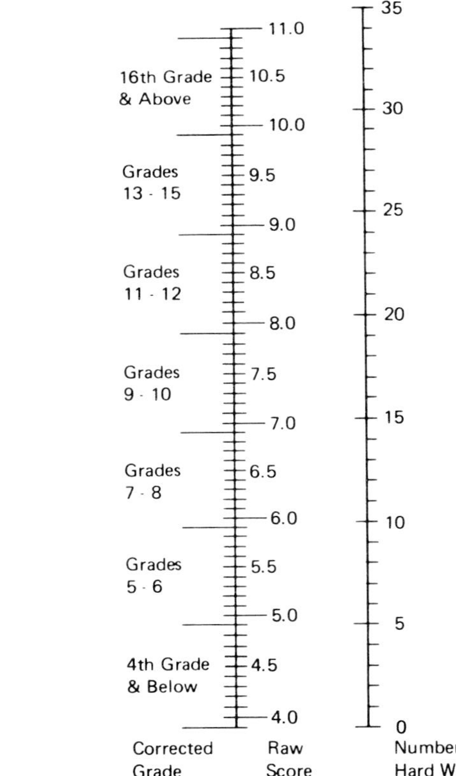

COMPUTATION EASE DIRECTIONS

To determine both the Dale-Chall raw readability score and the correspondent grade level placement:

1. Count a 100-word sample from the passage selected.
2. Count the number of sentences in the 100 words. Disregard the sentence in which the one hundredth word appears, i.e., count only those sentences which are completely within the 100-word sample.
3. Count the number of words in the 100-word sample which do not appear on the Dale List of 3,000 Words.
4. Lay a straight edge so that it touches (a) the number of sentences as shown on the left-hand column, and (b) the number of "Hard Words," i.e., those words not on Dale's list, as shown on the right-hand column.
5. Read (a) the Dale-Chall raw score and/or (b) the Grade Level at the point where the straight edge intersects the middle column.

Examples:

1. A 100-word sample with ten sentences and ten "Hard Words" has a raw score of 5.7 and a grade level designation of 5.6.
2. A sample with 20 sentences and seven "Hard Words" has approximately a 5.0 raw score and 5-6 grade level designation.

"Dale-Chall Readability Formula: A Computation Ease." (From "Another Practical Note on Readability Formulas," Karl Koenke, *Journal of Reading*, **15**, December 1971, p. 206. Reprinted with the permission of Karl Koenke and the International Reading Association.)

NOTES

1 George D. Spache. "The Spache Readability Formula." *Good Reading for Poor Readers*. Champaign, Illinois: Garrard Publishing, 1974, pp. 195–207.
2 Lou E. Burmeister. "A Chart for the New Spache Formula." *The Reading Teacher*, 29 (January 1976): 384–385.
3 Edgar Dale and Jeanne Chall. "A Formula for Predicting Readability." *Educational Research Bulletin* (January 21, 1948): 11–20, 28.
4. Karl Koenke. "Another Practical Note on Readability Formulas." *Journal of Reading*, 15 (December 1971): 206.

Phonics Charts: Research Information Used in Formulating Phonic Generalizations

Silent Consonants

Two unlike consonant letters are sometimes used to represent one consonant sound. Only those are listed which occured six or more times in Hanna's 17,310 words.*

Grapheme	Phoneme	Examples	Position in syllable	Number of instances in 17,310 words
bt	t	debt, doubt	final	11
dg	j	dodge, bridge	final	51
dj	j	a-djust	initial	13
gh	f	e-nough, laugh	final	8
gh	g	ghost, ghastly	initial	9
		burgh	final	1
gn	n	gnat, gnome	initial	5
		sign, reign	final	27
kn	n	kneel, knot	initial	37
lm	m	a-lmond	initial	2
		alms	medial	2
		calm, palm	final	13
lk	k	chalk, talk	final	14
mb	m	bomb, comb	final	27
mn	m	hymn, autumn	final	7
rh	r	rhyme, rhetoric	initial	16
ps	s	psalm, pseudo	initial	19
tch	ch	catch, witch	final	61
wh	h	who, whole	initial	12
wr	r	wrap, write	initial	48

*Lou E. Burmeister, "Content of a Phonics Program Based on Particularly Useful Generalizations," In Nila Banton Smith (ed.), *Reading Methods and Teacher Improvement*, Newark, Del.: International Reading Association, 1971, p. 34. Used by permission of the International Reading Association.

Single Vowels

Frequency and percent of occurrence of each phoneme for each single-vowel grapheme according to syllabic position and accent pattern. *All single vowels which occurred in Hanna's 17,310 words are included in total (Σ) listings, but only the most frequently occurring sounds are described.*

			Syllabic Position					
			Open Syllable						Closed Syllable					
			Total		Accented		Unaccented		Total		Accented		Unaccented	
			f	%	f	%	f	%	f	%	f	%	f	%
a	ā	halo	860	32.4	849	93.0	11	.6	142	2.8	139	4.1	3	.2
a	â	vary	0	0	0	0	0	0	64	1.3	64	1.9	0	0
a	ă	baboon	304	11.5	1	.1	303	17.4	3888	76.6	2485	73.4	1403	82.7
a	ä	arm	58	2.2	49	5.4	9	.5	460	9.1	383	11.3	77	4.5
a	ə	canal	1418	53.4	0	0	1418	81.5	19	.4	0	0	19	1.1
Σa			2654		913		1741		5078		3382		1696	
e	ē	senior	1740	90.4	345	97.7	1395	88.8	25	.4	18	.6	7	.2
e	e	hero	0	0	0	0	0	0	64	1.0	63	2.2	1	.03
e	ĕ	bet	44	2.3	1	.3	43	2.7	3272	48.3	2419	85.2	853	21.7
e	e	after	6	.3	1	.3	5	.3	1660	24.5	0	0	1660	42.2
e	ə	angel	115	6.0	0	0	115	7.3	648	9.6	1	.04	647	16.5
e	û	her	0	0	0	0	0	0	313	4.6	288	10.1	25	.6
le	′l	able	0	0	0	0	0	0	620	9.2	0	0	620	15.8
Σe			1924		353		1571		6772		2840		3932	
i	ĭ	china	395	14.2	294	94.8	101	4.1	159	3.4	158	5.7	1	.1
i	i	in	1039	37.3	0	0	1039	41.9	4307	91.5	2417	86.9	1890	98.0
i	ə	pencil	1332	47.8	0	0	1332	53.7	15	.3	0	0	15	.8
i	ē	ski	23	.8	16	5.2	7	.3	15	.3	13	.5	2	.1
Σi			2789		310		2479		4709		2781		1928	
o	ō	so	1629	92.0	545	97.0	1084	89.7	247	5.8	208	9.5	39	1.9
o	ô	cord	0	0	0	0	0	0	312	7.4	262	12.0	50	2.4
o	ŏ	dot	0	0	0	0	0	0	1557	36.7	1425	65.0	132	6.4
o	ô	off	0	0	0	0	0	0	123	2.9	102	4.7	21	1.0
o	ə	carton	114	6.4	0	0	114	9.4	1497	35.3	0	0	1497	73.0
o	e	humor	0	0	0	0	0	0	268	6.3	0	0	268	13.1
o	ŭ	son	0	0	0	0	0	0	112	2.6	110	5.0	2	.1
Σo			1770		562		1208		4243		2192		2051	
u	ū	union	770	82.6	320	82.3	450	82.0	44	2.3	29	2.3	15	2.3
u	û	burn	0	0	0	0	0	0	203	10.6	188	14.7	15	2.3
u	ŭ	cup	2	.2	0	0	2	.4	1210	62.9	996	77.8	214	33.3
u	ə	submit	42	4.5	0	0	42	7.7	255	13.3	0	0	255	39.7
u	o͞o	truth	82	8.8	69	17.7	13	2.4	11	.6	11	.9	0	0
u	o͝o	put	36	3.9	0	0	36	6.6	164	8.6	51	4.0	113	17.6
Σu			932		389		543		1923		1280		643	

*Lou E. Burmeister, "The Effect of Syllabic Position and Accent Pattern on the Phonemic Behavior of Single Vowel Graphemes," in J. Allen Figurel (ed.), *Reading and Realism*, Newark, Del.: International Reading Association, 1969, p. 648. Used by permission of the International Reading Association.

Vowel Pairs

Frequency and percent of occurrence of each phoneme for each single vowel-pair grapheme in the Hanna, *et. al.*, list of the 17,310 most common English words.*

Grapheme			Phonemic Behavior		
Name	*Frequency*	*Pronunciation key*	*Example*	*Frequency*	*Percent (%)*
first vowel long, second vowel silent					
ai	(309)	ā	abstain	230	74.4
		â	air	49	15.5
		ĭ	mountain	15	4.9
		ə	villain	9	2.9
		ĕ	again	4	1.3
		ă	plaid	1	.3
		ī	aisle	1	.3
ay	(137)	ā	gray	132	96.4
		ī	kayak	3	2.2
		ĕ	says	1	.7
		ĭ	yesterday	1	.7
ea	(545)	ē	east	275	50.5
		ĕ	weapon	140	25.7
		ē	ear	49	9.0
		û	earth	31	5.7
		â	bear	13	2.4
		ä	hearty	18	3.3
		ā	great	14	2.6
		ĭ	guinea	2	.4
		ə	sergeant	3	.5
ee	(290)	ē	sleet	248	85.5
		ē	peer	36	12.4
		ĭ	been	6	2.1
ey	(69)	ĭ **	honey	40	58.0
		ā	convey	14	20.3
		ī	geyser	8	11.6
		ē	key	6	8.7
		â	eyrie	1	1.4
oa	(138)	ō	road	129	93.5
		ô	broad	9	6.5
ow	(250)	ō	own	125	50.0
		ou	town	121	48.4
		ŏ	knowledge	4	1.6

*Lou E. Burmeister, "Vowel Pairs," *The Reading Teacher* 21 (February 1968): 448–449. Used by permission of the International Reading Association.
**Reclassified long e (ē)

Grapheme		Phonemic Behavior			
Name	*Frequency*	*Pronunciation key*	*Example*	*Frequency*	*Percent (%)*
diphthongs					
oi	(102)	oi	moist	100	98.0
		ə	porpoise	2	2.0
oy	(50)	oi	convoy	49	98.0
		ī	coyote	1	2.0
ou	(803)	ə	rigorous	336	41.2
		ou	out	285	35.0
		oo	soup	54	6.6
		ō	four	47	5.8
		ŭ	touch	30	3.7
		oo	your	25	3.1
		û	journey	22	2.7
		ĕ	glamour	1	.1
ow	(250)	ō	own	125	50.0
		ou	town	121	48.4
		ŏ	knowledge	4	1.6
broad a (ô) (or diphthongs)					
au	(178)	ô	auction	167	93.8
		ō	chauffeur	5	2.8
		ä	laugh	4	2.2
		ə	epaulet	1	.6
		ā	gauge	1	.6
aw	(77)	ô	lawn	77	100
long and short oo					
oo	(315)	oo	lagoon	185	58.7
		oo	wood	114	36.2
		ō	floor	9	2.9
		ŭ	blood	7	2.2
ei and ie					
ei	(86)	ā	reign	34	40.0
		ē	deceit	22	25.6
		ĭ	foreign	11	12.8
		ī	seismic	9	10.5
		â	their	5	5.8
		ə	sovereignty	2	2.3
		ē	weird	2	2.3
		ĕ	heifer	1	1.2
ie	(156)	ē	thief	56	35.9
		ĭ*	lassie	30	19.2
		ī	die	26	16.7
		ə	patient	23	14.7
		ȩ̄	cashier	17	10.9
		e	friend	4	2.6

*Reclassified long e (ē)

Grapheme			Phonemic Behavior		
Name	*Frequency*	*Pronunciation key*	*Example*	*Frequency*	*Percent (%)*
miscellaneous and rare combinations					
ae	(6)	ē	algae	5	83.3
		ĕ	aesthetic	1	16.7
ao	(2)	ô	extraordinary	2	100
eo	(15)	ə	pigeon	10	66.7
		ĕ	leopard	3	20.0
		ē	people	2	13.3
eu	(40)	ū	feud	29	72.5
		û	amateur	6	15.0
		oo	sleuth	4	10.0
		oo	pleurisy	1	2.5
ew	(64)	ū	news	39	60.9
		oo	flew	22	34.4
		ō	sew	3	4.7
ia	(5)	ĭ	carriage	3	60
		ə	parliament	2	40
oe	(22)	ō	foe	13	59.1
		ē	amoeba	5	22.7
		oo	shoe	4	18.2
ue	(43)	ū	due, cue	27	62.8
		oo	clue	16	37.2
ui	(34)	ĭ	build	16	47.1
		oo	fruit	10	29.4
		ū	suit	8	23.5
uo	(2)	oo	buoyant	2	100
uy	(3)	ī	buy	3	100

Children's Choices for 1981

This year's "Children's Choices" is the seventh annual bibliography of children's trade books (books other than textbooks) compiled under the direction of the Joint Committee of the International Reading Association and the Children's Book Council. The list reflects children's selections from among books published in the United States in 1980. It is meant to aid the teacher, librarian, and parent in identifying books that children themselves like.

Of the nearly 3,000 children's books published in 1980, approximately 500 were preselected, from publishers' suggestions, by the IRA educators who oversaw the testing. They chose as many different types of books as possible, in a range of subjects for all K-8 grade levels. Publishers sent multiple copies of these 500 books to each of five teams that tested them in classrooms.

Each team—consisting of a children's literature specialist and classroom teachers—involved a minimum of 2,000 children in field testing. Thus, at least 10,000 children throughout the United States selected these books. A voting system recorded the children's choices and ballots were collected to preserve their reactions. At the 1981 IRA Annual Convention in May, the team leaders met, tabulated the children's votes and, on the basis of the children's preferences, determined the 1981 "Children's Choices" list.

To make "Children's Choices" more useful, the book review teams have prepared annotations. Each annotation is followed by the number of the team that wrote it. The reviewers have also grouped books under appropriate headings and age levels. These designations are not intended to be restrictive. Many of the titles transcend their assigned group. Information concerning paper editions has been provided when known; the symbol "F" indicates that the paper edition is forthcoming. Prices of hardcover editions were accurate as of June 1981 but are subject to change without notice.

The 1980 book review teams were: # 1, Texas: Dick Abrahamson, team leader, University of Houston; Betty Carter, Spring Branch Independent School District, Houston; Rosemary O. Ingham, University of Houston; Molly McLaurin, Klein Independent School District, Spring; Frank Talbot, Houston Independent School District, Houston. # 2, Michigan: Patricia Cianciolo, team leader, Michigan State University, East Lansing, and six schools from the area. # 3, California: Norma Dick, team leader, Clovis Unified School District, Clovis, and 26 teachers from that district. # 4, Missouri: Linnea D. Lilja, team leader, University of Missouri, Columbia, and 17 schools from the Columbia area. # 5, New York: Karel Rose, team leader, Brooklyn College, City University of New York, Brooklyn, and 8 schools.

Single copies of "Children's Choices for 1981" may be obtained free by sending a self-addressed 6 1/2" x 9 1/2" (16 x 24 cm) envelope, stamped with first class postage for two ounces, to: The Children's Book Council, 67 Irving Place, New York, New York 10003, USA, Attn: Children's Choices. (Requests from outside the U.S. should include an envelope, but postage is not required.)

Beginning independent reading

Animals Should Definitely Not *Act Like People.* Judi Barrett. Ill. by Ron Barrett. Atheneum. Unpaged (30 pp.). US$9.95.

A delightful book for beginning readers to develop comprehension skills by "reading" the pictures and the large type text. Also a good book to develop oral language by talking about the pictures. This was a favorite for teachers to read aloud to small groups of children, who laughed loudly when they "figured out" the illustrations. # 3

Bear Hunt. Anthony Browne. Ill. by the author. Atheneum. Unpaged (24 pp.). US$7.95.

Bear takes his pencil and draws his way out of a series of situations. Large, bright, colorful pictures show the creative ways he uses to escape the hunters. # 4

Benjamin's Dreadful Dream. Alan Baker. Ill. by the author. Lippincott. 32 pp. US$7.95.

Full-color, realistic illustrations detail Benjamin's nightmares—the predictable result of his eating a ludicrous assortment of food. # 2

Boo! Bernard Most. Ill. by the author. Prentice. 32 pp. US$7.95.

A delightful turnabout—the monster is afraid of the children. And children will learn how to overcome their own fears by seeing how the monster overcomes its own fear. # 2

Bullfrog and Gertrude Go Camping. Rosamond Dauer. Ill. by Byron Barton. Greenwillow. 40 pp. US$5.95.

A Read-Alone book about a non-sexist, nontraditional family. Bullfrog and Gertrude go camping and adopt lonely but lovable Itsa Snake, a delightful character. # 4

Double-Decker. Double-Decker. Double-Decker Bus. Patty Wolcott. Ill. by Bob Barner. Addison-Wesley. Unpaged (24 pp.). US$4.95.
A delightful First Read-By-Myself Book with a vocabulary of only 10 words. Beginning readers love the clever repetition of words and bright colorful illustrations. Many teachers commented on the fun they had teaching the song at the end. # 3

George and Martha Tons of Fun. James Marshall. Ill. by the author. Houghton. 48 pp. US$6.95.
George and Martha, the funniest pair of hippos ever to overflow the pages of a picture book, are back. These five very short stories humorously remind young readers that true friendship persists in the face of such gargantuan failings as gluttony, conceit, and carelessness. # 1

Good Morning. Chick. Mirra Ginsburg. Ill. by Byron Barton. Greenwillow. Unpaged (32 pp.). US$7.95.
A day in the life of a brand new chick is told through simple text and brightly colored pictures. The repetitive use of "like this" on each righthand page gives an extra sense of structure to the story. # 4

Honk Honk! Anne Rockwell. Ill. by the author. Dutton. 32 pp. US$6.95.
Gray Goose bites the tails of a pig, a dog, a cow, and finally Billy Boy's shirt so they will chase her. The chase ends in the pond where everyone gets wet and mad at Gray Goose. Repetition of animal sounds and bold pictures make this a favorite. # 1

Humphrey, the Dancing Pig. Arthur Getz. Ill. by the author. Dial. Unpaged (32 pp.). US$7.95. Paper ed., Dial.
Simple, cartoon-like watercolor pictures outlined in black tell the story of Humphrey, the pig who doesn't like being fat. Dancing makes him slim like the cat, but when the farmer has him chasing mice, Humphrey eats himself back to his former self. # 3

The Last Puppy. Frank Asch. Ill. by the author. Prentice. 32 pp. US$8.95.
The puppy who was last at everything becomes the very first puppy a little boy ever had and both are delighted to be together. The pastel, cartoon-style drawings highlight nicely the emotions evoked by this pleasant and satisfying story. # 2

Matilda Hippo Has a Big Mouth. Dennis Panek. Ill. by the author. Bradbury. 32 pp. US$7.95.
Action-filled, humorous cartoon-style pictures add depth to the sketchy text about Matilda's misfortunes as she skates past various other animals. When she sees "Matilda Hippo has a big mouth" written on a wooden fence she bursts into tears. The animals replace "has" with "had" and Matilda can smile again. # 2

Mildred and the Mummy. Lady McCrady. Ill. by the author. Holiday. 32 pp. US$7.95.
This action-filled fantasy is about the midnight adventures of Mildred and a mummy in a display case in the library. Detailed illustrations depict how Mildred hid in the library until it closed, opened the mummy case, and took her friend, the mummy, home. # 2

Mine Will, Said John. Helen V. Griffith. Ill. by Muriel Batherman. Greenwillow. Unpaged (32 pp.). US$7.95.
A clever little book about how John gets the puppy he wants so badly. His parents think a gerbil would be better because they don't make any noise at all. But John says, "Mine will," and it did. Eventually his parents concede and he gets his puppy. # 3

Mr. Miller The Dog. Helme Heine. Ill. by the author. McElderry/ Atheneum. 64 pp. US$8.95.
The fantastic notion of a man and his dog becoming like one another is played out in this serious/ridiculous book. Mr. Miller and his dog ultimately exchange roles through the skillful juxtaposition of illustrations and text. # 5

The Mystery of the Flying Orange Pumpkin. Steven Kellogg. Ill. by the author. Dial. 32 pp. US$6.95.
Delicate drawings illustrate a delightful Halloween story about how the Patterson Pumpkin Club foils mean Mr. Klug, who is determined to make the children's pumpkin into a pie rather than a jack-o'-lantern. All the characters get what they want as Mr. Klug, wearing a devil's suit, joins the club. # 3

The Night Before Christmas. Clement Moore. Ill. by Tomie de Paola. Holiday. 32 pp. US$10.95. Paper ed., Holiday.
Clear, precise, watercolor paintings, suggestive of naive art, detail the events of this classic narrative poem. The borders of each page are patterns from antique quilts. # 2

Poofy Loves Company. Nancy Winslow Parker. Ill. by the author. Dodd. Unpaged (32 pp.) US$7.95.
When Sally and her mother visit Poofy's mistress, Sally doesn't mind the overly friendly maneuvers of the big shaggy dog. But when Sally's possessions disappear, the battle is on. The illustrations capture the humorous one-liners of Poofy's owner. # 3

Positively No Pets Allowed. Nathan Zimelman. Ill. by Pamela Johnson. Dutton. 32 pp. US$7.95.
"A gorilla is not a pet; a gorilla is a visitor," Mrs. Goldberg tells the landlord when he refuses to allow her son to keep the animal. This amusing story of the perfect pet has appealing illustrations of urban life. # 5

Q Is for Duck: An Alphabet Guessing Game. Mary Elting and Michael Folsom. Ill. by Jack Kent. Houghton/Clarion. Unpaged (64 pp.). US$8.95.
This unusual alphabet book matches various animals with unexpected letters. The alphabet is made into an associative guessing game. Example: "Q is for Duck . . . because a duck quacks." # 4

The Shopping Basket. John Burningham. Ill. by the author. Crowell. 32 pp. US$9.95.
An array of mathematical concepts is explored in this story about Steven's experiences with a series of beasts on his way home from the store. Line and wash illustrations help readers differentiate between the boy's real world and his flights into fantasy. # 2

Space Case. Edward Marshall. Ill. by James Marshall. Dial. Unpaged (40 pp.). US$5.95.
A "thing" from outer space lands on earth and joins a group of trick-or-treating children. Upon learning that Halloween comes only once a year and it must go to school, the "thing" takes off for parts unknown. Children wish the story would continue and love the bold illustrations. # 3

Strong John. Joan Chase Bowden. Ill. by Sal Murdocca. Macmillan. 64 pp. US$6.95.
This easy reader follows John as he goes out to earn money for his poor mother. Three years' work yields a skinny goose, a piece of rope, and a rusty cannon. Dejected, he goes to the Queen, who just happens to need his three items and pays with gold and silver. Bold illustrations depict the action of this simple story. # 1

Super Bowl. Leonard Kessler. Ill. by the author. Greenwillow. 56 pp. US$5.95.
A very popular Read-Alone book with a high interest level. Cartoon-style illustrations depict the super bowl game of the Animal Champs against the Super Birds. # 3

Ten Copycats in a Boat and Other Riddles. Alvin Schwartz. Ill. by Marc Simont. Harper. 64 pp. US$6.95. Paper ed., Scholastic.
"Ten Copycats were sitting in a boat, and one jumped out. How many were left? None. They were all copycats." So begins Alvin Schwartz' collection of 28 riddles culled from folklore and aimed at beginning readers. Children always have room for another riddle book, and the simple sentences and corny punch lines of this one are successful. # 1

Uproar on Hollercat Hill. Jean Marzollo. Ill. by Steven Kellogg. Dial. 32 pp. US$7.95.

As reported by the young readers, "This is a cheerful book." Rhymed text with a repeated chorus tells of the misadventures of a feline family. Kellogg's pictures are lively, full of personality, and require careful study for all the fun details. # 4

We're in Big Trouble, Blackboard Bear. Martha Alexander. Ill. by the author. Dial. 32 pp. US$6.95

In this fourth book about Anthony and the bear he drew that comes to life, while Anthony sleeps, the bear steps off the blackboard, out through the window and consumes a basket of blackberries, six goldfish, and a jar of honey. When Anthony's friends discover what the bear has done, Anthony draws the items on the blackboard and is able to return them to his friends. # 2

What a Good Lunch! Shigeo Watanabe. Ill. by Yasuo Ohtomo. Philomel. 32 pp. US$6.95.

Big print, easy concepts, simple language, and clear, large pictures combine to show a bear's efforts to eat lunch. He tries soup, bread and jam, and spaghetti and makes a delicious mess in the end. # 4

Who's Afraid of the Dark? Crosby Bonsall. Ill. by the author. Harper. 32 pp. US$5.95.

Stella the dog is afraid of night noises and the dark, or so her young master tells his older friend. The friend gives good advice and the master's fears are alleviated by hugs and love. # 1

Whose Birthday Is It? Bill Woodman. Ill. by the author. Crowell. 48 pp. US$7.95.

Green and yellow cartoons detail the slapstick story of a bear's search for the party to which he was invited but about which he had no information. Only by accident does Bob Bear quite predictably discover the party is for him. # 2

Witches Four. Marc Brown. Ill. by the author. Parents. Unpaged (40 pp.). US$4.95.

Four witches riding their brooms lose their hats. The hats rain down on four homeless cats. Who gets to keep the hats? The pictures and rhyming words combine to make the book enjoyable. # 1.

Younger readers

Amanda and the Giggling Ghost. Steven Kroll. Ill. by Dick Gackenbach. Holiday. Unpaged (40 pp.). US$8.95.

Amanda's encounter with a giggling ghost leads to a chase through town as she attempts to retrieve her possessions. Amanda has a hard time convincing the townfolk that it is a ghost, not she, who is responsible for all the humourous misdeeds. An "I told you so" ending makes the book especially satisfying to children. # 1

Anybody Home? Aileen Fisher. Ill. by Susan Bonners. Crowell. Unpaged (32 pp.). US$6.95.

A gentle, poetic fantasy of a young girl who wishes she could see the inside of the homes of certain woodland animals. Both the dreamlike script and soft black-and-white illustrations combine to create the aura of childhood wonder. # 4

Arthur's Valentine. Marc Brown, Ill. by the author. Atlantic/Little, Brown. 32 pp. US$7.95. Paper ed., Avon. F.

Arthur has been getting a lot of valentines from a secret admirer. Arthur puts together the clues from each valentine, decides who has sent them and sends a valentine to the wrong person. # 4

The Bear on the Doorstep. Jane Flory. Ill. by

Carolyn Croll. Houghton. 32 pp. US$6.95.

A young bear, adopted by a rabbit family, soon outgrows their home. What to do? The logical and heartwarming conclusion is to combine two homes so all are content. # 4

The Berenstain Bears and the Missing Dinosaur Bone. Stan Berenstain and Jan Berenstain. Ill. by the authors. Random. Unpaged (48 pp.). US$3.95.

Another clever, rhyming tale about the three bear detectives who try to find a dinosaur bone missing from a display in the museum. The bears come to the aid of the distraught keeper of the museum by using their trusty detective kit and their hound dog, Snuff. # 3

Bonzo Beaver. Arthur Crowley. Ill. by Annie Gusman. Houghton. 32 pp. US$7.95.

Bonzo runs away after a day of older brother Boo's continual taunts. Bonzo makes friends with a crabby old lady and together they plot to teach Boo a lesson. The full-page, simple and colorful illustrations and the rhyming verse make this an excellent book for reading aloud. # 3

Boris and the Monsters. Elaine Macmann Willoughby. Ill. by Lynn Munsinger. Houghton. 32 pp. US$7.95.

Boris has a common complaint. He is afraid of the dark and the monsters that hide there. A scared new puppy overcomes the problem and brings out bravery in Boris. Children understand the problem and love the solution. "I could read it over and over," commented one child. # 1

The Day I Was Born. Marjorie Sharmat and Mitchell Sharmat. Ill. by Diane Dawson. Dutton. Unpaged (32 pp.). US$7.95.

At Alexander's sixth birthday party, his three guests looked bored as they listen to Alexander tell about all the important events that happened the day he was born. On each facing page, his older brother has another version of what really happened. The story ends with the older brother saying, "In the last six years, I got to like my turtle a lot. But I like Alexander even better." Black-and-white pencil sketches illustrate this humorous, yet positive and loving story. # 3

The Day Jimmy's Boa Ate the Wash. Trinka Hakes Noble. Ill. by Steven Kellogg. Dial. 32 pp. US$7.95.

The full-color, cartoon-style pictures embellish this action-filled tall tale of Jimmy's boa's escape from the school bus and the havoc it caused during a class visit to a farm. The matter-of-fact narration combined with the utterly nonsensical and zany events make for a vigorous and memorable story. # 2

The Discontented Mother. Ben Shecter. Ill. by the author. Harcourt. Unpaged (32 pp.). US$6.95.

It all started the day Orin's mother asked him, "Won't you ever change?" That night he wished he could be different and in the morning he was a cat. Orin continues to change magically until the surprise ending. # 4

First Grade Takes a Test. Miriam Cohen. Ill. by Lillian Hoban. Greenwillow. Unpaged (32 pp.). US$7.95.

A first grader's view of the processes and results of standardized testing is gained through the use of realistic dialogue. How can you mark a little box when the answer you want isn't on the page? A wise, compassionate teacher finally convinces her students that a test can't measure everything. Good reading for parents and students. # 1

The Great Valentine's Day Balloon Race. Adrienne Adams. Ill. by the author. Scribner. Unpaged (32 pp.). US$9.95.

An unusual holiday book for Valentine's Day about a hot air balloon race. Rabbit Orson Abbott and his neighbor Connie build and navigate the winning balloon. The story has strong appeal because a wish is granted, a contest is won, and a great accomplishment is achieved. # 3

Gregory, the Terrible Eater. Mitchell Sharmat. Ill. by Jose Aruego and Ariane Dewey. Four Winds. Unpaged (32 pp.). US$7.95.

Gregory, a finicky goat, frustrates his parents by eating only "junk food." The twist is that "junk food" for a goat is vegetables, eggs, and fruit. Bold illustrations highlight the absurdity of the situation and delight young readers as the family struggles to effect a compromise. # 1

Grumley the Grouch. Marjorie Weinman Sharmat. Ill. by Kay Chorao. Holiday. Unpaged (32 pp.). US$7.95.
The delicate black-and-white cross-hatched illustrations, washed with soft greens, offer a delightful contrast to the negative conversations of Grumley Badger, "the biggest grouch in the neighborhood." Grumley is so challenged by negative Brunhilda Badger that he encourages her to notice pleasant things. A romance develops and they are happily married. # 3

Hang On, Hester! Wende Devlin and Harry Devlin. Ill. by Harry Devlin. Lothrop. 48 pp. US$6.95.
Hester becomes a celebrity after she bravely hangs on to the weather vane as her house floats down the river. This fast-moving account of Hester's adventure is heightened with the repetition of the phrase, "Hang on, Hester," and eye-catching illustrations. # 1

Hansel and Gretel. The Brothers Grimm. Ill. by Susan Jeffers. Dial. 32 pp. US$9.95.
Large-scale, realistic pictures in soft, fresh colors add considerable depth of action and feeling to this simplified version of the well-known fairy tale of two lost children who find a witch's house made of cake and candy. # 2

Hush Up! Jim Aylesworth. Ill. by Glen Rounds. Holt. 32 pp. US$6.95.
This hilarious tall tale is embellished by exaggerated pen-and-ink sketches. One hot, lazy day Jasper Walker tilted his chair back, propped up his feet, and snoozed. The barnyard animals decided to nap, too. A chain reaction of incredible slapstick events occurs when a huge, nasty horsefly bites the sleeping mule's nose. # 2

I Know an Old Lady Who Swallowed a Fly. Retold by Nadine Bernard Westcott. Ill. by the author. Atlantic/Little, Brown. 40 pp. US$8.95. Paper ed., Atlantic/Little, Brown.
Children love this retelling of the favorite folksong where each cure is worse than the last. Colorful illustrations help tell the tale. # 2

If You Say So, Claude. Joan Lowery Nixon. Ill. by Lorinda Bryan Cauley. Warne. Unpaged (48 pp.). US$9.95.
Claude wants to leave the noisy mining town and Shirley agrees to go with him to find peace and quiet in Texas. Circumstances favor Shirley when she has interesting encounters with the native animals. The illustrations are large, detailed, and colorful. # 1

Jenny Learns a Lesson. Gyo Fujikawa. Ill. by the author. Grosset. Unpaged (32 pp.). US$4.95.
Jenny learns that cooperation, sharing, and apologizing are a part of being and keeping friends. The events of the story are common to childhood and allow the reader to empathize with the characters. # 4

King Rollo and the Bread. King Rollo and the Birthday. King Rollo and the New Shoes. David McKee. Ill. by the author. Atlantic/Little, Brown. 32 pp. each. US$6.95 (set of three).
Each of these child-sized books tells a story about King Rollo, an ingenious character. The brightly colored illustrations catch the eyes of children. # 3

The Little Worm Book. Janet Ahlberg and Allan Ahlberg. Ill. by the authors. Viking. 32 pp. US$2.95.
This tiny book, illustrated with humorous drawings, provides a wealth of information about worms: a brief history of the worm, superstitions about worms, worms that can be pets, food, trained performers, and much more. # 2

Maude and Claude Go Abroad. Susan Meddaugh. Ill. by the author. Houghton. 32 pp. US$7.95.
Brother and sister foxes, reckless Claude and older, protective Maude, set sail

across the ocean for a visit with their aunts. When Claude falls into the ocean, dutiful Maude jumps in after, and the adventure begins. # 3

Mean Maxine. Barbara Bottner. Ill. by the author. Pantheon. Unpaged (32 pp.). US$5.99.
Ralph's life has been made miserable by the name-calling neighborhood bully, Maxine. Ralph imagines himself in a number of fantasy roles in which he scares Maxine, but he learns that his best weapon is simply to be himself. # 3

Mrs. Peloki's Snake. Joanne Oppenheim. Ill. by Joyce Audy dos Santos. Dodd. Unpaged (32 pp.). US$6.95.
Mrs. Peloki's classroom erupts when a student reports a snake in the boys' bathroom. Mrs. Peloki musters up courage and takes her yardstick to fight the serpent, but it is fearless Stephie who uncovers the gray mop string masquerading as a snake. The funny classroom illustrations and comic captions are an integral and popular part of this favorite. # 1

Molly and the Slow Teeth. Pat Ross. Ill. by Jerry Milord. Lothrop. 48 pp. US$6.95.
"Molly Davis had not lost one tooth yet. And she was already in second grade." An easy story of how one child goes to almost any length to get her name on the tooth chart in the front of the room. # 4

A Mouse Called Junction. Julia Cunningham. Ill. by Michael Hague. Pantheon. Unpaged (32 pp.). US$7.95.
The beauty of the language and the full-page illustrations make this tale of Junction's search for adventure a winner. When the harsh realities of life in the outside world threaten to overwhelm this pampered mouse, he is befriended by a stuffy, old rat and a warm friendship develops between them. # 1

My Mother Didn't Kiss Me Goodnight. Charlotte Herman. Ill. by Bruce Degen. Dutton. Unpaged (32 pp.). US$7.95.
Leon wonders why his mother didn't kiss him goodnight. Maybe he did some-

thing wrong. Leon discovers at the end that it's because Mama's catching a cold and doesn't want him to get it. She blows him a kiss, he catches it, and she hugs him with her eyes. # 3

My Very Own Octopus. Bernard Most. Ill. by author. Harcourt. 32 pp. US$7.95.
When your brother is allergic to lots of animals, an octopus seems to be the perfect pet. All those arms would have lots of advantages, especially when it comes to being hugged. # 4

Next Year I'll Be Special. Patricia Reilly Giff. Ill. by Marylin Hafner. Dutton. Unpaged (32 pp.) US$7.95.
One child opined, "It has very good pictures and it shows the way a first grader might feel about going into second grade. It tells how you feel in school sometimes. But don't expect too much from next year or you might be disappointed." # 4

Nobody Stole the Pie. Sonia Levitin. Ill. by Fernando Krahn. Harcourt. Unpaged (32 pp.). US$7.95.
A village celebration centering around a huge pie is jeopardized when pieces begin disappearing. The pie dwindles to one slice, and still no one will admit guilt. The mayor finally proclaims that nobody stole the pie and eats the last piece himself. Cartoon-like drawings add zest and humor to the lesson on community responsibility found in this tale. # 1

Oliver and Alison's Week. Jane Breskin Zalben. Ill. by Emily Arnold McCully. Farrar. 40 pp. US$9.95.
A delightful collection of short stories about the trials and triumphs of childhood friendships. Oliver and Alison are best friends and, even though friends can argue a lot, it's nice to have them around in case someone tells you that you have big ears and you need another opinion. The full-color illustrations and the short, short stories help make this a good book for sharing with children when you have three minutes before the bell rings. # 3

One Big Wish. Jay Williams. Ill. by John

O'Brien. Macmillan. Unpaged (32 pp.). US$7.95.
An outlandish tale illustrated in cinnamon brown and green in which a kind-hearted farmer helps to free a woman's dress from a bramble bush. In gratitude she grants him wish fulfillment which results in unpredictable consequences and a humorous conclusion. # 3

One, Two, Three—A-Choo! Marjorie N. Allen. Ill. by Dick Gackenbach. Coward. 64 pp. US$6.59.
Poor Wally Springer, everyone else has a pet but him. He has to be allergic to furry things. But when Harold the hermit crab crawls into the scene, Wally stops crabbing. # 4

Peace at Last. Jill Murphy. Ill. by the author. Dial. Unpaged (32 pp.). US$7.95.
Mr. Bear could not find a quiet place to sleep until dawn when he found "peace at last"—just in time to get up. The use of common night noises and the humor in the homey illustrations add to the reader's empathy with the frustrated bear. # 4

Pig Pig Grows Up. David McPhail. Ill. by the author. Dutton/Unicorn. Unpaged (24 pp.). US$8.95.
Pig Pig doesn't want to grow up. He sleeps in his crib but his feet hang over. He wears his sleep suit although it's too tight. When Pig Pig saves a real baby from a disastrous collision, he finally grows up. McPhail's action-packed, watercolor illustrations are the key to this book's popularity. # 1

Rainy Rainy Saturday. Jack Prelutsky. Ill. by Marylin Hafner. Greenwillow. 48 pp. US$5.95.
Poems about things one might do on a rainy day: clean one's room, make fudge, color in a coloring book. Illustrations in browns and purple are appropriate to the rainy day theme. # 2

The Runaway Pancake. P. Chr. Asbjornsen and Jorgen Moe. Trans. from the Danish by Joan Tate. Ill. by Svend Otto S. Larousse. Unpaged (32 pp.). US$7.95.
Here's a new version of an old folktale about the pancake who runs away from the hungry family in order to save his life. The repetitive phrases and the colorful illustrations make this book a favorite with children. # 1

729 Curious Creatures. Helen Oxenbury. Ill. by the author. Harper. 18 pp., cut in thirds. US$3.95.
A heads, bodies, and legs book in which the pages are cut into thirds and the object is to make amusing combinations of the heads, bodies, and legs and the words that go with them. # 3

Taking Care of Melvin. Marjorie Weinman Sharmat. Ill. by Victoria Chess. Holiday. Unpaged (32 pp.). US$6.95.
Melvin Dog, who is "kind, generous, thoughtful, dear, and altogether wonderful," collapses of fatigue from doing so many kind chores for his friends. When he discovers how pleasant it is to be waited on, he becomes the worst kind of ogre. The delightful black-and-white drawings on pink pages offer the simple message that it is best to reach a happy medium in our willingness to help our friends. # 3

The Tale of Meshka the Kvetch. Carol Chapman. Ill. by Arnold Lobel. Dutton. 32 pp. US$8.95.
Told in the tradition of a folktale and illustrated in a style that suggests an Eastern European peasant community, this story tells how Meshka, the best complainer (kvetch) in the village, woke up one morning with an itching tongue and suffered all the disasters she complained about so frequently in the past. # 2

The Tale of Thomas Mead. Pat Hutchins. Ill. by the author. Greenwillow. 32 pp. US$5.95.
A Read-Alone book which points out, in rhyme, the hazards of being a nonreader—or as a child said, "It tells that you should learn to read or else." The repeated phrase "Why should I?" even appears on the last page, but happily this time it refers to Thomas not wanting to stop reading. # 4

That Terrible Halloween Night. James Stevenson. Ill. by the author. Greenwillow. Unpaged (32 pp.). US$7.95.
The lovable old grandpa of *Could Be Worse!* comes up with a winner for Halloween. Louie and Mary Ann want to scare grandpa, but not too much because "Grandpa's pretty old." But the joke is on the children when Grandpa is unruffled by their attempts to frighten him. *The New Yorker* cartoonist's ghostly color-washed drawings brought comments of "scary and good" from the voting children. The last picture shows Grandpa enjoying the whopper of a story with children huddled on his lap. # 3

Those Terrible Toy-Breakers. David McPhail. Ill. by the author. Parents. Unpaged (48 pp.). US$4.95.
When Walter forgets to bring in some of his toys at night, he awakes the next day to find them broken. A lion, a tiger, and an elephant are the midnight marauders. Walter and his friend, Bernie, catch the culprits who admit the deed, fix the toys, and all part as friends. McPhail's animal illustrations add the humor to this tale of friendship. # 1

Today Was a Terrible Day. Patricia Reilly Giff. Ill. by Susanna Natti. Viking. 32 pp. US$6.95.
Ever have one of those days when nothing goes right? Well, second grader Ronald Morgan did. One child said, "It made me feel at home in class." # 4

Troll Country. Edward Marshall. Ill. by James Marshall. Dial. 56 pp. US$5.89. Paper ed., Dial.
An easy-to-read book about Elsie Fay who, after hearing about her mother's adventure years earlier, sets out to meet a troll in the deep, dark woods. Clear illustrations capture the personality of this unusual troll. # 4

Tyler Toad and the Thunder. Robert L. Crowe. Ill. by Kay Chorao. Unpaged (32 pp.). US$9.95.
No explanation for the origin of thunder appeases T. Tyler Toad, who sits frightened in a hole waiting for the storm to pass. One explanation finally draws him out of the hole until an absolutely gigantic clap of thunder finds T. Tyler Toad jumping back into the hole on top of John Bluejay, Mrs. Raccoon, C.C. Chipmunk, Mr. Badger, and Reginald P. Merriweather-Fieldmouse. Chorao's delicate pastel animals delight young readers. # 3

Welcome Is a Wonderful Word. Gyo Fujikawa. Ill. by the author. Grosset. Unpaged (32 pp.). US$4.95.
Jenny and her friends prepare a welcome for the new girl, Mei Su. The children share their "treasures" as the way to make their new friend feel at home. # 4

The Werewolf Family. Jack Gantos. Ill. by Nicole Rubel. Houghton. 32 pp. US$8.95.
The Werewolf family reunion occurs on the night of a full moon which prompts much bizarre behavior from the group. The colorful art work illustrates the humorous antics of the Werewolf family at the gathering. # 1

Where Does the Sun Go at Night? Mirra Ginsburg. Ill. by Jose Aruego and Ariane Dewey. Greenwillow. 32 pp. US$7.95.
Clear, crisp, cartoon-style drawings add a humorous element to this rhythmic tale of animals watching the sun set and speculating about where the sun goes at night. # 2

The Wuggie Norple Story. Daniel M. Pinkwater. Ill. by Tomie de Paola. Four Winds. Unpaged (40 pp.). US$9.95.
Wuggie Norple is a big, orange cat who grows bigger than a bulldog, bigger than a hog, bigger than a horse, and bigger than an elephant. The vibrant illustrations are the real strength of this book, along with the crazy names of the characters. # 1

Middle grades

Chester. Mary Francis Shura. Ill. by Susan Swan. Dodd. 96 pp. US$6.95.

Chester, a boy new to the neighborhood, is eventually accepted into a tight group of five friends. This tale of how their jealousy of Chester gradually gives way to acceptance is humorous and believable. # 2

Cookie Becker Casts a Spell. Lee Glazer. Ill. by Margot Apple. Little, Brown. 48 pp. US$6.95.

When Cookie loses the lead in the class play, she puts a curse on it. When the play actually does fail and the kids blame Cookie, she finds out it's not always satisfying to ruin other people's fun. # 4

Crazy in Love. Richard Kennedy. Ill. by Marcia Sewall. Dutton/Unicorn. 64 pp. US$7.95.

A captivating tale of love and enchantment in rhythmic style tells the story of lonely young Diana who wishes for a husband to share her life. She finds an enchanted woman in the woods who promises her a husband if she will visit her each day. The secret visits endanger Diana's new marriage and the spell must be broken. # 3

Dracula. Bram Stoker. Adapted by Alice Schick and Joel Schick. Ill. by the adapters. Delacorte. 48 pp. US$8.44. Paper ed., Delacorte.

This retelling of the classic horror story is in a colorful comic strip format. # 2

Fanny's Sister. Penelope Lively. Ill. by Anita Lobel. Dutton. 64 pp. US$7.95.

Sibling rivalry and the fear of losing affection distress young Fanny when another child is born into her large family. Like the character in a fairy tale, she makes a ghastly wish which she regrets when it seems possible that it might come true. # 5

The Gift-Giver. Joyce Hansen. Houghton/ Clarion. 128 pp. US$7.95.

An urban ghetto not only presents harsh realities but is also a place where people learn to love and grow. Ten-year-old Doris and her new friend Amir help each other withstand peer pressure and family difficulties in this positive story. # 5

The Green Man. Gail E. Haley. Ill. by the author. Scribner. 32 pp. US$9.95.

The strong colored pictures of medieval clothing and architecture firmly establish the era in which this legendary story occurred. An arrogant youth, whose clothes are stolen while he is swimming, finds shelter in a cave, plants and reaps his harvest, cares for creatures of the wild and becomes a kindly and generous person. # 2

The Hand-Me-Down Kid. Francine Pascal. Viking. 172 pp. US$9.95.

Ari is the youngest in her family, the hand-me-down kid. Middle graders delight in the contemporary language which expresses Ari's typical concerns: her suspicions that she is adopted, her fear of peer rejection, and her need to look grownup. # 5

The Housekeeper's Dog. Jerry Smath. Ill. by the author. Parents. Unpaged. (48 pp.). US$4.95.

A cute pet story with a funny twist: A dog bosses his owner around, but only for a while. The story has a moral which is subtly presented and with which children can easily identify. # 4

Left-Handed Shortstop. Patricia Reilly Giff. Ill. by Leslie Morrill. Delacorte. 128 pp. US$7.95. Paper ed., Dell.

Walter Moles must save face with his friends who can't understand his preference for ecology over baseball. This typical but insecure fourth grader found many admiring fans. A welcome story about an appealing young person who is unable or unwilling to conform to the stereotype. # 5

Leprechauns Never Lie. Lorna Balian. Ill. by the author. Abingdon. Unpaged (32 pp.). US$7.95.

A humorous and charming story of how

Lazy Ninny Nanny tries to find a captured leprechaun's gold. The text is catchy and children particularly like the green leprechaun. # 4

Mice on Ice. Jane Yolen. Ill. by Lawrence DiFiori. Dutton. 72 pp. US$7.95.
The star of the Mice on Ice show is kidnapped and the formula for making ice demanded as ransom. Using mouse initiative, Horace and little Ruby find the kidnappers, rescue the star, and toss the crooks in jail. Easy text and fun illustrations add dash to the story. # 4

The Robot and Rebecca: The Mystery of the Code-Carrying Kids. Jane Yolen. Ill. by Jürg Obrist. Knopf. 128 pp. US$4.99. Paper ed., Knopf.
Rebecca lives in Bosyork in the year 2121. On her ninth birthday she is given a robot as a gift and together the two solve a futuristic space mystery. # 5

Rosie's Double Dare. Robie H. Harris. Ill. by Tony De Luna. Knopf. 128 pp. US$4.99. Paper ed., Knopf.
Rosie is shorter than the rest of the kids and in order to gain acceptance she accepts two secret dares. A lot of laughter is the result of Rosie's efforts. # 5

The Sick of Being Sick Book. Jovial Bob Stine and Jane Stine. Ill. by Carol Nicklaus. Dutton. 80 pp. US$7.95. Paper ed., Scholastic. F.
This is a manual for the sick and not-so-sick on how to make the most of the situation. A veritable encyclopedia of information with advice on such topics as "How to Get the Most Sympathy from Your Illness" and "How to Survive Daytime Television." # 5

Something Queer on Vacation. Elizabeth Levy. Ill. by Mordicai Gerstein. Delacorte. Unpaged (48 pp.). US$6.95. Paper ed., Delacorte.
One child observed, "This book is funny and if you were to read it you would be stuck in anticipation." Gwen and Jill are determined to win the weekly sandcastle contest on the beach but something always seems to hamper their efforts. The cartoon-like drawings present clues to help solve the mystery. # 4

Superfudge. Judy Blume. Dutton. 166 pp. US$7.95. Paper ed., Dell. F.
This sequel to *Tales of a Fourth Grade Nothing* continues the hilarious experiences of Peter Hatcher. With his younger brother in the first grade in the same school as Peter and another baby on the way, Peter thinks the only solution is to pack his bag and leave home. # 5

Things Won't Be the Same. Kathryn Ewing. Harcourt. 96 pp. US$6.95.
A simple, well-written book for the younger reader about a young girl's response to the changes that will result from her mother's impending remarriage. Each character must slowly adjust to the unexpected events that life presents. # 5

The Worst Witch. Jill Murphy. Ill. by the author. Allison and Busby. (Distributed by Schocken). 72 pp. US$6.95.
Mildred's incompetence in the basic skills of witchery gain her the reputation of being the "worst" witch at Miss Cackle's Academy. Readers alternately laugh and squirm at the accounts of her misadventures. Pen-and-ink drawings enhance the warmth of this tale. # 1

Older readers

Accident. Hila Colman. Morrow. 192 pp. US$7.95. Paper ed., Archway/Pocket.
Fifteen-year-old Jenny is invited by her classmate Adam to ride with him on his motorcycle. There is an accident which leaves Jenny paralyzed and Adam unhurt. Two major themes are emphasized in this realistic story: the friendship between two young people despite the fact that they are from different socio-

economic backgrounds and the trauma resulting from the accident. # 2

Cute Is a Four-Letter Word. Stella Pevsner. Houghton/Clarion. 190 pp. US$7.95. Paper ed., Archway/Pocket.

A sixth-grade reader wrote: "Clara Conrad decided the eighth grade would be her best year ever. She soon found out that being in Pom Pon and having the cutest boy in the school wasn't everything. I enjoyed this book because I wanted the same things Clara did and I sometimes acted like her." # 1

The Face at the Window. Wolfgang Ecke. Trans. from the German by Stella Humphries and Vernon Humphries. Ill. by Rolf Rettich. Prentice. 134 pp. US$7.95.

Pen-and-ink drawings combined with short, solve-it-yourself mystery stories offer challenging and exciting reading fare. Each story is about a different character and the stories take place in different locales in England, Germany, Turkey, Denmark, and Antibes. The solutions are grouped at the end of the book; all the clues needed to solve the mysteries are in the stories themselves. # 2

From Prison to the Major Leagues: The Picture Story of Ron LeFlore. Ron Knapp. Ill. with photographs. Messner. 64 pp. US$7.95.

Excellent black-and-white photographs and a brief but adequate text are combined to tell the life story of Ron LeFlore, the well-known Detroit Tigers player who got his start on the state prison baseball team. # 2

Haunted. Judith St. George. Putnam. 160 pp. US$7.95. Paper ed., Bantam. F.

Sixteen-year-old Alex and college sophomore Bruce have accepted a summer job house-sitting in Pennsylvania. But this is no ordinary house, for the previous occupants have committed suicide and seem to have left behind a weird legacy. # 5

The Headless Roommate and Other Tales of Terror. Daniel Cohen. Ill. by Peggy Brier. Evans. 128 pp. US$7.95. Paper ed., Bantam. F.

Some children's comments were: "Part of the book was gory, but it had a lot of interesting stories"; "it always kept you in suspense and it was exciting"; "part of it was gross but it made you stay awake"; "I really like spooky stories and this is a real collection." The black-and-white charcoal drawings lend an eerie tone to the book. # 3

How to Eat Fried Worms and Other Plays. Thomas Rockwell. Ill. by Joel Schick. Delacorte. 144 pp. US$7.95. Paper ed., Dell.

This book offers fun for the performers and for the audiences attending the performances. The dialogues for the plays in this collection are easy to read and the staging directions easy to follow. # 2

In Our House Scott Is My Brother. C.S. Adler. Macmillan. 144 pp. US$7.95. Paper ed., Bantam. F.

When Jodi's father remarries, 13-year-old Jodi must confront her distrust of family life, especially as her new stepmother, Donna, is unstable. In time she learns to enjoy being part of a family and comes to like and respect Donna's son, Scott. When the marriage disintegrates, Jodi must once again examine her feelings about family living. # 5

Into the Unknown: Nine Astounding Stories. Stephen Mooser. Ill. with photos, line drawings and lithographs. Lippincott. 128 pp. US$7.95.

This fascinating collection of mysterious events that defy explanation (a young girl's ability to see through walls, the sighting of a flying saucer, a man's disappearance into thin air) appeals to even the most reluctant reader. A challenge to think critically about possible explanations. # 2

Jokes to Read in the Dark. Scott Corbett. Ill. by Annie Gusman. Dutton/Unicorn. 80 pp. US$7.95. Paper ed., Dutton.

This collection of limericks, dog stories, knock-knocks, puns, and jokes results in lots of fun reading. # 5

Just Between Us. Susan Beth Pfeffer. Ill. by Lorna Tomei. Delacorte. 120 pp. US$7.95. Paper ed., Dell.

When is a secret a secret? Cass needs to learn when to respect a confidence. Through the use of behavior modification, she learns how, and is able to help her two best friends. # 4

Kate Alone. Patricia Lee Gauch. Putnam. 112 pp. US$7.95. Paper ed., Archway/Pocket. F.

Fourteen-year-old Kate, devoted to her dog McDuff who has just returned from an extended stay at the veterinarian's, is horrified when the dog growls at her mother and bites a family friend. The girl's love for McDuff and the conflict of feelings that she has about ending the dog's life create an intense, emotional reading experience. # 2

The Last Monster. Jane Annixter and Paul Annixter. Harcourt. 84 pp. US$6.95.

Ron must deal with his hate and fear of a grizzly bear: hate because the grizzly has crippled his father and his dog, and fear for his own safety. He stalks the grizzly for the kill, but learns great respect for this wise and ancient creature of the mountains. # 1

The Lemon Meringue Dog. Walt Morey. Dutton. 176 pp. US$9.95. Paper ed., Scholastic.

Chris, a Coast Guard trainer, and Mike, his dog trained to sniff out heroin, turn their first drug bust into a slapstick routine. When Mike is dishonorably discharged, Chris purchases him, and together they track down Miami's largest narcotics dealer in this action-filled adventure story. # 1

Like Everybody Else. Barbara Girion. Scribner. 176 pp. US$8.95.

Twelve-year-old Sam is the daughter of a writer and often plays mother to her mother. But when Mom writes a book about marital infidelity and other things Sam would rather not know about, a great deal of anxiety results. It takes real family strength and affection to dispel the disturbances. # 5

Love Is Like Peanuts. Betty Bates. Holiday. 128 pp. US$7.95. Paper ed., Archway/Pocket.

Marianne, 14, accepts a summer job babysitting a brain-damaged 8 year old named Catsy Kranz. Caring for Catsy matures Marianne; Catsy's older brother, Toby, who is in prep school, provides the love interest. # 3

Man from the Sky. Avi. Ill. by David Wiesner. Knopf. 120 pp. US$4.95. Paper ed., Knopf.

"An adventure story which has just enough details to make it interesting and the middle is the best part," reported a reader. A man parachutes from a plane with a great deal of stolen money. But 11-year-old Jamie Peters witnesses the act and the chase is on. # 4

Masquerade. Kit Williams. Ill. by the author. Schocken. Unpaged (32 pp.). US$9.95.

Where is the lost jewel which the Moon gave to the Sun and which Jack Hare carried to earth? This series of 15 verbal and visual riddles gives you the answer. Or does it? Nobody-yet-knows. # 1

Maudie and Me and the Dirty Book. Betty Miles. Knopf. 160 pp. US$6.95. Paper ed., Avon.

When two sixth graders read a story to first graders about how a puppy is born, some parents in their school accuse them of exposing little children to a "dirty book." A good book for exploring the problems of censorship. # 5

My Brother, the Thief. Marlene Fanta Shyer. Scribner. 138 pp. US$8.95.

Told from the viewpoint of 12-year-old Carolyn Desmond, this story realistically presents the pressures on her 16-year-old half-brother, Richard, which result in his arrest for theft and trial in juvenile court. The crisis brings Richard and his stepfather closer together. # 4

The Night Swimmers. Betsy Byars. Delacorte. 144 pp. US$7.95. Paper ed., Dell.

The eldest of three motherless children, Retta, is left to care for her two younger brothers while their father is on the road performing as a country-and-western singer. Retta entertains the boys with night swims in a neighbor's pool, a recreation which leads to near-disaster. # 5

Only Love. Susan Sallis. Harper. 256 pp. US$8.95. Paper ed., Dell. F.
Sixteen-year-old Fran Adamson may be confined to a wheelchair, but her spirit is livelier than most. She is determined not to let her disability interfere with experiencing life to its fullest. # 5

A Ring of Endless Light. Madeleine L'Engle. Farrar. 356 pp. US$9.95. Paper ed., Dell. F.
Another book about the Austin family in which Vicky, who was 12 in *Meet the Austins*, is now 16. Her telepathic powers permit her to communicate with dolphins. This relationship with the dolphins eventually allows her to recover from her depression over her beloved grandfather's terminal cancer and a family friend's death while rescuing a would-be suicide. # 2

Someone Slightly Different. Judy Frank Mearian. Dial. 192 pp. US$8.95.
Twelve-year-old Marty cherishes memories of her father and dreams of his return. Though her hopes are never realized, her father's mother does come to live with Marty and her mother. Fortunately, this fun-loving, unconventional grandma has the capacity to pull together the distraught family. # 5

There's a Rat in Bunk Five. Paula Danziger. Delacorte. 150 pp. US$7.95. Paper ed., Dell.
Fourteen-year-old Marcy Lewis jumps at the chance to work as a counselor at Ms. Finney's art camp in upstate New York. The humorous antics of a dozen preteen bunkmates combined with a summer romance will ensure this easy-to-read sequel to *The Cat Ate My Gymsuit* a special cubby all its own. # 1

What If They Knew? Patricia Hermes. Harcourt. 132 pp. US$6.95.
Ten-year-old Jeremy has epilepsy and fears that her secret will be discovered. Hermes has written a sympathetic, realistic novel which is a sensitive introduction for youngsters to the personal anguish of physical disabilities. # 5

What's the Matter with the Dobsons? Hila Colman. Crown. 120 pp. US$7.95. Paper ed., Archway/Pocket. F.
Neither Dobson parent is able to show equal affection toward both their daughters. Mrs. Dobson and Amanda pair up against Mr. Dobson and Lisa and their bitter arguments force an unhappy separation. Although the Dobsons eventually remarry, their reconciliation comes through serious efforts by all rather than with a simplistic, happy-ever-after solution. # 1

Who Stole Kathy Young? Margaret Goff Clark. Dodd. 192 pp. US$6.95.
"This story has a lot of excitement and a lot of danger and suspense," one reader reported. When Kathy, a deaf girl, is kidnapped, her friends Meg and Julian try to find her. The suspense mounts and the mystery is logically resolved. # 4

With a Wave of the Wand. Mark Jonathan Harris. Lothrop. 192 pp. US$7.95.
In this first-person narrative, Marlee, a sixth grader, tells her readers what her thoughts and feelings were when her parents separated and divorced. Included in this impressionistic statement are the girl's comments about the supportive friendship that developed between her and an old man next door, a magician who helped her differentiate between tricks and real human powers. # 2

Informational books

Dragons and Other Fabulous Beasts. Richard Blythe. Ill. by Fiona French and Joanna Troughton. Grosset. 64 pp. US$5.95.
This anthology of folktales about unusual creatures from different cultures is organized around the theme that "most fabulous beasts have some origin in truth." Each chapter is introduced with an explanation of how the stories might

have begun. Attractive illustrations fit the country and time of origin. # 4

Halloween. Joyce K. Kessel. Ill. by Nancy L. Carlson. Carolrhoda. 48 pp. US $5.95.
This easy-to-read book traces Halloween customs from the days of the early Celts to today's trick-or-treaters. # 4

Movie Stunts and the People Who Do Them. Gloria D. Miklowitz. Ill. with photographs. Harcourt. 64 pp. US$7.95. Paper ed., Harcourt.
An interesting look at the people who perform the stunts for films and television, the techniques they use, and the preparations they make for performing stunts. Information on some of the earliest-known stunt people is included. # 5

Ocean Frontiers. Eryl Davies. Ill. with photographs and diagrams. Viking. 64 pp. US$5.95.
An informational book about ocean exploration, oceanography, fishing, ocean research, and conservation. Terms are defined, "know-how boxes" explain how things work, and projects are suggested. # 4

The Sea World Book of Sharks. Eve Bunting. Ill. with photographs by Flip Nicklin. Harcourt. 80 pp. US$8.95.
A concise, interesting text and colorful, clear photographs blend to present in vivid detail the world of sharks. Readers will develop a sense of appreciation for this often-misunderstood creature. # 4

The Story of Nim: The Chimp Who Learned Language. Anna Michel. Ill. with photographs by Susan Kuklin and Herbert S. Terrace. Knopf. 60 pp. US$6.95.

An interesting book about Nim, a chimpanzee who is taught to use sign language to communicate. The black-and-white photographs show all the facets of Project Nim: living with a family, being loved, wearing clothes, learning a language, and being raised like a child. # 4

Two Kittens Are Born. Betty Schilling. Ill. with photographs by the author. Holt. Unpaged (44 pp.). US$6.95.
This photographic record and factual account of the birth and early life of two kittens attracts all age groups. Even non-animal lovers are fascinated by the black-and-white photographs of the delivery and the developmental stages of the offspring. # 1

Unbuilding. David Macaulay. Ill. by the author. Houghton. 80 pp. US$9.95.
This book focuses on the "unbuilding" of the Empire State Building. Readers are treated to a floor-by-floor description of the dismantling, augmented by superb, detailed pen-and-ink drawings of the process. A glossary provides needed information which enhances the value of this creative book. # 5

The Wild Rabbit. Oxford Scientific Films. Ill. with photographs by George Bernard. Putnam. Unpaged (32 pp.). US$7.95.
Here's a fine, introductory, nonfiction book on rabbits. Beautiful, full-page color photographs are accompanied by a single sentence each that provides young readers with facts about the life cycle of rabbits, what they eat, where they live, and how they deal with danger. # 1